Semantic Web Technologies and Applications in Artificial Intelligence of Things

Fernando Ortiz–Rodriguez
Tamaulipas Autonomous University, Mexico

Amed Leyva–Mederos
Universidad Central "Marta Abreu" de Las Villas, Cuba

Sanju Tiwari
Tamaulipas Autonomous University, Mexico

Ania R. Hernandez–Quintana
Universidad de La Habana, Cuba

Jose L. Martinez–Rodriguez
Autonomous University of Tamaulipas, Mexico

A volume in the Advances in Web Technologies and Engineering (AWTE) Book Series

Published in the United States of America by
IGI Global
Engineering Science Reference (an imprint of IGI Global)
701 E. Chocolate Avenue
Hershey PA, USA 17033
Tel: 717-533-8845
Fax: 717-533-8661
E-mail: cust@igi-global.com
Web site: http://www.igi-global.com

Library of Congress Cataloging-in-Publication Data

CIP DATA PROCESSING

Semantic Web Technologies and Applications in Artificial Intelligence of Things
 Fernando Ortiz-Rodriguez, Amed Leyva-Mederos, Sanju Tiwari, Ania Hernandez-Quintana, Jose L. Martinez-Rodriguez
  2024 Engineering Science Reference

ISBN: 9798369314876(hc) | ISBN: 9798369347737(sc) | eISBN: 9798369314883

This book is published in the IGI Global book series Advances in Web Technologies and Engineering (AWTE) (ISSN: 2328-2762; eISSN: 2328-2754)

British Cataloguing in Publication Data
A Cataloguing in Publication record for this book is available from the British Library.

For electronic access to this publication, please contact: eresources@igi-global.com.

Advances in Web Technologies and Engineering (AWTE) Book Series

Ghazi I. Alkhatib
The Hashemite University, Jordan
David C. Rine
George Mason University, USA

ISSN:2328-2762
EISSN:2328-2754

MISSION

The **Advances in Web Technologies and Engineering (AWTE) Book Series** aims to provide a platform for research in the area of Information Technology (IT) concepts, tools, methodologies, and ethnography, in the contexts of global communication systems and Web engineered applications. Organizations are continuously overwhelmed by a variety of new information technologies, many are Web based. These new technologies are capitalizing on the widespread use of network and communication technologies for seamless integration of various issues in information and knowledge sharing within and among organizations. This emphasis on integrated approaches is unique to this book series and dictates cross platform and multidisciplinary strategy to research and practice.

The **Advances in Web Technologies and Engineering (AWTE) Book Series** seeks to create a stage where comprehensive publications are distributed for the objective of bettering and expanding the field of web systems, knowledge capture, and communication technologies. The series will provide researchers and practitioners with solutions for improving how technology is utilized for the purpose of a growing awareness of the importance of web applications and engineering.

COVERAGE

- Security, integrity, privacy, and policy issues
- Web systems performance engineering studies
- Web user interfaces design, development, and usability engineering studies
- Human factors and cultural impact of IT-based systems
- Knowledge structure, classification, and search algorithms or engines
- Quality of service and service level agreement issues among integrated systems
- Metrics-based performance measurement of IT-based and web-based organizations
- Ontology and semantic Web studies
- Mobile, location-aware, and ubiquitous computing
- Web Systems Architectures, Including Distributed, Grid Computer, and Communication Systems Processing

IGI Global is currently accepting manuscripts for publication within this series. To submit a proposal for a volume in this series, please contact our Acquisition Editors at Acquisitions@igi-global.com or visit: http://www.igi-global.com/publish/.

Titles in this Series

For a list of additional titles in this series, please visit: http://www.igi-global.com/book-series/advances-web-technologies-engineering/37158

Decentralizing the Online Experience With Web3 Technologies
Dina Darwish (Ahram Canadian University, Egypt)
Engineering Science Reference • copyright 2024 • 422pp • H/C (ISBN: 9798369315323) • US $300.00 (our price)

Digital Technologies, Ethics, and Decentralization in the Digital Era
Balraj Verma (Chitkara Business School, Chitkara University, India) Babita Singla (Chitkara Business School, Chitkara University, Punjab, India) and Amit Mittal (Chitkara Business School, Chitkara University, Punjab, India)
Engineering Science Reference • copyright 2024 • 365pp • H/C (ISBN: 9798369317624) • US $300.00 (our price)

Infrastructure Possibilities and Human-Centered Approaches With Industry 5.0
Mohammad Ayoub Khan (University of Bisha, Saudi Arabia) Rijwan Khan (Galgotias University, India) Pushkar Praveen (Govind Ballabh Pant Institute of Engineering and Technology, India) Agya Ram Verma (Govind Ballabh Pant Institute of Engineering and Technology, India) and Manoj Kumar Panda (Govind Ballabh Pant Institute of Engineering and Technology, India)
Engineering Science Reference • copyright 2024 • 318pp • H/C (ISBN: 9798369307823) • US $300.00 (our price)

Internet of Behaviors Implementation in Organizational Contexts
Luísa Cagica Carvalho (Instituto Politécnico de Setúbal, Portugal) Clara Silveira (Polytechnic Institute of Guarda, Portugal) Leonilde Reis (Instituto Politecnico de Setubal, Portugal) and Nelson Russo (Universidade Aberta, Portugal)
Engineering Science Reference • copyright 2023 • 471pp • H/C (ISBN: 9781668490396) • US $270.00 (our price)

Supporting Technologies and the Impact of Blockchain on Organizations and Society
Luís Ferreira (Polytechnic Institute of Cávado and Ave, Portugal) Miguel Rosado Cruz (Polytechnic Institute of Viana do Castelo, Portugal) Estrela Ferreira Cruz (Polytechnic Institute of Viana do Castelo, Portugal) Hélder Quintela (Polytechnic Institute of Cavado and Ave, Portugal) and Manuela Cruz Cunha (Polytechnic Institute of Cavado and Ave, Portugal)
Engineering Science Reference • copyright 2023 • 337pp • H/C (ISBN: 9781668457474) • US $270.00 (our price)

Concepts, Technologies, Challenges, and the Future of Web 3
Pooja Lekhi (University Canada West, Canada) and Guneet Kaur (University of Stirling, UK & Cointelegraph, USA)
Engineering Science Reference • copyright 2023 • 602pp • H/C (ISBN: 9781668499191) • US $360.00 (our price)

Perspectives on Social Welfare Applications' Optimization and Enhanced Computer Applications

701 East Chocolate Avenue, Hershey, PA 17033, USA
Tel: 717-533-8845 x100 • Fax: 717-533-8661
E-Mail: cust@igi-global.com • www.igi-global.com

Table of Contents

Preface.. xix

Chapter 1
Achieving Balance Between Innovation and Security in the Cloud With Artificial Intelligence of
Things: Semantic Web Control Models 1
*R. Sundar, Department of Computer Science and Engineering, Madanapalle Institute of
    Technology and Science, Madanapalle, India*
*P. Balaji Srikaanth, Department of Networking and Communications, SRM Institute of
    Science and Technology, Kattankulathur, India*
*Darshana A. Naik, Department of Computer Science and Engineering, Ramaiah Institute of
    Technology, Bengaluru, India*
V. P. Murugan, Department of Mathematics, Panimalar Engineering College, Chennai, India
*Madhavi Karumudi, Department of Computer Science and Engineering, St. Peter's
    Engineering College, Hyderabad, India*
*Sampath Boopathi, Department of Mechanical Engineering, Muthayammal Engineering
    College, Namakkal, India*

Chapter 2
Industrial Supply Chain Coordination Based on Real-Time Web Service 27
Kamalendu Pal, University of London, UK

Chapter 3
Traffic: An Intelligent System for Detecting Traffic Events Based on Ontologies 53
Hayder Luis Endo Pérez, Universidad Central "Marta Abreu" de Las Villas, Cuba
Amed Abel Leiva Mederos, Universidad Central "Marta Abreu" de Las Villas, Cuba
José Antonio Senso-Ruíz, University of Granada, Spain
Ghislain Auguste Atemezing, Mondeca, France
Daniel Gálvez Lio, Universidad Central "Marta Abreu" de Las Villas, Cuba
Jose Luis Sánchez-Chávez, Universidad Central " Marta Abreu" de Las Villas, Cuba
Alfredo Simón Cueva, Universidad Tecnologica de la Habana, Cuba

Chapter 4

Multi-Factor Authentication Web Security System Based on Facial Recognition, One Time
Password, and Hashed Secure Question 66

    Graveth Uzoma Ejekwu, NYSC Secretariat Bayelsa, Nigeria
    Samson Ajodo, Nigerian Defence Academy, Nigeria
    O. Mashood Lawal, Air Force Institute of Technology, Nigerian Air Force Base, Mando,
        Nigeria
    Oluwafemi S. Balogun, University of Eastern Finland, Finland

Chapter 5

Developing Industry 4.0 Smart Parking Through Deep Learning and IoT-Based for Electric Vehicle 86

    Marwa Ben Arab, Electrical Systems and Renewable Energies Laboratory, National
        Engineering School of Sfax, University of Sfax, Tunisia
    Mouna Rekik, Electrical Systems and Renewable Energies Laboratory, National Engineering
        School of Sfax, University of Sfax, Tunisia
    Lotfi Krichen, Electrical Systems and Renewable Energies Laboratory, National Engineering
        School of Sfax, University of Sfax, Tunisia

Chapter 6

Study on Integrated Neural Networks and Fuzzy Logic Control for Autonomous Electric Vehicles 104

    J. Vimala Devi, Department of Computer Science Engineering, Dayananda Sagar College of
        Engineering, India
    Rajesh Vyankatesh Argiddi, Department of Computer Science and Engineering, Walchand
        Institute of Technology, Solapur, India
    P. Renuka, Department of Mathematics, KPR Institute of Engineering and Technology, India
    K. Janagi, Department of Mathematics, KPR Institute of Engineering and Technology, India
    B. S. Hari, Department of Mechanical Engineering, Kongu Engineering College, India
    S. Boopathi, Muthayammal Engineering College, India

Chapter 7

Securing Web Data and Privacy in AIoT Systems 128

    Marius Iulian Mihailescu, Universitatea Spiru Haret Bucureşti, Romania
    Stefania Loredana Nita, Military Technical Academy "Ferdinand I", Romania

Chapter 8

Leveraging Ethics in Artificial Intelligence Technologies and Applications: E-Learning
Management Systems in Namibia 173

    Gabriel N. Uunona, University of South Africa, South Africa
    Leila Goosen, University of South Africa, South Africa

Chapter 9

Enhancing Usability and Control in Artificial Intelligence of Things Environments (AIoT)
Through Semantic Web Control Models 186

    D.S. Dayana, Department of Networking and Communications, College of Engineering and
        Technology, SRM Institute of Science and Technology, Kattankulathur, India
    T. S. Shanthi, Department of Computer Science, S.A.V. Sahaya Thai Arts and Science
        (Women) College, Tirunelveli, India
    Girish Wali, Citibank, Bangalore, India
    P. V. Pramila, Department of Computer Science Engineering, Saveetha Institute of Medical
        and Technical Sciences, Saveetha University, Chennai, India
    T. Sumitha, Department of Computer Science Engineering, R.M.K. Engineering College,
        India
    M. Sudhakar, Department of Mechanical Engineering, Sri Sai Ram Engineering College,
        Chennai, India

Chapter 10

Emerging Trends in Artificial Intelligence of Things With Machine Learning and Semantic Web
Convergence 207

    A. Revathi, VISTAS, India
    S. Poonguzhali, VISTAS, India

Chapter 11

Cloud Computing Adoption for Small and Medium Enterprises in Mechanical Engineering 219

    K. C. Sekhar, Department of Mechanical Engineering, Lendi Institute of Engineering and
        Technology, Vizianagaram, India
    L. Ranganathan, Department of Mechanical Engineering, Cambridge Institute of
        Technology, Ranchi, India
    S. Bathrinath, Department of Mechanical Engineering, Kalasalingam Academy of Research
        and Education, Krishnankoil, India
    D. Premnath, Department of Mechanical Engineering, SRM Institute of Science and
        Technology, Kattankulathur, India
    B. Yuvasri, Department of Computer Science and Engineering, R.M.K. College of
        Engineering and Technology, Puduvoyal, India
    Sampath Boopathi, Department of Mechanical Engineering, Muthayammal Engineering
        College, Namakkal, India

Chapter 12

Semantic Web Technologies and Its Applications in Artificial Intelligence of Things 248

    Shalini Roy, VIT Bhopal University, India
    Harshit Gautam, VIT Bhopal University, India
    D. Lakshmi, VIT Bhopal University, India

Chapter 13

Sugarcane Disease Detection Using Data Augmentation 284

    Abhishek Verma, Centre for Advanced Studies, Lucknow, India
    Jagrati Singh, Indira Gandhi Delhi Technical University for Women, Delhi, India

Chapter 14
Oil and Gas Industry Challenges for the Next Decade: Strategies to Face Them From the
Education of Future Petroleum Engineers 311
    Rosario Cruz, UAT UAMRR, Mexico

Chapter 15
Classification of Indian Native English Accents 320
    A. Aadhitya, Anna University, Chennai, India
    K. N. Balasubramanian, Anna University, Chennai, India
    J. Dhalia Sweetlin, Anna University, Chennai, India

Chapter 16
Analyzing Fuel Cell Vehicles Through Intelligent Battery Management Systems (BMS): AI and
ML Technologies for E-Mobility 335
    Putchakayala Yanna Reddy, Department of Electrical & Electronics Engineering
        Department, Bharath Institute of Engineering and Technology, India
    Balpreet Singh Madan, Department of Art and Design, School of Design, Architecture, and
        Planning, Sharda University, Greater Noida, India
    Harishchander Anandaram, Department of Artificial Intelligence, Amrita Vishwa
        Vidyapeetham, Coimbatore, India
    Praveen Rathod, Department of Mechanical Engineering, Vishwakarma Institute of
        Information Technology, Pune, India
    S. Vasanthaseelan, Department of Mechanical Engineering, Sri Krishna College of
        Technology, Coimbatore, India
    S. Boopathi, Muthayammal Engineering College, India

Chapter 17
AI-Enabled Data Processing for Real-World Applications of IoT: A Review-Based Approach 356
    Suresh Santhanagopalan, St. Joseph's College (Autonomous), India
    Murali Ramachandran, St. Joseph's College (Autonomous), India
    A. Pappu Rajan, St. Joseph's College (Autonomous), India

Chapter 18
Advancements in Electric Vehicle Management System: Integrating Machine Learning and
Artificial Intelligence 371
    D. Godwin Immanuel, Department of Electrical and Electronics Engineering, Sathyabama
        Institute of Science and Technology, India
    Gautam Solaimalai, U.S. Bank, USA
    B. M. Chandrakala, Department of Information Science and Engineering, Dayananda Sagar
        College of Engineering, Bengaluru, India
    V. G. Bharath, Vessels Engineers, Bangalore, India
    Mukul Kumar Singh, Department of Electrical Engineering, MJP Rohilkhand University,
        Bareilly, India
    Sampath Boopathi, Department of Mechanical Engineering, Muthayammal Engineering
        College, Namakkal, India

Chapter 19
A Comprehensive Exploration of Mathematical Programming and Optimization Techniques in
Electrical and Electronics Engineering..392
    S. Nagarani, Department of Mathematics, Sri Ramakrishna Institute of Technology,
        Coimbatore, India
    A. Arivarasi, Department of Electronics and Communication Engineering, Sri Sairam
        College of Engineering, Bangalore, India
    L. Ancelin, Department of Mathematics, Madras Christian College, Chennai, India
    R. Naveeth Kumar, Department of Biomedical Engineering, Dr. NGP Institute of
        Technology, Coimbatore, India
    Arvind Sharma, Department of Electronics and Communication Engineering, Government
        Women Engineering College, Ajmer, India
    Sureshkumar Myilsamy, Bannari Amman Institute of Technology, India

Compilation of References 419

About the Contributors 470

Index..475

Detailed Table of Contents

Preface xix

Chapter 1

Achieving Balance Between Innovation and Security in the Cloud With Artificial Intelligence of
Things: Semantic Web Control Models 1

R. Sundar, Department of Computer Science and Engineering, Madanapalle Institute of
Technology and Science, Madanapalle, India

P. Balaji Srikaanth, Department of Networking and Communications, SRM Institute of
Science and Technology, Kattankulathur, India

Darshana A. Naik, Department of Computer Science and Engineering, Ramaiah Institute of
Technology, Bengaluru, India

V. P. Murugan, Department of Mathematics, Panimalar Engineering College, Chennai, India

Madhavi Karumudi, Department of Computer Science and Engineering, St. Peter's
Engineering College, Hyderabad, India

Sampath Boopathi, Department of Mechanical Engineering, Muthayammal Engineering
College, Namakkal, India

This chapter explores the integration of Semantic Web control models, innovation, and security in cloud computing, especially in the context of AIoT integration. The Semantic Web provides machine-understandable data and offers sophisticated control models that enhance innovation and security in cloud environments. Technologies like RDF, OWL, and SPARQL enable semantic interoperability, while control models focus on access control mechanisms and authentication strategies. The chapter introduces the concept of AIoT, integrating AI with IoT devices and discusses the potential of Semantic Web control models in managing security risks and fostering innovation.

Chapter 2

Industrial Supply Chain Coordination Based on Real-Time Web Service 27

Kamalendu Pal, University of London, UK

Integrating and coordinating supply chain business operations using intelligent wireless web (IWW) technology has been appreciated in many industries. In the IWW operational environment, real-time business process data collection using the internet of things (IoT) technology, web service, and artificial intelligence (AI) techniques play an enormous role in practical deployment purposes. This chapter explains how the IWW services and capabilities can be deployed in real-time coordination in supply chain management, and the feasibility of semantic technology has been depicted with the help of a business scenario. This chapter presents the main concepts of ontology-based semantic web service architecture for interconnecting distributed business operations in supply chain management. An ontology-based Semantic Web service discovery architecture (SWSDA) for the industrial supply chain is described as a business case. The concept of description logic (DL) and a service concept similarity assessment based on an algorithm are presented in this chapter.

Chapter 3

Traffic: An Intelligent System for Detecting Traffic Events Based on Ontologies 53

Hayder Luis Endo Pérez, Universidad Central "Marta Abreu" de Las Villas, Cuba
Amed Abel Leiva Mederos, Universidad Central "Marta Abreu" de Las Villas, Cuba
José Antonio Senso-Ruíz, University of Granada, Spain
Ghislain Auguste Atemezing, Mondeca, France
Daniel Gálvez Lio, Universidad Central "Marta Abreu" de Las Villas, Cuba
Jose Luis Sánchez-Chávez, Universidad Central " Marta Abreu" de Las Villas, Cuba
Alfredo Simón Cueva, Universidad Tecnologica de la Habana, Cuba

Traffic event detection is a multidisciplinary field that includes information retrieval, automatic, big data, etc. The absence of tools that integrate the detection of traffic events with the annotation, grouping, and location of events on transport routes led to the conception and implementation of this intelligent system based on ontologies for the management of streams, which facilitates the grouping of traffic data. As a result of the application of the system, it was possible to identify the speed events of a road in real-time and validate its efficiency through clustering algorithms.

Chapter 4

Multi-Factor Authentication Web Security System Based on Facial Recognition, One Time
Password, and Hashed Secure Question 66

Graveth Uzoma Ejekwu, NYSC Secretariat Bayelsa, Nigeria
Samson Ajodo, Nigerian Defence Academy, Nigeria
O. Mashood Lawal, Air Force Institute of Technology, Nigerian Air Force Base, Mando, Nigeria
Oluwafemi S. Balogun, University of Eastern Finland, Finland

Web application authentication is a critical aspect of digital security, serving as both the first and last line of defense for safeguarding sensitive information. Unfortunately, traditional text-based passwords are susceptible to a variety of attacks, leaving many web apps vulnerable to data theft by unauthorized users. As a solution, this study developed a multi-factor authentication technique to bolster the conventional username and password method. Utilizing Agile methodology, the proposed solution examined current authentication practices and evaluated the feasibility of multi-factor authentication. The system generates a one-time password (OTP) using the user's login credentials and incorporates additional steps such as face recognition and secure hashed questions for user authentication. To enhance security and user flexibility, the system was implemented using Python programming language, various Python libraries, and an image processing library.

Chapter 5

Developing Industry 4.0 Smart Parking Through Deep Learning and IoT-Based for Electric Vehicle 86

Marwa Ben Arab, Electrical Systems and Renewable Energies Laboratory, National
Engineering School of Sfax, University of Sfax, Tunisia
Mouna Rekik, Electrical Systems and Renewable Energies Laboratory, National Engineering
School of Sfax, University of Sfax, Tunisia
Lotfi Krichen, Electrical Systems and Renewable Energies Laboratory, National Engineering
School of Sfax, University of Sfax, Tunisia

Object detection is central to computer vision, drawing significant attention lately. Deep learning techniques shine for their precision, robustness, and speed. Their integration into Industry 4.0 is widely recognized, especially in AI-powered smart parking systems. This fusion is swiftly advancing, bolstering Industry 4.0 smart parking management and security. This chapter introduces a comprehensive framework presenting both software and hardware components, along with a mixing methodology, to enhance industry smart parking through detecting electric vehicles. The foundation of this approach lies in the application of deep learning, specifically utilizing the YOLOv3 methodology. In addition, the internet of things (IoT) is leveraged, employing a Raspberry Pi4 platform. The methodology for the development and execution of the system is outlined step by step to provide a clear understanding. This integrated solution showcases the detailed practical implementation. As a result, the detection of two vehicles has achieved confidence scores exceeding 0.7.

Chapter 6

Study on Integrated Neural Networks and Fuzzy Logic Control for Autonomous Electric Vehicles 104

J. Vimala Devi, Department of Computer Science Engineering, Dayananda Sagar College of
Engineering, India
Rajesh Vyankatesh Argiddi, Department of Computer Science and Engineering, Walchand
Institute of Technology, Solapur, India
P. Renuka, Department of Mathematics, KPR Institute of Engineering and Technology, India
K. Janagi, Department of Mathematics, KPR Institute of Engineering and Technology, India
B. S. Hari, Department of Mechanical Engineering, Kongu Engineering College, India
S. Boopathi, Muthayammal Engineering College, India

This chapter presents a comprehensive study on the integration of neural networks and fuzzy logic control techniques for enhancing the autonomy of electric vehicles (EVs). The integration of these two paradigms aims to overcome the limitations of traditional control approaches by leveraging the complementary strengths of neural networks in learning complex patterns and fuzzy logic in handling uncertainty and imprecision. The chapter discusses the design, implementation, and evaluation of an autonomous EV control system that utilizes neural networks for learning vehicle dynamics and fuzzy logic for decision-making in various driving scenarios. Through extensive simulations and experiments, the effectiveness and robustness of the proposed integrated approach are demonstrated, showcasing its potential for improving the safety, efficiency, and adaptability of autonomous EVs in real-world environments.

Chapter 7

Securing Web Data and Privacy in AIoT Systems..128

Marius Iulian Mihailescu, Universitatea Spiru Haret București, Romania
Stefania Loredana Nita, Military Technical Academy "Ferdinand I", Romania

The exponential growth of Artificial Intelligence of Things (AIoT) has resulted in an unparalleled fusion of AI with IoT technologies, giving rise to intricate systems that present vast opportunities for automation, productivity, and data-centric decision-making. Nevertheless, this amalgamation also poses substantial obstacles regarding safeguarding online information and upholding confidentiality. The chapter extensively examines the difficulties associated with these issues and the tactics employed to surmount them. The chapter commences by delineating the distinctive susceptibilities inherent in AIoT systems, with a particular emphasis on how the interconnection of AI and IoT technologies gives rise to novel avenues for data breaches and privacy infringements. It then explores the most recent approaches and technologies used to protect data sent over AIoT networks. These include improved encryption methods, secure data transfer protocols, and solutions based on blockchain technology. A substantial chunk of the chapter focuses on privacy-preserving strategies in AIoT. The text examines the equilibrium between data usefulness and privacy protection. It delves into techniques like anonymization, differential privacy, and federated learning as means to safeguard user data while ensuring the effectiveness of AIoT systems. The chapter also examines regulatory and ethical factors, thoroughly examining current and developing legislation and regulations that oversee data security and privacy in AIoT. The content incorporates case studies and real-world examples to demonstrate the pragmatic implementation of theoretical principles. Ultimately, the chapter predicts forthcoming patterns and difficulties in this swiftly progressing domain, providing valuable perspectives on possible AIoT security and privacy protocol advancements. This resource is vital for professionals, researchers, and students engaged in AIoT, cybersecurity, and data privacy. It provides them with the necessary information and tools to protect against the ever-changing threats in this dynamic field.

Chapter 8
Leveraging Ethics in Artificial Intelligence Technologies and Applications: E-Learning
Management Systems in Namibia... 173
    Gabriel N. Uunona, University of South Africa, South Africa
    Leila Goosen, University of South Africa, South Africa

The purpose of the study reported on is to establish ways in which ethics in artificial intelligence (AI) technologies and applications can be leveraged towards improved, standardized and safe e-learning management systems (eLMSs) at higher education institutions (HEIs) in Namibia, against the background of semantic web technologies and applications in artificial intelligence, the internet of things (IoT), and artificial intelligence of things (AIoT).

Chapter 9
Enhancing Usability and Control in Artificial Intelligence of Things Environments (AIoT)
Through Semantic Web Control Models 186
    D.S. Dayana, Department of Networking and Communications, College of Engineering and
        Technology, SRM Institute of Science and Technology, Kattankulathur, India
    T. S. Shanthi, Department of Computer Science, S.A.V. Sahaya Thai Arts and Science
        (Women) College, Tirunelveli, India
    Girish Wali, Citibank, Bangalore, India
    P. V. Pramila, Department of Computer Science Engineering, Saveetha Institute of Medical
        and Technical Sciences, Saveetha University, Chennai, India
    T. Sumitha, Department of Computer Science Engineering, R.M.K. Engineering College, India
    M. Sudhakar, Department of Mechanical Engineering, Sri Sai Ram Engineering College,
        Chennai, India

The chapter discusses the usability of artificial intelligence of things (AIoT) applications, emphasizing the complexity of these systems and the need for intuitive interfaces. It emphasizes the need to address system complexity, user interaction issues, and interface design hurdles for effective AIoT deployment. The chapter introduces Semantic Web control models, leveraging technologies like RDF, OWL, and SPARQL, to enhance usability in AIoT environments. It presents real-world case studies and successful implementations, highlighting the effectiveness of these models. The chapter also discusses future directions and challenges in AIoT usability, including emerging trends, obstacles, and research opportunities. The chapter concludes that usability is crucial in AIoT applications, and addressing these challenges and leveraging Semantic Web technologies can promote widespread adoption and unlock the full potential of AIoT.

Chapter 10
Emerging Trends in Artificial Intelligence of Things With Machine Learning and Semantic Web Convergence 207

A. Revathi, VISTAS, India
S. Poonguzhali, VISTAS, India

This chapter explores the dynamic convergence of artificial intelligence of things (AIoT), machine learning algorithms, and the semantic web. The fusion of AI and the internet of things (IoT) creates context-aware applications with transformative potential. Machine learning enhances AIoT capabilities, empowering systems to process IoT data effectively. Simultaneously, the semantic web, with its knowledge representation frameworks, augments adaptability. Delving into deep learning, reinforcement learning, and ensemble methods, the chapter elucidates how machine learning drives autonomous decision-making in AIoT. In the semantic web, the integration of machine learning introduces dynamic knowledge adaptation. Case studies in smart environments, predictive maintenance, and recommendation systems highlight practical implementations. The chapter addresses challenges, including scalability, security, and ethical implications. Emerging trends, interdisciplinary approaches, and societal impacts are explored, emphasizing the transformative potential of AIoT and semantic web integration.

Chapter 11
Cloud Computing Adoption for Small and Medium Enterprises in Mechanical Engineering 219

K. C. Sekhar, Department of Mechanical Engineering, Lendi Institute of Engineering and Technology, Vizianagaram, India
L. Ranganathan, Department of Mechanical Engineering, Cambridge Institute of Technology, Ranchi, India
S. Bathrinath, Department of Mechanical Engineering, Kalasalingam Academy of Research and Education, Krishnankoil, India
D. Premnath, Department of Mechanical Engineering, SRM Institute of Science and Technology, Kattankulathur, India
B. Yuvasri, Department of Computer Science and Engineering, R.M.K. College of Engineering and Technology, Puduvoyal, India
Sampath Boopathi, Department of Mechanical Engineering, Muthayammal Engineering College, Namakkal, India

This chapter delves into the adoption of cloud computing in small and medium-sized enterprises (SMEs) in mechanical engineering, highlighting its transformative potential. It discusses the benefits of cloud infrastructure, such as improved operational efficiency and innovation, but also addresses security and privacy challenges. The chapter provides strategies to mitigate these risks and emphasizes the importance of tailoring cloud solutions to meet the unique needs of SMEs. It also discusses the future of cloud technology, focusing on emerging trends and innovations. It also examines regulatory compliance and adherence strategies for a secure and compliant cloud integration journey. The chapter concludes with a comprehensive roadmap for SMEs in mechanical engineering, offering practical strategies, lessons learned, and a forward-looking perspective on the ever-evolving intersection of cloud computing and mechanical engineering.

Chapter 12
Semantic Web Technologies and Its Applications in Artificial Intelligence of Things 248
Shalini Roy, VIT Bhopal University, India
Harshit Gautam, VIT Bhopal University, India
D. Lakshmi, VIT Bhopal University, India

Semantic web transforms web search, enhancing data retrieval and storage. It enables machines to interpret online content through diverse technologies for data integration, knowledge representation, and intelligent search. This paradigm revolutionizes information organization, supporting AI, data analysis, and knowledge management. The chapter focuses on AIoT, covering data representation, integration, semantic web applications, control models, and recommendations. Practical case studies illustrate the application of semantic web tools, highlighting real-world scenarios.

Chapter 13
Sugarcane Disease Detection Using Data Augmentation 284
Abhishek Verma, Centre for Advanced Studies, Lucknow, India
Jagrati Singh, Indira Gandhi Delhi Technical University for Women, Delhi, India

Sugarcane is an important crop for the Indian economy, providing employment opportunities for millions of farmers. Nevertheless, the cultivation of sugarcane faces challenges from pests and diverse diseases. The detection and segmentation of plant diseases using deep learning have shown promising results in simple environments with abundant data. However, in complex environments with limited samples, the performance of existing models suffers. This study introduces an innovative method that addresses the challenges of complex environments and sample scarcity, aiming to enhance disease recognition accuracy. The highest accuracy showcased by model is 98% on testing data. Comparative study was done on the same dataset by employing various ML algorithms and achieved the highest accuracy of 70%. An Android app has been created to serve as the user interface for this model. This app enables farmers to either take pictures using their phone's camera or choose images from their gallery.

Chapter 14
Oil and Gas Industry Challenges for the Next Decade: Strategies to Face Them From the
Education of Future Petroleum Engineers 311
Rosario Cruz, UAT UAMRR, Mexico

Hydrocarbons are one of the most important sources of energy globally. The processing, use, and commercialization of these resources are the basis of the world economy, even in an era of energy transition like the one experienced today, in which alternative energies are developing rapidly. Activities carried out in the hydrocarbon industry contribute a large amount of energy-related CO_2 emissions, in addition to other environmental risks such as hydrocarbon spills, soil and groundwater contamination, and fires. As a result, the importance of the industry has been overshadowed, even though because of these same activities, engineering and scientific advances have been achieved to optimize the production of hydrocarbons to satisfy global demand. Consequently, it is expected that the oil and gas industry will face challenges in the environmental, operational, and social context during the next decade.

Chapter 15
Classification of Indian Native English Accents.. 320

    A. Aadhitya, Anna University, Chennai, India

    K. N. Balasubramanian, Anna University, Chennai, India

    J. Dhalia Sweetlin, Anna University, Chennai, India

The accent spoken by the people is generally influenced by their native mother tongue language. People located at various geographical locations speak by adding flavors to their native language. Various Indian native English accents are classified to bring out a classic difference between these accents. To bring a solution to this problem, a comparative classification model has been built to classify the accents of five distinct native Indian languages such as Tamil, Malayalam, Odia, Telugu, and Bangla from English accents. Firstly, the features of the five-second audio samples each from different accents are obtained and converted to images. The consolidated attributes are gathered. The VGG16 pre-trained model is fused with support vector model to classify accents accurately. Secondly, along with these features, mel frequency cepstral coefficient is added and trained. Then, the features obtained from VGG16 were reduced using principal component analysis. Highest accuracy obtained was 98.46%. Further analysis could be made to produce automated speech recognition for various aspects.

Chapter 16
Analyzing Fuel Cell Vehicles Through Intelligent Battery Management Systems (BMS): AI and ML Technologies for E-Mobility 335

    Putchakayala Yanna Reddy, Department of Electrical & Electronics Engineering Department, Bharath Institute of Engineering and Technology, India

    Balpreet Singh Madan, Department of Art and Design, School of Design, Architecture, and Planning, Sharda University, Greater Noida, India

    Harishchander Anandaram, Department of Artificial Intelligence, Amrita Vishwa Vidyapeetham, Coimbatore, India

    Praveen Rathod, Department of Mechanical Engineering, Vishwakarma Institute of Information Technology, Pune, India

    S. Vasanthaseelan, Department of Mechanical Engineering, Sri Krishna College of Technology, Coimbatore, India

    S. Boopathi, Muthayammal Engineering College, India

Integrating artificial intelligence (AI), internet of things (IoT), and machine learning (ML) technologies into fuel cell systems offers numerous benefits, applications, and opportunities for advancement across various sectors. This chapter explores the synergistic potential of AI, IoT, and ML in fuel cell integration, outlining their advantages, applications, challenges, and potential solutions. By leveraging AI for predictive maintenance, optimizing operating conditions through IoT sensors, and employing ML algorithms for efficiency enhancements, fuel cell systems can achieve higher performance and reliability. Real-world case studies and examples demonstrate successful integration in sectors such as transportation, energy production, and manufacturing. Moreover, this chapter discusses future prospects, including advancements in data analytics, system optimization, and scalability, driving innovation in fuel cell technology integration with AI, IoT, and ML.

Chapter 17

AI-Enabled Data Processing for Real-World Applications of IoT: A Review-Based Approach 356
Suresh Santhanagopalan, St. Joseph's College (Autonomous), India
Murali Ramachandran, St. Joseph's College (Autonomous), India
A. Pappu Rajan, St. Joseph's College (Autonomous), India

This is a digitally inclined era. The government support across all the countries in the globe and its associated initiatives on this IoT are commendable. In this chapter, the authors studied the research papers related to big data, IoT, and AI. The research papers were fetched from the Scopus database using Boolean operators (AND, OR) with the keywords, "IoT", "Big Data", "H IoT", and "AI". The chapter is presented in two parts. The first part is about the synthesis of the major papers related to this study. The second part is about the leverage of AI in various sectors like healthcare, education, finance, smart cities, energy, telecommunication, and agriculture. After studying from the vast literature, it shows that that IoT, big data, and ML are indispensable in the years to come. In this chapter, the authors call for government, industries, and academicians to collaborate together for conferences, seminars, and joint projects to digitalize all the premises and bring a data driven decisions.

Chapter 18

Advancements in Electric Vehicle Management System: Integrating Machine Learning and Artificial Intelligence 371
D. Godwin Immanuel, Department of Electrical and Electronics Engineering, Sathyabama Institute of Science and Technology, India
Gautam Solaimalai, U.S. Bank, USA
B. M. Chandrakala, Department of Information Science and Engineering, Dayananda Sagar College of Engineering, Bengaluru, India
V. G. Bharath, Vessels Engineers, Bangalore, India
Mukul Kumar Singh, Department of Electrical Engineering, MJP Rohilkhand University, Bareilly, India
Sampath Boopathi, Department of Mechanical Engineering, Muthayammal Engineering College, Namakkal, India

The chapter discusses the advancement of electric vehicle (EV) management systems, emphasizing the role of machine learning and artificial intelligence in optimizing vehicle dynamics, battery management, charging infrastructure, and user preferences. These technologies can enhance performance, efficiency, and user experience by adapting to dynamic driving conditions, optimizing energy consumption, and providing personalized experiences. The chapter also addresses challenges like data privacy, computational complexity, and interoperability, suggesting solutions and highlighting the need for collaborative research initiatives and regulatory frameworks for responsible ML and AI deployment in the EV industry.

Chapter 19

A Comprehensive Exploration of Mathematical Programming and Optimization Techniques in Electrical and Electronics Engineering 392

S. Nagarani, Department of Mathematics, Sri Ramakrishna Institute of Technology, Coimbatore, India

A. Arivarasi, Department of Electronics and Communication Engineering, Sri Sairam College of Engineering, Bangalore, India

L. Ancelin, Department of Mathematics, Madras Christian College, Chennai, India

R. Naveeth Kumar, Department of Biomedical Engineering, Dr. NGP Institute of Technology, Coimbatore, India

Arvind Sharma, Department of Electronics and Communication Engineering, Government Women Engineering College, Ajmer, India

Sureshkumar Myilsamy, Bannari Amman Institute of Technology, India

This chapter delves into the use of mathematical programming techniques in electrical and electronics engineering, highlighting their significance in enhancing efficiency, resource allocation, and decision-making processes. Techniques like linear programming, nonlinear programming, and integer programming are utilized for optimal power system resource allocation, design optimization, and discrete decision variables in circuit design. Mixed-integer programming is used for network optimization, dynamic programming for trajectory optimization, quadratic programming for control strategies, stochastic programming for uncertainties in electrical grid operations, and convex programming for structural optimization.

Compilation of References 419

About the Contributors 470

Index 475

Preface

In an era where technological advancements shape the landscape of industry, research, and society, the convergence of Artificial Intelligence of Things (AIoT) and Semantic Web technologies stands out as a pivotal development. As editors of *Semantic Web Technologies and Applications in Artificial Intelligence of Things*, we are delighted to present this comprehensive reference book that delves into the synergistic relationship between these two domains.

Our team, comprising Fernando Ortiz-Rodriguez, Amed Leyva-Mederos, Sanju Tiwari, Ania Hernández Quintana, and José Martinez-Rodriguez, hails from diverse academic backgrounds, uniting our expertise to curate a collection that reflects the essence of innovation driving the future society.

This book serves as a beacon for those navigating the complex terrain of Semantic Web technologies within the realm of Industry 4.0 and AIoT. Our aim is clear: to provide a repository of knowledge that not only captures the current state of the field but also illuminates pathways for future developments.

Designed with academics, students, and industry professionals in mind, this compilation covers a spectrum of topics including smart agriculture, manufacturing, healthcare, governmental applications, and more. It is our fervent belief that the insights presented within these pages will empower readers to harness the transformative potential of Semantic Web technologies in their respective domains.

The breadth of coverage within this book is expansive, touching upon crucial themes such as interoperability, usability, data representation, control models, architectures, machine learning, and information retrieval. While these topics serve as the backbone of our exploration, they are by no means exhaustive, as the landscape of AIoT and Semantic Web continues to evolve.

As editors, we extend our gratitude to the contributors whose dedication and expertise have enriched this volume. Their scholarly contributions have not only enhanced the depth of our discussions but have also inspired further inquiry and exploration.

In closing, we invite readers to embark on a journey through the pages of *Semantic Web Technologies and Applications in Artificial Intelligence of Things*. May this book serve as a compass guiding you through the intricate interplay of technologies shaping our collective future.

Chapter 1: Achieving Balance Between Innovation and Security in the Cloud With Artificial Intelligence of Things: Semantic Web Control Models

Authored by R. Sundar, P. Balaji Srikaanth, Darshana A Naik, V. P. Murugan, Madhavi Karumudi, and Sampath Boopathi, this chapter explores the integration of Semantic Web control models, innovation, and security in cloud computing, especially in the context of AIoT integration. The chapter discusses how Semantic Web technologies, such as RDF, OWL, and SPARQL, enhance innovation and security in cloud environments, focusing on access control mechanisms and authentication strategies. It introduces the concept of AIoT and discusses the potential of Semantic Web control models in managing security risks and fostering innovation.

Chapter 2: Industrial Supply Chain Coordination Based on Real-Time Web Service

This chapter, written by Kamalendu Pal, introduces an ontology-based Semantic Web Service Discovery Architecture (SWSDA) for industrial supply chain coordination. It discusses real-time business process data collection using IoT technology, web services, and AI techniques, highlighting the feasibility of semantic technology in coordinating supply chain management operations.

Chapter 3: Traffic: An Intelligent System for Detecting Traffic Events Based on Ontologies

Hayder Endo Pérez, Amed Leiva Mederos, José Senso-Ruíz, Ghislain Atemezing, Daniel Gálvez Lio, and Jose Sánchez-Chávez present an intelligent system based on ontologies for detecting and managing traffic events. It addresses the absence of tools for integrating traffic event detection with annotation and grouping, facilitating real-time traffic data management.

Chapter 4: Multi-Factor Authentication Web Security System Based on Facial Recognition, One Time Password, and Hashed Secure Question

Authored by Graveth Ejekwu, Samson Ajodo, O lawal, and Oluwafemi Balogun, this chapter focuses on enhancing web application security through multi-factor authentication. It proposes a technique incorporating facial recognition, one-time passwords, and hashed secure questions to bolster traditional text-based password authentication.

Chapter 5: Developing Industry 4.0 Smart Parking Through Deep Learning and IoT-Based for Electric Vehicle

In this chapter, Marwa Ben Arab, Mouna Rekik, and Lotfi Krichen introduce a framework for developing Industry 4.0 smart parking systems using deep learning and IoT. The chapter outlines the software and hardware components of the framework, along with a mixing methodology, to detect electric vehicles in smart parking environments.

Chapter 6: Study on Integrated Neural Networks and Fuzzy Logic Control for Autonomous Electric Vehicles

Authored by J. Vimala Devi, Rajesh Argiddi, P. Renuka, K Janagi, Hari B. S., and Murugan S., this chapter presents a study on integrating neural networks and fuzzy logic control techniques for autonomous electric vehicles. It discusses the design, implementation, and evaluation of an autonomous EV control system leveraging neural networks for learning vehicle dynamics and fuzzy logic for decision-making.

Chapter 7: Securing Web Data and Privacy in AIoT Systems

Written by Marius Iulian Mihailescu, Stefania Loredana Nita, and Jose Sánchez-Chávez, this chapter explores the application of semantic web, IoT, and machine learning in detecting meteorological events. The chapter discusses handling meteorological data using ontology-based semantic web technologies and machine learning models, focusing on prediction and analysis.

Chapter 8: Leveraging Ethics in Artificial Intelligence Technologies and Applications: E-Learning Management Systems in Namibia

In this chapter, Gabriel Uunona and Leila Goosen investigate leveraging ethics in AI technologies for improved e-Learning Management Systems in Namibia. It explores ways to integrate ethical considerations into AI applications, particularly in e-learning environments, to ensure standardized and safe systems.

Chapter 9: Enhancing Usability and Control in Artificial Intelligence of Things Environments (AIoT) Through Semantic Web Control Models

Dayana D. S., T. S. Shanthi, Girish Wali, P. V. Pramila, Sumitha T., and Subhi B. discuss enhancing usability in AIoT applications using Semantic Web control models in this chapter. The chapter addresses system complexity, user interaction issues, and interface design hurdles, leveraging Semantic Web technologies for effective AIoT deployment.

Chapter 10: Emerging Trends in Artificial Intelligence of Things With Machine Learning and Semantic Web Convergence

Revathi A. and Poonguzhali S. explore the convergence of AIoT, machine learning, and Semantic Web in this chapter. They delve into how machine learning algorithms and Semantic Web technologies enhance AIoT capabilities, driving transformative applications in various domains.

Chapter 11: Cloud Computing Adoption for Small and Medium Enterprises in Mechanical Engineering

Authored by K. Ch. Sekhar, L. Ranganathan, S. Bathrinath, D. Premnath, Yuvasri B., and Sampath Boopathi, this chapter examines cloud computing adoption in SMEs in mechanical engineering. The chapter discusses the benefits of cloud infrastructure, strategies to mitigate security risks, and future trends in cloud technology adoption for SMEs.

Chapter 12: Semantic Web Technologies and Its Applications in Artificial Intelligence of Things

In this chapter written by Shalini Roy, Harshit Gautam, and Lakshmi D., provides an overview of semantic web technologies and their applications in AIoT. It discusses data representation, integration, and control models based on the Semantic Web, highlighting practical applications and case studies.

Chapter 13: Sugarcane Disease Detection Using Data Augmentation

In this book, Abhishek Verma and Jagrati Singh present a method for detecting sugarcane diseases using deep learning and data augmentation. The chapter addresses challenges in disease recognition accuracy and scarcity of samples, proposing an innovative approach to enhance disease recognition accuracy in sugarcane crops.

Chapter 14: Oil and Gas Industry Challenges for the Next Decade: Strategies to Face Them From the Education of Future Petroleum Engineers

Rosario Cruz discusses challenges facing the oil and gas industry in the next decade and strategies to address them. It explores environmental, operational, and social challenges, emphasizing the role of education in preparing future petroleum engineers.

Chapter 15: Classification of Indian Native English Accents

In this chapter, Aadhitya A., Balasubramanian K.N., and J. Dhalia Sweetlin proposes a model for classifying Indian native English accents using machine learning. The chapter addresses the influence of native languages on English accents, presenting a comparative classification model to distinguish between different Indian native English accents.

Chapter 16: Analyzing Fuel Cell Vehicles Through Intelligent Battery Management Systems (BMS): AI and ML Technologies for E-Mobility

In this chapter authored by Putchakayala Yanna Reddy, Balpreet Singh Madan, Harishchander Anandaram, Praveen Rathod, Vasanthaseelan S, and Boopa S. B., explores AI and ML technologies in optimizing fuel cell vehicles. The chapter discusses leveraging AI for predictive maintenance, optimizing operating conditions, and enhancing efficiency in fuel cell systems.

Chapter 17: AI-Enabled Data Processing for Real-World Applications of IoT: A Review-Based Approach

Suresh Santhanagopalan, Murali Ramachandran, and Pappu Rajan A. review research papers on AI, IoT, and big data processing in this chapter. They synthesizes major research findings and discusses AI applications in sectors such as healthcare, education, finance, smart cities, energy, telecommunications, and agriculture.

Chapter 18: Advancements in Electric Vehicle Management System: Integrating Machine Learning and Artificial Intelligence

Authored by Godwin Immanuel D., Gautam Solaimalai, Chandrakala B. M., Bharath V. G., Mukul Kumar Singh, and Sampath Boopathi explore the integration of machine learning and AI in electric vehicle management systems. The chapter discusses optimizing vehicle dynamics, battery management, charging infrastructure, and user preferences using AI and ML technologies.

Chapter 19: A Comprehensive Exploration of Mathematical Programming and Optimization Techniques in Electrical and Electronics Engineering

In this concluding chapter, S. Nagarani, A. Arivarasi, Ancelin L., Naveeth Kumar R., Arvind Sharma, and Sureshkumar Myilsamy examine mathematical programming techniques in electrical and electronics engineering. They discuss their applications in resource allocation, design optimization, trajectory optimization, control strategies, and structural optimization.

As editors of *Semantic Web Technologies and Applications in Artificial Intelligence of Things*, we are honored to present this compendium of knowledge that illuminates the dynamic interplay between Semantic Web technologies and the burgeoning field of Artificial Intelligence of Things (AIoT). Through the collaborative efforts of our esteemed contributors and our dedicated editorial team, this volume encapsulates the essence of innovation driving the future of society.

In an era defined by rapid technological advancement, the convergence of AIoT and Semantic Web technologies offers unparalleled opportunities for transformative change across industries. From smart agriculture to manufacturing, healthcare, governmental applications, and beyond, the insights shared within these pages serve as a beacon for those navigating the complex terrain of Industry 4.0.

Our aim in curating this collection was twofold: to capture the current state of the field and to chart a course for future developments. Through a diverse array of chapters covering topics such as security, usability, data representation, control models, machine learning, and more, we have endeavored to provide readers with a comprehensive understanding of the vast potential inherent in this convergence.

We extend our deepest gratitude to the contributors whose scholarly contributions have enriched this volume, inspiring further inquiry and exploration. Their dedication and expertise have been instrumental in shaping this book into a repository of knowledge that will empower academics, students, and industry professionals alike to harness the transformative power of Semantic Web technologies in their respective domains.

In closing, we invite readers to embark on a journey through the pages of *Semantic Web Technologies and Applications in Artificial Intelligence of Things*. May this book serve as a compass guiding you through the intricate interplay of technologies shaping our collective future.

Fernando Ortiz-Rodriguez
Tamaulipas Autonomous University, Mexico

Amed Leyva-Mederos
Universidad Central "Marta Abreu" de Las Villas, Cuba

Sanju Tiwari
Tamaulipas Autonomous University, Mexico

Ania Hernandez-Quintana
Universidad Central "Marta Abreu" de Las Villas, Cuba

Jose L. Martinez-Rodriguez
Autonomous University of Tamaulipas, Mexico

Chapter 1
Achieving Balance Between Innovation and Security in the Cloud With Artificial Intelligence of Things:
Semantic Web Control Models

R. Sundar

Department of Computer Science and Engineering, Madanapalle Institute of Technology and Science, Madanapalle, India

P. Balaji Srikaanth

(iD) https://orcid.org/0000-0003-4717-7367

Department of Networking and Communications, SRM Institute of Science and Technology, Kattankulathur, India

Darshana A. Naik

(iD) https://orcid.org/0000-0001-5103-3089

Department of Computer Science and Engineering, Ramaiah Institute of Technology, Bengaluru, India

V. P. Murugan

Department of Mathematics, Panimalar Engineering College, Chennai, India

Madhavi Karumudi

Department of Computer Science and Engineering, St. Peter's Engineering College, Hyderabad, India

Sampath Boopathi

(iD) https://orcid.org/0000-0002-2065-6539

Department of Mechanical Engineering, Muthayammal Engineering College, Namakkal, India

ABSTRACT

This chapter explores the integration of Semantic Web control models, innovation, and security in cloud computing, especially in the context of AIoT integration. The Semantic Web provides machine-understandable data and offers sophisticated control models that enhance innovation and security in cloud environments. Technologies like RDF, OWL, and SPARQL enable semantic interoperability, while control models focus on access control mechanisms and authentication strategies. The chapter introduces the concept of AIoT, integrating AI with IoT devices and discusses the potential of Semantic Web control models in managing security risks and fostering innovation.

DOI: 10.4018/979-8-3693-1487-6.ch001

INTRODUCTION

The Semantic Web, a concept by Tim Berners-Lee, has revolutionized data management and information retrieval on the internet. It aims to improve the meaning of data, enabling machines to better understand and interpret information. Semantic Web control models govern access, manipulation, and dissemination of semantic data, fostering semantic interoperability, innovation, and security within digital ecosystems. Semantic Web control models use semantic enrichment to annotate data with metadata, enhancing querying, reasoning, and inference, enabling machines to perform complex tasks autonomously(Anwar, 2022). Key technologies include RDF (Resource Description Framework) and OWL (Web Ontology Language), which standardize data representation and linking, and SPARQL (SPARQL Protocol and RDF Query Language) for querying and manipulating RDF data, facilitating seamless access to semantic information (Martinez-Rodriguez et al., 2020).

Semantic Web control models aim to establish robust access control mechanisms for semantic data dissemination. By implementing fine-grained access policies based on user roles, privileges, and contextual attributes, organizations can safeguard sensitive information, promote collaboration, and ensure data integrity constraints and provenance tracking, ensuring the reliability and trustworthiness of semantic data sources. Semantic Web control models are essential for driving innovation by promoting semantic interoperability across diverse data sources and applications (Yahya et al., 2021a). They standardize data representations, enabling seamless integration and facilitating the development of new applications. These models also enable organizations to utilize emerging technologies like artificial intelligence, machine learning, and IoT by providing a coherent framework for data integration and analysis. By leveraging these models, organizations can navigate digital ecosystems confidently, driving value creation and fostering a culture of data-driven decision-making.

The integration of cloud computing has revolutionized the way businesses operate, offering agility, scalability, and cost-effectiveness. However, this has also brought risks such as data breaches, cyberattacks, and compliance violations. To mitigate these risks, organizations must strike a delicate balance between innovation and security. Cloud-native technologies like serverless computing, containerization, and microservices architectures enable rapid application development and deployment, allowing businesses to respond quickly to market changes (Costa Lima et al., 2023; Yahya et al., 2021a). Therefore, organizations must balance their pursuit of innovation with robust security measures to protect against these threats. Cloud environments present inherent security challenges, necessitating proactive risk management strategies. The shared responsibility model, where service providers and customers share responsibility for securing assets, emphasizes collaboration and transparency. Implementing a multi-layered approach to security, including network security, identity and access management, encryption, and continuous monitoring, can fortify defenses against evolving threats while preserving cloud technologies' agility and flexibility.

Achieving a balance between innovation and security in the cloud is crucial for maintaining data integrity and regulatory compliance, especially in highly regulated industries like finance, healthcare, and government. Data privacy regulations like GDPR, CCPA, and HIPAA require robust security controls and privacy-enhancing technologies to safeguard sensitive information and uphold consumer trust (Sepasgozar et al., 2020). Failure to comply can lead to financial penalties, legal liabilities, and eroded brand reputation, emphasizing the importance of prioritizing security alongside innovation The relationship between innovation and security is crucial for maximizing cloud computing's potential while safeguarding critical assets and ensuring regulatory compliance. By embracing a security culture and integrating security considerations into cloud-native architectures and DevOps practices, organizations can create a resilient security posture that allows innovation without compromising data integrity or customer trust. A commitment to security and risk management is essential for confident innovation and leveraging the transformative power of cloud technologies (Hansen & Bøgh, 2021).

The integration of Artificial Intelligence (AI) and the Internet of Things (IoT) holds great potential for revolutionizing various industries. This section explores the drivers, benefits, and challenges of AIoT integration, highlighting its potential to improve operational efficiency, enable predictive maintenance, and unlock new innovation opportunities. AIoT uses AI algorithms and machine learning to analyze IoT device data, extracting valuable insights and actionable intelligence in real-time. By integrating cognitive capabilities, organizations can transform sensor data into meaningful information, enabling proactive decision-making and operational excellence (Wu et al., 2020). AIoT optimizes resource utilization, minimizes downtime, and enhances productivity across various domains, enabling predictive analytics, anomaly detection, autonomous decision-making, and adaptive control.

The rapid growth of IoT devices and the vast amount of data they generate have led to the rise of AIoT. With billions of connected devices in various environments, the need for intelligent data processing and analysis is pressing. AI algorithms help organizations utilize IoT data to identify hidden patterns, correlations, and trends, enabling strategic decision-making and driving business innovation. AIoT offers significant potential for predictive maintenance and proactive asset management, reducing downtime, optimizing performance, and extending asset lifecycles. By using AI-driven predictive analytics, organizations can anticipate equipment failures, schedule preventive maintenance, and optimize schedules based on real-time performance data, enhancing equipment reliability, reducing operational costs, and boosting customer satisfaction (Kuzlu et al., 2021).

The integration of AI with IoT presents challenges such as data privacy, security vulnerabilities, and interoperability issues. Organizations must prioritize cybersecurity measures, implement robust authentication and encryption mechanisms, and adhere to industry best practices for IoT devices and data. Ensuring interoperability between disparate IoT devices and AI algorithms requires standardized protocols, data formats, and communication frameworks for seamless integration and collaboration across diverse environments (Adly et al., 2020; Kuzlu et al., 2021). The integration of Artificial Intelligence with the Internet of Things (IoT) has significant potential for innovation, operational efficiency, and new business models. By analyzing real-time IoT data, AI algorithms can provide actionable insights, optimize resource utilization, and transform operations. However, addressing challenges like data privacy, security, and interoperability is crucial for achieving full potential of AIoT integration and implementation.

SEMANTIC WEB TECHNOLOGIES

Semantic Web Technologies

Semantic Web technologies are a set of standards and protocols aimed at enhancing the meaning and understanding of data on the World Wide Web. Unlike traditional web technologies that primarily focus on the presentation of information, Semantic Web technologies aim to enable machines to comprehend the semantics or meaning of data, facilitating more intelligent data processing and interaction. At its core, the Semantic Web is based on the principles of annotating data with metadata that describe its meaning and relationships in a machine-readable format. This metadata enables automated reasoning, inference, and integration of disparate data sources, thereby enabling more sophisticated applications and services (Rhayem et al., 2020a).

RDF (Resource Description Framework)

RDF, or Resource Description Framework, is a foundational technology in the Semantic Web stack that provides a standard data model for representing and linking data on the web. At its essence, RDF represents information in the form of subject-predicate-object triples, where the subject denotes the resource being described, the predicate represents the property or relationship, and the object specifies the value or target resource. This graph-based data model enables the creation of interconnected semantic networks, allowing for the representation of complex relationships and knowledge structures. RDF provides a flexible and extensible framework for expressing diverse types of metadata and ontologies, making it a fundamental building block for Semantic Web applications and services (Patel & Jain, 2021).

OWL (Web Ontology Language)

OWL, or Web Ontology Language, is a semantic markup language designed to represent ontologies, which define formal vocabularies and conceptual frameworks for describing domains of knowledge. OWL enables the specification of classes, properties, and relationships within a domain, allowing for the creation of rich, expressive ontologies that capture the semantics of a particular domain. By providing a standardized language for defining ontologies, OWL facilitates interoperability and knowledge sharing across different systems and applications. OWL supports advanced features such as class hierarchies, property restrictions, and logical axioms, enabling sophisticated reasoning and inference capabilities within Semantic Web environments (Dadkhah et al., 2020a).

SPARQL (SPARQL Protocol and RDF Query Language)

SPARQL, or SPARQL Protocol and RDF Query Language, is a query language and protocol for querying and manipulating RDF data on the Semantic Web. SPARQL provides a powerful and expressive syntax for formulating queries that retrieve, filter, and transform RDF data according to specified criteria. It supports a wide range of query capabilities, including pattern matching, graph traversal, aggregation, and inferencing, making it suitable for a variety of data retrieval tasks. SPARQL queries can be executed against remote RDF data sources using the SPARQL protocol, enabling distributed querying and federated search across heterogeneous data repositories. SPARQL plays a crucial role in enabling data access and integration within Semantic Web applications, allowing users to extract meaningful insights from interconnected semantic data sources (Patel & Jain, 2021; Rhayem et al., 2020a).

CONTROL MODELS IN SEMANTIC WEB

Control models in the Semantic Web are frameworks and mechanisms that govern the access, manipulation, and dissemination of semantic data in distributed environments, enforcing security policies, managing data integrity, and ensuring regulatory compliance within Semantic Web applications and services. Control models in the Semantic Web focus on access control, which regulates who can access, modify, or delete semantic data resources. These models may include authentication, authorization, and audit functionalities to ensure only authorized users have access to sensitive information (Hema et al., 2023; Rahamathunnisa et al., 2023; Syamala et al., 2023; Venkateswaran, Vidhya, et al., 2023). Data integrity management is crucial, ensuring the accuracy, consistency, and reliability of semantic data sources. These models may include mechanisms for data validation, versioning, and provenance tracking, ensuring a trusted and authoritative data environment (Dadkhah et al., 2020a; Wagner et al., 2020). The figure 1 illustrates the connection between various access control mechanisms and authorization/ authentication methods.

Control models in the Semantic Web address privacy and confidentiality concerns by enabling data anonymization, encryption, and pseudonymization techniques. These measures protect sensitive information from unauthorized disclosure or misuse, fostering trust and compliance with data protection regulations. Control models ensure secure and effective management of semantic data assets, providing access control, data integrity management, and privacy protection, allowing organizations to leverage semantic technologies while mitigating risks.

The Semantic Web uses various access control mechanisms to regulate the access to semantic data resources, ensuring only authorized users or entities have appropriate access to sensitive information. Common mechanisms included as (Patel & Jain, 2021; Wagner et al., 2020):

i.   Role-Based Access Control (RBAC): RBAC is a widely used access control model that assigns permissions to users based on their roles within an organization. In the Semantic Web, RBAC can be implemented using ontologies to define roles and access permissions, allowing administrators to manage access control policies centrally.

ii. Attribute-Based Access Control (ABAC): ABAC is a flexible access control model that considers various attributes, such as user attributes, resource attributes, and environmental attributes, to make access control decisions. In the Semantic Web, ABAC can be implemented using RDF triples to represent policies that specify conditions based on attributes.

iii. Access Control Lists (ACLs): ACLs are lists associated with resources that enumerate the users or entities authorized to access those resources and their corresponding permissions. In the Semantic Web, ACLs can be represented using RDF triples or linked data structures, enabling fine-grained access control at the resource level.

The Semantic Web relies on authorization and authentication methods to verify user identities and determine access rights to semantic data resources (A. A. Kumar, 2021).

i.   Single Sign-On (SSO): SSO is a authentication method that allows users to authenticate once and access multiple resources or services without needing to re-authenticate. In the Semantic Web, SSO can be implemented using standards such as OAuth or OpenID Connect to enable secure and seamless authentication across distributed environments.

Figure 1. Relationship between different access control mechanisms and authorization/authentication methods

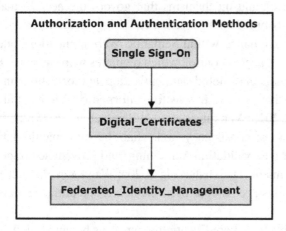
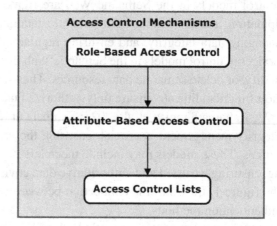

ii.   Digital Certificates: Digital certificates are cryptographic credentials that authenticate the identity of users or entities and enable secure communication over the internet. In the Semantic Web, digital certificates can be used to authenticate users, validate digital signatures, and establish secure connections between clients and servers.

iii. Federated Identity Management: Federated identity management allows users to access resources or services across multiple domains using a single set of credentials. In the Semantic Web, federated identity management can be achieved through standards such as SAML (Security Assertion Markup Language) or LDAP (Lightweight Directory Access Protocol), enabling seamless authentication and authorization across distributed environments.

INNOVATION IN CLOUD COMPUTING

The evolution of cloud computing traces back to the early 2000s when internet-based services began to gain traction, leading to the emergence of utility computing and grid computing paradigms. However, the term "cloud computing" as we understand it today was coined in the mid-2000s, marking the beginning of a transformative journey that has reshaped the IT landscape (El-Haddadeh, 2020; Mokhtar et al., 2020).

- **Early Concepts**: The concept of utility computing, proposed by John McCarthy in the 1960s, laid the groundwork for cloud computing by envisioning computing as a public utility. Grid computing emerged in the late 1990s, emphasizing the aggregation of computing resources to solve large-scale problems collaboratively.

- **Emergence of Cloud Services**: The advent of Amazon Web Services (AWS) in 2006 marked a significant milestone in the evolution of cloud computing, offering scalable infrastructure services on a pay-as-you-go basis. Other major players such as Google Cloud Platform and Microsoft Azure entered the market, further driving innovation and competition.

- **Key Innovations**: Virtualization technologies played a pivotal role in enabling the efficient utilization of hardware resources by abstracting physical infrastructure into virtual machines (VMs) or containers. Platform as a Service (PaaS) and Software as a Service (SaaS) models emerged, allowing developers to build and deploy applications without worrying about underlying infrastructure management.

- **Expansion of Cloud Offerings**: Cloud providers expanded their offerings beyond infrastructure services to include a wide array of managed services such as databases, analytics, machine learning, and Internet of Things (IoT) platforms (Boopathi, 2024c; BOOPATHI et al., 2024; Malathi et al., 2024). Hybrid and multi-cloud architectures gained prominence, allowing organizations to leverage a combination of on-premises, private cloud, and public cloud resources based on their specific requirements.

- **Advancements in Technologies**: Innovations in networking, storage, and computing technologies, such as Software-Defined Networking (SDN), Storage Area Networks (SANs), and serverless computing, have further enhanced the scalability, agility, and performance of cloud environments.

Edge computing and 5G networks are set to revolutionize cloud computing by bringing computing resources closer to end-users and IoT devices (Agrawal, Shashibhushan, et al., 2023; Venkateswaran, Vidhya, et al., 2023). Quantum computing has the potential to solve complex problems beyond classical computing, opening new frontiers for innovation. The evolution of cloud computing has seen innovation, expansion, and increased adoption across industries. The figure 2 showcases the various innovations driving cloud adoption and their significant impact on businesses and industries (Atieh, 2021; M. Sharma et al., 2020).

Innovations Driving Cloud Adoption

a) **Scalability and Elasticity**: Cloud computing offers scalable and elastic resources that can be easily adjusted to meet changing demands. Innovations in auto-scaling and dynamic resource provisioning enable businesses to efficiently handle fluctuations in workload without overprovisioning infrastructure.

b) **Cost Efficiency**: Pay-as-you-go pricing models and resource optimization techniques have revolutionized cost management in the cloud. Innovations such as spot instances, reserved instances, and serverless computing enable businesses to optimize costs by paying only for the resources they consume (Rahamathunnisa et al., 2024; Ravisankar et al., 2023).

c) **Flexibility and Agility**: Cloud-native technologies and DevOps practices enable rapid application development, deployment, and iteration. Innovations such as containerization, microservices architectures, and continuous integration/continuous deployment (CI/CD) pipelines empower businesses to deliver new features and updates at unprecedented speeds.

d) **Global Reach**: Cloud providers offer geographically distributed data centers that provide global reach and low-latency access to resources. Innovations in content delivery networks (CDNs) and edge computing technologies enable businesses to deliver content and services to users worldwide with minimal latency.

e) **Security and Compliance**: Cloud providers invest heavily in security and compliance measures to protect customer data and ensure regulatory compliance. Innovations such as encryption, iden-

Figure 2. Innovations driving cloud adoption and impact of cloud innovation

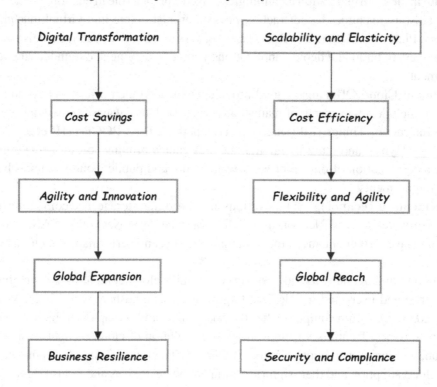

tity and access management (IAM), and security monitoring tools provide businesses with robust security solutions to safeguard their assets in the cloud.

Impact of Cloud Innovation on Businesses and Industries

a) **Digital Transformation**: Cloud computing has become a cornerstone of digital transformation initiatives, enabling businesses to modernize their IT infrastructure, adopt agile business practices, and innovate at scale. Cloud-based services empower organizations to leverage emerging technologies such as AI, IoT, and big data analytics to drive business growth and competitiveness (Agrawal, Pitchai, et al., 2023; Boopathi, 2024b; Suresh et al., 2024).

b) **Cost Savings**: By shifting from capital expenditures (CapEx) to operational expenditures (OpEx) and optimizing resource usage, businesses can achieve significant cost savings in the cloud. Cloud adoption eliminates the need for upfront investments in hardware and infrastructure, allowing organizations to allocate resources more efficiently and invest in strategic initiatives.

c) **Agility and Innovation**: Cloud computing fosters a culture of innovation and experimentation, enabling businesses to rapidly prototype, test, and launch new products and services. The agility and scalability of cloud resources empower organizations to respond quickly to market changes, customer feedback, and emerging opportunities, driving continuous innovation and competitive advantage.

Figure 3. Relationship between the main security challenges in cloud computing

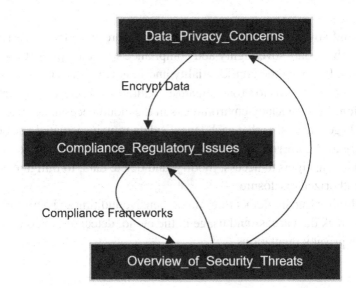

d) **Global Expansion**: Cloud computing facilitates global expansion by providing a scalable and accessible platform for reaching new markets and customers. Businesses can leverage cloud infrastructure to deploy applications and services worldwide, localize content and experiences, and adapt to regional preferences and regulations, accelerating international growth and market penetration.

e) **Business Resilience**: Cloud computing enhances business resilience by providing robust disaster recovery and business continuity solutions. Cloud-based backup and recovery services, coupled with redundant infrastructure and data replication across multiple regions, ensure high availability and reliability, mitigating the impact of outages, disasters, and unforeseen disruptions on business operations.

SECURITY CHALLENGES IN CLOUD COMPUTING

The figure 3 showcases the various innovations driving cloud adoption and their significant impact on businesses and industries. Security challenges in cloud computing encompass a range of threats, vulnerabilities, and regulatory concerns that organizations must address to safeguard their data and infrastructure in cloud environments. Cloud data breaches pose a significant threat, allowing unauthorized access to sensitive information, leading to data theft, financial loss, and reputational damage (Tabrizchi & Kuchaki Rafsanjani, 2020). Malicious actors exploit vulnerabilities to deploy malware and ransomware attacks. Insider threats, both intentional and unintentional, pose a significant risk to cloud security, potentially allowing sensitive data to be accessed or leaking. Denial of Service (DoS) attacks disrupt availability and cause service degradation, while misconfigured cloud services or security controls can expose sensitive data to unauthorized access, leading to data leaks or breaches (Alouffi et al., 2021).

Data Privacy

- **Data Location and Sovereignty**: Cloud providers may store data in multiple geographic locations, raising concerns about data sovereignty and compliance with data protection regulations.
- **Data Encryption**: Ensuring the confidentiality and integrity of data stored in the cloud requires robust encryption mechanisms to protect against unauthorized access or interception.
- **Data Segregation**: Multi-tenancy environments in the cloud necessitate strict data segregation to prevent data leakage and ensure that each tenant's data remains isolated and secure.
- **Data Ownership and Control**: Organizations must clarify ownership and control of data stored in the cloud, including rights to access, modify, and delete data, to mitigate risks associated with data loss or unauthorized disclosure.
- **Auditing and Monitoring**: Implementing comprehensive auditing and monitoring solutions enables organizations to track data access and usage in the cloud, detect anomalous activities, and ensure compliance with privacy regulations.

Compliance and Regulatory Issues

- **GDPR (General Data Protection Regulation)**: Organizations storing or processing personal data in the cloud must comply with GDPR requirements, including data protection, consent management, and breach notification obligations (Butt et al., 2020).
- **HIPAA (Health Insurance Portability and Accountability Act)**: Healthcare organizations must ensure that cloud services comply with HIPAA regulations governing the privacy and security of protected health information (PHI).
- **PCI DSS (Payment Card Industry Data Security Standard)**: Organizations handling payment card data must adhere to PCI DSS requirements when using cloud services to ensure the security of cardholder data.
- **Industry-Specific Regulations**: Various industries, such as finance, government, and telecommunications, have specific regulatory frameworks governing data privacy, security, and compliance requirements that apply to cloud deployments.
- **Data Residency Requirements**: Some jurisdictions impose restrictions on the storage and processing of data, requiring organizations to adhere to specific data residency requirements when using cloud services.

BALANCING INNOVATION AND SECURITY

Balancing innovation and security in the cloud is essential for organizations seeking to leverage the benefits of emerging technologies while mitigating associated risks. This delicate equilibrium requires a strategic approach that fosters innovation while prioritizing the protection of sensitive data and infrastructure (Yahya et al., 2021a). The relationship diagram illustrates strategies for achieving balance, risk management approaches, and the significance of proactive security measures in innovation as shown in Figure 4.

Strategies for Achieving Balance

a. **Adopt a Risk-Based Approach**: Organizations should assess the risks associated with innovative initiatives and prioritize security measures accordingly. By conducting comprehensive risk assessments and identifying potential vulnerabilities, businesses can allocate resources effectively to mitigate the most significant risks.

b. **Implement Defense in Depth**: Adopting a layered security approach, known as defense in depth, helps organizations defend against a wide range of threats by deploying multiple security controls at different layers of the IT infrastructure. This strategy involves combining preventive, detective, and responsive security measures to create a robust security posture.

c. **Embrace Security by Design**: Integrating security into the development lifecycle from the outset, known as security by design, ensures that security considerations are embedded into every stage of the innovation process. By implementing security controls, conducting security testing, and fostering a culture of security awareness, organizations can minimize the likelihood of security breaches and vulnerabilities.

d. **Promote Collaboration Between IT and Business Units**: Collaboration between IT and business units is essential for aligning innovation initiatives with security objectives. By involving security professionals early in the innovation process, organizations can identify potential security risks and implement appropriate controls without hindering the pace of innovation.

Risk Management Approaches

Identify and Assess Risks: Conducting thorough risk assessments helps organizations identify potential threats, vulnerabilities, and impacts associated with innovative projects. By analyzing the likelihood and potential consequences of risks, businesses can prioritize mitigation efforts and allocate resources effectively.

Implement Controls and Countermeasures: Once risks are identified, organizations should implement controls and countermeasures to mitigate them effectively. This may include implementing access controls, encryption, intrusion detection systems, and other security measures to protect data and infrastructure.

Monitor and Respond to Threats: Continuous monitoring of cloud environments enables organizations to detect and respond to security threats in real-time. Implementing security monitoring tools, threat intelligence feeds, and incident response procedures helps organizations detect and mitigate security incidents promptly.

Importance of Proactive Security Measures in Innovation

Proactive security measures are essential for fostering a culture of innovation while safeguarding sensitive data and infrastructure. By implementing security controls, conducting regular security assessments, and prioritizing security in the innovation process, organizations can minimize the risk of security breaches and protect their reputation, customer trust, and competitive advantage. Proactive security measures also enable organizations to demonstrate compliance with regulatory requirements and industry standards, enhancing their credibility and trustworthiness in the eyes of customers, partners, and stakeholders.

Figure 4. Relationship diagram: Strategies for achieving balance, risk management approaches, and the importance of proactive security measures in innovation

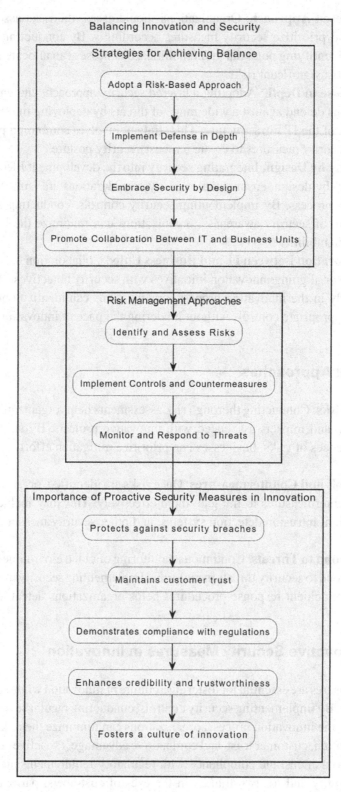

Ultimately, proactive security measures enable organizations to embrace innovation with confidence, knowing that their data and assets are protected against emerging threats and vulnerabilities (Elagib & Al-Saidi, 2020; Rejeb et al., 2021).

ARTIFICIAL INTELLIGENCE OF THINGS (AIOT)

Artificial Intelligence of Things (AIoT) is an emerging paradigm that combines the capabilities of Artificial Intelligence (AI) with Internet of Things (IoT) devices to create intelligent systems capable of collecting, analyzing, and acting upon data in real-time. AIoT leverages machine learning algorithms, deep learning techniques, and predictive analytics to enable IoT devices to make autonomous decisions, adapt to changing environments, and optimize performance without human intervention- (Zhang & Tao, 2020).

Integration of AI With IoT Devices

The integration of AI with IoT devices enhances their capabilities by enabling them to process and analyze data locally, make intelligent decisions, and communicate insights to other devices or cloud-based platforms (Boopathi, 2024c; Koshariya, Kalaiyarasi, et al., 2023; M. Kumar et al., 2023; Maguluri et al., 2023; Pachiappan et al., 2024). AI algorithms deployed on IoT devices can detect patterns, anomalies, and trends in sensor data, predict future outcomes, and trigger automated actions or alerts based on predefined rules or thresholds. Additionally, AIoT enables edge computing, where data processing and analysis occur closer to the data source, reducing latency, bandwidth requirements, and dependence on cloud infrastructure (Wang et al., 2023).

Applications and Benefits of AIoT in Various Domains (de Freitas et al., 2022; Pise et al., 2022)

1. **Smart Cities**: AIoT enables the creation of intelligent urban infrastructure, including smart transportation systems, energy management solutions, and environmental monitoring networks. AI-powered IoT devices can optimize traffic flow, reduce energy consumption, and detect and respond to environmental hazards in real-time, enhancing the quality of life for residents and reducing the ecological footprint of cities.
2. **Healthcare**: In healthcare, AIoT facilitates remote patient monitoring, personalized treatment recommendations, and predictive maintenance of medical equipment. Wearable devices equipped with AI algorithms can monitor vital signs, detect early signs of health problems, and provide timely interventions or alerts to healthcare providers. AIoT also enables the integration of medical devices and electronic health records, improving patient outcomes and reducing healthcare costs (Boopathi & Khang, 2023; Malathi et al., 2024; Satav et al., 2023; Venkateswaran, Kumar, et al., 2023).
3. **Manufacturing**: AIoT revolutionizes manufacturing processes by enabling predictive maintenance, quality control, and supply chain optimization. AI-powered sensors installed on manufacturing equipment can monitor performance metrics, detect abnormalities, and schedule maintenance activities to prevent costly downtime. AIoT also facilitates the implementation of smart factories,

where interconnected machines communicate and collaborate autonomously to optimize production efficiency and product quality (Boopathi, 2022; Boopathi & Sivakumar, 2013; Mohanty, Jothi, et al., 2023).

4. **Agriculture**: In agriculture, AIoT supports precision farming practices such as crop monitoring, irrigation management, and pest detection. IoT sensors deployed in fields collect data on soil moisture levels, temperature, and crop health, which AI algorithms analyze to optimize irrigation schedules, identify nutrient deficiencies, and predict crop yields. AIoT enables farmers to make data-driven decisions, conserve resources, and increase agricultural productivity sustainably (Boopathi, 2024c; Koshariya, Kalaiyarasi, et al., 2023; Pachiappan et al., 2024).

5. **Retail**: AIoT transforms the retail industry by enabling personalized customer experiences, inventory management, and supply chain optimization. IoT devices equipped with AI algorithms can analyze customer behavior, preferences, and purchase history to deliver targeted promotions, recommendations, and discounts in real-time. AIoT also enables retailers to optimize inventory levels, streamline logistics operations, and reduce costs through predictive analytics and demand forecasting.

Thus, Artificial Intelligence of Things (AIoT) represents a convergence of AI and IoT technologies that promises to revolutionize various domains, including smart cities, healthcare, manufacturing, agriculture, and retail. By harnessing the power of AI to augment IoT devices with intelligence and autonomy, AIoT enables organizations to unlock new opportunities for innovation, efficiency, and sustainability, paving the way for a smarter, more connected future.

SEMANTIC WEB CONTROL MODELS IN AIOT

Semantic Web control models in Artificial Intelligence of Things (AIoT) represent a convergence of Semantic Web technologies and IoT devices, enabling intelligent control and management of IoT ecosystems. These control models leverage Semantic Web standards such as RDF (Resource Description Framework), OWL (Web Ontology Language), and SPARQL (SPARQL Protocol and RDF Query Language) to enable semantic interoperability, enhance security, and drive innovation in AIoT environments (Rhayem et al., 2020b).

Utilizing Semantic Web Technologies for AIoT Control

Semantic Web technologies provide a standardized framework for representing, integrating, and reasoning over data in AIoT environments, facilitating intelligent control and management of interconnected IoT devices. RDF enables the representation of IoT data and metadata in a structured, machine-readable format, allowing devices to communicate and exchange information seamlessly. OWL enables the creation of ontologies that define domain-specific concepts, relationships, and rules, enabling devices to interpret and reason over data semantics. SPARQL provides a powerful query language for retrieving and manipulating IoT data stored in Semantic Web repositories, enabling sophisticated data analytics and decision-making (Franco da Silva & Hirmer, 2020).

By leveraging Semantic Web technologies for AIoT control, organizations can achieve semantic interoperability, enabling seamless communication and collaboration between heterogeneous IoT devices

Figure 5. Applications and benefits of AIoT in various domains

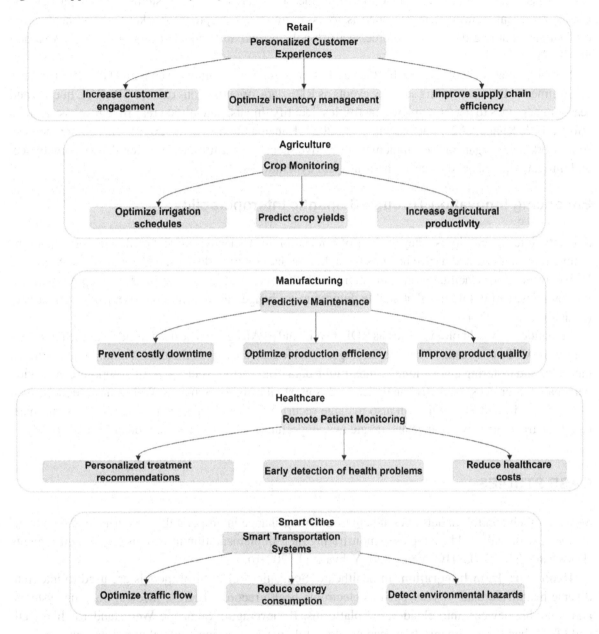

and systems. This enables the integration of diverse data sources, devices, and applications, facilitating the development of intelligent AIoT solutions that can adapt to changing environments and requirements.

Managing Security Risks in AIoT Environments

Semantic Web control models in AIoT play a crucial role in managing security risks and ensuring the integrity, confidentiality, and availability of IoT data and resources. By incorporating security policies, access controls, and encryption mechanisms into Semantic Web ontologies, organizations can enforce fine-grained access control and data protection measures across IoT ecosystems. RDF triples can be used to represent security metadata, such as access permissions, cryptographic keys, and authentication credentials, enabling devices to enforce security policies and authenticate users or entities (Amara et al., 2022).

Semantic Web technologies enable the integration of security monitoring and threat detection in AIoT environments. By representing security events as RDF data, organizations can use SPARQL queries and reasoning engines to detect suspicious activities, identify threats, and initiate real-time response actions (Boopathi & Khang, 2023; Pachiappan et al., 2024; Rahamathunnisa et al., 2024). This comprehensive framework helps organizations implement proactive security measures, enforce regulatory compliance, and mitigate the impact of security breaches and cyberattacks.

Enhancing Innovation Through Semantic Interoperability

Semantic interoperability is a key enabler of innovation in AIoT environments, allowing organizations to integrate, analyze, and derive insights from diverse data sources, devices, and applications. Semantic Web control models facilitate semantic interoperability by providing standardized data representations, vocabularies, and ontologies that enable devices to exchange and interpret data semantics effectively (Pliatsios et al., 2020).

Semantic Web technologies, such as RDF, OWL, and SPARQL, can be used to enhance the interoperability of AIoT ecosystems. These technologies enable data sharing and collaboration, breaking down data silos and fostering innovation. By integrating data from various sources, AIoT solutions can provide personalized services, predictive analytics, and contextual insights. Semantic Web control models, such as RDF, OWL, and SPARQL, can also manage security risks and enhance innovation. This approach can drive transformative change and create new opportunities for businesses, industries, and society.

CASE STUDIES

Semantic Web control models in cloud environments enhance interoperability, security, and data management, with real-world examples demonstrating their implementation in various cloud environments (Dadkhah et al., 2020b; Hyvönen, 2020; Yahya et al., 2021b).

Healthcare Data Integration: In healthcare, Semantic Web control models are used to integrate diverse healthcare data sources, such as electronic health records (EHRs), medical imaging systems, and wearable devices, into cloud-based platforms. By leveraging Semantic Web standards like RDF and OWL, healthcare organizations can create ontologies that define medical concepts, relationships, and protocols. These ontologies enable interoperability between disparate data sources, facilitating the exchange and analysis of healthcare data in cloud environments. For example, platforms like Health Level Seven International (HL7) FHIR (Fast Healthcare Interoperability Resources) use Semantic Web technologies to standardize data exchange formats and enable seamless interoperability between healthcare systems and applications.

Supply Chain Management: In supply chain management, Semantic Web control models are used to integrate and analyze data from multiple supply chain partners, including suppliers, manufacturers, distributors, and retailers. By representing supply chain data using Semantic Web standards such as RDF and SPARQL, organizations can create semantic models that capture the relationships and dependencies between different entities in the supply chain (Mohanty, Venkateswaran, et al., 2023; Verma et al., 2024). These semantic models enable organizations to track inventory levels, monitor logistics operations, and optimize supply chain processes in cloud-based platforms. For example, companies like IBM use Semantic Web technologies to create blockchain-based supply chain networks that provide real-time visibility into product movement, provenance, and authenticity.

Financial Risk Management: In the financial services industry, Semantic Web control models are used to analyze and manage financial risk factors, such as market fluctuations, credit defaults, and regulatory compliance requirements. By representing financial data using Semantic Web standards like RDF and OWL, financial institutions can create semantic models that capture the relationships between financial instruments, market indicators, and risk factors (Babu et al., 2022; Ravisankar et al., 2023; Venkateswaran, Vidhya, et al., 2023). These semantic models enable organizations to perform complex risk analysis and scenario planning in cloud-based risk management platforms. For example, companies like RiskLens use Semantic Web technologies to create risk quantification models that help organizations assess and prioritize cybersecurity risks based on their potential impact on business operations and financial performance.

Smart City Infrastructure: In smart city initiatives, Semantic Web control models are used to integrate data from various urban systems, such as transportation networks, energy grids, and environmental sensors, into cloud-based platforms. By representing urban data using Semantic Web standards like RDF and OWL, city governments can create semantic models that capture the relationships between different urban entities, such as roads, buildings, and public utilities (Boopathi, 2024a). These semantic models enable cities to optimize resource allocation, improve service delivery, and enhance quality of life for residents in cloud-based smart city platforms. For example, projects like the European Union's City-Pulse use Semantic Web technologies to create interoperable platforms that integrate data from multiple smart city applications, such as traffic management, energy efficiency, and air quality monitoring.

Thus, implementing Semantic Web control models in cloud environments offers a powerful means of integrating, analyzing, and managing data across diverse domains and industries. By leveraging Semantic Web standards and technologies, organizations can create semantic models that enable interoperability, enhance security, and drive innovation in cloud-based platforms and applications.

Successful Deployment of AIoT Solutions

The successful deployment of AIoT solutions necessitates a balanced approach that combines innovation and security to ensure system effectiveness, reliability, and trustworthiness, requiring several key aspects (Pliatsios et al., 2020; Yahya et al., 2021b).

Innovative Design and Development: A successful AIoT solution begins with innovative design and development practices that leverage cutting-edge technologies and methodologies. This includes the use of advanced AI algorithms, machine learning techniques, and IoT devices capable of capturing, processing, and analyzing data in real-time. By embracing innovation in design and development, organizations can create AIoT solutions that deliver actionable insights, predictive capabilities, and adaptive functionalities to address evolving business needs and challenges.

Robust Security Measures: Security is paramount in AIoT deployments to protect sensitive data, ensure user privacy, and safeguard against cyber threats and attacks. Implementing robust security measures, such as encryption, authentication, access controls, and intrusion detection systems, helps mitigate security risks and vulnerabilities in AIoT ecosystems. Additionally, adopting security-by-design principles ensures that security considerations are integrated into every stage of the AIoT solution lifecycle, from design and development to deployment and maintenance (Boopathi, 2024b, 2024a; Nanda et al., 2024).

Data Privacy and Compliance: With the proliferation of data collected and processed by AIoT solutions, maintaining data privacy and compliance with regulatory requirements is imperative. Organizations must implement measures to anonymize, encrypt, and securely store sensitive data to protect user privacy and comply with data protection regulations such as GDPR, HIPAA, and CCPA. By prioritizing data privacy and compliance, organizations can build trust with users and stakeholders and avoid potential legal and reputational risks associated with data breaches or non-compliance.

Continuous Monitoring and Maintenance: AIoT solutions require ongoing monitoring and maintenance to ensure optimal performance, reliability, and security over time. Implementing robust monitoring tools, performance metrics, and automated alerts enables organizations to detect and respond to issues proactively, minimizing downtime and service disruptions. Additionally, regular software updates, patches, and security audits help mitigate emerging threats and vulnerabilities, ensuring the long-term viability and effectiveness of AIoT deployments (Hussain et al., 2023; Ingle et al., 2023).

User Education and Training: User education and training are essential aspects of successful AIoT deployments, empowering users to understand the capabilities, limitations, and security best practices associated with AIoT solutions. Providing comprehensive training programs, user guides, and support resources helps users make informed decisions, mitigate risks, and maximize the value of AIoT technologies. Additionally, fostering a culture of security awareness and accountability among employees and stakeholders promotes responsible use of AIoT solutions and enhances overall cybersecurity posture (Das et al., 2024; D. M. Sharma et al., 2024).

By addressing these important aspects—innovative design and development, robust security measures, data privacy and compliance, continuous monitoring and maintenance, and user education and training—organizations can successfully deploy AIoT solutions that combine innovation with security, driving business growth, efficiency, and competitiveness in today's digital landscape.

FUTURE DIRECTIONS

As we look ahead, several emerging trends are poised to shape the future of Semantic Web, cloud computing, and AIoT, paving the way for continued innovation and advancements in technology (de Freitas et al., 2022; Rhayem et al., 2020b, 2020a; M. Sharma et al., 2020).

Emerging Trends in Semantic Web, Cloud Computing, and AIoT

Semantic Interoperability: The Semantic Web will continue to evolve, with a focus on enhancing interoperability between heterogeneous data sources and systems. Ontology-driven approaches and semantic technologies will play a crucial role in enabling seamless integration and interoperability across diverse domains and applications.

Edge Computing: Edge computing will gain prominence as organizations seek to leverage AIoT solutions closer to the data source, reducing latency, bandwidth usage, and dependence on centralized cloud infrastructure. Edge AI capabilities will enable real-time decision-making and analysis at the edge, empowering IoT devices to operate autonomously and intelligently (Das et al., 2024).

Explainable AI (XAI): With the growing adoption of AI technologies, there will be increased emphasis on explainable AI (XAI) to enhance transparency, accountability, and trustworthiness in AIoT systems. XAI techniques will enable users to understand and interpret the decisions made by AI models, facilitating better decision-making and risk management in complex environments (Rahamathunnisa et al., 2023; Venkateswaran, Vidhya, et al., 2023).

Predictions for the Future of Innovation and Security in the Cloud

Hybrid and Multi-Cloud Architectures: Organizations will increasingly adopt hybrid and multi-cloud architectures to leverage the strengths of different cloud providers and optimize performance, scalability, and cost-effectiveness. This trend will drive innovation in cloud management tools, orchestration platforms, and interoperability standards to enable seamless integration and management of diverse cloud environments.

AI-driven Security: AI and machine learning will play a pivotal role in enhancing cloud security by enabling proactive threat detection, anomaly detection, and automated incident response. AI-driven security solutions will continuously analyze vast amounts of data to identify emerging threats and vulnerabilities, empowering organizations to stay ahead of cyber threats and protect their cloud assets effectively (Koshariya, Kalaiyarasi, et al., 2023; Koshariya, Khatoon, et al., 2023; Ramudu et al., 2023).

Final Thoughts on Achieving Balance and Maximizing Benefits

Achieving balance between innovation and security is essential for organizations to maximize the benefits of emerging technologies while mitigating associated risks. By adopting a proactive approach to security, embracing industry best practices, and fostering a culture of collaboration and accountability, organizations can effectively navigate the complexities of the evolving technological landscape (El-Haddadeh, 2020). In conclusion, the convergence of Semantic Web, cloud computing, and AIoT holds immense potential to drive innovation, efficiency, and transformation across industries. By staying abreast of emerging trends, embracing new technologies, and prioritizing security and compliance, organizations can capitalize on the opportunities presented by the evolving technological landscape, achieving sustainable growth and competitive advantage in the digital age.

CONCLUSION

In conclusion, the chapter has explored the dynamic intersection of Semantic Web control models, cloud computing, and Artificial Intelligence of Things (AIoT), highlighting their potential to drive innovation while ensuring robust security measures. Throughout the discussion, key concepts such as utilizing Semantic Web technologies for AIoT control, managing security risks, and enhancing innovation through semantic interoperability have been examined. Semantic Web control models provide a standardized framework for managing data in AIoT environments, enabling seamless communication and interoperability among devices. Leveraging Semantic Web standards like RDF, OWL, and SPARQL, organizations can enhance security, drive innovation, and mitigate security risks. Addressing security risks, data privacy safeguards, and regulatory compliance is crucial for mitigating threats, protecting sensitive data, and building trust with users and stakeholders.

Emerging trends like edge computing, explainable AI, and hybrid multi-cloud architectures are shaping the future of Semantic Web, cloud computing, and AIoT. These technologies offer opportunities for organizations to innovate, optimize performance, and enhance security in AIoT environments. Balancing innovation and security is crucial in AIoT deployments, allowing organizations to harness technology's full potential while safeguarding against cyber threats. By adopting a proactive approach, embracing industry best practices, and staying updated, organizations can drive sustainable growth and competitiveness in the digital era.

ABBREVIATIONS

AIoT - Artificial Intelligence of Things
RDF - Resource Description Framework
OWL - Web Ontology Language
SPARQL - SPARQL Protocol and RDF Query Language
IoT - Internet of Things
GDPR - General Data Protection Regulation
CCPA - California Consumer Privacy Act
HIPAA - Health Insurance Portability and Accountability Act
AI - Artificial Intelligence
RBAC - Role-Based Access Control
ABAC - Attribute-Based Access Control
ACLs - Access Control Lists
SSO - Single Sign-On
LDAP - Lightweight Directory Access Protocol
SAML - Security Assertion Markup Language
AWS - Amazon Web Services
PaaS - Platform as a Service
SaaS - Software as a Service
SDN - Software-Defined Networking
SANs - Storage Area Networks
CI/CD - Continuous Integration/Continuous Deployment
CDNs - Content Delivery Networks
IAM - Identity and Access Management
CapEx - Capital Expenditure
OpEx - Operational Expenditure
DoS - Denial of Service
PHI - Protected Health Information
PCI DSS - Payment Card Industry Data Security Standard
EHRs - Electronic Health Records
HL7 - Health Level Seven International
FHIR - Fast Healthcare Interoperability Resources

REFERENCES

Adly, A. S., Adly, A. S., & Adly, M. S. (2020). Approaches based on artificial intelligence and the internet of intelligent things to prevent the spread of COVID-19: Scoping review. *Journal of Medical Internet Research*, 22(8), e19104. doi:10.2196/19104 PMID:32584780

Agrawal, A. V., Pitchai, R., Senthamaraikannan, C., Balaji, N. A., Sajithra, S., & Boopathi, S. (2023). Digital Education System During the COVID-19 Pandemic. In Using Assistive Technology for Inclusive Learning in K-12 Classrooms (pp. 104–126). IGI Global. doi:10.4018/978-1-6684-6424-3.ch005

Agrawal, A. V., Shashibhushan, G., Pradeep, S., Padhi, S., Sugumar, D., & Boopathi, S. (2023). Synergizing Artificial Intelligence, 5G, and Cloud Computing for Efficient Energy Conversion Using Agricultural Waste. In Sustainable Science and Intelligent Technologies for Societal Development (pp. 475–497). IGI Global.

Alouffi, B., Hasnain, M., Alharbi, A., Alosaimi, W., Alyami, H., & Ayaz, M. (2021). A systematic literature review on cloud computing security: Threats and mitigation strategies. *IEEE Access : Practical Innovations, Open Solutions*, 9, 57792–57807. doi:10.1109/ACCESS.2021.3073203

Amara, F. Z., Hemam, M., Djezzar, M., & Maimour, M. (2022). Semantic web technologies for internet of things semantic interoperability. *Advances in Information, Communication and Cybersecurity: Proceedings of ICI2C'21*, 133–143.

Anwar, A. A. (2022). A survey of semantic web (Web 3.0), its applications, challenges, future and its relation with Internet of things (IoT). *Web Intelligence, Preprint*, 1–30.

Atieh, A. T. (2021). The next generation cloud technologies: A review on distributed cloud, fog and edge computing and their opportunities and challenges. *ResearchBerg Review of Science and Technology*, 1(1), 1–15.

Babu, B. S., Kamalakannan, J., Meenatchi, N., Karthik, S., & Boopathi, S. (2022). Economic impacts and reliability evaluation of battery by adopting Electric Vehicle. *IEEE Explore*, 1–6.

Boopathi, S., Karthikeyan, K. R., Jaiswal, C., Dabi, R., Sunagar, P., & Malik, S. (2024). *IoT based Automatic Cooling Tower*. Academic Press.

Boopathi, S. (2022). An extensive review on sustainable developments of dry and near-dry electrical discharge machining processes. *ASME: Journal of Manufacturing Science and Engineering*, 144(5), 050801–1.

Boopathi, S. (2024a). Advancements in Machine Learning and AI for Intelligent Systems in Drone Applications for Smart City Developments. In *Futuristic e-Governance Security With Deep Learning Applications* (pp. 15–45). IGI Global. doi:10.4018/978-1-6684-9596-4.ch002

Boopathi, S. (2024b). Balancing Innovation and Security in the Cloud: Navigating the Risks and Rewards of the Digital Age. In Improving Security, Privacy, and Trust in Cloud Computing (pp. 164–193). IGI Global.

Boopathi, S. (2024c). Sustainable Development Using IoT and AI Techniques for Water Utilization in Agriculture. In Sustainable Development in AI, Blockchain, and E-Governance Applications (pp. 204–228). IGI Global. doi:10.4018/979-8-3693-1722-8.ch012

Boopathi, S., & Khang, A. (2023). AI-Integrated Technology for a Secure and Ethical Healthcare Ecosystem. In *AI and IoT-Based Technologies for Precision Medicine* (pp. 36–59). IGI Global. doi:10.4018/979-8-3693-0876-9.ch003

Boopathi, S., & Sivakumar, K. (2013). Experimental investigation and parameter optimization of near-dry wire-cut electrical discharge machining using multi-objective evolutionary algorithm. *International Journal of Advanced Manufacturing Technology, 67*(9–12), 2639–2655. doi:10.1007/s00170-012-4680-4

Butt, U. A., Mehmood, M., Shah, S. B. H., Amin, R., Shaukat, M. W., Raza, S. M., Suh, D. Y., & Piran, M. J. (2020). A review of machine learning algorithms for cloud computing security. *Electronics (Basel), 9*(9), 1379. doi:10.3390/electronics9091379

Costa Lima, V., Alves, D., Andrade Bernardi, F., & Charters Lopes Rijo, R. P. (2023). Security approaches for electronic health data handling through the Semantic Web: A scoping review. *Semantic Web, 14*(4), 771–784. doi:10.3233/SW-223088

Dadkhah, M., Araban, S., & Paydar, S. (2020a). A systematic literature review on semantic web enabled software testing. *Journal of Systems and Software, 162*, 110485. doi:10.1016/j.jss.2019.110485

Das, S., Lekhya, G., Shreya, K., Shekinah, K. L., Babu, K. K., & Boopathi, S. (2024). Fostering Sustainability Education Through Cross-Disciplinary Collaborations and Research Partnerships: Interdisciplinary Synergy. In Facilitating Global Collaboration and Knowledge Sharing in Higher Education With Generative AI (pp. 60–88). IGI Global.

de Freitas, M. P., Piai, V. A., Farias, R. H., Fernandes, A. M., de Moraes Rossetto, A. G., & Leithardt, V. R. Q. (2022). Artificial intelligence of things applied to assistive technology: A systematic literature review. *Sensors (Basel), 22*(21), 8531. doi:10.3390/s22218531 PMID:36366227

El-Haddadeh, R. (2020). Digital innovation dynamics influence on organisational adoption: The case of cloud computing services. *Information Systems Frontiers, 22*(4), 985–999. doi:10.1007/s10796-019-09912-2

Elagib, N. A., & Al-Saidi, M. (2020). Balancing the benefits from the water–energy–land–food nexus through agroforestry in the Sahel. *The Science of the Total Environment, 742*, 140509. doi:10.1016/j.scitotenv.2020.140509 PMID:33167296

Franco da Silva, A. C., & Hirmer, P. (2020). Models for internet of things environments—A survey. *Information (Basel), 11*(10), 487. doi:10.3390/info11100487

Hansen, E. B., & Bøgh, S. (2021). Artificial intelligence and internet of things in small and medium-sized enterprises: A survey. *Journal of Manufacturing Systems, 58*, 362–372. doi:10.1016/j.jmsy.2020.08.009

Hema, N., Krishnamoorthy, N., Chavan, S. M., Kumar, N., Sabarimuthu, M., & Boopathi, S. (2023). A Study on an Internet of Things (IoT)-Enabled Smart Solar Grid System. In *Handbook of Research on Deep Learning Techniques for Cloud-Based Industrial IoT* (pp. 290–308). IGI Global. doi:10.4018/978-1-6684-8098-4.ch017

Hussain, Z., Babe, M., Saravanan, S., Srimathy, G., Roopa, H., & Boopathi, S. (2023). Optimizing Biomass-to-Biofuel Conversion: IoT and AI Integration for Enhanced Efficiency and Sustainability. In Circular Economy Implementation for Sustainability in the Built Environment (pp. 191–214). IGI Global.

Hyvönen, E. (2020). Using the Semantic Web in digital humanities: Shift from data publishing to data-analysis and serendipitous knowledge discovery. *Semantic Web*, *11*(1), 187–193. doi:10.3233/SW-190386

Ingle, R. B., Swathi, S., Mahendran, G., Senthil, T., Muralidharan, N., & Boopathi, S. (2023). Sustainability and Optimization of Green and Lean Manufacturing Processes Using Machine Learning Techniques. In *Circular Economy Implementation for Sustainability in the Built Environment* (pp. 261–285). IGI Global. doi:10.4018/978-1-6684-8238-4.ch012

Koshariya, A. K., Kalaiyarasi, D., Jovith, A. A., Sivakami, T., Hasan, D. S., & Boopathi, S. (2023). AI-Enabled IoT and WSN-Integrated Smart Agriculture System. In *Artificial Intelligence Tools and Technologies for Smart Farming and Agriculture Practices* (pp. 200–218). IGI Global. doi:10.4018/978-1-6684-8516-3.ch011

Koshariya, A. K., Khatoon, S., Marathe, A. M., Suba, G. M., Baral, D., & Boopathi, S. (2023). Agricultural Waste Management Systems Using Artificial Intelligence Techniques. In *AI-Enabled Social Robotics in Human Care Services* (pp. 236–258). IGI Global. doi:10.4018/978-1-6684-8171-4.ch009

Kumar, A. A. (2021). Semantic memory: A review of methods, models, and current challenges. *Psychonomic Bulletin & Review*, *28*(1), 40–80. doi:10.3758/s13423-020-01792-x PMID:32885404

Kumar, M., Kumar, K., Sasikala, P., Sampath, B., Gopi, B., & Sundaram, S. (2023). Sustainable Green Energy Generation From Waste Water: IoT and ML Integration. In Sustainable Science and Intelligent Technologies for Societal Development (pp. 440–463). IGI Global.

Kuzlu, M., Fair, C., & Guler, O. (2021). Role of artificial intelligence in the Internet of Things (IoT) cybersecurity. *Discover Internet of Things*, *1*(1), 1–14. doi:10.1007/s43926-020-00001-4

Maguluri, L. P., Ananth, J., Hariram, S., Geetha, C., Bhaskar, A., & Boopathi, S. (2023). Smart Vehicle-Emissions Monitoring System Using Internet of Things (IoT). In Handbook of Research on Safe Disposal Methods of Municipal Solid Wastes for a Sustainable Environment (pp. 191–211). IGI Global.

Malathi, J., Kusha, K., Isaac, S., Ramesh, A., Rajendiran, M., & Boopathi, S. (2024). IoT-Enabled Remote Patient Monitoring for Chronic Disease Management and Cost Savings: Transforming Healthcare. In Advances in Explainable AI Applications for Smart Cities (pp. 371–388). IGI Global.

Martinez-Rodriguez, J. L., Hogan, A., & Lopez-Arevalo, I. (2020). Information extraction meets the semantic web: A survey. *Semantic Web*, *11*(2), 255–335. doi:10.3233/SW-180333

Mohanty, A., Jothi, B., Jeyasudha, J., Ranjit, P., Isaac, J. S., & Boopathi, S. (2023). Additive Manufacturing Using Robotic Programming. In *AI-Enabled Social Robotics in Human Care Services* (pp. 259–282). IGI Global. doi:10.4018/978-1-6684-8171-4.ch010

Mohanty, A., Venkateswaran, N., Ranjit, P., Tripathi, M. A., & Boopathi, S. (2023). Innovative Strategy for Profitable Automobile Industries: Working Capital Management. In Handbook of Research on Designing Sustainable Supply Chains to Achieve a Circular Economy (pp. 412–428). IGI Global.

Mokhtar, S. S. S., Mahomed, A. S. B., Aziz, Y. A., & Rahman, S. A. (2020). Industry 4.0: The importance of innovation in adopting cloud computing among SMEs in Malaysia. *Polish Journal of Management Studies, 22*.

Nanda, A. K., Sharma, A., Augustine, P. J., Cyril, B. R., Kiran, V., & Sampath, B. (2024). Securing Cloud Infrastructure in IaaS and PaaS Environments. In Improving Security, Privacy, and Trust in Cloud Computing (pp. 1–33). IGI Global. doi:10.4018/979-8-3693-1431-9.ch001

Pachiappan, K., Anitha, K., Pitchai, R., Sangeetha, S., Satyanarayana, T., & Boopathi, S. (2024). Intelligent Machines, IoT, and AI in Revolutionizing Agriculture for Water Processing. In *Handbook of Research on AI and ML for Intelligent Machines and Systems* (pp. 374–399). IGI Global.

Patel, A., & Jain, S. (2021). Present and future of semantic web technologies: A research statement. *International Journal of Computers and Applications, 43*(5), 413–422. doi:10.1080/1206212X.2019.1570666

Pise, A. A., Almuzaini, K. K., Ahanger, T. A., Farouk, A., Pareek, P. K., Nuagah, S. J., & ... (2022). Enabling artificial intelligence of things (AIoT) healthcare architectures and listing security issues. *Computational Intelligence and Neuroscience, 2022*, 2022. doi:10.1155/2022/8421434 PMID:36911247

Pliatsios, A., Goumopoulos, C., & Kotis, K. (2020). A review on iot frameworks supporting multi-level interoperability—The semantic social network of things framework. *Int. J. Adv. Internet Technol, 13*(1), 46–64.

Rahamathunnisa, U., Sudhakar, K., Murugan, T. K., Thivaharan, S., Rajkumar, M., & Boopathi, S. (2023). Cloud Computing Principles for Optimizing Robot Task Offloading Processes. In *AI-Enabled Social Robotics in Human Care Services* (pp. 188–211). IGI Global. doi:10.4018/978-1-6684-8171-4.ch007

Rahamathunnisa, U., Sudhakar, K., Padhi, S., Bhattacharya, S., Shashibhushan, G., & Boopathi, S. (2024). Sustainable Energy Generation From Waste Water: IoT Integrated Technologies. In Adoption and Use of Technology Tools and Services by Economically Disadvantaged Communities: Implications for Growth and Sustainability (pp. 225–256). IGI Global.

Ramudu, K., Mohan, V. M., Jyothirmai, D., Prasad, D., Agrawal, R., & Boopathi, S. (2023). Machine Learning and Artificial Intelligence in Disease Prediction: Applications, Challenges, Limitations, Case Studies, and Future Directions. In Contemporary Applications of Data Fusion for Advanced Healthcare Informatics (pp. 297–318). IGI Global.

Ravisankar, A., Sampath, B., & Asif, M. M. (2023). Economic Studies on Automobile Management: Working Capital and Investment Analysis. In Multidisciplinary Approaches to Organizational Governance During Health Crises (pp. 169–198). IGI Global.

Rejeb, A., Rejeb, K., & Keogh, J. G. (2021). Cryptocurrencies in modern finance: A literature review. *Etikonomi*, *20*(1), 93–118. doi:10.15408/etk.v20i1.16911

Rhayem, A., Mhiri, M. B. A., & Gargouri, F. (2020). Semantic web technologies for the internet of things: Systematic literature review. *Internet of Things : Engineering Cyber Physical Human Systems*, *11*, 100206. doi:10.1016/j.iot.2020.100206

Satav, S. D., Hasan, D. S., Pitchai, R., Mohanaprakash, T., Sultanuddin, S., & Boopathi, S. (2023). Next generation of internet of things (ngiot) in healthcare systems. In *Sustainable Science and Intelligent Technologies for Societal Development* (pp. 307–330). IGI Global.

Sepasgozar, S., Karimi, R., Farahzadi, L., Moezzi, F., Shirowzhan, S. M., Ebrahimzadeh, S., Hui, F., & Aye, L. (2020). A systematic content review of artificial intelligence and the internet of things applications in smart home. *Applied Sciences (Basel, Switzerland)*, *10*(9), 3074. doi:10.3390/app10093074

Sharma, D. M., Ramana, K. V., Jothilakshmi, R., Verma, R., Maheswari, B. U., & Boopathi, S. (2024). Integrating Generative AI Into K-12 Curriculums and Pedagogies in India: Opportunities and Challenges. *Facilitating Global Collaboration and Knowledge Sharing in Higher Education With Generative AI*, 133–161.

Sharma, M., Gupta, R., & Acharya, P. (2020). Analysing the adoption of cloud computing service: A systematic literature review. *Global Knowledge. Memory and Communication*, *70*(1/2), 114–153.

Suresh, S., Natarajan, E., Boopathi, S., & Kumar, P. (2024). Processing of smart materials by additive manufacturing and 4D printing. In A. Kumar, P. Kumar, N. Sharma, & A. K. Srivastava (Eds.), *Digital Manufacturing, Artificial Intelligence, Industry 4.0* (pp. 181–196). De Gruyter. doi:10.1515/9783111215112-008

Syamala, M., Komala, C., Pramila, P., Dash, S., Meenakshi, S., & Boopathi, S. (2023). Machine Learning-Integrated IoT-Based Smart Home Energy Management System. In *Handbook of Research on Deep Learning Techniques for Cloud-Based Industrial IoT* (pp. 219–235). IGI Global. doi:10.4018/978-1-6684-8098-4.ch013

Tabrizchi, H., & Kuchaki Rafsanjani, M. (2020). A survey on security challenges in cloud computing: Issues, threats, and solutions. *The Journal of Supercomputing*, *76*(12), 9493–9532. doi:10.1007/s11227-020-03213-1

Venkateswaran, N., Kumar, S. S., Diwakar, G., Gnanasangeetha, D., & Boopathi, S. (2023). Synthetic Biology for Waste Water to Energy Conversion: IoT and AI Approaches. *Applications of Synthetic Biology in Health. Energy & Environment*, 360–384.

Venkateswaran, N., Vidhya, K., Ayyannan, M., Chavan, S. M., Sekar, K., & Boopathi, S. (2023). A Study on Smart Energy Management Framework Using Cloud Computing. In *5G, Artificial Intelligence, and Next Generation Internet of Things: Digital Innovation for Green and Sustainable Economies* (pp. 189–212). IGI Global. doi:10.4018/978-1-6684-8634-4.ch009

Verma, R., Christiana, M. B. V., Maheswari, M., Srinivasan, V., Patro, P., Dari, S. S., & Boopathi, S. (2024). Intelligent Physarum Solver for Profit Maximization in Oligopolistic Supply Chain Networks. In *AI and Machine Learning Impacts in Intelligent Supply Chain* (pp. 156–179). IGI Global. doi:10.4018/979-8-3693-1347-3.ch011

Wagner, A., Bonduel, M., Pauwels, P., & Rüppel, U. (2020). Representing construction-related geometry in a semantic web context: A review of approaches. *Automation in Construction, 115*, 103130. doi:10.1016/j.autcon.2020.103130

Wang, Y., Zhang, B., Ma, J., & Jin, Q. (2023). Artificial intelligence of things (AIoT) data acquisition based on graph neural networks: A systematical review. *Concurrency and Computation, 35*(23), e7827. doi:10.1002/cpe.7827

Wu, H., Han, H., Wang, X., & Sun, S. (2020). Research on artificial intelligence enhancing internet of things security: A survey. *IEEE Access : Practical Innovations, Open Solutions, 8*, 153826–153848. doi:10.1109/ACCESS.2020.3018170

Yahya, M., Breslin, J. G., & Ali, M. I. (2021). Semantic web and knowledge graphs for industry 4.0. *Applied Sciences (Basel, Switzerland), 11*(11), 5110. doi:10.3390/app11115110

Zhang, J., & Tao, D. (2020). Empowering things with intelligence: A survey of the progress, challenges, and opportunities in artificial intelligence of things. *IEEE Internet of Things Journal, 8*(10), 7789–7817. doi:10.1109/JIOT.2020.3039359

Chapter 2
Industrial Supply Chain Coordination Based on Real-Time Web Service

Kamalendu Pal

ⓘ https://orcid.org/0000-0001-7158-6481

University of London, UK

ABSTRACT

Integrating and coordinating supply chain business operations using intelligent wireless web (IWW) technology has been appreciated in many industries. In the IWW operational environment, real-time business process data collection using the internet of things (IoT) technology, web service, and artificial intelligence (AI) techniques play an enormous role in practical deployment purposes. This chapter explains how the IWW services and capabilities can be deployed in real-time coordination in supply chain management, and the feasibility of semantic technology has been depicted with the help of a business scenario. This chapter presents the main concepts of ontology-based semantic web service architecture for interconnecting distributed business operations in supply chain management. An ontology-based Semantic Web service discovery architecture (SWSDA) for the industrial supply chain is described as a business case. The concept of description logic (DL) and a service concept similarity assessment based on an algorithm are presented in this chapter.

INTRODUCTION

Today's business appreciates the value and consequence of building an effective supply chain as part of organizational proliferation and profitability (Pal, 2018). A supply chain is a network of facilities and distribution options that performs material procurement functions, transforming these materials into intermediate and finished products and distributing these finished products to customers (Ganeshan & Harrison, 1995). A research group introduces the concept of supply chain by defining it as integrating key business processes from end users through original suppliers that provide products, services, and information that add value for customers and other stakeholders (Liu et al., 2005). Supply Chain Manage-

DOI: 10.4018/979-8-3693-1487-6.ch002

ment's main objective is effectively integrating the information and material flows within the demand and supply process. In other words, supply chain management (SCM) aims to improve logistical resource allocation, management, and control. In this way, it provides the potential for improved productivity, cost reduction, and efficient customer service (Pal, 2019). In addition, the benefits of SCM are based on effectively employing the right processes and supporting information and communication technologies.

With its origins in manufacturing, SCM relies on business operations to achieve a competitive advantage (Vrijhoef & Koskela, 1999). The first signs of SCM were perceptible in Toyota Motor Manufacturing's Just-In-Time (JIT) procurement system (Shingo, 1988). Mainly, JIT was used to control supplies to the factory just in the right quantities, to the correct location, and at the right time in order to optimize system-wide costs and customer affordability. The main goal was to drastically reduce inventory levels and regulate the suppliers' interaction with the production line more effectively. It consists of material and information flowing through the supply chain organizations. The scope of the supply chain begins with the source of supply and ends at the point of consumption. It extends much further than simply a concern with the physical movement of material. Equal emphasis is given to supplier management, purchasing, material management, manufacturing management, facilities planning, customer service, information flow, transport, and physical distribution.

Supply chain management tries to bring suppliers and customers together in one concurrent business process. Its main objective is to synchronize the customer's needs with the flow of raw materials from purchasers. It balances the constraint satisfaction problem (CSP) with reasonable customer service, minimum inventory holding cost, and optimal unit cost. In this complex CSP environment, the design and operation of an effective supply chain is of fundamental importance. It is also worth noting that the purchasing process does not finish when the customer orders using an existing sales channel. Customers' queries, before or after order placement, are inevitable. At the same time, the seller might want to contact customers with purchase confirmation and shipping information. Customer service encompasses all points of contact between the seller and the customer and is an essential output of SCM. It results from the accumulated value of all business processes along the supply chain. These business processes are responsible for offering an acceptable level of customer service. Moreover, these business processes are also interdependent; if one business function fails to provide the expected level of customer service, the chain is disrupted, and the scheduled workload in other areas is destabilized. Customer satisfaction is the casualty.

In order to provide better customer service at no additional cost or workload, all business processes along the supply chain have to be balanced. It requires trade-offs throughout the supply chain. When considering practical trade-offs, thinking of a single interconnected chain rather than narrow functional business processes is essential. Seamless integration along the supply chain is challenged when there is a conflict between a company's functional behaviours and objectives, as is often the case. For example, suppliers typically want manufacturers to purchase in bulk quantities, in stable volumes, and with flexible delivery dates. However, although most manufacturers desire long production shifts, they must be flexible to their customers' requirements and fluctuating market demands. Thus, the suppliers' objectives directly contradict the manufacturers' wish for flexibility. Indeed, since manufacturing decisions are typically made without accurate information about customer demand, the ability of manufacturers to match supply and demand depends mainly on their ability to change supply volume as information about demand arrives. In the same way, the manufacturers' goal of making bulk production batches typically conflicts with the objectives of distribution and warehouse facility layouts to reduce materials inventory. To worsen the situation, this latter goal of reducing inventory typically implies an extra cost in transportation and distribution.

System fluctuations over time are also critical criteria that need to be considered. Even when the requisition is accurately known because of prior contractual agreements, strategic decisions need to consider demand and cost variations due to changes in market trends, market and sales logistics, competitive movement, and the like. These time-varying demand and cost criteria make it more complex to figure out the most appropriate supply chain strategy that optimizes system-wide management costs and complies with customer needs. Global optimization indicates that it is essential to optimize supply chain resource provisions and business activities connected with the supply chain. In addition, SCM captures, stores, and analyzes data with high volume and incredible velocity and comes from various sources (e.g., machines, radio frequency identification tags, geographical positioning system data, text files, etc.). These data sources are putting high demand on SCM for robust data infrastructure, the right analytical tools to manipulate it, and people skilled in analytics. Hence, determining which business activities and plans optimize both chains concurrently is essential. In this way, companies recognize the strategic importance of well-managed supply chains. For example, companies like Dell, Toyota, and Wal-Mart have based their corporate strategy on achieving supply chain superiority over their competitors (Copacino & Anderson, 2003). These multinational corporations have gained competitive advantages by effectively managing the complex web of supply chain business process interactions that extend across continents and enterprises in product procurement, manufacturing, and distribution.

Accomplishing supply chain superiority in today's globalized world is challenging for many companies. Effective SCM can be a competitive advantage that needs synergistic relationships between distributed corporate partners to maximize customer experience and provide a profit for each supply chain partner (Fugate et al., 2006); (Kalakota & Whinston, 1997). The design of a collaborative business process is vital for successful SCM and is enabled by information and communication technologies (ICT) (Li, 2002). The main objectives of supply chain management can be categorized as follows:

- Lowering material holding cost by using appropriate Material Requirement Planning (MRP), which needs to reflect JIT inventory management in the production line;
- Reducing overall production costs by streamlining the product flow within the production process and enhancing information flow between corporate business partners and
- Improving customer satisfaction by offering quick delivery and flexibility through seamless cooperation with distributors, warehouse operators, and other customer-centric services.

Success in an increasingly competitive global supply chain marketplace relies heavily on the quality of data, information, and knowledge that enterprises use in day-to-day business operations. Notably, manufacturing supply chains use purchasing, distribution, material management (or inventory management), picking and packing items, and production control information in assembly lines and at the end-user service. Integrated business information systems are the lifeblood of manufacturing chains. For example, any manufacturer's profitability depends heavily on effective inventory management systems, which help reduce stock-holding costs and streamline assembly line production processes. Inventory replenishment based on classical forecast methods, where safety stock is determined based on past sales and procurement data, is no longer adequate to handle globalized manufacturing processes. The correct information at the right time makes manufacturing chain operations much more effective. Therefore, today's globalized manufacturing business relies heavily on advanced Information and Communication

Technologies (ICT), such as electronic data interchange (Lambert & Cooper, 2000), multi-agent technologies (Pal & Karakostas, 2014); (Woodridge & Jennings, 19995); and in particular web service-based computing applications (Zhang et al., 2009); (Cai et al., 2010).

Web service-based business applications have developed a new paradigm of communication revolution in heterogeneous data source connectivity applications (e.g., global supply chains). However, the increasing use of web services has raised new research challenges. These challenges have attracted considerable research efforts on enhancing service description semantics and service composition algorithms (Matskin et al., 2007). In the research on the semantic enhancement of web services, different approaches have been used to provide appropriate business system architectures and specific languages that permit easy information systems integration of distributed business applications. In particular, one attractive theme is emerging from the service community research that shows how to enhance Business Process Execution Language (BEPL) by enhancing the semantics of the workflow-based service composition approach (Laliwala et al., 2006). However, most of this research matches the static behavior of web services with functional and non-functional properties. While these properties are likely to be semantically similar to the candidate web service, it is the execution values for such functional and non-functional properties that provide valuable guidelines for selecting appropriate web services.

Hence, the problem requires a methodical approach with specific knowledge for capturing the web service execution experiences and appropriate reasoning mechanisms based on the enhanced service descriptions. Semantic web services empower web services with semantics. Moreover, the popularity of semantic web service-based computing (Berners-Lee et al., 2001) has attracted particular attention to service modeling. For example, one of the leading research projects includes the US-based initiative – Ontology Web Language Service (OWL-S) (Martin et al., 2004). European projects include DIP (Data, Information, and Process Integration with Semantic Web Services), SUPER (a security-focused research project using social media in emergency management), and SOA4All (a project that provides a comprehensive global service delivery platform) (Roman et al., 2015). In these and other projects, researchers have proposed several frameworks for semantic web services, especially WSDL-S (Web Service Description Language – Semantics) (McIlraith et al., 2003) (Martin et al., 2004) and WSMO (Web Service Modeling Ontology) (Romana et al., 2005).

Despite these efforts, web service discovery is still a complex task and is difficult to implement manually. Hence, Semi-automated or fully dynamic web service discovery presents a real research challenge. To address the problem, this chapter describes the functionalities of a hybrid knowledge-based service matchmaking framework, SWSDF, which uses Structured Case-Base Reasoning (S-CBR) and Rule-Based Reasoning (RBR). The remainder of the chapter is organized as follows. Section 2 outlines the overview and motivations of this chapter. It includes a brief introduction to the semantic enrichment of web service using ontology, semantic web service frameworks, and ontology-based service description of a business scenario. In addition, it also provides a formal web service description for the business case using Description Logic (DL). Section 3 describes the overview of S-CBR and its relevance for semantic web services research. Section 4 presents briefly the system architecture of SWSDF and its service similarity assessment algorithm. This includes a material management business scenario and the service concept similarity assessment algorithm, including its evaluation procedure. Section 5 presents a review of relevant research approaches for web service discovery. Section 6 ends with concluding remarks.

OVERVIEW AND MOTIVATION

Web services have become the popular choice for the implementation of service delivery systems, which are distributed and interoperable. These services are built by a set of core technologies that provide these functionalities for communication, description, and discovery of services. The standards that cater these functionalities are Simple Object Access Protocol (SOAP), Web Services Description Language (WSDL), and Universal Description, Discovery, and Integration (UDDI) (OASIS, 2004). These XML-based standards use common Internet Protocols for the exchange of service requests and responses. (Extensible Markup Language, XML, is a common platform-independent data format across the enterprise) Figure 1 shows the relationship of these technologies as standards stack for web services; and Figure 2 describes briefly service publishing, service requesting and service finding mechanisms using a simple diagrammatic representation.

When a service provider creates a new service, it describes the service using standard WSDL, which defines a service in terms of the messages to be exchanged between services and how they can be found by specifying the location of the service with an appropriate Universal Resource Locater (URL). To make the service available to consumers, the provider registers the service in a UDDI registry by supplying the details of the service provider, the category of the service, and technical details on how to bind to the service. The UDDI registry will then maintain pointers to the WSDL description and to the service. When a consumer wants to use a service, it queries the UDDI registry to find the service that matches its needs and obtains the WSDL description of that service, as well as the access point of the service. The consumer uses the WSDL description to construct a SOAP message to be transported over HTTP (Hyper Text Transmission Protocol) with which to communicate with the service.

Web services are loosely coupled software components that are published, located and invoked across a network-computing infrastructure. Software-based web services are the building blocks for Service Oriented Computing (SOC), and they can be composed to provide a coarse-grained functionality and to automate business processes. In addition, technological improvements are providing more advanced communication facilities (e.g. online vendor managed inventory replenishment, payment using mobile hand-held devices). Business service facilities are providing more flexibility to its end-users and at the same time managing these business processes are becoming more complex. In SCM, many applications can be built by calling different web services available on the web or corporate intranets. These applications are highly dependent on discovering of correct web services. In particular, the description of web service consists of the technical parameters, constraints and policies that define the terms to invoke the web service. A web service definition needs four important things – *name, description, input* and *output*. Name provides business service name and it is used as a unique identifier; description represents the brief outline of the service; the input consists of number of parameters; and the output is also represented by a set of service parameters. SOAP based protocol provides the mechanism to exchange structured information in a decentralized and distributed information system.

In this way, web services aim to use the Web as a worldwide infrastructure for distributed computation purposes in order to carry out seamless integration of business processes. However, as the set of available web services increases, it becomes crucial to have automated service discovery mechanisms to help in finding services that match a requester's requirement. Finding appropriate web services depends on the facilities available for service providers to describe the capabilities of their services and for service requesters to describe their needs in an unambiguous form that is ideally machine-readable. In order to achieve this objective, ordinary web service description need to be enriched using domain

Figure 1. Web service standards stack

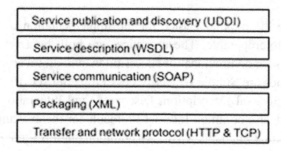

Figure 2. Web service relationships diagram

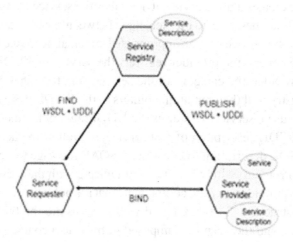

ontology (or semantic markup). The next section introduces the concept of ontology and semantic annotation mechanisms of web services.

Semantic Enrichment of Web Service Using Ontology

The word ontology has its origin in philosophy, and it relates the philosophical study of the nature of existence. In information management, the term ontology has a particular meaning: "An ontology is an explicit specification of a conceptualization" (Gruber, 1993). Studer et al. (Studer et al., 1998) advocated that this specification is also formal, i.e. an ontology is an *explicit* and formal specification of conceptualizing an environment (Antoniou & Harmelen, 2008) for a particular area of interest in a human understandable, and machine-readable format, which consists of objects, concepts, relationships, axioms, individuals and assertions (Guarino & Giaretta, 1995).

Ontologies are often considered as bare building blocks for heterogeneous software system integration. The use of ontologies in computing has gained popularity in recent decades for two specific reasons: they facilitate interoperability, and they enhance computer-based reasoning practice. Particularly in computer science and information science, knowledge reuse is facilitated by the use of explicit ontology, as opposed to implicit ontology (i.e. knowledge encoded into software systems). Hence, suitable ontology languages are required to realize explicit ontologies with respect to three important aspects:

- *Conceptualization*: The language should choose an appropriate reference model, such as Unified Modelling Language (UML) based class model (OMG, 2009), and provide corresponding ontology constructs to represent factual knowledge. For example, defining the classes and related relationships in a particular area of interest, and asserting relations among classes.
- *Vocabulary*: In addition to factual knowledge, the language needs to have vocabulary (i.e. assigning symbols to concepts) and grammar rules in order to represent the vocabulary explicitly.
- *Axiomatization*: In order to capture the semantics for inference, rules and constraints are required in addition to factual knowledge. One can use these rules to produce new facts from existing knowledge.

Information sharing among supply chain business partners using information systems is an important enabler for SCM. Many research works are devoted to answering the question of 'what information to share'. Li and co-researchers (Li et al, 2006) offer four types of data to be shared across the supply chain, namely, *order*, *demand, inventory,* and *shipment.* Lambert and his fellow researcher (Lambert & Cooper, 2000) suggest supply chain issues that need to be managed, such as customer service management, inventory management, and so on. In addition, they emphasize the importance of focusing on business processes, rather than individual functions. Consequently, information about these issues needs to be shared in order to achieve efficiency and effectiveness in the supply chain. In this way, information sharing activities require that human and/or machine agents agree on common and explicit ontologies (or business related taxonomies) so as to exchange information and derive knowledge to achieve collaborative objectives of business operations. In order to share knowledge across different communities, three requirements need to be considered when developing explicit ontologies: *extensibility* – reuse existing concepts and develop ontologies in an incremental way; *visibility* – publishing information and knowledge on the Web based on common ontological grounds between information publishers and consumers; and *inferenceability* – enable logical inference on facts through axiomatization.

The semantic web inherits the power of interoperability, and it can function as a distributed collaborative knowledge-base for a particular application domain. Moreover, to encode the ontology in information systems different knowledge representation techniques (e.g. graph-based, logic-based representation and other formal representation mechanisms) are used. A part of supply chain inventory management ontologies is shown in Figure 3.

In this diagrammatic representation, a procurement officer is a managerial role aimed on sourcing, procurement, and supply management for an enterprise. Corporate procurement can take place globally due to the economic benefits of the described supply chain. In this process, product costing, transportation facilities, country specific risk associated for a procurement process are all part of the procurement manager's decision-making activities. The top-level basic concepts (i.e. relevant entities or classes) are *country, profile, description, material,* and so on. The concept *profile* is further specialized as *costing* and *resource.* In the same way, concept *material* is specialized as *metatl bar*, and *ceramics pallet*. A supply chain business process may be atomic, composed of only one logistical service, or it may be a composite process, containing a series of services that together form a workflow.

These ontologies are presented in OWL (Ontology Web Language) description format; and they can form as the basis for the semantic representation of supply chain related services. The details of logi-

Figure 3. A partial state of the world represented by supply chain inventory management ontology

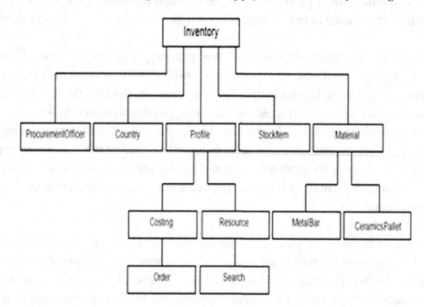

cal formalism and consistency checking mechanisms are beyond the scope of this chapter. However, a part of the inventory management ontology formalism is described in Table 1, using description logics (Baader & Nutt, 2003); and some of its core concepts are adopted from the service modeling approach, which has been used for the semantic service description in SWSDF. The objective of the ontology-based semantic similarity algorithm, discussed in the later part of this chapter, is to support the discovery of relevant web services.

A Formal Definition of Web Service Ontology

The semantic web service ontology can be described as follows:

$$\theta s_{ervice}\{\alpha fp, \beta nfp, \gamma ip, \delta o\}$$

where $\theta servi_{ce}$ symbolizes semantic web service in a prescribed representation;

αfp expresses functional characteristic attributes of service (it comprises of syntax attributes, static semantics which includes messages and operation semantics, service mediator and dynamic semantics;

βnfp corresponds to non-functional attributes of service (it includes unique *service identification, service name, service type, quality of service, economic properties, and* so on);

γip stands for a collection of interface attributes (consisting of input interfaces sets, output interfaces sets, pre-condition interfaces sets, post-condition interfaces sets, and so on) for a semantic web service; and

δo denotes ontology of service.

An ontology ()comprises of six constituent parts and it can be defined as follows:

$$\delta o \{C, AC, R, AR, H, X\}$$

where C symbolizes a set of concepts;

AC ^{e}xpresses a collection of attribute sets, one of each concept;

R represents a set of relationships;

A^R denotes a collection of attribute sets, one for each relationship;

H corresponds to a concept hierarchy; and

X stands for a set of axioms.

In this formalism, every concept C_i in C stands for a collection of similar object types, and can be described by the same collection of characteristic properties denoted by $A^C(C_i)$. Each relationship $r_i(c_p, c_q)$ in R denotes a binary association between concepts c_p and c_q, and the instances of such a relationship are pairs of (c_p, c_q) concept objects. The characteristic properties of r_i can be symbolized by $A^R(r_i)$. In this representation formalism, H is a concept hierarchy derived from C and it is a set of parent-child (or superclass – subclass) relationships between concepts in C. Each axiom in X is a constraint on the concepts and relationships attribute values or a constraint on the relationships between concept objects. Each constraint can be expressed in a logic programming rule format. Contextual information that establishes relationships between the data and the real world aspects it applies to forms rich metadata. In this way, academic research has investigated approaches of semantic annotations in web services (Cardoso & Sheth, 2003) (Patil et al, 2004) and offers different semantic web service frameworks.

Semantic Web Service Frameworks

The new breed of web semantic annotated web service is ushering the realization process of having data on the Web defined and linked in such a way that it can be used by matching not just for display purposes, but for automation, integration, and reuse of data across various applications. In this section, three main approaches, to bring semantics to web services, are discussed: WSDL-S, OWL-S, and WSMO.

WSDL-S: Initially this approach was originated by a research group at the University of Georgia, USA. In this approach, the expressivity of web service description (WSDL specification) is augmented with semantics by employing ontological concepts; and it is termed as WSDL-S (WSDL-S, 2005). The idea of establishing mappings between service, task, or activity descriptions and ontological concepts was first proposed by Cardoso and Sheth (Cardoso & Sheth, 2003). In this approach, one can specifically define the semantics of a web service for an area of interest. With the help of ontologies, the semantics or the meaning of service data and functionality can be described. In this way, integration can be accomplished in an automated way and with a higher degree of success. The WSDL elements that can be marked up with metadata are operations, messages, preconditions and effects, since all the elements are specifically described in a WSDL description.

- **Operations**: Each WSDL description may have a number of operations with different functionalities. In order to add semantics, the operations must be mapped to ontological concepts to describe their functionality.
- **Message**: Message parts, which are input and output parameters of operations, are defined in WSDL using the XML Schema. Ontologies – which are more expressive than the XML Schema – can be used to annotate WSDL message parts.
- **Preconditions and Effects**: Each WSDL operation may have a number of preconditions and effects. The preconditions are usually logical conditions, which must be evaluated to be true in order

to execute a specific operation. Effects are changes in the world that occur after the execution of an operation.

OWL-S: OWL-S (formally DAML-S) is emerging as a description language that semantically describes web services using OWL ontologies. OWL-S consists of three parts expressed with OWL ontologies: the service profile, the service model, and the service grounding. The profile is used to describe "what a service does", with advertisement and discovery as its objective. The service model describes "how a service works", to enable invocation, enactment, composition, monitoring and recovery. Finally, the grounding maps the constructs of the process model onto detailed specifications of message formats and protocols. In this approach, the ontology itself defines the top-level concept "Service" and three OWL-S sub-ontologies known as the "Service Profile" (SP), "Service Model" (SM), and "Service Grounding" (SG), as shown in Figure 4.

Service Profile (SP): Every instance of the service class *presents* zero or more service profiles. A service profile expresses the purposes of advertising and serves as a template for service requests, thus enabling service discovery and matchmaking in a better way. The profile consists of non-functional properties - such as references to existing categorization schemes or ontologies, service provider information, and the quality rating of the service. In addition, the specification of functionality of the service is the most important information in the service profile.

Service Model (SM): A service capability needs to be described by a service model which tells "how a service works". The essential purpose of a service model is to enable invocation, enactment, composition, monitoring, and recovery. The service model views the interactions of the service as a process. A process is not necessarily a program to be executed, but rather, a specification of ways in which a client may interact with a service.

Service Grounding (SG): The grounding of a given OWL-S service description provides a pragmatic binding between the logic-based and XMLS-based service definitions for the purpose of facilitating

Figure 4. OWL-S conceptual model

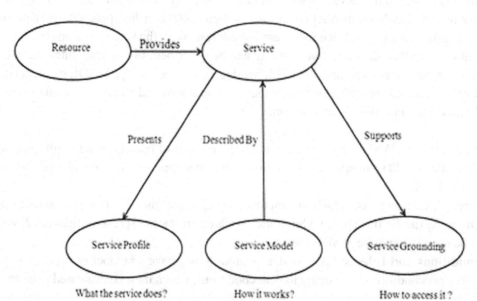

service execution. In order to map to the web service world, an OWL service can support a grounding which maps the constructs of the process model to detailed specifications of message formats, protocols, and so on. Unlike OWL-S, WSDL cannot be used to express pre-conditions or effects of executing services. Any atomic or composite OWL-S service with a grounding in WSDL is executable either by direct invocation of the (service) program that is referenced in the WSDL file, or by a BPEL engine, which processes the WSDL groundings of semantic web services.

WSMO: The third approach, Web Service Modelling Ontology (WSMO), provides ontological specifications for the description of semantic web services. WSMO has been developed by the Digital Enterprise Research Institute (DERI), a European research organization that targets the integration of the semantic web with web services. The WSMO approach is based on the Web Service Modeling Framework (WSMF) (Fensel & Bussler, 2002), a framework that provides the appropriate conceptual model for developing and describing web services and their composition.

Web service modelling ontology discovery framework (WSMO-DF) is based on the WSMO framework (Roman et al, 2005) for web service discovery. In WSMO-DF, a web service is a computational entity which is able, by invocation, to achieve a goal. A *service,* in contrast, is the actual value provided by this invocation, to achieve a goal. Therefore, there are abstract web service and concrete service descriptions. The former describes web services in terms of its abstract functionality, whereas the latter contains more detailed information about the service. For example, a metal trading merchant offers an abstract service for supplying different types of metals, and requesters provide concrete descriptions of their requirements, e.g. number of pallets of a particular metal, its dimensions, quality specification, date of requirement to a particular manufacturing plant, and so on.

Web Service Description of a Business Scenario

In an inventory management system, different materials need to be procured for manufacturing supply chain management purposes. Material attribute ontology design can be viewed from higher perspectives, such as semantic meanings or logical reasoning. However, in this chapter, the main focus is on one pragmatic perspective: as a definition of concepts (or taxonomies) in the domain and associated relations. To illustrate the functionalities of domain ontologies, a simple business scenario has been used to demonstrate the activities.

Business Scenario: Table 1 presents four web services advertisements using the complex concepts and the OWL-S service profile approach. The advertisement one (i.e. adv1) is classified in the Order class and requires a description and an account as inputs in order to return a *metal bar* that can be sent to South Africa (SA). In a similar way, the advertisement two (i.e. adv2) is classified in the Order class and requires a description and an account in order to return a *ceramics pallet* that can be sent to South Africa. The advertisement three (i.e. adv3) is also classified in the Order class and requires a *stock item* and an account in order to return a *ceramics pallet* that can be sent to UK. Finally, the advertisement four (i.e. adv4) is classified in the Search class and returns a *metal bar* based on the *stock item*. The above characteristic properties are expressed in the complex concept model by defining appropriate classes that describe services as a whole, whereas in the OWL-S service profile model each advertisement is expressed as an instance of the appropriate Profile subclass.

The scheme, as shown in Table 1, provides skeletons of instances for web services in material management of a global supply chain. In SWSDF, object-oriented structural matching techniques have been used in the domain of Structural Case-Based Reasoning (Bergmann & Schaaf, 2003), with Description

Table 1. Web service description examples using description logic syntax

Domain Ontology Axioms
$Order \sqsubseteq Costing \sqcap \exists StockItem._\top \sqcap \exists account._\top \sqcap \exists material._\top \sqcap \exists to._\top,$ $Search \sqsubseteq Resource \sqcap \exists StockItem. \sqcap \exists StockItem._\top,$ $Costing \sqsubseteq Profile, Resource \sqsubseteq Profile, MetalBar \sqsubseteq Material,$ $CeramicsPallet \sqsubseteq Material, sa : Country, uk : Country,$

Complex Concept
[1] $adv1 \equiv Order \sqcap stockitem.StockItem \sqcap \forall material.MetalBar \forall account.ProcurementOfficer \sqcap \exists to.\{sa\}$ [2] $adv2 \equiv Order \sqcap stockitem.StockItem \sqcap \forall material.CeramicsPallet \sqcap \forall account.ProcurementOfficer \sqcap \exists to.\{sa\}$ [3] $adv3 \equiv Order \sqcap \forall stockitem.StockItem \sqcap \forall material.CeramicPallets \sqcap \forall account.ProcurementOfficer \sqcap \exists to.\{uk\}$ [4] $adv4 \equiv Search \sqcap \forall stockitem.StockItem \sqcap \forall material.MetalBar$

OWL-S Service Profile Instances
[1] $adv1 : Order, < adv1, StockItem >: hasInput,$ $< adv1, ProcurementOfficer >: hasInput, < adv1, MetalBar >: hasOutput, < adv1, sa >: to$
[2] $adv2 : Order, < adv2, StockItem >: hasInput,$ $< adv2, ProcurementOfficer >: hasInput, < adv2, CeramicPallet >: hasOutput, < adv2, sa >: to$
[3] $adv3 : Order, < adv3, StockItem >: hasInput,$ $< adv3, ProcurementOfficer >: hasInput, < adv3, CeramicPallet >: hasOutput, < adv3, uk >: to$
[4] $adv4 : Search, < adv4, StockItem >: hasInput, < adv4, Metal >: hasOutput$

Logic (DL) based reasoning over Profile instances. Structural CBR (S-CBR) and ontology based semantic web service management are widely used by the research community.

Semantic Web Services and Case Based Reasoning

Semantic web service initiatives define information systems infrastructure, which enrich the human-readable data on the Web with machine-readable annotations thereby allowing the Web to evolve into the world's biggest information repository which can be accessible from anywhere, at anytime. In order to achieve these objectives, one main issue would be the *markup* of web services to make them computer-interpretable. Within this markup and semantically enhanced service descriptions, powerful tools should be facilitated across the *web service lifecycle* (Papazoglou, 2012). In particular, web services lifecycle includes automatic web service discovery to find either a web service that offers a particular service, or a web service to be used that is sufficiently similar to the current service request; and automatic web service composition and interoperation that involves the run-time service selection, composition, and interoperation of appropriate web services to complete some business activity, given a high-level abstraction of service description.

At the same time, another research community has been working on similarity based *retrieval* and *adaptation* of past solutions to match new problems: two main aspects in the working semantic web service lifecycle. Case-Based Reasoning (CBR) is thriving in the applied computing community and is propagating the idea of finding a solution to a problem based on past experience of similar problems. CBR systems are a particular type of analogical reasoning system (Liang & Konsynski, 1993). It has diverse applications in many fields, such as classification systems for credit card transactions (Reategui & Campbell, 1994) and decision support systems for business acquisitions (Pal & Palmer, 1999). Attempting to imitate human reasoning, this technique solves new problems by using or adopting solutions of previously-solved old problems. A CBR system consists of a case base, which is the set of all previously solved cases that are known to the system. The case base can be thought of as a specific kind of knowledge that contains only *cases* and their *solutions*. There are four main stages in the CBR life cycle and they are:

- **Case Representation**: A case is a contextualized piece of knowledge representing an experience. Since a problem is solved by recalling a past experience suitable for solving the new problem at hand, the case search and matching processes need to be both effective and reasonably time efficient. Moreover, since the experience from a problem just solved has to be retained in some way, these need to apply to the method of integrating a new case into the case collection, too. In this way, CBR is heavily dependent on the structure and content of its collection of cases.
- **Case Storage and Indexing**: Cases are assigned indices that express information about their content, then stored in a case library. This is an important aspect for the design of CBR systems because it reflects the conceptual view of what is represented in the case. The indexing problem is central and a much focused problem in CBR.
- **Case Retrieval**: An important step in the CBR cycle is the retrieval of previous cases that can be used to solve the target problem. Whenever a new problem needs to be solved, the case library index is searched for cases which can be a potential solution. The first phase of this search is case retrieval with the aim of finding the cases which are contextually similar to the new problem. The case retrieval task starts with a problem description, and ends when a suitable matching previous case has been found. Its subtasks are referred to as Identify Features, Search, and Select best possible cases from the system's repository.
- **Case Matchmaking and Use**: Matchmaking performs comparison between the similar cases and the new request to verify if the possible solution is the one applied to prior cases. The past solutions may be reused, directly or through adaptation, in the current situation.

CBR systems typically apply retrieval and matching algorithms to a case base of past problem-solution pairs. Many successful research and industry results are paving the way of CBR in software development and deployment practice. In recent years, *ontologies and descriptive logics* (DLs) have become systems of interest for the CBR community. Many multinational organizations (e.g. IBM, British Airways, Volkswagen, NASA, and so on) are using CBR techniques for their knowledge intensive business operations (Watson, 1997). Moreover, some real-world CBR applications are taking advantage of the Descriptive Logics (DLs) reasoning mechanisms for the processes involved in the CBR cycle. However, among the different approaches considered, all focus on the fact that the formal semantics and the capabilities of the DLs maintain terminological taxonomy. These are interesting properties to measure similarity and to manage a case base.

In SWSDF, efforts of the semantic web services lifecycle management and CBR cycle are trying to find synergies between both of them. Given a certain requirement describing the user goals, automatic web service discovery typically uses a dedicated inference mechanism in order to answer queries conforming to the logic formalism and the terms defined in the ontology.

PROPOSED SYSTEM FRAMEWORK

This section briefly presents the overall architecture of the SWSDF system and illustrates the interplay of the different components. The computational framework of SWSDF is shown in Figure 4. It uses a relational similarity assessment measure between implicitly stated concepts. The proposed framework accepts the service consumer request which consists of the requirements of a new service (e.g. input, output, precondition, and so on). Next, the user requirement information is parsed for further processing; and finally semantically ranked web services are presented to the consumer. The dynamics of SWSDF are as follows:

- Initially, the service repository is populated with semantically enriched web service descriptions for specific application areas within a supply chain.
- The service requester inputs the service requirements using SWSDF's interface.
- The service matchmaking module takes the retrieved cases and the annotation of the problem description from the semantic description generator module (within the system framework), runs them through a matchmaking algorithm and forwards the closest match web service to the requester.

The ontologically enhanced web service descriptions are manually encoded in the SWSDF service repository. In the processing of ontological concept matching, when dealing with similarity between concepts, it not only considers inheritance (i.e. the relationship between supper-class and subclass) relations, but also considers the distance relationship between concepts. In SWSDF, on the basis of the comprehensive consideration of the inheritance relations and semantic distance between concepts, a concept similarity matching method based on semantic distance has been used. The SWSDF uses structural case-based reasoning (S-CBR) for services and the relevant ontological concepts storage purpose; and it uses a rule-based reasoning (RBR) for service similarity assessment. The algorithm, as shown in Figure 5, is used to discover semantic web services advertised within SWSDF.

Model of Concept Similarity for SWSDF

This section describes the method for measuring the degree of similarity of two OWL concepts. This measure will then be used in the next section for determining the degree of functional similarity of two services.

Definition 1 (*Concept Similarity*): A similarity $\sigma: C \times C \rightarrow [0,1]$ is a function from a pair of concepts to a real number between zero and one expressing the degree of similarity between two concepts such that:

(1) $\forall x \in C, \ \sigma(x,x) = 1$

(2) $\forall x, y \in C, \ \sigma(x,y) = \sigma(y,x)$

(3) $\forall x, y, z: \ if \ SimDistance \ (x,y) > SimDistance(x,z), \ then \ \sigma(x,y) < \sigma(x,z)$

Figure 5. Diagrammatic representation of the SWSDF

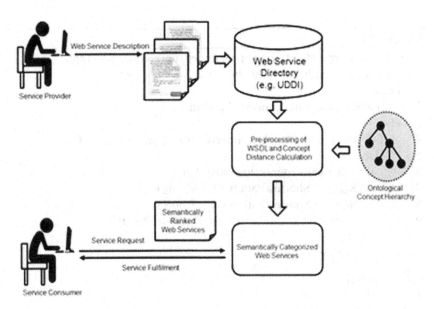

The above properties provide the range of semantic similarity function $\sigma(x,x)$. For exactly similar concepts the similarity is $\sigma(x,x)=1$; and when two concepts have nothing in common, their similarity is $\sigma(x,y)=0$. In this way, the output of similarity function should be in closed interval [0,1] and it is a reflexive relation. In SWSDF, the following semantic similarity function has been used for computation purposes:

$$f_{similarity} = p^{SimDistance+1}$$

In the above similarity function, the value of $p(0<p\leq1)$ and *SimDistance* decide the impact degree of semantic distance to semantic similarity. In SWSDF, the similarity between two ontological concepts C_i and C_j can be expressed by a number S_{ij} which can be expressed by the semantic distance among any two concepts. Given two concepts C_i and C_j, the SWSDF calculates the distance as weight allocation function as follows:

$$\omega[sub(C_i andC_j)] = 1 + \frac{1}{k^{depth\ (C_j)}}$$

where depth (C_j) represents the depth of concept (C_j) from the root concept to node C_j in ontology hierarchy, and k is a predefined factor larger than 1 showing the rate at which the weight values decrease along the ontology hierarchy.

The above function has got two important properties: (1) the semantic differences between higher concepts are more in comparison to lower level concepts, and (2) the distance between sibling concepts is

Table 1. Similarity measure of two concepts (C_1, C_2)

Algorithm I

input: two concepts (C_1, C_2), the root node (root), concepts graph (G)
output: semantic similarity value between two concepts
1: begin
2: if C_1 and C_2 are same concept then $Sim_d = 0$
3: else
4:    if C_1 and C_2 are directly connected then $Sim_d = w(C_1, C_2)$
5:    else
6:       if idirect path connection exist then
7:          $S_{path01} = ShortestPath(G, C_1, Root_N)$
8:          $S_{path02} = ShortestPath(G, C_2, Root_N)$
9:          $Sim_d = w(S_{path01}) + w(S_{path02}) - 2*w(CSPath]$
10:      end if
11:         $\partial(C_1, C_2) = \dfrac{1}{deg \cdot Sim_d + 1}$
12:   end if
13: end if
14: return ∂
15: end

---

greater than the distance between parent and child concepts. In particular, the depth of topmost concept is considered be zero, and the lower level other concepts are related to their path length to root concept node.

The algorithm, as shown in Figure 5, takes two concepts as input and computes a semantic similarity as output based on the ALGORITHM1.

The part of the type of hierarchy in the matchmaker ontology and all instances used in this example are shown in Figure 6. In the experimental comparison, semantic similarity among Copper, Glass, Metal, Steel and Material are considered.

In Table 2 tabulates the results of synonymy similarity (Giunchiglia et al, 2004), Table 3 tabulates the results of Jian and Conrath similarity (Jiang & Conrath, 1997) results, Table 4 tabulates the results of path similarity (Varelas et al, 2005), and Table 6 tabulates the results of algorithm used in SWSDF – concept similarity measure based on semantic distance.

The Results of Various Similarity Measures

As shown in Tables 3-5, the synonymy similarity measure can only find similarity between the same concepts, and Jian and Conrath' similarity measure is better than the synonymy similarity measure. The path similarity measure and SWSDF's used method are better than the above two methods. The path similarity measure can find the semantic similarity between concepts, but the similarity score is low. The SWSDF's similarity method can also get the semantic similarity between concepts, and the similarity score is high.

Figure 6. The hierarchical concept relationships

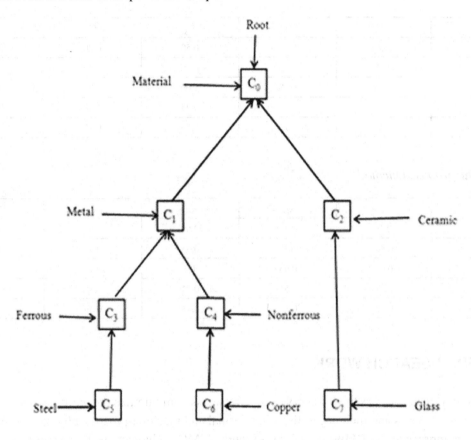

Table 2. Synonymy similarity

	C_1	C_2	C_3	C_4	C_5
C_1	1.00	0.00	0.00	0.00	0.00
C_2	0.00	1.00	0.00	0.00	0.00
C_3	0.00	0.00	1.00	0.00	0.00
C_4	0.00	0.00	0.00	1.00	0.00
C_5	0.00	0.00	0.00	0.00	1.00

Table 3. Jian and Conrath similarity

	C_1	C_2	C_3	C_4	C_5
C_1	1.00	0.60	0.41	0.97	0.52
C_2	0.42	1.00	0.81	0.60	0.36
C_3	0.97	0.81	1.00	0.68	0.44
C_4	0.60	0.60	0.68	1.00	0.53
C_5	0.52	0.36	0.44	0.53	1.00

Table 4. Path similarity

	C_1	C_2	C_3	C_4	C_5
C_1	1.00	0.25	0.50	0.20	0.20
C_2	0.25	1.00	0.50	0.33	0.16
C_3	0.50	0.50	1.00	0.25	0.16
C_4	0.20	0.33	0.25	1.00	0.20
C_5	0.20	0.16	0.16	0.20	1.00

Table 5. The proposed method

	C_1	C_2	C_3	C_4	C_5
C_1	1.0	0.48	0.65	0.51	0.38
C_2	0.48	1.0	0.65	0.51	0.38
C_3	0.65	0.65	1.0	0.71	0.48
C_4	0.51	0.51	0.71	1.0	0.59
C_5	0.38	0.38	0.48	0.59	1.0

RELATED RESEARCH WORK

The semantic web approaches to web services give business communities the ability to describe the semantics of web services and their capabilities in a formal and machine-processable manner. A majority of the current approaches (e.g. OWL-S, WSDL-S, and WSMO) enhancing web services using semantic tagged descriptions. However, these approaches have several limitations. First, it is impractical to expect all new services to have semantic tagged descriptions. Second, descriptions of the vast majority of existing web services are specified using WSDL and do not have associated semantics. Also, from the service requestor's perspective, the requestor may not be aware of all the knowledge that constitutes the domain. Specifically, the service requestor may not be aware of all the terms related to the service request. As a result, many services relevant to the request may not be considered in the service discovery process. Akkiraju and his research group (Akkiraju et al, 2005), conjectured an attempt to design a system which can create semantic web services is by mapping concepts in a web service description (WSDL specification) to ontological concepts. This approach is known as WSDL-S. The idea of establishing mappings between service, task, or activity description and its enrichment using domain specific ontological concepts was first introduced by Cardoso (Cardoso & Sheth, 2003). Martin has also concentrated on enhancement of service descriptions, in work with other researchers on OWL-S (Martin et al, 2007), which is an important attempt to use lightweight web service description based on inputs, outputs and non-functional properties, in order to find an initial set of candidate web services for a request. Fensel has also concentrated on service enrichment and modelling, in work with Bussler on the system WSMF (Fensel & Bussler, 2002), a framework that provides the appropriate conceptual model for developing and describing web services and their composition.

Web service modelling ontology discovery framework (WSMO-DF), also contributed to semantic enrichment of web services, and is based on the WSMO framework (Roman et al, 2005) for web service discovery. In the semantic web service paradigm, discovery is performed over semantic descriptions of web services. WSMO-DF and OWL-S SP (service profile) are two frameworks that are generally used for service description purposes.

While these are a few main styles of service enrichment in semantic web service descriptions, they are by no means the only research conducted in the recent past. Later work by Pengwei and his colleagues on their semantic enhancement web service research (Wang et al, 2008) has used WSMO-DF for rich web service representation purposes. In contrast to Pengwei and his research partners (Weang et al, 2008) work, SWSDF follows the Service Profile (SP) model and uses structural ontology information.

In IRS-III (Domingue et al, 2008), an extended approach of the WSMO conceptual model is used, where OCML (Options Configuration Modeling Language) has provided internal description of service and an appropriate OCML reasoner. In contrast to SWSDF, IRS-III follows an enhanced WSMO model and a frame-based rule language for representing domain ontologies.

Li and his colleagues advocated the use of a mechanism based on the Rough sets theory to discover grid services (Li et al, 2008). The implemented software system, known as ROSSE, builds on the Rough sets theory to dynamically reduce uncertain properties when matching grid services. The evaluation results have shown that ROSSE significantly improves the precision and recall of services compared with keyword-based service matching techniques and OWL-S matching. The novelty of ROSSE is in its capability to deal with uncertain properties, that is, properties that are explicitly used by one advertisement but do not appear in another service of the same category. In SWSDF, only the common properties of an advertisement have been used.

Li and Horrocks have distinguished a number of things in a service matchmaking research porotype (Li & Horrocks, 2003), which uses a DL reasoner to match service advertisements and requests based on ontology enhanced service descriptions. In this particular project, web service descriptions are defined as Complex Concepts (CCs) in OWL and the matchmaking mechanism examines the subsumption relationships. FC-MATCH research project (Bianchini et al, 2006) uses a similar type of approach, performing text similarity matching using WordNet. In some research (Grimm et al., 2006), a software framework has been used to annotate web services using DLs. Similar to SWSDF, it follows the abstract web service model.

In the DAML-S/UDDI matchmaker (Sycara et al, 2003), OWL-S SP advertisements and requests refers to DAML concepts and the matching process that performs inferences on the subsumption hierarchy. It uses a different definition of web service filters from SWSDF and it does not consider profile taxonomies, roles or group filtering.

LARKS (Sycara et al, 2002) uses both syntactic and semantic matching. It uses five matchmaking filters, namely context matching, profile comparison, similarity matching, signature matching and constant matching. LARKS uses its own capability description and DL language in contrast to the SWSDF approach.

OWLS-MX (Klusch et al, 2008) utilizes both logic-based reasoning and content-based IR techniques for web services in OWL-S. It cannot handle profile taxonomies and it follows the static SP paradigm, unable to use dynamic ontology roles. iMatcher2 (Kiefer & Bernstein, 2008) follows the OWLS-MX approach, also applying learning algorithms in order to predict similarities. Like OWLS-MX, it uses a DL reasoner in order to unfold the annotation concepts, creating a vector on which the IR techniques are applied. iMatcher2 does not follow a standard matchmaking algorithm, which is defined through an iSPARQL strategy. WSMO-MX (Kaufer & Klusch, 2006) is a hybrid approach based on rich WSMO service descriptions.

In the DAML-S/UDDI matchmaker (Sycara et al, 2003), OWL-S SP advertisements and requests refers to DAML concepts and the matching process performs inferences on the subsumption hierarchy. It uses a different definition of web service filters from SWSDF and it does not consider profile taxonomies, roles or group filtering.

LARKS (Sycara et al, 2002) use both syntactic and semantic matching. It uses five matchmaking filters, namely context matching, profile comparison, similarity matching, signature matching and constant matching. LARKS uses its own capability description and DL language in contrast to the SWSDF approach.

In a hybrid semantic web service matchmaker for OWL-S services, known as OWLS-MX (Klusch et al, 2008), researchers have used both logic-based reasoning and content-based information retrieval techniques. Experimental evaluation results show strong justification in favor of the proposition that the performance of logic-based matchmaking can be considerably improved by incorporating non-logic based information retrieval techniques into the matchmaking algorithms. However, OWLS-MX cannot handle profile taxonomies and it follows the static SP paradigm, unable to use dynamic ontology roles. iMatcher2 (Kiefer & Bernstein, 2008) follows the OWLS-MX approach, applying also learning algorithms in order to predict similarities. Like OWLS-MX, it uses a DL reasoner in order to unfold the annotation concepts, creating a vector on which the IR techniques are applied. iMatcher2 does not follow a standard matchmaking algorithm, which is defined through an iSPARQL strategy. WSMO-MX (Kaufer & Klusch, 2006) is a hybrid approach based on rich WSMO service descriptions.

There are plenty of other approaches that are based on inputs/outputs, for example (Cardoso, 2006) (Pathak et al, 2005) (Skoutas et al, 2007). These approaches retrieve directly the input/output annotations and any taxonomical knowledge from special properties, such as service categorization. Moreover, they do not consider roles, using static annotation concepts, and do not apply further filtering on results (group filtering). METEOR-S (Verma et al, 2005) follows the WSDL-S approach, where WSDL constructs point to ontology concepts.

Thakker, Osman and Al-Dabass have reported their research in which the web service execution experiences are modeled as cases that represent the web service properties in a specific area described using OWL semantic description (Osman et al, 2006a) (Osman et al, 2006b). In this research, the service repository administrator performs the storing of service descriptions using ontology enhanced semantics for case representation. This representation is used to semantically annotate the users' queries looking for adequate services as well as the web service execution experiences in the given area. The proposed system uses frame structures to model its cases. These structures are not generalized and depend heavily on the application domain so that the constituent elements of these structures more precisely 'slots' differ from one application to another.

Lamjmi and co-researchers have proposed the WeSCo_CBR approach based mainly on ontologies and case-based reasoning meant for the web service composition (Lajmi et al, 2006a) (Lajmi et al, 2006b). They have created an ontology that describes various features of a web service using OWL representation formalism in order to bring a semi-automatic guidance for the user. In order to facilitate the processing, they proceed by transforming the user's query into an ontological formulation combining a set of ontology concepts. For each received new query, the reuse process consists on retrieving similar prior stored cases and eventually evaluating and storing the new case. In WeSCo_CBR, a case comprises the following three elements: a problem, a solution and an evaluation. The discovery of web service meeting the client's needs is accomplished by using similarity measures designed in accordance with the formalization of the problem. The most relevant case is usually determined according to its similarity with the new problem case.

In order to improve the web service discovery, Wan and Cao (Wang & Cao, 2007) have introduced an additional case-based reasoning component called CBR/OWL-S Matching Engine (Wang & Cao, 2007). In order to find out the desired web service, this matching engine uses ontologies for semantic similarity measure.

The SWSDF work has been motivated by object-oriented structural matching techniques that are used in the domain of Structural Case-Based Reasoning (SCBR) (Bergman & Schaaf, 2003), with the use of a DL reasoner to handle semantic web service descriptions and to apply an extended matchmaking algorithm. In addition, the method of allocating the weight value to concept node has been used for similarity assessment purposes.

CONCLUSION

This chapter reviews some of the business and technology challenges that companies are facing today in supply chain information sharing between business partners, and describes how a number of these difficulties could be overcome with the use of semantic web service. However, in order for semantic web service to be adopted within a global supply chain network there must be tools, which will help to automate heterogeneous data sources existing in this networked enterprise. In this chapter, a supply chain information sharing architecture between business partners is described using the semantic web service framework. The architecture is based on a hybrid knowledge-based service matchmaking framework, which uses Structural Case-Based Reasoning (S-CBR) and Rule-Based Reasoning (RBR). It uses ontology enhanced web service descriptions; object-oriented S-CBR knowledge representation, description logic (DL) for service formalization, and an algorithm to measure ontological concept similarity based on semantic distance. This algorithm considers not only the inheritance relation between concepts, but also the level of concepts in the ontology hierarchy. An experimental evaluation of the proposed algorithm is presented. In this architecture, ontological concepts play an important role in the development of the semantic web as a means for defining shared terms in web resources in SCM automation. Today, business partners within global supply chains are generating huge amounts of raw-data; and they are collecting some of this data for business intelligence purposes. This data is commonly referred to as 'big data' – because of its *volume*, the *velocity* with which it arrives in global supply chain environments, and the *variety* of forms it takes. Big data is ushering in a new era of corporate business intelligence promise; but one of main bottlenecks is how to capture this raw-data and analyze it to generate meaningful information. In the future, this research will extend the current concept-based ontological reasoning framework and investigate additional mapping techniques in order to express service descriptions in a much more enhanced form. This will allow a richer service discovery for globalized supply chain world. Particularly, one of the challenging tasks is how to handle *big data* in global supply chain environments, and how to use these untapped corporate *cyber-physical* resources to come up with better service provisions for its stakeholders. Cyber-physical systems enable new types of interconnected information service provisions by connecting networked systems with services of the automated system infrastructure. This in turn enables interaction with extended capabilities of physical business world through computation, communication and control. This infrastructure is going to be the source of next generation big data driven global supply chain information systems integration and coordination of global power houses.

REFERENCES

Akkiraju, R., Farrell, J., Miller, J., Nagarajan, M., Schmidt, M., Sheth, A., & Verma, K. (2005). *Web Service Semantics - WSDL-S*. A joint UGA-IBM Technical Note, version 1.0. http://lsdis.cs.uga.edu/projects/METEOR-S/WSDL-S

Antoniou, G., & Harmelen, F. V. (2008). *A Semantic Web Primer*. The MIT Press.

Baader, F., & Nutt, W. (2003). *Basic Description Logics, The description logic handbook*. Cambridge University Press.

Bergmann, R., & Schaaf, M. (2003). Structural Case-Based Reasoning and Ontology-Based Knowledge Management: A Perfect Match? *Journal of Universal Computer Science, UCS, 9*(7), 608–626.

Berners-Lee, T., Hendler, J., & Lassila, O. (2001). The Semantic Web. *Scientific American, 284*(May), 34–43. doi:10.1038/scientificamerican0501-34 PMID:11323639

Bianchini, D., Antonellis, V. A., Melchiori, M., & Salvi, D. (2006). Semantic Enriched Service Discovery. *International Conference in Data Engineering Workshop,* 38.

Cai, M. Zhang, W. Y., Zhang, K. & Li, S. T. (2010). SWMRD: A Semantic Web-based manufacturing resource discovery system for cross-enterprise collaboration. *International Journal of Production Research, 48*(120), 3445-3460.

Cardoso, J. (2006). Discovering Semantic Web Services with and without a Common Ontology Commitment. *IEEE Service Computing Workshop*, 183-190.

Cardoso, J., & Sheth, A. (2003). Semantic e-Workflow Composition. *Journal of Intelligent Information Systems, 21*(3), 191–225. doi:10.1023/A:1025542915514

Copacino, W., & Anderson, D. (2003). Connecting with the Bottom Line: A Global Study of Supply Chain Leadership and its Contribution to the High Performance Business. *Accenture,* 1.

Domingue, J., Cabral, L., Galizia, S., Tanasescu, V., Gugliotta, A., Norton, B., & Pedrinaci, C. (2008). IRS-III: A Broker-based Approach to Semantic Web Service. *Journal of Web Semantics, 6*(2), 109–132. doi:10.1016/j.websem.2008.01.001

Fensel, D., & Bussler, C. (2002). The Web Service Modeling Framework WSMF. *Electronic Commerce Research and Applications, 1*(2), 113–137. doi:10.1016/S1567-4223(02)00015-7

Fugate, B., Sahin, F., & Mentzer, J. T. (2006). Supply Chain Management Coordination Mechanisms. *Journal of Business Logistics, 27*(2), 129–161. doi:10.1002/j.2158-1592.2006.tb00220.x

Ganeshan, R., & Harrison, T. P. (1995). *An introduction to supply chain management*. Supply Chain Management, Version 1. Available from http://silmaril.smeal.psu.edu/misc/supply_chain_ intro.html

Giunchiglia, F., Shvaiko, P., & Yatskevich, M. (2004). S-Match: an algorithm and an implementation of semantic matching. *Proceedings of 1st European Semantic Web Symposium (ESWS),* 3053, 61-75. 10.1007/978-3-540-25956-5_5

Grimm, S., Monk, B., & Preist, C. (2006). Matching Semantic Service Descriptions with Local Closed-World Reasoning. *European Semantic Web Conference*, 575-589. 10.1007/11762256_42

Gruber, T. R. (1993). *A Translation Approach to Portable Ontology Specifications.* Stanford University, Computer Science Department, Knowledge Systems Laboratory, Technical Report KSL 92-71.

Guarino, N., & Giaretta, P. (1995). *Ontologies and Knowledge Base: Towards a Terminological Classification Toward Very Large Knowledge Base: Knowledge Building and Knowledge Sharing.* IOS Press.

Jiang, J. J., & Conrath, D. W. (1997). Semantic Similarity Based on Corpus Statistics and Lexical Taxonomy. *Proceedings of International Conference Research on Computational Lingustics.*

Kalakota, R., & Whiston, A. (1997). *Electronic commerce: a manager's guide.* Addison Wesley.

Kaufer, F., & Klusch, M. (2006). WSMO-MX: A Logic Programming Based Hybrid Service Matchmaker. *European Conference on Web Services*, 161-170. 10.1109/ECOWS.2006.39

Kiefer, C., & Bernstein, A. (2008). The Creation and Evaluation of iSPARQL Strategies for Matchmaking. *European Semantic Web Conference*, 463-477. 10.1007/978-3-540-68234-9_35

Klusch, M., Fries, B., & Sycara, K. (2008). OWLS-MX: A Hybrid Semantic Web Service Matchmaker for OWL-S Services. *Journal of Web Semantics.*

Lajmi, S., Ghedira, C., & Ghedira, K. (2006a). How to apply CBR method in web service composition. *Second International Conference on Signal-Image Technology and Internet Based Systems (SITI'2006).* Springer Verlag.

Lajmi, S., Ghedira, C., Ghedira, K., & Benslimane, D. (2006b). Web_CBR: How to compose web service via case based reasoning. *IEEE International Symposium on Service-Oriented Applications, Integration and Collaboration held with the IEEE International Conference on eBusiness Engineering (ICEBE 2006).*

Laliwala, Z., Khosla, R., Majumdar, P., & Chaudhary, S. (2006). Semantic and Rule Based Event-Driven Dynamic Web Service Composition for Automation of Business Processes. *Proceedings of the IEEE Service Computing Workshop (SCW06).*

Lambert, D. M., & Cooper, M. C. (2000). Issues in Supply Chain Management. *Industrial Marketing Management*, 29(1), 65–83. doi:10.1016/S0019-8501(99)00113-3

Li, J., Sikora, R., Shaw, M. J., & Woo Tan, G. A. (2006). Strategic analysis of inter-organizational information sharing. *Decision Support Systems*, 42(1), 251–266. doi:10.1016/j.dss.2004.12.003

Li, L., & Horrocks, I. (2003). A Software Framework for Matchmaking Based on Semantic Web Technology. *International Conference in World Wide Web*, 331-339. 10.1145/775152.775199

Li, M., Yu, B., Rana, O. F., & Wang, Z. (2008). Grid Service Discovery with Rough Sets. *IEEE Transactions on Knowledge and Data Engineering*, 20(6), 851–862. doi:10.1109/TKDE.2007.190744

Li, S. H. (2002). *An Integrated Model for Supply Chain Management Practice, Performance and Competitive Advantage* [PhD Dissertation]. University of Toledo, Toledo, OH.

Liang, T., & Konsynski, B. R. (1993). Modeling by analogy: Use of analogical reasoning in model management systems. *Decision Support Systems, 9*(1), 113–125. doi:10.1016/0167-9236(93)90026-Y

Martin, D., Burstein, M., Mcdermott, D., Mcilraith, S., Paolucci, M., Sycara, K., Mcguinness, D. L., Sirin, E., & Srinivasan, N. (2007). Bringing Semantics to Web Services with OWL-S. *World Wide Web (Bussum), 10*(3), 243–277. doi:10.1007/s11280-007-0033-x

Martin, D., Paolucci, M., McIlraith, S., Burstein, M., McDermott, D., McGunness, D., Barsia, B., Payne, T., Sabou, M., Solanki, M., Srinivasan, N., & Sycara, K. *(2004).* Bringing Semantics to Web Services: The OWL-S Approach, *Proceeding of First International Workshop Semantic Web Services and Web Process Composition.*

Matskin, M., Maigre, R., & Tyugu, E. (2007). Computational logical semantics for business process language. *Proceedings of second international conference on Internet and Web applications and services (ICIW 2007),* 526-531.

McIlraith, S., & Martin, D. (2003). Bringing Semantics to Web Services. *IEEE Intelligent Systems, 18*(1), 90–93. doi:10.1109/MIS.2003.1179199

OASIS. (2004). *Introduction to UDDI: Important Features and Functional Concepts.* Organization for the Advancement of Structured Information Standards.

OMG. (2009). *Business Process Model and Notation.* http://www.omg.org/spec/BPMN/1.2/(2009)

Osman, T., Thakker, D., & Al-Dabass, D. (2006a). *Semantic-Driven Matching of Web services using Case-Based Reasoning.* In The Fourth IEEE International Conference on Web Services (ICWS 2006), Chicago, USA.

Osman, T., Thakker, D., & Al-Dabass, D. (2006b). S-CBR: Semantic Case Based Reasoner for Web services discovery and matchmaking. *20th European Conference on Modeling and Simulation (ECMS2006),* 723-729.

Pal, K., & Karakostas, B. (2014). A Multi Agent-based Service Framework for supply Chain Management. *Procedia Computer Science, 32,* 53-60.

Pal, K., & Palmer, O. (2000). A decision-support systems for business acquisition. *Decision Support Systems, 27*(4), 411–429. doi:10.1016/S0167-9236(99)00083-4

Pal, K. (2018). Ontology-Based Web Service Architecture for Retail Supply Chain Management, in the 8th International Conference on Ambient Systems, Networks, and Technologies (ANT 2018), Procedia Computer Science 985 - 990, May 8 - May 11, Porto, Portugal.

Pal, K. (2019). Algorithmic Solutions for RFID Tag Anti-Collision Problem in Supply Chain Management, in the 9th International Symposium on Frontiers in Ambient and Mobile Systems (FAMS 19), Procedia Computer Science, 929-934, April 29 - May 2, 2019, Leuven, Belgium.

Papazoglou, M. (2012). *Web Services and SOA: Principles and Technology.* Pearson.

Pathak, J., Koul, N., Caragea, D., & Honavar, V. G. (2005). A Framework for Semantic Web Services Discovery. *ACM International Workshop on Web Information and Data Management*, 45-50. 10.1145/1097047.1097057

Patil, A., Oundhaka, S., Sheth, A., & Verma, K. (2004). METEOR-S Web service Annotation Framework. *Proceedings of the Thirteenth International World Wide Web Conference*, 553-562.

Reategui, E. B., & Campbell, J. A. (1995). A Classification System for Credit Card Transactions. *Advances in Case-Based Reasoning: Second European Workshop (EWCBR-94)*, 280-291. 10.1007/3-540-60364-6_43

Roman, D., Keller, U., Lausen, H., de Bruijn, J., Lara, R., Stollberg, M., Polleres, A., Feier, C., Bussler, C., & Fensel, D. (2005). Web service modeling ontology. *Applied Ontology, 1*(1), 77–106.

Roman, D., Kopecky, J., Vitvar, T., Domingue, J., & Fensel, D. (2015). WSMO-Lite and hRESTS: Lightweight semantic annotations for Web services and RESTful APIs. *Journal of Web Semantics, 31*, 39–58. doi:10.1016/j.websem.2014.11.006

Shingo, S. (1988). *Non-Stock Production*. Productivity Press.

Skoutas, D., Simitsis, A., & Sellis, T. (2007). A Ranking Mechanism for Semantic Web Service Discovery. *IEEE Congress on Services*, 41-48.

Studer, R., Benjamins, V. R., & Fensel, D. (1998). Knowledge engineering: Principles and methods. *Data & Knowledge Engineering, 25*(1-2), 161–197. doi:10.1016/S0169-023X(97)00056-6

Sycara, K., Widoff, S., Klusch, M., & Lu, J. (2002). LARKS: Dynamic Matching Among Heterogeneous Software Agents in Cyberspace. *Autonomous Agents and Multi-Agent Systems, 5*(2), 173–203. doi:10.1023/A:1014897210525

Sycara, K. P., Paolucci, M., Ankolekar, A., & Srinivasan, N. (2003). Automated Discovery, Interaction and Computation of Semanticmweb Services. *Journal of Web Semantics, 1*(1), 27–46. doi:10.1016/j.websem.2003.07.002

Varelas, G., Voutsakis, E., Raftopoulou, P., Petrakis, E. G. M., & Milios, E. (2005). Semantic Similarity methods in WordNet and their application to information retrieval on the Web. *Proceedings of the 7th annual ACM international workshop on web information and data management*. 10.1145/1097047.1097051

Verma, K., Sivashanmugam, K., Sheth, A., Patil, A., Oundhakar, S., & Miller, J. (2005). METEOR-S WSDI: A Scalable P2P Infrastructure of Registries for Semantic Publication and Discovery of Web Services. *Information Technology and Management, 6*(1), 17–39. doi:10.1007/s10799-004-7773-4

Vrijhoef, R., & Koskela, L. (1999). Role of supply chain management in construction. *Proceedings of the Seventh Annual Conference of the International Group for Lean Construction*, 133-146.

Wang, L., & Cao, J. (2007). Web Services Semantic Searching enhanced by Case Based Reasoning. *18th International Workshop on Database and Expert Systems Applications*.

Wang, P., Jin, Z., Liu, L., & Cai, G. (2008). Building Toward Capability Specifications of Web Services Based on an Environment Ontology. *IEEE Transactions on Knowledge and Data Engineering, 20*(4), 547–561. doi:10.1109/TKDE.2007.190719

Watson, I. (1997). *Applying Case-Based Reasoning: Techniques for Enterprise Systems.* Morgan Kaufman.

Wooldridge, M., & Jennings, N. (1995). Intelligent Agents: Theory and Practice. *The Knowledge Engineering Review, 10*(2), 115–152. doi:10.1017/S0269888900008122

WSDL-S. (2005). https://www.w3.org/Submission/WSDL-S/

Zhang, W. Y., Cai, M., Qiu, J., & Yin, J. W. (2009). Managing distributed manufacturing knowledge through multi-perspective modelling for Semantic Web applications. *International Journal of Production Research, 47*(23), 6525–6542. doi:10.1080/00207540802311114

Chapter 3
Traffic:
An Intelligent System for Detecting Traffic Events Based on Ontologies

Hayder Luis Endo Pérez
Universidad Central "Marta Abreu" de Las Villas, Cuba

Amed Abel Leiva Mederos
Universidad Central "Marta Abreu" de Las Villas, Cuba

José Antonio Senso-Ruíz
University of Granada, Spain

Ghislain Auguste Atemezing
https://orcid.org/0000-0003-1562-6922
Mondeca, France

Daniel Gálvez Lio
https://orcid.org/0000-0002-9245-0214
Universidad Central "Marta Abreu" de Las Villas, Cuba

Jose Luis Sánchez-Chávez
Universidad Central " Marta Abreu" de Las Villas, Cuba

Alfredo Simón Cueva
Universidad Tecnologica de la Habana, Cuba

ABSTRACT

Traffic event detection is a multidisciplinary field that includes information retrieval, automatic, big data, etc. The absence of tools that integrate the detection of traffic events with the annotation, grouping, and location of events on transport routes led to the conception and implementation of this intelligent system based on ontologies for the management of streams, which facilitates the grouping of traffic data. As a result of the application of the system, it was possible to identify the speed events of a road in real-time and validate its efficiency through clustering algorithms.

INTRODUCTION

Prediction of traffic events has been one of the research fields in the development of smart cities. Sensors are one of the most important data sources available for these purposes. Thanks to the semantic

DOI: 10.4018/979-8-3693-1487-6.ch003

web and Internet *of Things* (IoT) applications, sensor data can be published and reused, interpreted and integrated into public service applications. The Open Geospatial Consortium (OGC) provides standards for the management of sensor networks and provides a means to annotate their observations. However, these standards are not integrated or aligned with the W3C (*World Wide Web Consortium),* Semantic Web and linked data technologies Linked Data (2005). With the development of the IoT (Trialog, 2021), smart cities and buildings, the data produced by sensors are stored and increasingly used by citizens. With this data, multiple information can be recovered, the detection of traffic events has become a multidisciplinary field that includes information recovery, automatic, big data, etc. Although the current conception of traffic event detection has a strategic nature, it has not yet had a parallel development to the possibilities offered for storing information in RDF. If we truly want to move towards development with this strategic approach, it will be necessary to first develop tools that automatically assist users in detecting these events. These reasons alone determine the need to develop tools that allow applications to be made for end users in this area.

Currently, methods and techniques have been developed for each of the areas of the semantic web in isolation and there are few tools that integrate them for the development of research in this field. For this reason, a computational solution is required that allows, at least, the integration of semantic web techniques in the detection of traffic events. Based on the above, the general objective of this work is established to develop a tool that facilitates the detection of traffic events and that integrates elements of Artificial Intelligence and the Semantic Web (Villazon et al, 2020) in its conception.

DEVELOPMENT

Next, the architecture of the Traffic system is introduced, describing its components, the communication between these components and with other domain definitions and finally, how to semantically query the annotated data using the SPARQL language will be exemplified.

Ontologies

An ontology refers to a document or file that formally defines the relationships between terms. A typical ontology is composed of:

- A taxonomy that defines all classes of objects and the relationships established between them; For example: an address can be defined as a type of location.

- A set of inference rules that allows applications to make decisions based on the provided classes, without the need to understand the provided information. For example, an ontology can express the following rule: if a city code is associated with a state code, and an address uses that city code, then that address code has the associated state code.

Then ontologies allow establishing semantic relationships between the elements of their taxonomy and also making logical deductions by manipulating that information combined with the set of predetermined rules and in this way inferring logical conclusions about the data.

There are ontologies for different areas, particularly in the IoT area, the Time, SSN, SOSA (2018) ontologies (Janowicz, Krzysztof et al., 2021) among others are commonly used (Ortiz et al, 2006) . For the development of the Traffic system, the management of a new ontology called Traffic Store [1]was conceived that contains the attributes of IoTStream and geographical ontologies that allow capturing data (latitude, longitude, and altitude) in vehicles.

In Traffic Store, the StreamObservations class is used to handle historical observations . Since the streams are generated by sensors, the SOSA ontology was used. Through the properties of the objects defined in IoT -Lite, the concepts qu:QuantityKind and qu:Unit of the QU ontology are linked. The IoT -Lite class provides the IoTService subclass that contains fields related to the address of a Sparql service . For data analysis and quality of knowledge it is very important to apply measurements that can be applied when necessary. For this reason, the ontology is used for the quality of information (QoI) that provides the system with subclasses oriented to the quality of the data, they are qoi:Timeliness and qoi:Completeness . Table 1 offers the list of namespaces for the linked ontologies and their prefixes.

TRAFFIC SYSTEM COMPONENTS

Figure 2 shows the main components of the Traffic system, numbered 1 to 6 with green circles. Component number 1, called Producer, is responsible for recording the streams and publishing the observations generated by the sensors. Additionally, this component stores proprietary information about the sensors and streams that are still open. In this implementation variant, it has been decided to obtain the information related to the sensors and their observations from third sources and not from physical sensors. However, the implementation can be abstracted from such situations and is capable of, with minimal changes, moving from one to the other. For the system presented, the API was chosen [2]. The sensors offered by this service are located in lanes of different roads in the city of Brussels in Belgium and, for each sensor, its observations are offered at variable intervals of 1, 5, 15 and 60 minutes. Once service 1 has started, a first request to the aforementioned API is managed and the necessary information about the sensors is obtained to then register it in component 6 and thus enrich the streams.

This service is also responsible for associating each stream with its corresponding sensor and keeping the stream updated with the observations produced by its sensors. The API offers three data

Table 1. System namespaces

Prefix	Namespace
iot-lite	http://purl.oclc.org/NET/UNIS/fiware/iot-lite#
iot-stream	http://purl.org/iot/ontology/iot-stream#
owl	http://www.w3.org/2002/07/owl#
qoi	https://w3id.org/iot/qoi#
what	http://purl.oclc.org/NET/ssnx/qu/qu#
rdf	http://www.w3.org/1999/02/22-rdf-syntax-ns#
rdfs	http://www.w3.org/2000/01/rdf-schema#
sosa	http://www.w3.org/ns/sosa/
wgs84_pos	http://www.w3.org/2003/01/geo/wgs84_pos#
xml	http://www.w3.org/XML/1998/namespace
xsd	http://www.w3.org/2001/XMLSchema#
traff	http://sem.uclv.cu/def/trafficstore#

Figure 1. Traffic system components

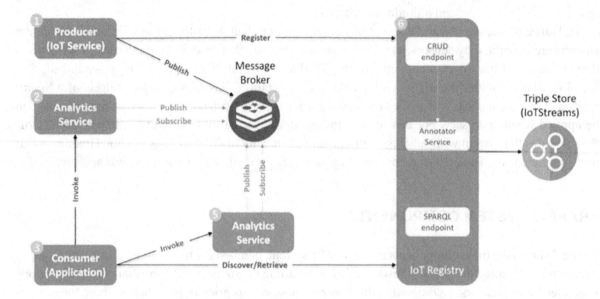

in real time: number of cars, average speed and percentage of time the sensor is busy; For our system, only the first two were used to later perform the data analysis. This component was written entirely using the Java language and the Vertx ³toolkit, an essential requirement for an IoT -based system . Components 2 and 6 are responsible for the analysis and pre-processing of the data respectively. For the operation of the system, component 6 can be omitted because its purpose is aimed at refining the data that component 2 will later consume. Deciding whether or not to include component 6 depends on the quality of the data; If the data is provided by a service that has already been responsible for purifying it or the amount of data is large enough to ignore small impurities, then it does not make sense to include it.

Component 2 must have a previously built classifier to be able to detect the events of the streams to which it was subscribed. To build this component, data from all the sensors offered by the API were collected every 5 min for a period of one week. Once the collection was completed, said data was used to form groups (clusters) using the GMM (Gaussian Mixture Models) algorithm and then, to each group, a label was associated depending on the traffic state that said group represented: LOW, NORMAL or HIGH. Then a classifier was built with said previously labeled data. This is responsible for detecting traffic events on demand. These services, in addition to data analysis, are responsible for publishing their discoveries in component 4 to later be consumed by other services. Component 3 is also optional and there may be several implementations and instances of it, everything depends on how you want to present the detected events and sensor observations. If what you want is to use the system to offer these events to other systems, then there are two variants, first do not implement component 3 and consume the events directly from component 4 or restrict the consumption of said events through a GATEWAY API4 . The entire semantic weight of the system resides in component 6. It is an intermediary system that provides a REST API or WebSocket interface to act as a router from a single entry point, the API Gateway, to a group of microservices and/or third-party APIs defined streams . The metadata is stored in a triplestore . In this case Stardog was used . In this component, you can see the existence of a subcomponent (the annotation service), which is responsible for transforming the data received from the sensors and streams into RDF documents to then be supplied to the triplestore . The component also provides the Iris corresponding to the domain definitions exposed in the domain ontologies. Component 4 is designed to allow communication between the other components of the system. It consists of a Redis database to which observations and events are published and consumed. This database was chosen for its great efficiency and speed (because the data persists in memory) and for the facilities it provides for using the publish – subscribe pattern. This component is essential for the operation of the system, since without it the detection and publication of events in real time would not be possible.

Annotation system

The annotation system is shown in Figure 3. The frequency of data generation by the sensors is 5 minutes. This frequency can be adjusted in two ways:
  → Request a different frequency than the consumed API to obtain sensor observations
  → Group observations into time windows of size according to the desired frequency.
    Note that this process occurs when the registry is requested to save or modify an entity; For example, when you request to start an analytics service, it will automatically instantiate a new stream that will be sent to the registry. In said request, the analytics service will send all the information necessary to annotate said stream appropriately, including the stream from which it is derived.
    In Figure 2, the direct flow of data is represented by blue arrows, while the flow of annotations is represented by gray arrows. This indirect process occurs when any of the following events are generated:
  → Some sensor is registered
    stream is recorded

Figure 2. Annotation system

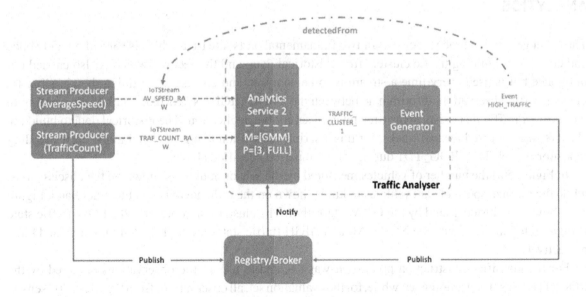

→ It is indicated that some stream no longer receives observations

→ Some analytics service is started

In the case of the system presented, it was decided not to include either the observations or the events in the annotations because the frequency of generation of said entities is very high and doing so would generate a significant load in the processing of the queries made to the triplestore by the unstructured nature in which you store your data. For streams derived from other streams ; That is, those that are produced as a result of some analytics service through the application of a certain algorithm and a certain set of parameters in the annotation process, the method and parameters used in the analytics component are included as metadata. Here M and P refer to said method and said parameters respectively. For the particular instance of the system, M would refer to the Gaussian Mixture Models method, which would be responsible for forming the clusters and P would refer to the number of expected clusters, which for the purposes of the system would be 3.

DATA FLOW

IoT data needs to employ some type of data analysis. Amazon libraries defined for popular programming languages have enabled the creation of tools that deal with data based on its nature. Depending on the application, the tools involve facilities for pre-processing data, machine learning, or correlation. The result of techniques has been used to enrich the semantic knowledge graph of the application. Knowledge Reception (CR) in the service allows the consumption of IoT data from remote sources where different methods are used. RC queries IoT data streams through SPARQL queries with a predefined format for performance variables. In turn, the service will generate a new stream of data based on the selected methods and their corresponding parameters. The new Stream Observations are then annotated and joined to a new IoT Stream, with the analytics details used, and then sent back to the Consumer. Figure 4 illustrates the process.

ANALYTICS

The event generation process consists of two fundamental parts: the first, which is carried out only once and consists of building traffic clusters from historical data; and the second, which is also carried out only once but is used every time a stream is to be analyzed and consists of building the classifier to, given a traffic observation, discriminate between the labels: HIGH, NORMAL and LOW according to the level. of traffic that exists in the time interval set for the application. The historical data to build the clusters was collected for two weeks, for this a script was written that is attached in the corresponding repository: CIN_TD1, ROG_TD1 during the time period specified above.

In Figure 5 a) the number of vehicles measured by the sensor in units is shown on the abscissa axis, while the average speed of said vehicles in km is shown on the ordinate axis. On the other hand, Figure 5 b) shows the clusters found by the GMM algorithm; The cluster that represents the LOW traffic state is highlighted in green, and the NORMAL and HIGH traffic states are highlighted in orange and blue, respectively.

For the classifier construction process, it was decided to use all the observations obtained by the ROG_TD1 sensor as a training set; while, for the evaluation set, all observations from the ARL_203 sensor.

Figure 3. Data flow

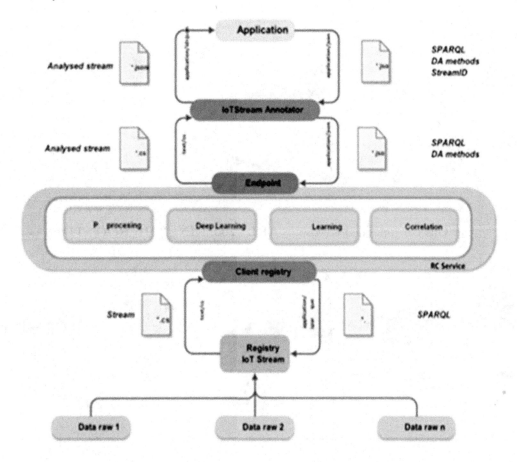

Once the training set and the evaluation set were established, the classifier began to be built, experimenting with different methods. In the validation and evaluation of the classifiers obtained, the precision and the confusion matrix were taken into account to be able to locally assess the behavior of the classifier with respect to the classes. Table 2 shows the results obtained regarding the precision of the classifiers, while Table 3 shows the confusion matrices of said classifiers. As can be seen, in general the precision of the classifiers obtained is quite good, in particular, the classifier obtained using logistic regression was the one that presented the best result in this category. Because this method is generally used for binary classification problems, the multinomial value had to be specified in the multi_class parameter to use the generalization of this method for multiclass problems: multinomial logistic regression . In addition, a greater number of iterations had to be specified because those used by the default method (100) did not allow convergence to be achieved. On the other hand, if the confusion matrices of the last two classifiers are observed, it can be seen that the classifier obtained using vector regression support is a better classifier for the high class than the one obtained using logistic regression; but generally both proved to be good enough. Consequently, the last classifier was chosen to build the analytics component.

Figure 4. Data flow and its processing

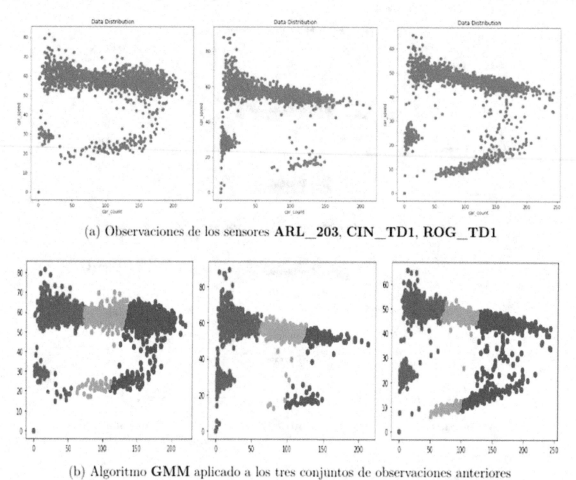

(a) Observaciones de los sensores **ARL_203**, **CIN_TD1**, **ROG_TD1**

(b) Algoritmo **GMM** aplicado a los tres conjuntos de observaciones anteriores

Table 2. Efficiency of the different classifiers used

Método	Parámetros	Precisión
k-nearest neighbors	$k \leftarrow 3$	95,70 %
k-nearest neighbors	$k \leftarrow 5, weights \leftarrow distance$	94,88 %
k-nearest neighbors	$k \leftarrow 7$	93,63 %
random forests	*Parámetros por defecto*	95,90 %
support vector regression	*Parámetros por defecto*	96,82 %
logistic regression	$multiclass \leftarrow multinomial, maxiter \leftarrow 110$	97,99 %

INFORMATION RECOVERY

Said component can be queried in two ways: 1. Through the REST API offered by said component, 2. Through the SPARQL query language. Option 1 allows you to consult specific information about the

Table 3. Confusion matrices for the classifiers shown

KNN, $k \leftarrow 3$				KNN, $k \leftarrow 5, weights \leftarrow distance$			
	high	low	normal		high	low	normal
high	1931	0	0	high	1931	0	0
low	0	1621	16	low	0	1621	16
normal	133	61	1123	normal	218	16	1083

KNN, $k \leftarrow 3$				Random Forests			
	high	low	normal		high	low	normal
high	1931	0	0	high	1922	0	9
low	0	1621	16	low	0	1637	0
normal	133	61	1123	normal	165	26	1126

SVR				Logistic regression			
	high	low	normal		high	low	normal
high	1931	0	0	high	1910	0	21
low	0	1637	0	low	0	1637	0
normal	81	74	1162	normal	8	69	1240

sensors and streams individually, always in RDF format; while option 2 offers greater flexibility when retrieving information. For the first case it would only be necessary to make an HTTP request using the GET verb towards the required route; For example, if you wanted to obtain information regarding all the sensors stored by the system, the request would be made to the route /api/v1/ sensors, while if what you want is to obtain information regarding the streams, the request would be made to the path /api/v1/ streams . For the second case, it would be necessary to create a SPARQL query that expresses what you want to obtain.

For example, suppose you want:

a) Know when the stream started784fb2df-cc95-41f4-bf95-259515a06fc0speed
b) Obtain the URIs of the streams generated by the ARL_103 sensor.

The corresponding queries are shown below:

PREDICTION

Finally we show the predictions of the previously trained models, for this we execute the SPARQL code. The query would return the class with the original data, the predicted value. You can examine these values to verify whether the predictions are consistent and make sense in relation to the data and the classification problem you are addressing. In the following image we will see a visualization of this data. In the output provided, the original and predicted values are displayed. Each row represents an example, where:

- OriginalValue - This is the original value of the node 's typeEvent attribute .
- PredictedValue – is the value predicted by the model

Figure 5. Examples of queries

```
1   PREFIX              http://purl.org/iot/ontology/iot-stream/
2
3   SELECT ?started
4   WHERE {
5       http://localhost:9987/api/v1/streams/784fb2df-cc95-41f4-bf95-259515a06fc0-speed          windowStart ?started.
6   }
7
```

(a) Consulta para obtener la fecha de inicio del stream **784fb2df-cc95-41f4-bf95-259515a06fc0-speed**

```
1   PREFIX iot-stream: http://purl.org/iot/ontology/iot-stream/
2   PREFIX sosa: http://www.w3.org/ns/sosa/
3
4   SELECT ?stream
5   WHERE {
6       { ?stream rdf:type iot-stream:IotStream;
7                 iot-stream:generatedBy http://localhost:9987/api/v1/sensors/ARL_103_SPEED }
8       UNION
9       { ?stream rdf:type iot-stream:IotStream;
10                iot-stream:generatedBy http://localhost:9987/api/v1/sensors/ARL_103_COUNT }
11  }
12
```

(b) Consulta para obtener los streams generados por el sensor **ARL_103**

Figure 6. Predicted values

In most cases, the predicted value matches the original value. For example, rows 1, 2, 3, 4, 5, 7, 8, 9, 10 indicate that the prediction was correct. However, in row 6 the predicted value differs from the original value.

GRAPHIC INTERFACE

A graphical interface was developed in Python using the Folium library to display the events detected in Brussels. The interface (Quinter at al 2018, Quintero et al 2022) will allow users to define a time window and display on a map the traffic events indicated by the model in that period. Legend:

- Green marker: Normal traffic level.
- White marker: Low traffic level.
- Orange marker: High level of traffic with good speed.
- Red marker: Agglomeration of cars

CONCLUSION

Based on the research work carried out and presented in this report, the following conclusions are presented:

- Traffic system was developed for the detection of traffic events that enables the grouping of streams from homogeneous groups of data in RDF, with an integration approach, thus fulfilling

Figure 7. Graphical interface developed in Python

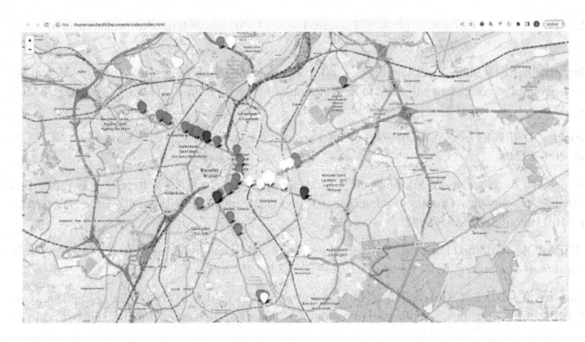

the general objective set. This system can be used in various environments due to its flexibility and architecture.

- The design of the system components explains and substantiates a general methodological procedure that allows data to be grouped to obtain streams from homogeneous groups of related data, with an integration approach that contributes to the development of research in the field of the semantic web and the IOT . The software definition contains the premises, procedures and principles that characterize the IoT scenario . It is a flexible and extensible tool.
- The validation of the proposed system was carried out using linked data from the Brussels traffic collection representative of the investigated universe. The results were obtained from the proposed software. The application of non-parametric statistical tests for the study of clustering methods allowed us to determine that the algorithms used in the experiment have good results, but the one with the highest percentage of efficiency is the logistic regression developed specifically for IoT environments .

RECOMMENDATIONS

Taking into consideration that the proposed software is extensible, it is recommended:

- Implement the proposed software in other similar systems.
- Incorporate hierarchical clustering methods that allow initializing SKWIC and Fuzzy SKWIC and also determining proximity between the formed clusters.

REFERENCES

ACTIVAGE. (2021). *About ACTIVAGE*. Retrieved May 11, 2021 from https://www.activageproject.eu/activage-project/ #About-ACTIVAGE

Berners-Lee, T., Hendler, J., & Lassila, O. (2001). The Semantic Web: A new form of Web content that is meaningful to computers will unleash a revolution of new possibilities. *Scientific American*, *284*(5), 34–43.

Brickley, D. (n.d.). *Geospatial ontology*. Available. https://www.w3.org/2005/Incubator/geo/XGR-geo-ont-20071023/

Elsaleh, T., Bermudez-Edo, M., Enshaeifar, S., Acton, S.T., Rezvani, R., & Barnaghi, P. (2019). IoT-Stream: A Lightweight Ontology for Internet of Things Data Streams. *2019 Global IoT Summit (GIoTS)*. doi:10.1109/giots.2019.8766367

EPSPARQL: A Unified Language for Event Processing and Stream Reasoning. (n.d.). In *The 20th International Conference*. ACM Press. doi:10.1145/1963405.1963495

Janowicz, K., Haller, A., Cox, S., Phuoc, D. L., & Lefrancois, M. (2018). SOSA: A Lightweight Ontology for Sensors, Observations, Samples, and Actuators. *Journal of Web Semantics*. doi:10.2139/ssrn.3248499

Ortiz-Rodríguez, F., Palma, R., & Villazón-Terrazas, B. (2006). Semantic based P2P System for local e-Government. In Proceedings of Informatik 2006. GI-Edition- Lecture Notes in Informatics (LNI).

Quintero, J. M., Abrego-Almazán, D., & Ortiz-Rodríguez, F. (2018). Use and usefulness of the information systems measurement. a quality approach at the Mexican northeastern region. *Cuadernos de Administración, 31*(56), 7-30. doi:10.11144/javeriana.cao.31-56.ubwm

Quintero, J. M. M., Echeverría, O. R., & Rodríguez, F. O. (2022). Trust and information quality for the customer satisfaction and loyalty in e-Banking with the use of the mobile phone. *Contaduría y Administración, 67*(1), 283–304.

Trialog. (2021). *IoT systems and interoperability*. Retrieved June 5, 2021 from https://www.trialog.com/en/IoT-systems-and-interoperability

Villazón-Terrazas, B., Ortiz-Rodríguez, F., Tiwari, S. M., & Shandilya, S. K. (2020). Knowledge graphs and semantic web. *Communications in Computer and Information Science, 1232*, 1–225.

W3C. (2013). *SPARQL Query Language for RDF*. Retrieved June 9, 2021 from https://www.w3.org/TR/rdf-sparql-query/

W3C. (n.d.-a). *Semantic Sensor Network Ontology*. Available. https://www.w3.org/TR/vocab-ssn/

W3C. (n.d.-b). *SSN*. Available at https://bioportal.bioontology.org/ontologies/SSN

Weyrich & Ebert. (2016). Reference Architectures for the Internet of Things. *IEEE Software, 33*(1), 112–116. . 1109/MS.2016.20 doi:https://doi.org/10

What is Linked Data? (2015). Retrieved June 9, 2021 from https://www.w3.org/standards/semanticweb/data

Zeadally, S., & Bello, O. (2021). Harnessing the power of Internet of Things based connectivity to improve healthcare. *Internet of Things : Engineering Cyber Physical Human Systems, 14*, 100074. doi:10.1016/j.IoT.2019.100074

ENDNOTES

[1]   http://linkedvocabs.org/onto/trafficstore/trafficstore.html
[2]   https://data.mobility.brussels/traffic/api/counts/
[3]   https://vertx.io/

Chapter 4
Multi–Factor Authentication Web Security System Based on Facial Recognition, One Time Password, and Hashed Secure Question

Graveth Uzoma Ejekwu
(iD) https://orcid.org/0000-0002-0698-6718
NYSC Secretariat Bayelsa, Nigeria

O. Mashood Lawal
(iD) https://orcid.org/0000-0002-1312-944X
Air Force Institute of Technology, Nigerian Air Force Base, Mando, Nigeria

Samson Ajodo
(iD) https://orcid.org/0000-0002-4845-1682
Nigerian Defence Academy, Nigeria

Oluwafemi S. Balogun
(iD) https://orcid.org/0000-0002-8870-9692
University of Eastern Finland, Finland

ABSTRACT

Web application authentication is a critical aspect of digital security, serving as both the first and last line of defense for safeguarding sensitive information. Unfortunately, traditional text-based passwords are susceptible to a variety of attacks, leaving many web apps vulnerable to data theft by unauthorized users. As a solution, this study developed a multi-factor authentication technique to bolster the conventional username and password method. Utilizing Agile methodology, the proposed solution examined current authentication practices and evaluated the feasibility of multi-factor authentication. The system generates a one-time password (OTP) using the user's login credentials and incorporates additional steps such as face recognition and secure hashed questions for user authentication. To enhance security and user flexibility, the system was implemented using Python programming language, various Python libraries, and an image processing library.

DOI: 10.4018/979-8-3693-1487-6.ch004

1. INTRODUCTION

The world wide web as an entity is been seen my business owners and online vendors and most organizations as a place to carry out businesses and transactions. Individuals and companies perform many tasks on the web such as fetching emails and sending emails, getting access to various gate for making payments of all kinds and also generating reports of various kinds, also having access to contacts information stored on the cloud either google cloud or yahoo cloud via computer systems or mobile phones, this requests are sent through the web browser which in turn returns a response from the host server. Website authentication being the first protective measure for a website user to secure his/her data and to make sure the data is higher secured and restricted from authorized users.

Mostly users navigating the website will need to verify his/her login details, this login details are usually setup at the early stage of creating account with a website or desktop application as well android applications, this verification is done by the user either by statically inputting the login details or automatically inputted by the web browser password manager or google password saver like Authenticator, LastPass etc. This authentication is performed during login process of the website or android applications.

Text-based authentication has been the most common approach used by websites and mobile applications, however this approach or partner of authenticating users is not sufficient enough to provide protection against authorized users from getting information of another user, this is because the approach is open to multiple cyber-attacks example brute force password guessing, phishing attack and the rest of it.

The word authentication is the process or method of confirming a user identity or a request coming from a system that is providing certain types of services to the entity (user) requesting the service. This is done to make sure a user making the request is actually a valid user as they said. In other words, authentication is making sure user supplies the system he/she is making request from with a classified detail agreed between the two entity (user and system) Singh, Charanjeet, & singh, Tripat Deep (2019).

Multi-factor authentication needs more than one verification level to be available. These layers or levels of verification can be user password, which is what the inputted during registration or creating of an account the said system, this is known by the user only on less he or she chooses to share with friends and family, a guarded token or one time password that is sent to user on each login, hashed secure question and Facial Recognition feature. If user provides all the four layers of authentication there will be a higher level of authentication assurance and high level of security, Aldwairi, Monther & Aldhanhani, Saoud (2017, August). The reasons for integrating multiple authentication or security into an application is for the protection of data or what we call data privacy.

Data privacy, this denotes how organizations handle user information or personal information such as transactions, financial data, health records, academic records and many more. Data privacy gives room for organizations to protect user information and keep it from been public else permitted by the said owner of the data. Why data privacy is important, and why every web applications or desktop application should protect customer data from been accessed by unauthorized users.

Knowing fully well that the information mentioned above is important to users and should be kept secret and not be made public, because if this unique identities are compromised it could lead to identity theft or something worse than that, it could lead to user losing their lives or property because their data has been compromised.

Here are some of the reasons why data privacy is important:

(a) It safeguards private information since someone could start credit card accounts in your name, steal your identity, or pass themselves off as you if they have access to your financial information or social security number. These are very dangerous behaviors that may have severe repercussions.

(b) It fosters trust because, as we've already discussed, businesses can learn a lot from the information they collect about their consumers. However, customers will only give their information to a business they have complete faith in. Client interactions reflect a company's commitment to data protection.

(c) It complies with national and international laws: Because data security is so crucial, the great majority of nations and international regulatory agencies have put strong restrictions in place regarding how businesses must handle and retain customer data.

Peoples private information are very important and is therefore necessary for every organizations, web applications, etc to protect user data Juliette Erath (2023). Al Abdulwahid, Abdulwahid & Clarke, Nathan & Stengel, Ingo & Furnell, Steven & Reich, Christoph (2016) made a critical point about authentication, regardless of the process: though user data is protected or secured it is important that user is required to authenticate him or herself when trying to access their information on the system, this is done to establish a level of answerability or accountability for that user. As they stated, Answerability or accountability is kept in place in other to store user activities as the perform them, to keep tracks of them, in other to revisit it later if need be.

This study applies to all online authentication systems, especially those used by websites that handle sensitive data. Many common cyberattacks, including keyloggers, brute-force attacks, and social engineering, can be stopped by installing this authentication method. Through this study, authentication security is increased with little user experience loss. This study allows users to execute multi-factor authentication with a touch of a finger, making the system much more secure than other existing systems that simply require a password and one-time password (OTP). Although heavily advocated and more secure than one-factor authentication, two-factor authentication has not been generally used for web authentication, Xie, Mengjun & Li, Yanyan & Yoshigoe, K. & Seker, Remzi & Bian, Jiang (2015, January).

2. LITERATURE REVIEW

Authentication is a verification setup that the user must complete in other to confirm their identity in a web application. In a network security confidentiality and authentication are two major components required in securing a network. Thomas, Princy & Mathew, K. (2023) according to their research paper described Authentication as the practice of maintaining the confidentiality of user data in digital applications. Additionally, the digital platform's user identification procedure uses techniques like voice recognition and biometrics to confirm the identity of its own users. For user authentication in the past, a one-time login based credential verification mechanism was used. Recently, several fresh ideas to improve the user authentication framework were put forth, however the execution of the authentication process revealed inconsistencies with those ideas.

However, most web applications or mobile applications that serves a security system recommend biometric powered quick fix, that would be easily misled via duplicating fingerprints using clay Byoung Wook Kwon., Pradip Kumar Sharma and Jong Hyuk Park (2019). Despite the ease with which image-based security may stand compromised, it is a solution for which further user training may not require. In this work, we propose a three-step multi-factor user authentication method.

The presence of malware on a PC is no longer unusual. A single legitimate credential, like a password, may not be enough for user authentication, making it difficult to determine the legitimacy of a user. Two-factor authentication, a technique of authentication based on the presentation of two factors by the user, is a common solution to this issue. The first factor is often entered into a computer, and the second into a smartphone. However, by requiring the user to provide numerous factors for each authentication, this diminishes usability. User authentication consists of three security components that distinguish between authorized and unauthorized users in order to "confirm the claimed identity of a human user."

- Confidentiality, which makes sure that unauthorized users cannot access the information.
- Integrity verifies that no uninvited human user has altered the data.
- Achieving availability is making the computer systems accessible to authorized persons when needed. Nozaki, Shinnosuke., Serizawa, Ayumi., Yoshihira, Muzuho., Fujita, Masahiro., Shibata, Yoichi., Yamanaka, Tadakazu., Matsuda, Nori., Ohki, Tetsushi & Nishigaki, Masakatu (2022, August).

Identification is the first stage of authentication, followed by Authentication and Authorization. The explanation of these three phases continues. Identification is the process by which the system first establishes a user's identity and defines who they are. At this step, users typically enter a username or other form of identification, and the system then examines the database to determine if the value retrieved corresponds to the information provided by the user. As a result, this stage alone is insufficient, and that is when user authentication enters the picture. The fundamental procedure for determining if a user's inputs are correct or wrong is user authentication. At this point, the user enters a secret key that is specific to them, such as a password, pin, or number. If the authentication and identification steps are successful, only then does the user permission stage allow the user access to the secure website.

Cybersecurity is important in today's e-commerce applications, Tang, Chenyu., Cui, Ziang., Chu, Meng., Lu, Yujiao., Zhou, Fugiang., & Gao, Suo (2022). In this paper, we describe an identity authentication method based on keystroke dynamics and piezoelectric touch sensing that enables safe smartphone access.

2.1 Authentication Factors

2.1.1 Single Factor Authentication (SFA)

The traditional security approach for controlling and securing access to a network or system is single-factor authentication. By requesting a specific category of credentials for verification, the approach identifies and confirms that the party attempting to get access is truly authorized to do so. The most popular Single-Factor Authentication technique is password-based authentication. Before giving access, the approach requires users to input the proper login and password. The technique strongly depends on the user's or network administrator's attention in choosing a secure password and keeping it hidden from prying eyes.

According to the majority of experts and CISA (Cyber-security & Infrastructure Security Agency), single-factor authentication is a weak authentication method. SFA has been exposed to a variety of password compromise methods, including phishing, social engineering, network sniffing, keylogging, etc. James Moutsos (2022).

2.1.2 Two-Factor Authentication (2FA)

It was determined that SFA could not provide reliable security because of a number of security issues. Two-factor authentication (2FA) boosts security by combining representative data (username/password combination) with a different form of identity, such as a personal ownership factor, which could include a secure token using a One Time Password (OTP). Figure 1 illustrates three different types of factor groups from which 2FA can be derived.

1. Possession of an item, such as a mobile phone, gives a user ownership.
2. Knowledge factor: something the user is aware of, like a password.
3. A biometric factor, or fact, this is a characteristic of a user.

2FA has its be benefits and draw backs as every system does, one of the benefits been that the use of two or more factors is an improved user identification mechanism that increases security. The user may additionally select a second authentication method in addition to the default one, Rani, C.H. Jhansi, & Munnisa, S.K. Sammi (2016). This increases the security of the user's personal data because if some-one steals a user's password, they will also need access to the second authentication mechanism, which may not be accessible by the user who is trying to access your detail without your permission. While one of its drawbacks is that as the number of authentication methods increases the complexity of the authentication procedure. 2FA requires additional hardware, which raises costs and frequently impairs usability, Shteingart H., Gordon A.N., Gazit J. (2016).

2.1.3 Multi-Factor Authentication (MFA)

Multifactor Authentication (MFA), also known as Multi-Step Verification, is a security mechanism that requires users to supply two or more distinct and independent authentication factors in order to access a system, application, or account. In a variety of settings, such as online banking, email services, social media, and corporate networks, MFA is frequently used. It adds a further layer of security in a world that is becoming more digital and connected, assisting in the protection of sensitive data and preventing unauthorized access. Unique biological characteristics of the user, such as fingerprint or facial express, iris scans, etc., are frequently included in MFA because they are frequently extremely accurate in both their creation and use Tsai, Chien-Hua & Su, Pin-Chang. (2021). Combining at least three different types of credentials enables a higher level of security to protect computer systems and other important services from unauthorized access Azrour, M., Mourade Azrour., Jamal Mabrouki., Azidine Guezzaz & Yousef Farhaoui (2021).

The benefit of using multi-factor authentication in a system or web application is that by combining knowledge and ownership factors with biometric factors to increase identity proofing, it makes it more difficult for threat actors to fool a system through impersonation. The multi-factor authentication system's performance can be significantly enhanced by evaluating a variety of biologically related characteristics to determine an individual's identity, Dasgupta, Dipankar, Roy, Arunava & Nag, Abhijit (2017). In terms of user experience, the fingerprint scanner has emerged as the biometric interface that is used the most frequently. The widespread adoption by smartphone manufacturers is primarily to blame for this. Pre-integrated ones make the authentication system more affordable and simpler for end users to use. The trade-off between usability and security in contemporary authentication systems is one of the most important factors to take into account. The MFA approach permits a variety of circumstances where security is paramount, Velásquez, Ignacio, Caro, Angelica & Rodríguez, Alfonso (2018). Using biological components has several disadvantages, primarily in terms of usability, which has a significant impact on the usefulness of the MFA system, Vinoth Kumar M.I., K. Venkatachalam, Prabu P., Abdulwahab Almutairi, Mohamed Abouhawwash (2023).

A discrepancy between the measured biometric presentation and the information recorded at the initial biometric registration can be problematic from the perspective of biometric authentication, especially when using cheap and unreliable equipment, Tran, Quang Nhat., Turnbull, Benjamin P. & Hu, Jiankun. (2021). Issues with biometric authentication include False Accept Rates (FAR) and False Reject Rates (FRR), Yuan, Chengsheng., Zhang, Qianyue., Wu, Sheng. Q.M. & Wu, Jonathan (2023). "The false acceptance rates (FAR) is a unit used to measure the average number of false acceptances within a biometric security system. It measures and evaluates the efficiency and accuracy of a biometric system by determining the rate at which unauthorized or illegitimate users are verified on a particular system" Margaret Rouse (2018), while False rejection rate (FRR) is "the probability of touch actions performed by the legitimate user, which were falsely detected as touch actions performed by illegitimate users. A low FRR indicates the scheme rejects less legitimate users and is convenient for the user in terms of usability" Zaidi, Ahmad & Chong, Chun Yong & Jin, Zhe & Parthiban, R. & Sadiq, Ali (2021). The MFA operation depends heavily on FAR and FRR because it is virtually impossible to achieve perfect accuracy for these two metrics.

3. METHODOLOGY

3.1 User Authentication Workflow

Upon attempting to access the system, users will be prompted to input their login credentials. These credentials consist of a variety of factors, such as a traditional password, a one-time password (OTP) sent to their registered device, biometric authentication through facial recognition, and a secure hashed question or challenge-response mechanism. This authentication process has been specifically crafted to ensure multi-factor authentication (MFA) for heightened security. The traditional password and OTP serve as a knowledge factor, while facial recognition acts as the inherence factor. Additionally, the secure hashed question or challenge-response mechanism provides a possession factor.

By combining these different factors, the system can offer an extra layer of security, ultimately preventing unauthorized access. This multi-factor authentication (MFA) workflow is a powerful tool for keeping potential security breaches and unauthorized access attempts at bay.

3.2 Agile

Agile Methodology was the development life cycle methodology utilized to produce this project. A framework for the software development process, the agile methodology includes an iterative approach, open communication, and process flexibility. According to Amanda Teixeira Barbosa., César Carriço da Silva., Rebecca Leal Caetano., Deborah Paredes Soares da Silva., Júlio Vianna Barbosa. & Zeneida Teixeira Pinto, (2022). The Agile development life circle have been used in the business and in software development for some time now, but they are increasingly common in public relations and communication firms.

Agile Development Iterations

The Agile methodology is a project management approach that aims to streamline the development process by breaking it down into iterative cycles. These cycles, known as "sprints," allow for the continuous improvement of the authentication process. Each sprint is dedicated to implementing and refining specific authentication factors and integrating them within the system. By breaking down the development process into smaller, more manageable cycles, the Agile methodology allows for a more flexible and adaptive approach to authentication. This approach enables us to assess the effectiveness of each factor and make necessary adjustments based on feedback received. As a result, the authentication process becomes more robust and efficient over time.

In addition to improving the authentication process, the Agile methodology also promotes collaboration and communication among team members. By working together in short sprints, team members can better coordinate their efforts and ensure that everyone is on the same page. This collaborative approach helps to minimize misunderstandings and errors, leading to a more successful and efficient development process overall.

Figure 1. Diagram showing agile methodology (agile benefits for businesses may be found at https:// devcom.com/tech-blog/)

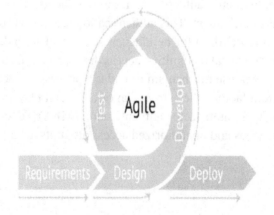

3.3 Implementation Steps

Password Integration: When users create an account, they are prompted to choose a strong password that follows best practices for password security. This includes using a combination of uppercase and lowercase letters, numbers, and symbols, and avoiding easily guessable information like common words or dates. To ensure that stored passwords are protected, the passwords are securely hashed using robust algorithms like Bcrypt.

This process converts the passwords into a unique string of characters that cannot be reversed to reveal the original password. This way, even in the event of a data breach, an attacker would not be able to access the plaintext passwords and use them to gain unauthorized access to user accounts. Overall, these measures help to ensure that user credentials are kept safe and secure, protecting both users and the platform itself from potential security threats.

One-time Password (OTP) Integration: One-time Passwords (OTPs) are a type of authentication mechanism commonly used by online services to verify the identity of users. These passwords are generated and delivered to the user's registered device via email, SMS, or authenticator app. OTPs are usually time-based, meaning they expire after a single use or within a short time window to prevent replay attacks and enhance security. This authentication method is increasingly popular because of its effectiveness in preventing unauthorized access to user accounts, particularly in scenarios where traditional passwords are weak or compromised.

Facial Recognition Integration: Our system relies on advanced computer vision technologies, specifically OpenCV and Haar Cascaded Classifier algorithms, to accurately detect and recognize facial features. During the registration process, users' facial features are captured and securely stored in our database for future authentication. This ensures that only authorized individuals have access to the system and provides an additional layer of security against unauthorized access. Our facial recognition technology is constantly improving, allowing for faster and more accurate identification of users even in challenging lighting conditions or with partial facial obstructions.

Secure Hashed Question Integration: When users sign up for an account on a website or application, they are often required to select security questions and provide answers as a form of identity verification. These security questions are then securely hashed and stored in the backend of the system. During the authentication process, users are prompted to answer one of their pre-defined security questions to verify their identity. The system matches the answer provided by the user with the stored hashed answer to determine if the user is the authentic account owner. This process helps to ensure that only authorized users can access their accounts and protects against unauthorized access and potential fraud.

3.4 Testing and Validation

The security of this system heavily relies on a dependable authentication process. To confirm its reliability, security, and usability, each authentication factor undergoes extensive testing. These tests involve various scenarios, including incorrect inputs and potential security risks, to assess the effectiveness of each factor. The main goal is to test the authentication process in different edge cases, ensuring its reliability and security in unexpected situations. Moreover, User Acceptance Testing (UAT) is a critical part of the testing process. UAT involves real users who validate the effectiveness and user experience of the authentication process. This guarantees that the authentication process is not only secure and reliable but also user-friendly and easy to use.

By subjecting each authentication factor to rigorous testing, including edge cases and user acceptance testing, the authentication process can be designed to be highly dependable, secure, and user-friendly. This way, the system's safety and security are ensured.

3.5 Continuous Improvement

The Agile methodology is a software development approach that emphasizes the iterative and incremental delivery of software products. One of the key advantages of this approach is its ability to facilitate continuous improvement through user feedback, emerging security threats, and technological advancements. As a result, the authentication system can always remain up-to-date and resilient. To achieve this, Agile development employs regular retrospectives and feedback loops to gather input and insights from stakeholders, users, and team members. These insights are then used to inform future iterations, ensuring that the system is constantly evolving and improving in response to changing needs and requirements.

By adopting the Agile approach, the development team is better equipped to respond to emerging security threats and adapt to new technologies as they emerge. This helps to ensure that the authentication system remains effective and secure in the face of evolving challenges.

3.6 Tools, Dataset and Algorithms

3.6.1 Selection of Tools and Libraries

➤ **Python:** Python is a powerful, adaptable, and all-purpose programming language. It reads clearly and easily, which makes it a great first language, Srinath, K. R. (2017). Due to its wide-ranging capabilities, user-friendly syntax, and a broad selection of libraries and frameworks, Python is the preferred programming language for this project. Its adaptability, readability, and widespread adoption in the developer community make it the perfect choice for bringing our proposed project to life. Additionally, its expansive ecosystem enables developers to create robust, scalable, and secure solutions with ease and efficiency.

➤ **Django:** A high-level Python web framework known as Django enables the quick creation of trustworthy and secure websites. Almost every sort of website, including web wallets, content management systems, social medias, and news websites etc can be developed with Django Framework. Ramesh, B Nithya., Amballi, Aashay R. & Mahanta Vivekananda, (2018).

➤ **OpenCv:** OpenCV is a fantastic tool for work in image processing and computer vision. It is an open-source library that may be used for an assortment of tasks, including face recognition, object tracking, landmark detection, and many more. It supports a wide variety of languages, including Python, Java, and C++, Ma, Qingyun & Huang, Xubin (2022).

➤ **Numpy:** NumPy is a Python library used for manipulation of arrays. There are also functions for working with linear algebra, matrix operations, and the Fourier transform, Harris, Charles., Millman, K., Walt, Stéfan., Gommers, Ralf., Virtanen, Pauli., Cournapeau, David., Wieser, Eric., Taylor, Julian., Berg, Sebastian., Smith, Nathaniel., Kern, Robert., Picus, Matti., Hoyer, Stephan., Kerkwijk, Marten., Brett, Matthew. et al. (2020).

➤ **Pandas:** Python Pandas package is use to alter data sets. It offers tools for examining, categorizing, analyzing, and modifying data. The term "Pandas" was created in 2008 by Wes McKinney and stands for both "Panel Data" and "Python Data Analysis." Pandas allow us to analyze massive volumes of data and make inferences based on statistical principles. Pandas can also clean large, complex data sets to make them relevant and intelligible. Vagizov, M., Potapov, A., Konzhgoladze, K., Stepanov, S & Martyn, I. (2021).

➤ **Pillow:** Utilizing the Pillow Python Imaging Library, the Python interpreter can now handle pictures. a variety of file format compatibility options, an effective intrinsic resemblance, and relatively powerful image manipulation functions are all provided by this package. The main picture library exists organized to provide easy access to data held in a few fundamental pixel formats. This acts as a reliable base for an all-encompassing image manipulation tool, Asaad, Renas., Ali, Rasan., Ali, Zeravan & Shaaban, Awaz (2023).

3.6.2 Dataset Generation

A dataset is a collection of instances, datasets are used in machine learning to analysis a system, or to build artificial intelligence base software, Wikipedia (2023). The dataset used in this work was generated by the system itself. The system captures user images during registration and process it then retrain the system to adopt the new user.

3.6.3 Algorithms and Techniques

Haar Cascaded Classifier: In still images or moving movies, this makes use of an Object Detection Algorithm to locate faces Madan, Arnav (2021). The approach constructs the use of the edge or line detection characteristics, as published in 2001 by Viola and Jones in their paper "Rapid Object Detection using a Boosted Cascade of Simple Features" The algorithm is trained using a large number of both positive images with faces and negative images without any faces, Alto, V. (2019). No matter where an object is in an image or how big they are, it can be detected using the Haar cascade algorithm. This algorithm is simple and real-time capable. We can program a Haar-cascade detector to recognize a variety of objects, including cars, bikes, structures, fruits, etc. When using the cascading window, Haar cascade attempts to compute features in each window and determine whether it might be an object, Abhishek Jaiswal, (2023).

The need for security based on face detection requires the development of a more robust security framework. Face detection systems can be particularly useful in locations like airports and line intersections where differentiating proof confirmation is essential Jiang, Huaizu & Learned-Miller, Erik (2017, May).

Face Recognition: Due to recent security-related developments, rapid advancements in mobile technology, and PC system development, face detection has become a popular research topic Ranjan, Rajeev & Patel, Vishal & Chellappa, Rama (2017). Access control, personality verification, security frameworks, observation frameworks, and web-based entertainment companies are just a few of the many applications that face detection is frequently used in. Similar arguments can be made regarding observation frameworks if lawbreakers are assumed to be at large. In efforts to find these people, surveillance cameras with face detection capabilities can be helpful, Zhang, Tao & Li, Jingjing & Jia, Wenjing & Sun, Jun & Yang, Huihua (2018).

The basis for face recognition and face verification is face detection. Hu, Xizhi & Huang, Bingyu (2020, December) stated that face detection is simply the system's capacity to recognize the presence of a human face when it is simultaneously exposed to a variety of different items. Face detection seeks to identify any faces in a given image (typically in gray scale) and, if any are found, to return the location and content of each face in the image. Any fully automatic system that examines the data present in faces must start here, Li, Xiaochao., Yang, Zhenjie. & Wu, Andhongwei (2020). The need for security based on face detection requires the development of a more robust security framework. Face detection frameworks can be useful, particularly in locations like airports and line intersections where differentiating proof confirmation is essential Hou, Shaoqi., Fang, Dongdong, Pan, Yixi., Li, Ye., & Yin corresponding, Guangqiang (2021). To achieve this in real life, face detection must be added, and rigorous work must be done on its extraction, training, and testing within a model, Sawat, Dattatray & Hegadi, Ravindra (2017).

Bycrypt Algorithm: Bcrypt password hashing algorithm, which lives based on the Blowfish cipher, was devised by Niels Provos and David Mazières. It stood initially introduced in 1999 at USENIX. Bcrypt is a cross-platform program for file encryption. Access to encrypted data is possible on all supported operating systems and processors. Passwords are internally hashed to a 448-bit key and must be 8 to 56 characters long. Each character offered, nevertheless, is significant. The more secure your passphrase, the safer your data will be, Kunal Jain, kunalkj. (2021), Bcrypt is an appropriate hashing algorithm because it allows us to create a unique hash for each password by adding a random salt to the beginning of each one. The advantage of the bcrypt hashing algorithm over other algorithms is its capacity to control the speed of hashing. Attackers can brute force password hashes using other algorithms, like SHA-256, which can be calculated very quickly, Victor Wu, (2021).

"The bcrypt algorithm runs in two phases, In the first phase, EksBlowfishSetup is called with the cost, the salt, and the password, to initialize eksblowfish's state. Most of bcrypt's time is spent in the expensive key schedule. Following that, the 192-bit value "OrpheanBeholderScryDoubt" is encrypted 64 times using eksblowfish in ECB mode with the state from the previous phase. The output is the cost and 128-bit salt concatenated with the result of the encryption loop." Provos, N.

Bcrypt is preferable because SHA-256 hashing algorithms are quicker but more vulnerable to simple attacks like brute force, Skanda, C., Srivatsa, B., & Premananda, B. S. (2022, November).

Passwords and plain text are changed into an original and irreversible form using the cryptographic technique of hashing. By doing this, it is made sure that hackers cannot convert the hashed value back to the original password. Although hashing is a key component of password security, it does have a flaw that can be exploited. When fed the same input, a good hashing algorithm makes sure the hash value produced is always the same. This means that an attacker could use the rainbow table to brute force his way into sensitive data. Developers will use salts to increase the difficulty of obtaining the password in order to prevent this. Before hashing, a salt, which is a random string, is added to the original password. As a result, it becomes nearly impossible for the attacker to reverse the password because the hash value generated will always be different, J4y J3ff, (2023).

Figure 2. Architectural design of the system

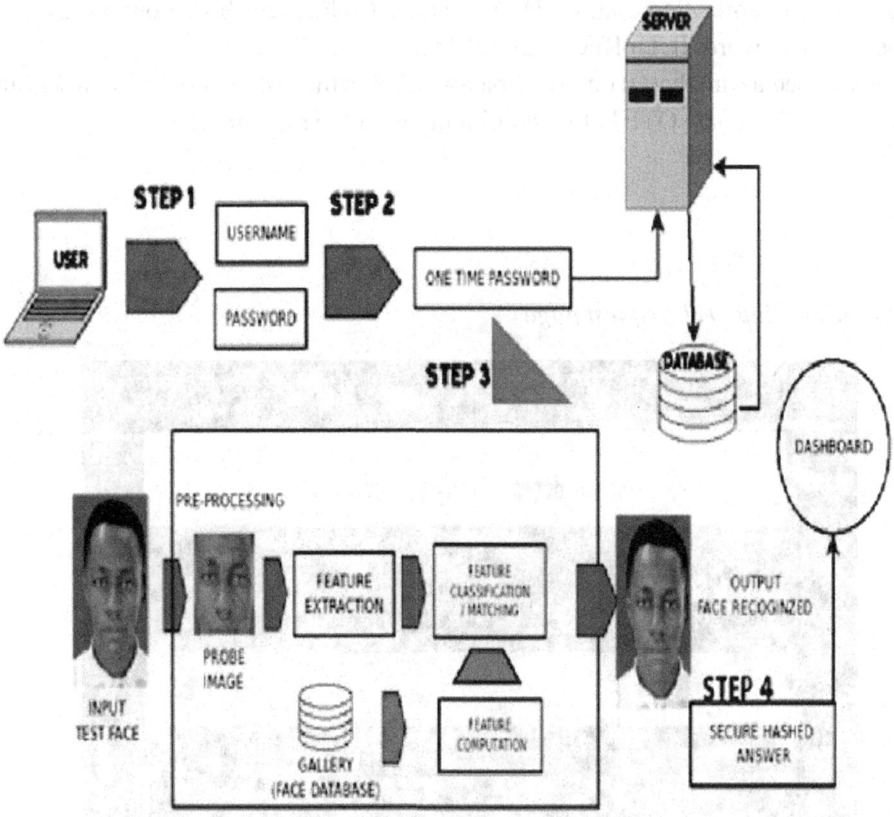

4. IMPLEMENTATION, RESULT, AND DISCUSSION

4.1 Architectural Diagram of the System Developed

After the user logins with his or her username and password, then proceeds to the execute the other three authentications mentioned earlier in this study.

4.1.1 The One-Time Password (OTP) Algorithm Process

In order to protect the system, the generated OTP must be difficult to decode, recover, or track. Therefore, building a secured one-time password generating system is important. The one-time password approach may utilize different factors to generate a harrowing key. The system generates a one-of-a-kind OTP and emails it to the user. The system will make use of some special data to generate the pin. The server will use the same information to validate the OTP. To ensure the guarantee of the system, the unique OTP must be challenging for hackers to decipher. A timestamp will stand applied to generate an OTP that is one-of-a-kind and only valid once.

There are many types of OTP MFA solutions, which includes: seed value-based one-time password; hash-based message authentication codes (HMAC)-based OTP; event-based one-time password; and time-based one-time password, IETF RFC 4226 (2015).

In this study, we used a time-based one-time password, this means it expires after a set time and will require user to request for a new OTP before continuing with the system.

Figure 3. Diagram showing OTP request page

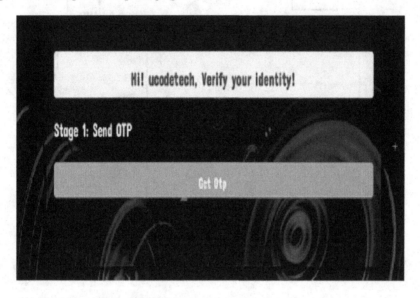

Figure 4. Diagram showing OTP verification page

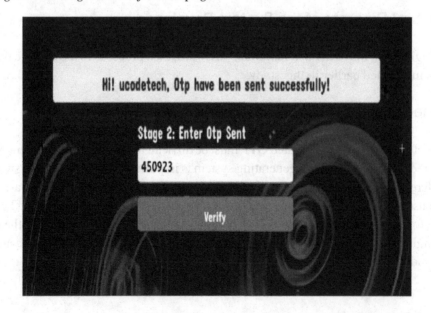

Figure 5. Diagram showing OTP confirmation page

4.2 Facial Recognition Process

Facial recognition is a technology that identifies or verifies individuals by analyzing their facial features. The process involves several steps and technologies.

4.2.1 Image Preprocessing

Preprocessing the image to remove unwanted noise is the first stage in image analysis. These elements are then deleted by preprocessing since they are harmful to the analysis of the image. Down sampling is used for all photos larger than 96 by 84 pixels.

All colored photos are then turned into grayscale after this. The photos' outputs are divided into training and test sets. With 20% serving as the test set, 80% of the photos are thought of as training sets. This preprocessing will reduce the elaborateness while lengthening the computation span.

4.2.2 Feature Extraction

The feature extraction strategy utilized in this study is further explained in this section. One of the dreams of the project is to implement an offline face recognition system with an improved and trustworthy feature extraction approach using optimization techniques.

4.2.3 Dimensionality Reduction and Feature Selection

Given that the mean face of the training data has been determined, the binary singleton evolution function is utilized as an element-wise operator. In order to reduce the coefficient that was onetime used to characterize the picture, the single-value decomposition function is utilized to break down the final image.

4.3 Hashed Secure Question

You've undoubtedly used the method of identity identification known as security questions before. When creating an account or signing up for a service online, users supply providers with their replies to private questions. Security questions are primarily used for self-service password recovery, even though they may stand utilized as an extra authentication factor for logins. By providing the appropriate response, users are verified and presented with the option to reset their password.

The security of the security answers we utilized on our system was ensured using the following advice, Swaroop Sham (2021).

1. **Restricting answers:** We compared responses to a deny list for frequent responses, like the user's current password, the username or email address, and character sequences that are easy to guess, including "123" and "password." A minimum answer length requirement can also aid in preventing such responses, Justinha et al. (2023).
2. **Renewing questions:** We ask the user to examine their security questions from time to time to make sure they still know the answers. In addition to making it more likely that they will remember their most recent response if they need to regain access to their account, this should enable them to amend any retorts that might have changed, Optimal IdM (2022).
3. **No user-written questions:** The system lived made to prevent users from writing their questions to lower risk. Having people contribute queries may result in powerful, innovative questions that

Figure 6. Diagram showing extraction and recognition processes

are difficult for hackers to answer and may also result in weak, readily vulnerable queries. Because self-written questions depend on the user's security behavior, inviting users with lesser security knowledge to establish their questions can broadly increase the risk of account takeover, Optimal IdM (2022).

4. **Create many security queries:** The confidence level of the security questions can be enhanced by asking numerous users the same questions at once, specifically if their answers differ and need more specialized knowledge from an attacker. Covering questions that the user created and questions that the system defined is one potential remedy for this. In any possibility, if a user is asked a question from a list of possibilities, don't allow them to choose another until they have correctly answered the first. As a result, it is less likely that attackers will be able to guess or locate the answers they need to gain access to accounts.

5. **User encrypted storage:** This method is essential. Answers may contain hidden attributes of the user and stand used by many accounts. The system constructs the usage of secure hashing techniques to stop hackers from obtaining security responses from it, Yuxiang, Chen., Guishan, Dong., Chunxiang, Xu., Yao, Hao & Yue, Zhao (2023).

5. CONCLUSION

The purpose of the system developed is to minimize the level of insecurity on web applications and to prevent intruders from accessing authorized user information on the web applications. And to achieve this we have used OTP, Hashed Secure Question and Face Recognition couple with the traditional username and password to make the web application secure, we also used bycrpyt hashing algorithm to make password authentication is secure and inaccessible to hackers, in general the developed system will serve users better if adopted. Using precisely something familiar as a password leaves you open to typical hacking techniques, particularly social engineering. Multi-factor authentication procedures, however, are frequently tiresome. To spare themselves some bother, many users still choose not to implement multi-factor authentication on their accounts today. Even major technological businesses like Google and Facebook utilize MFA on a regular basis. However, these newly launched MFA cannot get away with demanding a user to go through numerous steps to configure and employ it.

In addition, OTP (One-time Password) is now the most often utilized MFA in the sector. When the OTP is sent while the user is surfing in a desktop client, OTP cannot prevent the user from typing it in again. System does not only use one time password but also include face recognition feature as proposed, this features allows user account to be accessed only by the authorized user thereby making our system very secure. This multi-factor authentication system offers a simple authentication option. This system uses a combination of your password (something you know), a one-time password (something you have), a facial feature (something you have), and a secure hashed question to confirm your identity. Even though these credentials come from four different categories, users are required to satisfy a few steps to verify themselves. This strategy can provide a secure authentication method while reducing the bother of using MFA.

REFERENCES

Al Abdulwahid, A., Clarke, N., Stengel, I., Furnell, S., & Reich, C. (2016). Continuous and transparent multimodal authentication: Reviewing the state of the art. *Cluster Computing*, *19*(1), 455–474. doi:10.1007/s10586-015-0510-4

Aldwairi, M., & Aldhanhani, S. (2017, August). Multi-factor authentication system. In *The 2017 International Conference on Research and Innovation in Computer Engineering and Computer Sciences (RICCES'2017)*. Malaysia Technical Scientist Association.

Alto, V. (2019). Face recognition with opencv: Haar cascade. *DataSeries Imagine the future of data*.

Asaad, R. R., Ali, R. I., Ali, Z. A., & Shaaban, A. A. (2023). Image Processing with Python Libraries. *Academic Journal of Nawroz University*, *12*(2), 410–416. doi:10.25007/ajnu.v12n2a1754

Azrour, M., Mabrouki, J., Guezzaz, A., & Farhaoui, Y. (2021). New enhanced authentication protocol for internet of things. *Big Data Mining and Analytics*, *4*(1), 1–9. doi:10.26599/BDMA.2020.9020010

Barbosa, A. T., da Silva, C. C., Caetano, R. L., da Silva, D. P. S., Barbosa, J. V., & Pinto, Z. T. (2022). Agile methodologies: And its applicability in the marketing area. *Revista Ibero-Americana de Humanidades. Ciência & Educação (Bauru)*, *8*(3), 1659–1669.

Benjamin Argyle-Ross. (2018). *Agile Methodology: An Overview, The art of iterative and incremental software development*. https://zenkit.com/en/blog/agile-methodology-an-overview/

Chen, Y., Dong, G., Xu, C., Hao, Y., & Zhao, Y. (2023). EStore: A User-Friendly Encrypted Storage Scheme for Distributed File Systems. *Sensors (Basel)*, *23*(20), 8526. doi:10.3390/s23208526 PMID:37896619

Dasgupta, D., Roy, A., & Nag, A. (2017). *Advances in user authentication*. Springer International Publishing. doi:10.1007/978-3-319-58808-7

Harris, C. R., Millman, K. J., Van Der Walt, S. J., Gommers, R., Virtanen, P., Cournapeau, D., Wieser, E., Taylor, J., Berg, S., Smith, N. J., Kern, R., Picus, M., Hoyer, S., van Kerkwijk, M. H., Brett, M., Haldane, A., del Río, J. F., Wiebe, M., Peterson, P., ... Oliphant, T. E. (2020). Array programming with NumPy. *Nature*, *585*(7825), 357–362. doi:10.1038/s41586-020-2649-2 PMID:32939066

Hou, S., Fang, D., Pan, Y., Li, Y., & Yin, G. (2021). Hybrid Pyramid Convolutional Network for Multiscale Face Detection. *Computational Intelligence and Neuroscience*, *2021*, 1–15. doi:10.1155/2021/9963322 PMID:34035802

Hu, X., & Huang, B. (2020, December). Face Detection based on SSD and CamShift. In *2020 IEEE 9th Joint International Information Technology and Artificial Intelligence Conference (ITAIC)* (Vol. 9, pp. 2324-2328). IEEE. 10.1109/ITAIC49862.2020.9339094

IETF RFC 4226. (2015). *HOTP: An HMAC-Based One-Time Password Algorithm, Anti Phishing Group, "Phishing Activity rends Report"*. http://www.antiphishing.org

Jaiswal, A. (2023). *Guide to Haar Cascade Algorithm with Object Detection Example*. https://www.analyticsvidhya.com/blog/2022/04/object-detection-using-haar-cascade-opencv/

Jiang, H., & Learned-Miller, E. (2017, May). Face detection with the faster R-CNN. In *2017 12th IEEE International Conference on Automatic Face & Gesture Recognition (FG 2017)* (pp. 650-657). IEEE. 10.1109/FG.2017.82

Juliette, E. (2023). *Data Privacy and Security: Safeguarding.* https://www.ironhack.com/gb/blog/data-privacy-and-security-safeguarding-information-in-the-digital-age

Justinha. (2023). *Authentication methods in Microsoft Entra ID - security questions.* https://learn.micro-soft.com/en-us/entra/identity/authentication/conceptauthentication-security-questions

Kunal Jain, K. (2021). *BCrypt Algorithm.* https://www.topcoder.com/thrive/articles/bcrypt-algorithm

Kwon, B. W., Sharma, P. K., & Park, J. H. (2019). CCTV-based multi-factor authentication system. *Journal of Information Processing Systems*, *15*(4), 904–919.

Li, X., Yang, Z., & Wu, H. (2020). *Face detection based on receptive field enhanced multi-task cascaded convolutional neural networks.* IEEE. doi:10.1109/ACCESS.2020.3023782

M, V. K., Venkatachalam, K., P, P., Almutairi, A., & Abouhawwash, M. (2021, July 30). Secure biometric authentication with de-duplication on distributed cloud storage. *PeerJ. Computer Science*, *7*, e569. doi:10.7717/peerj-cs.569

Ma, Q., & Huang, X. (2022). Research on recognizing required items based on opencv and machine learning. In *SHS Web of Conferences* (Vol. 140, p. 01016). EDP Sciences. 10.1051/shsconf/202214001016

Madan, A. (2021). Face recognition using Haar cascade classifier. *Int. J. Mod. Trends Sci. Technol*, *7*(01), 85–87. doi:10.46501/IJMTST070119

Margaret, R. (2018). *False Acceptance Ratio.* https://www.techopedia.com/definition/27569/false-acceptance-ratio-far

Moutsos, J. (2022). *Why You Need to Stop Using Single-Factor Authentication.* https://dynamixsolutions.com/stop-using-single-factor-authentication

Nozaki, S., Serizawa, A., Yoshihira, M., Fujita, M., Shibata, Y., Yamanaka, T., ... Nishigaki, M. (2022, August). Multi-observed Multi-factor Authentication: A Multi-factor Authentication Using Single Credential. In *International Conference on Network-Based Information Systems* (pp. 201-211). Cham: Springer International Publishing. 10.1007/978-3-031-14314-4_20

Optimal IdM. (2022). *Security Question Best Practices.* https://optimalidm.com/resources/blog/security-question-best-practices/

Ramesh, B. N., Amballi, A. R., & Mahanta, V. (2018). Django the python web framework. *International Journal of Computer Science and Information Technology Research*, *6*(2), 59–63.

Rani, C. J., & Munnisa, S. S. (2016). A survey on web authentication methods for web applications. *International Journal of Computer Science and Information Technologies*, *7*(4), 1678–1680.

Ranjan, R., Patel, V. M., & Chellappa, R. (2017). Hyperface: A deep multi-task learning framework for face detection, landmark localization, pose estimation, and gender recognition. *IEEE Transactions on Pattern Analysis and Machine Intelligence, 41*(1), 121–135. doi:10.1109/TPAMI.2017.2781233 PMID:29990235

Sawat, D.D., & Hegadi, R.S. (2017). Unconstrained face detection: a deep learning and machine learning combined approach. *CSI Transactions on ICT, 5*(2), 195-199.

Sham, S. (2021). *Security Questions: Best Practices, Examples, and Ideas*. https://www.okta.com/blog/2021/03/security-questions/

Shteingart, H., Gordon, A. N., & Gazit, J. (2016). Two-factor authentication. In Microsoft technology licensing. LLC.

Singh, C., & Singh, D. (2019). A 3-level multifactor Authentication scheme for cloud computing. *International Journal of Computer Engineering and Technology, 10*(1). Advance online publication. doi:10.34218/IJCET.10.1.2019.020

Skanda, C., Srivatsa, B., & Premananda, B. S. (2022, November). Secure Hashing using BCrypt for Cryptographic Applications. In *2022 IEEE North Karnataka Subsection Flagship International Conference (NKCon)* (pp. 1-5). IEEE. 10.1109/NKCon56289.2022.10126956

Srinath, K. R. (2017). Python–the fastest growing programming language. *International Research Journal of Engineering and Technology, 4*(12), 354–357.

Tang, C., Cui, Z., Chu, M., Lu, Y., Zhou, F., & Gao, S. (2022). Piezoelectric and Machine Learning Based Keystroke Dynamics for Highly Secure User Authentication. *IEEE Sensors Journal*.

Thomas, P. A., & Preetha Mathew, K. (2023). A broad review on non-intrusive active user authentication in biometrics. *Journal of Ambient Intelligence and Humanized Computing, 14*(1), 339–360. doi:10.1007/s12652-021-03301-x PMID:34109006

Tran, Q. N., Turnbull, B. P., & Hu, A. J. (2021). Biometrics and Privacy-Preservation: How Do They Evolve? *IEEE Open Journal of the Computer Society, 2*, 179–191. doi:10.1109/OJCS.2021.3068385

Tsai, C. H., & Su, P. C. (2021). The application of multi-server authentication scheme in internet banking transaction environments. *Information Systems and e-Business Management, 19*(1), 77–105. doi:10.1007/s10257-020-00481-5

Vagizov, M., Potapov, A., Konzhgoladze, K., Stepanov, S., & Martyn, I. (2021, October). Prepare and analyze taxation data using the Python Pandas library. *IOP Conference Series. Earth and Environmental Science, 876*(1), 012078. doi:10.1088/1755-1315/876/1/012078

Velásquez, I., Caro, A., & Rodríguez, A. (2018). Authentication schemes and methods: A systematic literature review. *Information and Software Technology, 94*, 30–37. doi:10.1016/j.infsof.2017.09.012

Wikipedia. (2023). *Dataset*. Wikipedia The Free Encyclopedia.

Wu, V. (2021). *Hashing passwords and authenticating users with bcrypt.* https://medium.com/@wu.victor.95/hashing-passwords-and-authe nticating-users-with-bcrypt-dc2fdd978568

Xie, M., Li, Y., Yoshigoe, K., Seker, R., & Bian, J. (2015, January). CamAuth: securing web authentication with camera. In *2015 IEEE 16th International Symposium on High Assurance Systems Engineering* (pp. 232-239). IEEE. 10.1109/HASE.2015.41

Yuan, C., Zhang, Q., & Wu, S. (2023). A real time fingerprint liveness detection method for fingerprint authentication systems. *Advances in Computers*, *131*, 149–180. doi:10.1016/bs.adcom.2023.04.004

Zaidi, A. Z., Chong, C. Y., Jin, Z., Parthiban, R., & Sadiq, A. S. (2021). Touch-based continuous mobile device authentication: State-of-the-art, challenges and opportunities. *Journal of Network and Computer Applications*, *191*, 103162. doi:10.1016/j.jnca.2021.103162

Zhang, T., Li, J., Jia, W., Sun, J., & Yang, H. (2018). Fast and robust occluded face detection in ATM surveillance. *Pattern Recognition Letters*, *107*, 33–40. doi:10.1016/j.patrec.2017.09.011

Chapter 5
Developing Industry 4.0 Smart Parking Through Deep Learning and IoT– Based for Electric Vehicle

Marwa Ben Arab

Electrical Systems and Renewable Energies Laboratory, National Engineering School of Sfax, University of Sfax, Tunisia

Mouna Rekik

Electrical Systems and Renewable Energies Laboratory, National Engineering School of Sfax, University of Sfax, Tunisia

Lotfi Krichen

Electrical Systems and Renewable Energies Laboratory, National Engineering School of Sfax, University of Sfax, Tunisia

ABSTRACT

Object detection is central to computer vision, drawing significant attention lately. Deep learning techniques shine for their precision, robustness, and speed. Their integration into Industry 4.0 is widely recognized, especially in AI-powered smart parking systems. This fusion is swiftly advancing, bolstering Industry 4.0 smart parking management and security. This chapter introduces a comprehensive framework presenting both software and hardware components, along with a mixing methodology, to enhance industry smart parking through detecting electric vehicles. The foundation of this approach lies in the application of deep learning, specifically utilizing the YOLOv3 methodology. In addition, the internet of things (IoT) is leveraged, employing a Raspberry Pi4 platform. The methodology for the development and execution of the system is outlined step by step to provide a clear understanding. This integrated solution showcases the detailed practical implementation. As a result, the detection of two vehicles has achieved confidence scores exceeding 0.7.

DOI: 10.4018/979-8-3693-1487-6.ch005

INTRODUCTION

The fusion of deep learning with Internet of Things (IOT) technologies has become crucial in the quickly developing field of smart buildings (Jan & Ahsan, 2021). While object detection focuses on locating and identifying certain objects within visual data, deep learning, a subset of artificial intelligence, has proven to be a game-changer in managing complex data (Pal et al., 2021; Sharma & Naaz, 2020). In the context of the smart industry, this technological synergy improves automation, security, and overall efficiency.

Deep learning and the IOT have been the focus of many researchers (Lakshmanna et al., 2022). (Babangida et al., 2022) focus on a review of implementation strategies for activity recognition by looking at various sensor's technologies. These technologies were used to gather useful data from IOT devices, reviewing preprocessing and feature extraction techniques. In addition, classification algorithms are used to identify human activities in smart homes. Finally, the study hypothesizes that combining IOT sensor data with a variety of activity labels depending on time might help reduce computational overhead and enhance activity detection. (Sujith et al., 2022) gave a thorough analysis of smart health monitoring, recent developments, and ongoing difficulties. Deep learning and machine learning have been used to evaluate health data to achieve a number of goals, including managing patient mortality and providing preventative healthcare. This has made it feasible to diagnose chronic illnesses early on, which was previously impossible. to improve the efficiency and responsiveness of the services at the hospital and at home. Additionally, cloud computing and cloud storage have been combined. (Franco et al., 2021) presented an invasive load monitoring solution based on IoT architecture for power monitoring and activity detection in smart homes. A machine learning based appliance recognition system first identifies the appliances. This is examined using three alternative models: a support vector machine classifier, a long short-term memory neural network, and a simple feed-forward neural network. Comparisons are made between the three models' accuracy, precision, recall, and F1-score. The most effective model is then applied. To offer a Deep-learning-based framework for intelligent energy management, (Han et al., 2021) concentrated on the needs of today's smart households, industries, and grids. We offer an effective channel of communication between energy distributors and consumers, as well as short-term predictions of future energy use. They used several preprocessing strategies to handle the variety of electrical data before implementing an effective decision-making algorithm for short-term forecasting on devices with limited resources. A new security architecture and an attack detection method that effectively detects devices are presented by (Kumar Sahu et al., 2021). The suggested approach extracts the precise feature representation of the data using a convolution neural network, and then further categorizes it using a long-term memory model. Twenty Raspberry Pi-based IoT devices that were infected provided the dataset for the experimental evaluation. In a Face Detection Dataset, which has 9205 photos of samples wearing masks and three categories, (Jiang et al., 2021) suggested the face detection method. In addition, they suggested Squeeze and Excitation (SE)-YOLOv3, a mask detector with balanced efficacy and efficiency. To gain the linkages between channels and incorporate the attention mechanism, also a block into Darknet 53 was introduced. This allowed the network to concentrate more on the key feature. Yet, a little amount of research has been done on object recognition in smart homes using deep learning to enforce energy control.

To achieve this, this research chapter proposes a comprehensive framework aimed at improving industry 4.0 smart parking with a focus on detecting electric vehicles. The proposed system integrates deep learning, specifically utilizing the YOLOv3 methodology for object detection, and leverages the IOT through the Raspberry Pi4 platform. The main contributions to this chapter are:

- The introduction of a detailed framework for an Industry 4.0 smart parking system, providing a structured approach for implementation.
- Utilization of deep learning, specifically the YOLOv3 methodology, showcasing the integration of advanced computer vision techniques for efficient vehicle detection.
- Leveraging the IOT and the "Raspberry Pi 4" platform to enable real-time monitoring and data collection within the smart parking system.
- A detailed presentation of the practical steps involved in implementing the proposed technologies, facilitating a clear understanding for future development and replication.
- Achievement of High Confidence Scores.

STUDIED SYSTEM

As depicted in Figure 1, the examined industry 4.0 smart parking facility integrates electric vehicles that support charging only or both charging and discharging functions through industrial charging sockets as part of an integrated energy management system. The industry 4.0 smart parking system that is being developed, permitting two-way flows of both power and information, to optimize energy distribution among various components. So, both of IOT and deep learning technologies are used to strengthen this system by detecting the availability of electric vehicles. By providing insightful information about the status of electric vehicles, this integration enhances the overall smart parking energy management system.

Figure 1. Industry 4.0 smart parking architecture

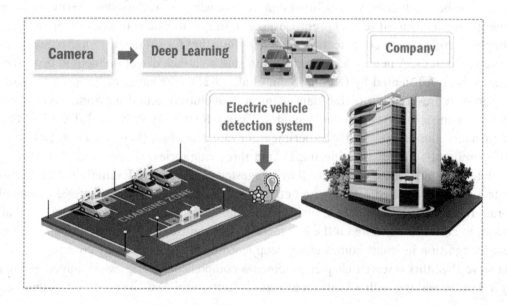

IMPORTANCE OF AN INDUSTRY 4.0 SMART PARKING

For industries specifically, the improvement of smart parking through electric vehicle detection with deep learning can bring several benefits. Here are some industry-specific improvements:

- Smart parking systems can contribute to cost savings by minimizing the time employees spend searching for parking. Additionally, optimized charging schedules can help reduce energy costs (Marwa et al., 2022).
- Utilize data from the parking system for predictive maintenance planning. For instance, if a significant number of vehicles are consistently using a specific charging station, predictive maintenance can be scheduled for that station to avoid potential downtime.
- Prioritizing the charging process of electric vehicles within the smart parking system (Marwa et al., 2023).
- Improve overall traffic flow within industrial premises by efficiently managing parking spaces. This can lead to a reduction in congestion and improved logistics
- Implement access control measures to secure parking facilities. This is crucial for industries where security is a top priority.
- Explore integration with Industrial Internet of Things devices for holistic facility management. The smart parking system can be part of a broader network of connected devices for comprehensive industrial automation.
- A convenient and well-managed parking system contributes to employee satisfaction and can be a factor in talent retention. Satisfied employees are more likely to stay with a company.

ENGINEERING

In this application, the effective execution of the practical phase is paramount, emphasizing the critical role of thoughtfully choosing hardware, software, and all tools employed in the vehicle detection system. This part presents all the used hardware and software designs and other used tools.

Hardware Design

Raspberry Pi

The Raspberry Pi is a compact-printed circuit board (PCB)-based single-board computer. This low-cost microcomputer is made to support research and experimentation in computer science (Venâncio et al., 2023). There are several types of this board, each with well-defined characteristics and functionalities. As mentioned earlier, since the studied application is based on the use of IoT, the Raspberry Pi 4 board is required. For a deeper understanding of the board's functionality, it is advisable to gain a comprehensive grasp of its architecture, depicted in Figure 2.

The Raspberry Pi showcases numerous characteristics, including:

- The board is equipped with a Quad-core Cortex A72 (ARM v8) 64-bit SoC processor operating at 1.5 GHz.

Figure 2. Raspberry Pi4 cart architecture

- It is equipped with an 8 GB of RAM (Random Access Memory). Storage is handled using the SD card.
- It provides internet access either through the Ethernet port or the built-in Wi-Fi.
- A camera module can be integrated through a specialized interface.
- Raspberry Pi is compatible with multiple operating systems, including Raspberry Pi OS (formerly Raspbian), Windows 10 IoT Core, and RetroPie, among others.
- Similar to conventional computers, you can manage the board using a screen, keyboard, and mouse, or opt for Secure Shell (SSH) connectivity through an Ethernet cable.
- The Raspberry Pi board natively supports programming languages like C, C++, Python 2/3, and Scratch. Nevertheless, it is adaptable to a wide range of programming languages. Additionally, the active and large Raspberry Pi community ensures ample resources, including forums and tutorials, making it likely that solutions to most complex issues have already been addressed.

Pi Camera

A compact camera is designed for integration with the Raspberry Pi board, illustrated in Figure 3. This camera facilitates the capture of reflected light from detected objects, transforming it into an image resembling that perceived by the human eye. This functionality empowers the generation of a significant volume of images and videos, suitable for diverse applications (Venâncio et al., 2023). In this application, the used Pi camera is a Pi V2. Table 1.

Ultrasonic Sensor

An Ultrasonic sensor is employed to identify the presence of an object. Once the sensor detects the object, it sends a signal to the camera, instructing it to capture an image. This integration enhances the

Figure 3. Pi camera

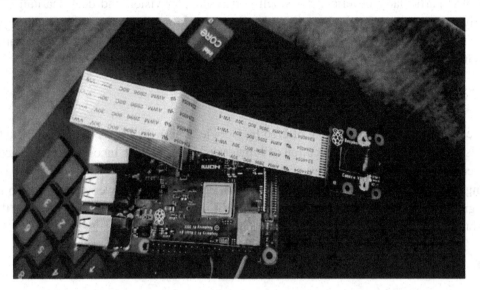

Table 1. Pi V2 camera specifications

Pi V2 Camera	
Resolution	**8 Megapixels**
Sensor Type	Sony IMX219
Sensor Size	1/4 inch
Field of View	62.2 degrees (horizontal)
Focal Length	3.04 mm
Video Sensor Support	Up to 1080p at 30 frames per second (FPS)
Image Sensor Support	JPEG, PNG, RAW
Connection Interface	CSI (Camera Serial Interface).
- Dimensions	25mm×23mm×9mm

system's ability to respond to the physical presence of objects, allowing for more precise and dynamic image capture based on real-time environmental conditions (Singh & Kapoor, 2021).

Software Design

Makesense AI

Makesense.ai offers a user-friendly, free-to-use online photo labeling tool that simplifies the process of annotating images for various computer vision and deep learning projects. With no need for complex installations, it is easy to access and utilize this tool through a web browser. Furthermore, it is designed to be compatible with multiple operating systems, ensuring a truly cross-platform experience.

This tool is particularly beneficial for small-scale computer vision and deep learning initiatives, significantly expediting and streamlining the dataset preparation phase. Once the labeling process is completed, the annotations can conveniently be downloaded in a variety of supported formats, such as YOLO, VGG, CSV, JSON and XML (Kaur & Singh, 2021).

Google Collaboratory

Colab is a complimentary cloud service offered by Google, where data processing occurs on Google's servers. It is utilized for the online execution of Jupyter notebooks. Colab incorporates interactive notebook files containing code, text, images, and other elements.

Building deep learning models demands substantial computational power. Hence, Colab is chosen because it grants access to Google's GPUs (such as INVIDIA Tesla K80) and TPUs, enabling the execution of resource-intensive tasks and complex computations (Le-Thanh et al., 2021).

Pycharm

PyCharm stands out as an integrated development environment crafted specifically for Python developers by JetBrains. Packed with a rich set of features, it offers an enhanced coding experience. Intelligent code completion, robust debugging tools, and seamless integration with version control systems like Git contribute to increased developer efficiency.

Putty

PuTTY is a software application that functions as an open-source terminal client, extensively used to connect to remote servers via protocols like Secure Shell (SSH) and Rlogin. Its primary use lies in remotely administering servers, network devices, and other computer systems by providing a command-line interface for remote management. PuTTY is available for operating systems including Windows, Linux, and various other platforms.

VNC Viewer

VNC Viewer is a software application serving as a client for Virtual Network Computing. It facilitates remote access to computers via the VNC protocol, allowing users to connect to a distant VNC server. Through VNC Viewer, users can both view and control the graphical interface of the remote computer.

Others

YOLOv3

Object detection from images has posed a persistent challenge in the field of computer vision. Despite the existence of various object detection algorithms, the standout performer in this domain is undeniably YOLO. It's an algorithm designed to detect objects in images, videos, or real-time camera streams. The implementation of YOLO utilizes the Keras and OpenCV libraries, in addition to deep learning libraries. Object classification systems are utilized to recognize specific items within images. These systems organize objects in the images into groups based on the similarity of their features, disregarding those that fall outside their established knowledge parameters.

In conventional detectors, the features learned by convolutional layers are transmitted to a classifier for making predictions. In contrast, YOLO exclusively employs 1x1 and 3x3 convolutional filters, earning its name "You Only Look Once" as it comprehensively analyzes the entire image in a single pass. Figure 4 provides a detailed illustration of the YOLOv3 architecture (Liua et al., 2021).

YOLO is an implementation of the Convolutional Neural Network (CNN) using the Darknet53 architecture. CNNs, being founded on classifiers adept at processing input images in the form of structured arrays and discerning their structure and relationships, showcase YOLO's unique advantage in speed without compromising precision. YOLO allows the model to comprehensively analyze the entire image at once. The image is partitioned into blocks based on precision and similarities with predefined classes. Regions with relatively high scores are identified as detections of related classes.

The first detection is carried out by the 82nd layer of the network, where the initial 81 layers subsample the image with a stride of 32, resulting in a feature map of 13 x 13 for an image of size 416 x 416. A 1 x 1 detection kernel yields a detection feature map of 13 x 13 x 255. Subsequently, the feature map of the 79th layer is down sampled by 2x to achieve a size of 26 x 26, and then concatenated with the feature map of the 61st layer in depth. This combined map undergoes multiple 1 x 1 convolutional layers to incorporate features from the previous layer (61), followed by a second detection performed by the 94th layer, generating a detection feature map of 26 x 26 x 255. A similar process is iterated, culminating in the final layers at the 106th layer and producing feature maps of size 52 x 52 x 255 (Diwan et al., 2021).

Figure 4. YOLOv3 architecture

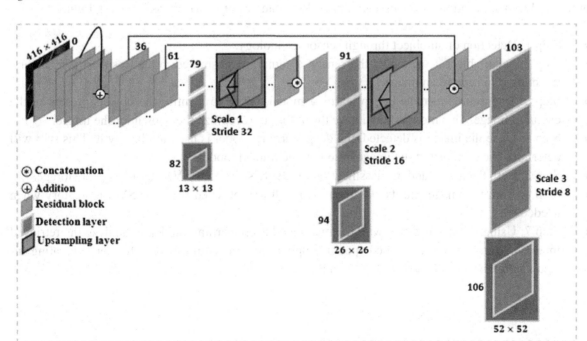

OpenCV

It is an immensely valuable library for image processing, crafted to excel in state-of-the-art computer vision tasks. This open-source library is feature-rich, especially in image processing functionalities, and incorporates a sub-library dedicated to YOLO model implementations. In this application, OpenCV is employed to visualize confidence values associated with detected objects, outline bounding boxes, and verify if all objects in the image have been successfully detected, contributing to the improvement of model development.

Raspberry Pi OS

Despite the multitude of operating systems, the preferred choice is determined by the product's manufacturer. The Raspberry Pi operating system, built on Debian-based Linux, is tailored for Raspberry Pi boards to seamlessly manage all components. A new 64-bit version is now available.

METHODOLOGY

In this section, the methodology for the development and execution of the system is outlined. Initially, the data flow within the system is elucidated to provide a clear understanding. Subsequently, the process is detailed step by step, encompassing the database preparation phase, the learning phase, the implementation phase, and the testing phase.

System Data Flow

In the analyzed application, seven essential data flows can be summarized, as shown in Figure 5:

- Step 1: Detection of an object through sensor technology.
- Step 2: Upon object detection by the sensor, a signal is transmitted to the Raspberry Pi camera, directing it to capture an image.
- Step 3: Using the pre-trained deep learning model, CNN, to identify the objects present in the captured image. This model should have the ability to recognize the content of the image.
- Step 4: Once the image is detected, the deep learning model is used to classify it. This step will determine the category of the image based on the trained model.
- Step 5: Both the image and its classification result are sent to the SVN repository for storage.
- Step 6: Both the image and its classification result are retrieved from the SVN repository when needed.
- Step 7: Using PyCharm, along with the mentioned deep learning model, to analyze the retrieved image. Depending on the studied specific application, this could involve further generating insights or taking specific actions based on the image category.

Figure 5. System data flow

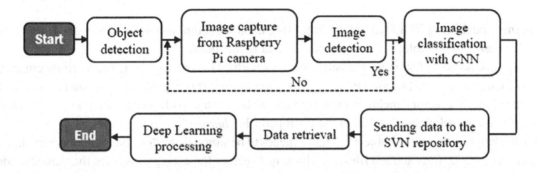

Database Preparing Phase

First and foremost, it is crucial to adequately prepare the database. The dataset used consists of 340 images collected from 'Unsplash.' Subsequently, to enhance and annotate our dataset in YOLO format, the Makesense AI software is employed, as illustrated in Figure 6.

Then, the collected data was split into training and test sets. The training set is employed to facilitate the CNN model's learning of distinctive features of various vehicle types, while the test set is utilized to assess the accuracy of the model's learning from the training data. The testing dataset in a deep learning project typically constitutes around 20–25% of the total original data.

Figure 6. Makesense AI vehicles database annotation

Training Phase

Training the model using YOLOv3 entails importing an architecture through the transfer learning approach. As presented in Table. 2, nine steps are crucial in this phase.

At first, the Google Collaboratory session connects with a GPU to accelerate the learning computations, and then an access to Google Drive is established to import the database generated by the initial phase. Indeed, each directory includes images along with annotations linked to the coordinates of the objects depicted in each image located in the unzipped file *"Images"*.

Then, the label for the studied object "Vehicle" needs to be stored in the *"custom_data/custom.names"* file. After constructing train and test files and a backup directory for storing weights of the trained model, a *"detector.data"* file that contains the three previous files paths was made in the *"custom data"* directory.

Later on, and using the git command, the Darknet project and the architecture of the CNN network Darknet53 were downloaded. Then, the file located at *"darknet/cfg/yolov3.cfg"* was duplicated to *"custom_data/cfg/yolov3-custom.cfg"*.

Upon completing these steps, the resulting hierarchy should mirror the one depicted in Figure 7.

As soon as all the necessary files and annotated photographs are in place, the last step remaining is to train the model. At the conclusion of model setup, it is imperative to retrieve the weights file *"yolov3-custom-100.weights"*. The resultant model is stored in the directory referenced in the 'backup' section of the *"backup"* file.

Implementation Phase

This part covers the implementation steps on the Raspberry Pi 4 as indicated in Table 3, providing a detailed overview of the environment setup and the installation of the required modules.

Prior to implementation, the Raspberry Pi OS was installed on the memory card using the Raspberry Pi Imager, with the activation of SSH connectivity. Then, after installing PuTTY.exe basing on the computer operating system (64-bit, Windows), a connection to the *"raspberrypi.local"* server was established as indicated in Figure 8.

It is crucial to note that, the SSH option was configured with the following settings:

- Enable compression: yes.
- Preferred SSH protocol version: 2.
- Encryption cipher selection policy: AES (SSH 2 only).

Table 2. Training phase steps

Enabling and testing the GPU
Mounting the drive to store and load file
Developing the image directory "Images"
Constructing the object name file *"custom.names"*
Constructing the train and valid file *"train.txt"* and *"test.txt"*
Constructing the backup directory *"Backup"*
Adding the three previous files paths in Yolo data file *"detector.data"*
Importing the Darknet project *"darknet"*
Downloading the CNN network configuration *"Cfg"*
Training the model

Figure 7. The training phase

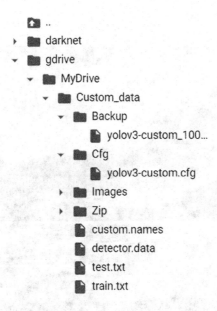

Table 3. Implementation phase steps

Installation of the Raspberry Pi OS
Installation of the Putty network file transfer application
Establishing a connection
Activating the VNC and installing library

Figure 8. The training phase

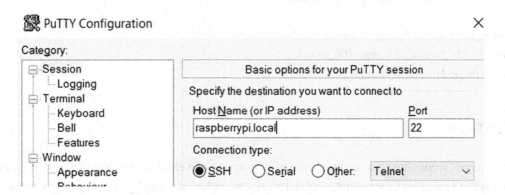

After establishing the connection, the Raspberry Pi 4 was connected to the computer using VNC. Figure 9 shows the graphical interface of the Raspberry Pi in VNC.

Lastly, the Raspberry Pi 4 must have the OpenCV and NumPy libraries installed using the VNC interface terminal to manage resources, resolve dependencies, facilitate use, and enable remote accessibility.

Figure 9. Interface of the Raspberry Pi

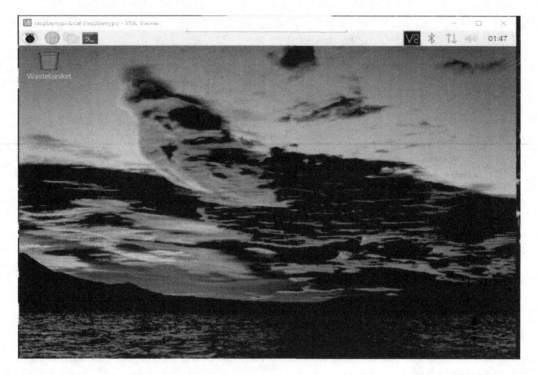

Test Phase

After the installation of PyCharm and essential libraries such as pip, numpy, and opencv-python, the code was developed as indicated in Table. 4, and a segment of it is illustrated in Figure 10. As is written in the code, three necessaries' files are needed:

- Configuration file "*yolov3-custom.cfg*".
- Weight file "*yolov3-custom-100.weights*".
- Class name file "*custom.names*".

SIMULATION

Initially, images were chosen to evaluate the effectiveness of vehicle detection utilizing the computer camera. Figure 11 displays the outcomes of detecting two vehicles using PyCharm with the implemented

Table 4. Test phase steps

Test Phase
Downloading Pycharm and library Developing code using Yolov3

Figure 10. Part of the Developed Code in PyCharm.

```
import cv2
import numpy as np

camera = cv2.VideoCapture(0)

classNames = ['Vehicle']
confThreshold = 0.1
modelConfiguration = 'yolov3-custom.cfg'
modelWeights = 'yolov3-custom_100.weights'
wht = 416
#net = cv2.dnn.readNetFromDarknet(modelConfiguration,modelWeights)
net = cv2.dnn.readNet("dnn_model/yolov3-custom.cfg.cfg", "dnn_model/yolov3-custom_100.weights")
```

YOLOv3 method. As depicted in the figure, both vehicles were successfully detected. To assess the system's performance, scores, and bounding boxes (Bboxes) are generated, as detailed in Table 5. To clear that:

- The scores are confidence values attributed to each identified object. These values reflect the degree of certainty the YOLOv3 model has in its predictions (Alsanad et al., 2022).
- Boxes are rectangular frames delineating detected objects and specifying their positions in the image. The values within the brackets denote the coordinates of the bounding boxes in the [x_{min}, y_{min}, x_{max}, y_{max}] format (Ho & Kim., 2023). From this result, and to assess the accuracy of the vehicles' detection algorithms, the Intersection over Union (IoU) is calculated as in the following equation:

$$IoU = \frac{Area\ of\ Intersection(Vehicle1, Vehicle2)}{Area\ of\ Union(Vehicle1, Vehicle2)} \tag{1}$$

The vehicle 1 score is approximately 0.871, which means the model is quite confident in the first detection. And the second score is approximately 0.787, indicating a high level of confidence in the second detection. Also, the results generate an IoU equal to 0.227 between the Bboxes of two vehicles, which indicates that the model has successfully identified and localized both vehicles as there is an overlap between their Bboxes. So, these results prove the effectiveness of the Yolov3 method and Makesense AI software.

Finally, the practical implementation of the application has been executed, as exemplified by the wiring illustrated in Figure 12. As depicted, it incorporates a Pi V2 camera, an ultrasonic sensor, and a Raspberry Pi 4 connected to the PyCharm software.

To install the card, a test was conducted on the wiring, yielding the following practical results, presented in Figure 13.

Figure 11. Part of the developed code in PyCharm

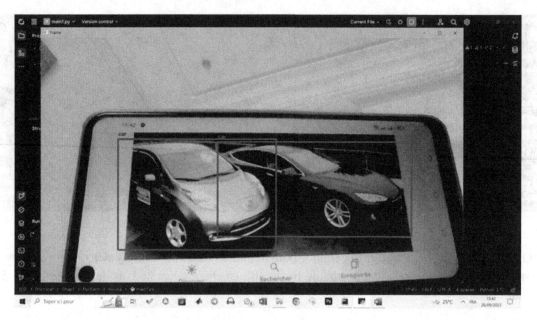

Table 5. Two vehicles detection deep learning results

	Vehicle 1	**Vehicle 2**
Score	0.87091005	0.78728944
Bboxes	[527 324 267 124]	[700 328 139 90]
IoU	≈ 0.227	

Figure 12. Circuit wiring

Figure 13. Vehicle detection test

CONCLUSION

This chapter introduces a holistic framework designed to enhance industry 4.0 smart parking, with a specific emphasis on the detection of electric vehicles. The proposed system seamlessly integrates deep learning, employing the YOLOv3 methodology for precise object detection, and harnesses the capabilities of the IOT through the Raspberry Pi 4 platform. The primary focus of the chapter is to detail the methodology for establishing the detection system, spanning from dataset preparation to practical implementation. As a result, the system demonstrates a remarkable success in vehicle detection, achieving high scores attributed to the utilization of the YOLOv3 method and Makesense AI software for image enhancement and annotation.

REFERENCES

Alsanad, H., Sadik, A., Ucan, O., Ilyas, M., & Bayat, O. (2022). YOLO-V3 based real-time drone detection algorithm. *Multimedia Tools and Applications*, *81*, 26185–26198.

Anand, G., & Kumawat, A. (2021). Object detection and position tracking in real time using Raspberry Pi. *Materials Today: Proceedings*, *47*, 3221–3226. doi:10.1016/j.matpr.2021.06.437

Babangida, L., Perumal, T., Mustapha, N., & Yaakob, R. (2022). Internet of Things (IoT) Based Activity Recognition Strategies in Smart Homes: A Review. *IEEE Sensors Journal*, *22*(9), 8327–8336. doi:10.1109/JSEN.2022.3161797

Diwan, T., Anirudh, G., & Tembhurne, J. (2023). Object detection using YOLO: Challenges, architectural successors, datasets and applications. *Multimedia Tools and Applications*, *82*, 9243–9275.

Franco, P., Martínez, J. M., Kim, Y., & Ahmed, M. (2021). IoT Based Approach for Load Monitoring and Activity Recognition in Smart Homes. *IEEE Access : Practical Innovations, Open Solutions*, *9*, 45325–45339. doi:10.1109/ACCESS.2021.3067029

Han, T., Muhammad, K., Hussain, T., Jaime, L., & Wook Baik, S. (2021). An Efficient Deep Learning Framework for Intelligent Energy Management in IoT Networks. *IEEE Internet of Things Journal*, *8*(5), 3170–3179. doi:10.1109/JIOT.2020.3013306

Jan Saleem, T., & Ahsan Chishti, M. (2021). Deep learning for the internet of things: Potential benefits and use-cases. *Digital Communications and Networks*, *7*(4), 526–542. doi:10.1016/j.dcan.2020.12.002

Jiang, X., Gao, T., Zhu, Z., & Zhao, Y. (2021). Real-Time Face Mask Detection Method Based on YO-LOv3. *Electronics, 10*, 837.

Kang, Ho., & Kim, Y. (2023). *Real-time object detection and segmentation technology: an analysis of the YOLO algorithm*. JMST Advances.

Kaur, J., & Singh, W. (2022). Tools, techniques, datasets and application areas for object detection in an image: A review. *Multimedia Tools and Applications*, *81*(27), 38297–38351. doi:10.1007/s11042-022-13153-y PMID:35493415

Kumar, S., Chandra, J., Alshamrani, S., Chaudhari, V., Dumka, A., Singh, R., Rashid, M., Gehlot, A., & AlGhamdi, S. (2022). Automatic Vehicle Identification and Classification Model Using the YOLOv3 Algorithm for a Toll Management System. *Sustainability*, *14*, 9163.

Kumar Sahu, A., Sharma, S., Tanveer, M., & Raja, R. (2021). Internet of Things attack detection using hybrid Deep Learning Model. *Computer Communications*, *176*, 146–154. doi:10.1016/j.comcom.2021.05.024

Le-Thanh, L., Nguyen-Thi-Viet, H., Lee, J., & Nguyen-Xuan, H. (2022). Machine learning-based real-time daylight analysis in buildings. *Journal of Building Engineering*, *52*, 104374. doi:10.1016/j.jobe.2022.104374

Liua, S., Xua, Y., Guoa, L., Shaoa, M., Yuea, G., & An, D. (2021). Multi-scale personnel deep feature detection algorithm based on Extended-YOLOv3. *Journal of Intelligent & Fuzzy Systems*, *40*(1), 773–786. doi:10.3233/JIFS-200778

Pal, S., Pramanik, A., Maiti, J., & Pabitra, M. (2021). Deep learning in multi-object detection and tracking: State of the art. *Applied Intelligence*, *51*(9), 6400–6429. doi:10.1007/s10489-021-02293-7

Sharma, V., & Naaz Mir, R. (2020). A comprehensive and systematic look up into deep learning based object detection techniques: A review. *Computer Science Review, 38*, 100301.

Singh, B., & Kapoor, M. (2021). A Framework for the Generation of Obstacle Data for the Study of Obstacle Detection by Ultrasonic Sensors. *IEEE Sensors Journal*, *21*(7), 1558–1748. doi:10.1109/JSEN.2021.3055515

Sujith, A., Sekhar Sajja, G., Mahalakshmi, V., Nuhmani, S., & Prasanalakshmi, B. (2022). Systematic review of smart health monitoring using deep learning and Artificial intelligence. *Neuroscience Informatics (Online)*, *2*(3), 100028. doi:10.1016/j.neuri.2021.100028

Venâncio Adriano, P., Lisboa, A., & Barbosa, A. (2022). An automatic fire detection system based on deep convolutional neural networks for low-power, resource-constrained devices. *Neural Computing & Applications*, *34*(18), 15349–15368. doi:10.1007/s00521-022-07467-z

Chapter 6
Study on Integrated Neural Networks and Fuzzy Logic Control for Autonomous Electric Vehicles

J. Vimala Devi

Department of Computer Science Engineering, Dayananda Sagar College of Engineering, India

Rajesh Vyankatesh Argiddi

iD https://orcid.org/0000-0002-4227-2384

Department of Computer Science and Engineering, Walchand Institute of Technology, Solapur, India

P. Renuka

Department of Mathematics, KPR Institute of Engineering and Technology, India

K. Janagi

iD https://orcid.org/0000-0001-6492-0939

Department of Mathematics, KPR Institute of Engineering and Technology, India

B. S. Hari

iD https://orcid.org/0000-0002-4778-3802

Department of Mechanical Engineering, Kongu Engineering College, India

S. Boopathi

Muthayammal Engineering College, India

ABSTRACT

This chapter presents a comprehensive study on the integration of neural networks and fuzzy logic control techniques for enhancing the autonomy of electric vehicles (EVs). The integration of these two paradigms aims to overcome the limitations of traditional control approaches by leveraging the complementary strengths of neural networks in learning complex patterns and fuzzy logic in handling uncertainty and imprecision. The chapter discusses the design, implementation, and evaluation of an autonomous EV control system that utilizes neural networks for learning vehicle dynamics and fuzzy logic for decision-making in various driving scenarios. Through extensive simulations and experiments, the effectiveness and robustness of the proposed integrated approach are demonstrated, showcasing its potential for improving the safety, efficiency, and adaptability of autonomous EVs in real-world environments.

DOI: 10.4018/979-8-3693-1487-6.ch006

INTRODUCTION

Autonomous electric vehicles (AEVs) represent a transformative paradigm in the automotive industry, merging cutting-edge technology with sustainable mobility solutions. At their core, AEVs are vehicles equipped with advanced sensors, computing systems, and artificial intelligence algorithms, enabling them to navigate and operate independently without human intervention. These vehicles rely on a plethora of sensors such as LiDAR, radar, cameras, and GPS to perceive their surroundings and make informed decisions in real-time. By harnessing the power of electric propulsion systems, AEVs not only reduce reliance on fossil fuels but also contribute to mitigating environmental pollution and combating climate change (Phan, Bab-Hadiashar, Fayyazi, et al., 2020).

One of the primary objectives of AEVs is to enhance road safety by minimizing human errors and distractions, which are major contributors to accidents on roads. Through sophisticated perception algorithms and advanced control systems, AEVs can detect and respond to dynamic environments, including detecting pedestrians, cyclists, and other vehicles, with a level of precision and speed unmatched by human drivers. Moreover, AEVs hold the promise of revolutionizing urban mobility by offering on-demand transportation services, reducing traffic congestion, and optimizing travel routes for efficiency. Additionally, AEVs have the potential to redefine the concept of vehicle ownership, with the rise of autonomous ride-hailing services and shared mobility platforms, leading to a shift from individual car ownership towards mobility-as-a-service models (Angundjaja et al., 2021). As the automotive industry continues to embrace autonomy and electrification, AEVs are poised to play a pivotal role in shaping the future of transportation, ushering in an era of safer, cleaner, and more efficient mobility solutions for society.

The relentless march of technological advancement has propelled the automotive industry into a new era, characterized by the emergence of autonomous vehicles and electric propulsion systems. As the capabilities of these vehicles evolve, so too must the control techniques that govern their behavior. The need for advanced control techniques in this context stems from the unprecedented complexity and dynamism of the autonomous electric vehicle (AEV) environment (Phan, Bab-Hadiashar, Hoseinnezhad, et al., 2020). Unlike traditional vehicles, which rely primarily on human drivers to interpret and respond to changing road conditions, AEVs must navigate a multifaceted landscape of sensors, algorithms, and decision-making processes to operate safely and efficiently.

At the heart of the demand for advanced control techniques lies the inherent intricacy of AEV systems. These vehicles are equipped with an array of sensors, including LiDAR, radar, cameras, and GPS, which generate vast amounts of data about the surrounding environment in real-time. Managing and interpreting this data requires sophisticated control algorithms capable of processing complex sensor inputs, identifying relevant features, and making rapid decisions to ensure safe navigation. Moreover, the transition to electric propulsion introduces additional layers of complexity, as AEVs must dynamically manage power distribution, battery state-of-charge, and energy efficiency while navigating diverse driving conditions (Guo et al., 2021). Conventional control approaches are ill-equipped to handle such multifaceted challenges, underscoring the imperative for advanced techniques that can adapt and evolve alongside the evolving landscape of AEV technology.

Furthermore, the push towards autonomy necessitates control techniques that can accommodate uncertainty, variability, and ambiguity in the AEV environment. Unlike deterministic systems where inputs and outputs are precisely defined, AEVs operate in a world characterized by inherent unpredictability, including variability in road conditions, weather patterns, and human behavior. In such dynamic environments, traditional rule-based control approaches often fall short, as they struggle to account for the myriad of possible scenarios and responses (Ahmed & Alshandoli, 2020). Herein lies the promise of advanced control techniques such as neural networks and fuzzy logic, which excel at learning complex patterns, modeling uncertainty, and making decisions in ambiguous situations. By leveraging the power of artificial intelligence and machine learning, these techniques enable AEVs to adapt and learn from experience, continuously improving their performance and reliability in the face of uncertainty. Thus, the need for advanced control techniques in the realm of AEVs transcends mere technological innovation; it represents a fundamental shift towards intelligent, adaptive systems capable of navigating the complexities of the modern transportation landscape (Al Sumarmad et al., 2022).

In the pursuit of developing robust and efficient control systems for autonomous electric vehicles (AEVs), there exists a compelling motivation to integrate neural networks and fuzzy logic. This integration is driven by the unique strengths of each approach and the synergistic benefits that arise from their combination. Neural networks excel at learning complex patterns and relationships from data, while fuzzy logic is adept at handling uncertainty and imprecision in decision-making. By integrating these two paradigms, we aim to harness the complementary advantages of both techniques to create a control system that is not only capable of navigating the complexities of the AEV environment but also adaptable to varying conditions and robust against uncertainties (Taghavifar et al., 2020).

Neural networks have emerged as powerful tools for modeling complex systems and extracting meaningful information from large datasets. In the context of AEVs, neural networks can be employed to learn the intricate dynamics of vehicle behavior, including factors such as acceleration, steering, and braking, from sensor data collected during operation. By training neural networks on real-world driving scenarios, we can develop models that accurately capture the nonlinear relationships between input signals and vehicle responses, enabling precise control and optimization of AEV performance. Furthermore, neural networks have the ability to learn from experience and adapt to changing conditions over time, making them well-suited for dynamic and evolving environments encountered by AEVs on the road (Suhail et al., 2021).

On the other hand, fuzzy logic provides a formal framework for reasoning under uncertainty, allowing for the representation of vague and imprecise information in a systematic manner. In the context of AEV control, fuzzy logic can be utilized to incorporate human-like reasoning and decision-making capabilities into the system, enabling it to handle situations where the available information is incomplete or ambiguous. By defining fuzzy rules and membership functions that capture the inherent uncertainty in the AEV environment, we can create a fuzzy inference system that can make informed decisions based on a combination of sensor data, expert knowledge, and heuristics. This enables the AEV to adapt its behavior in real-time to respond to changing conditions and unexpected events on the road (Al Sumarmad et al., 2022; Taghavifar et al., 2020).

The motivation for integrating neural networks and fuzzy logic in AEV control stems from their complementary nature and the potential synergies that arise from their combination. Neural networks excel at learning complex patterns and dynamics from data, while fuzzy logic provides a formal framework for reasoning under uncertainty. By integrating these two approaches, we can create a control system that is not only capable of learning from experience and adapting to changing conditions but also robust against uncertainties and capable of making informed decisions in ambiguous situations. This integrated approach holds the promise of enhancing the autonomy and intelligence of AEVs, enabling them to operate safely and efficiently in a wide range of real-world scenarios.

FUNDAMENTALS OF NEURAL NETWORKS AND FUZZY LOGIC

Neural networks and fuzzy logic are two distinct paradigms in the field of artificial intelligence and control systems, each with its own set of principles, techniques, and applications. Understanding the fundamentals of neural networks and fuzzy logic is essential for appreciating their role in designing advanced control systems for autonomous electric vehicles (AEVs) (Wilamowski, 2018).

Neural Network Architecture and Learning Algorithms: Neural networks are computational models inspired by the structure and function of biological neural networks in the human brain. At their core, neural networks consist of interconnected nodes organized into layers, including input, hidden, and output layers. These nodes, or neurons, perform computations on incoming data, applying activation functions to produce output signals (Gurney, 2018). The architecture of a neural network can vary widely depending on the specific task and complexity of the problem it aims to solve. Neural networks learn from data through a process known as training, wherein the network adjusts its internal parameters (weights and biases) to minimize the difference between predicted and actual outputs. This optimization process is typically achieved using various learning algorithms, such as backpropagation, gradient descent, and stochastic optimization methods. Through iterative training on labeled datasets, neural networks can learn complex patterns and relationships in the data, enabling them to make accurate predictions and classifications in novel situations.

Fuzzy Logic Principles and Membership Functions: Fuzzy logic is a mathematical framework for representing and reasoning with uncertainty and imprecision in decision-making. Unlike traditional binary logic, which operates on precise true or false values, fuzzy logic allows for degrees of truth between 0 and 1, reflecting the inherent vagueness in human reasoning. At the heart of fuzzy logic are fuzzy sets and membership functions, which describe the degree of membership of an element in a set. In fuzzy logic systems, input variables are mapped to linguistic terms (e.g., low, medium, high) using membership functions that define the degree of membership of a given input value to each term. Fuzzy rules, expressed in the form of IF-THEN statements, capture the relationship between input variables and output actions. These rules are combined using fuzzy inference mechanisms, such as Mamdani or Sugeno methods, to generate crisp output values based on fuzzy inputs (de Campos Souza, 2020).

Advantages and Limitations of Each Technique: Both neural networks and fuzzy logic offer unique advantages and limitations in the context of control systems for AEVs (Gurney, 2018; Nauck & Kruse, 2020a; Tabbussum & Dar, 2021).

- **Advantages of Neural Networks:** Neural networks excel at learning complex patterns and relationships from data, making them well-suited for tasks such as sensor fusion, trajectory prediction, and adaptive control. They can generalize from training data to make predictions in novel situations and are capable of learning from experience to improve performance over time.

- **Advantages of Fuzzy Logic:** Fuzzy logic provides a formal framework for representing and reasoning with uncertainty, enabling robust decision-making in ambiguous situations. Fuzzy logic systems are interpretable and can incorporate expert knowledge and heuristics into the control process. They are particularly useful for handling imprecise inputs and non-linear relationships in control tasks.

- **Limitations:** Neural networks can be computationally intensive and require large amounts of training data to achieve optimal performance. They may also suffer from overfitting or generalization issues if not properly trained or validated. Fuzzy logic systems rely heavily on expert knowledge and may struggle in situations where precise mathematical models are required or when faced with highly dynamic or unpredictable environments.

Understanding the advantages and limitations of neural networks and fuzzy logic is crucial for designing effective control systems that leverage the strengths of each approach in the context of AEV autonomy and intelligence. By integrating these techniques, researchers can develop hybrid control systems that combine the learning capabilities of neural networks with the reasoning and interpretability of fuzzy logic, enabling AEVs to navigate complex real-world environments with precision and reliability.

INTEGRATION OF NEURAL NETWORKS AND FUZZY LOGIC

Conceptual Framework for Integration

The integration of neural networks and fuzzy logic represents a powerful approach for developing advanced control systems capable of handling the complexities and uncertainties inherent in autonomous electric vehicles (AEVs). A conceptual framework for integrating these two techniques involves combining their respective strengths to create a hybrid control system that leverages the complementary advantages of both paradigms (Garud et al., 2021). At the heart of the integration is the fusion of neural networks and fuzzy logic into a unified architecture that exploits their synergies. The conceptual framework consists of several important components:

- **Data-driven Learning with Neural Networks:** Neural networks are employed to learn complex patterns and relationships from data collected from AEV sensors. This includes modeling vehicle dynamics, environment perception, and decision-making processes based on input-output mappings learned from training data. The neural network component serves as a flexible and adaptive system that can capture the nonlinearities and uncertainties inherent in the AEV environment.
- **Fuzzy Logic for Decision-making and Control:** Fuzzy logic is utilized to incorporate human-like reasoning and decision-making capabilities into the control system. Fuzzy rules are defined to encode expert knowledge and heuristics, allowing the system to make informed decisions based on fuzzy inputs representing uncertain or imprecise information. Fuzzy inference mechanisms combine the fuzzy rules to generate crisp control actions that govern the behavior of the AEV in real-time.
- **Integration Layer:** The integration layer acts as the bridge between the neural network and fuzzy logic components, facilitating communication and information exchange between the two paradigms. This layer encompasses techniques for mapping neural network outputs to fuzzy inputs and vice versa, enabling seamless integration of learned patterns and fuzzy reasoning in the control process.
- **Adaptation and Learning:** The integrated control system incorporates mechanisms for adaptation and learning, allowing it to continuously improve and refine its performance over time. Neural networks can adapt their internal parameters based on feedback from the environment, while fuzzy logic rules can be refined or adjusted based on observed outcomes and expert feedback. This adaptive learning process enables the control system to evolve and adapt to changing conditions and uncertainties encountered during AEV operation.

By combining neural networks and fuzzy logic within a unified conceptual framework, researchers can develop hybrid control systems that leverage the strengths of both techniques to achieve robust, adaptive, and intelligent control of AEVs. This integration enables AEVs to navigate complex and dynamic environments with precision, reliability, and human-like decision-making capabilities, paving the way for safer, more efficient, and more autonomous transportation systems of the future (Melin et al., 2023).

Hybrid Control Architecture Design

Designing a hybrid control architecture that effectively integrates neural networks and fuzzy logic is crucial for developing robust and adaptive control systems for autonomous electric vehicles (AEVs). This architecture encompasses a structured procedure and implementation strategy to seamlessly combine the strengths of both neural networks and fuzzy logic, enabling the AEV to navigate complex real-world environments with precision and reliability. The Figure 1 depicts a hybrid control architecture, combining neural networks and fuzzy logic (Garud et al., 2021; Guo et al., 2021; Tabbussum & Dar, 2021).

Procedure

- **Requirement Analysis:** The first step in designing the hybrid control architecture is to conduct a comprehensive analysis of the control requirements and objectives for the AEV. This includes defining the desired performance metrics, identifying critical tasks such as perception, decision-making, and control, and specifying the inputs and outputs of the control system.
- **Component Selection:** Based on the requirements analysis, suitable neural network and fuzzy logic components are selected for integration into the control architecture. This involves choosing neural network architectures that are well-suited for learning complex patterns and dynamics from sensor data, as well as fuzzy logic systems capable of handling uncertainty and imprecision in decision-making.
- **Interface Definition:** Next, interfaces between the neural network and fuzzy logic components are defined to facilitate communication and data exchange. This includes specifying the format and structure of inputs and outputs for each component, as well as establishing protocols for transmitting data between them.

Figure 1. Designing a hybrid control architecture: Neural networks and fuzzy logic

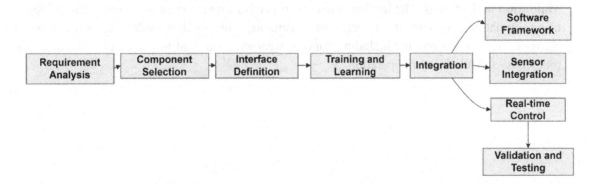

- **Training and Learning:** Neural networks are trained using labeled data collected from AEV sensors to learn the underlying patterns and dynamics of the environment. This involves preprocessing the data, selecting appropriate training algorithms, and fine-tuning the network parameters to optimize performance. Meanwhile, fuzzy logic rules are defined based on expert knowledge and heuristics to encode decision-making logic for the control system (Prabhuswamy et al., 2024; Sharma et al., 2024; Venkatasubramanian et al., 2024).
- **Integration:** The trained neural network and fuzzy logic components are integrated into a unified control architecture. This involves developing mechanisms for mapping neural network outputs to fuzzy inputs and vice versa, as well as coordinating the decision-making and control processes between the two components.

Implementation

By following this procedure and implementation strategy, researchers can design and deploy a hybrid control architecture that effectively integrates neural networks and fuzzy logic for autonomous electric vehicles. This architecture enables the AEV to navigate complex environments autonomously while adapting to uncertainties and making informed decisions in real-time, ultimately enhancing safety, efficiency, and reliability on the road(Ahmed & Alshandoli, 2020).

- **Software Framework:** The hybrid control architecture is implemented within a software framework that provides the necessary infrastructure for data processing, communication, and control. This framework may be built using programming languages such as Python, C++, or MATLAB, along with libraries and tools for neural network training (e.g., TensorFlow, PyTorch) and fuzzy logic modeling (e.g., MATLAB Fuzzy Logic Toolbox).
- **Sensor Integration:** Sensor data from various sources, including LiDAR, radar, cameras, and GPS, are integrated into the control architecture to provide real-time information about the AEV's surroundings. This involves developing interfaces to capture and preprocess sensor data before feeding it into the neural network and fuzzy logic components for analysis and decision-making (Pachiappan et al., 2024; Rahamathunnisa et al., 2024; Venkateswaran et al., 2023).
- **Real-time Control:** The integrated control architecture operates in real-time to process sensor data, make decisions, and generate control commands for the AEV. This involves implementing algorithms for perception, localization, path planning, and trajectory tracking using a combination of neural network predictions and fuzzy logic reasoning.
- **Validation and Testing:** The implemented control architecture is rigorously validated and tested using simulation environments and real-world scenarios. This involves evaluating its performance across a range of conditions, including varying weather, road, and traffic conditions, to ensure robustness and reliability in operation.

Integration Challenges and Solutions

The integration of neural networks and fuzzy logic into a unified control architecture for autonomous electric vehicles (AEVs) presents several challenges, including ensuring system effectiveness and reliability, and potential solutions(Rezaee et al., 2018).

- **Data Integration:** One of the primary challenges is integrating data from diverse sources, including sensors, into the control architecture. Different sensors may provide data in different formats and resolutions, making it challenging to preprocess and feed into both neural networks and fuzzy logic components. A solution to this challenge involves developing standardized data interfaces and preprocessing techniques to harmonize sensor data before inputting it into the control system (Hussain et al., 2023; Kumar et al., 2023).
- **Model Complexity:** Neural networks and fuzzy logic models can be highly complex, requiring significant computational resources and memory to train and execute. Integrating these models into a real-time control system while maintaining acceptable performance can be challenging. One solution is to optimize the architecture and parameters of neural networks and fuzzy logic systems to reduce computational complexity while preserving accuracy and reliability.
- **Mapping Neural Outputs to Fuzzy Inputs:** Another challenge is mapping the outputs of neural networks to inputs of fuzzy logic systems and vice versa. This requires careful design of interfaces and conversion mechanisms to ensure seamless communication between the two components. Solutions may involve defining clear mappings between neural network outputs and fuzzy input variables and developing algorithms to convert between different data representations (Agrawal, Shashibhushan, et al., 2023; Veeranjaneyulu et al., 2023).
- **Robustness and Adaptability:** AEVs operate in dynamic and uncertain environments, requiring control systems to be robust and adaptable to varying conditions. Integrating neural networks and fuzzy logic can enhance robustness and adaptability by leveraging the learning capabilities of neural networks and the reasoning abilities of fuzzy logic. Solutions include incorporating mechanisms for online learning and adaptation, as well as designing fuzzy logic rules to handle uncertainty and ambiguity effectively.
- **Validation and Testing:** Finally, validating and testing the integrated control system poses a significant challenge due to the complexity and interconnectedness of neural networks and fuzzy logic components. Solutions involve rigorous testing in simulation and real-world environments, as well as the development of validation frameworks to evaluate system performance across a range of scenarios.

Researchers are developing robust control architectures for autonomous vehicles (AEVs) using innovative solutions to overcome integration challenges, enhancing autonomy, safety, and efficiency on the road.

MODELING VEHICLE DYNAMICS WITH NEURAL NETWORKS

Data Collection and Preprocessing: Data collection is a crucial first step in modeling vehicle dynamics with neural networks. Various sensors such as accelerometers, gyroscopes, wheel speed sensors, and GPS units can be used to gather data on vehicle motion, including acceleration, steering, and braking.

Additionally, environmental factors such as road conditions and weather may also be considered. Once collected, the data undergoes preprocessing to remove noise, outliers, and irrelevant information. This may involve filtering, normalization, and feature extraction techniques to ensure the data is suitable for input into the neural network model (Phan, Bab-Hadiashar, Hoseinnezhad, et al., 2020; Rezaee et al., 2018).

Neural Network Modeling of EV Dynamics: Neural networks offer a powerful approach to modeling the complex dynamics of electric vehicles (EVs). Depending on the specific application, different neural network architectures such as feedforward, recurrent, or convolutional networks may be used. The neural network is trained to learn the relationship between input variables (e.g., sensor readings) and output variables (e.g., vehicle behavior). This may include predicting vehicle trajectory, estimating state-of-charge (SoC) of the battery, or optimizing energy consumption. The neural network model is designed to capture the nonlinear relationships and dynamics of the EV system, allowing it to adapt and generalize to various driving conditions (Ahmed & Alshandoli, 2020; Guo et al., 2021; Phan, Bab-Hadiashar, Hoseinnezhad, et al., 2020). The implementation procedure for Neural Network Modeling of EV Dynamics is depicted in Figure 2.

- **Data Preparation:** Begin by collecting a comprehensive dataset containing input-output pairs that represent the dynamics of the electric vehicle (EV). Inputs may include sensor readings such as accelerometer data, steering angle, wheel speed, battery voltage, and current. Corresponding

Figure 2. Implementation procedure for neural network modeling of EV dynamics

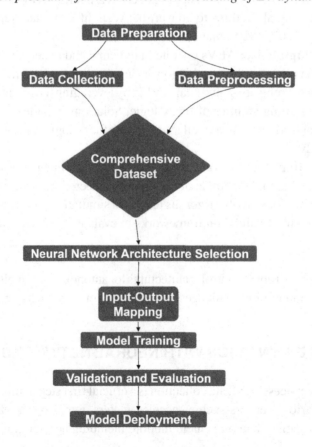

outputs may include vehicle acceleration, steering angle changes, and battery state-of-charge (SoC). Ensure the dataset covers a wide range of driving conditions, including various speeds, road types, and environmental factors (Babu et al., 2022; Chandrika et al., 2023).

- **Data Preprocessing:** Preprocess the collected data to ensure it is suitable for training the neural network model. This may involve normalization to scale the input features, handling missing or erroneous data points, and removing outliers. Additionally, consider augmenting the dataset through techniques such as data interpolation or perturbation to increase its diversity and robustness.

- **Neural Network Architecture Selection:** Choose an appropriate neural network architecture for modeling the EV dynamics. This may include feedforward neural networks, recurrent neural networks (RNNs), convolutional neural networks (CNNs), or hybrid architectures depending on the complexity of the task and the characteristics of the data. Consider factors such as the number of layers, activation functions, and connectivity patterns to design an architecture that can effectively capture the nonlinear relationships in the data.

- **Input-Output Mapping:** Define the input and output layers of the neural network based on the selected architecture. Map the input features to the corresponding output variables to establish the relationship between sensor readings and vehicle dynamics. Ensure the input layer size matches the dimensionality of the input data, and the output layer size aligns with the number of output variables to be predicted.

- **Model Training:** Train the neural network model using the preprocessed dataset. Split the data into training and validation sets to monitor the model's performance during training and prevent overfitting. Utilize optimization algorithms such as stochastic gradient descent (SGD) or Adam to minimize the loss function and update the network parameters iteratively. Experiment with different hyperparameters such as learning rate, batch size, and regularization techniques to optimize model performance (Anitha et al., 2023; Sundaramoorthy et al., 2024; Zekrifa et al., 2023).

- **Validation and Evaluation:** Evaluate the trained model's performance using the validation dataset. Calculate metrics such as mean squared error (MSE), root mean squared error (RMSE), or coefficient of determination (R-squared) to assess the model's accuracy and generalization ability. Visualize the predicted outputs against the ground truth to identify any discrepancies and areas for improvement. Iterate on the model architecture and training process as needed to enhance performance.

- **Model Deployment:** Once the neural network model achieves satisfactory performance on the validation dataset, deploy it for real-world applications. Integrate the trained model into the overall control system of the electric vehicle to facilitate tasks such as autonomous driving, energy management, or predictive maintenance. Continuously monitor and update the model as new data becomes available to ensure its reliability and effectiveness in operation.

Researchers have developed reliable neural network models for electric vehicle dynamics, enabling applications in autonomous driving and intelligent transportation systems.

Training and Validation Strategies: Training and validation are critical steps in developing a reliable neural network model for vehicle dynamics. Training data is divided into training and validation sets, with the former used to adjust the network parameters through optimization algorithms such as backpropagation. Validation data is then used to evaluate the performance of the trained model and ensure it generalizes well to unseen data. Strategies such as cross-validation, data augmentation, and early stopping may be employed to improve the robustness and generalization ability of the model. Additionally, techniques such as transfer learning, where pre-trained models are fine-tuned for specific tasks, may also be utilized to accelerate the training process and improve overall performance (Satav et al., 2023; Verma et al., 2024).

In summary, modeling vehicle dynamics with neural networks involves data collection, preprocessing, neural network modeling, and training/validation strategies. By leveraging the capabilities of neural networks, researchers can develop accurate and reliable models that capture the complex dynamics of electric vehicles, enabling applications such as autonomous driving, energy management, and predictive maintenance.

FUZZY LOGIC DECISION-MAKING SYSTEM

Design of Fuzzy Inference System (FIS)

The Fuzzy Inference System (FIS) is a crucial component of a fuzzy logic decision-making system, consisting of several important elements (Jane & Ganeshi, 2019).

i.   **Input Variables:** Define the input variables relevant to the decision-making process. These variables represent the inputs to the system and may include factors such as speed, distance, or environmental conditions.
ii. **Membership Functions:** Assign membership functions to each input variable to quantify the degree of membership or truthfulness of a given input value to each linguistic term (e.g., low, medium, high).
iii. **Fuzzy Rules:** Formulate a set of fuzzy rules that encode the relationship between the input variables and the output actions. These rules typically take the form of IF-THEN statements and are based on expert knowledge or heuristics.
iv. **Inference Engine:** Implement an inference mechanism that combines the fuzzy rules to determine the appropriate output actions based on the current input values. Common inference methods include Mamdani and Sugeno.
v.   **Output Variables:** Define the output variables representing the actions or decisions to be taken by the system. These variables may include control commands, set points, or recommendations.
vi. **Defuzzification:** Convert the fuzzy output values obtained from the inference engine into crisp output values suitable for implementation. This process involves aggregating and averaging the fuzzy output values to derive a single, actionable output.

Rule Base Construction

A fuzzy logic system's rule base comprises fuzzy IF-THEN rules, based on expert knowledge or empirical observations, that dictate the decision-making process. These rules specify antecedents and consequents based on input variables' current states. An example of a rule base for controlling the speed of an autonomous vehicle is provided (Wu et al., 2020). Figure 3 depicts the construction of a rule base for the decision-making process.

- IF distance is close AND speed is high THEN decrease speed
- IF distance is moderate AND speed is moderate THEN maintain current speed
- IF distance is far AND speed is low THEN increase speed

Membership Function Selection

The selection of membership functions involves several steps, as illustrated in Figure 4. By following these steps, designers can develop an effective fuzzy logic decision-making system with a well-defined Fuzzy Inference System (FIS), a robust rule base, and carefully selected membership functions tailored to the specific application domain (Ghani et al., 2018; Jane & Ganeshi, 2019).

- **Variable Identification:** Identify the input and output variables relevant to the decision-making process. These variables represent the factors influencing the system's behavior and the actions to be taken.
- **Partitioning:** Divide the range of each input and output variable into linguistic terms or fuzzy sets. Choose appropriate linguistic terms that capture the relevant characteristics of the variables.
- **Membership Function Design:** Select suitable membership functions for each linguistic term. Common types of membership functions include triangular, trapezoidal, Gaussian, and sigmoidal. Consider factors such as the shape, slope, and spread of the membership functions to accurately represent the input-output relationships.
- **Validation:** Validate the selected membership functions through simulation, experimentation, or expert evaluation. Ensure that the membership functions effectively capture the fuzzy relationships between the input and output variables and provide meaningful interpretations for decision-making.

Figure 3. Rule base construction for decision-making process

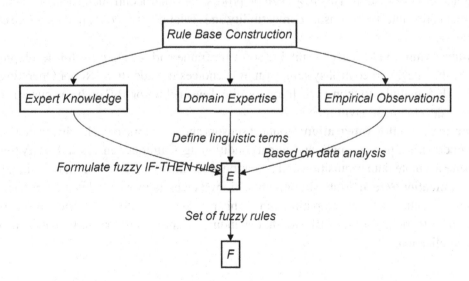

Figure 4. Procedure for selecting membership functions

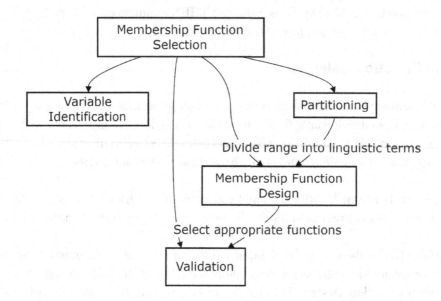

IMPLEMENTATION OF INTEGRATED CONTROL SYSTEM

Software and Hardware Setup

The figure 5 illustrates the integration of a neural network and fuzzy logic modules in both software and hardware setups (Nauck & Kruse, 2020b; Rezaee et al., 2018). Developers can construct efficient integrated control systems for various applications like autonomous vehicles, robotics, industrial automation, and smart infrastructure by adhering to specific implementation guidelines and control strategies.

- **Hardware Selection:** Choose appropriate hardware components based on the requirements of the integrated control system. This may include processors, microcontrollers, sensors, actuators, and communication interfaces. Ensure compatibility and scalability to accommodate future expansions or upgrades.
- **Software Framework:** Select a suitable software framework or platform for developing and deploying the integrated control system. Common choices include ROS (Robot Operating System), MATLAB/Simulink, Python with libraries like TensorFlow or PyTorch, or custom embedded software development environments.
- **Sensor and Actuator Integration:** Connect sensors and actuators to the hardware platform, ensuring proper wiring, power supply, and signal conditioning. Calibrate sensors and verify functionality to ensure accurate data acquisition and actuation (Hussain et al., 2023; Kumar et al., 2023).
- **Communication Setup:** Establish communication channels between hardware components, including sensors, actuators, and computing units. This may involve wired or wireless protocols such as CAN bus, Ethernet, Wi-Fi, or Bluetooth, depending on the specific requirements and constraints of the application.

- **Testing and Validation:** Conduct comprehensive testing and validation of the hardware setup to ensure reliability, stability, and compatibility with the integrated control system. Verify sensor accuracy, actuator responsiveness, and data transmission integrity under various operating conditions.

Integration of Neural Network and Fuzzy Logic Modules (Rezaee et al., 2018; Suhail et al., 2021)

- **Parallel Integration:** Run neural network and fuzzy logic modules in parallel on the computing platform. Each module processes sensor data independently and generates control commands or recommendations based on its respective algorithms and logic.
- **Sequential Integration:** Implement a sequential integration approach where sensor data is first processed by one module (e.g., neural network) to generate intermediate outputs, which are then fed into the subsequent module (e.g., fuzzy logic) for further processing and decision-making.
- **Hybrid Integration:** Explore hybrid integration strategies that combine elements of both neural networks and fuzzy logic within a unified control architecture. This may involve using neural networks for perception and prediction tasks, while fuzzy logic is utilized for decision-making and control actions (Boopathi et al., 2021; KAV et al., 2023; Nishanth et al., 2023).

Real-Time Control Strategies

- **Feedback Control:** Implement feedback control loops that continuously monitor the system's state and adjust control actions in response to deviations from desired trajectories or set points. This may involve PID (Proportional-Integral-Derivative) controllers, state feedback controllers, or model predictive control (MPC) algorithms.

Figure 5. Software and hardware setup: Integration of neural network and fuzzy logic modules

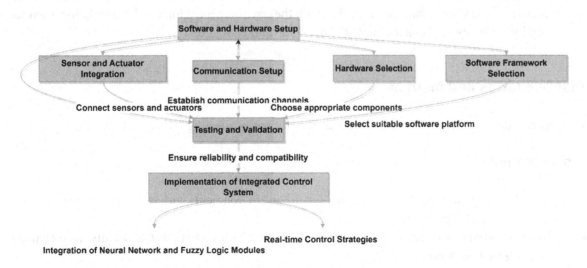

- **Feedforward Control:** Utilize feedforward control techniques to anticipate and compensate for disturbances or external factors that may affect the system's behavior. This involves precomputed control actions based on known system dynamics or predictive models to achieve desired performance without relying solely on feedback.
- **Adaptive Control:** Employ adaptive control strategies that dynamically adjust control parameters or algorithms based on changes in the system or environment. This may include adaptive PID control, model reference adaptive control (MRAC), or reinforcement learning-based approaches that continuously learn and adapt to evolving conditions.
- **Safety and Redundancy:** Implement safety mechanisms and redundancy strategies to ensure fail-safe operation and mitigate potential risks or failures. This may involve redundant sensor configurations, fault detection and isolation (FDI) algorithms, and emergency stop mechanisms to safeguard against unexpected events or malfunctions (Selvakumar et al., 2023; Sengeni et al., 2023).

PERFORMANCE EVALUATION

Simulation Environment Description

- **Setup Simulation Environment:** Define the simulation environment using suitable simulation software such as MATLAB/Simulink, Gazebo, or CARLA. Specify the virtual environment parameters such as road layout, traffic density, weather conditions, and obstacles (Jane & Ganeshi, 2019).
- **Model Integration:** Integrate the developed control system model into the simulation environment. This involves connecting the control system to the virtual vehicle model, sensors, actuators, and other simulation components.
- **Sensor Data Generation:** Simulate sensor data generation based on the vehicle's dynamics, environment, and control inputs. Generate realistic sensor readings such as LiDAR, camera images, GPS, and inertial measurements to mimic real-world scenarios.
- **Real-time Simulation:** Run the simulation in real-time or accelerated mode to emulate the dynamic behavior of the vehicle and its interaction with the environment. Monitor the simulation to ensure stability, accuracy, and consistency of results (Revathi et al., 2024).

Test Scenarios and Metrics

The Figure 6 depicts various scenarios and matrices for various testing (Qiao et al., 2019).

Test Scenarios

- Urban Driving: Simulate driving scenarios in urban environments with intersections, traffic lights, pedestrians, and other vehicles.
- Highway Driving: Evaluate performance on highways with varying traffic density, lane changes, and merging maneuvers.

Figure 6. Various testing scenario and matrices

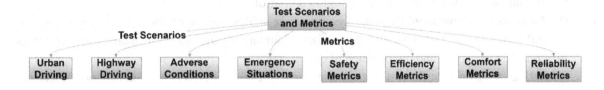

- Adverse Conditions: Test the system's robustness under adverse conditions such as rain, fog, low visibility, or slippery roads.
- Emergency Situations: Assess the system's response to emergency scenarios such as sudden obstacles, collision avoidance, or vehicle malfunctions.

Metrics

- Safety: Measure safety-related metrics such as collision rate, distance to obstacles, and adherence to traffic rules.
- Efficiency: Evaluate efficiency metrics including fuel consumption, energy usage, and travel time.
- Comfort: Assess passenger comfort metrics such as smoothness of acceleration, braking, and steering.
- Reliability: Quantify reliability metrics such as system uptime, error rate, and robustness to sensor noise or failures.

COMPARATIVE ANALYSIS WITH BASELINE APPROACHES

Researchers can evaluate the integrated control system's effectiveness, efficiency, and reliability in various simulated scenarios using these performance evaluation procedures, making informed decisions for further improvements and optimizations (de Campos Souza, 2020; Jane & Ganeshi, 2019).

- **Baseline Selection:** Choose appropriate baseline approaches for comparison, such as traditional PID control, rule-based systems, or other existing control algorithms relevant to the application domain.

Figure 7. Comparative analysis with baseline approaches

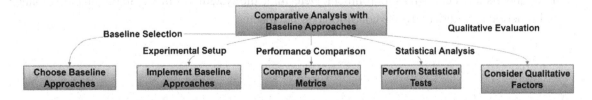

- **Experimental Setup:** Implement the baseline approaches in the same simulation environment and test scenarios used for evaluating the integrated control system.
- **Performance Comparison:** Conduct a comparative analysis of the performance of the integrated control system against the baseline approaches. Compare significant performance metrics across different test scenarios and environmental conditions.
- **Statistical Analysis:** Perform statistical tests such as t-tests or ANOVA to determine if there are significant differences in performance between the integrated control system and the baseline approaches (Yupapin et al., 2023).
- **Qualitative Evaluation:** Consider qualitative factors such as ease of implementation, scalability, and adaptability when comparing the integrated control system with baseline approaches.

Results and Discussion

Researchers can evaluate the performance of an integrated control system by analyzing simulation results, assessing effectiveness, and gaining insights into system performance, enabling informed decision-making for further enhancement (de Campos Souza, 2020; Garud et al., 2021).

Analysis of Simulation Results

- **Interpretation of Metrics:** Analyze the simulation results obtained from various test scenarios and metrics. Interpret the performance of the integrated control system based on safety, efficiency, comfort, and reliability metrics. Identify trends, patterns, and areas of improvement revealed by the simulation data.
- **Comparison with Baseline Approaches:** Compare the performance of the integrated control system with baseline approaches. Assess the effectiveness and superiority of the proposed system in achieving the desired objectives and outperforming traditional control methods.
- **Identification of Strengths and Weaknesses:** Identify the strengths and weaknesses of the integrated control system based on the simulation results. Highlight areas where the system performs well and areas where improvements or optimizations are needed.

Effectiveness and Robustness

- **Effectiveness:** Evaluate the effectiveness of the integrated control system in achieving its intended goals and objectives. Measure how well the system performs in terms of safety, efficiency, comfort, and reliability compared to predefined benchmarks or performance targets.
- **Robustness:** Assess the robustness of the integrated control system in handling uncertainties, variations, and disturbances in the environment. Determine the system's ability to maintain performance and functionality under adverse conditions or unexpected events.

Insights into Integrated Control System Performance

- **Simulation-Based Insights:** Gain insights into the performance of the integrated control system based on the simulation results. Identify significant factors influencing system performance, such as sensor accuracy, control algorithms, environmental conditions, and vehicle dynamics.
- **Root Cause Analysis:** Conduct a root cause analysis to understand the underlying reasons for any observed limitations or failures of the integrated control system. Identify potential sources of errors, bottlenecks, or inefficiencies that may impact system performance.
- **Feedback Loop:** Use insights from the simulation results to iteratively improve and optimize the integrated control system. Incorporate feedback from the analysis into the design, development, and validation processes to enhance system performance and robustness over time.

CHALLENGES AND FUTURE DIRECTIONS

Researchers and industry stakeholders can accelerate the development and adoption of autonomous electric vehicles by addressing current challenges, securing improvement opportunities, and embracing future research directions (Suhail et al., 2021; Tabbussum & Dar, 2021).

Current Challenges in Autonomous EV Control

- **Sensor Fusion and Perception:** Integrating data from multiple sensors and achieving robust perception capabilities remains a challenge. Different sensor modalities may have varying levels of accuracy and reliability, leading to difficulties in accurately interpreting the environment and making informed decisions (Agrawal, Magulur, et al., 2023; Jeevanantham et al., 2022; Karthik et al., 2023).
- **Real-time Decision-making:** Ensuring real-time decision-making capabilities in complex and dynamic environments poses a significant challenge. Autonomous electric vehicles (AEVs) must process large volumes of sensor data and execute control actions within tight time constraints while maintaining safety and efficiency (Revathi et al., 2024).
- **Safety and Regulatory Compliance:** Ensuring the safety of AEVs and complying with regulatory standards are ongoing challenges. Addressing edge cases, unpredictable scenarios, and potential failures in the control system requires rigorous testing, validation, and certification processes.
- **Energy Efficiency and Range Optimization:** Maximizing energy efficiency and optimizing range are critical for the widespread adoption of electric vehicles. Developing intelligent control strategies to optimize energy consumption, manage battery health, and plan efficient routes remains a challenge (Boopathi et al., 2023; Boopathi & Sivakumar, 2013; Domakonda et al., 2022; Saravanan et al., 2022).

Opportunities for Improvement

- **Advancements in Sensor Technology:** Continued advancements in sensor technology, including LiDAR, radar, cameras, and inertial sensors, offer opportunities to enhance perception capabilities and improve the reliability of AEV control systems (Al Sumarmad et al., 2022).
- **Artificial Intelligence and Machine Learning:** Leveraging artificial intelligence (AI) and machine learning (ML) techniques can improve decision-making and control capabilities of AEVs. AI algorithms can learn from data and adapt to changing environments, enabling more robust and adaptive control strategies.
- **Connectivity and V2X Communication:** Expanding vehicle-to-everything (V2X) communication capabilities can enhance situational awareness and enable cooperative control strategies among vehicles, infrastructure, and other road users. V2X communication facilitates real-time exchange of information about traffic conditions, road hazards, and vehicle intentions, improving overall safety and efficiency.
- **Autonomous Fleet Management:** Developing autonomous fleet management systems can optimize the operation of large fleets of AEVs. Centralized control algorithms can dynamically allocate vehicles, optimize routing, and schedule maintenance tasks to maximize fleet efficiency and minimize operational costs.

Future Research Directions (2030 - Developments)

- **Autonomous Mobility-as-a-Service (MaaS):** Research in autonomous MaaS systems aims to revolutionize urban transportation by providing on-demand, shared mobility services using fleets of AEVs. Future developments may focus on seamless integration with public transit, dynamic ride-sharing algorithms, and personalized mobility experiences (de Campos Souza, 2020).
- **AI-driven Predictive Control:** Advancements in AI-driven predictive control algorithms can enable AEVs to anticipate future events, plan proactive actions, and optimize long-term objectives such as energy efficiency, passenger comfort, and traffic flow management.
- **Energy Harvesting and Storage:** Research into energy harvesting technologies, such as solar panels and regenerative braking systems, can enhance the energy autonomy of AEVs. Future developments may focus on integrating energy harvesting mechanisms with advanced battery technologies to extend range and reduce reliance on external charging infrastructure.
- **Ethical and Social Implications:** Addressing ethical and social implications of autonomous EV control systems will become increasingly important. Research may explore ethical decision-making frameworks, human-machine interaction, and societal acceptance of autonomous technologies to ensure equitable and responsible deployment of AEVs.

CONCLUSION

In this chapter, we have presented a comprehensive study on the integration of neural networks and fuzzy logic control techniques to enhance the autonomy of electric vehicles (EVs). Our aim was to overcome the limitations of traditional control approaches by leveraging the complementary strengths of neural networks in learning complex patterns and fuzzy logic in handling uncertainty and imprecision. The proposed integrated approach for autonomous EV control systems, utilizing neural networks for vehicle dynamics learning and fuzzy logic for decision-making, has been demonstrated to enhance safety, efficiency, and adaptability in real-world environments through design, implementation, and evaluation.

The integrated approach of neural networks and fuzzy logic in autonomous electric vehicles (EVs) has shown efficacy in accurately detecting the environment, making timely decisions, and adapting to changing conditions. Future research may focus on optimizing the control system, exploring advanced AI techniques like reinforcement learning, and integrating with emerging technologies like V2X communication and energy harvesting.

The chapter highlights the potential of integrating neural networks and fuzzy logic control techniques to enhance the autonomy of electric vehicles, paving the way for safer, more efficient, and adaptable transportation systems.

ABBREVIATIONS

AEV: Autonomous Electric Vehicle
FIS: Fuzzy Inference System
PID: Proportional-Integral-Derivative
MPC: Model Predictive Control
AI: Artificial Intelligence
ML: Machine Learning
V2X: Vehicle-to-Everything
MaaS: Mobility-as-a-Service

REFERENCES

Agrawal, A. V., Magulur, L. P., Priya, S. G., Kaur, A., Singh, G., & Boopathi, S. (2023). Smart Precision Agriculture Using IoT and WSN. In *Handbook of Research on Data Science and Cybersecurity Innovations in Industry 4.0 Technologies* (pp. 524–541). IGI Global. doi:10.4018/978-1-6684-8145-5.ch026

Agrawal, A. V., Shashibhushan, G., Pradeep, S., Padhi, S., Sugumar, D., & Boopathi, S. (2023). Synergizing Artificial Intelligence, 5G, and Cloud Computing for Efficient Energy Conversion Using Agricultural Waste. In Sustainable Science and Intelligent Technologies for Societal Development (pp. 475–497). IGI Global.

Ahmed, A. A., & Alshandoli, A. S. (2020). Using of neural network controller and fuzzy pid control to improve electric vehicle stability based on a14-dof model. *2020 International Conference on Electrical Engineering (ICEE)*, 1–6. 10.1109/ICEE49691.2020.9249784

Al Sumarmad, K. A., Sulaiman, N., Wahab, N. I. A., & Hizam, H. (2022). Energy management and voltage control in microgrids using artificial neural networks, PID, and fuzzy logic controllers. *Energies*, *15*(1), 303. doi:10.3390/en15010303

Angundjaja, C. Y., Wang, Y., & Jiang, W. (2021). Power management for connected EVs using a fuzzy logic controller and artificial neural network. *Applied Sciences (Basel, Switzerland)*, *12*(1), 52. doi:10.3390/app12010052

Anitha, C., Komala, C., Vivekanand, C. V., Lalitha, S., & Boopathi, S. (2023). Artificial Intelligence driven security model for Internet of Medical Things (IoMT). *IEEE Explore*, 1–7.

Babu, B. S., Kamalakannan, J., Meenatchi, N., Karthik, S., & Boopathi, S. (2022). Economic impacts and reliability evaluation of battery by adopting Electric Vehicle. *IEEE Explore*, 1–6.

Boopathi, S., Balasubramani, V., Kumar, R. S., & Singh, G. R. (2021). The influence of human hair on kenaf and Grewia fiber-based hybrid natural composite material: An experimental study. *Functional Composites and Structures*, *3*(4), 045011. doi:10.1088/2631-6331/ac3afc

Boopathi, S., Kumar, P. K. S., Meena, R. S., Sudhakar, M., & Associates. (2023). Sustainable Developments of Modern Soil-Less Agro-Cultivation Systems: Aquaponic Culture. In Human Agro-Energy Optimization for Business and Industry (pp. 69–87). IGI Global.

Boopathi, S., & Sivakumar, K. (2013). Experimental investigation and parameter optimization of near-dry wire-cut electrical discharge machining using multi-objective evolutionary algorithm. *International Journal of Advanced Manufacturing Technology*, *67*(9–12), 2639–2655. doi:10.1007/s00170-012-4680-4

Chandrika, V., Sivakumar, A., Krishnan, T. S., Pradeep, J., Manikandan, S., & Boopathi, S. (2023). Theoretical Study on Power Distribution Systems for Electric Vehicles. In *Intelligent Engineering Applications and Applied Sciences for Sustainability* (pp. 1–19). IGI Global. doi:10.4018/979-8-3693-0044-2.ch001

de Campos Souza, P. V. (2020). Fuzzy neural networks and neuro-fuzzy networks: A review the main techniques and applications used in the literature. *Applied Soft Computing*, *92*, 106275. doi:10.1016/j.asoc.2020.106275

Domakonda, V. K., Farooq, S., Chinthamreddy, S., Puviarasi, R., Sudhakar, M., & Boopathi, S. (2022). Sustainable Developments of Hybrid Floating Solar Power Plants: Photovoltaic System. In Human Agro-Energy Optimization for Business and Industry (pp. 148–167). IGI Global.

Garud, K. S., Jayaraj, S., & Lee, M.-Y. (2021). A review on modeling of solar photovoltaic systems using artificial neural networks, fuzzy logic, genetic algorithm and hybrid models. *International Journal of Energy Research*, *45*(1), 6–35. doi:10.1002/er.5608

Ghani, U., Bajwa, I. S., & Ashfaq, A. (2018). A fuzzy logic based intelligent system for measuring customer loyalty and decision making. *Symmetry*, *10*(12), 761. doi:10.3390/sym10120761

Guo, J., Li, K., Fan, J., Luo, Y., & Wang, J. (2021). Neural-fuzzy-based adaptive sliding mode automatic steering control of vision-based unmanned electric vehicles. *Chinese Journal of Mechanical Engineering*, *34*(1), 1–13. doi:10.1186/s10033-021-00597-w

Gurney, K. (2018). *An introduction to neural networks*. CRC Press. doi:10.1201/9781315273570

Hussain, Z., Babe, M., Saravanan, S., Srimathy, G., Roopa, H., & Boopathi, S. (2023). Optimizing Biomass-to-Biofuel Conversion: IoT and AI Integration for Enhanced Efficiency and Sustainability. In Circular Economy Implementation for Sustainability in the Built Environment (pp. 191–214). IGI Global.

Jane, J. B., & Ganeshi, E. (2019). A review on big data with machine learning and fuzzy logic for better decision making. *Int. J. Sci. Technol. Res*, *8*, 1121–1125.

Jeevanantham, Y. A., Saravanan, A., Vanitha, V., Boopathi, S., & Kumar, D. P. (2022). Implementation of Internet-of Things (IoT) in Soil Irrigation System. *IEEE Explore*, 1–5.

Karthik, S., Hemalatha, R., Aruna, R., Deivakani, M., Reddy, R. V. K., & Boopathi, S. (2023). Study on Healthcare Security System-Integrated Internet of Things (IoT). In Perspectives and Considerations on the Evolution of Smart Systems (pp. 342–362). IGI Global.

KAV, R. P., Pandraju, T. K. S., Boopathi, S., Saravanan, P., Rathan, S. K., & Sathish, T. (2023). Hybrid Deep Learning Technique for Optimal Wind Mill Speed Estimation. *2023 7th International Conference on Electronics, Communication and Aerospace Technology (ICECA)*, 181–186.

Kumar, M., Kumar, K., Sasikala, P., Sampath, B., Gopi, B., & Sundaram, S. (2023). Sustainable Green Energy Generation From Waste Water: IoT and ML Integration. In Sustainable Science and Intelligent Technologies for Societal Development (pp. 440–463). IGI Global.

Melin, P., Sánchez, D., Monica, J. C., & Castillo, O. (2023). Optimization using the firefly algorithm of ensemble neural networks with type-2 fuzzy integration for COVID-19 time series prediction. *Soft Computing*, *27*(6), 3245–3282. doi:10.1007/s00500-020-05549-5 PMID:33456340

Nauck, D., & Kruse, R. (2020). Neuro–Fuzzy Systems. In *Handbook of Fuzzy Computation* (pp. 319–D2). CRC Press. doi:10.1201/9780429142741-50

Nishanth, J., Deshmukh, M. A., Kushwah, R., Kushwaha, K. K., Balaji, S., & Sampath, B. (2023). Particle Swarm Optimization of Hybrid Renewable Energy Systems. In *Intelligent Engineering Applications and Applied Sciences for Sustainability* (pp. 291–308). IGI Global. doi:10.4018/979-8-3693-0044-2.ch016

Pachiappan, K., Anitha, K., Pitchai, R., Sangeetha, S., Satyanarayana, T., & Boopathi, S. (2024). Intelligent Machines, IoT, and AI in Revolutionizing Agriculture for Water Processing. In *Handbook of Research on AI and ML for Intelligent Machines and Systems* (pp. 374–399). IGI Global.

Phan, D., Bab-Hadiashar, A., Fayyazi, M., Hoseinnezhad, R., Jazar, R. N., & Khayyam, H. (2020). Interval type 2 fuzzy logic control for energy management of hybrid electric autonomous vehicles. *IEEE Transactions on Intelligent Vehicles*, *6*(2), 210–220. doi:10.1109/TIV.2020.3011954

Phan, D., Bab-Hadiashar, A., Hoseinnezhad, R. N., Jazar, R., Date, A., Jamali, A., Pham, D. B., & Khayyam, H. (2020). Neuro-fuzzy system for energy management of conventional autonomous vehicles. *Energies*, *13*(7), 1745. doi:10.3390/en13071745

Prabhuswamy, M., Tripathi, R., Vijayakumar, M., Thulasimani, T., Sundharesalingam, P., & Sampath, B. (2024). A Study on the Complex Nature of Higher Education Leadership: An Innovative Approach. In *Challenges of Globalization and Inclusivity in Academic Research* (pp. 202–223). IGI Global. doi:10.4018/979-8-3693-1371-8.ch013

Qiao, Y., Song, Y., & Huang, K. (2019). A novel control algorithm design for hybrid electric vehicles considering energy consumption and emission performance. *Energies*, *12*(14), 2698. doi:10.3390/en12142698

Rahamathunnisa, U., Sudhakar, K., Padhi, S., Bhattacharya, S., Shashibhushan, G., & Boopathi, S. (2024). Sustainable Energy Generation From Waste Water: IoT Integrated Technologies. In Adoption and Use of Technology Tools and Services by Economically Disadvantaged Communities: Implications for Growth and Sustainability (pp. 225–256). IGI Global.

Revathi, S., Babu, M., Rajkumar, N., Meti, V. K. V., Kandavalli, S. R., & Boopathi, S. (2024). Unleashing the Future Potential of 4D Printing: Exploring Applications in Wearable Technology, Robotics, Energy, Transportation, and Fashion. In Human-Centered Approaches in Industry 5.0: Human-Machine Interaction, Virtual Reality Training, and Customer Sentiment Analysis (pp. 131–153). IGI Global.

Rezaee, M. J., Jozmaleki, M., & Valipour, M. (2018). Integrating dynamic fuzzy C-means, data envelopment analysis and artificial neural network to online prediction performance of companies in stock exchange. *Physica A*, *489*, 78–93. doi:10.1016/j.physa.2017.07.017

Saravanan, M., Vasanth, M., Boopathi, S., Sureshkumar, M., & Haribalaji, V. (2022). Optimization of Quench Polish Quench (QPQ) Coating Process Using Taguchi Method. *Key Engineering Materials*, *935*, 83–91. doi:10.4028/p-z569vy

Satav, S. D., Lamani, D., Harsha, K., Kumar, N., Manikandan, S., & Sampath, B. (2023). Energy and Battery Management in the Era of Cloud Computing: Sustainable Wireless Systems and Networks. In Sustainable Science and Intelligent Technologies for Societal Development (pp. 141–166). IGI Global.

Selvakumar, S., Shankar, R., Ranjit, P., Bhattacharya, S., Gupta, A. S. G., & Boopathi, S. (2023). E-Waste Recovery and Utilization Processes for Mobile Phone Waste. In *Handbook of Research on Safe Disposal Methods of Municipal Solid Wastes for a Sustainable Environment* (pp. 222–240). IGI Global. doi:10.4018/978-1-6684-8117-2.ch016

Sengeni, D., Padmapriya, G., Imambi, S. S., Suganthi, D., Suri, A., & Boopathi, S. (2023). Biomedical waste handling method using artificial intelligence techniques. In *Handbook of Research on Safe Disposal Methods of Municipal Solid Wastes for a Sustainable Environment* (pp. 306–323). IGI Global. doi:10.4018/978-1-6684-8117-2.ch022

Sharma, D. M., Ramana, K. V., Jothilakshmi, R., Verma, R., Maheswari, B. U., & Boopathi, S. (2024). Integrating Generative AI Into K-12 Curriculums and Pedagogies in India: Opportunities and Challenges. *Facilitating Global Collaboration and Knowledge Sharing in Higher Education With Generative AI*, 133–161.

Suhail, M., Akhtar, I., Kirmani, S., & Jameel, M. (2021). Development of progressive fuzzy logic and ANFIS control for energy management of plug-in hybrid electric vehicle. *IEEE Access : Practical Innovations, Open Solutions*, *9*, 62219–62231. doi:10.1109/ACCESS.2021.3073862

Sundaramoorthy, K., Singh, A., Sumathy, G., Maheshwari, A., Arunarani, A., & Boopathi, S. (2024). A Study on AI and Blockchain-Powered Smart Parking Models for Urban Mobility. In *Handbook of Research on AI and ML for Intelligent Machines and Systems* (pp. 223–250). IGI Global.

Tabbussum, R., & Dar, A. Q. (2021). Performance evaluation of artificial intelligence paradigms—Artificial neural networks, fuzzy logic, and adaptive neuro-fuzzy inference system for flood prediction. *Environmental Science and Pollution Research International*, *28*(20), 25265–25282. doi:10.1007/s11356-021-12410-1 PMID:33453033

Taghavifar, H., Hu, C., Qin, Y., & Wei, C. (2020). EKF-neural network observer based type-2 fuzzy control of autonomous vehicles. *IEEE Transactions on Intelligent Transportation Systems*, *22*(8), 4788–4800. doi:10.1109/TITS.2020.2985124

Veeranjaneyulu, R., Boopathi, S., Kumari, R. K., Vidyarthi, A., Isaac, J. S., & Jaiganesh, V. (2023). Air Quality Improvement and Optimisation Using Machine Learning Technique. *IEEE Explore*, 1–6.

Venkatasubramanian, V., Chitra, M., Sudha, R., Singh, V. P., Jefferson, K., & Boopathi, S. (2024). Examining the Impacts of Course Outcome Analysis in Indian Higher Education: Enhancing Educational Quality. In Challenges of Globalization and Inclusivity in Academic Research (pp. 124–145). IGI Global.

Venkateswaran, N., Kumar, S. S., Diwakar, G., Gnanasangeetha, D., & Boopathi, S. (2023). Synthetic Biology for Waste Water to Energy Conversion: IoT and AI Approaches. *Applications of Synthetic Biology in Health. Energy & Environment*, 360–384.

Verma, R., Christiana, M. B. V., Maheswari, M., Srinivasan, V., Patro, P., Dari, S. S., & Boopathi, S. (2024). Intelligent Physarum Solver for Profit Maximization in Oligopolistic Supply Chain Networks. In *AI and Machine Learning Impacts in Intelligent Supply Chain* (pp. 156–179). IGI Global. doi:10.4018/979-8-3693-1347-3.ch011

Wilamowski, B. M. (2018). Neural networks and fuzzy systems. In *Microelectronics* (pp. 18–1). CRC Press. doi:10.1201/9781315220482-18

Wu, B., Cheng, T., Yip, T. L., & Wang, Y. (2020). Fuzzy logic based dynamic decision-making system for intelligent navigation strategy within inland traffic separation schemes. *Ocean Engineering*, *197*, 106909. doi:10.1016/j.oceaneng.2019.106909

Yupapin, P., Trabelsi, Y., Nattappan, A., & Boopathi, S. (2023). Performance improvement of wire-cut electrical discharge machining process using cryogenically treated super-conductive state of Monel-K500 alloy. *Iranian Journal of Science and Technology. Transaction of Mechanical Engineering*, *47*(1), 267–283. doi:10.1007/s40997-022-00513-0

Zekrifa, D. M. S., Kulkarni, M., Bhagyalakshmi, A., Devireddy, N., Gupta, S., & Boopathi, S. (2023). Integrating Machine Learning and AI for Improved Hydrological Modeling and Water Resource Management. In *Artificial Intelligence Applications in Water Treatment and Water Resource Management* (pp. 46–70). IGI Global. doi:10.4018/978-1-6684-6791-6.ch003

Chapter 7
Securing Web Data and Privacy in AIoT Systems

Marius Iulian Mihailescu

ⓘD https://orcid.org/0000-0001-9655-9666
Universitatea Spiru Haret București, Romania

Stefania Loredana Nita
Military Technical Academy "Ferdinand I", Romania

ABSTRACT

The exponential growth of Artificial Intelligence of Things (AIoT) has resulted in an unparalleled fusion of AI with IoT technologies, giving rise to intricate systems that present vast opportunities for automation, productivity, and data-centric decision-making. Nevertheless, this amalgamation also poses substantial obstacles regarding safeguarding online information and upholding confidentiality. The chapter extensively examines the difficulties associated with these issues and the tactics employed to surmount them. The chapter commences by delineating the distinctive susceptibilities inherent in AIoT systems, with a particular emphasis on how the interconnection of AI and IoT technologies gives rise to novel avenues for data breaches and privacy infringements. It then explores the most recent approaches and technologies used to protect data sent over AIoT networks. These include improved encryption methods, secure data transfer protocols, and solutions based on blockchain technology. A substantial chunk of the chapter focuses on privacy-preserving strategies in AIoT. The text examines the equilibrium between data usefulness and privacy protection. It delves into techniques like anonymization, differential privacy, and federated learning as means to safeguard user data while ensuring the effectiveness of AIoT systems. The chapter also examines regulatory and ethical factors, thoroughly examining current and developing legislation and regulations that oversee data security and privacy in AIoT. The content incorporates case studies and real-world examples to demonstrate the pragmatic implementation of theoretical principles. Ultimately, the chapter predicts forthcoming patterns and difficulties in this swiftly progressing domain, providing valuable perspectives on possible AIoT security and privacy protocol advancements. This resource is vital for professionals, researchers, and students engaged in AIoT, cybersecurity, and data privacy. It provides them with the necessary information and tools to protect against the ever-changing threats in this dynamic field.

DOI: 10.4018/979-8-3693-1487-6.ch007

1. INTRODUCTION TO AIOT AND WEB SECURITY

The combination of Artificial Intelligence (AI) and the Internet of Things (IoT), referred to as the Artificial Intelligence of Things (AIoT), is a significant transformation in the technological field. Integrating AI technology into IoT systems enhances their capabilities, facilitating more efficient, autonomous, and intelligent decision-making processes. Nevertheless, as these systems grow more intricate and interconnected, primarily through web technologies, they become more susceptible to cyber dangers. This requires a robust and comprehensive approach to security, namely in protecting web data and preserving user privacy.

AIoT systems can efficiently handle substantial amounts of data (Ramos et al., 2022), frequently in real-time, to extract essential insights and execute automated actions. These systems are utilized in diverse domains like healthcare, smart cities, industrial, and home automation. The widespread management of data presents the difficulty of guaranteeing data integrity, confidentiality, and availability. Furthermore, because of the frequent interconnection of AIoT devices via the internet, they are susceptible to the inherent weaknesses of web technologies. This encompasses potential hazards such as unlawful data breaches, data tampering, and diverse cyber assaults.

This chapter delves into the complexities of protecting web data and preserving privacy in AIoT systems. We want to equip readers with the essential knowledge and skills to manage cybersecurity challenges in this quickly evolving sector successfully. This book offers a comprehensive guide for anyone looking to improve the security of AIoT systems. This course encompasses the fundamental principles of Artificial Intelligence of Things (AIoT) and internet security, sophisticated defense tactics, and adherence to regulatory standards. At the outset of our voyage, we will analyze the field's current state and estimate the future challenges and opportunities in this rapidly evolving subject.

Web security in the context of AIoT encompasses more than just protecting data from unwanted access. It also involves preventing any manipulation of the AI components. Manipulation of AI models might result in erroneous judgments, potentially resulting in substantial damage, particularly in vital domains such as healthcare or self-driving vehicles. Furthermore, ensuring the privacy of users is of utmost importance. AIoT systems frequently manage sensitive personal information, and it is essential to guarantee the anonymity and privacy of this data. This is important to preserve user confidence and adhere to increasingly strict global data protection standards.

The convergence of Artificial Intelligence of Things (AIoT) and web technologies gives rise to a dynamic and intricate cybersecurity landscape. Conventional security measures are frequently insufficient to tackle the distinct problems presented by these linked systems. Hence, it is crucial to possess knowledge of AIoT designs and online security concepts. This encompasses expertise in network security, application security, data encryption, access control, and the ethical and legal aspects of data privacy.

Comprehending AIoT can be exciting, contingent upon the specific case study and practical circumstances. To address this obstacle, let us consider a hypothetical scenario where our residential thermostat can acquire knowledge about our tastes and autonomously regulate the temperature accordingly. Similarly, envision a scenario where factory equipment can anticipate and avert future malfunctions. The power of AIoT lies in the ability of physical devices to gather data, connect, and utilize AI algorithms to carry out intelligent actions. Nevertheless, the extensive array of interconnected gadgets, frequently equipped with restricted computational capabilities and security attributes, generates a substantial vulnerability for malevolent individuals.

Web security becomes paramount as AIoT devices rely on internet connectivity and web-based platforms for data exchange and control. This encompasses various aspects, including:

- **Secure communication protocols.** Protecting data transmission between devices and platforms using encryption and authentication.
- **Robust authentication and authorization.** Implementing strong passwords, multi-factor authentication, and access control mechanisms to prevent unauthorized access.
- **Vulnerability management.** Regularly patching software vulnerabilities in devices and platforms to address known security risks.
- **Data privacy and compliance.** Ensuring adherence to data privacy regulations like the General Data Protection Regulation (GDPR) and California Consumer Privacy Act (CCPA), especially when handling sensitive personal information.

Most professionals, industries, and academics face different vital challenges and considerations when it comes to practice, such as:

- *The wide range of AIoT devices*, ranging from limited-resource sensors to high-performance smart devices, necessitates adaptable and scalable security solutions.
- *AI algorithms* are prone to manipulation and attacks, so additional security measures must be implemented to address these weaknesses.
- *Striking a balance between security and usability.* The implementation of stringent security measures might occasionally cause inconvenience for users. Achieving equilibrium is paramount.

The future of AIoT and web security can be seen as an:

- With AIoT's increasing acceptance, strong online security is crucial to establish trust and promote the responsible advancement of this technology.
- Continuous research and innovation are necessary to create AIoT devices that are inherently safe, establish sophisticated systems for detecting and preventing advanced threats, and promote cooperation among relevant parties to tackle emerging security issues.

The importance of data security and privacy in Artificial Intelligence of Things (IoT) systems cannot be overstated, as these systems have increasingly become integral to our daily lives, business operations, and critical infrastructure. Here are the key reasons why data security and privacy are paramount in AIoT systems:

1. **Sensitive data handling.** AIoT systems often process and store sensitive information, from personal user data to critical business information. This data can include personal identifiers, financial details, health records, and more. Ensuring the security and privacy of this data is crucial to protect individuals and organizations from identity theft, financial fraud, and other malicious activities.
2. **Decision-making impact.** AIoT systems frequently make automated decisions based on the data they collect and analyze. If this data is compromised, the resulting decisions could be flawed, leading to potentially harmful consequences, especially in sectors like healthcare, transportation (e.g., autonomous vehicles), and public safety.

3. **Compliance and legal obligations**. Numerous regulations and laws, such as the General Data Protection Regulation (GDPR) in the European Union, mandate the protection of personal data. Non-compliance with these regulations can lead to substantial fines, legal penalties, and damage to the organization's reputation.

4. **Trust and reputation**. Users' trust in AIoT systems is essential for their widespread adoption. Data security and privacy concerns can deter individuals and organizations from utilizing these technologies, hindering technological advancement and innovation. Maintaining robust security and privacy measures is vital for building and preserving this trust.

5. **Vulnerability to cyber-attacks**. AIoT systems, being interconnected and often reliant on the Internet, are vulnerable to a range of cyber threats, including hacking, phishing, ransomware, and denial-of-service attacks. These threats can lead to data breaches, unauthorized access, and manipulation of AIoT systems, resulting in data integrity and availability loss.

6. **Ethical considerations**. The ethical implications of AIoT data usage are significant. The handling of personal data must respect user privacy and consent, avoiding unauthorized surveillance and data misuse. Ethical data practices in AIoT are not only a legal obligation but also a moral one.

7. **Long-term data security**. AIoT systems often collect data continuously over long periods. Ensuring this data's long-term security and privacy is crucial as threats evolve. The systems must be resilient to future vulnerabilities and adapt to new security challenges.

8. **Network security**. Given the interconnected nature of AIoT devices, a breach in one device can potentially compromise the entire network. Secure communication protocols and network security measures are essential to prevent cascading failures.

Ultimately, AIoT and web security are intricately interconnected. To fully harness AIoT's promise and safeguard our interconnected world, it is crucial to comprehend the distinct obstacles and establish extensive security protocols.

2. VULNERABILITIES AND THREATS IN AIOT SYSTEMS

The amalgamation of Artificial Intelligence (AI) with the Internet of Things (IoT), resulting in the formation of the Artificial Intelligence of Things (AIoT), has given rise to inventive applications in many fields. Nevertheless, this integration also brings forth distinct weaknesses and exposes these systems to attacks. This study aims to thoroughly examine the vulnerabilities and dangers inherent in AIoT systems.

2.1. Architecture and Vulnerabilities of AIoT Systems

The vulnerabilities in the AIoT architectures and systems can be summarized as follows:

1. *Device vulnerabilities*. AIoT devices frequently exhibit constrained processing capacity and may possess inadequate security features. These vulnerabilities render them prone to physical manipulation and cyber-attacks, such as firmware hacking or device impersonation.

2. *Network vulnerabilities*. These vulnerabilities arise due to the constant communication of AIoT devices over networks, making them susceptible to exploitation. Data interception and network

penetration can result from vulnerabilities such as unsecured wireless connectivity and miscon-figured APIs.

3. *Data processing and storage vulnerabilities.* AIoT systems produce substantial volumes of data, which are stored and processed locally and remotely in the cloud. Data breaches can occur because of insufficient data encryption and inadequate access control.

4. *AI models* utilized in AIoT are prone to adversarial attacks, model poisoning, and biased decision-making if the dataset is not sufficiently safeguarded and vetted.

AIoT systems exhibit a complicated security environment characterized by distinct vulnerabilities and threats. This study emphasizes the necessity of implementing a comprehensive security strategy that includes device security, network security, data protection, and AI model security. Ensuring the security and privacy of AIoT systems is crucial as AIoT technologies progress.

2.1.1. Device Vulnerabilities

Within the Artificial Intelligence of Things (AIoT) domain, 'device vulnerabilities' denote the inherent weaknesses or defects present in the physical objects comprising these systems. AIoT devices, encom-passing a broad spectrum from basic sensors to intricate processors, typically serve at the forefront of the network of interconnected components. A comprehensive understanding of these vulnerabilities is paramount to effectively protecting AIoT systems from potential attackers.

1. Insufficient computational capacity and memory

Several AIoT devices are engineered to be economical and energy-conserving, resulting in restricted processing capabilities and memory (see Figure 2). This constraint can hinder the deployment of strong security measures, such as sophisticated encryption algorithms or complete security protocols, hence increasing the susceptibility of these devices to assaults.

The constraint of computational capacity and memory in AIoT (Artificial Intelligence of Things) devices is a notable issue, as it directly affects the device's capability to carry out intricate activities, such as implementing sophisticated security measures. Below is an in-depth examination of this restric-tion and its consequences:

*   Resource limitations might hinder the implementation of robust security measures. Complex security protocols typically demand significant processing resources to perform encryption, decryption, and execution of advanced algorithms. AIoT devices with constrained processing power and memory may face challenges in effectively implementing these security features without adversely affecting their primary functioning.
*   *Lack of capacity to sustain sophisticated AI models.* AIoT devices are anticipated to handle and examine data, occasionally employing intricate AI models. However, the device's processing and memory capacity is limited, hindering its ability to run these models locally. This may require simpler, less efficient models or reliance on cloud processing. However, this introduces delays and possible security risks during data transmission.
*   *Challenges in managing large data volumes.* AIoT devices frequently produce and accumulate substantial amounts of data. The device's limited memory and processing capabilities can impede

its capacity to efficiently store and process this data, which may result in data loss or necessitate regular data offloading to external storage solutions.

- *Challenges in executing real-time processing.* Real-time data processing and decision-making are crucial in several AIoT applications, such as driverless vehicles or industrial automation. The device's limited processing capabilities can hinder its ability to conduct these activities in real time, impacting the system's overall responsiveness and efficiency.
- *Software updates and patch management* are essential for preserving security. Nevertheless, devices with restricted memory and processing capabilities may encounter difficulties while attempting to download and install these updates, mainly if the upgrades are extensive or need significant computational resources for implementation.
- *Energy efficiency concerns.* Numerous AIoT devices are specifically engineered to prioritize energy conservation and function on batteries or restricted power sources. Utilizing intricate security algorithms or AI models necessitates additional power, resulting in an accelerated depletion of the device's energy reserves and presenting operational difficulties.
- *Scalability challenges.* As AIoT networks expand, the volume of data processed and the intricacy of processes rise correspondingly. Devices with restricted processing capabilities and memory may hinder the performance of scalable systems, as they are unable to handle the growing demands.
- *Striking a balance between functionality and security.* Manufacturers of AIoT devices frequently encounter a dilemma regarding improving device functionality while incorporating strong security measures. When faced with limited resources, prioritizing one aspect can compromise the other, a significant worry in systems requiring high-security levels.

AIoT devices sometimes include interfaces that let users communicate with or configure the device, such as web interfaces, USB ports, or wireless connections. If these interfaces are not adequately secured, they can have vulnerabilities that may lead to illegal access or data leaking.

2. Vulnerabilities in firmware and software

The firmware embedded in AIoT devices, serving as the enduring software integrated into the hardware, may possess vulnerabilities. Attackers can exploit outdated or poorly designed firmware to seize control of the device or utilize it as a gateway into the network.

Likewise, the software applications operating on these devices may possess vulnerabilities, mainly if they are not frequently updated or have subpar coding.

3. Vulnerabilities in physical security

AIoT devices are frequently installed in insecure or public settings, rendering them vulnerable to physical manipulation or theft. Physical access to a gadget enables one to manipulate its functioning or exploit its data directly.

4. Insufficient frequency of updates

AIoT devices, in contrast to conventional computing devices, may not receive periodic software updates or patches to address known vulnerabilities. This problem is exacerbated when devices are installed in inaccessible or isolated regions.

5.   Insufficient authentication and authorization mechanisms

Inadequate authentication and authorization systems can enable unauthorized actors to gain access to or manipulate AIoT devices. The risk is significantly elevated when default credentials are employed or shared among many devices.

6.   Vulnerabilities in network connectivity

AIoT devices that establish wireless connections are vulnerable to interception or unauthorized access if the communication lacks sufficient encryption or the network is insecure.

7.   Compromises in the supply chain

Weaknesses may arise during the production phase or due to the supply chain. Devices can be preloaded with malicious components or backdoors prior to reaching users.

2.2. Analysis of the Potential Risks and Dangers Present in AIoT Systems

The potential risks and dangers that are at the AIoT systems can be summarized as:

1.   *Cyber-assaults*. Phishing, ransomware, and Distributed Denial of Service (DDoS) assaults are frequently seen. These attacks can potentially impair AIoT operations and compromise access to essential data.
2.   *Physical attacks* involve physically manipulating AIoT devices, which can result in unauthorized access and control over the device's functions.
3.   *Data privacy threats* encompass the peril of unauthorized intrusion into confidential data, including personal information and usage habits, posing a substantial risk to user privacy.
4.   *AI Model threats* encompass the risks of model theft, adversarial assaults, and model inversion attacks. These threats involve malicious actors manipulating AI decision-making or extracting sensitive information from AI models.

2.3. Case Studies of AIoT Security Breaches

This section aims to analyze real-world situations in which vulnerabilities in AIoT systems were exploited, examining the causes, repercussions, and reactions to these breaches.

At the nexus of the Internet of Things (IoT) and Artificial Intelligence (AI), AIoT is the integration of AI technologies with IoT infrastructure to optimize IoT operations, foster better human-machine interactions, and boost data analytics and management. Regarding automation, efficiency, and intelligence, AIoT has several advantages, but it also brings new security risks and difficulties. These are a few noteworthy case studies of AIoT security lapses that demonstrate the need for solid security controls in these systems:

1. The 2016 Mirai Botnet Attack

Even while the Mirai botnet event was primarily focused on IoT, it highlights the possibility of AIoT systems being infiltrated. The Mirai malware used default username and password combinations to infect Internet of Things devices (such as DVRs and IP cameras). These devices were compromised by malware, which used them as a botnet to perform enormous Distributed Denial of Service (DDoS) attacks, most famously against Dyn, a significant DNS provider. This led to widespread internet disruptions that impacted well-known websites, including PayPal, Netflix, and Twitter. Such vulnerabilities could be used in AIoT scenarios to control AI functions and interfere with services.

2. Voice Assist Listening In

Researchers have shown how to use AI-powered voice assistants, such as Google Home and Amazon Echo, to listen in on conversations surreptitiously. These incidents have brought attention to vulnerabilities in these AIoT ecosystems. These hacks frequently took advantage of software bugs in the devices or used malicious skills or programs intended to keep the device listening after its activation phase was entered. This instance emphasizes how AIoT devices pose privacy hazards and how important it is to have strong security measures to safeguard sensitive data.

3. Hacks Using Smart Home Devices

IoT and AI technologies are frequently combined in smart home gadgets, which have been the subject of numerous security lapses. For instance, by taking advantage of security flaws, security experts have shown that they can remotely turn off home security systems or control smart locks and thermostats. These instances emphasize the need for secure communication methods and frequent software upgrades by highlighting the possible dangers of unauthorized access to and control of AIoT devices.

4. IoT Security Incidents in Healthcare

AIoT security issues in the healthcare industry have been raised, mainly related to linked medical devices. For example, malicious setups or commands could be delivered through vulnerabilities in insulin pumps or pacemakers. Strict security protocols are vital for AIoT healthcare applications since these breaches directly endanger patient health and pose privacy problems.

5. Theft of Surveillance Cameras

With AI powering facial recognition and event detection more and more, surveillance systems have seen security breaches where hackers could access recorded or live feeds. This jeopardizes security and privacy because video can be altered or removed. These events highlight the dangers of shoddy authentication procedures and the requirement for end-to-end encryption in AIoT devices.

These case studies of IoT and AI security breaches highlight the challenging security environment when combining these technologies. They emphasize the necessity of all-encompassing security plans that incorporate strong encryption, safe authentication techniques, frequent software upgrades, and knowledge of the weaknesses of AI capabilities. The methods used to secure these networked systems must change as AIoT does.

Several important lessons for improving the security posture of AIoT systems are highlighted by the case studies of security breaches involving AIoT. For companies and developers involved in creating, implementing, and managing AIoT systems, these lessons are essential:

1. Robust Access Control and Authentication

Lesson. One significant risk is weak or default authentication techniques. Devices and systems must have robust authentication and access controls to prevent unwanted access.

Application. To guarantee that only authorized people and devices may access and interact with AIoT systems, implement multi-factor authentication (MFA), strong password rules, and access management protocols.

2. Frequent Patch Management and Software Updates

Lesson. Many security breaches exploit well-known flaws that have not been fixed. Patch management and routine software upgrades are essential for repairing security holes and improving system security.

Application. Create a regular procedure for quickly updating AIoT systems and devices with security patches and software upgrades.

3. Protocols for Secure Communication

Lesson. Insecure data transport might result in data tampering and interception. Secure communication techniques are necessary to safeguard data while it's in transit.

Application. Make sure that all communications between AIoT devices and servers are encrypted by using encryption standards like TLS/SSL for data transmission.

4. Protection and Privacy of Data

Lesson. Because AIoT systems often handle and gather sensitive data, they are high-risk targets for security breaches. Protecting and preserving data privacy ought to come first.

Application. Use data encryption while data is at rest, follow privacy laws (such as the CCPA and GDPR), and use data minimization and anonymization techniques whenever feasible.

5. Monitoring and Segmenting Networks

Lesson: A single device breach can compromise the network as a whole. Segmentation helps limit the scope of breaches and their effects.

Application. Use network segmentation to separate AIoT devices from vital network resources. Use ongoing surveillance to identify and address any unusual activity quickly.

6. Design for Security

Lesson. Rather than being an afterthought, security should be incorporated into the design of AIoT systems.

Application. When designing AIoT projects, consider security. Conduct threat modeling and security assessments early in the development lifecycle and throughout.

7. Knowledge and Instruction

Lesson. Even the most secure systems can be compromised by carelessness and human mistakes. Continuous training and education are essential.

Application. Run frequent security awareness and training campaigns for developers, operators, end users, and all other parties participating in the AIoT ecosystem.

8. Reconstruction and Incident Handling

Lesson. It is essential to be ready to respond and recover from a breach since they do occur.

Application. Create and maintain an incident response strategy regularly. Practice exercises to ensure your team is ready to react quickly and effectively to security problems.

9. Working Together and Exchanging Best Practices

Lesson. The field of AIoT security is constantly changing. Stakeholder cooperation and information exchange can improve security posture.

Application. Take part in industry forums, exchange knowledge, and best practices, and keep up with the most recent developments in AIoT security trends and risks.

While combining AI with IoT opens up new possibilities, it poses new security risks. More secure and robust AIoT systems should be developed and implemented using the lessons discovered from previous breaches. By adopting these lessons, organizations may reduce risks, improve security, and realize the full potential of AIoT technology.

2.4. Measures to Reduce or Prevent the Impact of Adverse Events and the Most Effective Methods

Several measures are essential to prevent such events' negative impact. A couple of measures can be summarized as follows:

1. *Device level security*. It enforces security measures at the hardware level by incorporating features based on physical components, implementing secure boot procedures, and ensuring regular updates to the device's firmware.
2. *Ensuring secure communication,* implementing encryption during data transmission, and employing secure communication methods.
3. *Ensuring data security and privacy*, employing robust encryption techniques to protect data when it is stored and sent, and utilizing algorithms that safeguard privacy throughout data processing.

4. *AI model security.* Employing adversarial training, model hardening, and robust validation methodologies to safeguard AI models from potential assaults.
5. *Regular security assessments.* Performing regular security assessments and penetration testing to detect and address problems.

2.5. Prospects and Emerging Patterns in AIoT Security

Integrating Artificial Intelligence (AI) and the Internet of Things (IoT), referred to as AIoT, transforms how devices establish connections and communicate, providing unparalleled levels of intelligent automation and effectiveness in diverse industries. Nevertheless, this amalgamation also brings up novel challenges and prospects in security. A comprehensive summary of the potential outcomes and trends in AIoT security is provided.

1. Improved Detection and Response to Potential Threats

- *AI-powered security analysis.* AI's capacity to swiftly evaluate large volumes of data allows for the identification of intricate patterns and anomalies that may suggest a security risk. AI algorithms may utilize past data to discern and promptly address potential risks in real-time, greatly enhancing the security stance of IoT networks.
- *Predictive security.* By harnessing AI for predictive analysis, prospective security breaches can be anticipated by finding weaknesses and forecasting attack paths. By adopting a proactive approach, companies can strengthen their defenses in preparation for expected attacks.

2. Implementation of Automated Security Policies and Adherence to Compliance Regulations

- *Dynamic security policies.* Artificial intelligence can automatically generate and implement security policies in response to the evolving environment and threat landscape. The security measures can be dynamically adjusted, providing a defense mechanism that is both flexible and robust.
- *Compliance Monitoring.* AI technologies can consistently monitor IoT environments to guarantee adherence to industry standards and regulatory obligations. These systems automatically detect any inconsistencies and enforce the necessary compliance actions.

3. Ensuring the Secure Integration and Administration of Devices

- *AIoT enhances device authentication and management* by employing sophisticated techniques to guarantee that only authorized devices may establish connections with networks. This is especially crucial in IoT environments, where large devices present a substantial administrative obstacle.
- *Continuous device assessment.* Utilizing artificial intelligence, continuous assessment of device behavior, and security posture can promptly detect potential vulnerabilities or indications of compromise in IoT devices, facilitating fast remedial actions.

4. Ensuring the Confidentiality and Protection of Personal Information

- *Improved privacy measures.* AIoT systems can utilize AI's efficient data processing capabilities to build sophisticated data anonymization and encryption mechanisms, thereby safeguarding user privacy. This is of utmost importance in consumer IoT applications, as they frequently entail handling sensitive personal data.
- *Ensuring secure data processing.* AI algorithms can be specifically developed to process data securely, guaranteeing the preservation of data integrity and the protection of sensitive information throughout its lifespan.

5. Current Obstacles and Resolutions

- With the expansion of AIoT into edge computing, it is crucial to *prioritize the security of edge devices.* Possible solutions involve implementing security standards specifically designed for edge devices and utilizing artificial intelligence to continuously monitor and control their security in real-time.
- *Quantum computing threats.* The emergence of quantum computing poses possible risks to existing encryption techniques. AIoT security research is investigating quantum-resistant algorithms as a proactive measure to address forthcoming difficulties.
- *Ethical and legal considerations.* The incorporation of AI in IoT raises ethical and legal concerns about protecting data privacy, surveillance practices, and decision-making autonomy. The ongoing endeavor involves establishing ethical principles and legal frameworks for AIoT applications.

6. Frameworks for Collaborative Security

- *Collaboration between technology companies, governments, and academic institutions* is essential to establish standardized security procedures for AIoT and facilitate the exchange of threat intelligence.
- Promoting open standards and interoperability across IoT devices can promote a single security approach, simplifying the implementation of comprehensive security measures across various devices.

The progress of Artificial Intelligence of Things (AIoT) technologies, although providing substantial advantages in effectiveness, mechanization, and intellect, nevertheless brings about a range of hazards. The main threats are predominantly linked to privacy, security, and ethics issues. Below is an in-depth analysis of these potential dangers and the proactive measures required to minimize their impact:

Rising Hazards Associated With Advancements in Artificial Intelligence of Things (AIoT)

1. *Risks related to the privacy and security of data.* AIoT devices produce and analyze immense quantities of data, including extremely sensitive data. If this data is not well secured, its collection

and examination can present substantial privacy hazards. Furthermore, AIoT devices expand the potential targets for cybercriminals, creating weaknesses at multiple stages, including device-level security, data transmission, and storage.

2. *Sophisticated methods of attack.* Integrating artificial intelligence (AI) with Internet of Things (IoT) devices engender intricate systems that pose difficulties in ensuring security. Adversaries can utilize AI algorithms, manipulate data to influence AI judgments or compromise the reliability and accessibility of AI systems, resulting in potentially disastrous consequences.

3. *Attacks' ability to scale up. AI technologies can automate processes on a large scale, including harmful processes. AI-driven automated assaults can exploit weaknesses in IoT devices with greater* efficiency, resulting in extensive security breaches. The inherent scalability of IoT devices enables the exploitation of a single vulnerability to propagate across a vast number of devices, perhaps reaching millions.

4. *Absence of uniformity or standardization.* The AIoT ecosystem faces a dearth of standardization, which hampers the implementation of consistent security protocols. Many device kinds, operating systems, and communication protocols add complexity to developing all-encompassing security solutions.

5. *. Obstacles related to regulations and adherence to rules.* The rapid progress of AIoT technologies frequently surpasses the establishment of legal frameworks and standards, resulting in deficiencies in compliance and security requirements. This can lead to insufficient safeguards and privacy protocols.

Preemptive Measures to Minimize Risks

1. *Strengthened data protection measures.* Utilizing resilient data encryption, anonymization, and privacy-preserving computation approaches can safeguard data privacy. Moreover, it is imperative to implement secure methods for both storing and transmitting data.

2. *Sophisticated security architectures.* It is crucial to create security frameworks that can flexibly adjust to threats and integrate multiple layers of security techniques. This includes security measures at the device level, such as secure communication channels and robust AI-powered systems for detecting and responding to threats.

3. *Periodic security audits and updates.* To reduce vulnerabilities, it is crucial to regularly perform security audits and promptly upgrade and patch AIoT devices. Additionally, this entails closely observing the devices and systems for any abnormal behaviors that may suggest a security compromise.

4. *Conformity and adherence to established standards.* Striving for universal standards within the industry and ensuring that devices and systems adhere to these standards can improve security. Engagement in formulating regulations and strict adherence to established standards and norms are essential for establishing a robust and safe environment for Artificial Intelligence of Things (AIoT).

5. *The promotion of knowledge and consciousness.* Educating developers, consumers, and stakeholders regarding security concerns and optimal strategies for AIoT is crucial. Increased awareness can promote the implementation of secure development methods and knowledgeable utilization of AIoT technology.

6. *Ethical utilization of Artificial Intelligence.* Establishing ethical principles for the development and utilization of AI is imperative, particularly when making decisions related to privacy, surveillance, and data management. Utilizing ethical AI guarantees trust and transparency in the applications of AIoT.

7. *Joint security endeavors.* Promoting cooperation among technology firms, cybersecurity experts, regulatory entities, and other involved parties can result in exchanging information about potential risks, implementing effective strategies, and creating strong security measures.

8. *Implementing security via design.* By incorporating security considerations from the outset of AIoT device and system development, one can guarantee that security is neither neglected nor treated as an afterthought. This encompasses doing risk assessments, implementing secure coding techniques, and evaluating the security ramifications of AI algorithms.

Ultimately, as AIoT technologies progress, the corresponding hazards likewise escalate. To address these dangers, proactive initiatives that include technology solutions, legislative measures, and collaborative activities are necessary. By directly confronting these problems, it is feasible to leverage the advantages of AIoT while guaranteeing the sufficient safeguarding of privacy, security, and ethical concerns.

The potential impact of new technologies, particularly quantum computing, on the security of AIoT (Artificial Intelligence of Things) is significant and complex. Quantum computing holds the potential to significantly improve processing power, hence bolstering AIoT's capabilities. However, it also presents unique security challenges that have not been encountered before. In the following discussion, we will examine the effects of AIoT on security and how the security landscape is changing in the quantum era.

Advancements in Artificial Intelligence of Things (AIoT) Capabilities

1. *Data processing and analysis.* Quantum computing can process and analyze data at unprecedented speeds, surpassing the capabilities of conventional computers. This advancement greatly enhances artificial intelligence's potential to acquire knowledge from and comprehend data created by the Internet of Things (IoT). This can result in AIoT systems that are more intelligent, efficient, and responsive, with the ability to make real-time decisions and perform predictive analytics.

2. *Optimization challenges.* Numerous AIoT applications, including logistics and smart grids, entail intricate optimization challenges. Quantum algorithms demonstrate exceptional performance in these areas, potentially transforming route planning, energy distribution, and other domains and greatly enhancing the efficiency of AIoT systems.

Issues Related to Security

The primary and noteworthy risk that quantum computing presents is its potential to compromise existing encryption protocols. Quantum algorithms like Shor's algorithm can compromise encryption techniques like RSA and ECC, safeguarding the data exchanged between IoT devices and networks. AIoT systems are susceptible to eavesdropping, data breaches, and manipulation.

1. *Data Privacy.* Quantum computers' capacity to compromise existing encryption standards presents a significant threat to data confidentiality. AIoT systems, which frequently manage sensitive per-

sonal and commercial data, may become vulnerable to adversaries possessing quantum computing capabilities, resulting in substantial privacy breaches.

2. *Revamping security mechanisms.* The emergence of quantum computing requires a comprehensive reworking of the security mechanisms employed in AIoT. The development of post-quantum cryptography (PQC) aims to protect communications from quantum attacks. However, incorporating these measures into the varied and disjointed IoT environment is a significant problem.

Strategies and Factors to Consider in Taking the Initiative

The current focus is on creating cryptographic algorithms that can withstand attacks from quantum and classical computers to ensure long-term security. In order to protect against any future threats, AIoT systems should include these quantum-resistant standards.

Quantum Key Distribution (QKD) employs the principles of quantum mechanics to safeguard communication channels, providing an additional level of security for IoT networks. Implementing Quantum Key Distribution (QKD) makes it possible to guarantee secure communication between devices, even when faced with potential threats from quantum computing.

Adopting a security-by-design strategy is paramount in the quantum era, especially for AIoT. This encompasses the timely incorporation of algorithms resistant to quantum attacks and the careful evaluation of potential risks posed by quantum technology during the planning and creation stages of AIoT solutions.

The security landscape of quantum computing is undergoing rapid and continuous changes. AIoT systems require ongoing surveillance for potential vulnerabilities and adaptable architectures capable of integrating new security technologies and protocols as they emerge.

Collaboration and standardization are essential for developing quantum-resistant technologies and their smooth integration into AIoT. This necessitates cooperation among several sectors, including companies, academia, and governments. The collective endeavor is vital in developing a robust groundwork for the future of AIoT.

To conclude, the future of AIoT security appears to be quite favorable since AI offers robust capabilities to bolster security in IoT settings. Nevertheless, this swiftly progressing domain necessitates ongoing ingenuity to tackle emerging risks and a collaborative endeavor from all parties involved to develop a robust and impervious AIoT ecosystem.

The advent of quantum computing brings forth both prospects and obstacles for AIoT security. As AIoT capabilities are improved, it is necessary to reassess and reinforce security policies to safeguard against quantum attacks. It is crucial to address these difficulties proactively by developing and adopting quantum-resistant cryptography and implementing a security-by-design approach to protect the future of AIoT. Adopting quantum-safe AIoT systems will be intricate and necessitates collaborative endeavors from all participants engaged in the IoT ecosystem.

3. DATA ENCRYPTION AND PROTECTION TECHNIQUES

Encryption techniques are essential for safeguarding data's secrecy, accuracy, and legitimacy in AIoT (Artificial Intelligence of Things) systems during its transmission across networks and devices. Securing AIoT systems against unauthorized access and cyber threats is paramount due to their diversified and distributed nature. These systems combine AI with IoT devices to improve decision-making and operational efficiencies. Below, we are describing the most crucial encryption techniques and tactics that are particularly applicable to AIoT data:

1. Encryption Using Symmetric Algorithms

Advanced Encryption technology (AES) is a highly utilized encryption technology that safeguards AIoT data. Due to its ability to maintain great security while still delivering good performance, AES is a viable encryption algorithm for IoT devices with limited processing capabilities. It is frequently employed to encrypt data stored and transferred inside AIoT ecosystems.

2. Asymmetric Encryption Refers to a Cryptographic Method That Uses Different Keys for the Encryption and Decryption Processes

RSA (Rivest-Shamir-Adleman) is a widely used asymmetric encryption technique that ensures strong security by utilizing two keys, namely the public key and the private key. Although RSA offers strong security measures, its computational demands render it unsuitable for IoT devices with limited resources. However, it is highly suitable for establishing secure communication between AIoT systems and back-end services.

Elliptic Curve Cryptography (ECC) provides security comparable to RSA but with smaller key sizes, rendering it more efficient and appropriate for AIoT devices with constrained processing capabilities. Elliptic Curve Cryptography (ECC) ensures communications security in Artificial Intelligence of Things (AIoT) systems, encompassing tasks such as device authentication and data transmission.

3. Encryption That Is Resistant to Attacks Using Quantum Computers

The progress of quantum computing presents a peril to conventional encryption techniques. Researchers are currently developing quantum-resistant or post-quantum cryptography techniques to protect AIoT systems from potential quantum attacks in the future. The following items are included:

Lattice-based cryptography is a cryptographic technique based on the use of lattice problems, which are considered resistant to attacks from quantum computers. Encrypting data in AIoT systems is advisable to provide enduring security.

Hash-based cryptography employs robust hash functions to generate digital signatures, offering a quantum-resistant approach to validating the integrity and authenticity of AIoT data.

4. Homomorphic Encryption Refers to a Cryptographic Technique That Allows Computations to Be Performed on Encrypted Data Without the Need for Decryption

Homomorphic encryption enables the execution of calculations on encrypted data, producing an encrypted output that, when decrypted, corresponds to the outcome of operations as if they were conducted on the original unencrypted data. This is especially advantageous in the field of AIoT as it protects privacy when analyzing data in cloud-based AI analytics. This enables the extraction of valuable information without compromising the confidentiality of the original data.

5. SMPC (Secure Multi-Party Computation)

Secure Multi-Party Computation (SMPC) allows multiple participants to collaboratively calculate a function using their respective inputs while ensuring the privacy of those inputs. Within Artificial Intelligence of Things (AIoT), Secure Multi-Party Computation (SMPC) safeguards collaborative AI operations conducted on various devices while ensuring that confidential information remains undisclosed. This technology is precious in situations involving federated learning.

6. QKD (Quantum Key Distribution)

Quantum Key Distribution (QKD) employs the principles of quantum mechanics to safeguard a communication channel. It enables the secure exchange of cryptographic keys that are resistant to any computational attacks, even those launched by quantum computers. This is a proactive method for ensuring the security of AIoT communications.

The are some factors that must be taken into account during the implementation process; when incorporating encryption into AIoT systems, it is crucial to take into account multiple factors:

- *Resource limitations.* Numerous IoT devices possess restricted processing capabilities and energy resources. It is imperative to have lightweight cryptographic algorithms or efficient versions of established methods.
- *Scalability.* AIoT systems can accommodate many devices, ranging from thousands to millions. Scalable solutions for managing and distributing keys are crucial.
- *Interoperability.* Due to the wide range of devices and platforms in AIoT ecosystems, encryption methods and protocols must guarantee compatibility across many systems.
- *Regulatory compliance.* Adhering to data protection standards such as GDPR and CCPA necessitates using encryption techniques to safeguard data during transmission and storage and implementing measures to ensure data integrity and regulate access.

Data security throughout its transmission and storage is essential for protecting information confidentiality, integrity, and availability in any digital ecosystem, including AIoT (Artificial Intelligence of Things) environments. Cryptographic methods, network security measures, and data management practices are employed to ensure data security during these stages. Here is a method to efficiently safeguard data:

Securing Data During Transmission

Utilization of secure communication protocols. TLS/SSL (Transport Layer Security/Secure Sockets Layer) is a cryptographic protocol that ensures the secure transmission of data over the internet. It achieves this by encrypting the data and maintaining confidentiality and integrity between two communicating apps.

IPSec is a collection of protocols to secure Internet Protocol (IP) communications. It achieves this by verifying the authenticity and encrypting each IP packet in a data stream.

End-to-end encryption (E2EE) is a security measure that guarantees data encryption on the sender's device and allows only the intended recipient to decode it. This effectively prevents any middlemen from gaining access to the original, unencrypted data.

A VPN, or Virtual Private Network, establishes a secure and encrypted pathway for data transmission over the Internet, safeguarding it from interception by unauthorized individuals and potential attacks by intermediaries.

Quantum Key Distribution (QKD) is a secure technique that distributes encryption keys, safeguarding encrypted data from potential quantum computing threats.

Data Security in Storage

Data Encryption. At-rest encryption refers to the process of encrypting data stored on any device or storage medium. This encryption renders the data unreadable without the corresponding encryption key. AES, also known as the Advanced Encryption Standard, is frequently employed for this objective.

Database Encryption. Dedicated encryption solutions for databases guarantee the security of stored data, offering features such as transparent data encryption (TDE) that encrypts data without modifying the application.

Access control. Implementing robust access control methods guarantees that only authorized people and systems can access or modify stored data. This encompasses the utilization of multi-factor authentication (MFA), role-based access control (RBAC), and most minor privilege concepts.

Data masking and tokenization. Data masking refers to concealing confidential data stored in a database, ensuring that the information presented to data users does not reveal any sensitive details.

Tokenization is substituting sensitive data pieces with non-sensitive equivalents called tokens. These tokens can later be linked to the original sensitive data via tokenization.

Data backup and redundancy measures are implemented to safeguard against potential data loss caused by hardware malfunctions, cybercrime, or natural calamities. By utilizing encryption, backups are guaranteed to maintain their security, safeguarding the backup data.

Data sanitization. When data becomes obsolete, securely erasing it guarantees its irretrievability. This encompasses the physical destruction of storage media and the cryptographic erasure, which involves the destruction of encryption keys, rendering the data permanently inaccessible.

Optimal Guidelines for Overall Performance

Periodic security audits and compliance assessments. Regular audits of security measures and evaluating compliance with applicable data protection rules (such as GDPR and HIPAA) guarantee continuous data safeguarding during transmission and storage.

Continuous monitoring and threat detection. Deploying a security information and event management (SIEM) system enables the real-time surveillance and examination of security alarms produced by applications and network devices.

Training and raising awareness among employees. Providing staff with information on security protocols and potential risks can mitigate data breaches resulting from human mistakes.

To ensure data security in an AIoT environment, it is essential to adopt a complete strategy that incorporates encryption, secure communication protocols, access control, and continuous monitoring. As technology advances continuously, the accompanying risks also progress. Therefore, it is crucial for enterprises to be well-informed and implement sophisticated security measures to protect their data properly.

4. PRIVACY PRESERVATION IN AIOT

AIoT systems, which combine Artificial Intelligence (AI) with the Internet of Things (IoT), present distinct privacy challenges. These issues emerge from the immense quantities of data that these systems gather, analyze, and retain, frequently encompassing personal and confidential information. It is essential to tackle these privacy concerns to uphold user confidence and adhere to worldwide data protection rules. The following are the primary privacy challenges that are unique to AIoT systems:

1. *Extensive data aggregation.* AIoT devices are specifically engineered to efficiently gather extensive data from their surroundings to operate optimally. The data may encompass personal information, including user activity, location data, biometrics, and even recordings of conversations. If the data obtained is not managed appropriately, the large amount and sensitivity of information can result in significant privacy problems.
2. *Intrusive surveillance and monitoring.* AIoT systems' continuous monitoring ability has the potential to result in intrusive surveillance, hence raising concerns over individuals' right to privacy. Smart home devices and wearables can monitor various elements of an individual's life, potentially without their complete comprehension or agreement.
3. *Data collection and analysis involves collecting and combining data from various sources and then analyzing and categorizing it to create profiles or summaries.* AIoT systems frequently collect data from various sources to construct full user profiles. Although advantageous for customized services, this method can unintentionally disclose sensitive information, subject users to privacy vulnerabilities, and potentially result in discrimination or exclusion based on the generated profiles.
4. *Lack of transparency in decision-making processes.* AI algorithms can make judgments or provide ideas by analyzing the obtained data. However, these procedures generally lack transparency and are not easily understood. Users may lack comprehension regarding the utilization of their data, the deductions drawn about them, and the derivation of decisions that impact them. This lack of understanding might result in privacy apprehensions and the possibility of biases in decision-making.
5. *Vulnerabilities in data security.* The interconnectivity of AIoT systems expands the attack surface, increasing their vulnerability to potential cyber threats. Data breaches can potentially reveal confidential personal data, resulting in privacy infringements. Protecting these systems from threats while guaranteeing privacy is a substantial task.
6. *Sharing data with external parties. AIoT ecosystems sometimes entail data exchange with external entities, including service providers, advertisers, and analytics firms. Without stringent regulations and clear visibility, this* sharing might result in the illicit utilization of personal information, heightening the risks associated with privacy.
7. *Absence of user autonomy and consent.* Preserving user autonomy and obtaining informed permission pose difficulties with AIoT systems. Users may lack awareness regarding the timing and kind of data collection and its utilization and may face difficulties in opting out, thus compromising their privacy rights.

Approaches to Tackle Privacy Obstacles

Implementing privacy considerations into the initial design and structure of AIoT systems, known as Privacy by Design, can help alleviate numerous issues. Data minimization involves gathering only the essential data required for a particular purpose, which aids in mitigating privacy hazards.

1. *Improved transparency and user empowerment.* Offering users comprehensive details regarding data collecting procedures and granting them authority over their data, encompassing consent protocols and the ability to opt-out.
2. *Ensuring data security.* Strong data protection methods, such as encryption and safe data storage, must be enforced to prevent unwanted access and breaches. Anonymization and pseudonymization can safeguard individual privacy while enabling valuable data analysis.
3. *Regulatory Compliance.* Ensuring compliance with worldwide data protection rules, such as GDPR in Europe or CCPA in California, which provide guidelines for safeguarding privacy and data.

A comprehensive strategy is needed to effectively tackle the privacy issues associated with AIoT systems. This strategy should encompass a range of measures, including technological advancements, adherence to regulations, and ethical concerns. By doing so, individual privacy can be safeguarded while reaping the advantages AI and IoT technologies offer.

To guarantee user privacy, particularly in the realm of AIoT (Artificial Intelligence of Things) systems, it is necessary to implement a blend of technical, legal, and organizational precautions. These systems combine artificial intelligence capabilities with the Internet of Things devices, gathering, handling, and examining immense quantities of data, frequently encompassing personal and sensitive information. Below are numerous essential strategies and optimal methods for guaranteeing user privacy:

1. Implementation of privacy by design principles
    *   Integration of privacy. Infuse privacy into the system architecture from the outset rather than as an afterthought. This strategy guarantees that privacy concerns dictate the development process.
2. Minimization of data
    *   Minimize data collection. Gather only the data that is essential for the desired objective. Refrain from gathering unnecessary data that may heighten the likelihood of privacy vulnerabilities.
3. The process of anonymization and pseudonymization
    *   Data anonymization involves eliminating or altering personal identifiers inside data sets to limit the possibility of connecting the information to specific individuals, thereby ensuring anonymity.
    *   *Pseudonymize data.* Substituting private identifiers with pseudonyms or tokens to avoid direct identification while maintaining data utility for specific procedures.
4. The process of converting information into a coded form to prevent unauthorized access or understanding.
    *   *Secure data.* Employ robust encryption protocols to protect data both when stored and during transmission. This ensures the security of the data by preventing unauthorized individuals from accessing it, rendering it incomprehensible without the appropriate decryption key.

- End-to-end encryption. Establish end-to-end encryption for communications, guaranteeing that data is securely encoded throughout its transmission without any intermediates being able to access it.

5. Security measures for controlling access and verifying user identity
    - Deploy robust authentication. Employ robust authentication technologies like multi-factor authentication (MFA) to authenticate user identification.
    - Role-Based Access Control (RBAC) restricts access to resources based on the roles assigned to users. Implement strict access controls to restrict users' access to only the specific data and functions essential for their designated position, thereby reducing the potential for unauthorized access to sensitive information.

6. Ensuring the protection of data during storage and transmission
    - *Secure Storage Solutions.* Safely store data by utilizing encrypted databases and secure storage solutions.
    - *Ensure secure transmission.* To safeguard data throughout its transfer across networks, employ robust transmission methods such as HTTPS, TLS, and VPNs.

7. Periodic security audits and compliance checks
    - *Perform security audits.* Conduct periodic assessments of security and privacy protocols to detect and address potential weaknesses.
    - *Adherence to regulations.* Ensure adherence to pertinent data protection legislation and regulations, such as GDPR, CCPA, and HIPAA, establishing guidelines for safeguarding user privacy.

8. Clarity and approval
    - *Transparent privacy policies.* Offer transparent and comprehensible privacy policies that elucidate the data collection, utilization, sharing, and safeguarding methods for users.
    - *Informed consent.* Acquire express consent from users regarding the gathering and utilization of their data, offering choices to decline or manage their privacy preferences.

9. Management of data lifecycle
    - *Enact data retention policies.* Establish and uphold guidelines on the duration for which data is stored and the timing of its deletion, guaranteeing that it is not preserved beyond its mandatory period.
    - *Secure data deletion.* When data becomes obsolete or at the user's request, it is ensured that it is thoroughly erased in a manner that prevents any possibility of retrieval.

10. PETs (Privacy Enhancing Technologies)
    - *Utilize privacy-enhancing technologies (PETs). Employ advanced technological solutions aimed at augmenting user privacy, such as implementing* federated learning for Artificial Intelligence (AI). This approach enables model training to occur directly on individual devices, minimizing the need to exchange sensitive data.

11. User education and awareness
    - *Inform users.* Offer resources and training to users regarding privacy protocols and the significance of safeguarding their data, enabling them to assert authority over their privacy.

To ensure user privacy, a proactive and comprehensive strategy that combines robust technical measures with policies and practices that uphold user rights and adhere to data protection standards is necessary. By implementing these methodologies, enterprises can safeguard user privacy and cultivate confidence in their AIoT systems.

5. AUTHENTICATION AND ACCESS CONTROL

Securing authentication techniques is of utmost importance in AIoT (Artificial Intelligence of Things) because of the interconnectedness of devices and systems. AIoT integrates the extensive network of IoT devices with AI's data processing and analysis skills, giving rise to notable security problems. Below are a few robust authentication techniques that are well-suited for AIoT contexts, emphasizing their significance and practicality:

1. Multi-factor authentication (MFA) is a security measure that requires users to provide multiple forms of identification in order to access a system or application. MFA strengthens security measures by necessitating the use of two or more authentication factors, such as a combination of knowledge-based (password), possession-based (security token, mobile phone), and biometric-based (biometric verification) factors. AIoT Application: Multi-factor authentication (MFA) can significantly enhance user access control in AIoT systems, providing extra protection while accessing confidential data or control panels.
2. Biometric Authentication refers to verifying an individual's identity using unique physical or behavioral characteristics, such as fingerprints, facial recognition, or voice patterns. Utilizes distinct physical or behavioral attributes for verification, such as fingerprints, facial recognition, voice patterns, or iris scans. This approach provides a superior level of security and ease.
3. Application of Artificial Intelligence of Things (AIoT): This is designed for personal devices inside the AIoT ecosystem, such as smart home systems or healthcare equipment, that necessitate a robust level of security and tailored customisation for individual users.
4. The topic of discussion is Digital Certificates and Public Key Infrastructure (PKI). Digital certificates, administered via PKI, verify the identification of devices or users. PKI employs asymmetric cryptography to safeguard communications, guaranteeing that the designated recipient can decipher the transmitted data.
5. *AIoT Application.* Digital certificates are crucial for authenticating devices in AIoT, ensuring the security of communication and data transmission between devices over networks.
6. *OAuth and Token-Based Authentication.* OAuth is a widely accepted protocol that enables users to authorize websites or applications to access their information on other services without disclosing their passwords. Token-based authentication ensures the security of API transactions and user sessions by using tokens granted after successful authentication.
7. *AIoT Application.* Beneficial for services that necessitate access to user data across several platforms, guaranteeing that AIoT apps can securely retrieve essential information without compromising user credentials.
8. *FIDO (Fast Identity Online) standards.* The FIDO Alliance establishes open standards for more straightforward and robust authentication techniques that decrease the dependence on passwords. FIDO2 allows users to authenticate using ubiquitous devices, such as smartphones or hardware tokens.

9. *AIoT Application.* Using FIDO standards in AIoT devices allows for safe and passwordless authentication, improving security and user experience by eliminating the weaknesses associated with password-based authentication. *Behavioral Authentication* refers to verifying a user's identity based on their unique behavioral patterns and characteristics. This approach utilizes artificial intelligence to continuously verify users' identities by analyzing their distinct behavior profiles, including typing rhythm, mouse motions, and walking patterns. Application of Artificial Intelligence of Things (AIoT): Behavioral authentication is highly advantageous in continuous monitoring systems within AIoT as it provides a non-intrusive and continual verification process that improves security while maintaining user ease.

10. *Quantum Cryptography.* Quantum cryptography, specifically Quantum Key Distribution (QKD), is a secure encryption technique rooted in quantum mechanics. While it is not yet widely used, it promises to provide an encryption approach that is theoretically impossible to break.

11. *AIoT Application.* Quantum cryptography has the potential to provide robust security for communication between AIoT devices, protecting against eavesdropping, including by quantum computers. This ensures the utmost confidentiality of data while it is being transmitted.

Obstacles in Execution

Deploying robust authentication mechanisms in AIoT contexts presents inherent difficulties:

- *Resource limitations.* Internet of Things (IoT) devices frequently have restricted processing capabilities and energy resources, which can restrict the application of intricate authentication techniques.
- *Scalability.* The authentication technique should demonstrate efficient scalability when accommodating new devices and users within the AIoT ecosystem.
- *Interoperability* is of utmost importance when dealing with a wide variety of devices and protocols, as it is essential to ensure that authentication systems can work seamlessly together.
- Striking a balance between robust security measures and user comfort is crucial to promote universal acceptance and adherence.

Robust authentication is essential for safeguarding AIoT systems against illegal entry and cybersecurity risks. As the field of Artificial Intelligence of Things (AIoT) progresses, the techniques for ensuring its security will also advance, necessitating continuous focus on the newest developments and standards in cybersecurity.

Enforcing efficient access control policies is essential for preserving the security and reliability of any information system, particularly in intricate contexts such as AIoT (Artificial Intelligence of Things). Access control rules enforce restrictions to guarantee that only individuals or systems with proper authorization can access specific data or functionality. This reduces the likelihood of unauthorized access, data breaches, and other security vulnerabilities. Below are essential tactics for developing efficient access control policies in AIoT systems:

Establish Precise Criteria for Accessing

1. *Analyze and classify data.* Determine and categorize data according to its level of sensitivity and secrecy. Understanding the many categories of data at hand and their significance can aid in establishing precise degrees of access.
2. *Perform user and device identification.* Unambiguously determine the specific individuals and devices that require access to various categories of data or systems. This involves classifying them according to their positions, departments, or functions.

Implement the Principle of Least Privilege (PoLP)

1. *Principle of minimum necessary access.* Ensure that users and devices are only given access to carry out their specific jobs or functions. This reduces the likelihood of harm resulting from unintentional or intentional abuse.

Implement Role-Based Access Control (RBAC) for Enhanced Security

1. *Responsibilities and permissions.* Establish distinct responsibilities within your organization or system and allocate permissions accordingly. Subsequently, users are allocated roles that bestow upon them the necessary permissions.
2. *Periodic evaluations and assessments.* Roles and permissions necessitate regular scrutiny and modification in response to alterations in responsibilities, work conditions, or the system's functionality.

Deploy Robust Authentication Mechanisms

1. *Multi-factor authentication (MFA)* is a security measure that mandates users to confirm their identity by providing numerous pieces of evidence before being granted access. This practice dramatically enhances security.
2. *Biometrics, tokens, and passwords.* Employ a multifactor authentication approach incorporating biometrics (such as fingerprint or facial recognition), physical tokens, and robust passwords.

ABAC (Attribute-Based Access Control) for Dynamic Environments

1. *Dynamic Access Decisions.* Attribute-Based Access Control (ABAC) employs policies that assess attributes (traits) of users, devices, and resources to determine access permissions. This is especially advantageous in AIoT (Artificial Intelligence of Things) contexts, where access requirements vary dynamically based on contextual factors, such as location or time.

Implement Temporal and Geographical Limitations

1. *Time restrictions* involve restricting access to sensitive systems or data during specified periods of the day or week by operational hours or specific usage patterns.
2. *Geofencing* refers to utilizing location-based controls to limit access to data or systems based on the user's geographical position or device.

Ongoing Surveillance and Examination

1. *Monitor access patterns.* Use monitoring tools to observe and record the individuals accessing certain data and the precise timing of their access. Deviation from normal access patterns can indicate possible security vulnerabilities.
2. *Audit and compliance.* Periodic examinations of access restrictions and usage records are essential for guaranteeing policy adherence and detecting opportunities for enhancement.

Deploy Access Control Lists (ACLs) and Network Segmentation

1. *Resource Access Control Lists (ACLs).* Establish ACLs to determine the authorized users or devices that can access particular resources.
2. Network Segmentation. Divide your network into separate segments to isolate and protect sensitive data and systems. Only authorized users and devices will have access to these parts.

Academic and Instructional Programs

1. Training and awareness programs should be conducted regularly to educate users about the significance of access control and security practices. Train people to effectively identify and respond to social engineering attacks, such as phishing, that attempt to circumvent access constraints.

Utilization of Access Management Tools and Solutions

1. *Centralized management.* Employ access management systems that provide centralized authority over user identities, rights, and access policies, simplifying the administration and implementation of access controls.

A thorough strategy is necessary to successfully implement access control policies in AIoT. This strategy involves integrating technical measures, organizational regulations, and user education. By implementing these measures, enterprises can greatly improve the security of their AIoT systems against unauthorized access and other security concerns.

6. SECURE COMMUNICATION PROTOCOLS

Robust and effective communication protocols are necessary to integrate AI capabilities with IoT devices in the Artificial Intelligence of Things (AIoT) ecosystem. These protocols guarantee uninterrupted data transmission between devices, facilitating intelligent decision-making and automation. Below is a comprehensive summary of essential communication protocols that have a crucial impact on AIoT systems, emphasizing their distinct characteristics and practical uses:

1. *MQTT (Message Queuing Telemetry Transport)* is a communication protocol. It is a lightweight, publish-subscribe network protocol specifically developed to establish connections with remote places that have a tiny code footprint or limited network capacity. MQTT is useful for Internet of Things (IoT) situations that demand immediate and effective communication, such as smart homes, industrial monitoring, and car telematics.

2. *CoAP (Constrained Application Protocol)*. CoAP is a web transfer protocol specifically intended for restricted devices. It allows for easy translation to HTTP, enabling seamless interaction with the web. Additionally, CoAP provides an efficient communication mechanism with minimal overhead. It is ideal for IoT devices with limited resources in settings such as smart cities and environmental monitoring, where optimizing energy and bandwidth utilization is crucial.

3. *HTTP/HTTPS (Hypertext Transfer Protocol/Secure)* is the communication protocol for transmitting data over the Internet. HTTP is the standard protocol, while HTTPS is the secure version that encrypts the data to ensure confidentiality and integrity. HTTP/HTTPS serves as the fundamental framework for transmitting data on the Internet. It is adaptable, extensively used, and ensures security with HTTPS. This makes it appropriate for intricate inquiries and seamless integration with web services. This technology benefits AIoT applications that necessitate secure and dependable communication with web-based services and cloud computing, where compatibility with current web infrastructure is essential.

4. *WebSocket* is a communication protocol that provides full-duplex communication channels over a single TCP connection. It facilitates bidirectional communication between a web browser (or any other client program) and a server by establishing a single TCP connection that supports full-duplex communication channels. This is especially advantageous for AIoT applications that require instantaneous data sharing, such as real-time monitoring systems, gaming, and interactive dashboards.

5. *BLE (Bluetooth Low Energy)*. Tailored for minimal energy usage, BLE is an optimal communication protocol for IoT devices powered by batteries, providing adequate data transfer over limited distances. This technology is extensively utilized in wearable technology, healthcare devices, and smart home items, where energy efficiency and proximity-based communication are crucial.

6. *Zigbee* is a wireless communication protocol that utilizes low-power digital radios. It was specifically developed for secure networking, extended battery life, and low-data rate transmission. Zigbee is frequently employed in home automation, smart energy management, and healthcare monitoring systems. It facilitates mesh networking, enabling a wide range of devices to connect to each other.

7. *Long-Term Evolution for Machines (LTE-M) and Narrowband Internet of Things (NB-IoT)*. Cellular IoT solutions provide extensive coverage, minimal energy usage, and enhanced penetration in urban and interior settings. LTE-M offers enhanced data transmission speeds and improved mobility capabilities, while NB-IoT is designed explicitly for stationary applications that require

lower data rates. Ideal for various AIoT applications, such as smart metering, asset tracking, and smart agriculture, that necessitate cellular connectivity across extensive geographical regions.

8. *LoRaWAN* is an acronym for Long Range Wide Area Network. The features of this protocol include its ability to manage communication between LPWAN devices and network gateways at the media access control (MAC) layer. It is specifically designed to optimize power consumption and facilitate long-range communication. Utilized in the context of smart cities, industrial Internet of Things (IoT), and environmental monitoring, where equipment necessitates long-range communication while minimizing energy consumption.

The selection of an appropriate communication protocol for AIoT applications is contingent upon various factors:

1. *Power consumption.* Protocols such as BLE and LoRaWAN are specifically engineered to minimize energy usage, making them well-suited for devices that rely on batteries.
2. *Data rate requirements.* Protocols such as Wi-Fi or LTE-M can optimize high-bandwidth applications, whereas CoAP or MQTT are more suitable for low-bandwidth transfers. LoRaWAN and cellular IoT technologies are well-suited for long-range communication, while BLE and Zigbee are more appropriate for short-range applications.
3. *Security requirements.* Protocols like HTTPS and those with inherent security features (such as TLS encryption) are essential for apps that manage sensitive data.

The selection of a protocol should be based on the demands of the AIoT application, considering aspects such as the capabilities of the devices, the network infrastructure, the security needs, and the limitations on expenses.

7. LEGAL AND ETHICAL CONSIDERATIONS

Comprehending and adhering to compliance and regulatory obligations is essential for firms operating across many sectors, particularly those involved in handling sensitive data, safeguarding customer privacy, conducting financial transactions, or managing health-related information. Compliance guarantees that firms conform to laws, regulations, standards, and ethical norms pertinent to their operations. This not only aids in reducing legal and financial liabilities but also fosters confidence among customers and stakeholders. Here is a comprehensive summary of the main areas where compliance and regulatory requirements are especially relevant:

1. *Safeguarding and confidentiality of data.* The General Data Protection Rule (GDPR) is a legal rule in the European Union (EU) and the European Economic Area (EEA) that focuses on safeguarding data protection and privacy. Furthermore, it deals with transferring personal data across the European Union (EU) and the European Economic Area (EEA) geographical boundaries. The California Consumer Privacy Act (CCPA) is a state law designed to strengthen privacy rights and provide consumer protection for inhabitants of California, USA. The Health Insurance Portability and Accountability Act (HIPAA) is a United States law that establishes regulations to protect the privacy and security of medical information.

2. *Adherence to financial regulations and standards.* The Sarbanes-Oxley Act (SOX) is a federal law in the United States that seeks to safeguard investors from deceptive financial reporting conducted by firms. The Payment Card Industry Data Security Standard (PCI DSS) is a set of regulations that govern payment card data security. The Payment Card Industry Data Security Standard (PCI DSS) is a comprehensive collection of regulations to guarantee that every organization that handles credit card data adheres to strict security measures to maintain a secure environment.

3. *Regulations specific to the industry.* The International Traffic in Arms Regulations (ITAR) and Export Administration Regulations (EAR) are United States regulations that govern the export and import of defense-related commodities and services and commercial and dual-use items, respectively. The Federal Information Security Management Act (FISMA) is a U.S. federal law that mandates federal agencies to create, record, and execute a program for safeguarding and securing information.

4. *Global standards and frameworks. ISO/IEC 27001* is a globally recognized standard that provides guidelines for effectively managing information security. This document outlines the criteria for creating, executing, upholding, and consistently enhancing an information security management system (ISMS). *IST Framework.* The National Institute of Standards and Technology has created a computer security policy framework that offers direction to private sector businesses in the US. This framework helps these organizations evaluate and enhance their capacity to avoid, detect, and respond to cyber threats.

Methods for Guaranteeing Adherence

1. *Perform routine audits.* Regular compliance audits are essential for detecting and resolving deficiencies before they escalate into problems.
2. *Stay updated.* Laws and regulations constantly change, and it is essential to stay updated to ensure compliance.
3. *Employee training.* Implementing regular training programs for employees helps them comprehend compliance rules and the significance of adherence.
4. *Deploy compliance management systems.* These systems facilitate the monitoring of compliance with various regulations and standards.
5. *Interact with legal professionals.* Specialized legal consultants in compliance can offer essential expertise and counsel to ensure complete adherence to regulatory obligations.

Compliance and regulatory standards exhibit significant variation across different areas and industries, and possessing a comprehensive awareness of these regulations is crucial for conducting a legal and ethical firm. Organizations must regularly oversee compliance practices to reduce risks, prevent penalties, and establish confidence with customers and partners. Efficient compliance management entails periodic assessment of legal responsibilities, employee training, and implementation of thorough security and privacy protocols customized to the organization's unique requirements and regulatory environment.

Legal and ethical considerations for AIoT (Artificial Intelligence of Things) systems are paramount to ensure that these technologies are developed, deployed, and used to benefit society and not infringe upon individual rights or safety. AIoT combines AI (Artificial Intelligence) with IoT (Internet of Things), integrating machine learning algorithms with IoT devices to create intelligent systems capable of autonomous decision-making based on data collected from their environment. This integration raises several legal and ethical issues that must be addressed:

1. Privacy and Data Protection

- *Data collection*: AIoT devices can collect vast amounts of personal data, raising concerns about privacy and the potential for surveillance.
- *Data storage and access*: How and where data is stored and who has access to it must comply with data protection laws, such as the GDPR in the European Union, which mandates strict guidelines on data handling and privacy.

2. Security

- *Vulnerability to Attacks*: The interconnected nature of AIoT devices increases the risk of cyber-attacks. Ensuring the security of these devices is critical to protect against unauthorized access and data breaches.
- *Data Integrity*: Protecting data integrity from manipulation is essential, especially when decisions are made based on this data.

3. Ethical Use and Bias

- *Decision-making*: AIoT systems can make autonomous decisions that impact people's lives. It's important that these decisions are fair, transparent, and explainable.
- *Bias in AI*: AI systems can inherit biases in their training data, leading to discriminatory outcomes. Ethical considerations must ensure that AIoT systems are fair and unbiased.

4. Regulatory Compliance

- *Standards and regulations*: Compliance with existing regulations and standards is necessary. As AIoT is a relatively new domain, regulations may need to be updated or created to address specific issues related to AIoT systems.
- *Liability*: Determining liability in cases where AIoT systems fail or cause harm is complex. Clear guidelines and legal frameworks are needed to address these issues.

5. Transparency and Accountability

- Understanding AI Decisions: Ensuring that AIoT system decisions can be understood and justified is essential for accountability.
- Public Trust: Building public trust in AIoT systems is crucial for their acceptance and ethical use.

6. Environmental Impact

- *Resource consumption*: The production and operation of AIoT devices consume resources and generate waste, contributing to environmental issues.
- *Sustainability*: Developing sustainable AIoT systems that minimize environmental impact is an ethical consideration that should not be overlooked.

The amalgamation of Artificial Intelligence (AI) and the Internet of Things (IoT), resulting in AIoT, offers many advantages, such as improved effectiveness, customized experiences, and more intelligent decision-making in many industries. Nevertheless, this integration also presents noteworthy ethical data security and privacy considerations. Given that AIoT systems gather, handle, and evaluate significant quantities of data, frequently in real-time, it is imperative to address these ethical challenges to uphold user confidence and comply with societal standards. Below are several significant ethical ramifications of data security and privacy in the realm of Artificial Intelligence of Things (AIoT):

1. Agreement and Clarity

Problem. Numerous AIoT devices regularly gather personal data, although users may be unaware of the data types collected, their utilization, and the entities they are shared with.

Ethical implications. Without explicit agreement and open disclosure, users relinquish authority over their personal information, raising questions regarding autonomy and the ability to make informed decisions.

2. Minimization of Data

Problem. AIoT systems frequently gather excessive amounts of data beyond what is required to enhance services or customize user experiences.

Ethical implication. Gathering excessive data might violate individuals' rights to privacy and heighten the potential for harm if the data is misused or insufficiently safeguarded.

3. Prejudice and Inequality

Problem. AI systems can potentially acquire or magnify biases in their training data or design, resulting in biased results.

Ethical implications. AIoT devices that make judgments relying on biased data can perpetuate or intensify inequality and injustice, impacting domains such as personal finance, healthcare, and law enforcement.

4. Observation and Supervision

Problem. The widespread presence of AIoT devices allows for a high degree of surveillance and monitoring that can be obtrusive and ever-present.

Ethical implication. Unrestricted and unregulated continuous monitoring can result in establishing a surveillance society, undermining privacy and potentially restricting freedom of expression and association.

5. Measures to Ensure Security and Mitigate Data Breaches

Problem. AIoT devices, due to their networked nature and occasional lack of solid security measures, are susceptible to cyberattacks, resulting in unauthorized access and data leaks.

Ethical implication. Failure to adequately protect personal and sensitive data not only infringes upon private rights but can also lead to substantial injury to persons, such as identity theft, financial detriment, and emotional anguish.

6. Ensuring That Individuals Are Held Accountable and Responsible for Their Actions

Problem. Establishing responsibility for data breaches or harm resulting from AIoT systems can be intricate, particularly when numerous entities are engaged in creating, implementing, and administrating such systems.

Ethical implication. Without transparent responsibility, individuals who suffer from privacy breaches or unfair judgments may lack the means to seek remedy, compromising the principles of justice and equity.

7. Effects in the Long Run

Problem. The comprehensive comprehension of the enduring societal consequences resulting from extensive data gathering and analysis via AIoT, encompassing alterations to social norms and expectations of privacy, remains incomplete.

Ethical implication. The steady erosion of privacy poses a risk of normalizing this trend, which could shift society's values and potentially facilitate more intrusive data practices in the future.

8. Examining the Ethical Ramifications. In Order to Address These Ethical Challenges, Participants in the AIoT Ecosystem Must

- Enforce resilient data security measures and employ secure communication protocols.
- Guarantee openness and well-informed agreement for the gathering and utilization of data.
- Implement the principles of reducing data collection and limiting data usage to specific purposes.
- Consistently evaluate and minimize biases in AI algorithms.
- Implement robust systems to ensure transparent responsibility for safeguarding data security and privacy.
- Continuously communicate with authorities, civic society, and the public to assess and tackle the societal effects of AIoT technology.

It is crucial to consider the ethical consequences of data security and privacy in AIoT to develop systems that effectively utilize AI and IoT technology while upholding individual rights and social values.

8. CASE STUDIES AND REAL-WORLD APPLICATIONS

The convergence of Artificial Intelligence (AI) with the Internet of Things (IoT), AIoT, transforms various sectors by facilitating intelligent and more effective operations, improved decision-making procedures, and customized user interactions. Presented below is a collection of case studies and practical examples that demonstrate the profound influence of AIoT in several industries:

8.1. Intelligent Healthcare: Remote Patient Monitoring

Summary. To monitor patients remotely, a platform combining artificial intelligence and the Internet of Things (AIoT) was created. This platform uses wearable devices to gather real-time health data, including heart rate, blood pressure, and activity levels (Ju & Park, 2023; see also Judith et al., 2023; Alvi et al., 2024; Chang et al., 2020; Lee et al., 2023).

Implementation. AI algorithms analyze data anomalies, forecast health problems, and offer tailored suggestions. The system notifies healthcare providers when medical attention is urgently needed.

Impact. Timely identification and action enhanced patient outcomes, decreased hospital readmissions, and increased healthcare providers' ability to oversee patient care remotely.

Critical Determinants of Success

- Interoperability refers to the capacity to seamlessly integrate with existing healthcare systems, enabling smooth and uninterrupted data flow.
- Design that prioritizes the needs and preferences of the user, specifically the patient, emphasizing ease of use and active participation.
- *Privacy and security*. Stringent data protection procedures are implemented to adhere to regulations such as HIPAA.

Result. Improved quality of patient care, hospital readmissions, and financial savings.

8.2. Intelligent Urban Areas: A System for Managing Traffic

Summary. A municipality has deployed an AIoT-driven traffic management system that utilizes cameras and sensors to gather up-to-the-minute information on traffic conditions and the movement of vehicles (Cob-Parro et al., 2024; see also Kong et al., 2024; Ju & Park, 2023).

Implementation. AI algorithms analyze the data to light schedules, forecast areas of congestion, and suggest route modifications to drivers via a mobile application (Shin et al., 2024; see also Lauria & Azzalin, 2024; Ülkü et al., 2024; Umer et al., 2024; Fera & Spandonidis, 2024; Lampropoulos et al., 2024).

Effect. By giving priority to emergency vehicles through traffic control systems, there has been a decrease in traffic congestion, a reduction in emission levels, and an improvement in emergency response times.

Critical Determinants of Success (Wiryasaputra et al., 2024; See Also Hadad et al., 2024)

- Scalability refers to the capacity to effectively handle and accommodate the increasing volume of data generated by additional sensors and sources (Ni et al., 2020).
- Real-time Data Processing: Utilization of edge computing to reduce delay in traffic management replies (Yang et al., 2024).

- Public-private Partnerships refer to the collaborative efforts of local authorities and technology companies to facilitate the sharing of resources (Sun et al., 2021).

Result: Decreased traffic congestion, excellent air quality, and improved public safety (Zhu et al., 2022; see also Oh et al., 2022; Chang et al., 2020).

8.3. Precision Farming in Agriculture

Summary. A precision farming AIoT solution employs drones and ground-based sensors to observe crop well-being, measure soil moisture levels, and monitor environmental variables (Vandervelden et al., 2023; see also Xu et al., 2023; Hung, 2021).

Implementation. Artificial intelligence utilizes the gathered data to offer farmers precise guidance on the most favorable periods for planting, efficient water administration, effective insect management, and strategic crop rotation techniques.

Effect. Enhanced agricultural productivity, diminished utilization of resources (such as water, fertilizers, pesticides), and decreased operational expenses, resulting in the adoption of more environmentally friendly farming methods.

Critical Determinants of Success

- *Data accuracy*. We can gather exact and reliable data regarding crop health and environmental conditions using state-of-the-art sensors and advanced drone technology.
- *Custom AI Models*. Creation of artificial intelligence models designed specifically for individual crop varieties and agricultural environments.
- *Farmer engagement*. Training initiatives aim to equip farmers with the necessary skills to utilize technology and accurately understand artificial intelligence findings.

Result. Enhanced agricultural productivity, optimized resource utilization, and minimized ecological footprint.

8.4. Predictive Maintenance in the Manufacturing Industry

Summary. A manufacturing plant implemented an AIoT system that utilized machine sensors to monitor operational parameters and identify indications of wear or malfunction (Canavese et al., 2024; see also Bakhshi et al., 2024; Altulaihan et al., 2024).

Implementation. AI algorithms anticipate equipment malfunctions in advance, enabling prompt maintenance and repairs and reducing downtime to a minimum.

Effects. Reducing unexpected periods of inactivity, prolonging the operational lifespan of equipment, and optimizing the timing of maintenance activities can achieve substantial financial benefits.

Critical Determinants of Success

- *Seamless integration with legacy systems*. Efficiently integrating with pre-existing machinery and ERP systems.

- *Workforce training and acceptance.* Ensuring that employees comprehend and embrace novel technologies.
- Continuous improvement involves utilizing AIoT data not only for maintenance purposes but also for optimizing processes.

Result. Decreased periods of inactivity, prolonged lifespan of equipment, and financial savings in operations.

8.5. Energy: Efficient Grid Control

Summary: An AIoT-enabled innovative grid system incorporates sensors and smart meters throughout the energy network to monitor energy usage, distribution, and grid conditions in real time (Hossain et al., 2024; see also Bobde et al., 2024; Zhang et al., 2024; Ożadowicz, 2024; Qu et al., 2024; Raja et al., 2023).

Implementation: Artificial intelligence enhances the efficiency of energy distribution by utilizing demand projections, rapidly detecting and isolating defects, and effectively integrating renewable energy sources.

Effects: Enhanced energy efficiency, decreased operational expenses, and heightened reliability of the energy provision. Additionally, it facilitates the shift towards renewable energy by effectively handling fluctuations and storage.

Critical Determinants of Success

- Cybersecurity protects computer systems, networks, and data from unauthorized access, attacks, and damage. Security measures: Implementation of sophisticated security processes to safeguard against cyber threats.
- Demand Response Management: Utilizing AI algorithms to regulate energy delivery dynamically by real-time demand.
- Stakeholder Collaboration effectively coordinates and collaborates among energy providers, customers, and regulatory agencies.

Result. Enhanced energy efficiency facilitated the integration of renewable energy and improved grid resilience.

8.6. Retail: Customized Shopping Experience

Summary. A retail chain has adopted an AIoT platform that utilizes sensors within its stores and consumer mobile devices to improve the shopping experience (Nadhan & Jacob I, 2023; see also Lin et al., 2024; Rekeraho et al., 2024; Joshua et al., 2024).

Implementation. Artificial intelligence (AI) utilizes advanced algorithms to examine and interpret consumer behavior (Lee et al., 2023), preferences, and up-to-date location data. This enables the AI system to provide tailored recommendations, promotions, and guidance for customers while they are in the business (Mimboro et al., 2021).

Impact. Enhanced customer happiness and engagement, augmented sales through tailored marketing strategies, and optimized inventory management utilizing customer behavior information.

Critical Determinants of Success

- Customization Algorithms refer to artificial intelligence models that can anticipate customer preferences and provide product recommendations effectively.
- Omnichannel Integration ensures a smooth, uninterrupted consumer experience across online and physical retail outlets.
- Data-Driven Decisions: Utilizing AIoT insights to enhance inventory management, optimize shop layout, and implement targeted marketing strategies.

Result: Enhanced revenue, elevated client contentment, and optimized operational effectiveness.

These case studies exemplify AIoT's extensive versatility and capacity to revolutionize businesses through efficiency enhancement, predictive analytics facilitation, and tailored user experiences. As technology advances, the potential for innovation and influence in different industries will grow, presenting substantial opportunities for businesses and society.

The successful integration of AI with IoT, known as AIoT (Artificial Intelligence of Things), across many sectors, demonstrates the promise of this combination and offers significant insights into the crucial variables that contribute to their success. Examining these implementations facilitates the identification of optimal methodologies, the obstacles surmounted, and the strategic approaches that resulted in favorable results. Below is an examination of accomplished AIoT deployments in several domains:

Notable Insights and Optimal Methods

Stakeholder engagement. Engaging all stakeholders, including end-users, from the initial phases of project design to execution guarantees that the solution aligns with actual requirements and achieves broader acceptance.

Data governance is crucial for safeguarding privacy and ensuring adherence to regulations. It involves formulating explicit guidelines on the collection, storage, and utilization of data.

Scalability and flexibility are crucial in system design to ensure adaptability to evolving requirements, avoid obsolescence, and promote long-term success.

Implementing security measures from the beginning, rather than as an afterthought, is crucial for protecting against ever-changing cyber threats.

Continuous Monitoring and Optimization. By establishing feedback loops, AIoT systems may be consistently monitored, and the insights gained can be utilized to optimize performance and increase return on investment (ROI) over time.

Successful AIoT implementations showcase the need for strategic design, active stakeholder involvement, and continuous management. These implementations can bring substantial advantages in many industries, emphasizing the revolutionary power of combining AI with IoT efficiently.

Advanced technology applications in the real world, such as the Internet of Things (IoT) and artificial intelligence (AI), may teach us a lot about navigating the challenges of digital transformation. These insights are derived from the triumphs and setbacks experienced in several sectors. Through analyzing these situations, valuable insights can be gained regarding risk mitigation methods, best practices, and the essential elements that facilitate the efficient implementation and utilization of AI and IoT technologies. The following are some critical lessons from actual situations:

1. The Value of Flexibility and Scalability

Lesson: Systems must be built to scale effectively with growing data quantities and change with time. Flexible technology infrastructure enables adding new tools and procedures without extensive redesigns.

As a demonstration, IoT installations in intelligent cities have demonstrated that flexible and scalable designs can handle the long-term expansion of connected devices and data analytics requirements.

2. Prioritizing Data Security and Privacy

Lesson. Ensuring system security and safeguarding user data are critical since flaws can result in serious breaches that damage user confidence and may even be illegal.

Example. Data breaches in consumer IoT goods have highlighted the need for robust security measures like encryption, authentication, and frequent security upgrades.

3. Enhanced Adoption Through User-Centric Design

Lesson. User needs and experiences should be the center of technology implementation efforts to ensure that solutions are clear, easily accessible, and solve problems for users.

Example. Higher adoption rates and user engagement have been observed for wearable health devices, which focus on user-friendly designs and offer actionable health insights.

4. Interdisciplinary Cooperation Is Essential

Lesson. Domain-specific knowledge, data science, engineering, cybersecurity, and other disciplines are often needed to integrate AI and IoT solutions. Working together across different domains encourages creativity and more comprehensive solutions.

As a demonstration, productive AIoT initiatives in the manufacturing sector have used cross-functional teams to forecast maintenance requirements, enhance production processes, and guarantee worker safety.

5. Ongoing Education and Adjustment

Lesson. Because technology is advancing so quickly, it is necessary to continuously learn about and adjust to new developments in the technology itself and the ethical and legal issues surrounding its use.

As a demonstration, AI algorithms used in predictive healthcare analytics need to be updated regularly to consider the most recent medical findings and adhere to shifting legal requirements.

6. Open Communication Fosters Confidence

Lesson. By being transparent about the capabilities, constraints, and data use of AI and IoT systems, stakeholders and users may develop trust, which promotes wider adoption and support.

Example. Businesses have been able to manage privacy issues more successfully when they openly disclose how customer data is used in AI models for customized suggestions.

7. Adherence to Regulations Is a Changing Objective

Lesson. The laws about AI and IoT are constantly changing. Organizations need to be watchful and flexible regarding new rules to guarantee continuous compliance.

Example. The implementation of GDPR in Europe necessitated considerable changes in how businesses manage and process personal data, affecting the global deployment of AI and IoT.

8. Ethical Issues Must Be Taken Into Account

Lesson. To ensure responsible innovation, ethical concerns about bias, justice, and the societal impact of technology deployments must be addressed proactively, in addition to legal compliance.

For instance, the use of AI in recruiting and hiring has brought attention to the need for systems to detect and reduce bias in automated decision-making.

Scalability, security, user-centricity, interdisciplinary cooperation, and ethical considerations are all important lessons learned from real-world applications of AI and IoT technologies. Organizations may successfully negotiate the challenges of technology adoption by internalizing these principles, which will result in deployments that meet social norms and ethical standards and yield observable advantages.

9. EMERGING TRENDS AND FUTURE DIRECTIONS

The quick development of the Internet of Things (IoT) has led to significant developments in security techniques and technology. Protection of the enormous volumes of data generated and processed by these increasingly intricate networks of linked devices depends on these developments. An examination of current developments in AIoT security is provided below:

1. Advanced Methods of Encryption

Quantum-resistant encryption. Conventional encryption techniques are vulnerable to the emergence of quantum computing. The development of quantum-resistant algorithms is underway to protect AIoT communications from potential quantum attacks in the future (Soroceanu et al., 2023; see also Wang et al., 2024).

Homomorphic encryption makes AI analysis possible, which enables computations on encrypted data without disclosing the underlying data. It's beneficial in AIoT applications where data privacy is essential, like in the medical field (Nita & Mihailescu, 2023).

2. SMPC (Secure Multi-Party Computation)

SMPC protects the privacy of the inputs by enabling multiple parties to compute a function over them jointly. In the context of AIoT, this can improve security and privacy in situations like federated learning across IoT devices by enabling collaborative AI without disclosing sensitive data (Liu et al., 2023).

3. Blockchain Technology for Integrity and Device Identity

Device IDs are securely managed, and unchangeable logs of device actions are produced with the help of blockchain technology. In AIoT ecosystems, this can guard against unwanted device access and guarantee the accuracy of data supplied by devices (Kerrison et al., 2023; see also Jia et al., 2020).

4. Threat Detection and Response Powered by AI

Real-time identification of anomalies and possible assaults on AIoT networks is made possible by machine learning models or deep learning (Chang et al., 2000), which are increasingly skilled at spotting patterns suggestive of cyber threats.

Automated response. AI-powered systems can lessen the need for human intervention by automatically responding to attacks in real-time and detecting threats.

5. Architectures of Zero Trust

Zero Trust security models verify each request as if it were coming from an open network because they consider that threats may come from internal and external sources. In AIoT environments, this strategy is becoming essential for ensuring strict access control and verification (Thantharate & Thantharate, 2023; see also Dhiman et al., 2024; Daah et al., 2024).

6. Security of Edge Computing

Decentralized security. By relocating data processing to the edge, networks are exposed to fewer assaults since there is less critical data traveling through them. Security protocols that are specific to edges are being developed to safeguard these decentralized networks (Alamsyah et al., 2024; see also Din et al., 2024).

7. Service Edge for Secure Access (SASE)

SASE frameworks, which are particularly helpful in managing the heterogeneous and scattered nature of AIoT devices, integrate network security features with WAN capabilities to suit the dynamic, secure access demands of enterprises (Alrubayyi et al., 2024; see also (Shen et al., 2016)).

8. Design-Based Security

Including security during the design phase: Adding security concerns from the outset of AIoT system development is becoming more and more important to mitigate potential vulnerabilities prior to deployment (Kim et al., 2024; see also Zhang et al., 2024).

9. Innovation in Regulatory and Compliance

Automated compliance provides more advanced tools and platforms that automatically verify that AIoT deployments adhere to applicable laws and standards, such as the GDPR for data protection (Taylor et al., 2021).

10. Techniques for Privacy-Preserving AI

Differential privacy. By incorporating differential privacy into AI algorithms, it is possible to ensure that AIoT systems can identify patterns without jeopardizing the protection of personal information (Arafeh et al., 2023).

Federated learning eliminates the need to exchange or centralize sensitive data by enabling AI models to be trained across numerous decentralized devices that contain local data samples.

AIoT security concerns are becoming more sophisticated as it grows. But improvements in privacy-preserving methods, blockchain, AI-driven security, and encryption are opening the door to more robust and safer AIoT ecosystems. These developments provide a reliable basis for the ongoing development of AIoT applications by improving the security of AIoT networks and guaranteeing the confidentiality and integrity of the data they use.

Rapid technological breakthroughs create opportunities and difficulties for the future of web data and privacy in the artificial intelligence of things (AIoT) space. The data management and privacy field is anticipated to undergo substantial change as AIoT devices proliferate and generate ever-increasing volumes of data. The following are a few forecasts regarding web data and privacy in the context of AIoT:

1. A rise in the production and use of data. *Forecast*: As AIoT devices proliferate, data generation will expand exponentially, providing deeper insights into user preferences, habits, and interactions with the environment. Implication: This will make services more individualized and effective, but it will also give rise to serious privacy issues since more specific portions of people's lives are being captured and examined.
2. Improved technologies for preserving privacy. *Forecast* - Due to technological advancements like secure multi-party computation, homomorphic encryption, and differential privacy, data processing will become more commonplace without compromising privacy. *Implication* - although these technologies will allay specific privacy worries, their execution will necessitate processing power and complex planning.
3. Tighter regulations regarding data protection. *Forecast* - Stricter limitations on data collecting, processing, and sharing will be implemented internationally in response to growing privacy concerns. These regulations will resemble the CCPA in California and the GDPR in the EU. *Implication* – businesses will have to spend money on compliance systems, which might impede innovation but boost customer confidence.
4. The development of decentralized data structures. *Forecast* - Decentralized data architectures, such as federated learning and blockchain, will become more popular as ways to improve data security and privacy in AIoT ecosystems. *Implication* - New data management and analytics methods will be needed due to this change, which will put old, centralized data processing and storage models to the test.

5. The impact of quantum computing. *Forecast* - The emergence of quantum computing will force the creation of quantum-resistant cryptography algorithms since it will present new difficulties for existing encryption approaches. *Implication* - there will be a competition to protect AIoT communications from quantum attacks, which will have a big impact on data security and privacy.

6. AIoT devices as protectors of privacy. *Forecast* – AI-driven privacy protection features will become more prevalent in AIoT devices themselves, actively controlling data processing and sharing in accordance with user choices and legal requirements. *Implication* - Although it also raises concerns about the regularity and dependability of these measures, this could provide users with more direct control over their data.

7. Development of Ethical AI. *Forecast* - Fairness, accountability, and transparency will be the guiding principles for AIoT applications, and ethical considerations in AI research will become a primary priority. *Implication* - By concentrating on this area, privacy protections will be strengthened; yet AIoT developers may face additional operational and regulatory difficulties.

8. Data economies focused on users. *Forecast* - The existing data economy may change as models such as data trusts and personal data marketplaces that give people greater control over their data become more prevalent. *Implication* - These models will necessitate robust frameworks for permission and compensation, even while they may improve privacy and give consumers a stake in their data.

AIoT's complicated future for web data and privacy is characterized by technical developments that simultaneously strengthen and undermine privacy laws. It will be crucial to strike a balance between ethical issues, legal compliance, and innovation. To effectively traverse this changing terrain, organizations and stakeholders need to be flexible in order to adjust to new technology and societal expectations.

10. CONCLUSION

The study of AIoT (Artificial Intelligence of Things) from a variety of angles, including future projections, practical applications, ethical considerations, and security developments, reveals a complex environment influenced by both the rapid advancement of technology and the growing consciousness of society. The main conclusions are outlined as follows:

AIoT Security Developments. Creating homomorphic and quantum-resistant encryption methods is essential for protecting data from future attacks and facilitating safe data processing. Blockchain technology is improving real-time security monitoring and device identity management using AI-powered threat detection methods. In order to guarantee strong access control and data integrity in decentralized networks, zero-trust architectures, and edge computing security are essential.

Implications for ethics. Three main ethical issues are permission and privacy, data reduction, bias, and discrimination. To tackle these, open data policies, moral AI development, and the application of fairness principles are necessary. Clear legal frameworks and moral standards are required in light of the concerns raised by surveillance and monitoring over the invasion of privacy and individuality.

Practical uses. The Internet of Things (IoT) is revolutionizing various industries with its applications in intelligent traffic management, precision farming, smart grids, predictive maintenance, and remote patient monitoring. Interoperability, user-centric design, cross-disciplinary cooperation, scalability, and ongoing learning are examples of success factors.

Prospective forecasts. The future of web data and privacy will be shaped by an exponential rise in data generation and the implementation of privacy-preserving solutions. Security and privacy standards will be redefined by tighter data protection laws, decentralized data architectures, and the effects of quantum computing. AIoT gadgets might develop into privacy protectors, and the development of ethical AI will play a more significant role in the application of technology.

The field at the nexus of AI and IoT is active and offers ample opportunity for efficiency and innovation. However, it also raises complex issues with privacy, security, and moral application. AIoT improvements in the future will hinge on striking a careful balance between utilizing technology capabilities and abiding by legal and ethical obligations.

AIoT technologies improve social well-being while protecting individual rights and privacy; success in this field demands not just technological innovation but also a commitment to ethical values, user participation, and proactive governance.

REFERENCES

Alamsyah, A., Kusuma, G. N. W., & Ramadhani, D. P. (2024, February 26). A Review on Decentralized Finance Ecosystems. *Future Internet, 16*(3), 76. doi:10.3390/fi16030076

Alrubayyi, H., Alshareef, M. S., Nadeem, Z., Abdelmoniem, A. M., & Jaber, M. (2024, February 29). Security Threats and Promising Solutions Arising from the Intersection of AI and IoT: A Study of IoMT and IoET Applications. *Future Internet, 16*(3), 85. doi:10.3390/fi16030085

Altulaihan, E., Almaiah, M. A., & Aljughaiman, A. (2024, January 22). Anomaly Detection IDS for Detecting DoS Attacks in IoT Networks Based on Machine Learning Algorithms. *Sensors (Basel), 24*(2), 713. doi:10.3390/s24020713 PMID:38276404

Alvi, A. N., Ali, M., Saleh, M. S., Alkhathami, M., Alsadie, D., Alghamdi, B., & Alenzi, B. (2024, February 5). TMPAD: Time-Slot-Based Medium Access Control Protocol to Meet Adaptive Data Requirements for Trusted Nodes in Fog-Enabled Smart Cities. *Applied Sciences (Basel, Switzerland), 14*(3), 1319. doi:10.3390/app14031319

Arafeh, M., Wazzeh, M., Ould-Slimane, H., Talhi, C., Mourad, A., & Otrok, H. (2023, October 16). Efficient Privacy-Preserving ML for IoT: Cluster-Based Split Federated Learning Scheme for Non-IID Data. *2023 7th Cyber Security in Networking Conference (CSNet).* 10.1109/CSNet59123.2023.10339772

Bakhshi, T., Ghita, B., & Kuzminykh, I. (2024, January 22). A Review of IoT Firmware Vulnerabilities and Auditing Techniques. *Sensors (Basel), 24*(2), 708. doi:10.3390/s24020708 PMID:38276399

Bobde, Y., Narayanan, G., Jati, M., Raj, R. S. P., Cvitić, I., & Peraković, D. (2024, February 7). Enhancing Industrial IoT Network Security through Blockchain Integration. *Electronics (Basel), 13*(4), 687. doi:10.3390/electronics13040687

C., Qureshi, A., Awan, I., & Konur, S. (2024, February 23). Enhancing Zero Trust Models in the Financial Industry through Blockchain Integration: A Proposed Framework. *Electronics, 13*(5), 865. doi:10.3390/electronics13050865

Canavese, D., Mannella, L., Regano, L., & Basile, C. (2024, January 17). Security at the Edge for Resource-Limited IoT Devices. *Sensors (Basel)*, *24*(2), 590. doi:10.3390/s24020590 PMID:38257680

Chang, W. J., Chen, L. B., Chen, M. C., Chiu, Y. C., & Lin, J. Y. (2020). ScalpEye: A Deep Learning-Based Scalp Hair Inspection and Diagnosis System for Scalp Health. *IEEE Access : Practical Innovations, Open Solutions*, *8*, 134826–134837. doi:10.1109/ACCESS.2020.3010847

Chang, W. J., Chen, L. B., Chen, M. C., Lin, J. Y., Su, J. P., Hsu, C. H., & Ou, Y. K. (2020, October 13). A Deep Learning-Based Intelligent Anti-Collision System for Car Door. *2020 IEEE 9th Global Conference on Consumer Electronics (GCCE)*. 10.1109/GCCE50665.2020.9291741

Cob-Parro, A. C., Lalangui, Y., & Lazcano, R. (2024, January 25). Fostering Agricultural Transformation through AI: An Open-Source AI Architecture Exploiting the MLOps Paradigm. *Agronomy (Basel)*, *14*(2), 259. doi:10.3390/agronomy14020259

Fera, F. T., & Spandonidis, C. (2024, February 6). An Artificial Intelligence and Industrial Internet of Things-Based Framework for Sustainable Hydropower Plant Operations. *Smart Cities*, *7*(1), 496–517. doi:10.3390/smartcities7010020

Hadad, M., Attarsharghi, S., Dehghanpour Abyaneh, M., Narimani, P., Makarian, J., Saberi, A., & Alinaghizadeh, A. (2024, February 14). Exploring New Parameters to Advance Surface Roughness Prediction in Grinding Processes for the Enhancement of Automated Machining. *Journal of Manufacturing and Materials Processing*, *8*(1), 41. doi:10.3390/jmmp8010041

Hossain, M., Kayas, G., Hasan, R., Skjellum, A., Noor, S., & Islam, S. M. R. (2024, January 24). A Holistic Analysis of Internet of Things (IoT) Security: Principles, Practices, and New Perspectives. *Future Internet*, *16*(2), 40. doi:10.3390/fi16020040

Hung, L. L. (2021, November 16). Adaptive Devices for AIoT Systems. *2021 International Symposium on Intelligent Signal Processing and Communication Systems (ISPACS)*. 10.1109/ISPACS51563.2021.9651095

Jia, X., Hu, N., Su, S., Yin, S., Zhao, Y., Cheng, X., & Zhang, C. (2020, April 11). IRBA: An Identity-Based Cross-Domain Authentication Scheme for the Internet of Things. *Electronics (Basel)*, *9*(4), 634. doi:10.3390/electronics9040634

Joshua, S. R., Park, S., & Kwon, K. (2024, January 8). Knowledge-Based Modeling Approach: A Schematic Design of Artificial Intelligence of Things (AIoT) for Hydrogen Energy System. *2024 IEEE 14th Annual Computing and Communication Workshop and Conference (CCWC)*. 10.1109/CCWC60891.2024.10427681

Ju, S., & Park, Y. (2023, December 11). Provably Secure Lightweight Mutual Authentication and Key Agreement Scheme for Cloud-Based IoT Environments. *Sensors (Basel)*, *23*(24), 9766. doi:10.3390/s23249766 PMID:38139612

Judith, A., Kathrine, G. J. W., Silas, S., & J, A. (2023, December 24). Efficient Deep Learning-Based Cyber-Attack Detection for Internet of Medical Things Devices. *RAiSE-2023*. doi:10.3390/engproc2023059139

Kerrison, S., Jusak, J., & Huang, T. (2023, May 6). Blockchain-Enabled IoT for Rural Healthcare: Hybrid-Channel Communication with Digital Twinning. *Electronics (Basel)*, *12*(9), 2128. doi:10.3390/electronics12092128

Kim, H., Park, S., Hong, H., Park, J., & Kim, S. (2024, February 28). A Transferable Deep Learning Framework for Improving the Accuracy of Internet of Things Intrusion Detection. *Future Internet*, *16*(3), 80. doi:10.3390/fi16030080

Kong, S. M., Yoo, C., Park, J., Park, J. H., & Lee, S. W. (2024, January 25). AIoT Monitoring Technology for Optimal Fill Dam Installation and Operation. *Applied Sciences (Basel, Switzerland)*, *14*(3), 1024. doi:10.3390/app14031024

Lampropoulos, G., Garzón, J., Misra, S., & Siakas, K. (2024, February 7). The Role of Artificial Intelligence of Things in Achieving Sustainable Development Goals: State of the Art. *Sensors (Basel)*, *24*(4), 1091. doi:10.3390/s24041091 PMID:38400249

Lauria, M., & Azzalin, M. (2024, February 1). Digital Twin Approach in Buildings: Future Challenges via a Critical Literature Review. *Buildings*, *14*(2), 376. doi:10.3390/buildings14020376

Lee, H. M., Ham, S. M., Moon, H., Kwon, H. M., Rho, J. H., & Seo, J. (2023, June). A Metaverse Emotion Mapping System with an AIoT Facial Expression Recognition Device. *2023 IEEE International Conference on Metaverse Computing, Networking and Applications (MetaCom)*. 10.1109/MetaCom57706.2023.00132

Lin, S., Cui, L., & Ke, N. (2024, January 10). End-to-End Encrypted Message Distribution System for the Internet of Things Based on Conditional Proxy Re-Encryption. *Sensors (Basel)*, *24*(2), 438. doi:10.3390/s24020438 PMID:38257530

Liu, X., Kong, J., Peng, L., Luo, D., Xu, G., Chen, X., & Liu, X. (2023, December 1). A Secure Multi-Party Computation Protocol for Graph Editing Distance against Malicious Attacks. *Mathematics*, *11*(23), 4847. doi:10.3390/math11234847

Mimboro, P., Lumban Gaol, F., Lesie Hendric Spits Warnars, H., & Soewito, B. (2021, November 24). Weather Monitoring System AIoT Based for Oil Palm Plantation Using Recurrent Neural Network Algorithm. *2021 IEEE 5th International Conference on Information Technology, Information Systems and Electrical Engineering (ICITISEE)*. 10.1109/ICITISEE53823.2021.9655818

Nadhan, A. S., & Jacob, I. J. (2023, December 12). A Secure Lightweight Cryptographic Algorithm for the Internet of Things (IoT) Based on Deoxyribonucleic Acid (DNA) Sequences. *RAiSE*, *2023*, 31. Advance online publication. doi:10.3390/engproc2023059031

Ni, M., Chen, L., Hao, X., Sun, H., Liu, C., Zhang, Z., Wu, L., & Pan, L. (2020, October 24). A Novel Prefetching Scheme for Non-Volatile Cache in the AIoT Processor. *2020 5th International Conference on Universal Village (UV)*. 10.1109/UV50937.2020.9426214

Nita, S. L., & Mihailescu, M. I. (2023). *Advances to Homomorphic and Searchable Encryption*. Springer., doi:10.1007/978-3-031-43214-9

Oh, J., Lee, J., Park, Y., & Park, Y. (2022, December 18). A Secure Data Processing System in Edge Computing-Powered AIoT. *2022 IEEE Asia-Pacific Conference on Computer Science and Data Engineering (CSDE)*. 10.1109/CSDE56538.2022.10089302

Ożadowicz, A. (2024, February 3). Generic IoT for Smart Buildings and Field-Level Automation—Challenges, Threats, Approaches, and Solutions. *Computers*, *13*(2), 45. doi:10.3390/computers13020045

P., Saini, N., Gulzar, Y., Turaev, S., Kaur, A., Nisa, K. U., & Hamid, Y. (2024, February 19). A Review and Comparative Analysis of Relevant Approaches of Zero Trust Network Model. *Sensors, 24*(4), 1328. https://doi.org/ doi:10.3390/s24041328Daah

Qu, Q., Hatami, M., Xu, R., Nagothu, D., Chen, Y., Li, X., Blasch, E., Ardiles-Cruz, E., & Chen, G. (2024, February 13). The Microverse: A Task-Oriented Edge-Scale Metaverse. *Future Internet, 16*(2), 60. doi:10.3390/fi16020060

Raja, G., Essaky, S., Ganapathisubramaniyan, A., & Baskar, Y. (2023, August). Nexus of Deep Reinforcement Learning and Leader–Follower Approach for AIoT Enabled Aerial Networks. *IEEE Transactions on Industrial Informatics, 19*(8), 9165–9172. doi:10.1109/TII.2022.3226529

Ramos, E. J., Montpetit, M. J., Skarmeta, A. F., Boussard, M., Angelakis, V., & Kutscher, D. (2022, November 29). Architecture Framework for Intelligence Orchestration in AIoT and IoT. *2022 International Conference on Smart Applications, Communications and Networking (SmartNets)*. 10.1109/SmartNets55823.2022.9994029

Rekeraho, A., Cotfas, D. T., Cotfas, P. A., Tuyishime, E., Balan, T. C., & Acheampong, R. (2024, February 13). Enhancing Security for IoT-Based Smart Renewable Energy Remote Monitoring Systems. *Electronics (Basel), 13*(4), 756. doi:10.3390/electronics13040756

Shen, C., Yu, T., Yuan, S., Li, Y., & Guan, X. (2016, March 9). Performance Analysis of Motion-Sensor Behavior for User Authentication on Smartphones. *Sensors (Basel), 16*(3), 345. doi:10.3390/s16030345 PMID:27005626

Shin, D. H., Han, S. J., Kim, Y. B., & Euom, I. C. (2024, January 29). Research on Digital Forensics Analyzing Heterogeneous Internet of Things Incident Investigations. *Applied Sciences (Basel, Switzerland), 14*(3), 1128. doi:10.3390/app14031128

Soroceanu, T., Buchmann, N., & Margraf, M. (2023, October 6). On Multiple Encryption for Public-Key Cryptography. *Cryptography, 7*(4), 49. doi:10.3390/cryptography7040049

Su, J. (1668). H., Ali, S., & Salman, M. (2024, March 4). Research on Blockchain-Enabled Smart Grid for Anti-Theft Electricity Securing Peer-to-Peer Transactions in Modern Grids. *Sensors (Basel), 24*(5), 1668. Advance online publication. doi:10.3390/s24051668

Sun, Z., Zhu, M., Zhang, Z., Chen, Z., Shi, Q., Shan, X., & Lee, C. (2021, January 25). Smart Soft Robotic Manipulator for Artificial Intelligence of Things (AIOT) Based Unmanned Shop Applications. *2021 IEEE 34th International Conference on Micro Electro Mechanical Systems (MEMS)*. 10.1109/MEMS51782.2021.9375221

Taylor, S., Surridge, M., & Pickering, B. (2021, May 10). Regulatory Compliance Modelling Using Risk Management Techniques. *2021 IEEE World AI IoT Congress (AIIoT)*. 10.1109/AIIoT52608.2021.9454188

Thantharate, P., & Thantharate, A. (2023, October 17). ZeroTrustBlock: Enhancing Security, Privacy, and Interoperability of Sensitive Data through ZeroTrust Permissioned Blockchain. *Big Data and Cognitive Computing, 7*(4), 165. doi:10.3390/bdcc7040165

Ülkü, M. A., Bookbinder, J. H., & Yun, N. Y. (2024, February 4). Leveraging Industry 4.0 Technologies for Sustainable Humanitarian Supply Chains: Evidence from the Extant Literature. *Sustainability (Basel), 16*(3), 1321. doi:10.3390/su16031321

Umer, M. A., Belay, E. G., & Gouveia, L. B. (2024, February 5). Leveraging Artificial Intelligence and Provenance Blockchain Framework to Mitigate Risks in Cloud Manufacturing in Industry 4.0. *Electronics (Basel), 13*(3), 660. doi:10.3390/electronics13030660

Vandervelden, T., Deac, D., Van Glabbeek, R., De Smet, R., Braeken, A., & Steenhaut, K. (2023, December 22). Evaluation of 6LoWPAN Generic Header Compression in the Context of an RPL Network. *Sensors (Basel), 24*(1), 73. doi:10.3390/s24010073 PMID:38202935

Wang, X., Chen, Y., Zhu, X., Li, C., & Fang, K. (2024, January 18). A Redactable Blockchain Scheme Supporting Quantum-Resistance and Trapdoor Updates. *Applied Sciences (Basel, Switzerland), 14*(2), 832. doi:10.3390/app14020832

Wiryasaputra, R., Huang, C. Y., Lin, Y. J., & Yang, C. T. (2024, February 11). An IoT Real-Time Potable Water Quality Monitoring and Prediction Model Based on Cloud Computing Architecture. *Sensors (Basel), 24*(4), 1180. doi:10.3390/s24041180 PMID:38400338

Xu, J., Liu, X., Pan, W., Li, X., Yao, A., & Yang, Y. (2023, September 11). EXPRESS 2.0: An Intelligent Service Management Framework for AIoT Systems in the Edge. *2023 38th IEEE/ACM International Conference on Automated Software Engineering (ASE).* 10.1109/ASE56229.2023.00020

Yang, Z., Xiong, B., Chen, K., Yang, L. T., Deng, X., Zhu, C., & He, Y. (2024, January 1). Differentially Private Federated Tensor Completion for Cloud–Edge Collaborative AIoT Data Prediction. *IEEE Internet of Things Journal, 11*(1), 256–267. doi:10.1109/JIOT.2023.3314460

Zhang, C., Liang, Y., Tavares, A., Wang, L., Gomes, T., & Pinto, S. (2024, February 21). An Improved Public Key Cryptographic Algorithm Based on Chebyshev Polynomials and RSA. *Symmetry, 16*(3), 263. doi:10.3390/sym16030263

Zhang, R., Liu, L., Dong, M., & Ota, K. (2024, February 2). On-Demand Centralized Resource Allocation for IoT Applications: AI-Enabled Benchmark. *Sensors (Basel), 24*(3), 980. doi:10.3390/s24030980 PMID:38339696

Zhu, H., Tiwari, P., Ghoneim, A., & Hossain, M. S. (2022, May). A Collaborative AI-Enabled Pretrained Language Model for AIoT Domain Question Answering. *IEEE Transactions on Industrial Informatics, 18*(5), 3387–3396. doi:10.1109/TII.2021.3097183

Chapter 8

Leveraging Ethics in Artificial Intelligence Technologies and Applications:
E–Learning Management Systems in Namibia

Gabriel N. Uunona

 https://orcid.org/0000-0003-3859-6033
University of South Africa, South Africa

Leila Goosen

 https://orcid.org/0000-0003-4948-2699
University of South Africa, South Africa

ABSTRACT

The purpose of the study reported on is to establish ways in which ethics in artificial intelligence (AI) technologies and applications can be leveraged towards improved, standardized and safe e-learning management systems (eLMSs) at higher education institutions (HEIs) in Namibia, against the background of semantic web technologies and applications in artificial intelligence, the internet of things (IoT), and artificial intelligence of things (AIoT).

INTRODUCTION

This section will describe the general perspective of the chapter and end by specifically stating the objectives.

Semantic Web Technologies and Applications in Artificial Intelligence of Things

The value that Artificial Intelligence (AI), the Internet of Things (IoT), Artificial Intelligence of Things (AIoT) and the Semantic Web had contributed to the development of industry, research, and society, in

DOI: 10.4018/979-8-3693-1487-6.ch008

general, is relevant for a future society. As part of this book, the chapter could serve as a reference for the development of Semantic Web technologies in Industry 4.0 and the AIoT.

Leveraging Ethics in Artificial Intelligence Technologies and Applications at Higher Education Institutions: E-Learning Management Systems in Namibia

According to a previous chapter by Uunona and Goosen (2023, p. 310) on leveraging ethical standards in artificial intelligence technologies as a guideline for responsible teaching and learning applications in the *Handbook of Research on Instructional Technologies in Health Education and Allied Disciplines,* AI "is revolutionizing the field of education by providing new opportunities for online learning. However, as with any technology, there are ethical" implications that must be considered. With the commencement of the conversation on AI, the awareness of such ethical considerations needed to be kept in mind. Such a conversation should trigger the possibility of considering a logical culturally-sensitive framework that will be used to provide guidelines for national policy development on AI.

Recommended Topics

From the recommended topics for the book, this chapter will cover the following (although it is not limited to these):

- Usability and user experience in Semantic Web and AIoT application environments
- AIoT-based Semantic Web applications and public services
- Use of model and learning algorithms and machine learning in AIoT and Semantic Web

Target Audience

As part of this book, the chapter is aimed at academics, students, and industry, around topics such as the manufacturing industry, health and sciences, as well as e-government.

Objectives

The objective of this quality chapter is to contribute to the book on topics related to cutting-edge technologies and serve as a knowledge base in terms of future research directions. Some of the objectives of the study reported on in this chapter include to:

- Explore current and future-projected developments in AI autonomy and how these could impact education, and
- Establish the extent to which the Namibian government had considered AI implications in its strategic plans and associated policies.

BACKGROUND

This section of the chapter will provide broad definitions and discussions of the topic on Leveraging Ethics in AI Technologies and Applications at Higher Education Institutions (HEIs) via e-Learning Management Systems (e-LMSs) in Namibia and incorporate the views of others (in the form of a literature review) into the discussion to support, refute, or demonstrate the authors' position on the topic.

"Marginalias are the reading marks found in different types of documents" (Hernández-Quintana & Trinquete, 2022, p. 111). The way in which the latter are approached by "research in different fields of science is a growing phenomenon and therefore" required a proposal from the digital humanities regarding TAXChe, an online taxonomy for Che's marginalias, which was described in the chapter by the latter authors in a book on *knowledge organization across disciplines, domains, services and technologies*.

Citizen information "is treated in the local media" (press) as being "of upmost importance for the" decision making of "citizens, and it is also relevant because of its impact" (Madruga, Roche, & Hernández Quintana, 2017, p. 11). The journal article by the latter authors therefore provided a content analysis of the *Tribuna de La Habanas* newspaper for the period 2008-2014

The journal article by Borges, Hernández Quintana and Roche (2017, p. 19) "identified the principal universities that prepare Digital Humanities curricula." This also decided the position of such universities in academic rankings. Towards a necessary diagnosis, the latte authors looked at curricular production academic stages in the Digital Humanities.

Folksonomies were considered by Hernández-Quintana (2014a) to be the most recent (at the time) ecological evidence in the information industry.

Use of Modelling and Learning Algorithms, as Well as Machine Learning in Artificial Intelligence of Things and the Semantic Web

In answer to the question: 'What is machine learning?', a chapter by El Naqa and Murphy (2015) in a book on *machine learning in radiation oncology* explained that a "machine learning algorithm is a computational process", the "process of adaptation is called training" and such training is the 'learning' part of machine learning. Machine Learning (ML) can therefore be described as computer algorithms that mimic human intelligence capable of learning from the patterns of events happening in the surrounding environment.

On the interpretations, illustrations, and implications of artificial intelligence, the journal article by Kaplan and Haenlein (2019, p. 15) explained that AI can be defined as a "system's ability to correctly interpret external data, to learn from such data, and to use those learnings to achieve specific goals and tasks through flexible adaptation".

An international journal article on information management debated 'big data' concepts, methods, and analytics, where for 'big data', the volume and variety are relatively high such that these exert pressure on cost and innovation for storage and processing (Gandomi & Haider, 2015). Similarly, the chapter by Ngugi and Goosen (2021) investigated innovation, entrepreneurship, and sustainability for Information and Communication Technology (ICT) students towards the post-COVID-19 era.

Artificial Intelligence in Education (AIED) refers to the understanding and application of AI in education for the improvement of teaching and learning, as well as developing expertise in AI (Paek & Kim, 2021).

Educational Technology (EdTech) is the use of technological resources for the enhancement of teaching and learning processes (Byrnes & Etter, 2008), while e-learning is the use of digital media and information communication technologies for the development, management and delivery of educational content and processes (Thomas & Pachaiyappan, 2022).

Learning Management Systems (LMSs) are computerized web-based applications designed for administering and managing teaching, learning and assessment (Fry, 2022), whereas LMS 'plugins' are applications that enhance the ability of the LMS to create, innovate, host and manage online teaching and learning (Nabilla, 2023).

Finally, for the sake of the study discussed in this chapter, a policy is defined as a "law, regulation, procedure, administrative action, incentive, or voluntary practice of government and other institutions" (Centres for Disease Control and Prevention, 2015).

MAIN FOCUS OF THE CHAPTER

Issues, Problems

This section of the chapter will present the authors' perspectives on the issues, problems, etc., as these relate to the main theme of the book on Semantic Web Technologies and Applications in Artificial Intelligence of Things, and arguments supporting the authors' position on Leveraging Ethics in AI Technologies and Applications at HEIs via e-LMSs in Namibia. It will also compare and contrast with what had been, or is currently being, done as it relates to the specific topic of the chapter.

While Dumbrava (2021) provided an overview of the applications and key issues related to artificial intelligence at European Union (EU) borders, a chapter by Sahagun, Ortiz-Rodriguez and Medina-Quintero (2023, p. 193) indicated that in "today's global economy, emerging economies play a very important role in the production chain." The latter authors therefore considered the salary and wage inequality effect on productivity at the Mexico-United States border from a Mexican middle management supervisor perspective.

A book with regard to *Global Perspectives on the Strategic Role of Marketing Information Systems* edited by Medina-Quintero, Sahagun, Alfaro and Ortiz-Rodriguez (2023) indicated that a "level of decision making is concerned with deciding the organization s objectives, resources, and policies. A significant problem at this decision-making level is predicting the organization's future".

The chapter by Barrera, Martinez-Rodriguez, Tiwari and Barrera (2023, p. 118) in the latter book "addressed what smartphones, mobile applications, programming languages, and mobile operating systems are. The development, implementation, and results obtained" were related to a political marketing application (app) based on citizens.

Usability and User Experience in Semantic Web and Artificial Intelligence of Things Application Environments

A chapter by Medina-Quintero, Ortiz-Rodriguez, Tiwari and Saenz (2023, p. 87) in the book described earlier in this section on trust in electronic banking with the use of cell phones for user satisfaction pointed out that mobile "technologies play a transcendental role in the development of organizations. The banking industry has become the world's economic engine".

An end-user perspective on e-government success was shown in the chapter by Ortiz, Tiwari, Amara and Sahagun (2023, p. 168) in the same book. The objective of the latter research was "to determine the critical success factors of a tax collector website in a country with an emerging economy."

"Cybersecurity is one of the main concerns of most organizations, derived from the violation of their cybersecurity." The objective of the chapter by Morales-Sáenz, Medina-Quintero and Ortiz-Rodriguez (2023, p. 115) was "the development of a bibliometric study of organizational *cybersecurity*".

Rationale for the Study

Like other nations, the Namibian education sector would want to keep up with the pace and emerging trends with regard to educational technologies and is thus likely to continue adopting educational technologies as they continue evolving. While technologies are widely adopted even in sectors beside education, and they can undoubtedly be beneficial, there are unique ethical implications which might only prevail on the background, whose impact may only be discovered late.

As emphasized by the World Economic Forum (2022), it is necessary to have an active and responsive regulatory and policy framework to guide the adoption, adaptation, and application of technologies. Such active and responsive regulatory or policies are missing in Namibia, and there are currently no visible practical efforts towards these calls. Even though Namibia has recently launched new and revised policies, such as the 'Public Sector Innovation' (Republic of Namibia, 2020) and the 'Science Technology and Innovation' (Ministry of Higher Education, Technology, and Innovation, 2021), none of these policies have addressed the aspects of AI either in wider sectors or in education. In addition, the Namibian ICT policy for education (Ministry of Education, 2005) is not only over-due for revision, but it also does not address any aspect relating to AI in education in general let alone ethical considerations.

Furthermore, besides the 'Windhoek statement on Artificial Intelligence in Southern Africa' (United Nations Educational, Scientific and Cultural Organisation (UNESCO), 2022), other research conferences and dialogues relating to AI, such as the "International Conference on Data Science, Machine Learning and Artificial Intelligence" that was hosted by Namibia University of Science and Technology in 2022 focused more on the advancement of knowledge, skills, and application of AI with little to no attention to the dimensions of ethics, policy, or regulation. Equally, research and curricula efforts, such as that of Shipepe, et al. (2021) significantly pointed out some ethical implications of AI-inspired learning, they could not address or at least mention how regulatory and policy framework could be an ultimate guide to the sector in adopting, adapting, or advancing AI inspired teaching and learning initiatives. This study is therefore crucial to the addressing of Namibia's void on the dialogues and research focused on the regulatory and policy framework on AI in education sector.

Research Methodology and Design

Research Approach

The study proposed will take an interactive qualitative approach with case studies and the Delphi technique as modes of inquiry. The Delphi technique is a systematic qualitative research method used to centrifuge diverse opinions into a converged opinion (Dell'Olio, Ibeas, de Ona, & de Ona, 2017).

Population and Sampling

With regard to the challenges and conditions applicable to developing a sampling frame for a case study, the world journal article on education by Ishak and Abu Bakar (2014) suggested that the primary purpose of qualitative sampling to be centered around the identification of unique cases which would enhance a better understanding of the subject being researched. Considering that the Delphi technique will be used to collect data, a panel of experts would be required, and a purposive sampling will therefore be used to identify members of the expert panel.

The first level of sampling documents will consider the systematic method presented by Gagnon and Barber (2018). Firstly, sources of documents will be identified, which will include public and institutional websites, national archives, newspaper archives and library collections. Secondly, the types of documents will be established, which will focus on both primary and secondary types. Thereafter, inclusionary and exclusionary criteria shall be employed by focusing on official documents and avoiding opinion-based documents. This will then result in the final list of sample documents. Data from documents analysis will be used to determine the extent to which Namibian government considers AI implications in their strategic documents and related policies.

To identify the world's best public policies from which Namibia will be able to benchmark an AI policy, firstly, the Global AI Index (GAII) (Tortoise Media, 2021) will be used to select the top 10 ranked countries on the GAII. The GAII ranks countries against three main pillars, which are further broken down into seven sub-pillars:

1. Implementation (talent, infrastructure, and operating environment)
2. Innovation (research, development)
3. Investment (commercial ventures and government strategies)

The operating environments sub-pillar focuses on government regulation, as well as the check and balances for the development and implementation of artificial intelligence initiatives. Four countries, who score high in this sub-pillar and have AI-focused policies will then make up the final sample cases to be considered in this study.

Instrumentation and Data Collection Techniques

Furthermore, a real-time Delphi technique will be applied (Gordon, 2009). Questionnaires will therefore be designed using either Microsoft or Google forms, and a link would be sent to the panelists through their email addresses. To achieve the goal of the real-time Delphi technique, links to summary of results will be shared with the panelists for their instant perusal before proceeding to the next round. The questionnaires will contain some statements to be rated by use of a Linkert scale plus text inputs for textual comments collection. The number of statements to be rated will reduce and vary in each round. Three rounds will be used.

To gather data from which the extent to which Namibian government considers AI implications in their strategic documents and related policies would be determined, a thematic analysis (Fereday and Muir-Cochrane, as cited in Chanda, 2021) will be used. Firstly, themes will be developed. Then the selected documents will be read to look for the phrases or points fitting in either of the developed themes, which will be extracted into the thematic table.

Given that the case study method, which will be used in this study, involves the analysis of policy documents, thematic analysis will also be applied in this context.

Data Analysis and Interpretation

Even though Delphi datasets analysis can branch into many methods (Beiderbeck, Frevel, von der Gracht, Schmidt, & Schweitzer, 2021), this study will take the qualitative and a basic quantitative analysis. For quantitative analysis, a descriptive analysis will be used to bring out the demographic features of the participants, as well as the datasets from the Linkert scale ratings. Data generated from the document analysis and policies will be subjected to qualitative content analysis (Mayring, 2014), whereby patterns will be established and evaluated (Warren, 2020).

Reliability and Validity/Credibility and Trustworthiness

This study will adopt the strategies for ensuring credibility suggested in the evidence-based nursing journal article by Noble and Smith (2015, pp. 34-35) with regard to issues of validity and reliability in qualitative research: "accounting for personal biases, acknowledging biases in sampling, meticulous record keeping, establishing comparisons, data triangulation and engaging with other researchers" among others. Thick descriptions and an audit trial (Korstjens & Moser, 2018) will be used to ensure transferability and confirmability. For validity, this study will ensure the alignment between the research objectives and the data collection methods and tools, furthermore, reliability will be ensured by maintaining consistency and standards in the methods of collecting data.

The reliability and credibility strategies can collectively lead to the trustworthiness of the study (Middleton, 2020). Trustworthiness will further be ensured by employing dependability, confirmability, and audit trials strategies (Nowell, Norris, White, & Moules, 2017).

Research Ethics

Ethics refer to standards of right and wrong, which serve as a yardstick of human actions and behaviors in consideration of rights, fairness, and societal benefits (Velasquez, Andre, Shanks, & Meyer, 1992).

Ensuring the ethical management of data and research integrity in the context of e-schools and community engagement is an essential part of any research study (Goosen, 2018).

There will be no significant ethical implications for the case studies because public domain documents will be used. Consent forms will be given to the Delphi expert panel members.

Autonomous AI refers to the ability of machines, systems, or computer applications to take actions independently, without the influence of human guidance. The journal article by Totschnig (2020) in the context of science and engineering ethics discussed fully autonomous AI.

Limitations and Delimitations of the Study

Limitation of the Study

Given that this qualitative study consists of three tiers (Delphi experts technique, document analysis and policies), it might need lots of time to analyze and interconnect the results.

Delimitation of the Study

The process of identifying experts for the Delphi technique will depend on the goodwill of the participants to recommend other experts for the purpose of snowball sampling to taking place. It will also depend on the goodwill of the participants to participate in all the three rounds of data collection. However, this will be managed by employing a big number of participants such that there will still be a good number after possible rejections and withdrawals.

SOLUTIONS AND RECOMMENDATIONS

This section of the chapter will discuss solutions and recommendations in dealing with the issues or problems presented in the preceding section.

Solutions

The education sector had experienced the most crucial challenge in hundreds of years with the recent global pandemic, everyone seemed to seek answers in technology for the continuation of educational systems. As observed by Davies, Eynon and Salveson (2021), AI is seen as the ultimate solution to educational problems. Despite the popular views of how AI can accelerate solutions to educational challenges, the associated risks and challenges are outpacing debates on policies and regulatory frameworks (Miao, Holmes, Huang, & Zhang, 2021).

Recommendations

Population and Sampling

The sampling process will start by identifying appropriate institutions from academia and Information Technology (IT) or Computer Science industries. The list will include at least 20 local and international institutions. The sampling will continue to identify at least two experts from each institution, which is hoped to bring the initial number of potential participants to thirty-two (considering the possibility of 20% rejection). This number will likely increase to at least fifty-two participants by further employing snow-ball sampling, which will be done by asking every participant in the initial list to make recommendations for at least two more potential participants.

FUTURE RESEARCH DIRECTIONS

This section of the chapter will discuss future and emerging trends, as well as provide insights about the future of the theme of the book on Semantic Web Technologies and Applications in Artificial Intelligence of Things from the perspective of the chapter focus on Leveraging Ethics in AI Technologies and Applications at HEIs via e-LMSs in Namibia. The viability of a paradigm, model, implementation issues of proposed programs, etc., may be included in this section. If appropriate, this section will suggest future research directions within the domain of the topic.

Both the chapters by Morales-Sáenz, et al. (2023) and Sahagun, et al. (2023) already discussed in a previous section appeared in a book on emerging trends regarding technologies and digital transformation in the manufacturing industry.

The philosophy of information and document convergence required inserting a theoretical paradigm in archival science (Hernández-Quintana, 2014b).

Artificial Intelligence of Things-Based Semantic Web Applications and Public Services

As part of a book on futuristic and emerging trends for sustainable development and ecosystems, the chapter by Ortiz-Rodriguez, Medina-Quintero, Tiwari and Villanueva (2022, p. 261) indicated that the "electronic government is a new application field for the Semantic Web, and the ontologies play a key role in the development of the Semantic Web." The e-Government Documentation (EGODO) ontology for sharing, retrieving, and exchanging legal documentation across e-government therefore plays an increasingly important role.

Population and Sampling

The expert panel will help in projecting future AI autonomy in educational technologies and the ethical implications of these.

Instrumentation and Data Collection Techniques

The Delphi technique had been found to be the effective type for idea generation and opinions exploration (Franklin & Hart, 2006). The Delphi technique will therefore be appropriate to use for gathering data on the future of AI autonomy in educational technologies and the ethical implications of these.

CONCLUSION

This section of the chapter will provide a discussion of the overall coverage of the chapter and concluding remarks.

The chapter covered the rationale and objectives of the research. It also presented the approaches that will be taken to collect, analyze, and ensure the credibility of the research. The chapter finally included a literature review, which provides the broader background of the field being studied.

REFERENCES

Barrera, R. M., Martinez-Rodriguez, J. L., Tiwari, S., & Barrera, V. (2023). Political Marketing App Based on Citizens. In *Global Perspectives on the Strategic Role of Marketing Information Systems* (pp. 118–147). IGI Global. doi:10.4018/978-1-6684-6591-2.ch008

Beiderbeck, D., Frevel, N., von der Gracht, H. A., Schmidt, S. L., & Schweitzer, V. M. (2021). Preparing, conducting, and analyzing Delphi surveys: Cross-disciplinary practices, new directions, and advancements. *MethodsX*, *8*, 101401. Advance online publication. doi:10.1016/j.mex.2021.101401 PMID:34430297

Borges, L. O., Hernández Quintana, A., & Roche, S. R. (2017). Curricular production academic stages on Digital Humanities: Towards a necessary diagnosis. *Ciencias de la Información*, *48*(1), 19–26.

Byrnes, L., & Etter, S. J. (2008). Student Response Systems for Active Learning. In *Encyclopedia of Information Technology Curriculum Integration* (pp. 803–807). IGI Global. doi:10.4018/978-1-59904-881-9.ch126

Centres for Disease Control and Prevention. (2015, May 29). *Definition of policy*. Retrieved March 19, 2023, from https://www.cdc.gov/policy/opaph/process/definition.html

Davies, H. C., Eynon, R., & Salveson, C. (2021). The mobilisation of AI in education: A Bourdieusean field analysis. *Sociology*, *55*(3), 539–560. doi:10.1177/0038038520967888

Dell'Olio, L., Ibeas, A., de Ona, J., & de Ona, R. (2017). *Public transportation quality of service: Factors, models, and applications*. Elsevier.

Dumbrava, C. (2021). *Artificial intelligence at EU borders. Overview of applications and key issues*. Brussels, Belgium: European Parliamentary Research Service. Retrieved 12 21, 2021, from https://www.europarl. europa. eu/RegData/etudes/IDAN/2021/690706/EPRS_IDA (2021) 690706_EN.pdf

El Naqa, I., & Murphy, M. J. (2015). What is machine learning? In *Machine Learning in Radiation Oncology* (pp. 3–11). Springer International Publishing. doi:10.1007/978-3-319-18305-3_1

Franklin, K. K., & Hart, J. K. (2006). Influence of web-based distance education on the academic department chair role. *Journal of Educational Technology & Society, 9*(1), 213-228. doi:https://www.jstor.org/stable/jeductechsoci.9.1.213

Fry, A. (2022, January 31). *What is an LMS? Learning management systems explained*. Retrieved from MOODLE: https://moodle.com/news/what-is-an-lms-learning-management-systems-explained/

Gagnon, J. C., & Barber, B. R. (2018). Feasibility. In *The SAGE encyclopaedia of educational research, measurement, and evaluation* (p. 668). SAGE. doi:10.4135/9781506326139.n259

Gandomi, A., & Haider, M. (2015). Beyond the hype: Big data concepts, methods, and analytics. *International Journal of Information Management*, *35*(2), 137–144. doi:10.1016/j.ijinfomgt.2014.10.007

Goosen, L. (2018). Ethical Data Management and Research Integrity in the Context of e-Schools and Community Engagement. In C. Sibinga (Ed.), *Ensuring Research Integrity and the Ethical Management of Data* (pp. 14–45). IGI Global. doi:10.4018/978-1-5225-2730-5.ch002

Gordon, T. J. (2009). The real-time Delphi method. *Futures Research Methodology Version 3, 19*. Retrieved from https://millennium-project.org/wp-content/uploads/2022/01/05-Real-Time-Delphi.pdf

Hernández-Quintana, A. (2014a). *Folksonomies: the most recent ecological evidence in the information industry*. Instituto de Información Científica y Tecnológica (IDICT).

Hernández-Quintana, A. (2014b). *The philosophy of information and document convergence: inserting a theoretical paradigm in the archive science.* Instituto de Información Científica y Tecnológica (IDICT).

Hernández-Quintana, A., & Trinquete, A. T. (2022, May). TAXChe: An Online Taxonomy for Che's Marginalias: A Proposal from the Digital Humanities. In Knowledge Organization across Disciplines, Domains, Services and Technologies (pp. 111-120). Ergon-Verlag.

Ishak, N. M., & Abu Bakar, A. Y. (2014). Developing Sampling Frame for Case Study: Challenges and Conditions. *World Journal of Education, 4*(3), 29-35. Retrieved from https://files.eric.ed.gov/fulltext/EJ1158705.pdf

Kaplan, A., & Haenlein, M. (2019). Siri, Siri, in my hand: Who's the fairest in the land? On the interpretations, illustrations, and implications of artificial intelligence. *Business Horizons, 62*(1), 15–25. doi:10.1016/j.bushor.2018.08.004

Korstjens, I., & Moser, A. (2018). Series: Practical guidance to qualitative research. Part 4: Trustworthiness and publishing. *The European Journal of General Practice, 24*(1), 120–124. doi:10.1080/138147 88.2017.1375092 PMID:29202616

Madruga, G. O., Roche, S. R., & Hernández Quintana, A. (2017). Citizen Information in the local press. A content analysis in the Tribuna de La Habanas Newspaper in the period 2008-2014. *Ciencias de la Información, 48*(1), 11–18.

Mayring, P. (2014). *Qualitative content analysis: theoretical foundation, basic procedures and software solution.* Retrieved from Klagenfurt: https://www.ssoar.info/ssoar/bitstream/handle/document/39517/ssoar-2014-mayring-Qualitative_content_analysis_theoretical_foundation.pdf

Medina-Quintero, J. M., Ortiz-Rodriguez, F., Tiwari, S., & Saenz, F. I. (2023). Trust in Electronic Banking With the Use of Cell Phones for User Satisfaction. In *Global Perspectives on the Strategic Role of Marketing Information Systems* (pp. 87–106). IGI Global. doi:10.4018/978-1-6684-6591-2.ch006

Medina-Quintero, J. M., Sahagun, M. A., Alfaro, J., & Ortiz-Rodriguez, F. (Eds.). (2023). *Global Perspectives on the Strategic Role of Marketing Information Systems.* IGI Global. doi:10.4018/978-1-6684-6591-2

Miao, F., Holmes, W., Huang, R., & Zhang, H. (2021). AI and education: A guidance for policymakers. United Nations Educational, Scientific and Cultural Organization (UNESCO).

Middleton, F. (2020, June 26). *Reliability vs Validity in Research| Differences, Types and Examples.* Retrieved from Scribbr: https://www.scribbr.com/author/fionamiddleton/

Ministry of Education. (2005, March). *ICT Policy for Education.* Windhoek: John Meinert Publications. Retrieved from https://www.moe.gov.na/files/downloads/155_Published%20ICT%20Policy%202005%20 -%2015%20March%202005.pdf

Morales-Sáenz, F. I., Medina-Quintero, J. M., & Ortiz-Rodriguez, F. (2023). Bibliometrics Study of Organizational Cybersecurity. In *Emerging Technologies and Digital Transformation in the Manufacturing Industry* (pp. 115–139). IGI Global. doi:10.4018/978-1-6684-8088-5.ch008

Nabilla, R. (2023). *9 best WordPress LMS plugins for your eLearning site.* Retrieved from Hostinger: https://www.hostinger.com/tutorials/wordpress-lms-plugins

Ngugi, J. K., & Goosen, L. (2021). Innovation, Entrepreneurship, and Sustainability for ICT Students Towards the Post-COVID-19 Era. In L. C. Carvalho, L. Reis, & C. Silveira (Eds.), *Handbook of Research on Entrepreneurship, Innovation, Sustainability, and ICTs in the Post-COVID-19 Era* (pp. 110–131). IGI Global. doi:10.4018/978-1-7998-6776-0.ch006

Noble, H., & Smith, J. (2015). Issues of validity and reliability in qualitative research. *Evidence-Based Nursing*, *18*(2), 34–35. doi:10.1136/eb-2015-102054 PMID:25653237

Nowell, L. S., Norris, J. M., White, D. E., & Moules, N. J. (2017). Thematic analysis: Striving to meet the trustworthiness criteria. *International Journal of Qualitative Methods*, *16*(1). Advance online publication. doi:10.1177/1609406917733847

Ortiz-Rodriguez, F., Medina-Quintero, J. M., Tiwari, S., & Villanueva, V. (2022). EGODO ontology: sharing, retrieving, and exchanging legal documentation across e-government. In *Futuristic Trends for Sustainable Development and Sustainable Ecosystems* (pp. 261–276). IGI Global. doi:10.4018/978-1-6684-4225-8.ch016

Ortiz-Rodriguez, F., Tiwari, S., Amara, F. Z., & Sahagun, M. A. (2023). E-Government Success: An End-User Perspective. In Global Perspectives on the Strategic Role of Marketing Information Systems (pp. 168-186). IGI Global.

Paek, S., & Kim, N. (2021). Analysis of worldwide research trends on the impact of artificial intelligence in education. *Sustainability (Basel)*, *13*(14), 7941. doi:10.3390/su13147941

Republic of Namibia. (2020). *Public Sector Innovation Policy*. Office of the Prime Minister.

Sahagun, M. A., Ortiz-Rodriguez, F., & Medina-Quintero, J. M. (2023). The Salary and Wage Inequality Effect on Productivity on the Mexico-US Border: Mexican Middle Management Supervisor Perspective. In Emerging Technologies and Digital Transformation in the Manufacturing Industry (pp. 193-212). IGI Global.

Shipepe, A., Uwu-Khaeb, L., Kolog, E. A., Apiola, M., Mufeti, K., & Sutinen, E. (2021, October). Towards the Fourth Industrial Revolution in Namibia: An Undergraduate AI Course Africanized. *Frontiers in Education (FIE) Conference* (pp. 1-8). IEEE.

Thomas, S., & Pachaiyappan, P. (2022). Role of E-Learning in Secondary Teacher Education. In P. Pachaiyappan (Ed.), *Current Trends in ICT and Education* (Vol. 1, pp. 67–77). AkiNik Publications.

Tortoise Media. (2021). *The Global AI Index*. Retrieved March 4, 2023, from https://www.tortoisemedia.com/intelligence/global-ai/

Totschnig, W. (2020). Fully autonomous AI. *Science and Engineering Ethics*, *26*(5), 2473–2485. doi:10.1007/s11948-020-00243-z PMID:32725298

United Nations Educational, Scientific and Cultural Organisation (UNESCO). (2022). *Windhoek statement on Artificial Intelligence in Southern Africa*. UNESCO.

Uunona, G. N., & Goosen, L. (2023). Leveraging Ethical Standards in Artificial Intelligence Technologies: A Guideline for Responsible Teaching and Learning Applications. In M. Garcia, M. Lopez Cabrera, & R. de Almeida (Eds.), *Handbook of Research on Instructional Technologies in Health Education and Allied Disciplines* (pp. 310–330). IGI Global. doi:10.4018/978-1-6684-7164-7.ch014

Velasquez, M., Andre, C., Shanks, S. J., & Meyer, M. (1992). Ethical relativism. *Issues in Ethics*, *5*(2). https://edwardwimberley.com/courses/IntroEnvPol/ethicalreal.pdf

Warren, K. (2020, May). *Qualitative data analysis methods 101: The "Big 6" methods + examples*. Retrieved March 12, 2023, from Grad Coach: https://gradcoach.com/qualitative-data-analysis-methods/

World Economic Forum. (2022). *Regulatory Technology for the 21st Century*. Retrieved from https://www3.weforum.org/docs/WEF_Regulatory_Tech_for_the_21st_Century_2022.pdf

KEY TERMS AND DEFINITIONS

Artificial Intelligence in Education (AIED): The understanding and application of AI in education for the improvement of teaching and learning, as well as developing expertise in AI.

Autonomous Artificial Intelligence (AI): The ability of machines, systems, or computer applications to take actions independently, without the influence of human guidance.

Big Data: Data, where the volume and variety are relatively high such that these exert pressure on cost and innovation for storage and processing.

Delphi Technique: A systematic qualitative research method used to centrifuge diverse opinions into a converged opinion.

E-Learning: The use of digital media and information communication technologies for the development, management and delivery of educational content and processes.

Educational Technology (EdTech): The use of technological resources for the enhancement of teaching and learning processes.

Ethics: Standards of right and wrong, which serve as a yardstick of human actions and behaviors in consideration of rights, fairness, and societal benefits.

Learning Management System (LMS): The computerized web-based applications designed for administering and managing teaching, learning and assessment.

LMS Plugin: Applications that enhance the ability of the LMS to create, innovate, host and manage online learning.

Machine Learning (ML): Computer algorithms that mimic human intelligence capable of learning from the patterns of events happening in the surrounding environment.

Chapter 9
Enhancing Usability and Control in Artificial Intelligence of Things Environments (AIoT) Through Semantic Web Control Models

D.S. Dayana

Department of Networking and Communications, College of Engineering and Technology, SRM Institute of Science and Technology, Kattankulathur, India

T. S. Shanthi

Department of Computer Science, S.A.V. Sahaya Thai Arts and Science (Women) College, Tirunelveli, India

Girish Wali

Citibank, Bangalore, India

P. V. Pramila

Department of Computer Science Engineering, Saveetha Institute of Medical and Technical Sciences, Saveetha University, Chennai, India

T. Sumitha

Department of Computer Science Engineering, R.M.K. Engineering College, India

M. Sudhakar

Department of Mechanical Engineering, Sri Sai Ram Engineering College, Chennai, India

ABSTRACT

The chapter discusses the usability of artificial intelligence of things (AIoT) applications, emphasizing the complexity of these systems and the need for intuitive interfaces. It emphasizes the need to address system complexity, user interaction issues, and interface design hurdles for effective AIoT deployment.

DOI: 10.4018/979-8-3693-1487-6.ch009

The chapter introduces Semantic Web control models, leveraging technologies like RDF, OWL, and SPARQL, to enhance usability in AIoT environments. It presents real-world case studies and successful implementations, highlighting the effectiveness of these models. The chapter also discusses future directions and challenges in AIoT usability, including emerging trends, obstacles, and research opportunities. The chapter concludes that usability is crucial in AIoT applications, and addressing these

INTRODUCTION

Enhancing usability and control in Artificial Intelligence of Things (AIoT) environments through Semantic Web Control Models represents a significant advancement in the field, offering a comprehensive framework for managing the complexity of interconnected devices and systems. Semantic Web Control Models leverage semantic technologies, such as ontologies and linked data, to enhance interoperability, discoverability, and understanding of web content within AIoT ecosystems. By providing a shared understanding of data semantics, these models enable more intelligent, context-aware interactions among diverse applications and devices. This overview explores how Semantic Web Control Models facilitate usability and control in AIoT environments by enabling personalized experiences, seamless integration, and efficient management of interconnected resources (Zhang & Tao, 2020). Through the integration of standardized ontologies and vocabularies, Semantic Web Control Models enable AIoT systems to interpret and contextualize information accurately, leading to more intuitive and effective user interfaces. Additionally, these models support the development of adaptive systems and intelligent assistants that can learn from user interactions and dynamically adjust their behavior to meet evolving user needs and preferences (Bibri et al., 2024). Moreover, Semantic Web Control Models enable the aggregation and fusion of data from disparate sources, facilitating seamless integration and interoperability among heterogeneous devices and systems. This unified view of data enhances decision-making, enables real-time monitoring and control, and fosters innovation in AIoT applications. Overall, Semantic Web Control Models offer a holistic approach to enhancing usability and control in AIoT environments, enabling organizations to realize the full potential of interconnected devices and systems in delivering personalized, context-aware experiences to users.

The Artificial Intelligence of Things (AIoT) is a combination of AI and the Internet of Things, offering transformative capabilities. However, as AIoT systems become more complex and interconnected, usability and control are crucial. The complexity of interconnected devices, sensors, and actuators can make it difficult for users to manage and control these systems effectively. The diversity of interfaces and interaction paradigms can also cause confusion and frustration. Therefore, simplifying the user experience and providing intuitive control mechanisms are essential for improving usability in AIoT environments (Tabuenca et al., 2024). User interface design is crucial for enhancing usability in AIoT environments. It should be intuitive, responsive, and accessible, facilitating user interactions. Human-centered design principles and user feedback can tailor interfaces to specific needs. Prioritizing usability empowers users to interact with complex systems. Accessibility and user experience issues are also essential for inclusivity and usability. Ensuring AIoT systems are accessible to diverse users can enhance engagement and satisfaction. Addressing accessibility and user experience considerations upfront can lead to more user-friendly and inclusive AIoT environments (Shi et al., 2021).

Semantic Web control models enhance usability and control in AIoT environments by leveraging semantic technologies like ontologies and linked data. They enable intelligent, context-aware interactions, seamless integration across devices, and simplified user control. These models capture and represent IoT data, resulting in more intuitive and personalized user experiences. They simplify management and management of AIoT environments. Enhancing usability and control in AIoT environments is crucial for maximizing the full potential of these technologies. By addressing device complexity, designing intuitive interfaces, and utilizing semantic Web control models, developers can create intelligent AIoT systems, leading to more accessible, inclusive, and satisfying user experiences (Tan et al., 2021). Artificial Intelligence of Things (AIoT) is a combination of Artificial Intelligence (AI) and the Internet of Things (IoT), enabling the integration of AI capabilities into IoT devices and systems. This synergy has the potential to revolutionize various industries by enabling smarter, more efficient, and responsive systems. The IoT, consisting of interconnected devices with sensors, actuators, and communication capabilities, forms the foundation of AIoT. By leveraging this data, AIoT systems can gain insights into real-world phenomena, make intelligent decisions, optimize processes, enhance services, and improve user experiences (Nahr et al., 2021).

Artificial Intelligence (AI) drives IoT applications by enabling devices to learn from data, recognize patterns, and make predictions autonomously. Machine learning algorithms play a central role in AIoT, allowing devices to adapt and become more intelligent and responsive to changing environments and user needs. This enables IoT systems to become more intelligent and responsive. AIoT offers advantages such as autonomous decision-making and action-taking at the network's edge, reducing latency, bandwidth requirements, and dependence on centralized cloud infrastructure. This makes AIoT systems more efficient, scalable, and resilient. By embedding intelligence directly into IoT devices, AIoT enables real-time responses and adaptive behaviors, unlocking new opportunities for automation and optimization across various applications (Zhu et al., 2022).

AIoT has applications in various sectors like smart cities, healthcare, transportation, agriculture, manufacturing, and home automation. It can optimize energy consumption, improve traffic management, and enhance public safety. In healthcare, AIoT can monitor patient health remotely, facilitate early disease detection, and personalize treatment plans. However, it also presents challenges like data privacy, security, interoperability, ethics, and regulatory compliance. A holistic approach is needed to address these issues (Sun et al., 2021). The Artificial Intelligence of Things (AIoT) is a significant advancement in our understanding and interaction with the world, enabling smarter, more autonomous, and responsive environments that enhance efficiency, decision-making, and enrich human experiences across various applications and domains.

Background

The rise of Artificial Intelligence of Things (AIoT) has sparked interest in academia, industry, and society. As the Internet of Things (IoT) expands, integrating AI capabilities into IoT systems opens up new opportunities for innovation and disruption. This chapter provides an overview of AIoT, exploring its foundational concepts, key technologies, applications, and implications. It delves into the synergistic relationship between AI and IoT, highlighting how AI enhances IoT devices' capabilities to analyze data, make decisions, and act autonomously (Bronner et al., 2021; Nahr et al., 2021; Shi et al., 2021). This chapter explores the evolution and potential of Artificial Intelligence and Machine Learning (AIoT) in the context of rapid technological advancements and societal transformations. It provides a comprehensive understanding of AIoT, including technical, social, ethical, and regulatory aspects. Drawing on interdisciplinary research and real-world applications, it elucidates the principles driving the convergence of AI and IoT, equipping readers with the knowledge and insights needed to navigate the complex landscape and harness its transformative potential (Zhang & Tao, 2020).

The chapter explores the role of AIoT in digital transformation, highlighting its impact on industries, business models, and everyday experiences. It examines its historical roots, current trends, and future trajectories, providing a roadmap for stakeholders to navigate the evolving landscape of intelligent, connected systems. The chapter contextualizes discussions on enhancing usability and control in AIoT environments, laying the groundwork for deeper exploration and analysis of AIoT's multifaceted dimensions and implications for society, economy, and technology.

Objectives

- **To Explore the Intersection of AI and IoT**: The fundamental concepts and principles underlying the convergence of artificial intelligence (AI) and the Internet of Things (IoT), providing readers with a deeper understanding of how AI enhances the capabilities of IoT devices and systems (Boopathi, 2024c; Malathi et al., 2024).
- **To Examine the Importance of Usability in AIoT Environments**: By examining the challenges and considerations related to usability in AIoT environments, the chapter seeks to highlight the critical role of user-friendly interfaces and intuitive control mechanisms in maximizing the effectiveness and acceptance of AIoT systems.
- **To Introduce Semantic Web Control Models**: The chapter aims to introduce readers to semantic web control models and their relevance in enhancing usability and control within AIoT environments. By exploring concepts such as ontologies, linked data, and semantic interoperability, the chapter provides insights into how these models can facilitate intelligent and context-aware interactions in AIoT systems.
- **To Provide Practical Insights and Case Studies**: Through the analysis of real-world applications and case studies, the chapter aims to offer practical insights into the implementation and impact of usability enhancements and semantic web control models in AIoT environments. By showcasing successful examples and lessons learned, the chapter aims to inspire and inform researchers, practitioners, and stakeholders in the field.
- **To Discuss Future Directions and Challenges**: The chapter seeks to stimulate discussion on the future directions and challenges in enhancing usability and control in AIoT environments. By identifying emerging trends, opportunities, and areas for further research, the chapter aims to contribute to the advancement of knowledge and innovation in the field of AIoT.
- **To Empower Stakeholders with Actionable Knowledge**: Ultimately, the chapter aims to empower stakeholders, including researchers, developers, policymakers, and end-users, with actionable knowledge and insights that can inform decision-making, shape strategies, and drive the adoption of AIoT technologies for positive societal impact.

USABILITY CHALLENGES IN AIOT ENVIRONMENTS

The complexity of AIoT environments, user interface design, and accessibility issues pose unique usability challenges, making it crucial to address these issues to ensure AIoT systems are user-friendly, intuitive, and accessible to a diverse user base (Shi et al., 2021; Tan et al., 2021).

Complexity of Interconnected Devices: AIoT environments typically comprise a multitude of interconnected devices, sensors, and actuators, each serving specific functions and interacting with one another. This complexity poses challenges for users in managing and controlling these interconnected systems effectively. Users may struggle to understand the relationships between different devices, navigate through complex configurations, and troubleshoot issues that arise. Moreover, interoperability issues between devices from different manufacturers further exacerbate the complexity, making it challenging for users to integrate disparate systems seamlessly.

User Interface Design Considerations: Designing intuitive and user-friendly interfaces is paramount in AIoT environments to enable users to interact with and control interconnected devices efficiently. However, designing interfaces for AIoT systems presents unique challenges due to the diversity of devices, interaction paradigms, and user contexts. Developers must consider factors such as screen size, input modalities, and interaction patterns when designing interfaces for various IoT devices, ranging from smartphones and tablets to smart speakers and wearable devices. Moreover, ensuring consistency across different interfaces and platforms is essential for providing a cohesive user experience.

Accessibility and User Experience Issues: Accessibility is a critical consideration in AIoT environments to ensure that users with diverse abilities and needs can access and interact with IoT devices and systems effectively. However, many IoT devices and interfaces may not adequately address accessibility requirements, posing barriers to users with disabilities. Issues such as small font sizes, lack of alternative input methods, and inaccessible controls can hinder the usability of AIoT systems for users with visual, motor, or cognitive impairments. Additionally, ensuring a positive user experience requires addressing factors such as responsiveness, reliability, and responsiveness to user input to minimize frustration and enhance satisfaction.

To improve usability in AIoT environments, developers should adopt a comprehensive approach that includes technical, design, and accessibility considerations. This includes simplifying complexity, streamlining user interfaces, and prioritizing inclusivity, which can boost user satisfaction and adoption.

ARTIFICIAL INTELLIGENCE OF THINGS (AIOT)

AIoT is the integration of AI and IoT, enabling intelligent, interconnected systems that analyze data, make decisions, and take autonomous actions. It extends the capabilities of traditional IoT systems by integrating AI algorithms, enhancing IoT devices' smarter, adaptive, and responsiveness to their environments (Wang et al., 2023). The conceptual framework of AIoT encompasses the following elements:

Internet of Things (IoT): The Internet of Things (IoT) forms the foundational infrastructure of AIoT, comprising a network of interconnected devices embedded with sensors, actuators, and communication capabilities. These IoT devices collect and transmit data from the physical world, creating vast streams of information that can be analyzed and acted upon (Pachiappan et al., 2024; Rahamathunnisa et al., 2024).

Artificial Intelligence (AI): Artificial Intelligence (AI) encompasses a range of technologies and techniques that enable machines to mimic human intelligence and perform cognitive tasks such as learning, reasoning, and decision-making. In the context of AIoT, AI algorithms and models are applied to analyze IoT data, extract insights, and derive actionable intelligence (Boopathi, 2024a; Pachiappan et al., 2024).

Integration and Interoperability: AIoT involves the seamless integration and interoperability of AI and IoT technologies, enabling bidirectional communication and interaction between AI algorithms and IoT devices. This integration allows IoT devices to leverage AI capabilities for data analysis, predictive modeling, and autonomous decision-making, while also enabling AI systems to interact with and control IoT devices in real-time.

Data Analytics and Machine Learning: Data analytics and machine learning play a central role in AIoT by enabling IoT devices to learn from data, recognize patterns, and make predictions or recommendations autonomously. Machine learning algorithms can be deployed at the edge of the network, within IoT devices themselves, or in centralized cloud platforms to analyze IoT data in real-time and derive actionable insights (Boopathi, 2024a; Veeranjaneyulu et al., 2023).

Autonomous Decision-Making and Action: AIoT systems enable autonomous decision-making and action-taking at the edge of the network, closer to where data is generated and where actions need to be performed. This edge intelligence reduces latency, bandwidth requirements, and dependence on centralized cloud infrastructure, making AIoT systems more efficient, scalable, and responsive to real-time events.

AIoT is a transformative paradigm that integrates AI and IoT technologies to create intelligent, adaptive, and autonomous systems. It opens up new opportunities for innovation and disruption across various industries and domains.

Integration of AI and IoT Technologies

The integration of Artificial Intelligence (AI) and the Internet of Things (IoT) technologies forms the cornerstone of the Artificial Intelligence of Things (AIoT) paradigm. This integration brings together the capabilities of AI algorithms with the vast network of interconnected IoT devices, creating intelligent systems capable of collecting, analyzing, and acting upon data in real-time. Several aspects characterize the integration of AI and IoT technologies: The figure 1 depicts the integration of AI and IoT technologies (Seng et al., 2022).

- *Data Acquisition and Sensing:* IoT devices are equipped with sensors and actuators that collect data from the physical world, including environmental parameters, user interactions, and device statuses. These sensors generate vast streams of data, which serve as the foundation for AI-driven analytics and decision-making (Rahamathunnisa et al., 2024).
- *Data Processing and Analysis:* AI algorithms are applied to process and analyze the data collected by IoT devices, extracting valuable insights, identifying patterns, and making predictions or recommendations. Machine learning techniques, such as supervised learning, unsupervised learning, and reinforcement learning, are commonly used to analyze IoT data and derive actionable intelligence.
- *Edge Computing and Edge AI:* Edge computing refers to the processing and analysis of data at the edge of the network, closer to where data is generated and where actions need to be performed. Edge AI extends this concept by deploying AI algorithms directly within IoT devices or at the network edge, enabling real-time data processing and autonomous decision-making without relying on centralized cloud infrastructure (Boopathi, 2024b).
- *Real-Time Decision-Making and Action:* The integration of AI and IoT technologies enables IoT devices to make autonomous decisions and take actions in real-time based on the insights derived

Figure 1. Schematic diagram: Integration of AI and IoT technologies

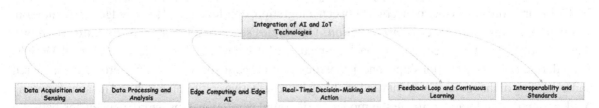

from data analysis. This capability allows AIoT systems to respond quickly to changing environmental conditions, user preferences, and business requirements, enhancing efficiency and agility.

- *Feedback Loop and Continuous Learning:* AIoT systems often incorporate feedback loops that enable continuous learning and improvement over time. By collecting feedback from IoT devices, user interactions, and environmental changes, AI algorithms can refine their models, adapt to evolving conditions, and optimize decision-making processes iteratively (Zainuddin et al., 2024).
- *Interoperability and Standards:* Effective integration of AI and IoT technologies requires interoperability and adherence to standards that facilitate seamless communication and interaction between diverse devices and platforms. Common standards, protocols, and interoperability frameworks ensure compatibility and interoperability across heterogeneous IoT ecosystems, enabling easier integration of AI capabilities.

AIoT systems, based on the integration of AI and IoT technologies, drive innovation and transformation across various industries. By leveraging their complementary strengths, organizations can unlock new opportunities for efficiency, optimization, and value creation in the digital era.

SEMANTIC WEB CONTROL MODELS

The Semantic Web is an evolution of the World Wide Web, aiming to improve interoperability, discoverability, and understanding of web content by adding semantics to web resources. It aims to enable machines to interpret web content meaning, facilitating intelligent interactions among applications and systems. The Semantic Web is centered on Linked Data, a framework for structuring and interconnecting web data in a standardized format. Linked Data principles use uniform resource identifiers (URIs) to uniquely identify entities and RDF (Resource Description Framework) to represent relationships and attributes (Rhayem et al., 2020).

Linked Data principles enable organizations and individuals to publish, share, and interlink data across various sources, creating a web of interconnected data that enhances the semantic richness and accessibility of web content. This enables efficient discovery, integration, and analysis of information, leading to new insights and opportunities for innovation. The Semantic Web fosters intelligent applications and services that can infer relationships, provide contextually relevant information, and personalize content, enhancing user experiences and fostering innovation. The Semantic Web and Linked Data are fundamental technologies that drive the evolution of the web towards a more intelligent, interconnected, and semantic-driven environment. They enable machines to understand and reason about web content, improving accessibility, interoperability, and usability of information on the web, thereby empowering users and organizations to extract more value from online data.

Semantic Web Control Models enhance usability and control in AIoT environments by incorporating ontologies and semantic interoperability and integration (Martinez-Rodriguez et al., 2020; Rhayem et al., 2020). Figure 2 illustrates the connection between integration, ontologies, and knowledge representation.

Ontologies and Knowledge Representation: Ontologies serve as foundational structures for representing knowledge in a structured and machine-readable format within Semantic Web Control Models. They define concepts, relationships, and properties in a domain-specific context, providing a shared understanding of the semantics of data and enabling more effective communication and reasoning among AIoT systems. Ontologies facilitate the modeling of complex relationships and dependencies between

Figure 2. The relationship integration, ontologies, and knowledge representation

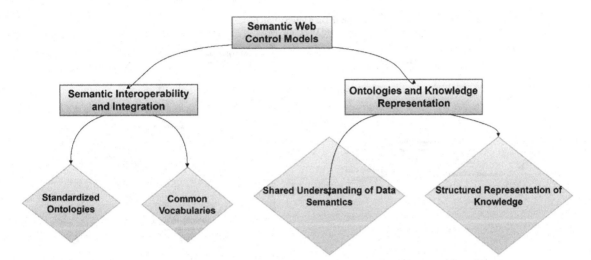

entities, allowing AIoT devices to interpret and contextualize information accurately. By utilizing ontologies for knowledge representation, Semantic Web Control Models enable AIoT systems to achieve a higher level of semantic understanding, leading to more intelligent and context-aware interactions.

Semantic Interoperability and Integration: Semantic interoperability and integration are essential aspects of Semantic Web Control Models, enabling seamless communication and collaboration among heterogeneous AIoT devices and systems. Semantic interoperability refers to the ability of different systems to exchange and interpret data meaningfully, regardless of differences in data formats, schemas, or vocabularies. By adopting standardized ontologies and vocabularies, Semantic Web Control Models facilitate semantic interoperability, allowing AIoT devices to exchange data in a common, machine-understandable format. Moreover, semantic integration enables the aggregation and fusion of data from diverse sources, enhancing the completeness and accuracy of information available to AIoT systems. Through semantic interoperability and integration, Semantic Web Control Models empower AIoT environments to overcome interoperability challenges and leverage the full potential of interconnected devices and data sources.

Semantic Web Control Models enhance AIoT usability and control by utilizing ontologies and semantic interoperability, facilitating seamless communication among diverse systems, enabling effective collaboration, informed decision-making, and personalized user experiences.

ENHANCING USABILITY THROUGH SEMANTIC WEB CONTROL MODELS

Semantic Data Integration for Improved User Interfaces

The figure 3 depicts the integration of semantic data to enhance user interfaces.

- **Semantic Data Integration**: Semantic data integration involves aggregating and harmonizing data from diverse sources, including IoT devices, databases, and external services, using standardized

Figure 3. Semantic data integration for improved user interfaces

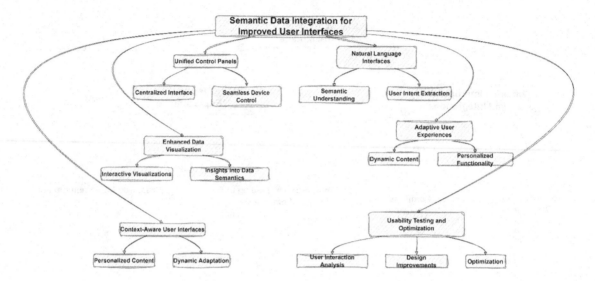

ontologies and vocabularies. By integrating data semantically, AIoT systems can achieve a unified view of information, enabling more comprehensive analysis and decision-making (Lampropoulos et al., 2020).

- **Context-Aware User Interfaces**: Semantic data integration facilitates the development of context-aware user interfaces that dynamically adapt to user preferences, environmental conditions, and task requirements. User interfaces can leverage semantic metadata to personalize content, recommend relevant actions, and anticipate user needs based on contextual information.
- **Enhanced Data Visualization**: Semantic data integration enables the visualization of complex data relationships and patterns through interactive and intuitive visualizations. User interfaces can use semantic metadata to generate visualizations that provide insights into data semantics, relationships, and trends, enhancing user understanding and decision-making.
- **Unified Control Panels**: Semantic data integration allows for the creation of unified control panels that provide a centralized interface for managing and controlling heterogeneous IoT devices and systems. Users can interact with AIoT systems through a single interface, leveraging semantic metadata to navigate and control interconnected devices seamlessly.
- **Natural Language Interfaces**: Semantic data integration enables the development of natural language interfaces that allow users to interact with AIoT systems using natural language commands and queries. These interfaces use semantic understanding to interpret user intent, extract relevant information, and execute commands or retrieve information from IoT devices.
- **Adaptive User Experiences**: Semantic data integration supports the creation of adaptive user experiences that tailor content, functionality, and interaction patterns to individual user preferences and behavior. User interfaces can leverage semantic metadata to adapt dynamically to changes in user context, device capabilities, and environmental conditions, providing personalized and contextually relevant experiences (KAV et al., 2023; Malathi et al., 2024).
- **Usability Testing and Optimization**: Semantic data integration enables usability testing and optimization by providing insights into user interactions, preferences, and behavior. User interfaces

can capture and analyze semantic metadata related to user interactions, allowing developers to identify usability issues, iterate on design improvements, and optimize the user experience over time (Durán & Ramírez, 2021).

Semantic data integration enhances usability in AIoT environments by creating context-aware, intuitive, and adaptive user interfaces. Semantic Web Control Models facilitate context-awareness, personalization, adaptive systems, and intelligent assistants, streamlining interactions and improving user experiences by leveraging semantic technologies (Rowland et al., 2020; Sobhkhiz et al., 2021).

a.   **Context-awareness and Personalization**: Semantic Web Control Models enable AIoT systems to be context-aware, meaning they can understand and respond to the specific circumstances and preferences of users. By leveraging semantic metadata and standardized ontologies, AIoT devices and applications can adapt their behavior based on factors such as user location, time of day, environmental conditions, and past interactions. This context-awareness enables personalized experiences tailored to individual user needs and preferences, enhancing usability by anticipating user actions and providing relevant information or services proactively.

b.   **Adaptive Systems and Intelligent Assistants**: Semantic Web Control Models facilitate the development of adaptive systems and intelligent assistants that can learn from user interactions, adapt to changing conditions, and provide proactive assistance. These systems leverage semantic understanding to interpret user intent, predict user preferences, and automate routine tasks, thereby enhancing usability by reducing cognitive load and streamlining user interactions. Adaptive systems can dynamically adjust their behavior based on feedback and user behavior, optimizing the user experience over time and improving overall usability (Verma et al., 2024).

c.   **Enhanced User Interfaces**: Semantic Web Control Models enable the creation of user interfaces that are more intuitive, interactive, and personalized. By integrating semantic data and knowledge representation, user interfaces can provide contextual information, recommend relevant actions, and adapt their layout and functionality to match user preferences and task requirements. This enhanced usability fosters a more seamless and enjoyable user experience, increasing user engagement and satisfaction with AIoT systems.

d.   **Efficient Decision-Making**: Semantic Web Control Models support efficient decision-making by providing a unified view of data and insights from heterogeneous sources. By integrating data from diverse IoT devices, databases, and external services using standardized ontologies, AIoT systems can analyze information more comprehensively and make informed decisions in real-time. This enhanced decision-making capability improves usability by enabling AIoT systems to respond quickly and accurately to user needs and changing conditions.

e.   **Personalized Recommendations and Assistance**: Semantic Web Control Models enable AIoT systems to deliver personalized recommendations and assistance tailored to individual user preferences and contexts. By analyzing user data and behavior using semantic techniques, intelligent assistants can anticipate user needs, suggest relevant actions, and provide helpful information or guidance. This personalized assistance enhances usability by reducing the cognitive burden on users and facilitating more efficient and effective interactions with AIoT systems (Lampropoulos et al., 2020).

Semantic Web Control Models enhance AIoT usability by improving context-awareness, personalization, adaptive systems, and intelligent assistants by using semantic technologies to automate tasks and provide personalized assistance.

IMPLEMENTATION OF SEMANTIC WEB CONTROL MODELS IN AIOT APPLICATIONS

Semantic Web Control Models are a framework that enhances usability and control in Artificial Intelligence of Things (AIoT) applications by leveraging semantic technologies like ontologies and linked data. Implementation involves defining specific needs, establishing data integration procedures, and deploying semantic-enabled systems to improve usability and control in AIoT applications. The figure 4 illustrates the implementation of semantic web control models in AIoT applications (Hu et al., 2023).

Identifying Needs and Requirements: The first step in implementing Semantic Web Control Models in AIoT applications is to identify specific needs and requirements. This involves understanding the challenges and limitations of existing systems, such as interoperability issues, lack of context-awareness, and difficulty in managing heterogeneous data sources. By conducting a thorough analysis of user needs, business objectives, and technical constraints, organizations can define clear goals and objectives for implementing Semantic Web Control Models.

Establishing Procedures for Data Integration: Semantic Web Control Models rely on the integration of heterogeneous data sources to provide a unified view of information within AIoT applications. Establishing procedures for data integration involves identifying relevant data sources, standardizing data formats and vocabularies, and mapping data to ontologies and semantic models. This process may involve data cleansing, transformation, and enrichment to ensure data quality and consistency. Additionally, organizations may need to establish data governance policies and mechanisms to manage data access, security, and privacy (Hussain et al., 2023; M. Kumar et al., 2023).

a) **Developing Semantic-enabled Systems**: Once data integration procedures are established, organizations can develop Semantic Web Control Models and integrate them into AIoT applications. This involves implementing ontologies, semantic models, and inference engines to enable semantic reasoning and decision-making. Semantic-enabled systems utilize semantic metadata to interpret user queries, infer relationships between entities, and provide context-aware recommendations and assistance. Development efforts may also involve integrating semantic technologies with existing AIoT platforms, middleware, and applications to enhance their functionality and usability (Huang et al., 2020).

b) **Realizing Overall Functions**: Semantic Web Control Models enable a range of functions that enhance usability and control in AIoT applications (Adli et al., 2023). These functions include:
   ◦ Context-awareness: AIoT systems can understand and respond to user context, such as location, time, and preferences, to provide personalized experiences and recommendations.
   ◦ Unified control: Users can interact with heterogeneous IoT devices and systems through a unified interface, simplifying management and control.
   ◦ Intelligent assistance: AIoT systems can provide proactive assistance and recommendations based on semantic understanding of user needs and preferences.

Figure 4. Implementation of semantic web control models in AIoT applications

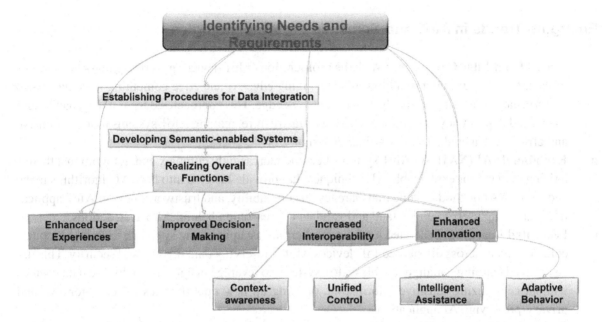

○ Adaptive behavior: AIoT systems can adapt their behavior dynamically based on changing conditions and user feedback, optimizing usability and performance over time.

c) **Outcomes**: The implementation of Semantic Web Control Models in AIoT applications yields several outcomes that improve usability and control:

  ○ Enhanced user experiences: Users benefit from more intuitive, personalized, and context-aware interactions with AIoT systems, leading to increased satisfaction and engagement.

  ○ Improved decision-making: AIoT systems can analyze data more comprehensively and make informed decisions in real-time, improving efficiency and effectiveness.

  ○ Increased interoperability: Semantic interoperability enables seamless integration and communication among heterogeneous devices and systems, reducing integration efforts and improving scalability.

  ○ Enhanced innovation: Semantic-enabled AIoT applications unlock new opportunities for innovation and value creation, enabling organizations to leverage data more effectively and deliver innovative services and solutions.

The use of Semantic Web Control Models in AIoT applications involves defining needs, establishing data integration procedures, developing semantic-enabled systems, and enhancing usability, control, and innovation. This approach allows organizations to fully utilize AIoT applications and deliver superior user experiences across various domains.

FUTURE DIRECTIONS AND CHALLENGES

Emerging Trends in AIoT and Semantic Web Technologies

i.   **Edge AI and Edge Computing**: With the proliferation of IoT devices generating massive amounts of data, there's a growing trend towards leveraging edge AI and edge computing technologies to perform data processing and analysis at the network edge. This approach reduces latency, bandwidth usage, and dependency on centralized cloud infrastructure, making AIoT systems more responsive and efficient (Hu et al., 2023; Martinez-Rodriguez et al., 2020).

ii. **Explainable AI (XAI)**: As AIoT systems become increasingly complex and autonomous, there's a rising demand for explainable AI techniques that provide insights into how AI algorithms make decisions. XAI methods enable transparency, accountability, and trustworthiness in AIoT applications, allowing users to understand and validate the reasoning behind AI-driven actions.

iii. **Federated Learning**: Federated learning is emerging as a promising approach to train AI models collaboratively across distributed IoT devices while preserving data privacy and security. This decentralized learning paradigm enables AIoT systems to leverage insights from diverse data sources without centralizing sensitive information, opening up new opportunities for collaborative and privacy-preserving AI applications.

iv. **Semantic Interoperability and Knowledge Graphs**: Semantic interoperability and knowledge graphs are gaining traction in AIoT applications, enabling seamless integration and interoperability among heterogeneous devices, platforms, and data sources. By leveraging standardized ontologies and linked data, AIoT systems can achieve a shared understanding of data semantics, facilitating more effective data integration, analysis, and decision-making (Das et al., 2024; Sharma et al., 2024).

v.   **Hybrid AI Models**: Hybrid AI models that combine different AI techniques, such as deep learning, machine learning, and symbolic reasoning, are emerging as a powerful approach to address the diverse challenges and requirements of AIoT applications. These hybrid models leverage the strengths of different AI paradigms to achieve robustness, scalability, and adaptability in dynamic and uncertain environments (Adli et al., 2023; Hu et al., 2023; Tanque, 2021).

vi. **Semantic Edge Computing**: Semantic edge computing integrates semantic technologies with edge computing infrastructure to enable context-aware and intelligent processing of IoT data at the network edge. By embedding semantic reasoning capabilities into edge devices and gateways, AIoT systems can perform real-time analysis, inference, and decision-making closer to where data is generated, enhancing responsiveness and scalability.

vii. **Ethical and Responsible AIoT**: As AIoT systems become more pervasive in everyday life, there's a growing focus on ensuring that AI-driven decisions and actions align with ethical principles, fairness, and societal values. Ethical and responsible AIoT practices encompass considerations such as privacy protection, bias mitigation, transparency, and accountability, aiming to mitigate potential risks and maximize the positive impact of AIoT technologies on individuals and society (Boopathi & Khang, 2023; Reddy et al., 2023).

Opportunities for Research and Development

Emerging AIoT and semantic web technologies offer promising research opportunities in privacy-preserving solutions, self-adaptive systems, interdisciplinary collaboration, explainable AIoT, human-centric design, ethical compliance, and sustainability. These advancements can help address societal challenges and unlock the full potential of AIoT technologies for positive impact (Bibri et al., 2024; Wang et al., 2023; Zainuddin et al., 2024). Figure 5 presents the latest trends and research in AIoT and Semantic Web Technologies.

a) **Privacy-preserving AIoT Solutions**: There's a need for research and development of privacy-preserving AIoT solutions that enable secure and confidential processing of sensitive data while preserving individual privacy rights. Techniques such as homomorphic encryption, differential privacy, and secure multi-party computation offer promising avenues for protecting privacy in AIoT environments.

b) **Self-adaptive AIoT Systems**: Research into self-adaptive AIoT systems aims to develop autonomous and self-optimizing systems that can dynamically adjust their behavior, configuration, and resource allocation in response to changing environmental conditions, user requirements, and performance objectives. Self-adaptive AIoT systems enhance scalability, resilience, and adaptability in dynamic and uncertain environments.

c) **Interdisciplinary Collaboration**: Opportunities exist for interdisciplinary collaboration between researchers and practitioners from diverse fields, including AI, IoT, semantic web, cybersecurity, and ethics. Collaborative research efforts can drive innovation, address complex challenges, and create holistic solutions that leverage the synergies between AIoT and semantic web technologies.

d) **Explainable and Trustworthy AIoT**: Research in explainable and trustworthy AIoT focuses on developing methods and techniques to enhance transparency, interpretability, and trustworthiness in AIoT systems. By providing explanations for AI-driven decisions and ensuring alignment with ethical and regulatory requirements, explainable and trustworthy AIoT solutions foster trust, acceptance, and adoption among users and stakeholders.

e) **Human-centric AIoT Design**: Human-centric AIoT design emphasizes the importance of designing AIoT systems with a focus on human needs, preferences, and values. Research in this area explores user-centered design approaches, usability testing methodologies, and participatory design practices to create AIoT solutions that are intuitive, accessible, and inclusive for diverse user populations.

f) **Ethical and Regulatory Compliance**: Research opportunities exist in exploring the ethical and regulatory implications of AIoT technologies and developing frameworks, guidelines, and standards to ensure ethical and responsible AIoT deployment. This includes considerations such as data privacy, fairness, accountability, transparency, and compliance with legal and regulatory requirements.

g) **Sustainability and Environmental Impact**: Research into the sustainability and environmental impact of AIoT technologies aims to mitigate their energy consumption, carbon footprint, and ecological footprint. Opportunities exist for developing energy-efficient algorithms, optimizing resource utilization, and promoting eco-friendly practices in AIoT design, deployment, and operation(Boopathi, 2022; Boopathi et al., 2023; Gowri et al., 2023).

Addressing Security and Privacy Concerns

Addressing security and privacy concerns in AIoT applications requires a comprehensive approach that includes privacy-preserving architectures, blockchain-based security mechanisms, secure authentication, threat detection, end-to-end encryption, regulatory compliance, and continuous monitoring and security updates. This integration enhances security, protects user privacy, and builds trust in AIoT technologies(Lampropoulos et al., 2020; Rhayem et al., 2020; Zainuddin et al., 2024).

- **Privacy-Preserving AIoT Architectures**: Developments in privacy-preserving AIoT architectures aim to safeguard sensitive data and protect user privacy in AIoT applications. Techniques such as homomorphic encryption, differential privacy, and federated learning enable data processing and analysis while preserving data confidentiality and anonymity, reducing the risk of privacy breaches and unauthorized access.
- **Blockchain-based Security Mechanisms**: Blockchain technology is increasingly being explored to enhance security and privacy in AIoT environments. Blockchain provides decentralized and im-

Figure 5. Emerging trends and research and developments in AIoT and semantic web technologies

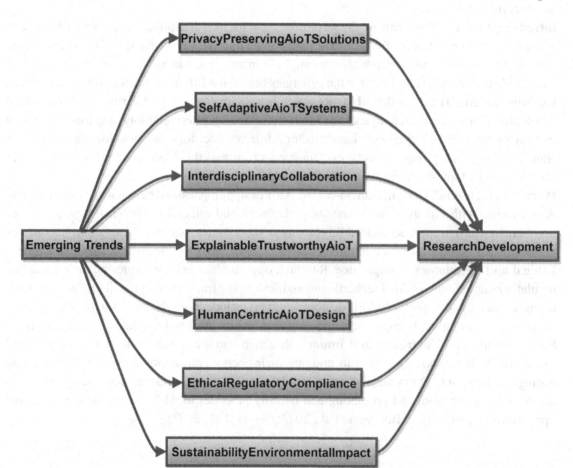

mutable data storage, enabling secure transaction recording, data provenance, and access control. By leveraging blockchain-based security mechanisms, AIoT systems can ensure data integrity, traceability, and auditability, mitigating the risk of data tampering and unauthorized modifications (P. R. Kumar et al., 2023; Sundaramoorthy et al., 2024).

- **Secure Device Authentication and Access Control**: Developments in secure device authentication and access control mechanisms strengthen the security of AIoT ecosystems by verifying the identities of devices and users and enforcing granular access policies. Techniques such as secure bootstrapping, mutual authentication, and attribute-based access control enable AIoT systems to authenticate devices and users securely, authorize access to resources based on predefined policies, and mitigate the risk of unauthorized access and malicious activities (Boopathi & Khang, 2023).
- **Threat Detection and Anomaly Detection**: Advances in threat detection and anomaly detection techniques enable AIoT systems to identify and mitigate security threats and anomalous behavior in real-time. Machine learning algorithms and AI-driven analytics can analyze IoT data streams for suspicious patterns, deviations from normal behavior, and potential security breaches. By proactively detecting and responding to security incidents, AIoT systems can enhance resilience and minimize the impact of cyber-attacks and data breaches.
- **End-to-End Encryption and Secure Communication Protocols**: Developments in end-to-end encryption and secure communication protocols ensure the confidentiality, integrity, and authenticity of data transmitted between IoT devices and cloud services. Protocols such as Transport Layer Security (TLS), Datagram Transport Layer Security (DTLS), and Message Queuing Telemetry Transport (MQTT) with Secure Sockets Layer (SSL) enable secure data exchange, encryption of sensitive information, and protection against eavesdropping and man-in-the-middle attacks.
- **Regulatory Compliance and Data Governance**: Efforts to address security and privacy concerns in AIoT applications include compliance with regulatory requirements and implementation of robust data governance practices. Organizations must adhere to relevant regulations such as the General Data Protection Regulation (GDPR), Health Insurance Portability and Accountability Act (HIPAA), and the California Consumer Privacy Act (CCPA) to protect user privacy, secure sensitive data, and ensure ethical and legal use of AIoT technologies.
- **Continuous Monitoring and Security Updates**: Continuous monitoring and security updates are essential for maintaining the security and resilience of AIoT systems in the face of evolving threats and vulnerabilities. Security monitoring tools, intrusion detection systems, and vulnerability management processes enable organizations to detect security incidents, assess risks, and deploy timely security patches and updates to mitigate potential security risks and vulnerabilities in AIoT deployments (Boopathi, 2021; Malathi et al., 2024; Subha et al., 2023).

CONCLUSION

The chapter discusses the use of Semantic Web Control Models in Artificial Intelligence of Things (AIoT) environments, focusing on improving usability, addressing security and privacy concerns, and exploring research opportunities. These models enhance interoperability, discoverability, and understanding of web content, enabling intelligent, context-aware interactions. The chapter emphasizes the importance of usability in enhancing user experiences and maximizing the value of interconnected devices. Semantic

Web Control Models offer mechanisms for representing knowledge, facilitating semantic interoperability, and enabling intuitive control of AIoT applications.

Emerging trends in AIoT and Semantic Web technologies, such as edge AI, explainable AI, federated learning, and semantic edge computing, present new opportunities for innovation and research. These technologies can address challenges like privacy preservation, security enhancement, and ethical considerations in AIoT applications. Implementing privacy-preserving architectures, blockchain-based security mechanisms, secure authentication, and access control can enhance security, protect user privacy, and build trust in AIoT technologies.

Future research in AIoT and Semantic Web technologies holds significant potential. Collaboration between academia, industry, and regulatory bodies is crucial for innovation, addressing emerging trends, and ethical deployment. Integrating Semantic Web Control Models in AIoT environments can transform interactions with interconnected devices, enabling intelligent, context-aware, and user-centric experiences. Organizations can unlock the full potential of AIoT technologies by leveraging semantic technologies and embracing emerging trends, achieving a smarter, more interconnected world.

ABBREVIATIONS

AI - Artificial Intelligence
AIoT - Artificial Intelligence of Things
CCPA - California Consumer Privacy Act
DTLS - Datagram Transport Layer Security
GDPR - General Data Protection Regulation
HIPAA - Health Insurance Portability and Accountability Act
IoT - Internet of Things
MQTT - Message Queuing Telemetry Transport
RDF - Resource Description Framework
SSL - Secure Sockets Layer
TLS - Transport Layer Security
URIs - Uniform Resource Identifiers
XAI - Explainable Artificial Intelligence

REFERENCES

Adli, H. K., Remli, M. A., Wan Salihin Wong, K. N. S., Ismail, N. A., González-Briones, A., Corchado, J. M., & Mohamad, M. S. (2023). Recent Advancements and Challenges of AIoT Application in Smart Agriculture: A Review. *Sensors (Basel)*, *23*(7), 3752. doi:10.3390/s23073752 PMID:37050812

Bibri, S. E., Krogstie, J., Kaboli, A., & Alahi, A. (2024). Smarter eco-cities and their leading-edge artificial intelligence of things solutions for environmental sustainability: A comprehensive systematic review. *Environmental Science and Ecotechnology*, *19*, 100330. doi:10.1016/j.ese.2023.100330 PMID:38021367

Boopathi, S. (2021). *Pollution monitoring and notification: Water pollution monitoring and notification using intelligent RC boat*. Academic Press.

Boopathi, S. (2022). Cryogenically treated and untreated stainless steel grade 317 in sustainable wire electrical discharge machining process: A comparative study. *Environmental Science and Pollution Research*, 1–10.

Boopathi, S. (2024a). Advancements in Machine Learning and AI for Intelligent Systems in Drone Applications for Smart City Developments. In *Futuristic e-Governance Security With Deep Learning Applications* (pp. 15–45). IGI Global. doi:10.4018/978-1-6684-9596-4.ch002

Boopathi, S. (2024b). Balancing Innovation and Security in the Cloud: Navigating the Risks and Rewards of the Digital Age. In Improving Security, Privacy, and Trust in Cloud Computing (pp. 164–193). IGI Global.

Boopathi, S. (2024c). Sustainable Development Using IoT and AI Techniques for Water Utilization in Agriculture. In Sustainable Development in AI, Blockchain, and E-Governance Applications (pp. 204–228). IGI Global. doi:10.4018/979-8-3693-1722-8.ch012

Boopathi, S., Alqahtani, A. S., Mubarakali, A., & Panchatcharam, P. (2023). Sustainable developments in near-dry electrical discharge machining process using sunflower oil-mist dielectric fluid. *Environmental Science and Pollution Research International*, 1–20. doi:10.1007/s11356-023-27494-0 PMID:37199846

Boopathi, S., & Khang, A. (2023). AI-Integrated Technology for a Secure and Ethical Healthcare Ecosystem. In *AI and IoT-Based Technologies for Precision Medicine* (pp. 36–59). IGI Global. doi:10.4018/979-8-3693-0876-9.ch003

Bronner, W., Gebauer, H., Lamprecht, C., & Wortmann, F. (2021). Sustainable AIoT: how artificial intelligence and the internet of things affect profit, people, and planet. *Connected Business: Create Value in a Networked Economy*, 137–154.

Das, S., Lekhya, G., Shreya, K., Shekinah, K. L., Babu, K. K., & Boopathi, S. (2024). Fostering Sustainability Education Through Cross-Disciplinary Collaborations and Research Partnerships: Interdisciplinary Synergy. In Facilitating Global Collaboration and Knowledge Sharing in Higher Education With Generative AI (pp. 60–88). IGI Global.

Durán, C. G., & Ramírez, C. M. (2021). Integration of open educational resources using semantic platform. *IEEE Access : Practical Innovations, Open Solutions*, 9, 93079–93088. doi:10.1109/AC-CESS.2021.3092315

Gowri, N. V., Dwivedi, J. N., Krishnaveni, K., Boopathi, S., Palaniappan, M., & Medikondu, N. R. (2023). Experimental investigation and multi-objective optimization of eco-friendly near-dry electrical discharge machining of shape memory alloy using Cu/SiC/Gr composite electrode. *Environmental Science and Pollution Research International*, 30(49), 1–19. doi:10.1007/s11356-023-26983-6 PMID:37126160

Hu, M., Cao, E., Huang, H., Zhang, M., Chen, X., & Chen, M. (2023). AIoTML: A Unified Modeling Language for AIoT-Based Cyber-Physical Systems. *IEEE Transactions on Computer-Aided Design of Integrated Circuits and Systems*, 42(11), 3545–3558. doi:10.1109/TCAD.2023.3264786

Huang, Y., Xue, X., & Jiang, C. (2020). Semantic integration of sensor knowledge on artificial internet of things. *Wireless Communications and Mobile Computing*, 2020, 1–8. doi:10.1155/2020/8815001

Hussain, Z., Babe, M., Saravanan, S., Srimathy, G., Roopa, H., & Boopathi, S. (2023). Optimizing Biomass-to-Biofuel Conversion: IoT and AI Integration for Enhanced Efficiency and Sustainability. In *Circular Economy Implementation for Sustainability in the Built Environment* (pp. 191–214). IGI Global.

KAV, R. P., Pandraju, T. K. S., Boopathi, S., Saravanan, P., Rathan, S. K., & Sathish, T. (2023). Hybrid Deep Learning Technique for Optimal Wind Mill Speed Estimation. *2023 7th International Conference on Electronics, Communication and Aerospace Technology (ICECA)*, 181–186.

Kumar, M., Kumar, K., Sasikala, P., Sampath, B., Gopi, B., & Sundaram, S. (2023). Sustainable Green Energy Generation From Waste Water: IoT and ML Integration. In *Sustainable Science and Intelligent Technologies for Societal Development* (pp. 440–463). IGI Global.

Kumar, P. R., Meenakshi, S., Shalini, S., Devi, S. R., & Boopathi, S. (2023). Soil Quality Prediction in Context Learning Approaches Using Deep Learning and Blockchain for Smart Agriculture. In *Effective AI, Blockchain, and E-Governance Applications for Knowledge Discovery and Management* (pp. 1–26). IGI Global. doi:10.4018/978-1-6684-9151-5.ch001

Lampropoulos, G., Keramopoulos, E., & Diamantaras, K. (2020). Enhancing the functionality of augmented reality using deep learning, semantic web and knowledge graphs: A review. *Visual Informatics*, *4*(1), 32–42. doi:10.1016/j.visinf.2020.01.001

Malathi, J., Kusha, K., Isaac, S., Ramesh, A., Rajendiran, M., & Boopathi, S. (2024). IoT-Enabled Remote Patient Monitoring for Chronic Disease Management and Cost Savings: Transforming Healthcare. In *Advances in Explainable AI Applications for Smart Cities* (pp. 371–388). IGI Global.

Martinez-Rodriguez, J. L., Hogan, A., & Lopez-Arevalo, I. (2020). Information extraction meets the semantic web: A survey. *Semantic Web*, *11*(2), 255–335. doi:10.3233/SW-180333

Nahr, J. G., Nozari, H., & Sadeghi, M. E. (2021). Green supply chain based on artificial intelligence of things (AIoT). *International Journal of Innovation in Management. Economics and Social Sciences*, *1*(2), 56–63.

Pachiappan, K., Anitha, K., Pitchai, R., Sangeetha, S., Satyanarayana, T., & Boopathi, S. (2024). Intelligent Machines, IoT, and AI in Revolutionizing Agriculture for Water Processing. In *Handbook of Research on AI and ML for Intelligent Machines and Systems* (pp. 374–399). IGI Global.

Rahamathunnisa, U., Sudhakar, K., Padhi, S., Bhattacharya, S., Shashibhushan, G., & Boopathi, S. (2024). Sustainable Energy Generation From Waste Water: IoT Integrated Technologies. In *Adoption and Use of Technology Tools and Services by Economically Disadvantaged Communities: Implications for Growth and Sustainability* (pp. 225–256). IGI Global.

Reddy, M. A., Reddy, B. M., Mukund, C., Venneti, K., Preethi, D., & Boopathi, S. (2023). Social Health Protection During the COVID-Pandemic Using IoT. In *The COVID-19 Pandemic and the Digitalization of Diplomacy* (pp. 204–235). IGI Global. doi:10.4018/978-1-7998-8394-4.ch009

Rhayem, A., Mhiri, M. B. A., & Gargouri, F. (2020). Semantic web technologies for the internet of things: Systematic literature review. *Internet of Things : Engineering Cyber Physical Human Systems*, *11*, 100206. doi:10.1016/j.iot.2020.100206

Rowland, A., Folmer, E., & Beek, W. (2020). Towards self-service gis—Combining the best of the semantic web and web gis. *ISPRS International Journal of Geo-Information*, *9*(12), 753. doi:10.3390/ijgi9120753

Seng, K. P., Ang, L. M., & Ngharamike, E. (2022). Artificial intelligence Internet of Things: A new paradigm of distributed sensor networks. *International Journal of Distributed Sensor Networks*, *18*(3), 15501477211062835. doi:10.1177/15501477211062835

Sharma, D. M., Ramana, K. V., Jothilakshmi, R., Verma, R., Maheswari, B. U., & Boopathi, S. (2024). Integrating Generative AI Into K-12 Curriculums and Pedagogies in India: Opportunities and Challenges. *Facilitating Global Collaboration and Knowledge Sharing in Higher Education With Generative AI*, 133–161.

Shi, Q., Zhang, Z., Yang, Y., Shan, X., Salam, B., & Lee, C. (2021). Artificial intelligence of things (AIoT) enabled floor monitoring system for smart home applications. *ACS Nano*, *15*(11), 18312–18326. doi:10.1021/acsnano.1c07579 PMID:34723468

Sobhkhiz, S., Taghaddos, H., Rezvani, M., & Ramezanianpour, A. M. (2021). Utilization of semantic web technologies to improve BIM-LCA applications. *Automation in Construction*, *130*, 103842. doi:10.1016/j.autcon.2021.103842

Subha, S., Inbamalar, T., Komala, C., Suresh, L. R., Boopathi, S., & Alaskar, K. (2023). A Remote Health Care Monitoring system using internet of medical things (IoMT). *IEEE Explore*, 1–6.

Sun, Z., Zhu, M., Zhang, Z., Chen, Z., Shi, Q., Shan, X., Yeow, R. C. H., & Lee, C. (2021). Artificial Intelligence of Things (AIoT) enabled virtual shop applications using self-powered sensor enhanced soft robotic manipulator. *Advancement of Science*, *8*(14), 2100230. doi:10.1002/advs.202100230 PMID:34037331

Sundaramoorthy, K., Singh, A., Sumathy, G., Maheshwari, A., Arunarani, A., & Boopathi, S. (2024). A Study on AI and Blockchain-Powered Smart Parking Models for Urban Mobility. In *Handbook of Research on AI and ML for Intelligent Machines and Systems* (pp. 223–250). IGI Global.

Tabuenca, B., Uche-Soria, M., Greller, W., Hernández-Leo, D., Balcells-Falgueras, P., Gloor, P., & Garbajosa, J. (2024). Greening smart learning environments with Artificial Intelligence of Things. *Internet of Things : Engineering Cyber Physical Human Systems*, *25*, 101051. doi:10.1016/j.iot.2023.101051

Tan, L., Yu, K., Ming, F., Cheng, X., & Srivastava, G. (2021). Secure and resilient artificial intelligence of things: A HoneyNet approach for threat detection and situational awareness. *IEEE Consumer Electronics Magazine*, *11*(3), 69–78. doi:10.1109/MCE.2021.3081874

Tanque, M. (2021). Knowledge Representation and Reasoning in AI-Based Solutions and IoT Applications. In *Artificial Intelligence to Solve Pervasive Internet of Things Issues* (pp. 13–49). Elsevier. doi:10.1016/B978-0-12-818576-6.00002-2

Veeranjaneyulu, R., Boopathi, S., Narasimharao, J., Gupta, K. K., Reddy, R. V. K., & Ambika, R. (2023). Identification of Heart Diseases using Novel Machine Learning Method. *IEEE Explore*, 1–6.

Verma, R., Christiana, M. B. V., Maheswari, M., Srinivasan, V., Patro, P., Dari, S. S., & Boopathi, S. (2024). Intelligent Physarum Solver for Profit Maximization in Oligopolistic Supply Chain Networks. In *AI and Machine Learning Impacts in Intelligent Supply Chain* (pp. 156–179). IGI Global. doi:10.4018/979-8-3693-1347-3.ch011

Wang, Y., Zhang, B., Ma, J., & Jin, Q. (2023). Artificial intelligence of things (AIoT) data acquisition based on graph neural networks: A systematical review. *Concurrency and Computation*, *35*(23), e7827. doi:10.1002/cpe.7827

Zainuddin, A. A., Zakirudin, M. A. Z., Zulkefli, A. S. S., Mazli, A. M., Wardi, M. A. S. M., Fazail, M. N., Razali, M. I. Z. M., & Yusof, M. H. (2024). Artificial Intelligence: A New Paradigm for Distributed Sensor Networks on the Internet of Things: A Review. *International Journal on Perceptive and Cognitive Computing*, *10*(1), 16–28. doi:10.31436/ijpcc.v10i1.414

Zhang, J., & Tao, D. (2020). Empowering things with intelligence: A survey of the progress, challenges, and opportunities in artificial intelligence of things. *IEEE Internet of Things Journal*, *8*(10), 7789–7817. doi:10.1109/JIOT.2020.3039359

Zhu, S., Ota, K., & Dong, M. (2022). Energy-efficient artificial intelligence of things with intelligent edge. *IEEE Internet of Things Journal*, *9*(10), 7525–7532. doi:10.1109/JIOT.2022.3143722

Chapter 10
Emerging Trends in Artificial Intelligence of Things With Machine Learning and Semantic Web Convergence

A. Revathi

VISTAS, India

S. Poonguzhali

ⓘ https://orcid.org/0000-0002-9118-9018

VISTAS, India

ABSTRACT

This chapter explores the dynamic convergence of artificial intelligence of things (AIoT), machine learning algorithms, and the semantic web. The fusion of AI and the internet of things (IoT) creates context-aware applications with transformative potential. Machine learning enhances AIoT capabilities, empowering systems to process IoT data effectively. Simultaneously, the semantic web, with its knowledge representation frameworks, augments adaptability. Delving into deep learning, reinforcement learning, and ensemble methods, the chapter elucidates how machine learning drives autonomous decision-making in AIoT. In the semantic web, the integration of machine learning introduces dynamic knowledge adaptation. Case studies in smart environments, predictive maintenance, and recommendation systems highlight practical implementations. The chapter addresses challenges, including scalability, security, and ethical implications. Emerging trends, interdisciplinary approaches, and societal impacts are explored, emphasizing the transformative potential of AIoT and semantic web integration.

I. INTRODUCTION

The dawn of the Artificial Intelligence of Things (AIoT) marks a pivotal moment in technological convergence. This paradigm brings together the realms of Artificial Intelligence (AI) and the Internet of

DOI: 10.4018/979-8-3693-1487-6.ch010

Things (IoT) to create a synergy that transcends traditional boundaries (Al-Amin et al., 2019; Kaundal et al., 2006). AI empowers machines with cognitive capabilities, endowing them with the capacity to analyze data, make informed decisions, and dynamically adapt to ever-changing environments (Das, Mallick, & Dutta, 2020). Concurrently, the IoT comprises a vast network of interconnected devices, sensors, and actuators, facilitating the seamless collection and exchange of data from the physical world (Hsieh et al., 2019). The fusion of AI and IoT in AIoT heralds a new era, characterized by intelligent, context-aware applications poised to revolutionize diverse industries (Krishnamoorthy et al., 2021). Applications range from healthcare, where AIoT systems can optimize patient care, to smart cities, where they can enhance urban planning and resource allocation. This paper embarks on a comprehensive exploration of the intricate relationship between machine learning algorithms, AIoT, and the Semantic Web. At its core, the study aims to elucidate how machine learning models amplify the capabilities of AIoT systems, enabling them to process and interpret data from IoT devices more effectively. Additionally, it investigates the symbiotic relationship between the Semantic Web and machine learning, demonstrating how knowledge representation frameworks benefit from such integration, fostering more adaptable and intelligent systems.

The overarching objective is to provide a nuanced understanding of how the integration of AIoT, machine learning, and the Semantic Web converges to create a robust framework for intelligent systems. By unraveling the intricacies of these intersections, this paper seeks to contribute valuable insights into the potential applications, challenges, and future trajectories of this dynamic field. A literature survey has been taken to analyse related works. Juihung Chang et al. (2022) replaced current medicine stations with a new IoT-based artificial intelligence system that can identify medicine bags using PP-OCR v2 and the most advanced OCR (optic character recognition) model. Healthcare staff who record data can be replaced by using OCR to identify drug bags. Furthermore, this study suggests a system's overseeing and tracking the system to keep an eye on the apparatus and offer a mobile application that allows patients to log their medication times and see the most recent state of their prescription bags in real time. The experiments' findings showed that the recognizing model performs admirably under many circumstances. Dmytro Chashyn et al. (2023) proposed model's main goal is to quickly rebuild destroyed and damaged structures. It accomplished through developing recovery strategies in post-conflict Ukraine and other nations. The strategy suggested utilizing artificial intelligence (AIoT) and building information modeling (BIM) to expedite, improve, and lower the cost of rehabilitation. By selecting retrofitting techniques, the author also obtained a decrease in energy usage and an extension of the building's lifespan. The efficiency of BIM and AIoT techniques made it possible to implement contemporary specifications to cut down on design time and expense, optimize design choices based on knowledge gained from creating new structures and buildings, and supply the information required to support a construction venture throughout its entire life cycle. Wen Tsai Sung et al. (2022) suggested an AIoT-based system which offered real-time flood analysis, enabling the authorities to keep an eye on locals living near mountainous regions and issue early warnings. With consideration for cost, time effectiveness, and safety measurement, this study focused on the flood monitoring system as a warning mechanism to effectively track the flood-prone slopes of mountains in real time. The suggested system design incorporates sensors into the microcontroller, and data is sent to the cloud server over the Internet via SIM900 and LoRa communication between the posts. Alerts are transmitted via SMS as well as the app, and all readings from sensors for every post are shown on the app.

II. ARTIFICIAL INTELLIGENCE OF THINGS (AIOT) AND SEMANTIC WEB: A CONVERGENCE

A. Definition and Concept of AIoT

The term "Artificial Intelligence of Things" encapsulates the fusion of AI technologies with the IoT ecosystem, leading to a transformative convergence of intelligence and connectivity (Patel & Sharaff, 2021). In AIoT, devices are endowed with localized intelligence, enabling them to process data autonomously, make real-time decisions, and communicate with other devices or central systems (Stephen et al., 2023). This symbiotic relationship allows devices not only to collect and transmit data but also to interpret and act upon it, fostering a paradigm shift in the capabilities of interconnected systems (Das et al., 2022). The essence of AIoT lies in its ability to create a harmonious interplay between artificial intelligence and the IoT. This convergence empowers devices to operate with heightened autonomy, extracting meaningful insights from data at the edge of the network (Patil & Kumar, 2021). As a result, AIoT systems excel in applications where real-time decision-making and contextual awareness are paramount, spanning domains from smart homes to industrial automation.

B. Semantic Web and Knowledge Representation

Central to the convergence of AIoT and the Semantic Web is the concept of knowledge representation. The Semantic Web, built on foundational technologies such as RDF (Resource Description Framework) and OWL (Web Ontology Language), provides a structured framework for organizing and linking information on the internet (Qiu et al., 2021). RDF serves as the backbone, allowing the expression of relationships between entities in the form of subject-predicate-object triples (Patil & Kumar, 2022). On the other hand, OWL enhances expressiveness, enabling the creation of intricate ontologies that capture complex relationships within a domain (Nettleton et al., 2019). These technologies facilitate the creation of a semantic layer, enabling machines not only to retrieve information but also to infer relationships and draw conclusions based on the semantic connections within the data (Das, Dutta, Das et al, 2020). The Semantic Web, through its knowledge representation mechanisms, establishes a foundation for reasoning and deriving insights from interconnected data sources (Malicdem & Fernandez, 2015).

C. Synergies between AIoT and Semantic Web

The convergence of AIoT and the Semantic Web represents a natural progression, combining the intelligence of AIoT with the semantic richness of the web. AIoT systems, empowered by machine learning models, can leverage semantic knowledge representations to enhance their understanding of the environment (Kim et al., 2017). This synergy equips AIoT applications with the capability to operate in more complex and dynamic contexts, offering advancements in areas such as smart environments, healthcare, and industrial automation (Jain & Ramesh, 2021). By unifying the capabilities of AIoT and the Semantic Web, applications gain the ability to derive higher-level insights from raw sensor data (Bashir et al., 2019). The Semantic Web provides the structural framework for organizing and interpreting information, while AIoT systems bring the power of machine learning to analyze this structured data (Kiratiratanapruk et al., 2022). This convergence empowers applications to not only react to events in real-time but also to understand the broader context in which they operate, ushering in a new era of intelligent and context-aware systems (Sethy et al., 2020).

III. MACHINE LEARNING ALGORITHMS IN AIOT

A. Deep Learning for Pattern Recognition

In the realm of AIoT, deep learning stands out as a potent tool for pattern recognition and feature extraction. Deep neural networks, particularly convolutional neural networks (CNNs) and recurrent neural networks (RNNs), excel in tasks that involve complex data patterns, making them well-suited for applications in image and speech recognition within AIoT systems (Verma & Dubey, 2021). CNNs, for instance, demonstrate remarkable capabilities in extracting hierarchical features from sensor data, enabling devices to discern intricate patterns that may signify specific events or anomalies (Bhartiya et al., 2022). The utilization of deep learning algorithms in AIoT extends beyond traditional data analytics. These algorithms empower devices to autonomously learn and adapt to evolving patterns, a critical capability in dynamic and unpredictable IoT environments (Sriwanna, 2022). As AIoT systems encounter new data, deep learning models continuously refine their understanding, enhancing the system's ability to recognize and respond to intricate patterns in real-time (Daud et al., 2013).

B. Reinforcement Learning for Autonomous Decision-Making

Reinforcement learning plays a pivotal role in enabling autonomous decision-making within AIoT systems. Markov Decision Processes (MDPs) provide a mathematical framework for modeling decision processes in dynamic environments, a common characteristic of IoT ecosystems (Rijal & Devkota, 2020). Algorithms such as Q-Learning and Policy Iteration enable devices to learn optimal strategies through interactions with their environment, allowing them to adapt and respond autonomously to changing conditions (Katsantonis et al., 2017). The adaptability of reinforcement learning is particularly valuable in AIoT scenarios where systems must make a series of decisions to achieve desired outcomes (Maneesha et al., 2021). This aligns with the inherent unpredictability of IoT environments, where devices and applications must dynamically adjust to varying conditions. By formulating problems as MDPs and applying reinforcement learning, AIoT systems gain the capability to learn effective strategies for tasks like resource allocation, energy optimization, and adaptive control (Chen et al., 2020).

C. Ensemble Methods for Robust Predictions

Ensemble methods, such as Random Forests and boosting algorithms like AdaBoost, play a crucial role in enhancing the predictive accuracy and stability of AIoT systems (Archana & Sahayadhas, 2018). These methods involve the combination of multiple models to improve decision-making by aggregating their outputs (Sengupta et al., 2022). Stacking and bagging techniques further exploit the diversity of models, making ensemble methods particularly effective in handling diverse data sources and mitigating noise (Rathore & Prasad, 2020). In AIoT scenarios, where data may be noisy or heterogeneous, ensemble methods prove invaluable for generating robust and accurate predictions (Hasan et al., 2019). The amalgamation of predictions from multiple models helps mitigate the impact of individual model weaknesses and enhances overall system reliability. This is especially critical in AIoT applications where data is sourced from diverse devices, each with its unique characteristics and challenges (Rehman & Atiq, 2022).

IV. MACHINE LEARNING INTEGRATION IN SEMANTIC WEB

The Semantic Web's foundation lies in RDF, a structure that facilitates the expression of information as subject-predicate-object triples (Sowmyalakshmi & Jayasankar, 2021). This structured representation allows for the effective organization of data, creating a semantic layer that enhances the interoperability and understanding of information (Limkar et al., 2020). OWL, an expressive language built on RDF, enables the creation of intricate ontologies, defining complex relationships between entities within a domain (Pallathadka et al., 2022). The representation of knowledge in the Semantic Web is pivotal for the system's ability to infer meaningful insights. RDF's simplicity and expressiveness provide a robust structure for defining relationships between entities, while OWL's capabilities elevate the Semantic Web's capacity to capture intricate ontological nuances (Du et al., 2008). This structured representation becomes the backbone for reasoning engines that perform logical inferences, allowing systems to deduce new knowledge from existing representations (Sharma & Kukreja, 2021).

The integration of machine learning introduces a dynamic dimension to knowledge representation within the Semantic Web. Ontology learning techniques enable systems to autonomously extract concepts and relationships from unstructured data (Vimala et al., 2021). Incremental learning mechanisms further enhance the adaptability of knowledge structures, allowing systems to update existing representations based on incoming data (Mathulaprangsan et al., 2020). Case-Based Reasoning (CBR) provides the ability to draw on past experiences, fostering context-aware decision-making within evolving knowledge domains (Singh & Singh, 2023). This marriage of machine learning and the Semantic Web introduces a new level of adaptability to knowledge representation. Ontology learning empowers systems to autonomously extract and refine knowledge from unstructured sources, enabling them to adapt to evolving domains (Liang et al., 2019). Incremental learning mechanisms ensure that knowledge structures remain up-to-date in the face of changing data landscapes. Additionally, Case-Based Reasoning enables systems to draw upon past experiences, providing valuable context for decision-making (Jiang et al., 2023).

Explainable AI techniques bridge the gap between complex models and human understanding (He et al., 2008). Contextual embeddings and knowledge graphs augment traditional machine learning approaches, providing a more nuanced understanding of data (Zhou et al., 2023). This integration enhances the Semantic Web's ability to infer context from diverse sources, enabling more precise and relevant information retrieval (Jain et al., 2022). Interpretability is crucial for building trust in AI models. Explainable AI techniques provide mechanisms for elucidating complex models, making them more accessible to human stakeholders (Daniya & Srinivasan, 2023). Contextual embeddings and knowledge graphs enhance traditional machine learning approaches, enabling systems to discern subtle nuances and context within data (Revathi & Poonguzhali, 2023). This heightened level of context-awareness empowers the Semantic Web to infer richer, more relevant insights from diverse information sources (Revathi & Poonguzhali, 2023).

V. CASE STUDIES: PRACTICAL IMPLEMENTATIONS OF AIOT AND SEMANTIC WEB INTEGRATION

A. Smart Environments: Enhancing Living Spaces

In the realm of smart environments, the integration of AIoT and the Semantic Web has demonstrated transformative effects. Consider an intelligent home equipped with interconnected devices. Machine learning algorithms, embedded in AIoT systems, can learn and predict user preferences, adjusting environmental parameters such as lighting and temperature. The Semantic Web, with its knowledge representation, enables these systems to understand the relationships between devices and user preferences, creating a truly adaptive and context-aware living space.

B. Predictive Maintenance in Industrial IoT

In the industrial Internet of Things (IoT), predictive maintenance is a critical application. Machine learning algorithms in AIoT systems analyze data from sensors embedded in machinery to predict potential failures before they occur. The Semantic Web aids in contextualizing this information by representing the relationships between different components of the industrial system. This integration allows for more accurate predictions, reduced downtime, and optimized maintenance schedules.

C. Recommendation Systems in E-Commerce

E-commerce platforms leverage AIoT and Semantic Web integration to enhance user experience. Machine learning algorithms analyze user behavior and preferences, generating personalized recommendations. The Semantic Web, through ontologies representing product categories and user preferences, refines these recommendations by understanding the nuanced relationships between products. This results in more accurate and contextually relevant suggestions, improving customer satisfaction and engagement.

VI. CHALLENGES AND CONSIDERATIONS IN AIOT AND SEMANTIC WEB INTEGRATION

A. Scalability and Resource Constraints

One of the primary challenges in the integration of AIoT and the Semantic Web is scalability. As the number of interconnected devices increases, AIoT systems must efficiently manage and process vast amounts of data. Similarly, the Semantic Web, with its knowledge representation, faces scalability concerns as ontologies grow in complexity and size. Addressing these challenges requires the development of scalable algorithms and architectures capable of handling the intricacies of large-scale data processing and semantic reasoning.

B. Security and Privacy Concerns

Ensuring the security and privacy of data is a paramount consideration in AIoT and Semantic Web integration. With interconnected devices transmitting sensitive information, securing communication channels and implementing robust authentication mechanisms become critical. The Semantic Web, relying on shared ontologies, must also address privacy concerns related to the representation of personal information. Techniques such as differential privacy and federated learning emerge as essential tools in preserving individual privacy while extracting meaningful insights from distributed data.

C. Ethical Implications of Autonomous Decision-Making

Empowering AIoT systems with autonomous decision-making capabilities introduces ethical considerations. Transparent and fair algorithmic outcomes become crucial as these systems interact autonomously with the physical world. Addressing biases in data collection and decision-making processes is imperative to prevent the reinforcement of existing disparities. Establishing ethical guidelines and governance frameworks for AIoT systems, along with mechanisms for human oversight, becomes essential in upholding ethical standards.

VII. FUTURE DIRECTIONS AND RESEARCH OPPORTUNITIES

A. Emerging Trends in AIoT and Semantic Web Integration

The integration of AIoT and the Semantic Web is a rapidly evolving field, and several emerging trends hold promise for further advancing the capabilities of intelligent systems. Edge computing, by bringing computation closer to the data source, enables real-time processing and decision-making, reducing latency and bandwidth requirements. Federated learning, as a decentralized approach to machine learning, allows models to be trained across multiple devices or servers while preserving data privacy. Hybrid AI models, combining symbolic reasoning with machine learning techniques, offer a powerful framework for context-aware and knowledge-driven applications. Exploring these emerging trends and their synergies with AIoT and Semantic Web technologies presents exciting avenues for future research and innovation.

B. Interdisciplinary Approaches and Cross-Domain Applications

The convergence of AIoT and the Semantic Web transcends traditional disciplinary boundaries, offering opportunities for interdisciplinary collaboration. Researchers from diverse fields, including computer science, engineering, cognitive science, and social sciences, can collaborate to address complex challenges and unlock new possibilities. Cross-domain applications of AIoT and Semantic Web technologies have the potential to revolutionize various industries. For instance, in healthcare, AIoT systems can enable personalized, context-aware treatment plans, while in smart cities, they can optimize resource allocation and improve urban planning. By fostering interdisciplinary collaboration and exploring cross-domain applications, researchers can drive innovation and create transformative solutions with far-reaching societal impact.

C. Implications for Industry and Societal Impact

The widespread adoption of AIoT and Semantic Web technologies has the potential to revolutionize industries and positively impact society at large. In healthcare, personalized AIoT systems can lead to enhanced patient care, optimized treatment plans, and early intervention. In the realm of manufacturing and Industry 4.0 initiatives, AIoT technologies can result in increased operational efficiency, reduced downtime, and improved quality control. Smart cities stand to benefit from AIoT solutions by optimizing resource allocation, fostering sustainable urban planning, and enhancing citizen services. These advancements hold the potential to elevate overall quality of life, drive economic growth, and address critical societal challenges. Recognizing the transformative potential of AIoT and Semantic Web technologies, industry stakeholders and policymakers must prioritize investment in research and development to realize their full impact.

VIII. CONCLUSION

This extended abstract has provided a comprehensive exploration of the integration of machine learning algorithms within the realms of AIoT and the Semantic Web. It has demonstrated how this synthesis empowers applications with the ability to learn, reason, and adapt, ultimately leading to more sophisticated and effective solutions in a wide range of domains. The challenges and opportunities outlined highlight the dynamic nature of this convergence and the potential for groundbreaking advancements in intelligent systems. The convergence of AIoT and the Semantic Web represents a paradigm shift in intelligent systems, opening up new possibilities for context-aware, adaptable applications. The enhanced capabilities of AIoT systems have the potential to revolutionize industries, improve quality of life, and address pressing societal challenges. By leveraging the synergies between AIoT, machine learning, and the Semantic Web, researchers and practitioners can pioneer innovative solutions with far-reaching implications. As the field of AIoT and Semantic Web integration continues to evolve, it is imperative to remain at the forefront of research and innovation. Addressing the challenges outlined, exploring emerging trends, and nurturing interdisciplinary collaboration will be pivotal in unlocking the full potential of this dynamic convergence. By pushing the boundaries of knowledge and technology, researchers can usher in a new era of intelligent systems that positively impact society, industry, and individual well-being.

REFERENCES

Al-Amin, M., Karim, D. Z., & Bushra, T. A. (2019, December). Prediction of rice disease from leaves using deep convolution neural network towards a digital agricultural system. In *2019 22nd International Conference on Computer and Information Technology (ICCIT)* (pp. 1-5). IEEE. 10.1109/IC-CIT48885.2019.9038229

Archana, K. S., & Sahayadhas, A. (2018). Automatic rice leaf disease segmentation using image processing techniques. *Int. J. Eng. Technol, 7*(3.27), 182-185.

Bashir, K., Rehman, M., & Bari, M. (2019). Detection and classification of rice diseases: An automated approach using textural features. *Mehran University Research Journal of Engineering & Technology*, *38*(1), 239–250. doi:10.22581/muet1982.1901.20

Bhartiya, V. P., Janghel, R. R., & Rathore, Y. K. (2022, March). Rice Leaf Disease Prediction Using Machine Learning. In *2022 Second International Conference on Power, Control and Computing Technologies (ICPC2T)* (pp. 1-5). IEEE. 10.1109/ICPC2T53885.2022.9776692

Chang, J., Ong, H., Wang, T., & Chen, H. H. (2022). A Fully Automated Intelligent Medicine Dispensary System Based on AIoT. *IEEE Internet of Things Journal*, *9*(23), 23954–23966. doi:10.1109/JIOT.2022.3188552

Chashyn, D., Khurudzhi, Y., & Daukšys, M. (2023). *Integration of Building Information Modeling and Artificial Intelligence of Things in Post-War Renovation and Retrofitting of Historical Buildings*. Academic Press.

Chen, J., Zhang, D., Nanehkaran, Y. A., & Li, D. (2020). Detection of rice plant diseases based on deep transfer learning. *Journal of the Science of Food and Agriculture*, *100*(7), 3246–3256. doi:10.1002/jsfa.10365 PMID:32124447

Daniya, T., & Srinivasan, V. (2023). Shuffled shepherd social optimization based deep learning for rice leaf disease classification and severity percentage prediction. *Concurrency and Computation*, *35*(4), e7523. doi:10.1002/cpe.7523

Das, A., Dutta, R., Das, S., & Sengupta, S. (2020). Feature selection using graph-based clustering for rice disease prediction. *Computational Intelligence in Pattern Recognition Proceedings of CIPR*, *2019*, 589–598.

Das, A., Mallick, C., & Dutta, S. (2020). Deep learning-based automated feature engineering for rice leaf disease prediction. *Computational Intelligence in Pattern Recognition Proceedings of CIPR*, *2020*, 133–141.

Das, S., Sengupta, S., & Das, P. (2022). Feature Selection Using Louvain Clustering Algorithm for Rice Disease Prediction. *Computational Intelligence in Pattern Recognition Proceedings of CIPR*, *2021*, 99–108.

Daud, S. M., Jozani, H. J., & Arab, F. (2013). A review on predicting outbreak of tungro disease in rice fields based on epidemiological and biophysical factors. *International Journal of Innovation, Management and Technology*, *4*(4), 447–450. doi:10.7763/IJIMT.2013.V4.439

Du, H., Wang, J., Hu, Z., Yao, X., & Zhang, X. (2008). Prediction of fungicidal activities of rice blast disease based on least-squares support vector machines and project pursuit regression. *Journal of Agricultural and Food Chemistry*, *56*(22), 10785–10792. doi:10.1021/jf8022194 PMID:18950187

Hasan, M. J., Mahbub, S., Alom, M. S., & Nasim, M. A. (2019, May). Rice disease identification and classification by integrating support vector machine with deep convolutional neural network. In *2019 1st international conference on advances in science, engineering and robotics technology (ICASERT)* (pp. 1-6). IEEE. 10.1109/ICASERT.2019.8934568

He, F., Zhang, Y., Chen, H., Zhang, Z., & Peng, Y. L. (2008). The prediction of protein-protein interaction networks in rice blast fungus. *BMC Genomics*, *9*(1), 1–12. doi:10.1186/1471-2164-9-519 PMID:18976500

Hsieh, J. Y., Huang, W., Yang, H. T., Lin, C. C., Fan, Y. C., & Chen, H. (2019). *Building the rice blast disease prediction model based on machine learning and neural networks*. EasyChair.

Jain, S., & Ramesh, D. (2021, July). AI based hybrid CNN-LSTM model for crop disease prediction: An ML advent for rice crop. In *2021 12th International Conference on Computing Communication and Networking Technologies (ICCCNT)* (pp. 1-7). IEEE.

Jain, S., Sahni, R., Khargonkar, T., Gupta, H., Verma, O. P., Sharma, T. K., Bhardwaj, T., Agarwal, S., & Kim, H. (2022). Automatic rice disease detection and assistance framework using deep learning and a Chatbot. *Electronics (Basel)*, *11*(14), 2110. doi:10.3390/electronics11142110

Jiang, Z., Gu, J., Liu, M., & Pan, D. Z. (2023, July). Delving into effective gradient matching for dataset condensation. In *2023 IEEE International Conference on Omni-layer Intelligent Systems (COINS)* (pp. 1-6). IEEE. 10.1109/COINS57856.2023.10189244

Katsantonis, D., Kadoglidou, K., Dramalis, C., & Puigdollers, P. (2017). Rice blast forecasting models and their practical value: A review. *Phytopathologia Mediterranea*, ●●●, 187–216.

Kaundal, R., Kapoor, A. S., & Raghava, G. P. (2006). Machine learning techniques in disease forecasting: A case study on rice blast prediction. *BMC Bioinformatics*, *7*(1), 1–16. doi:10.1186/1471-2105-7-485 PMID:17083731

Kim, Y., Roh, J. H., & Kim, H. Y. (2017). Early forecasting of rice blast disease using long short-term memory recurrent neural networks. *Sustainability (Basel)*, *10*(1), 34. doi:10.3390/su10010034

Kiratiratanapruk, K., Temniranrat, P., Sinthupinyo, W., Marukatat, S., & Patarapuwadol, S. (2022). Automatic Detection of Rice Disease in Images of Various Leaf Sizes. *arXiv preprint arXiv:2206.07344*.

Krishnamoorthy, N., Prasad, L. N., Kumar, C. P., Subedi, B., Abraha, H. B., & Sathishkumar, V. E. (2021). Rice leaf diseases prediction using deep neural networks with transfer learning. *Environmental Research*, *198*, 111275. doi:10.1016/j.envres.2021.111275 PMID:33989629

Liang, W. J., Zhang, H., Zhang, G. F., & Cao, H. X. (2019). Rice blast disease recognition using a deep convolutional neural network. *Scientific Reports*, *9*(1), 2869. doi:10.1038/s41598-019-38966-0 PMID:30814523

Limkar, S., Kulkarni, S., Chinchmalatpure, P., Sharma, D., Desai, M., Angadi, S., & Jadhav, P. (2020). Classification and prediction of rice crop diseases using CNN and PNN. In *Intelligent Data Engineering and Analytics: Frontiers in Intelligent Computing: Theory and Applications (FICTA 2020)* (Vol. 2, pp. 31–40). Springer Singapore.

Malicdem, A. R., & Fernandez, P. L. (2015). Rice blast disease forecasting for northern Philippines. *WSEAS Trans. Inf. Sci. Appl*, *12*, 120–129.

Maneesha, A., Suresh, C., & Kiranmayee, B. V. (2021). Prediction of rice plant diseases based on soil and weather conditions. In *Proceedings of International Conference on Advances in Computer Engineering and Communication Systems: ICACECS 2020* (pp. 155-165). Springer Singapore. 10.1007/978-981-15-9293-5_14

Mathulaprangsan, S., Lanthong, K., Jetpipattanapong, D., Sateanpattanakul, S., & Patarapuwadol, S. (2020, March). Rice diseases recognition using effective deep learning models. In *2020 Joint International Conference on Digital Arts, Media and Technology with ECTI Northern Section Conference on Electrical, Electronics, Computer and Telecommunications Engineering (ECTI DAMT & NCON)* (pp. 386-389). IEEE. 10.1109/ECTIDAMTNCON48261.2020.9090709

Nettleton, D. F., Katsantonis, D., Kalaitzidis, A., Sarafijanovic-Djukic, N., Puigdollers, P., & Confalonieri, R. (2019). Predicting rice blast disease: Machine learning versus process-based models. *BMC Bioinformatics*, *20*(1), 1–16. doi:10.1186/s12859-019-3065-1 PMID:31640541

Pallathadka, H., Ravipati, P., Sajja, G. S., Phasinam, K., Kassanuk, T., Sanchez, D. T., & Prabhu, P. (2022). Application of machine learning techniques in rice leaf disease detection. *Materials Today: Proceedings*, *51*, 2277–2280. doi:10.1016/j.matpr.2021.11.398

Patel, B., & Sharaff, A. (2021). Rice crop disease prediction using machine learning technique. *International Journal of Agricultural and Environmental Information Systems*, *12*(4), 1–15. doi:10.4018/IJAEIS.20211001.oa5

Patil, R. R., & Kumar, S. (2021). Predicting rice diseases across diverse agro-meteorological conditions using an artificial intelligence approach. *PeerJ. Computer Science*, *7*, e687. doi:10.7717/peerj-cs.687 PMID:34604518

Patil, R. R., & Kumar, S. (2022). Rice-fusion: A multimodality data fusion framework for rice disease diagnosis. *IEEE Access : Practical Innovations, Open Solutions*, *10*, 5207–5222. doi:10.1109/ACCESS.2022.3140815

Qiu, J., Lu, X., Wang, X., & Hu, X. (2021, March). Research on rice disease identification model based on migration learning in VGG network. *IOP Conference Series. Earth and Environmental Science*, *680*(1), 012087. doi:10.1088/1755-1315/680/1/012087

Rathore, N. P. S., & Prasad, L. (2020). Automatic rice plant disease recognition and identification using convolutional neural network. *Journal of Critical Reviews, 7*(15), 6076-6086.

Rehman, H. U., & Atiq, R. (2022). A disease predictive model based on epidemiological factors for the management of bacterial leaf blight of rice. *Brazilian Journal of Biology*, 84. PMID:35293481

Revathi, A., & Poonguzhali, S. (2023). IoT and Machine Learning Algorithm in Smart Agriculture. In *Futuristic Communication and Network Technologies: Select Proceedings of VICFCNT 2021, Volume 1* (pp. 355-369). Singapore: Springer Nature Singapore. 10.1007/978-981-19-8338-2_29

Revathi, A., & Poonguzhali, S. (2023). The Role of AIoT-Based Automation Systems Using UAVs in Smart Agriculture. In Revolutionizing Industrial Automation Through the Convergence of Artificial Intelligence and the Internet of Things (pp. 100-117). IGI Global.

Rijal, S., & Devkota, Y. (2020). A review on various management method of rice blast disease. *Malaysian Journal of Sustainable Agriculture*, *4*(1), 14–18.

Sengupta, S., Dutta, A., Abdelmohsen, S. A., Alyousef, H. A., & Rahimi-Gorji, M. (2022). Development of a Rice Plant Disease Classification Model in Big Data Environment. *Bioengineering (Basel, Switzerland)*, *9*(12), 758. doi:10.3390/bioengineering9120758 PMID:36550964

Sethy, P. K., Barpanda, N. K., Rath, A. K., & Behera, S. K. (2020). Nitrogen deficiency prediction of rice crop based on convolutional neural network. *Journal of Ambient Intelligence and Humanized Computing*, *11*(11), 5703–5711. doi:10.1007/s12652-020-01938-8

Sharma, R., & Kukreja, V. (2021, March). Rice diseases detection using convolutional neural networks: a survey. In *2021 International Conference on Advance Computing and Innovative Technologies in Engineering (ICACITE)* (pp. 995-1001). IEEE. 10.1109/ICACITE51222.2021.9404620

Singh, G., & Singh, R. (2023, April). Rice Leaf Disease Prediction: A Survey. In *2023 International Conference on Inventive Computation Technologies (ICICT)* (pp. 582-587). IEEE. 10.1109/ICICT57646.2023.10134267

Sowmyalakshmi, R., & Jayasankar, T., Pillai, V. A., Subramaniyan, K., Pustokhina, I. V., Pustokhin, D. A., & Shankar, K. (2021). An optimal classification model for rice plant disease detection. *Computers, Materials & Continua*, *68*, 1751–1767. doi:10.32604/cmc.2021.016825

Sriwanna, K. (2022). Weather-based rice blast disease forecasting. *Computers and Electronics in Agriculture*, *193*, 106685. doi:10.1016/j.compag.2022.106685

Stephen, A., Punitha, A., & Chandrasekar, A. (2023). Optimal deep generative adversarial network and convolutional neural network for rice leaf disease prediction. *The Visual Computer*, 1–18.

Sung, W. T., Devi, I. V., & Hsiao, S. J. (2022). Early warning of impending flash flood based on AIoT. *EURASIP Journal on Wireless Communications and Networking*, *2022*(1), 15. doi:10.1186/s13638-022-02096-5

Verma, T., & Dubey, S. (2021). Prediction of diseased rice plant using video processing and LSTM-simple recurrent neural network with comparative study. *Multimedia Tools and Applications*, *80*(19), 29267–29298. doi:10.1007/s11042-021-10889-x

Vimala, S., Gladiss Merlin, N. R., Ramanathan, L., & Cristin, R. (2021). Optimal routing and deep regression neural network for rice leaf disease prediction in IoT. *International Journal of Computational Methods*, *18*(07), 2150014. doi:10.1142/S0219876221500146

Zhou, C., Zhong, Y., Zhou, S., Song, J., & Xiang, W. (2023). Rice leaf disease identification by residual-distilled transformer. *Engineering Applications of Artificial Intelligence*, *121*, 106020. doi:10.1016/j.engappai.2023.106020

Chapter 11
Cloud Computing Adoption for Small and Medium Enterprises in Mechanical Engineering

K. C. Sekhar
Department of Mechanical Engineering, Lendi Institute of Engineering and Technology, Vizianagaram, India

D. Premnath
Department of Mechanical Engineering, SRM Institute of Science and Technology, Kattankulathur, India

L. Ranganathan
Department of Mechanical Engineering, Cambridge Institute of Technology, Ranchi, India

B. Yuvasri
Department of Computer Science and Engineering, R.M.K. College of Engineering and Technology, Puduvoyal, India

S. Bathrinath
iD https://orcid.org/0000-0002-5502-6203
Department of Mechanical Engineering, Kalasalingam Academy of Research and Education, Krishnankoil, India

Sampath Boopathi
iD https://orcid.org/0000-0002-2065-6539
Department of Mechanical Engineering, Muthayammal Engineering College, Namakkal, India

ABSTRACT

This chapter delves into the adoption of cloud computing in small and medium-sized enterprises (SMEs) in mechanical engineering, highlighting its transformative potential. It discusses the benefits of cloud infrastructure, such as improved operational efficiency and innovation, but also addresses security and privacy challenges. The chapter provides strategies to mitigate these risks and emphasizes the importance of tailoring cloud solutions to meet the unique needs of SMEs. It also discusses the future of cloud technology, focusing on emerging trends and innovations. It also examines regulatory compliance and adherence strategies for a secure and compliant cloud integration journey. The chapter concludes with a comprehensive roadmap for SMEs in mechanical engineering, offering practical strategies, lessons learned, and a forward-looking perspective on the ever-evolving intersection of cloud computing and mechanical engineering.

DOI: 10.4018/979-8-3693-1487-6.ch011

INTRODUCTION

Cloud computing has emerged as a transformative force across various industries, and its impact on mechanical engineering is profound. In the dynamic landscape of today's technological advancements, small and medium enterprises (SMEs) in the field of mechanical engineering are increasingly turning to cloud solutions to drive innovation, enhance efficiency, and remain competitive in a global market. This introduction provides a glimpse into the pivotal role that cloud computing plays in reshaping the traditional paradigms of how mechanical engineering tasks are executed and managed (Tao et al., 2011). Mechanical engineering, known for its intricate design processes, simulation models, and data-intensive tasks, faces the imperative of adapting to the digital era. Cloud computing offers a paradigm shift by providing a scalable and flexible infrastructure that enables engineers to access computational resources, software applications, and storage on-demand. This marks a departure from the traditional reliance on in-house servers and localized computing power, offering a more agile and cost-effective approach to handling the computational demands inherent in mechanical engineering projects (Wang et al., 2015).

The adoption of cloud computing is particularly relevant for SMEs in the mechanical engineering sector. Often constrained by limited resources, these enterprises stand to benefit immensely from the scalability and affordability that cloud solutions provide. Whether it's streamlining design processes, optimizing simulations, or collaborating on projects, cloud computing levels the playing field, empowering SMEs to access cutting-edge technologies and computational capabilities that were once exclusive to larger enterprises. Cloud infrastructure opens up a myriad of advantages and opportunities for SMEs in mechanical engineering. The ability to scale resources based on project requirements allows for cost-efficient operations, eliminating the need for large upfront investments in hardware (Taylor et al., 2014). Moreover, the cloud fosters collaboration by providing a centralized platform for teams to work on projects in real-time, irrespective of geographical locations. This collaborative environment not only accelerates project timelines but also enhances innovation through shared insights and expertise. The integration of cloud computing in mechanical engineering is not merely a matter of convenience; it represents a conduit for leveraging the latest technological advancements. From utilizing advanced simulation tools to incorporating artificial intelligence in design processes, cloud platforms enable SMEs to stay at the forefront of technological innovation without the burden of continuous infrastructure upgrades. The scalability inherent in cloud solutions ensures that as project demands fluctuate, the computational resources can seamlessly adjust to meet these requirements, ensuring optimal performance and resource utilization (Li et al., 2019).

This study explores the use of cloud computing in mechanical engineering, focusing on factors influencing adoption, the opportunities of cloud infrastructure, and security and privacy considerations. It provides real-world case studies and insights for SMEs looking to integrate into the cloud (Nanda et al., 2024). The goal is to provide a comprehensive understanding of how cloud computing is reshaping the landscape of mechanical engineering, offering strategic advantages for growth and innovation. Cloud computing offers a scalable and flexible computing environment, allowing engineers to access computational resources, software applications, and storage on-demand through the internet. This innovative approach addresses design processes, simulations, and data-intensive tasks in the field (Arita et al., 2012).

Relevance for Small and Medium Enterprises (SMEs)

Cloud computing is crucial for Small and Medium Enterprises (SMEs) in mechanical engineering due to resource constraints. Cloud solutions offer a cost-effective alternative to traditional on-premises systems, allowing SMEs to scale computing resources based on project requirements. This flexibility ensures optimal resource utilization and eliminates the need for significant upfront capital investments, democratizing access to high-performance computing resources. This makes cloud computing a valuable solution for SMEs in the field (Tamura et al., 2013). Potential Benefits for SMEs in Mechanical Engineering are explained below.

The cloud computing is not merely a technological evolution; it is a strategic enabler for SMEs in the field of mechanical engineering (Agrawal, Shashibhushan, et al., 2023; Hema et al., 2023). By offering cost efficiency, scalability, global collaboration, and access to advanced technologies, cloud computing empowers SMEs to innovate, compete, and thrive in an increasingly dynamic and digitally-driven industry landscape.

- Cloud computing allows SMEs to avoid the substantial initial costs associated with purchasing and maintaining on-premises servers. The pay-as-you-go model ensures that SMEs only pay for the resources they consume, making it a cost-effective solution.
- The ability to scale computing resources up or down based on project requirements is a significant advantage for SMEs. This adaptability ensures that SMEs can handle varying workloads without being burdened by excess capacity during periods of lower demand.
- Cloud computing facilitates collaboration on a global scale. Engineers and teams can work on projects in real-time, irrespective of their geographical locations. This not only enhances collaboration but also accelerates project timelines.
- Cloud platforms provide SMEs with access to cutting-edge technologies without the need for continuous infrastructure upgrades. Whether it's advanced simulation tools or incorporating artificial intelligence in design processes, cloud computing enables SMEs to stay technologically competitive.

FACTORS INFLUENCING CLOUD ADOPTION IN SMES:

The decision-making process for Small and Medium Enterprises (SMEs) considering cloud adoption is influenced by a multitude of factors, each playing a crucial role in shaping the path toward embracing cloud solutions (Tamura et al., 2013).

Cost Considerations

- **Upfront Investment vs. Ongoing Costs:** SMEs evaluate the balance between the initial investment required for on-premises infrastructure versus the ongoing operational costs associated with cloud services. Cloud adoption often eliminates the need for substantial upfront capital expenditures (Babu et al., 2022; Mohanty et al., 2023; Ravisankar et al., 2023).
- **Scalability and Pay-as-You-Go Model:** The pay-as-you-go pricing model of cloud services allows SMEs to scale resources based on demand, offering cost flexibility and efficiency.

Scalability and Flexibility

Adaptability to Workload Fluctuations: SMEs assess how well cloud solutions can adapt to varying workloads. The ability to scale resources up or down based on project requirements is crucial for maintaining efficiency and avoiding underutilization or over-provisioning (Cai et al., 2016).

Technical Compatibility

Integration with Existing Systems: Compatibility with existing systems and applications is a significant consideration. SMEs weigh the ease of integrating cloud services with their current infrastructure to ensure a smooth transition without disrupting ongoing operations.

Data Security and Privacy

Security Measures and Compliance: Ensuring the security of sensitive data is paramount. SMEs evaluate the security measures offered by cloud service providers, compliance with industry regulations, and the reliability of data protection protocols to mitigate risks associated with cloud adoption.

Reliability and Performance

Service Level Agreements (SLAs): The reliability and performance commitments outlined in SLAs are critical for SMEs. Factors such as uptime guarantees, data availability, and disaster recovery capabilities influence the decision-making process to ensure a dependable cloud service.

Staff Skillsets and Training

Technical Expertise: SMEs assess whether their existing staff possesses the necessary skills to manage and optimize cloud resources. The availability of training programs and the ease of acquiring cloud-related skills become key factors in determining the feasibility of cloud adoption.

Regulatory Compliance

Industry-Specific Regulations: SMEs operating in regulated industries evaluate whether cloud solutions align with industry-specific regulations. Ensuring compliance with data protection laws and standards is crucial for avoiding legal complications (Hui et al., 2019).

SMEs may face concerns about relinquishing control over their data and operations to a third-party cloud provider, which can be addressed by evaluating the level of control retained. However, cloud solutions can streamline operations and enhance collaboration, with centralized data storage, real-time collaboration tools, and improved accessibility significantly impacting operational efficiency. The reputation and quality of customer support from a cloud service provider are crucial factors for SMEs to consider in order to ensure reliability and prompt resolution of issues.

The decision-making process for SMEs considering cloud adoption involves evaluating factors like cost, technical compatibility, security, regulatory compliance, and operational efficiency. Balancing these factors is crucial for SMEs to fully utilize cloud computing while addressing their unique business needs.

Figure 1. Factors in cloud adoption in SME for mechanical engineering

Factors in Cloud Adoption

In the realm of cloud adoption, SMEs navigate a complex landscape where strategic decisions hinge on a careful examination of factors such as cost considerations, scalability options, and the integration of cutting-edge technological advancements. This exploration sheds light on how these factors influence the decision-making process for SMEs looking to harness the transformative power of cloud computing (Cai et al., 2016; Hui et al., 2019). The figure 1 illustrates the factors influencing the adoption of cloud technology in small and medium-sized enterprises (SMEs) in the field of mechanical engineering.

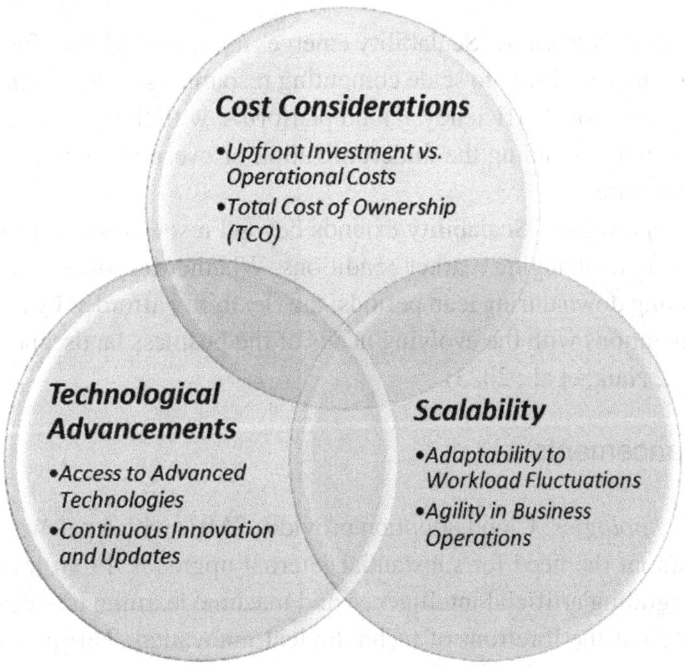

Cost Considerations

Upfront Investment vs. Operational Costs: SMEs scrutinize the financial implications of cloud adoption, weighing the initial upfront investment required for on-premises infrastructure against the ongoing operational costs associated with cloud services. The pay-as-you-go model, prevalent in most cloud service offerings, allows SMEs to allocate resources efficiently, aligning expenses with actual usage. This not only minimizes capital expenditures but also provides a predictable cost structure, aiding budgetary planning (Boopathi et al., 2018; Malathi et al., 2024).

Total Cost of Ownership (TCO): Beyond direct costs, SMEs delve into the total cost of ownership, factoring in expenses related to maintenance, upgrades, and potential downtime associated with on-premises solutions. Cloud services, with their inherent scalability and managed infrastructure, often present a more cost-effective alternative, particularly for SMEs with constrained budgets.

Scalability

Adaptability to Workload Fluctuations: Scalability emerges as a pivotal factor for SMEs seeking to optimize resource utilization. The ability to scale computing resources seamlessly in response to fluctuating workloads ensures operational efficiency. Cloud platforms, with their elasticity, empower SMEs to dynamically adjust resources, avoiding the underutilization or overprovisioning commonly associated with traditional infrastructure.

Agility in Business Operations: Scalability extends beyond resource allocation; it reflects the agility SMEs gain in adapting to changing market conditions. Whether responding to a sudden increase in project demands or scaling down during lean periods, the flexibility afforded by cloud solutions enables SMEs to align their operations with the evolving needs of the business landscape (Vanitha et al., 2023; Venkateswaran, Vidhya, Naik, et al., 2023).

Technological Advancements

Access to Advanced Technologies: Cloud adoption provides SMEs with a gateway to advanced technological capabilities without the need for substantial internal upgrades. From leveraging sophisticated simulation tools to integrating artificial intelligence and machine learning into design processes, cloud platforms position SMEs at the forefront of technological innovation. This access not only enhances competitiveness but also future-proofs SMEs against technological obsolescence.

Continuous Innovation and Updates: Cloud service providers routinely introduce updates and innovations to their platforms. SMEs benefit from this continuous cycle of improvement, gaining access to the latest features and security enhancements without the burden of managing the upgrade process internally. This ensures that SMEs remain technologically current and can readily adopt emerging trends (Mohanty et al., 2023).

The decision-making process for SMEs in cloud adoption is complex, involving factors like cost, scalability, and technological advancements. Strategic alignment of these factors is crucial for unlocking the full potential of cloud computing, driving operational efficiency, fostering innovation, and positioning organizations for sustained growth in a rapidly evolving business environment.

OPPORTUNITIES UNLEASHED BY CLOUD INFRASTRUCTURE:

Examining the Transformative Opportunities

Cloud infrastructure stands as a powerful catalyst for change, offering transformative opportunities that redefine how organizations operate, innovate, and compete in the digital landscape. This exploration delves into the myriad opportunities unleashed by cloud infrastructure, focusing on its capacity to enhance operational efficiency and drive innovation across diverse sectors (Sacco, 2020).

Operational Efficiency

- **Resource Optimization:** Cloud infrastructure enables organizations to optimize resource allocation dynamically. With the ability to scale computing resources up or down based on demand, organizations can ensure optimal utilization, eliminating the inefficiencies associated with maintaining excess capacity (Naveeenkumar et al., 2024; Paul et al., 2024).

- **Cost Reduction:** The pay-as-you-go model inherent in cloud services allows organizations to align costs directly with usage. This flexibility minimizes upfront investments in hardware and reduces operational expenses associated with maintaining on-premises infrastructure. The result is a cost-efficient operational model that particularly benefits small and medium enterprises (SMEs) with budget constraints.
- **Streamlined Processes:** Cloud services facilitate the automation of processes, streamlining workflows and reducing manual intervention. This operational agility enhances efficiency by accelerating time-to-market, responding swiftly to changing demands, and optimizing overall business processes.

Innovation Acceleration

- **Access to Cutting-Edge Technologies:** Cloud infrastructure provides organizations with on-demand access to a diverse array of cutting-edge technologies. From advanced analytics and artificial intelligence to machine learning and Internet of Things (IoT) capabilities, organizations can leverage these tools to drive innovation in product development, design, and customer engagement (Williams & Griffin, 2019).
- **Collaborative Ecosystems:** Cloud platforms foster collaboration by providing a centralized environment for teams to work on projects in real-time. This collaborative ecosystem transcends geographical boundaries, allowing diverse teams to contribute seamlessly. This not only enhances creativity but also accelerates the pace of innovation through shared insights and expertise (Boopathi, 2022; Boopathi & Sivakumar, 2012; Sampath et al., 2021).
- **Agile Development and Testing:** Cloud infrastructure supports agile development methodologies by providing scalable and flexible testing environments. This agility in development and testing processes allows organizations to iterate rapidly, experiment with new ideas, and bring innovative solutions to market more efficiently.

Scalable Growth

- **Global Expansion:** Cloud infrastructure facilitates global expansion without the need for significant upfront investments in new data centers. Organizations can scale their operations globally, tapping into new markets and opportunities while maintaining a consistent and reliable IT infrastructure (Williams & Griffin, 2019).
- **Elasticity for Peak Demands:** The scalability of cloud services enables organizations to handle peak demands effortlessly. Whether dealing with seasonal spikes or sudden increases in user activity, the elastic nature of the cloud allows organizations to scale up or down as needed, ensuring uninterrupted service delivery.

Cloud infrastructure offers numerous opportunities beyond technological advancements, enhancing operational efficiency and fostering innovation. It enables organizations to adapt, compete, and thrive in an ever-evolving business landscape. Strategic adoption of cloud infrastructure optimizes current operations, preparing organizations for sustained growth and agility in future challenges (Rahamathunnisa, Sudhakar, et al., 2023; Satav et al., 2023; Srinivas et al., 2023).

Illustrating Successful Utilization of Cloud Resources

Cloud infrastructure has become a game-changer in the field of mechanical engineering, offering a plethora of opportunities to enhance efficiency, innovation, and collaboration. By examining real-world case studies, we can gain insights into how organizations in mechanical engineering have successfully harnessed cloud resources to address challenges and unlock new possibilities- (Abraham et al., 2020).

Optimizing Simulation Workloads

- *Challenge:* Traditional on-premises infrastructure often struggles to handle the computational demands of complex simulations in mechanical engineering (Chen et al., 2014).
- *Solution:* A leading engineering firm migrated its simulation workloads to the cloud, leveraging scalable computing resources.
- *Outcome:* The firm achieved significant reductions in simulation time, enabling engineers to explore more design iterations within tight project timelines. The pay-as-you-go model also resulted in cost savings by avoiding the need for extensive in-house hardware.

Collaborative Design in a Global Context

- *Challenge:* Coordinating design efforts among geographically dispersed teams can be challenging and resource-intensive (Choobineh et al., 2022).
- *Solution:* An international manufacturing company adopted cloud-based collaboration tools and storage solutions.
- *Outcome:* Design teams across different continents could seamlessly collaborate in real-time on shared cloud platforms. This not only accelerated the design process but also ensured that all stakeholders had access to the latest design revisions, fostering a more cohesive and efficient workflow.

Agile Product Development

- *Challenge:* Traditional development cycles can be rigid, hindering the ability to respond quickly to market demands (Choobineh et al., 2022).
- *Solution:* A mid-sized engineering firm embraced cloud-based DevOps practices, integrating development and operations seamlessly.
- *Outcome:* The firm achieved faster time-to-market for new products by leveraging cloud-based continuous integration and deployment. This approach allowed for rapid testing, feedback, and iteration, enhancing the overall agility of the product development lifecycle.

Secure Data Management in Compliance-Driven Environments

- *Challenge:* Maintaining data security and compliance with industry regulations is paramount in certain mechanical engineering sectors.
- *Solution:* A defense contractor with stringent compliance requirements migrated its data management to a secure cloud environment.
- *Outcome:* The cloud infrastructure provided robust security features, including encryption and access controls, ensuring compliance with industry regulations. This allowed the contractor to focus on core engineering tasks while entrusting data security to the cloud provider.

Scalable High-Performance Computing (HPC)

- *Challenge:* Traditional HPC clusters may face limitations in scalability and flexibility.
- *Solution:* A research institution specializing in fluid dynamics adopted cloud-based HPC for its simulations.
- *Outcome:* The institution could scale its computational resources based on project demands, handling larger and more complex simulations without investing in additional on-premises hardware. This approach facilitated breakthroughs in fluid dynamics research.

The case studies demonstrate the benefits of cloud resources in mechanical engineering, including optimizing simulations, fostering global collaboration, enabling agile product development, and ensuring secure data management. These examples demonstrate how cloud solutions empower organizations to overcome challenges and embrace new opportunities (Boopathi, 2024a; Dhanalakshmi et al., 2024; Syamala et al., 2023; Venkateswaran, Vidhya, Ayyannan, et al., 2023).

SECURITY AND PRIVACY CONCERNS IN CLOUD ADOPTION

The migration of mechanical engineering operations to the cloud introduces a spectrum of security and privacy considerations that demand meticulous attention. This in-depth exploration delves into the specific issues associated with securing sensitive data in the cloud and outlines strategies along with best practices to mitigate risks and ensure robust data protection (Abdulsalam & Hedabou, 2021).

Security Concerns in Cloud Adoption

Data Encryption and Transmission

Issue: Transmitting sensitive mechanical engineering data over the network raises concerns about data interception and unauthorized access.

Mitigation Strategy: Implement end-to-end encryption for data in transit, ensuring that all communication between the client and cloud services is secured. Utilize industry-standard encryption protocols to safeguard data during transmission.

Data Residency and Jurisdiction

Issue: The geographic location of data storage in the cloud may conflict with legal and regulatory requirements, leading to uncertainties regarding jurisdiction and compliance.

Mitigation Strategy: Choose cloud providers with transparent data residency policies and compliance certifications. Implement data governance practices to track and control the geographical location of stored data in alignment with regulatory obligations.

Identity and Access Management (IAM)

Issue: Unauthorized access to sensitive engineering data poses a significant threat. Inadequate identity and access controls can lead to data breaches.

Mitigation Strategy: Implement robust IAM practices, including strong authentication mechanisms, role-based access controls, and regular access reviews. Ensure that only authorized personnel have access to critical data, minimizing the risk of insider threats.

Data Ownership and Control

Issue: The relinquishing of data control to a third-party cloud provider may create concerns regarding data ownership, governance, and control.

Mitigation Strategy: Clearly define data ownership and control agreements in service-level agreements (SLAs) with the cloud provider. Establish data governance policies to maintain visibility and control over how data is managed and accessed.

Privacy Concerns in Cloud Adoption

Regulatory Compliance

Issue: Compliance with data protection regulations, such as GDPR or industry-specific standards, becomes challenging when data is stored and processed in the cloud.

Mitigation Strategy: Conduct thorough assessments to ensure compliance with relevant regulations. Choose cloud providers with a proven track record in adhering to global and regional data protection standards.

Data Resilience and Availability

Issue: The potential for data loss or service outages may impact the availability of critical engineering data.

Mitigation Strategy: Implement robust backup and disaster recovery plans. Regularly test data recovery processes to ensure data resilience in the event of unforeseen incidents.

Vendor Security Practices

Issue: The security practices of the chosen cloud vendor may directly impact the overall privacy posture of the hosted data.

Mitigation Strategy: Evaluate and select cloud providers with comprehensive security certifications, transparent security practices, and a commitment to ongoing security improvements. Regularly assess and audit the security measures implemented by the cloud provider.

Best Practices for Ensuring Data Protection

Migrating mechanical engineering operations to the cloud requires a comprehensive approach to address security and privacy concerns. By combining technical measures with strategies and best practices, organizations can secure their cloud adoption journey (Pramila et al., 2023).

- **Data Classification and Sensitivity:** Classify data based on sensitivity levels and apply appropriate security measures accordingly.
- **Continuous Monitoring and Auditing:** Implement continuous monitoring of data access and activities, coupled with regular auditing to detect and respond to potential security incidents.
- **Employee Training and Awareness:** Provide comprehensive training to employees on security best practices and raise awareness about the importance of protecting sensitive data.
- **Incident Response Planning:** Develop and regularly test incident response plans to ensure a swift and effective response to security incidents, minimizing potential damages.
- **Encryption of Data at Rest:** Implement encryption for data at rest within the cloud environment to add an additional layer of protection.

TAILORING CLOUD SOLUTIONS FOR SMEs

Cloud computing has become a linchpin for innovation and efficiency across industries, and its application in small and medium-sized enterprises (SMEs) in the mechanical engineering domain is no exception. However, one size does not fit all, and tailoring cloud solutions to meet the specific needs and constraints of SMEs is crucial for unlocking the full potential of this transformative technology (Masood et al., 2020; Sheikh et al., 2020; Tabrizchi & Kuchaki Rafsanjani, 2020). The figure 2 depicts cloud computing as a key driver of innovation and efficiency across various industries.

Scalable and Cost-Effective Infrastructure

Customization Approach: SMEs often face budget constraints and varying workloads. Tailored cloud solutions should offer scalability to adjust resources dynamically, allowing SMEs to scale up during peak demand and scale down during lean periods.

Implementation: Adopting a pay-as-you-go model ensures cost efficiency, enabling SMEs to pay only for the resources consumed. This approach aligns with the budget constraints of SMEs and ensures optimal resource utilization.

Specialized Applications and Software

Customization Approach: Mechanical engineering involves the use of specialized software for design, simulation, and analysis. Cloud solutions should support the seamless integration and hosting of these applications (Rahamathunnisa, Subhashini, et al., 2023).

Implementation: Cloud providers can collaborate with software vendors to offer specialized packages tailored for mechanical engineering SMEs. This ensures that critical applications are accessible and optimized within the cloud environment, reducing the burden on SMEs to manage and maintain these tools locally.

Data Security and Compliance

Customization Approach: SMEs, particularly in regulated industries, need customized security measures and compliance features to meet industry-specific standards (Boopathi & Khang, 2023).

Implementation: Cloud solutions can provide configurable security settings and compliance features that align with the regulatory requirements of the mechanical engineering sector. This includes encryption options, access controls, and audit trails tailored to specific compliance frameworks.

Collaborative Workspaces

Customization Approach: Mechanical engineering projects often involve collaboration among cross-functional teams. Cloud solutions should provide collaborative workspaces that facilitate real-time collaboration and version control.

Figure 2. Cloud computing: Linchpin for innovation and efficiency across industries

Implementation: Integration of collaborative tools, such as document sharing, version tracking, and communication platforms, ensures that teams can work seamlessly on projects. Customization options may include role-based access controls and project-specific collaboration settings.

Data Backup and Disaster Recovery

Customization Approach: SMEs require reliable data backup and disaster recovery solutions tailored to the criticality of their engineering data.

Implementation: Cloud providers can offer customizable backup and recovery plans, allowing SMEs to define the frequency of backups, retention periods, and recovery time objectives based on the unique requirements of their projects.

Support and Training Programs

Customization Approach: SMEs may lack the in-house expertise to manage and optimize cloud resources. Customized support and training programs are essential (Rahamathunnisa, Sudhakar, et al., 2023; Sharma et al., 2024; Srinivas et al., 2023).

Implementation: Cloud providers can offer tailored support packages, including training sessions, documentation, and responsive customer support. These programs cater to the specific needs of SMEs, ensuring that they can leverage cloud resources effectively.

Flexible Contractual Agreements

Customization Approach: SMEs may require flexible contractual agreements that align with their changing business needs.

Implementation: Cloud providers can offer customizable subscription plans, allowing SMEs to adjust resource allocations, add or remove services, and scale their usage based on project demands. Flexible billing options provide SMEs with the agility to adapt to evolving business requirements.

Customized cloud solutions for SMEs in mechanical engineering can maximize the benefits of cloud computing by understanding their unique needs and constraints. These solutions empower them to innovate, collaborate, and compete effectively in the ever-evolving landscape of the industry (Agrawal, Magulur, et al., 2023; Srinivas et al., 2023). Customization ensures that cloud adoption becomes a strategic enabler, facilitating the growth and success of SMEs in the industry.

THE FUTURE LANDSCAPE: TRENDS AND INNOVATIONS IN CLOUD TECHNOLOGY

Exploration of Emerging Trends and Innovations

Cloud computing continues to evolve, and its impact on the field of mechanical engineering is continually shaped by emerging trends and innovations. This exploration delves into the latest developments in cloud computing that are particularly relevant to the needs and challenges of the mechanical engineering domain (Katuu & others, 2021; Singh et al., 2021). The figure 3 explores the latest trends and innovations in mechanical engineering.

Edge Computing Integration

Trend: Edge computing is gaining prominence, bringing computation closer to the data source to reduce latency and enhance real-time processing.

Relevance to Mechanical Engineering: In scenarios where real-time data analysis is critical, such as IoT-enabled sensors in manufacturing equipment, integrating edge computing with cloud solutions ensures rapid decision-making and improved efficiency in mechanical engineering processes.

AI and Machine Learning Integration

Trend: Cloud computing platforms are increasingly integrating artificial intelligence (AI) and machine learning (ML) services (M. Kumar et al., 2023; Puranik et al., 2024; Rebecca et al., 2024; Sharma et al., 2024).

Relevance to Mechanical Engineering: AI and ML algorithms can analyze vast datasets generated during design simulations, identify patterns, and optimize mechanical processes. This integration enhances predictive modeling, leading to more efficient designs and reduced time-to-market for products.

Figure 3. Exploration of emerging trends and innovations in mechanical engineering

Digital Twins for Simulation and Testing

Trend: Digital twins, virtual replicas of physical objects or systems, are gaining traction for simulation and testing purposes.

Relevance to Mechanical Engineering: Cloud-based digital twins allow engineers to simulate and analyze the performance of mechanical systems in a virtual environment. This trend facilitates more accurate testing, prototyping, and optimization, reducing the need for physical prototypes and experimentation.

Serverless Computing for Resource Optimization

Trend: Serverless computing abstracts infrastructure management, allowing developers to focus solely on code execution.

Relevance to Mechanical Engineering: In resource-intensive simulations or analyses, serverless computing ensures optimal resource utilization. Mechanical engineering tasks that require bursts of computing power can benefit from this pay-as-you-go model, reducing costs and improving scalability.

Multi-Cloud and Hybrid Cloud Strategies

Trend: Organizations are adopting multi-cloud and hybrid cloud strategies to leverage the strengths of different cloud providers and maintain flexibility (Domakonda et al., 2022; KAV et al., 2023; Nishanth et al., 2023).

Relevance to Mechanical Engineering: Multi-cloud strategies allow mechanical engineering firms to choose specialized services from different providers, optimizing costs and ensuring redundancy. Hybrid cloud setups offer a balance between on-premises infrastructure and cloud resources, accommodating specific security or regulatory requirements.

Blockchain for Secure Collaboration

Trend: Blockchain technology is being explored for secure and transparent collaboration in cloud environments (P. R. Kumar et al., 2023; Sundaramoorthy et al., 2024).

Relevance to Mechanical Engineering: Blockchain can enhance the security and traceability of design changes, collaboration records, and supply chain interactions. This innovation addresses concerns related to data integrity and intellectual property protection in collaborative mechanical engineering projects.

Quantum Computing Exploration

Trend: Quantum computing is in its exploratory stages, with cloud providers starting to offer quantum computing services (Agrawal, Shashibhushan, et al., 2023; Rahamathunnisa, Sudhakar, et al., 2023; Satav et al., 2023).

Relevance to Mechanical Engineering: Quantum computing has the potential to revolutionize complex simulations and optimization problems in mechanical engineering. It could significantly accelerate tasks such as material design and structural analysis.

5G Connectivity for Enhanced Mobility

Trend: The rollout of 5G networks provides faster and more reliable connectivity (Agrawal, Shashibhushan, et al., 2023; Venkateswaran, Vidhya, Ayyannan, et al., 2023).

Relevance to Mechanical Engineering: In mobile and remote scenarios, 5G connectivity ensures seamless access to cloud resources. This is particularly beneficial for engineers working on-site or in field operations, enabling them to access real-time data and cloud-based applications.

Advanced Data Analytics for Predictive Maintenance

Trend: Cloud platforms are integrating advanced analytics tools for predictive maintenance (P. R. Kumar et al., 2023; Ramudu et al., 2023; Sangeetha et al., 2023).

Relevance to Mechanical Engineering: By analyzing sensor data from machinery and equipment, cloud-based analytics can predict potential failures and schedule maintenance activities proactively. This trend enhances the reliability and lifespan of mechanical systems.

Cybersecurity Innovations for Data Protection

Trend: Cloud providers are continually improving cybersecurity measures, including advanced threat detection and encryption technologies (Agrawal, Magulur, et al., 2023; Gnanaprakasam et al., 2023).

Relevance to Mechanical Engineering: Enhanced cybersecurity measures ensure the protection of sensitive engineering data stored and processed in the cloud. This trend addresses concerns related to data breaches and unauthorized access.

The study explores emerging trends and innovations in cloud computing for mechanical engineering, highlighting the industry's dynamic landscape and the potential to reshape tasks, fostering innovation, efficiency, and collaboration in the pursuit of engineering excellence, as technology continues to evolve.

Predictions for the Future Evolution of Cloud Technology and Its Impact on SMEs

Cloud technology is poised for continued evolution, and its impact on Small and Medium Enterprises (SMEs) is expected to be transformative. The following predictions highlight key trends that are likely to shape the future of cloud technology and its role in empowering SMEs (Katuu & others, 2021; Tabrizchi & Kuchaki Rafsanjani, 2020):

Increased Focus on Industry-Specific Cloud Solutions

Prediction: Cloud providers will increasingly develop industry-specific solutions tailored to the unique needs of SMEs in various sectors, including manufacturing, healthcare, and finance (Subha et al., 2023; Ugandar et al., 2023; Venkateswaran, Kumar, et al., 2023).

Impact on SMEs: SMEs will benefit from specialized cloud solutions that address industry-specific challenges, providing tailored features, compliance measures, and optimized workflows.

Rise of Edge Computing Integration

Prediction: Edge computing will become more integrated with cloud services, enabling SMEs to process data closer to the source for faster decision-making and reduced latency (P. R. Kumar et al., 2023).

Impact on SMEs: SMEs, especially those in manufacturing and IoT-centric industries, will experience improved real-time analytics and operational efficiency with the integration of edge computing and cloud services.

Advancements in AI and Machine Learning Integration

Prediction: Cloud platforms will offer more advanced AI and machine learning services, allowing SMEs to harness these technologies for predictive analytics, automation, and decision support (Boopathi & Khang, 2023; Koshariya et al., 2023; Zekrifa et al., 2023).

Impact on SMEs: SMEs can leverage AI-driven insights to enhance product development, optimize supply chain management, and streamline operational processes, contributing to increased efficiency and competitiveness.

Proliferation of Serverless Computing

Prediction: Serverless computing models will gain popularity, enabling SMEs to focus on application development without the burden of managing underlying infrastructure.

Impact on SMEs: SMEs will benefit from cost-effective, scalable, and easy-to-manage solutions, allowing them to deploy applications rapidly and efficiently without the need for extensive infrastructure management.

Broader Adoption of Multi-Cloud Strategies

Prediction: Multi-cloud strategies will become more prevalent, with SMEs leveraging services from multiple cloud providers to optimize costs, enhance flexibility, and improve redundancy (Babu et al., 2022; Rahamathunnisa et al., 2024).

Impact on SMEs: Multi-cloud approaches will empower SMEs to choose the best-fit solutions for their specific needs, avoiding vendor lock-in and ensuring resilience in the face of potential service disruptions.

Quantum Computing Integration for Specialized Tasks

Prediction: Quantum computing will find applications in specialized tasks, offering SMEs the potential for solving complex optimization and simulation problems.

Impact on SMEs: SMEs in scientific research, material design, and advanced simulations can benefit from quantum computing's ability to process vast datasets and perform calculations beyond the capabilities of classical computers.

Enhanced Cybersecurity Measures

Prediction: Cloud providers will continually invest in advanced cybersecurity measures, including AI-driven threat detection, encryption, and secure collaboration tools.

Impact on SMEs: SMEs will enjoy heightened data security, reducing the risk of cyber threats and unauthorized access. This will foster trust in cloud adoption and encourage SMEs to leverage cloud solutions for critical operations.

Greater Integration of 5G Technology

Prediction: The widespread deployment of 5G networks will lead to greater integration with cloud services, offering SMEs faster and more reliable connectivity (Agrawal, Shashibhushan, et al., 2023).

Impact on SMEs: SMEs will experience improved mobility, enabling seamless access to cloud resources in remote or mobile environments. This is particularly beneficial for field operations and real-time data access.

Expanded Role of Cloud in Sustainability Initiatives

Prediction: Cloud providers will play a more significant role in supporting sustainability initiatives, offering energy-efficient solutions and carbon-neutral data centers (Boopathi, 2024c; Rahamathunnisa et al., 2024).

Impact on SMEs: SMEs adopting cloud services will contribute to environmental sustainability, benefiting from eco-friendly solutions while aligning with corporate social responsibility goals.

Customization of Cloud Services for Niche Industries

Prediction: Cloud services will evolve to offer more customizable solutions for niche industries, accommodating specific needs and compliance requirements.

Impact on SMEs: SMEs in specialized sectors, such as aerospace or biotechnology, will benefit from tailored cloud solutions that address unique challenges, allowing for efficient and compliant operations.

The future of cloud technology holds great promise for SMEs, offering a range of tools and services to boost productivity, innovation, and competitiveness. As predictions come true, SMEs will be better equipped to navigate the evolving business landscape and utilize cloud solutions for growth and success.

ENSURING REGULATORY COMPLIANCE IN CLOUD ENVIRONMENTS

The study explores the challenges faced by SMEs in mechanical engineering when implementing cloud solutions, focusing on regulatory frameworks and compliance requirements, and provides strategies for achieving compliance (Ali & Osmanaj, 2020).

Regulatory Frameworks Relevant to SMEs in Mechanical Engineering

a. **Data Protection Regulations:** *Relevance:* GDPR (General Data Protection Regulation) in the European Union, and other regional data protection laws, govern the handling of personal and sensitive data. - *Impact:* SMEs must ensure that cloud solutions comply with data protection regulations, especially when dealing with design data, employee information, or customer data.

b. **Industry-Specific Standards:** *Relevance:* Regulations such as ISO 9001 (Quality Management System) and ISO 27001 (Information Security Management System) are crucial for ensuring quality and security in mechanical engineering processes. - *Impact:* SMEs must align cloud solutions with industry-specific standards to maintain product quality, data security, and overall compliance.

c. **Intellectual Property Protection:** *Relevance:* Regulations related to intellectual property protection vary globally, impacting how SMEs manage and safeguard their design and innovation assets. - *Impact:* SMEs must ensure that cloud solutions do not compromise the confidentiality and ownership of intellectual property, requiring robust access controls and data encryption.

d. **Export Control Laws:** *Relevance:* International trade regulations and export control laws govern the transfer of certain technologies across borders. - *Impact:* SMEs operating globally need to ensure that cloud solutions comply with export control laws, especially when dealing with sensitive technologies or products.

Strategies for Maintaining Compliance in Cloud Environments

a. **Data Encryption and Access Controls:** *Strategy:* Implement strong encryption for data at rest and in transit. Utilize access controls to restrict data access based on user roles and responsibilities. - *Rationale:* Encryption ensures the confidentiality of sensitive data, while access controls limit unauthorized access, addressing data protection and intellectual property concerns (Ali & Osmanaj, 2020; Jaatun et al., 2020).

b. **Comprehensive Risk Assessments:** *Strategy:* Conduct regular risk assessments to identify potential compliance risks associated with the use of cloud services. - *Rationale:* Proactive risk assessments help SMEs anticipate and address compliance challenges, ensuring that cloud solutions align with regulatory requirements.

c. **Vendor Due Diligence:** *Strategy:* Perform thorough due diligence when selecting cloud service providers, evaluating their compliance certifications and adherence to industry standards. - *Rationale:* Choosing reputable cloud providers with a proven track record in compliance ensures that SMEs can trust the security and regulatory alignment of the chosen cloud solutions.

d. **Data Residency and Jurisdiction:** *Strategy:* Understand data residency requirements and the jurisdictional implications of storing data in the cloud. Choose cloud providers with transparent policies on data location. - *Rationale:* Adhering to data residency regulations is critical for SMEs to avoid legal and regulatory complications related to the geographical location of their data.

e. **Regular Compliance Audits:** *Strategy:* Conduct regular compliance audits, both internally and with the assistance of third-party auditors, to ensure ongoing adherence to regulatory requirements. - *Rationale:* Regular audits provide a systematic approach to monitoring and verifying compliance, identifying and addressing potential issues promptly.

f. **Clear Contractual Agreements:** *Strategy:* Establish clear contractual agreements with cloud service providers, outlining responsibilities, data protection measures, and compliance commitments. - *Rationale:* Well-defined contracts ensure that both parties understand their roles and responsibilities, providing a foundation for maintaining compliance throughout the partnership.

g. **Employee Training and Awareness:** *Strategy:* Provide ongoing training to employees on regulatory compliance, data protection, and the secure use of cloud resources. - *Rationale:* Well-informed employees are essential in ensuring that day-to-day operations within the cloud environment align with regulatory requirements, reducing the risk of human errors that may lead to compliance issues.

h. **Continuous Monitoring and Incident Response:** *Strategy:* Implement continuous monitoring of cloud environments for security and compliance. Develop a robust incident response plan to address and report any breaches promptly. - *Rationale:* Continuous monitoring and a well-defined incident response plan contribute to the early detection and mitigation of potential compliance breaches, minimizing the impact on SMEs (Boopathi, 2021, 2023; Kavitha et al., 2023).

SMEs in mechanical engineering face a challenge in ensuring regulatory compliance in cloud environments. By understanding relevant frameworks, implementing robust strategies, and fostering compliance awareness, they can leverage cloud technology while maintaining operational integrity and security while adhering to regulatory standards.

Figure 4. Strategies for enhancing cloud security in mechanical SMEs

STRATEGIES FOR ENHANCING CLOUD SECURITY IN MECHANICAL SMEs

The figure 4 outlines strategies for improving cloud security in Mechanical SMEs.

- **Robust Identity and Access Management (IAM):** Implementing a robust Identity and Access Management (IAM) strategy is foundational to enhancing cloud security for SMEs in mechanical engineering. Utilize IAM tools to enforce strong authentication measures, implement role-based access controls, and regularly audit user access. By ensuring that only authorized personnel have access to sensitive data and resources, SMEs can mitigate the risk of unauthorized access and data breaches (Han & Trimi, 2022).
- **Data Encryption Across the Lifecycle:** Deploy end-to-end encryption mechanisms for data both at rest and in transit within the cloud environment. Utilizing encryption tools ensures that even if unauthorized access occurs, the data remains unintelligible. Employing encryption for communication channels and stored data adds an additional layer of protection, safeguarding critical engineering data from potential cyber threats (Rebecca et al., 2024).
- **Continuous Security Monitoring and Threat Detection:** Implementing continuous security monitoring and threat detection tools is imperative for SMEs to promptly identify and respond to potential security incidents. Employ advanced security information and event management (SIEM) solutions that provide real-time monitoring, log analysis, and automated alerts. This proactive approach enables SMEs to detect and mitigate security threats before they escalate.
- **Regular Security Audits and Vulnerability Assessments:** Conducting regular security audits and vulnerability assessments is a proactive strategy to identify and address potential weaknesses in the cloud environment. Engage in penetration testing, code reviews, and systematic audits to assess the security posture of the infrastructure. By identifying and remedying vulnerabilities, SMEs can fortify their cloud infrastructure against potential cyber threats.
- **Secure Configuration Management:** Adopt secure configuration management practices to ensure that cloud resources are configured following industry best practices and security standards. Leverage configuration management tools to automate and enforce security configurations, reducing the likelihood of misconfigurations that could be exploited by malicious actors. A well-managed configuration minimizes the attack surface and enhances overall security.
- **Employee Training and Security Awareness:** Invest in comprehensive employee training programs focused on cloud security awareness. Educate staff about potential risks, social engineering tactics, and best practices for securely using cloud resources. By fostering a security-conscious culture, SMEs empower their workforce to become a first line of defense against common security threats, such as phishing attacks or unauthorized access attempts.
- **Secure DevOps Practices:** Integrate security into the DevOps lifecycle by adopting secure coding practices, automated security testing, and continuous security monitoring. Implementing DevSecOps principles ensures that security considerations are an integral part of the development and deployment process. This approach enables SMEs to deliver secure and resilient applications in their cloud environment.

Develop and regularly test an incident response plan that outlines the steps to be taken in the event of a security incident. Utilize incident response tools that facilitate quick detection, containment, and recovery. A well-prepared incident response plan helps SMEs minimize the impact of security breaches and ensures a swift return to normal operations (Narwane et al., 2020).

Leverage the security features provided by the chosen cloud service provider. Utilize built-in security services such as firewalls, encryption tools, and identity services. Stay informed about updates and new security features introduced by the cloud provider and implement them to enhance the overall security posture of the cloud environment (Boopathi, 2024b; Dhanalakshmi et al., 2024).

Invest in the training and certification of IT and security personnel to stay abreast of evolving security threats and best practices. Encourage employees to pursue certifications related to cloud security, such as Certified Cloud Security Professional (CCSP) or AWS Certified Security – Specialty. Well-trained and certified personnel are better equipped to implement and maintain robust security measures in the cloud (Revathi et al., 2024). In conclusion, a comprehensive approach to enhancing cloud security for SMEs in the mechanical engineering sector involves a combination of technical measures, employee training, and proactive strategies. By adopting these practical approaches and leveraging security tools, SMEs can create a resilient and secure cloud environment that safeguards critical engineering data and supports their business operations (Subramanian et al., 2021).

CONCLUSION

The book provides a comprehensive roadmap for small and medium-sized enterprises (SMEs) in mechanical engineering to successfully integrate cloud solutions, offering insights, strategies, and practical approaches to ensure successful growth in this dynamic industry. Understanding the cloud computing landscape is crucial for SMEs to make informed decisions about their cloud adoption strategy. This includes understanding cloud models and service delivery models. Key factors that shape decisions include cost implications, scalability requirements, and technological advancements. A nuanced understanding of these factors allows SMEs to make strategic choices that align with their unique needs and objectives, ensuring a successful transition to the cloud.

The chapters discuss the potential of cloud infrastructure in improving efficiency and innovation in mechanical engineering. They highlight real-world case studies showcasing successful use of cloud resources for simulation workloads, collaborative design, agile product development, secure data management, and high-performance computing. The chapter also addresses security and privacy concerns in the transition to the cloud, highlighting strategies and best practices to mitigate risks, ensure robust data protection, and address challenges related to data encryption, jurisdictional compliance, identity and access management, and secure collaboration.

This chapter discusses the importance of tailoring cloud solutions for SMEs in mechanical engineering, focusing on scalable infrastructure, specialized applications, data security, collaborative workspaces, and flexible contractual agreements. It also explores emerging trends and innovations in cloud computing, such as edge computing, artificial intelligence, quantum computing, and 5G connectivity, which could impact SMEs' operations and provide insights into the future of technology in the field. The chapter discusses the future of cloud technology and its impact on SMEs, including industry-specific solutions, AI integration, serverless computing, and sustainability initiatives. It emphasizes the importance of regulatory compliance in cloud environments, focusing on data protection regulations, industry standards, intellectual property protection, and export control laws. Practical strategies for improving cloud security in mechanical SMEs include robust identity and access management, data encryption, continuous security monitoring, regular audits, secure configuration management, employee training, and leveraging cloud provider security features.

In conclusion, this book serves as a comprehensive guide, equipping SMEs in mechanical engineering with the knowledge and strategies needed for a successful cloud integration journey. By navigating the complexities of cloud adoption, understanding regulatory landscapes, and embracing emerging technologies, SMEs can position themselves for innovation, efficiency, and sustained success in the dynamic realm of mechanical engineering. The roadmap presented here empowers SMEs to harness the full potential of cloud solutions and thrive in an era of technological advancement and digital transformation.

ABBREVIATIONS

SMEs: Small and Medium-sized Enterprises
Pay-as-You-Go: Pay-as-You-Go model in cloud computing
SLAs: Service Level Agreements
TCO: Total Cost of Ownership
IoT: Internet of Things
IT: Information Technology
DevOps: Development and Operations
IAM: Identity and Access Management
GDPR: General Data Protection Regulation
ML: Machine Learning
AI: Artificial Intelligence
5G: Fifth Generation (of mobile networks)
SIEM: Security Information and Event Management
DevSecOps: Development, Security, and Operations
CCSP: Certified Cloud Security Professional

REFERENCES

Abdulsalam, Y. S., & Hedabou, M. (2021). Security and privacy in cloud computing: Technical review. *Future Internet, 14*(1), 11. doi:10.3390/fi14010011

Abraham, A., Hörandner, F., Zefferer, T., & Zwattendorfer, B. (2020). E-government in the public cloud: Requirements and opportunities. *Electronic Government, an International Journal, 16*(3), 260–280.

Agrawal, A. V., Magulur, L. P., Priya, S. G., Kaur, A., Singh, G., & Boopathi, S. (2023). Smart Precision Agriculture Using IoT and WSN. In *Handbook of Research on Data Science and Cybersecurity Innovations in Industry 4.0 Technologies* (pp. 524–541). IGI Global. doi:10.4018/978-1-6684-8145-5.ch026

Agrawal, A. V., Shashibhushan, G., Pradeep, S., Padhi, S., Sugumar, D., & Boopathi, S. (2023). Synergizing Artificial Intelligence, 5G, and Cloud Computing for Efficient Energy Conversion Using Agricultural Waste. In Sustainable Science and Intelligent Technologies for Societal Development (pp. 475–497). IGI Global.

Ali, O., & Osmanaj, V. (2020). The role of government regulations in the adoption of cloud computing: A case study of local government. *Computer Law & Security Report, 36*, 105396. doi:10.1016/j.clsr.2020.105396

Arita, Y., Nozaki, N., & Demizu, K. (2012). Mechanical design platform on Engineering Cloud. *Fujitsu Scientific and Technical Journal*, 422–427.

Babu, B. S., Kamalakannan, J., Meenatchi, N., Karthik, S., & Boopathi, S. (2022). Economic impacts and reliability evaluation of battery by adopting Electric Vehicle. *IEEE Explore*, 1–6.

Boopathi, S. (2021). *Pollution monitoring and notification: Water pollution monitoring and notification using intelligent RC boat*. Academic Press.

Boopathi, S. (2022). Performance Improvement of Eco-Friendly Near-Dry wire-Cut Electrical Discharge Machining Process Using Coconut Oil-Mist Dielectric Fluid. *Journal of Advanced Manufacturing Systems*.

Boopathi, S. (2023). Internet of Things-Integrated Remote Patient Monitoring System: Healthcare Application. In *Dynamics of Swarm Intelligence Health Analysis for the Next Generation* (pp. 137–161). IGI Global. doi:10.4018/978-1-6684-6894-4.ch008

Boopathi, S. (2024a). Balancing Innovation and Security in the Cloud: Navigating the Risks and Rewards of the Digital Age. In Improving Security, Privacy, and Trust in Cloud Computing (pp. 164–193). IGI Global.

Boopathi, S. (2024b). Balancing Innovation and Security in the Cloud: Navigating the Risks and Rewards of the Digital Age. In Improving Security, Privacy, and Trust in Cloud Computing (pp. 164–193). IGI Global.

Boopathi, S. (2024c). Sustainable Development Using IoT and AI Techniques for Water Utilization in Agriculture. In Sustainable Development in AI, Blockchain, and E-Governance Applications (pp. 204–228). IGI Global. doi:10.4018/979-8-3693-1722-8.ch012

Boopathi, S., & Khang, A. (2023). AI-Integrated Technology for a Secure and Ethical Healthcare Ecosystem. In *AI and IoT-Based Technologies for Precision Medicine* (pp. 36–59). IGI Global. doi:10.4018/979-8-3693-0876-9.ch003

Boopathi, S., Saranya, A., Raghuraman, S., & Revanth, R. (2018). Design and Fabrication of Low Cost Electric Bicycle. *International Research Journal of Engineering and Technology, 5*(3), 146–147.

Boopathi, S., & Sivakumar, K. (2012). Experimental Analysis of Eco-friendly Near-dry Wire Electrical Discharge Machining Process. *Archives des Sciences, 65*(10), 334–346.

Cai, L., Tian, Y., Liu, Z., Cheng, Q., Xu, J., & Ning, Y. (2016). Application of cloud computing to simulation of a heavy-duty machine tool. *International Journal of Advanced Manufacturing Technology, 84*(1-4), 291–303. doi:10.1007/s00170-015-7916-2

Chen, K.-T., Huang, C.-Y., & Hsu, C.-H. (2014). Cloud gaming onward: Research opportunities and outlook. *2014 IEEE International Conference on Multimedia and Expo Workshops (ICMEW)*, 1–4. 10.1109/ICMEW.2014.6890683

Choobineh, M., Arab, A., Khodaei, A., & Paaso, A. (2022). Energy innovations through blockchain: Challenges, opportunities, and the road ahead. *The Electricity Journal, 35*(1), 107059. doi:10.1016/j.tej.2021.107059

Dhanalakshmi, M., Tamilarasi, K., Saravanan, S., Sujatha, G., Boopathi, S., & Associates. (2024). Fog Computing-Based Framework and Solutions for Intelligent Systems: Enabling Autonomy in Vehicles. In Computational Intelligence for Green Cloud Computing and Digital Waste Management (pp. 330–356). IGI Global.

Domakonda, V. K., Farooq, S., Chinthamreddy, S., Puviarasi, R., Sudhakar, M., & Boopathi, S. (2022). Sustainable Developments of Hybrid Floating Solar Power Plants: Photovoltaic System. In Human Agro-Energy Optimization for Business and Industry (pp. 148–167). IGI Global.

Gnanaprakasam, C., Vankara, J., Sastry, A. S., Prajval, V., Gireesh, N., & Boopathi, S. (2023). Long-Range and Low-Power Automated Soil Irrigation System Using Internet of Things: An Experimental Study. In Contemporary Developments in Agricultural Cyber-Physical Systems (pp. 87–104). IGI Global.

Han, H., & Trimi, S. (2022). Towards a data science platform for improving SME collaboration through Industry 4.0 technologies. *Technological Forecasting and Social Change, 174,* 121242. doi:10.1016/j.techfore.2021.121242

Hema, N., Krishnamoorthy, N., Chavan, S. M., Kumar, N., Sabarimuthu, M., & Boopathi, S. (2023). A Study on an Internet of Things (IoT)-Enabled Smart Solar Grid System. In *Handbook of Research on Deep Learning Techniques for Cloud-Based Industrial IoT* (pp. 290–308). IGI Global. doi:10.4018/978-1-6684-8098-4.ch017

Hui, E., Feng, B., Lee, C., Yang, J., & Chen, J. (2019). A design of CNC architecture based on cloud computing. *Proceedings of the Institution of Mechanical Engineers. Part B, Journal of Engineering Manufacture, 233*(4), 1260–1268. doi:10.1177/0954405418774601

Jaatun, M. G., Pearson, S., Gittler, F., Leenes, R., & Niezen, M. (2020). Enhancing accountability in the cloud. *International Journal of Information Management, 53,* 101498. doi:10.1016/j.ijinfomgt.2016.03.004

Katuu, S. (2021). Trends in the enterprise resource planning market landscape. *Journal of Information and Organizational Sciences, 45*(1), 55–75. doi:10.31341/jios.45.1.4

KAV, R. P., Pandraju, T. K. S., Boopathi, S., Saravanan, P., Rathan, S. K., & Sathish, T. (2023). Hybrid Deep Learning Technique for Optimal Wind Mill Speed Estimation. *2023 7th International Conference on Electronics, Communication and Aerospace Technology (ICECA),* 181–186.

Kavitha, C., Varalatchoumy, M., Mithuna, H., Bharathi, K., Geethalakshmi, N., & Boopathi, S. (2023). Energy Monitoring and Control in the Smart Grid: Integrated Intelligent IoT and ANFIS. In Applications of Synthetic Biology in Health, Energy, and Environment (pp. 290–316). IGI Global.

Koshariya, A. K., Kalaiyarasi, D., Jovith, A. A., Sivakami, T., Hasan, D. S., & Boopathi, S. (2023). AI-Enabled IoT and WSN-Integrated Smart Agriculture System. In *Artificial Intelligence Tools and Technologies for Smart Farming and Agriculture Practices* (pp. 200–218). IGI Global. doi:10.4018/978-1-6684-8516-3.ch011

Kumar, M., Kumar, K., Sasikala, P., Sampath, B., Gopi, B., & Sundaram, S. (2023). Sustainable Green Energy Generation From Waste Water: IoT and ML Integration. In Sustainable Science and Intelligent Technologies for Societal Development (pp. 440–463). IGI Global.

Kumar, P. R., Meenakshi, S., Shalini, S., Devi, S. R., & Boopathi, S. (2023). Soil Quality Prediction in Context Learning Approaches Using Deep Learning and Blockchain for Smart Agriculture. In Effective AI, Blockchain, and E-Governance Applications for Knowledge Discovery and Management (pp. 1–26). IGI Global. doi:10.4018/978-1-6684-9151-5.ch001

Li, Y., Wang, L., & Li, W. (2019). Key technologies of mechanical fault diagnosis system based on cloud computing. *International Journal of Mechatronics and Applied Mechanics*, 6, 107–119.

Malathi, J., Kusha, K., Isaac, S., Ramesh, A., Rajendiran, M., & Boopathi, S. (2024). IoT-Enabled Remote Patient Monitoring for Chronic Disease Management and Cost Savings: Transforming Healthcare. In Advances in Explainable AI Applications for Smart Cities (pp. 371–388). IGI Global.

Masood, A., Lakew, D. S., & Cho, S. (2020). Security and privacy challenges in connected vehicular cloud computing. *IEEE Communications Surveys and Tutorials*, 22(4), 2725–2764. doi:10.1109/COMST.2020.3012961

Mohanty, A., Venkateswaran, N., Ranjit, P., Tripathi, M. A., & Boopathi, S. (2023). Innovative Strategy for Profitable Automobile Industries: Working Capital Management. In Handbook of Research on Designing Sustainable Supply Chains to Achieve a Circular Economy (pp. 412–428). IGI Global.

Nanda, A. K., Sharma, A., Augustine, P. J., Cyril, B. R., Kiran, V., & Sampath, B. (2024). Securing Cloud Infrastructure in IaaS and PaaS Environments. In Improving Security, Privacy, and Trust in Cloud Computing (pp. 1–33). IGI Global. doi:10.4018/979-8-3693-1431-9.ch001

Narwane, V. S., Raut, R. D., Mangla, S. K., Gardas, B. B., Narkhede, B. E., Awasthi, A., & Priyadarshinee, P. (2020). Mediating role of cloud of things in improving performance of small and medium enterprises in the Indian context. *Annals of Operations Research*, 1–30.

Naveeenkumar, N., Rallapalli, S., Sasikala, K., Priya, P. V., Husain, J., & Boopathi, S. (2024). Enhancing Consumer Behavior and Experience Through AI-Driven Insights Optimization. In *AI Impacts in Digital Consumer Behavior* (pp. 1–35). IGI Global. doi:10.4018/979-8-3693-1918-5.ch001

Nishanth, J., Deshmukh, M. A., Kushwah, R., Kushwaha, K. K., Balaji, S., & Sampath, B. (2023). Particle Swarm Optimization of Hybrid Renewable Energy Systems. In *Intelligent Engineering Applications and Applied Sciences for Sustainability* (pp. 291–308). IGI Global. doi:10.4018/979-8-3693-0044-2.ch016

Paul, A., Thilagham, K., KG, J., Reddy, P. R., Sathyamurthy, R., & Boopathi, S. (2024). Multi-criteria Optimization on Friction Stir Welding of Aluminum Composite (AA5052-H32/B4C) using Titanium Nitride Coated Tool. Engineering Research Express.

Pramila, P., Amudha, S., Saravanan, T., Sankar, S. R., Poongothai, E., & Boopathi, S. (2023). Design and Development of Robots for Medical Assistance: An Architectural Approach. In Contemporary Applications of Data Fusion for Advanced Healthcare Informatics (pp. 260–282). IGI Global.

Puranik, T. A., Shaik, N., Vankudoth, R., Kolhe, M. R., Yadav, N., & Boopathi, S. (2024). Study on Harmonizing Human-Robot (Drone) Collaboration: Navigating Seamless Interactions in Collaborative Environments. In Cybersecurity Issues and Challenges in the Drone Industry (pp. 1–26). IGI Global.

Rahamathunnisa, U., Subhashini, P., Aancy, H. M., Meenakshi, S., Boopathi, S., & ... (2023). Solutions for Software Requirement Risks Using Artificial Intelligence Techniques. In *Handbook of Research on Data Science and Cybersecurity Innovations in Industry 4.0 Technologies* (pp. 45–64). IGI Global.

Rahamathunnisa, U., Sudhakar, K., Murugan, T. K., Thivaharan, S., Rajkumar, M., & Boopathi, S. (2023). Cloud Computing Principles for Optimizing Robot Task Offloading Processes. In *AI-Enabled Social Robotics in Human Care Services* (pp. 188–211). IGI Global. doi:10.4018/978-1-6684-8171-4.ch007

Rahamathunnisa, U., Sudhakar, K., Padhi, S., Bhattacharya, S., Shashibhushan, G., & Boopathi, S. (2024). Sustainable Energy Generation From Waste Water: IoT Integrated Technologies. In Adoption and Use of Technology Tools and Services by Economically Disadvantaged Communities: Implications for Growth and Sustainability (pp. 225–256). IGI Global.

Ramudu, K., Mohan, V. M., Jyothirmai, D., Prasad, D., Agrawal, R., & Boopathi, S. (2023). Machine Learning and Artificial Intelligence in Disease Prediction: Applications, Challenges, Limitations, Case Studies, and Future Directions. In Contemporary Applications of Data Fusion for Advanced Healthcare Informatics (pp. 297–318). IGI Global.

Ravisankar, A., Sampath, B., & Asif, M. M. (2023). Economic Studies on Automobile Management: Working Capital and Investment Analysis. In Multidisciplinary Approaches to Organizational Governance During Health Crises (pp. 169–198). IGI Global.

Rebecca, B., Kumar, K. P. M., Padmini, S., Srivastava, B. K., Halder, S., & Boopathi, S. (2024). Convergence of Data Science-AI-Green Chemistry-Affordable Medicine: Transforming Drug Discovery. In *Handbook of Research on AI and ML for Intelligent Machines and Systems* (pp. 348–373). IGI Global.

Revathi, S., Babu, M., Rajkumar, N., Meti, V. K. V., Kandavalli, S. R., & Boopathi, S. (2024). Unleashing the Future Potential of 4D Printing: Exploring Applications in Wearable Technology, Robotics, Energy, Transportation, and Fashion. In Human-Centered Approaches in Industry 5.0: Human-Machine Interaction, Virtual Reality Training, and Customer Sentiment Analysis (pp. 131–153). IGI Global.

Sacco, F. M. (2020). The Evolution of the Telecom Infrastructure Business: Unchartered Waters Ahead of Great Opportunities. *Disruption in the Infrastructure Sector: Challenges and Opportunities for Developers, Investors and Asset Managers*, 87–148.

Sampath, B., Sureshkumar, T., Yuvaraj, M., & Velmurugan, D. (2021). Experimental Investigations on Eco-Friendly Helium-Mist Near-Dry Wire-Cut EDM of M2-HSS Material. *Materials Research Proceedings*, *19*, 175–180.

Sangeetha, M., Kannan, S. R., Boopathi, S., Ramya, J., Ishrat, M., & Sabarinathan, G. (2023). Prediction of Fruit Texture Features Using Deep Learning Techniques. *2023 4th International Conference on Smart Electronics and Communication (ICOSEC)*, 762–768.

Satav, S. D., Lamani, D., Harsha, K., Kumar, N., Manikandan, S., & Sampath, B. (2023). Energy and Battery Management in the Era of Cloud Computing: Sustainable Wireless Systems and Networks. In *Sustainable Science and Intelligent Technologies for Societal Development* (pp. 141–166). IGI Global.

Sharma, M., Sharma, M., Sharma, N., & Boopathi, S. (2024). Building Sustainable Smart Cities Through Cloud and Intelligent Parking System. In *Handbook of Research on AI and ML for Intelligent Machines and Systems* (pp. 195–222). IGI Global.

Sheikh, M. S., Liang, J., & Wang, W. (2020). Security and privacy in vehicular ad hoc network and vehicle cloud computing: A survey. *Wireless Communications and Mobile Computing, 2020*, 1–25. doi:10.1155/2020/5129620

Singh, G., Bhardwaj, G., Singh, S. V., Chaturvedi, P., Kumar, V., & Gupta, S. (2021). Industry 4.0: The industrial revolution and future landscape in Indian Market. *2021 International Conference on Technological Advancements and Innovations (ICTAI)*, 500–505. 10.1109/ICTAI53825.2021.9673154

Srinivas, B., Maguluri, L. P., Naidu, K. V., Reddy, L. C. S., Deivakani, M., & Boopathi, S. (2023). Architecture and Framework for Interfacing Cloud-Enabled Robots. In *Handbook of Research on Data Science and Cybersecurity Innovations in Industry 4.0 Technologies* (pp. 542–560). IGI Global. doi:10.4018/978-1-6684-8145-5.ch027

Subha, S., Inbamalar, T., Komala, C., Suresh, L. R., Boopathi, S., & Alaskar, K. (2023). A Remote Health Care Monitoring system using internet of medical things (IoMT). *IEEE Explore*, 1–6.

Subramanian, G., Patil, B. T., & Gardas, B. B. (2021). Evaluation of enablers of cloud technology to boost industry 4.0 adoption in the manufacturing micro, small and medium enterprises. *Journal of Modelling in Management, 16*(3), 944–962. doi:10.1108/JM2-08-2020-0207

Sundaramoorthy, K., Singh, A., Sumathy, G., Maheshwari, A., Arunarani, A., & Boopathi, S. (2024). A Study on AI and Blockchain-Powered Smart Parking Models for Urban Mobility. In *Handbook of Research on AI and ML for Intelligent Machines and Systems* (pp. 223–250). IGI Global.

Syamala, M., Komala, C., Pramila, P., Dash, S., Meenakshi, S., & Boopathi, S. (2023). Machine Learning-Integrated IoT-Based Smart Home Energy Management System. In *Handbook of Research on Deep Learning Techniques for Cloud-Based Industrial IoT* (pp. 219–235). IGI Global. doi:10.4018/978-1-6684-8098-4.ch013

Tabrizchi, H., & Kuchaki Rafsanjani, M. (2020). A survey on security challenges in cloud computing: Issues, threats, and solutions. *The Journal of Supercomputing, 76*(12), 9493–9532. doi:10.1007/s11227-020-03213-1

Tamura, Y., Kawakami, M., & Yamada, S. (2013). Reliability modeling and analysis for open source cloud computing. *Proceedings of the Institution of Mechanical Engineers. Part O, Journal of Risk and Reliability, 227*(2), 179–186. doi:10.1177/1748006X12475110

Tao, F., Zhang, L., Venkatesh, V., Luo, Y., & Cheng, Y. (2011). Cloud manufacturing: A computing and service-oriented manufacturing model. *Proceedings of the Institution of Mechanical Engineers. Part B, Journal of Engineering Manufacture, 225*(10), 1969–1976. doi:10.1177/0954405411405575

Taylor, S. J., Kiss, T., Terstyanszky, G., Kacsuk, P., & Fantini, N. (2014). Cloud computing for simulation in manufacturing and engineering: Introducing the CloudSME simulation platform. *ANSS 14, Annual Simulation Symposium 2014, in Conjunction with 2014 Spring Simulation Multi-Conference (SpringSim'14), 46*(2).

Ugandar, R., Rahamathunnisa, U., Sajithra, S., Christiana, M. B. V., Palai, B. K., & Boopathi, S. (2023). Hospital Waste Management Using Internet of Things and Deep Learning: Enhanced Efficiency and Sustainability. In Applications of Synthetic Biology in Health, Energy, and Environment (pp. 317–343). IGI Global.

Vanitha, S., Radhika, K., & Boopathi, S. (2023). Artificial Intelligence Techniques in Water Purification and Utilization. In *Human Agro-Energy Optimization for Business and Industry* (pp. 202–218). IGI Global. doi:10.4018/978-1-6684-4118-3.ch010

Venkateswaran, N., Kumar, S. S., Diwakar, G., Gnanasangeetha, D., & Boopathi, S. (2023). Synthetic Biology for Waste Water to Energy Conversion: IoT and AI Approaches. *Applications of Synthetic Biology in Health. Energy & Environment*, 360–384.

Venkateswaran, N., Vidhya, K., Ayyannan, M., Chavan, S. M., Sekar, K., & Boopathi, S. (2023). A Study on Smart Energy Management Framework Using Cloud Computing. In 5G, Artificial Intelligence, and Next Generation Internet of Things: Digital Innovation for Green and Sustainable Economies (pp. 189–212). IGI Global. doi:10.4018/978-1-6684-8634-4.ch009

Venkateswaran, N., Vidhya, R., Naik, D. A., Raj, T. M., Munjal, N., & Boopathi, S. (2023). Study on Sentence and Question Formation Using Deep Learning Techniques. In *Digital Natives as a Disruptive Force in Asian Businesses and Societies* (pp. 252–273). IGI Global. doi:10.4018/978-1-6684-6782-4.ch015

Wang, P., Gao, R. X., & Fan, Z. (2015). Cloud computing for cloud manufacturing: Benefits and limitations. *Journal of Manufacturing Science and Engineering, 137*(4), 040901. doi:10.1115/1.4030209

Williams, K., & Griffin, J. A. (2019). Better security and encryption within cloud computing systems. In Cloud Security: Concepts, Methodologies, Tools, and Applications (pp. 812–823). IGI Global. doi:10.4018/978-1-5225-8176-5.ch041

Zekrifa, D. M. S., Kulkarni, M., Bhagyalakshmi, A., Devireddy, N., Gupta, S., & Boopathi, S. (2023). Integrating Machine Learning and AI for Improved Hydrological Modeling and Water Resource Management. In *Artificial Intelligence Applications in Water Treatment and Water Resource Management* (pp. 46–70). IGI Global. doi:10.4018/978-1-6684-6791-6.ch003

Chapter 12
Semantic Web Technologies and Its Applications in Artificial Intelligence of Things

Shalini Roy
VIT Bhopal University, India

Harshit Gautam
VIT Bhopal University, India

D. Lakshmi
ⓘ https://orcid.org/0000-0003-4018-1208
VIT Bhopal University, India

ABSTRACT

Semantic web transforms web search, enhancing data retrieval and storage. It enables machines to interpret online content through diverse technologies for data integration, knowledge representation, and intelligent search. This paradigm revolutionizes information organization, supporting AI, data analysis, and knowledge management. The chapter focuses on AIoT, covering data representation, integration, semantic web applications, control models, and recommendations. Practical case studies illustrate the application of semantic web tools, highlighting real-world scenarios.

TERMINOLOGIES

RDF (Resource Description Framework)
OWL (Web Ontology Language)
SPARQL (SPARQL Protocol and RDF Query Language)
W3C (World Wide Web Consortium)
BIM (Building Information Modeling)
AEC (Architecture, Engineering, and Construction)

DOI: 10.4018/979-8-3693-1487-6.ch012

JSON (JSON for Linking Data)
LDJ (Line Delimited JSON)
SSN (Semantic Sensor Network)
HVAC (Heating, Ventilation, and Air Conditioning)
ABAC (Attribute-Based Access Control)
RBAC (Role-Based Access Control)
IoT (Internet of Things)
AIoT (Artificial Intelligence for the Internet of Things)
SWRL (Semantic Web Rules Language)

1. INTRODUCTION

Semantic Web technology is well-known for its transformative capabilities, representing methods and approaches that empower machines to understand and interpret online content. This revolutionizes how we search, analyze, and comprehend information. By enabling machines to comprehend and interpret data, Semantic Web technology introduces groundbreaking possibilities in artificial intelligence, information integration, and information management. It supports data integration, knowledge representation, and intelligent search using technologies such as RDF, OWL, and SPARQL. The Semantic Web presents an innovative approach to organizing and sharing information, backing advanced applications in artificial intelligence, data analysis, and knowledge management. Leading companies like Google, Amazon, and NASA have leveraged Semantic Web technology for operational improvements. Google's Knowledge Graph utilizes semantic data to enhance search results, while Amazon employs semantic technology to improve product recommendations and elevate customer experiences. NASA depends on Semantic Web technology to integrate information from various sources and facilitate information sharing among scientists. These success stories highlight the transformative influence of Semantic Web technology across diverse industries. The inspiration for the Semantic Web traces back to a longstanding vision of the web, influenced by earlier concepts like Vannevar Bush's 'memex' machine from the 1940s, envisioning a universal library with a searchable catalog. Tim Berners-Lee initially imagined the World Wide Web with more detailed document descriptions and links. However, the pursuit of a simple, usable, and universally accessible system led to the present, more human-mediated web (Matthews, 2005). The overview of this chapter is illustrated in Figure 1 and Figure 2.

As Semantic Web technology progresses, it's crucial to consider several noteworthy future trends. These include the emergence of personal advisors utilizing semantic technology, the integration of blockchain with semantic web principles to ensure secure data management, and the development of AI-driven search engines that provide context-aware and precise results. Embracing these standards not only has the potential to revolutionize the industry but also opens up new possibilities for efficient data management and information sharing. In the age of interconnected devices, the integration of semantic web technology into IoT solutions has proven to be a game-changer. This innovative approach enhances the coordination, integration, and intelligence of IoT systems, covering a wide range of devices from everyday smart home appliances to sophisticated technology. A solid understanding of IoT fundamentals is essential to grasp the implications and advantages of incorporating Semantic Web technologies into IoT solutions. Semantic Web technology offers numerous advantages for the development of IoT solutions. Firstly, it facilitates enhanced communication and collaboration by enabling seamless data

Figure 1. Overview of semantic web technologies

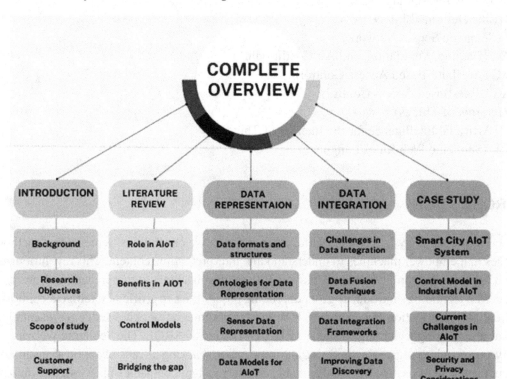

Figure 2. Overview of semantic web technologies

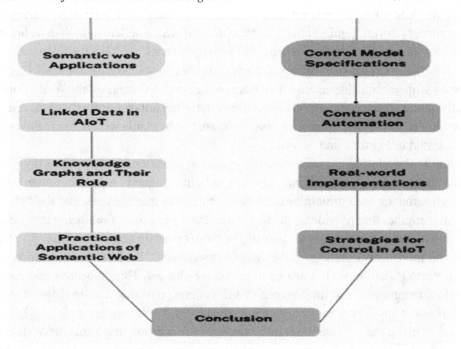

exchange across various devices and platforms. Secondly, it improves situational awareness, enabling IoT devices to understand and adapt to their surroundings. Thirdly, semantic reasoning plays a role in informed decision-making, enhancing the efficiency and effectiveness of IoT systems. Ultimately, it enables personalization and automation, making IoT devices more accessible and user-friendly (Janev & Vraneš, 2011).

The Semantic Web serves as an extension of the World Wide Web, empowering computers to intelligently search, link, and process web content based on its meaning to users. This is achieved by extracting the meaning or semantics of web resources, provided they are clearly expressed in a computer-processable format. This page delves into the content and semantics of the Web from a specific perspective, covering topics such as an introduction to Semantic Web technology, data analysis, data representation in AIoT, data integration in AIoT, Semantic Web applications in AIoT, control models in AIoT based on Semantic Web, case studies, challenges, and future direction.

1.1 Background

In the context of AIoT, the importance of semantic web technology is fundamental. It serves a crucial role in enabling devices and systems to understand, interpret, and share information in a meaningful and collaborative manner. The convergence of AI and IoT holds vast potential for reshaping various industries, including healthcare, smart cities, manufacturing, agriculture, and more. IoT involves connecting numerous devices and appliances to the Internet for data collection and transmission. However, the data often lacks completeness and clarity, leading to challenges in comprehension. Additionally, diverse information inputs and standards among different product manufacturers exacerbate issues of information fragmentation and interoperability. Semantic web technologies, incorporating standards like RDF, OWL, and SPARQL, provide a standardized framework for data representation and integration, ensuring not only machine readability but also practical utility.

In the realm of AIoT, the principle of connecting data by establishing links between diverse data sources is pivotal. Simultaneously, ontology emerges as a crucial tool for infusing semantic depth into IoT data. Ontologies, for example, can define concepts such as "temperature" and "humidity" and their interrelationships, enabling systems to recognize these associations. AIoT often requires the coordination of data from various sources, including sensors, libraries, and external services. Semantic web technologies address this challenge by creating content and structural models to describe and interconnect information, promoting collaboration and streamlining information sharing among different components of the AIoT system. Advanced technology ensures that AIoT systems can effectively sense and process data. For instance, a system might decide to activate machinery and water systems if the greenhouse temperature exceeds a threshold and humidity is low, facilitated by semantic network technology. SPARQL, a query language tailored for Semantic Web data, allows AIoT applications to efficiently retrieve and manage data from connected sources, simplifying the extraction of insights and informed decision-making based on AIoT data.

Semantic web technology enables AIoT applications to construct knowledge maps, revealing relationships among various IoT assets. These maps support advanced analytics and AI algorithms in identifying patterns, anomalies, and consensus. Designed with scalability in mind, semantic web technology effectively handles the increasing volume of data generated by IoT devices. Additionally, efforts in the IoT community to integrate web standards have improved data interoperability. Semantic network technology offers a structured framework for managing data generated by IoT devices in AIoT applications. By fostering data integration, collaboration, inference, and advanced analytics, it empowers AIoT processes to make informed decisions and drive innovation across industries. With substantial support from research organizations and industry, alongside numerous large-scale applications and recent technological advancements, the Semantic Web is quickly establishing itself as a widely recognized and essential field within computer science (Hitzler et al., 2009).

1.2 Research Objectives

This research seeks to explore the integration and application of semantic web technologies within the framework of AIoT, with a specific emphasis on assessing their influence on information interaction, knowledge representation, and the enhancement of decision-making processes. The primary objective is to scrutinize the existing status of semantic web technology and its prospective applications in AIoT systems, examining both its benefits and challenges. The study aims to propose viable solutions to address any identified issues, leveraging the capabilities of AIoT to advance and optimize IoT systems for increased efficiency and intelligence.

1.3 Scope of Study

Research on the integration of Semantic Web technologies within the AIoT context encompasses a vast and enduring field, offering numerous avenues for discovery and innovation. This domain presents several crucial issues that warrant further investigation. Initially, researchers can concentrate on enhancing the integration of diverse IoT data sources, addressing challenges related to data integration, ontology integration, and data issues to establish standards and facilitate meaningful information exchange in the AIoT ecosystem. Second, the creation of tailored ontologies and knowledge maps for AIoT applications can fortify knowledge representation, contributing to more profound and precise IoT data insights. Third, exploring semantic query and inference engines specifically crafted for AIoT systems is a promising avenue. This involves the development of efficient algorithms for querying extensive RDF data to streamline analysis and decision-making processes. Additionally, investigating the search for semantic data in the AIoT environment, ensuring capacity and efficiency, and tackling security, privacy, and ethical considerations are crucial aspects of Semantic Web technology research in AIoT. By contributing to these areas, researchers can enhance the capabilities and applications of AIoT systems while upholding ethical standards and security measures.

2. LITERATURE REVIEW

In current research, the integration of semantic network technology in the AIoT field is becoming increasingly important. This convergence brings significant benefits, including improved data integration and interoperability by aligning disparate data sources, often achieved through the use of ontologies. These ontologies can also serve as the basis for improved knowledge representation, enabling machines to understand the collected data and logically derive insights from it. Semantic query languages such as SPARQL enable complex data query and reasoning and enable advanced analytics capabilities within AIoT systems. Additionally, semantic-driven AIoT applications span diverse domains from smart cities to healthcare, providing insights, predictive capabilities, and real-time monitoring. The emergence of

BIM technology has also led to significant shifts in R&D within the AEC industry (Pauwels et al., 2017). Furthermore, as this field progresses, it faces challenges related to scalability, data privacy, security, and ethical considerations, emphasizing the need for ongoing research and standardization efforts to fully realize its potential.

2.1 The Role of Semantic Web in AIoT

Harnessing Semantic Web technologies plays a crucial role in advancing the capabilities of AIoT systems. The Semantic Web offers a standardized framework for representing, connecting, and reasoning about data and knowledge, a vital aspect in the AIoT context where the challenge lies in understanding and reconciling diverse data from IoT devices and sensors. Semantic technologies such as RDF and OWL facilitate the creation of ontologies, defining relationships and meanings within IoT data, fostering a shared understanding among machines. This enhances data interoperability, simplifying the integration and analysis of data from various sources. Additionally, the use of the SPARQL query language allows for more sophisticated data querying and reasoning, empowering AIoT systems to extract valuable insights and make informed decisions.

The application of Semantic Web technologies in online recruitment could significantly enhance market transparency, reduce transaction costs for employers, and reshape the business models of intermediaries involved, (Bizer et al., 2005). Going beyond data management, Semantic Web's impact on AIoT extends to areas like predictive maintenance, smart city solutions, and healthcare analytics, contributing to a more intelligent and interconnected IoT ecosystem. However, challenges related to scalability, data privacy, and the need for standardization efforts persist, necessitating ongoing attention to fully unlock the potential of Semantic Web technologies in AIoT. Moreover, the utilization of the SPARQL query language empowers AIoT systems to conduct advanced data querying and reasoning, enabling them to derive valuable insights and make well-informed decisions. The influence of the Semantic Web extends to various applications, fostering a more intelligent and interconnected IoT ecosystem in areas such as predictive maintenance, smart city solutions, and healthcare analytics. Nonetheless, challenges related to scalability, data privacy, and the imperative for standardization efforts persist, requiring sustained attention to fully exploit the potential of Semantic Web technologies in AIoT.

2.2 The Benefits of Semantic Web in AIoT

The application of Semantic Web technologies in the AIoT domain brings forth numerous advantages. By offering a standardized language and structure for data, these technologies empower machines to comprehend and reason about the extensive information generated by interconnected devices. A notable benefit is the enhancement of data interoperability. Semantic web standards, such as RDF and OWL, facilitate seamless data sharing and integration among different devices and systems. This interoperability, in turn, improves the effectiveness of data integration, analysis, and decision-making in AIoT applications. Another advantage is the augmentation of data discovery and search capabilities. Semantic web technologies enable machines to deduce relationships and identify pertinent information, transcending different domains or languages. This capability allows AIoT systems to better grasp and retrieve the requisite data for decision-making and problem-solving. Additionally, semantic web technologies support semantic reasoning and knowledge representation. Through the application of reasoning algorithms to semantic data, AIoT systems can derive new insights and make informed decisions based on context and predefined rules.

In essence, the incorporation of semantic web technologies into AIoT systems yields substantial benefits, including improved data interoperability, heightened data discovery and search capabilities, and more sophisticated reasoning and knowledge representation. These advantages significantly contribute to advancing the capabilities and autonomy of AIoT systems, ultimately fostering a smarter and more efficient interconnected world.

2.3 Control Models in Semantic Web AIoT

Control models in the realm of Semantic Web technologies within the context of AIoT hold a crucial position in overseeing, governing, and enhancing interactions and operations within IoT ecosystems. These models play an essential role in guaranteeing the efficient implementation and utilization of AIoT systems by offering mechanisms for access control, data management, and decision-making. This comprehensive overview explores the importance, components, and evolving patterns of control models

Figure 3. Overview of control models in semantic web

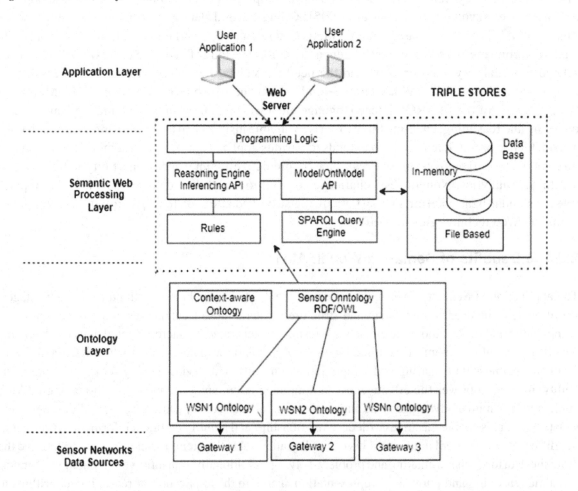

in the Semantic Web for AIoT, providing insights into their pivotal role in influencing the trajectory of IoT and AI convergence in the future (Barnaghi et al., 2012).

1. **Access Control and Authorization** for Control models in Semantic Web technologies for AIoT play a crucial role in ensuring the security and proper use of IoT data and services. With a focus on data interoperability and sharing, it's essential to regulate access, modification, and utilization of information. Common mechanisms include RBAC and ABAC, which establish roles and permissions or consider detailed attributes for nuanced control. These models safeguard sensitive data, allowing only authorized entities to interact with IoT devices and services.

2. **Data Governance and Provenance** in Semantic Web technologies empower the development of ontologies and semantic annotations, offering a robust context for IoT data. Control models play a significant role in extending their impact to data governance, ensuring the maintenance of data quality, lineage, and provenance. Notably, provenance information tracks the origin and transformation history of data, providing critical insights for data validation, compliance, and auditing purposes. Through the implementation of control models for data governance, AIoT systems can improve the reliability and traceability of data, essential elements for making informed decisions and upholding data integrity.

3. **Policy-Based Decision Making** in the Semantic Web for AIoT faciliates control models that frequently integrate decision-making mechanisms based on policies. Policies serve as the rules and regulations governing the behavior of IoT devices and services. Semantic representations of these policies enable the expression of intricate rules in a format readable by machines. When confronted with data or events, AIoT systems can consult these policies to ascertain the suitable actions or responses. This degree of automation plays a crucial role in streamlining the management and functioning of IoT ecosystems, diminishing the reliance on manual intervention and elevating overall system efficiency.

4. **Dynamic Adaptation and Self-Management** is a developing trend in control models for AIoT involving dynamic adaptation and self-management. Given the dynamic and ever-changing nature of IoT environments, the significance of control models capable of real-time adaptation is on the rise. With the utilization of Semantic Web technologies, AIoT systems can integrate knowledge reasoning and context-awareness to make intelligent decisions and adjust their behavior accordingly. For instance, an AIoT system might modify energy consumption patterns based on up-to-the-minute weather data or traffic conditions, thereby optimizing the utilization of resources.

5. **Interoperability and Semantic Mediation** with respect to control models play a role in tackling the interoperability challenge within diverse AIoT ecosystems. Through semantic mediation techniques, these models enable the integration of data and services by mapping distinct data models and ontologies to a shared semantic representation. Control models are instrumental in orchestrating the processes of semantic mediation, guaranteeing the smooth combination and utilization of data from different sources. This capability is crucial for establishing a cohesive perspective of IoT data and services, facilitating more comprehensive analytics and informed decision-making.

6. **Privacy-Preserving Control** with respect to amid rising concerns about data privacy, control models are evolving to incorporate privacy-centric mechanisms. Approaches like differential privacy and secure multi-party computation are being integrated to enable data analysis while safeguarding sensitive information. Within the context of the Semantic Web for AIoT, control models can deploy

these privacy-preserving measures, ensuring the judicious use of data and adherence to regulatory requirements.

Hence, control models in Semantic Web technologies play a pivotal role in the success of AIoT systems. They oversee access, improve data governance, facilitate policy-based decision-making, enable dynamic adaptation, foster interoperability, and address privacy considerations. As AIoT continues to progress, control models will be crucial in ensuring the efficient and secure functioning of IoT ecosystems, making them a focal point for ongoing research and development in this domain. Researchers and practitioners must consistently innovate and adapt control models to meet the evolving requirements and challenges of AIoT applications.

2.4 Bridging the Gap in AIoT Systems

Semantic interoperability in AIoT systems is crucial for ensuring seamless communication and data exchange among different devices and systems. It involves leveraging semantic web technologies, like ontologies, to establish a common understanding of data (Heiler, 1995).Ontologies serve as a standardized vocabulary that enables effective communication and data interpretation, enhancing decision-making in AIoT applications.By promoting shared data understanding, semantic interoperability contributes to the scalability and flexibility of AIoT systems, allowing for easy adaptation to dynamic environments and integration of new technologies.Ultimately, semantic interoperability plays a pivotal role in empowering the development of resilient and flexible AIoT applications.

3. DATA REPRESENTATION IN AIOT

In the realm of AIoT, knowledge representation involves utilizing Semantic Web technologies to create meaningful and valuable information. This facilitates seamless and interactive sharing among IoT devices and Artificial Intelligence systems, contributing to efficiency and effectiveness in the AIoT context. Essential Semantic Web technologies such as RDF, OWL, and SPARQL play a significant role in realizing this objective (Sharma & Jain, 2021). Here's a brief overview of these technologies and how they contribute to data representation:

a. **SPARQL** serves as a query language employed for the retrieval and manipulation of data stored in RDF format. Within the context of AIoT, SPARQL finds application in querying IoT objects, identifying relationships between these objects, and storing visual content. For instance, SPARQL can be utilized to inquire about all smart devices within a specific room or identify patterns within sensor data.

b. **Semantic Reasoning** in Semantic Web technologies provides a means to comprehend IoT data. Through the use of inference machines, it becomes possible to derive fresh insights from both existing data and ontologies. This capability proves beneficial for various tasks, including product integration, incident detection, and decision-making within the realm of AIoT.

c. **Interoperability** in Semantic Web technology promotes data interoperability by offering a means to describe and share data across various IoT platforms and diverse data sources. This capability facilitates the understanding and processing of data from multiple sources by AI systems.

d. **Security and Privacy** in Semantic Web technologies are applicable for modeling security and privacy within AIoT systems. By creating ontologies, it becomes possible to establish access rights and prioritize privacy settings for both IoT devices and data.

Hence, the utilization of Semantic Web technologies for data representation in AIoT entails constructing models of IoT data and devices that are rich in semantics. This enhances the ability of smart machines to comprehend, contemplate, and take action based on this information. Such an approach fosters improved collaboration, information sharing, and decision-making within the AIoT ecosystem.

3.1 Data Formats and Standards

Semantic web technologies play a crucial role in facilitating data integration and collaboration within the realms of the IoT and AIoT. This technology enables machines to comprehend and process data with the necessary context required for AIoT applications. Here are some important documents and standards regarding the Semantic Web and its application in AIoT:

a. **JSON-LDJ (JSON for data connectivity)**, a JSON-based format specifically crafted for conveying connection information, plays a pivotal role in the integration of RDF data into JSON, presenting a versatile approach for reporting. Within the realm of AIoT, JSON-LD serves as a valuable tool for effectively representing IoT data. By seamlessly combining JSON and RDF content, it provides a streamlined approach for interacting with AI processes. This integration enhances the consideration of IoT data within AI applications, fostering a more cohesive and interoperable environment for processing and analyzing information from interconnected devices (Sporny et al., 2018).

b. **Sensor Markup Language (SensorML)**, an XML-based standard, plays a crucial role in detailing the specifications and functionalities of sensors. Specifically within the context of the AIoT, SensorML serves the purpose of providing essential metadata pertaining to IoT sensors. This metadata is instrumental in enabling smart machines to perceive and comprehend the capabilities and characteristics of sensors within the network (Haller et al., 2019).

c. **Semantic Sensor Network (SSN) ontology** is purposefully crafted for detailing sensors and observations along with their intricate interconnections, and represents a significant advancement in the landscape of IoT ontologies. Specifically, within the domain of AIoT, the SSN ontology stands out as a valuable resource for modeling the network and its observations. Its design goes beyond existing IoT ontologies, offering an enriched framework that encapsulates the complex relationships between sensors and the data they generate. In the context of AIoT applications, the SSN ontology proves instrumental by simplifying the incorporation of sensor data into artificial intelligence applications. This streamlined integration enhances the adaptability and intelligence of the overall system, enabling more effective utilization of sensor-generated information in AI-driven decision-making processes (Janowicz et al., 2019).

d. **Schema.org**, a highly adopted language, functions as a versatile framework for structuring information on the internet, providing models that span diverse domains, including the realm of IoT devices. In the context of AIoT, Schema.org emerges as a valuable asset for documenting web content related to IoT devices. Its utility lies in simplifying the discoverability and comprehension of IoT device information by search engines and artificial intelligence systems. By employing Schema.org, data pertaining to IoT devices gains a standardized structure, making it more accessible and interpretable for both search engines and AI algorithms. This streamlined representation enhances the overall integration and utilization of IoT data in AIoT applications, contributing to more effective decision-making processes (Brickley, 2015).

These data structures and models empower AIoT applications to leverage web technologies in amalgamating data, logic, and decision-making processes. Their significance lies in enhancing the coordination and intelligence of IoT systems.

3.2 Ontologies for Data Representation

Ontologies play a vital role in AIoT systems by offering a structured framework for representing knowledge and information. They define concepts, relationships, and constraints within specific domains, enabling AIoT devices and systems to comprehend and analyze the collected data. A key benefit of employing ontologies in AIoT is the enhancement of data integration and interoperability. By establishing a common vocabulary and semantic structure, ontologies facilitate consistent data exchange and interpretation among diverse devices and systems. This ensures effective integration and analysis of data from various sources, leading to more precise insights and informed decision-making. The semantic web community emphasizes the importance of ontologies and reasoning. Additionally, ontologies empower AIoT systems to engage in reasoning and derive new knowledge from existing data. Through logical and semantic relationships defined in the ontology, machines can draw conclusions, make predictions, and generate novel insights. This capability boosts the autonomy of AIoT systems, enabling them to make intelligent decisions and adapt to changing circumstances.

Furthermore, ontologies facilitate efficient data discovery and retrieval in AIoT applications. Organizing data according to a structured ontology allows machines to navigate and search for relevant information with precision. This proves particularly valuable in large-scale AIoT deployments where vast amounts of data are generated and require quick access. Over the past two decades, ontologies have found widespread use in knowledge representation across various domains, including engineering, biomedical sciences, physics, and agriculture. There is a noticeable trend among scientists, and major tech companies like Google, Amazon, and Facebook, who are increasingly leveraging semantic technologies for data integration, interoperability, and semantic data search (Sheth & Ramakrishnan, 2003).

In conclusion, ontologies are integral to AIoT, offering a structured representation of knowledge that enhances data integration and interoperability, enables reasoning and inference, and facilitates efficient data discovery and retrieval. The incorporation of ontologies into AIoT systems not only boosts their capabilities but also contributes to the creation of more intelligent and autonomous interconnected devices.

3.3 Sensor Data Representation

Semantic web technology holds a significant role in the representation and analysis of sensor data within the framework of AIoT. Utilizing semantic web models like RDF and OWL, sensor data can be structured in formats that are both organized and machine-readable. This application of semantic web technologies enhances the interaction and integration of diverse data sources, allowing different devices, platforms, and applications to comprehend and share sensor data effectively (Davies et al., 2006). This facilitates the analysis of substantial data volumes generated by IoT devices. A key advantage of employing semantic web technology in AIoT lies in its capacity to derive decisions from sensor data and assess novel

Figure 4. Ontology adoption trend in big data application

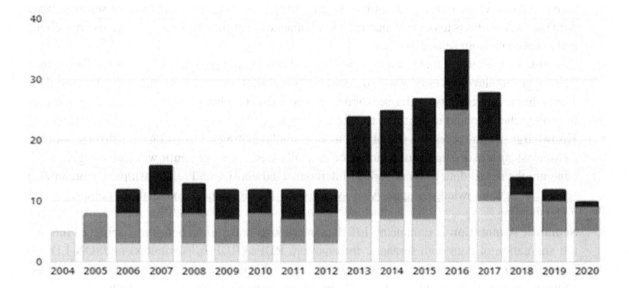

information. By identifying relationships between ontologies and sensor data, AI algorithms can reveal insights and patterns that may not be immediately apparent.

Semantic web technology enhances AIoT applications by enabling advanced analytics, predictive modeling, and decision-making capabilities. By combining sensor data with specific information like weather or geography, AI systems gain deep insights, facilitating accurate and personalized services. For instance, in smart cities, semantic web technologies integrate data from various sensors to optimize traffic flow and mitigate environmental impact. This integration results in more intelligent and efficient AIoT applications across diverse fields such as smart cities, healthcare, agriculture, and industrial automation.

3.4 Data Models for AIoT

Data models serve as a structure for expressing, combining, and validating sensor data within AIoT applications. Employing semantic web technologies empowers organizations to fully exploit the capabilities of sensor data, facilitating intelligent decision-making, automation, and the development of novel applications across various domains. Regarding data models tailored for semantic web technologies and their application in AIoT, numerous crucial models are commonly employed (Hendler et al., 2020). In this case, let's examine some important data structures:

1. **Resource Description Framework (RDF)** serves as the foundational data structure within the Semantic Web, presenting information in a triple format comprising subject, predicate, and object. This structure facilitates the interchange of sensor data and their interconnections, fostering relationships and integration among variables.
2. **Web Ontology Language (OWL)** functions as a language designed for articulating ontologies, encapsulating the elements, relationships, and constraints within a specific domain. It offers an extensive framework for depicting relationships and conducting logical reasoning on data.

3. **Sensor ontology** is a crucial component for representing sensor data in a standardized and inter-active manner. These ontologies outline the attributes, functionalities, and traits of sensors, along with their connections to other resources. They enhance the ability of AIoT systems to comprehend and assess data from sensor devices.

4. **File link** is an effective method for publishing and connecting design documents on the internet. The suggestion involves employing standard URIs and RDF to establish a network of linked data. Through this connectivity model, sensor data can be linked to other well-known sources, expanding the comprehension and insight into the data.

5. **Knowledge graph** serves as a potent data model, amalgamating information from diverse sources, encompassing sensor data and domain-specific details. Leveraging semantic web technology, knowl-edge graphs depict data as a network of interconnected entities and relationships. By organizing sensor data into knowledge graphs, AIoT systems can draw inferences and facilitate comprehensive understanding.

6. **Semantic Annotation** is Enhancing IoT data interaction and comprehension is achieved through the annotation of data with semantic information. RDFa (RDF in Attributes) or JSON-LD can be employed to integrate semantic annotations into IoT data streams. These annotations provide context and significance to the data, rendering it interpretable across various machines.

4. DATA INTEGRATION IN AIOT

The incorporation of semantic web technologies in AIoT systems entails linking content and processes from both domains, establishing connections between information derived from diverse sources. In this integration, IoT systems transmit data to AI technology, facilitating the amalgamation and interpretation of data, alongside capabilities such as image analysis and predictive modeling. Here are some important considerations regarding the use of Semantic Web technology for data integration in AIoT:

●   **Semantic interoperability,** including RDF and OWL, offer a structured framework for explicitly representing information with defined semantics. Through the application of ontologies and design principles, data sourced from diverse outlets can be systematically organized and aligned, fostering improved interoperability. This, in turn, enhances the comprehension, integration, and analytical capabilities of the information.

●   **Ontology mapping** facilitates Integrating data necessitates the mapping of concepts and rela-tionships across various ontologies, establishing semantic connections. Techniques like ontology alignment and matching algorithms play a crucial role in identifying and creating correspondences between distinct ontologies. This process facilitates the integration of objects originating from diverse sources that might employ disparate ontologies or schemas.

●   **Integrating related data** helps in Leveraging the principle of linked data, AIoT systems can amalgamate data from various sources using unique identifiers (URIs) and establish connections across the network. This approach ensures that data is not only linked but also supported by other correlated data, enhancing the content and value of the information.

●   **Design and Creativity** in Semantic Web technology empowers AIoT systems with thinking and reasoning capabilities that extend beyond basic data integration. By utilizing logical reasoning and rules defined in OWL, AIoT systems can extract new knowledge and insights from heterogeneous data. This, in turn, facilitates intelligent decision-making and automation that surpasses the capabilities of mere data integration.

● **Data fusion** in Semantic web technology facilitates the amalgamation of diverse data from various sources, offering a flexible and adaptable model. Through the integration of data from a multitude of sensors, devices, and other origins, AIoT systems can achieve a more comprehensive understanding of the environment, resulting in enhanced insights and value.

● **Data Quality Assurance** helps in Integrating data in AIoT entails implementing processes such as data cleansing, validation, and support to ensure data quality. AIoT systems adhere to data quality standards and best practices to uphold the accuracy and reliability of the integrated data.

By utilizing Semantic Web technologies for data integration in AIoT, organizations can harness the complete potential of their data, fostering collaboration, insight, and delivering valuable information (Prudhomme et al., 2020). This integration supports analytics, intelligent decision-making, and innovation across various sectors, including smart cities, healthcare, and manufacturing.

4.1 Challenges in Data Integration

Data integration in the realm of Semantic Web technologies presents numerous challenges, reflecting the intricacies of aligning diverse data sources and ensuring interoperability within a semantic framework (Sudairy, 2011). The key challenges include:

A. Data integration faces challenges due to the **Heterogeneity of Data Sources,** which include structural and semantic differences. Structural heterogeneity stems from varying structures, formats, and schemas, making integration difficult. Even with aligned structures, semantic heterogeneity presents another challenge. Differences in the meaning of terms across sources lead to conflicts at the semantic level, further complicating integration. Addressing these challenges requires advanced strategies and technologies tailored to heterogeneous environments.

B. Data integration faces a significant challenge due to the **Lack of Standardization**, particularly in vocabulary and ontology mismatch. Different sources use distinct vocabularies and ontologies, complicating mapping and alignment processes and hindering the establishment of a common vocabulary for integration. Ontology evolution presents another persistent challenge, as managing changes over time while ensuring backward compatibility is difficult. These challenges highlight the need for robust solutions and methodologies to navigate the complexities of integrating data with varied vocabularies and evolving ontologies.

C. Integrating data in AIoT faces challenges regarding **Data Quality and Trustworthiness**. Disparities in quality, such as accuracy, completeness, and consistency, among data from diverse sources must be addressed to maintain overall data quality. Provenance and trust are critical considerations; establishing the trustworthiness of data sources and determining data provenance are crucial for ensuring reliability. Comprehensive strategies and frameworks encompassing data quality assurance and trustworthiness analysis are needed to address these challenges in AIoT data integration.

D. **Scalability** is the challenge of large-scale integration in AIoT arises from the exponential growth in complexity as the number and size of data sources increase. This necessitates the development and implementation of efficient algorithms to ensure scalable integration processes. Effectively managing the intricacies associated with integrating a vast amount of data from diverse sources becomes imperative to maintain the overall efficiency and performance of AIoT systems.

E. **Dynamic Nature of Data** are Real-time updates present a challenge in AIoT, particularly with dynamic data sources that frequently update. The management of real-time updates requires careful consideration to ensure the timely incorporation of fresh data into the integrated datasets. Handling the dynamic nature of data streams in real-time is crucial for AIoT systems to provide accurate and up-to-date information, contributing to effective decision-making and overall system performance.

F. **Security and Privacy Concerns** integrating sensitive data in AIoT systems demands meticulous attention to privacy and security during the integration process. The nature of integrated data may involve confidential information, making it imperative to implement robust access control mechanisms. Effective access control ensures the regulation of who can access and modify integrated data, contributing to the overall security and confidentiality of sensitive information within the AIoT environment.

G. **Interoperability** challenges arise in protocols and formats, hindering seamless communication among diverse data sources. Achieving interoperability across tools and platforms for data creation, management, and querying is crucial. Overcoming these challenges is essential for creating a cohesive and interconnected system in the AIoT domain.

H. In Semantic Web technology for AIoT data integration, adopting a **User-Centered** approach is crucial. This involves actively involving end users in the integration process to understand their specific needs. By engaging users throughout the lifecycle, developers ensure that the resulting information meets user expectations. This user-centric integration approach creates more useful and user-friendly information, enhancing the effectiveness and acceptance of AIoT systems.

4.2 Data Fusion Techniques

Data fusion techniques play a pivotal role in Semantic Web technologies, aiming to integrate and combine information from diverse sources (Hunter et al., 2008). Commonly employed techniques include:

A. **Ontology Alignment and Integration** Ontology mapping aligns ontologies from different sources to identify equivalent concepts and relationships, ensuring semantic interoperability. By establishing correspondences between entities, seamless communication and data exchange across platforms are facilitated. Ontology integration consolidates aligned concepts into a unified ontology, harmonizing knowledge representation from multiple sources. This shared framework promotes standardized understanding of the domain. Both processes enhance efficiency and effectiveness of information systems, enabling cohesive operation in heterogeneous environments.

B. **Linking and Interlinking** Entity linking is vital for information integration, identifying and connecting similar entities across datasets or ontologies to enhance coherence and comprehensibility. Linked Open Data (LOD) is pivotal in creating an interconnected knowledge web, using common identifiers like URIs to link related data points across the Semantic Web. This interconnectedness facilitates seamless information traversal, enabling unified and standardized data retrieval from diverse sources. Both entity linking and LOD contribute to establishing a more interconnected and interoperable data landscape.

C. **RDF Data Integration** DF graph integration merges RDF graphs from diverse sources by aligning shared URIs and relationships, creating a consolidated knowledge representation. Named graphs, a technique within RDF, encapsulate information from various sources within a single dataset. Each named graph is identified and separated, facilitating the representation of heterogeneous data within a unified framework. This approach is valuable for managing and querying data from different contexts, providing a structured way to handle RDF graphs in a linked data environment.

D. **Semantic Annotation** Annotation fusion enriches information by integrating annotations and metadata, enhancing its semantic richness. This process consolidates diverse annotations linked to entities or relationships within a dataset, leading to a more comprehensive understanding of the information. Semantic tagging assigns standardized semantic tags to entities and relationships, facilitating easier data integration by providing a common language. Annotation fusion and semantic tagging together contribute to a more semantically aware and interoperable data environment, improving data discovery, retrieval, and comprehension across diverse applications and systems.

E. **Reasoning and Inference** play crucial roles in data integration, employing various approaches to enhance the overall understanding and coherence of integrated datasets. Rule-based reasoning involves the application of predefined rules to infer new knowledge from existing data, promoting seamless integration. Ontology reasoning, on the other hand, leverages logical reasoning over ontologies to derive implicit relationships, further enriching the semantic context of integrated information.

F. **Probabilistic and Statistical Approaches** are approaches that contribute to the accuracy of integrated datasets. Probabilistic data fusion involves assigning probabilities to different data sources or assertions and combining them for a more accurate representation. Statistical alignment utilizes statistical methods to align and merge information from diverse sources, ensuring a robust integration process.

G. **Machine Learning Techniques,** such as instance matching and classification/clustering, play pivotal roles in data integration by employing algorithms to identify instances referring to the same real-world entities and grouping similar entities or relationships, respectively.

H. **Quality Assessment and Trustworthiness** is ensuring the quality and trustworthiness of integrated data is critical. Data quality metrics assess the reliability of data from various sources, guiding the fusion process. Trustworthiness analysis incorporates trust and reliability measures to prioritize information from more trustworthy sources.

I. **Conflict Resolution** is essential for maintaining consistency in integrated datasets. Detecting conflicts or inconsistencies in information from different sources is the first step, followed by the application of conflict resolution strategies to harmonize conflicting data.

J. **Dynamic Fusion**, real-time integration adapts fusion techniques to handle dynamic data sources and updates, while incremental fusion involves updating integrated datasets incrementally as new data becomes available. These dynamic approaches ensure that integrated datasets remain relevant and up-to-date in evolving environments.

These techniques are often combined, with the specific choice depending on data characteristics, integration goals, and available resources. Ongoing research in data fusion within the context of Semantic Web technologies continues to refine and improve the efficiency of integration processes.

4.3 Data Integration Frameworks

Several information sharing systems and frameworks have been developed to facilitate data integration within the scope of Semantic Web technologies. Notable examples include:

I. **D2RQ (DB to RDF mapping)** forms the basis for virtually connecting data, introducing relational database schemas and data into RDF. It enables read-only RDF access and facilitates SPARQL queries on mapped data (Dhanapalan & Chen, 2007).

II. **On Top**,based on Ontology Data Access (OBDA), is an open platform enabling SPARQL queries in relational databases by converting them into SQL queries (Calvanese, 2015).

III. **R2RML (RDB to RDF Mapping Language)**, a W3C repository standard, defines a language for expressing graphs to map relational repositories to RDF triples, facilitating RDF-based data integration (Sequeda, 2013).

IV. **Silk Connection Framework** is a framework designed for discovering relationships between resources in networked environments. It provides tools for connecting data and links, supporting the creation of RDF links (Bizer et al., 2009).

V. **Gradoop** is a decentralized graph processing framework tailored for processing large datasets. It includes tools for graph-based data integration and analysis (Junghanns et al., 2015).

VI. **RDFpro** is a framework for parallel processing and distribution of RDF. It offers a set of operators for RDF data processing and integration, supporting operations such as filtering, mapping, and integration (Banane & Belangour, 2019).

VII. **MOMIS (Multiple Information Source Brokering Environment)** is an information sharing system supporting the creation of international standards. It provides ontology-based data integration and transformation tools (Bergamaschi et al., 2004).

VIII. **Morph-CSV** is a tool used to convert CSV files to RDF, enabling the integration of CSV data into the Semantic Web by providing annotations to clarify the mapping between CSV data and the RDF graph (Ruckhaus et al., 2021).

IX. **CARML (CSV to RDF Mapping Language)** is a language used to express data from CSV to RDF formats, allowing users to define how table data will be converted into RDF triples (Santipantakis et al., 2018).

X. **MapForce** is a comprehensive data mapping, transformation, and integration system. While not specific to Semantic Web technology, it supports various file formats, including XML and RDF, making it useful for data sharing operations (Kaykova et al., 2007).

These frameworks offer a range of features and functionality, with specific processes contingent on data nature, integration needs, and user or developer preferences. The ongoing development of these frameworks addresses the challenges associated with Semantic Web data integration.

4.4 Improving Data Discovery and Integration in AIoT

Managing the vast amount of data generated by interconnected devices in IoT and AI poses a significant challenge. Traditional methods of data discovery and integration are manual and complex. However, semantic web technologies offer an efficient and automated solution. They enable AIoT systems to seamlessly discover, understand, and integrate data from various sources by providing a common framework for describing and organizing data. With semantic web technologies, AIoT applications can leverage artificial intelligence and machine learning to automatically discover and integrate pertinent data (Perera et al., 2014).

For instance, in healthcare, semantic technologies can integrate patient data from different sources, such as electronic health records and wearables. This integrated data enables personalized and proactive healthcare services, improving patient outcomes. Moreover, semantic web technologies enhance AIoT systems' ability to handle data heterogeneity efficiently.

In conclusion, semantic web technologies play a pivotal role in overcoming challenges related to data discovery and integration in AIoT. They offer automated solutions that enhance efficiency and effectiveness, enabling AIoT applications to gain a holistic view of data and derive meaningful insights. By providing a standardized and automated approach to data organization and integration, semantic technologies empower AIoT applications to unlock their full potential.

4.5 Case Studies on Data Integration in AIoT

Technology plays a crucial role in expediting a wide range of activities, with IoT technology and intelligence standing out as a pivotal branch significantly influencing contemporary business operations. Here are some case studies that demonstrate the use of data integration in AIoT:

1. Smart City Infrastructure

Numerous smart city endeavors concentrate on aspects such as traffic flow, air quality, and waste management, utilizing interconnected devices to gather data. Data integration becomes imperative for amalgamating information from diverse sensors and systems, facilitating a comprehensive understanding of urban operations. In Barcelona, the CityOS initiative integrates data from sensors dispersed throughout the city to oversee and regulate urban operations, managing city services effectively. The amalgamated data contributes to enhancing traffic management, minimizing energy consumption, and optimizing overall city efficiency (Gharaibeh et al., 2017).

2. Industrial Internet of Things (IIoT) for Predictive Maintenance

Manufacturers utilize IoT sensors for equipment performance monitoring. AIoT solutions integrate sensor data with machine learning algorithms to predict equipment failures. General Electric applies AIoT for predictive maintenance in aircraft engines, utilizing sensor data to anticipate maintenance needs, minimize downtime, and optimize engine performance (Čolaković & Hadžialić, 2018).

3. Healthcare IoT for Patient Care

Within the healthcare sector, IoT devices like wearables and monitors are prolific in generating data for numerous patients. The fusion of this data with artificial intelligence algorithms holds the potential to offer personalized insights, facilitate early disease detection, and enhance overall patient care (Marcos et al., 2013). Philips Healthcare is at the forefront of providing AIoT solutions for patient care. Their platform seamlessly integrates data sourced from wearables, electronic health records, and various other channels, enabling real-time monitoring, predictive analytics, and timely interventions, especially for patients grappling with chronic diseases.

4. Smart Agriculture

Within agriculture, IoT sensors play a pivotal role in gathering data pertaining to soil conditions, weather patterns, and crop health. The amalgamation of this data with intelligent models presents an opportunity for farmers to optimize irrigation, forecast crop yields, and make well-informed decisions fostering sustainable agricultural practices. The John Deere Operations Center utilizes AIoT to gather data from a variety of sources including farm equipment, weather stations, and satellite imagery. This integrated approach empowers farmers to make informed decisions regarding crucial aspects such as planting, harvesting, and resource allocation in their agricultural operations (Zhang et al., 2018).

5. Retail and Customer Experience

Within the realm of retail, IoT devices like beacons and smart meters generate valuable data on customer behavior and inventory levels. Integrating this data with AI technologies facilitates personalized marketing, inventory optimization, and enhances overall customer service. Amazon Go stores serve as a notable example, employing IoT sensors and AI algorithms to seamlessly integrate data from cameras and sensors. This integration results in a cashierless store where the system autonomously tracks the products selected by customers, automatically charging their accounts during the checkout process (Dlamini & Johnston, 2016).

6. Energy Management in Smart Homes

IoT sensors embedded in smart homes are designed to monitor factors such as occupancy, temperature, and energy consumption. The integration of data with intelligent algorithms facilitates the implementation of smart energy management strategies, optimizing functions like lighting, heating, and cooling. It siemens' Desigo CC exemplifies an integrated control system that leverages AIoT to enhance energy efficiency. This system effectively integrates information from diverse building functions, encompassing HVAC and lighting, with the aim of boosting energy efficiency and curbing operational costs (Silva et al., 2018).

7. Semantic Web Applications in AIoT

Semantic web technology is a crucial driver in the evolution and progress of the AIoT. By offering a means to represent and interconnect data, semantic web technology enhances collaboration, fosters a deeper understanding of data semantics, and facilitates intelligent decision-making within AIoT applications. The integration of Semantic Web applications in AIoT contributes to the development of intelligent, context-aware, and integrated systems, ultimately boosting the efficiency and effectiveness of IoT applications. Some of the main web applications in AIoT are:

I.   **Ontology-Based Data Representation** Ontology serves as a method for systematically organizing and representing information and relationships within a specific domain. In the context of AIoT, ontologies are instrumental in modeling the content of IoT data, devices, and their interactions. It facilitates collaboration by enhancing the comprehension of data semantics. Enables deeper insights into IoT content, contributing to improved contextual information. Supports the analysis and reasoning of IoT data, thereby facilitating intelligent decision-making processes (Sheth & Ramakrishnan, 2003).

II. **Linked Data for Collaboration** Aligned with the principles of the Semantic Web, the Linked Data Policy involves the application of rules and standards to establish connections between information on the web. In the realm of AIoT, this entails the interlinking of data from diverse sources, encompassing IoT devices and platforms. It enables the creation of a comprehensive, interconnected perspective of IoT data on a global scale.Facilitates the seamless integration of data originating from various sources.It also promotes the exploration and discovery of knowledge pertinent to AI (Hendler et al., 2020).

III. **Semantic Sensor Network** The SSN is employed to delineate sensors, observations, and their corresponding Metadata ontology. In the context of AIoT, SSN offers a means to represent sensor data and enrich their information with semantic details. It enhances the interaction of sensor data by employing a standardized language by supporting thoughtful analysis and consideration of sensor context. It streamlines the integration of sensor data into comprehensive mapping systems (Janowicz et al., 2019).

IV. **Integration of IoT Data With RDF** Utilizing RDF to represent IoT data enables the establishment of a data link network. This methodology facilitates the integration of diverse IoT datasets into a cohesive semantic system. It facilitates the integration of varied and heterogeneous IoT data.Offers a flexible and extensible data model for the representation of IoT data within the Internet of Things. Also, it Simplifies the process of querying and analyzing intricate data through the use of SPARQL queries (Prudhomme et al., 2020).

V. **IoT Semantic Middleware** The IoT Semantic Middleware platform serves as an intermediary connecting IoT devices and applications, incorporating a data streaming Semantic layer. These middleware platforms commonly leverage ontology and semantic technologies. It includes Interpretation and coordination of diverse information and communication systems by facilitating the incorporation of semantic annotations into raw data files. It also supports the creation of intelligent applications by furnishing semantic content (Rodríguez, 2012).

VI. **AIoT Knowledge Graph** nowledge graphs serve as depictions of information concerning entities and their interconnections. Within the realm of AIoT, cognitive images can be formulated by amalgamating data from diverse IoT sources, enhancing comprehension of the surrounding environment. It enables reasoning about interconnected graphs of IoT information.Also, it facilitates context-aware decision-making by discerning relationships between entities (Gutiérrez & Sequeda, 2021). And it Contributes to the advancement of intelligent applications through an enhanced understanding of the IoT landscape.

VII. **Semantic Reasoning for IoT Analysis** Implementing semantic reasoning in IoT data processing presents a significant opportunity for extracting valuable insights. This approach is particularly beneficial in applications like predictive maintenance and troubleshooting within the IoT ecosystem. By incorporating semantic reasoning, the comprehension of IoT data improves, enabling the recognition of subtle patterns and relationships. This leads to more informed decision-making. Additionally, semantic reasoning supports the development of intelligent models for in-depth analysis, fostering innovation in various domains. Overall, leveraging semantic reasoning in IoT data processing enhances the utilization of information generated by IoT devices (Maarala et al., 2016).

5.1 Semantic Web Technologies

Semantic Web technology is a comprehensive system, process, and set of technologies meticulously designed to represent, link, and discover information on the World Wide Web in both machine-readable and human-understandable formats. Its primary goal is to facilitate the seamless sharing and integration of data across diverse domains and applications. The growing interest in the Semantic Web is evident in the notable surge in the number of semantic markups present on the Web and the proliferation of organizations dedicated to research and development in this field. The current landscape showcases a multitude of research projects and semantic web applications, indicating a substantial focus on the evolution of the Semantic Web since the early nineties. This suggests a promising trajectory toward the realization of a large-scale Semantic Web in the near future (Matthews, 2005).

5.2 Linked Data in AIoT

In AIoT systems, linked data is vital for semantic interoperability. It connects data across diverse sources, enabling access to extensive information pools. AIoT applications leverage linked data to tap into various sources, creating an interconnected network of information. This interconnectedness enhances insights, fostering intelligent decision-making and overall performance. For example, in a smart city AIoT application, linked data connects and analyzes information from traffic sensors, weather stations, and social media feeds to offer real-time updates and optimize energy consumption efficiently. Linked data also contributes to scalability and adaptability in AIoT applications (Hendler et al., 2020). It facilitates seamless integration and updates as new data sources emerge or existing ones evolve, ensuring ongoing relevance and currency of AIoT systems.

In summary, incorporating linked data into AIoT applications brings numerous benefits, including improved decision-making and heightened scalability. It empowers AIoT systems to extract valuable insights and navigate evolving environments adeptly.

5.3 Knowledge Graphs and Their Role in AIoT

A knowledge graph is a structured representation of information, containing entities, relationships, and attributes. Nodes represent entities, edges show relationships, and attributes provide additional details, organizing data graphically. This framework is vital for organizing data, enhancing information integration, semantic comprehension, and visual exploration (Gutiérrez & Sequeda, 2021). Knowledge graphs integrate ideas and technologies from various fields, fostering a comprehensive understanding of progress. In AIoT, they interpret and utilize data from IoT devices, providing standardized representations through entities, relationships, and attributes. They aid data modeling and contribute to AI applications by enabling pattern recognition, visualization, and decision-making.

Moreover, knowledge graphs enhance the robustness of AIoT systems by organizing and managing growing datasets. They support a connected ecosystem for intelligent algorithms to extract valuable information from IoT-generated data.

5.4 Practical Applications of Semantic Web in AIoT

The incorporation of semantic web technologies within the realm of AIoT opens up opportunities for numerous practical uses, enhancing the representation of knowledge, promoting interoperability, and augmenting semantic capabilities. Here are some useful applications where Semantic Web plays an important role in AIoT:

A. Smart Cities

The utilization of Semantic Network technology is instrumental in facilitating integration within smart city initiatives. Diverse IoT applications, including traffic management, environmental monitoring, and utility systems, benefit from this technology. Knowledge graphs play a crucial role in depicting relationships among entities like traffic patterns, air quality, and infrastructure. This enables informed decision-making in urban planning, resource development, and the provision of public services (Blomqvist, 2014).

B. Predictive Maintenance in Industrial IoT

The integration of semantic web technology proves invaluable in establishing connections between machines, sensor data, and historical maintenance knowledge graphs. This framework facilitates predictive maintenance by empowering intelligent algorithms to recognize patterns, identify anomalies, and forecast potential equipment failures. This not only results in cost savings but also enhances overall business performance by proactively addressing maintenance needs (Cao et al., 2022).

C. Healthcare IoT

Semantic Web technology is vital for seamlessly integrating patient data from diverse sources like wearable devices, electronic health records, and medical supplies. Knowledge graphs effectively capture relationships among patient information, treatments, and outcomes, advancing personalized medicine, precise treatment recommendations, and early diagnosis. This integration improves healthcare by enhancing understanding of patient health and optimizing medical decision-making (Malik & Malik, 2020).

D. Supply Chain Optimization

Within AIoT-driven supply chain management, the incorporation of semantic web technology contributes to the enhancement of different facets of the supply chain, including products, materials, and logistics. This implementation facilitates real-time tracking, accurate demand forecasting, and intelligent decision-making for efficient inventory management and optimization (Ye et al., 2008).

E. Energy Management in Smart Buildings

In smart buildings, semantic network technology models relationships among devices like smart thermostats, lighting systems, and energy meters. This enables AI applications to dynamically optimize energy consumption based on real-time patterns, weather conditions, and user preferences. This leads to increased energy efficiency and significant cost savings, highlighting the impactful role of semantic network technology in advancing building infrastructure intelligence and sustainability (Lork et al., 2019).

F. AgriTech (AgriTech)

Semantic web technology integrates data from sensors, weather updates, and crop information in precision agriculture. It creates knowledge maps showing relationships between soil characteristics, crop types, and environmental factors, aiding AI-driven decision-making for irrigation, fertilization, and crop management. Leveraging semantic web technology enhances precision agriculture, improving farming practices and resource utilization for increased crop yield (Triantafyllou et al., 2019).

G. Cross-Domain Integration of Personalized Services

Semantic Web technology integrates data from diverse sources like news, medical information, and user preferences, forming the basis for intelligent applications. These applications provide personalized services and recommendations, enhancing user experiences through a deeper understanding of relationships among different data sets. This fosters tailored interactions across various domains (Terziyan & Kononenko, 2003).

H. Traffic Management and Intelligence

Semantic networking technology in transportation assesses the connections among traffic signals, traffic data, and modeling. This enables AI applications to enhance traffic flow, anticipate collisions, and offer real-time suggestions for heightened efficiency (Toulni et al., 2015).

I. Environmental Monitoring

Semantic web technology is employed to depict the interconnections among environmental sensors, weather data, and geographic information. This aids in early warning and prevention initiatives for natural disasters by empowering artificial intelligence applications to detect and forecast environmental conditions (Donkers et al., 2022).

J. Cross-Domain Collaboration

Semantic Web technology facilitates collaboration and information exchange across diverse domains, proving particularly valuable in collaborative AIoT applications. In scenarios where data from disparate domains like healthcare, transportation, and energy must be integrated for analysis and decision-making, Semantic Web technology plays a crucial role (Rhayem et al., 2020).

In practical applications, the integration of semantic web technologies enhances the interactivity, situational awareness, and intelligence of AIoT systems, transforming them into valuable sources of accessible and decisive information.

6. CONTROL MODELS SPECIFICATIONS IN SEMANTIC WEB-BASED AIOT

Control standards and specifications play a crucial role in Semantic Web-Based AIoT, defining the parameters for interaction and management of devices, systems, and processes. Semantic Web technology serves as a robust foundation for instructing and conceptualizing control models within AIoT applications (Barnaghi et al., 2012). Important considerations for managing a model in Semantic Web-based AIoT are:

I. Ontology-Based Control Modeling

Ontologies provide an organized method for structuring elements, relationships, and attributes within a domain. They delineate concepts related to objects, controls, and their interconnections in a management model. Ontologies improve content management comprehension, fostering interoperability across devices and systems. Semantic annotations within the ontology enhance the understanding of control structures, making them more interpretable and machine-readable.

II. Semantic Representation of Control Actions

Semantic Web technologies, like RDF, express control actions in triple form, comprising subjects (e.g., devices), predicates (e.g., control actions), and objects (e.g., target values). Representing control actions in RDF adheres to Linked Data principles, allowing interlinking of control-related information across the web. RDF triples enable the use of SPARQL queries and semantic inference, enabling advanced control logic and reasoning capabilities.

III. Event-Driven Control Models

In AIoT, control models often use event-driven paradigms, where actions respond to specific events. Semantic Web technologies, like RDF (Resource Description Framework), allow modeling of events, conditions, and actions. RDF-based representation offers flexibility, accommodating various scenarios in AIoT. Events and conditions can dynamically link to control actions, enabling adaptive systems that adjust based on real-time changes.

IV. Rule-Based Control Systems

Semantic Web rule languages, such as SWRL, articulate complex control logic, enhancing control system sophistication. Standardized rule languages promote interoperability, enabling seamless sharing and reuse of control models across systems, enhancing efficiency and adaptability. Adoption of these languages elevates control model sophistication, fostering collaboration across domains.

V. Knowledge Graph for Control Context

Semantic Web technologies enable knowledge graph creation, modeling the context of control actions. They capture relationships between materials, the environment, and consumer preferences, supporting context-sensitive decision-making. Knowledge graphs provide a comprehensive overview of the management environment, aiding informed actions. Relationships in the graphs represent intricate dependencies, effectively capturing complex interactions impacting management processes.

VI. Queryable Control State

Semantic Web technology is capable of representing both the current and expected states of devices and systems. This data can be queried using SPARQL to assess the current state and initiate relevant checks. Event management enabled by Semantic Web technology facilitates real-time monitoring of equipment and systems, ensuring timely awareness of their status. The control system can dynamically adapt to problem conditions by responding to changes or deviations, enhancing overall system responsiveness.

VII. Device Semantic Annotation

Semantic annotation enhances interoperability and comprehension in the AIoT ecosystem. It annotates operations, effects, and control parameters, ensuring consistent device descriptions across platforms. Leveraging semantic information, the tool can automatically configure and adjust the control structure based on device capabilities, streamlining adaptation.

VIII. Communication Protocol

Semantic networking technology can be integrated with AIoT communication protocols, such as MQTT or CoAP, to enhance the efficiency and communication of equipment and management processes. The use of standardized communication protocols increases interoperability by establishing a common foundation for communication protocols. Communication can carry rich information, supporting interpretation and fostering a deeper understanding of the exchanged data.

In conclusion, Semantic Web technology offers a robust suite of tools and models for articulating, querying, and comprehending control models in AIoT. Through the utilization of ontologies, RDF, language conventions, and knowledge graphs, AIoT systems can attain heightened interoperability, adaptability, and semantic depth in management specifications. This integration fosters more intelligent and context-aware management processes, contributing to a sophisticated and responsive AIoT ecosystem.

6.1 Control and Automation in AIoT

Control and automation are transforming the AIoT landscape, using advanced algorithms and machine learning models for intelligent decision-making. Real-time audit data continuously enhances processes, increasing efficiency and productivity. Edge computing amplifies AIoT capabilities, enabling real-time decision-making at the network's edge (Domingue et al., 2011). Reduced latency allows swift responses to environmental changes, vital for scenarios like business automation and autonomous vehicles. Predictive maintenance powered by AI analytics minimizes downtime and extends equipment lifespan. Automation streamlines tasks, reducing errors and enhancing productivity, optimizing resource allocation in energy management for sustainable resource utilization.

Intelligent automation in AIoT incorporates features like natural language processing and computer vision, facilitating diverse functions. The fusion of control and automation prioritizes safety, enhancing efficiency and productivity. This evolution emphasizes the importance of intelligent decision-making and sustainable practices in contemporary systems.

6.2 Leveraging Semantic Web for Control Models

Leveraging semantic networking in AIoT control models enhances intelligence coordination and decision-making. Ontologies provide standardized frameworks for defining concepts and relationships, fostering communication among devices and promoting seamless integration and interoperability (Sabou, 2016). SWRL rules empower the expression and understanding of intricate controls through semantic relationships, encouraging logic and reasoning. This approach enhances control models' sophistication, allowing for nuanced decision-making based on semantic connections and logical rules. Knowledge graphs encapsulate contextual information about organizations and their interconnections, empowering informed decisions across various facets in AIoT systems. In the AIoT context, knowledge graphs specifically capture relationships among devices, environments, and user preferences, contributing to a comprehensive approach to decision-making.

SPARQL aids real-time monitoring and dynamic responses in control systems, facilitating seamless integration of IoT platforms. Implementing AIoT control models with Semantic Web technology enriches semantics, interactivity, and adaptability, enabling informed decision-making and data-driven strategies.

6.3 Strategies for Control in AIoT

Artificial Intelligence Governance in the Internet of Things entails the management and optimization of connected devices and systems through intelligent decision-making processes. Implementing a robust control strategy is crucial to ensuring compatibility, flexibility, and optimal performance within the AIoT environment. This strategic approach is essential for maintaining the efficiency and effectiveness of interconnected devices and systems in the rapidly evolving landscape of IoT and AI (Peter et al., 2023). The basic concepts of AIoT management are:

I. Adaptive Control System

The AIoT's adaptive control system exhibits responsiveness to variations and dynamically modifies the environment to adapt its actions. Utilizing real-time data and machine learning algorithms, these systems continuously tweak their parameters and responses. Adaptive control enables the system to adapt to unforeseen and uncertain alterations. The system has the potential to enhance its performance in response to changes.

II. Control Model

Predictive control encompasses forecasting the future state and behavior of a system in order to modify its current state. This involves the utilization of machine learning models, statistical methods, and historical data to anticipate upcoming trends. Anticipating the future empowers the system to proactively address potential risks, thereby preventing adverse outcomes. Predictive control aids in optimizing the allocation of resources to meet future needs effectively.

III. Rule Based Systems

Rule-Based Systems rely on predefined rules to govern the behavior of objects and structures, following a set standard. These rules are crafted to provide guidance in making decisions regarding specific situations or products. Rule-based systems are typically transparent and descriptive, rendering their actions more comprehensible and manageable. Clearly defined rules play a pivotal role in guiding and facilitating decision-making processes.

IV. Distributed Control Architecture

Distributed control architecture involves decentralized decision-making across a network, enabling devices to autonomously make decisions. This approach is well-suited for an extensive, decentralized AIoT environment. Distributed management facilitates the scalability of expansive and intricate systems. Decision-making at the local level can diminish communication latency, particularly in edge computing environments.

V. Event Management

The event management model initiates actions in response to particular events or conditions. Devices and systems promptly react to situations, enabling timely decision-making.Programs supported by the event management model can react swiftly to changing conditions.Efficient Resource .Adhering to specific conditions ensures the optimal utilization of resources.

VI. Fuzzy Logic Control

A fuzzy logic control system manages imprecise and uncertain information by employing diverse languages and fuzzy rules to model decisions with undefined inputs and out. Fuzzy logic systems exhibit robustness in handling uncertainty and variability. Fuzzy logic provides a mechanism for conveying information in situations where clarity or precision is lacking, resembling human-like decision-making processes.

VII. Hierarchical Control Structure

The hierarchical control structure arranges decisions into layers or hierarchies, where lower levels entail immediate actions, and upper levels focus on making well-informed decisions. The hierarchical arrangement offers a systematic approach to management and control.Managing diverse hierarchical functions enhances the allocation of resources in a more effective manner.

VIII. Machine Learning-Based Control

Machine learning algorithms, encompassing control, reinforcement learning, and neural networks, are employed for decision control in machines. These algorithms derive insights from data patterns, continuously enhancing decision-making capabilities.Machine learning models exhibit adaptability, consistently refining and enhancing their performance with the integration of new day. Control systems based on machine learning demonstrate superior performance, particularly when dealing with intricate, non-linear relationships.

IX. Security and Privacy-Aware Control

Control strategies in AIoT necessitate a careful consideration of security and privacy aspects. It is crucial to implement controls that safeguard data integrity, confidentiality, and user privacy. Employing security controls helps in reducing the risk of unauthorized access and potential cyber threats, thereby fostering user trust.

In conclusion, successful control in AIoT entails a blend of adaptive, predictive, and policy-based strategies tailored to the distinctive needs and features of the IoT environment. The selection of a management strategy is contingent upon factors such as the application's nature, deployment scale, and the desired level of decisional autonomy. It is imperative to incorporate security and privacy considerations to guarantee the reliable and responsible operation of AIoT systems.

6.4 Real-WORLD IMPLEMENTATIONS

Real-world applications showcase the extensive impact of Semantic Web technologies across industries, providing apt information representation for informed decision-making and enhanced application performance (Stephens, 2007). Noteworthy applications include:

a) Healthcare

Semantic Web aids in integrating diverse medical information, utilizing ontologies and RDF for improved understanding, decision-making, and information exchange in healthcare systems.

b) Electronics and Business

Semantic web is employed for product information display and recommendation systems in e-commerce, enhancing accuracy through semantic descriptions and ontologies, leading to personalized product recommendations.

c) Advertising and Media

Semantic Web technologies are utilized to enhance content discovery and link building in the advertising and media industry. RDF and linked content create knowledge maps, improving content navigation and understanding of digital relationships.

d) Smart Cities

Semantic Web plays a crucial role in integrating data from various sources in smart cities, employing ontologies for urban organization representation. This facilitates improved traffic management, public safety, and urban planning.

e) Cultural Heritage

Museums and archives use semantic web technology to organize and exhibit cultural works, creating infographics for comprehensive exploration and understanding of cultural heritage.

f) Financial Services

Semantic Web facilitates modeling relationships in financial services, aiding accurate risk assessment, fraud detection, and compliance, thereby contributing to a transparent and traceable financial ecosystem.

7. CASE STUDIES

7.1 Case Study 1: Data Representation and Integration in a Smart City AIoT

System

A. Title
   Enhancing Urban Intelligence: Data Representation and Integration in Smart City AIoT Systems (Alahi et al., 2023).
B. Introduction
   Investigates the implementation of smart city AIoT systems in "TechMetropolis," emphasizing data representation and integration for improved urban planning, public services, and resource development.
C. Goal
   Create a unified AIoT system extracting, processing, and representing data from various city products to enhance urban performance, public services, and contribute to sustainable development.
D. Activities
   Uses semantic web technology for improved coordination, harmonizing data from vehicle sensors, environmental monitoring, and utilities. Implements Linked Data Schema for seamless navigation, enabling urban planners to search for aggregated connections.Integrates IoT devices for effective municipal services, enhancing resource allocation and public awareness.

Applies machine learning algorithms to predict urban patterns and issues, aiding better decision-making for traffic and waste management. Addresses challenges through strong encryption and compliance with data protection laws.Ensures scalability via cloud-based infrastructure and distributed computing technology. Quick decisions, resource optimization, and improved public services. By focusing on robust data representation and integration, the integration of AIoT into TechMetropolis sets an example for smart city development.

7.2 Case Study 2 Implementing a Semantic Web-Based Control Model in Industrial

AIoT

A. Title

Orchestration Efficiency: Implementation of Semantic Web-Based Control Model in Industrial AIoT (Mehta et al., 2022).

B. Introduction

Explores the transformation of large-scale production in "TechManufacture" using a semantic web-based management model in the AIoT ecosystem.

C. Mission

Aims to provide a control model integrating information for optimizing business processes, reducing costs, and increasing productivity.

D. Activities

Develops business ontologies for common understanding in production processes. Represents data using RDF for dynamic knowledge graphs capturing relationships and dependencies. Adds semantic descriptions to machines for context-sensitive understanding. Uses SWRL rules for control changes based on sensor data and historical performance.

E. Competition

Addresses challenges through standard ontologies and semantic mapping tools. Manages real-time data processing using distributed computing resources. Improves efficiency, extends equipment life, and supports adaptive resource allocation. Tech manufacture's industrial AIoT ecosystem exemplifies the transformative power of semantic web technology in increasing operational excellence.

8. CHALLENGES AND FUTURE DIRECTIONS

Developing a unified understanding among stakeholders. Managing the increasing number of IoT devices with semantic models. Avoiding latency in AIoT applications. Ensuring data integrity, confidentiality, and protection in Semantic Web and AIoT integration. Collaborative creation of knowledge ontologies for interoperability. Enhancing AIoT capabilities with machine learning. Focusing on decentralized and edge-based semantic processing. Integrating encryption, self-distribution, and evolving standards.

8.1 Current Challenges in AIoT Data Management

Handling large and diverse data generated by connected devices. Ensuring reliability through data cleaning and prioritization. Managing instant decisions in applications like tracking or autonomous driving. Addressing cybersecurity threats and privacy breaches. Overcoming challenges in integrating different IoT devices and platforms. Balancing operations between edge and midstream for consistency and efficiency. Optimizing data transfer for sustainability. The challenges in AIoT data management call for integrated solutions involving data engineering, machine learning, cybersecurity, and compliance (Hou et al., 2023).

8.2 Emerging Trends and Future Applications in AIoT

Combining machine learning algorithms with semantic web technologies for pattern discovery. Using semantic web in smart cities for efficient resource management. Leveraging semantic technologies for intelligent data integration in healthcare. The future of AIoT is closely linked to advancements in semantic web technologies, promising innovative applications across industries (Yang et al., 2021).

8.3 Security and Privacy Considerations in AIoT

i) Security Measures

Protecting data during transmission and storage. Restricting data access to authorized individuals.Monitoring and tracking unauthorized activities.

ii) Privacy Measures

Protecting individual identities. Regulating responsible data use.

iii) Conclusion

Prioritizing security and privacy is crucial in utilizing semantic web technologies in AIoT applications (Xiong et al., 2021).

8.4 Discussion

A. Application

Semantic web technologies applied in various sectors for improved data representation and integration.

B. Challenges

Coherent semantic systems, scalability, real-time execution, security, and privacy.

C. Limitations

Balancing granular information needs with user privacy.

D. Advantages

Quick decisions, resource optimization, improved public services, and efficiency in industrial processes.

E. Future Directions

Collaboration for ontology model improvement, machine learning integration, decentralized and edge-based processing, and security solutions.

F. Overall Summarization

Semantic web technologies play a vital role in enhancing AIoT systems' efficiency and intelligence, addressing challenges and opening new possibilities for future applications.

9. CONCLUSION

Semantic Web technologies are indispensable in the AIoT landscape, providing the tools needed for effective organization, understanding, and analysis of vast interconnected data. The integration of semantic web technologies with AIoT not only addresses current challenges but also unlocks new avenues for innovation and intelligent connectivity. The collaboration of researchers, developers, and partners is crucial for realizing the full potential of these technologies and driving advancements that positively impact daily lives and fuel innovation across various domains.

REFERENCES

Al-Sudairy, M. T., & Vasista, T. G. K. (2011). Semantic Data Integration Approaches. *International Journal of Web & Semantic Technology*, 2(1), 12. doi:10.5121/ijwest.2011.2101

Alahi, M. E. E., Sukkuea, A., Tina, F. W., Nag, A., Kurdthongmee, W., Suwannarat, K., & Mukhopadhyay, S. C. (2023). Integration of IoT-Enabled Technologies and Artificial Intelligence (AI) for Smart City Scenario: Recent Advancements and Future Trends. *Sensors (Basel)*, 23(11), 5206. doi:10.3390/s23115206 PMID:37299934

Banane, M., & Belangour, A. (2019). A survey on RDF data stores based on NoSQL systems for the Semantic Web applications. In Advanced Intelligent Systems for Sustainable Development (AI2SD'2018) Volume 5: Advanced Intelligent Systems for Computing Sciences (pp. 444-451). Springer International Publishing. doi:10.1007/978-3-030-11928-7_40

Barnaghi, P., Wang, W., Henson, C., & Taylor, K. (2012). Semantics for the Internet of Things: Early progress and back to the future. *International Journal on Semantic Web and Information Systems*, 8(1), 1–21. doi:10.4018/jswis.2012010101

Bergamaschi, S., Beneventano, D., Guerra, F., & Vincini, M. (2004). Building a tourism information provider with the MOMIS system. *Information Technology & Tourism*, 7(3-4), 221–238.

Bizer, C., Heese, R., Mochol, M., Oldakowski, R., Tolksdorf, R., & Eckstein, R. (2005). The impact of semantic web technologies on job recruitment processes. In *Wirtschaftsinformatik 2005: eEconomy, eGovernment, eSociety* (pp. 1367–1381). Physica-Verlag HD. doi:10.1007/3-7908-1624-8_72

Bizer, C., Volz, J., Kobilarov, G., & Gaedke, M. (2009, April). Silk-a link discovery framework for the web of data. In *18th International World Wide Web Conference* (Vol. 122). Academic Press.

Blomqvist, E. (2014). The use of Semantic Web technologies for decision support–a survey. *Semantic Web*, *5*(3), 177–201. doi:10.3233/SW-2012-0084

Brickley, D., & Guha, R. (2015). RDFa Lite 1.1 - Third Edition. W3C Recommendation.

Calvanese, D., Cogrel, B., Kalayci, E. G., Komla-Ebri, S., Kontchakov, R., Lanti, D., . . . Xiao, G. (2015, June). OBDA with the Ontop Framework. In SEBD (pp. 296-303). Academic Press.

Cao, Q., Zanni-Merk, C., Samet, A., Reich, C., De Beuvron, F. D. B., Beckmann, A., & Giannetti, C. (2022). KSPMI: A knowledge-based system for predictive maintenance in industry 4.0. *Robotics and Computer-integrated Manufacturing*, *74*, 102281. doi:10.1016/j.rcim.2021.102281

Chaves-Fraga, D., Ruckhaus, E., Priyatna, F., Vidal, M. E., & Corcho, O. (2021). Enhancing virtual ontology based access over tabular data with Morph-CSV. *Semantic Web*, *12*(6), 869–902. doi:10.3233/SW-210432

Čolaković, A., & Hadžialić, M. (2018). Internet of Things (IoT): A review of enabling technologies, challenges, and open research issues. *Computer Networks*, *144*, 17–39. doi:10.1016/j.comnet.2018.07.017

Davies, J., Studer, R., & Warren, P. (Eds.). (2006). *Semantic Web technologies: trends and research in ontology-based systems*. John Wiley & Sons. doi:10.1002/047003033X

Dhanapalan, L., & Chen, J. Y. (2007). A case study of integrating protein interaction data using semantic web technology. *International Journal of Bioinformatics Research and Applications*, *3*(3), 286–302. doi:10.1504/IJBRA.2007.015004 PMID:18048193

Dlamini, N. N., & Johnston, K. (2016, November). The use, benefits and challenges of using the Internet of Things (IoT) in retail businesses: A literature review. In *2016 international conference on advances in computing and communication engineering (ICACCE)* (pp. 430-436). IEEE.

Domingue, J., Fensel, D., & Hendler, J. A. (Eds.). (2011). *Handbook of semantic web technologies*. Springer Science & Business Media. doi:10.1007/978-3-540-92913-0

Donkers, A., Yang, D., de Vries, B., & Baken, N. (2022). Semantic web technologies for indoor environmental quality: A review and ontology design. *Buildings*, *12*(10), 1522. doi:10.3390/buildings12101522

Fernández-Breis, J. T., Maldonado, J. A., Marcos, M., Legaz-García, M. D. C., Moner, D., Torres-Sospedra, J., Esteban-Gil, A., Martínez-Salvador, B., & Robles, M. (2013). Leveraging electronic healthcare record standards and semantic web technologies. *Journal of the American Medical Informatics Association : JAMIA*, *20*(e2), e288–e296. doi:10.1136/amiajnl-2013-001923 PMID:23934950

Gharaibeh, A., Salahuddin, M. A., Hussini, S. J., Khreishah, A., Khalil, I., Guizani, M., & Al-Fuqaha, A. (2017). Smart cities: A survey on data management, security, and enabling technologies. *IEEE Communications Surveys and Tutorials*, *19*(4), 2456–2501. doi:10.1109/COMST.2017.2736886

Gutiérrez, C., & Sequeda, J. F. (2021). Knowledge graphs. *Communications of the ACM*, *64*(3), 96–104. doi:10.1145/3418294

Haller, A., Janowicz, K., Cox, S. J., Lefrançois, M., Taylor, K., Le Phuoc, D., Lieberman, J., García-Castro, R., Atkinson, R., & Stadler, C. (2019). The modular SSN ontology: A joint W3C and OGC standard specifying the semantics of sensors, observations, sampling, and actuation. *Semantic Web*, *10*(1), 9–32. doi:10.3233/SW-180320

Heiler, S. (1995). Semantic interoperability. *ACM Computing Surveys*, *27*(2), 271–273. doi:10.1145/210376.210392

Hendler, J., Gandon, F., & Allemang, D. (2020). *Semantic web for the working ontologist: Effective modeling for linked data, RDFS, and OWL*. Morgan & Claypool.

Hitzler, P., Krotzsch, M., & Rudolph, S. (2009). *Foundations of semantic web technologies*. CRC Press. doi:10.1201/9781420090512

Hou, K. M., Diao, X., Shi, H., Ding, H., Zhou, H., & de Vaulx, C. (2023). Trends and Challenges in AIoT/IIoT/IoT Implementation. *Sensors (Basel)*, *23*(11), 5074. doi:10.3390/s23115074 PMID:37299800

Hunter, J., Little, S., & Schroeter, R. (2008). The application of semantic web technologies to multimedia data fusion within escience. In *Semantic Multimedia and Ontologies: Theory and Applications* (pp. 207–226). Springer London. doi:10.1007/978-1-84800-076-6_8

Janowicz, K., Haller, A., Cox, S. J., Le Phuoc, D., & Lefrançois, M. (2019). SOSA: A lightweight ontology for sensors, observations, samples, and actuators. *Journal of Web Semantics*, *56*, 1–10. doi:10.1016/j.websem.2018.06.003

Junghanns, M., Petermann, A., Gómez, K., & Rahm, E. (2015). Gradoop: Scalable graph data management and analytics with hadoop. *arXiv preprint arXiv:1506.00548*.

. Kaykova, O., Khriyenko, O., Kovtun, D., Naumenko, A., Terziyan, V., & Zharko, A. (2007). Challenges of General Adaptation Framework for Industrial Semantic Web. *Semantic Web-Based Information Systems: State-of-the-Art Applications, CyberTech Publishing*, 61-97.

Lork, C., Choudhary, V., Hassan, N. U., Tushar, W., Yuen, C., Ng, B. K. K., Wang, X., & Liu, X. (2019). An ontology-based framework for building energy management with IoT. *Electronics (Basel)*, *8*(5), 485. doi:10.3390/electronics8050485

Maarala, A. I., Su, X., & Riekki, J. (2016). Semantic reasoning for context-aware Internet of Things applications. *IEEE Internet of Things Journal*, *4*(2), 461–473. doi:10.1109/JIOT.2016.2587060

Malik, N., & Malik, S. K. (2020). Using IoT and semantic web technologies for the healthcare and medical sector. *Ontology-Based Information Retrieval for Healthcare Systems*, 91-115.

Matthews, B. (2005). Semantic web technologies. *E-learning*, *6*(6), 8.

Mehta, S., Tiwari, S., Siarry, P., & Jabbar, M. A. (Eds.). (2022). *Tools, Languages, Methodologies for Representing Semantics on the Web of Things*. John Wiley & Sons. doi:10.1002/9781394171460

Pauwels, P., Zhang, S., & Lee, Y. C. (2017). Semantic web technologies in the AEC industry: A literature overview. *Automation in Construction*, *73*, 145–165. doi:10.1016/j.autcon.2016.10.003

Perera, C., Zaslavsky, A., Christen, P., & Georgakopoulos, D. (2014). Sensing as a service model for smart cities supported by the internet of things. *Transactions on Emerging Telecommunications Technologies*, *25*(1), 81–93. doi:10.1002/ett.2704

Peter, O., Pradhan, A., & Mbohwa, C. (2023). Industrial internet of things (IIoT): Opportunities, challenges, and requirements in manufacturing businesses in emerging economies. *Procedia Computer Science*, *217*, 856–865. doi:10.1016/j.procs.2022.12.282

Prudhomme, C., Homburg, T., Ponciano, J. J., Boochs, F., Cruz, C., & Roxin, A. M. (2020). Interpretation and automatic integration of geospatial data into the Semantic Web: Towards a process of automatic geospatial data interpretation, classification and integration using semantic technologies. *Computing*, *102*(2), 365–391. doi:10.1007/s00607-019-00701-y

Rhayem, A., Mhiri, M. B. A., & Gargouri, F. (2020). Semantic web technologies for the internet of things: Systematic literature review. *Internet of Things : Engineering Cyber Physical Human Systems*, *11*, 100206. doi:10.1016/j.iot.2020.100206

Rodríguez Molina, J. (2012). *Semantic middleware development for the Internet of Things*. Academic Press.

Sabou, M. (2016). An introduction to semantic web technologies. *Semantic Web Technologies for Intelligent Engineering Applications*, 53-81.

Santipantakis, G. M., Kotis, K. I., Vouros, G. A., & Doulkeridis, C. (2018, June). Rdf-gen: Generating RDF from streaming and archival data. In *Proceedings of the 8th International Conference on Web Intelligence, Mining and Semantics* (pp. 1-10). 10.1145/3227609.3227658

Sequeda, J. F. (2013, October). On the Semantics of R2RML and its Relationship with Direct Mapping. In ISWC (Posters & Demos) (pp. 193-196). Academic Press.

Sharma, A., & Jain, S. (2021). Multilingual Semantic Representation of Smart Connected World Data. *Smart Connected World: Technologies and Applications Shaping the Future*, 125-138.

Sheth, A. P., & Ramakrishnan, C. (2003). Semantic (Web) technology in action: Ontology driven information systems for search, integration, and analysis. *A Quarterly Bulletin of the Computer Society of the IEEE Technical Committee on Data Engineering*, *26*(4), 40.

Silva, B. N., Khan, M., & Han, K. (2018). Internet of things: A comprehensive review of enabling technologies, architecture, and challenges. *IETE Technical Review*, *35*(2), 205–220. doi:10.1080/0256 4602.2016.1276416

Sporny, Longley, Kellogg, & Lehn. (2018). *JSON-LD 1.1*. W3C Recommendation.

Stephens, S. (2007). The enterprise semantic web: technologies and applications for the real world. In *The Semantic Web: Real-World Applications from Industry* (pp. 17–37). Springer US. doi:10.1007/978-0-387-48531-7_2

Terziyan, V., & Kononenko, O. (2003, September). Semantic Web enabled Web services: State-of-art and industrial challenges. In *International Conference on Web Services* (pp. 183-197). Springer Berlin Heidelberg. 10.1007/978-3-540-39872-1_15

Toulni, H., Nsiri, B., Boulmalf, M., & Sadiki, T. (2015). An ontology based approach to traffic management in urban areas. *International Journal of Systems Applications, Engineering & Development*, 9.

Triantafyllou, A., Sarigiannidis, P., & Bibi, S. (2019). Precision agriculture: A remote sensing monitoring system architecture. *Information (Basel)*, *10*(11), 348. doi:10.3390/info10110348

Xiong, Z., Cai, Z., Takabi, D., & Li, W. (2021). Privacy threat and defense for federated learning with non-iid data in AIoT. *IEEE Transactions on Industrial Informatics*, *18*(2), 1310–1321. doi:10.1109/TII.2021.3073925

Yang, C. T., Chen, H. W., Chang, E. J., Kristiani, E., Nguyen, K. L. P., & Chang, J. S. (2021). Current advances and future challenges of AIoT applications in particulate matters (PM) monitoring and control. *Journal of Hazardous Materials*, *419*, 126442. doi:10.1016/j.jhazmat.2021.126442 PMID:34198222

Ye, Y., Yang, D., Jiang, Z., & Tong, L. (2008). An ontology-based architecture for implementing semantic integration of supply chain management. *International Journal of Computer Integrated Manufacturing*, *21*(1), 1–18. doi:10.1080/09511920601182225

Zhang, L., Dabipi, I. K., & Brown Jr, W. L. (2018). Internet of Things applications for agriculture. *Internet of things A to Z: Technologies and applications*, 507-528.

Chapter 13
Sugarcane Disease Detection Using Data Augmentation

Abhishek Verma

(iD) https://orcid.org/0009-0002-2417-047X
Centre for Advanced Studies, Lucknow, India

Jagrati Singh
Indira Gandhi Delhi Technical University for Women, Delhi, India

ABSTRACT

Sugarcane is an important crop for the Indian economy, providing employment opportunities for millions of farmers. Nevertheless, the cultivation of sugarcane faces challenges from pests and diverse diseases. The detection and segmentation of plant diseases using deep learning have shown promising results in simple environments with abundant data. However, in complex environments with limited samples, the performance of existing models suffers. This study introduces an innovative method that addresses the challenges of complex environments and sample scarcity, aiming to enhance disease recognition accuracy. The highest accuracy showcased by model is 98% on testing data. Comparative study was done on the same dataset by employing various ML algorithms and achieved the highest accuracy of 70%. An Android app has been created to serve as the user interface for this model. This app enables farmers to either take pictures using their phone's camera or choose images from their gallery.

INTRODUCTION

India ranks as the second-largest sugarcane producer globally, following Brazil (Sakshi Srivastava et al., 2020). Sugarcane holds significant importance as a crop cultivated across numerous tropical and subtropical regions worldwide (Viswanathan et al., 2011). It is used to produce sugar, ethanol, and other products (Elsharif et al., 2019). However, the crop is susceptible to a wide range of diseases that can cause significant yield losses. Several common diseases can affect sugarcane as shown in Figure 1, including Red rot, which is a fungal infection caused by Colletotrichum falcatum (Ruchika Sharma and Sushma Tamta, 2015). This disease primarily targets the sugarcane stem, resulting in

DOI: 10.4018/979-8-3693-1487-6.ch013

reddish-brown lesions that darken over time, often turning black. Infected plants typically exhibit stunted growth, wilting, and premature death. Red rot thrives in warm and humid climates and can rapidly spread through contaminated plant debris, soil, and water. Another notable disease is Red rust, caused by the fungus Puccinia melanocephala. This disease predominantly affects sugarcane leaves, manifesting as orange-red rust pustules beneath the underside of the leaves. Red rust can hinder photosynthesis, leading to leaf yellowing and shedding, ultimately reducing cane yield. It tends to be prevalent in humid tropical regions and spreads through wind, water, and human activities. Lastly, Bacterial blight, induced by Xanthomonas albilineans (Rakesh Yonzone et al., 2018), affects sugarcane leaves by creating yellowish-white streaks that gradually turn brown. This disease can disrupt photosynthesis, resulting in stunted growth and reduced yield. Bacterial blight thrives in warm and humid environments and can spread through infected planting material, sap, or insect vectors. These diseases collectively pose significant challenges to sugarcane cultivation and necessitate vigilant management strategies. The occurrence of diseases in sugarcane plants poses a substantial challenge and risk to farmers, leading to economic repercussions by affecting both yield and production (Apan et al., 2004). Timely detection is crucial to mitigate these impacts. A decline in the cultivation of such crops can exert adverse effects on the overall economy. Not only the crop but fertilizers, water and seeds are also wasted (E. K. ratnasari et al., 2014). Detecting and identifying sugarcane diseases is crucial for maintaining competitive flexibility in crop production and preservation (Simon Strachan et al., 2022). However, relying solely on traditional techniques that involve naked eye observation by experts can be problematic, as they may not always be accurate and can lead to misidentification of diseases (Tisen Huang et al., 2018). Traditional methods require continuous observation which can be a laborious task and a large farm makes this task almost impossible (L. Li et al., 2021). In developing countries like India, it is costly and laborious to seek out an expert's assistance. Among the limited options at hand, machine learning techniques have been employed, but their performance often falls short of expectations, yielding merely satisfactory results. To attain enhanced outcomes, the transition to more advanced approaches, such as deep learning, becomes imperative. Deep learning has demonstrated its prowess as a leading methodology for image classification, a testament to its success across diverse domains (H. S. Malik et al., 2020). Particularly noteworthy is its effectiveness when applied to large datasets, as it has consistently delivered remarkable results. The work conducted by Sammy V. Militante et al. (2019) stands as an instance of employing Convolutional Neural Networks (CNNs) to develop a model aimed at recognizing sugarcane diseases. A dataset comprising 13,842 sugarcane images was employed for training purposes and achieved an accuracy of 95%. Wang et al. introduced a two-stage model known as DUNet, which combined DeepLabV3+ and U-Net architectures for cucumber leaf disease severity classification, particularly in challenging backgrounds. Remarkably, this approach achieved an impressive leaf segmentation accuracy of 93.27%. Adem et al. introduced a hybrid approach, combining Yolov4 deep learning and image processing, to automatically detect and classify leaf spot disease on sugar beets. With 1040 images, the method achieved a classification accuracy rate of 96.47%.

This paper presents a fresh perspective on improving the precision of sugarcane leaf disease classification by harnessing the power of data augmentation techniques. In our investigation, we harnessed a substantial dataset, consisting of 2099 images. This dataset encompasses not only three distinct categories of diseases but also includes a reference class of healthy sugarcane leaves. These images were thoughtfully curated for the purpose of training and rigorous experimentation.

(a) (b) (c) (d)

Figure 1. Illustrations showcasing instances from the three disease categories along with the healthy class: (a) bacterial blight, (b) red rot, (c) red rust, and (d) healthy

(a)   (b)   (c)   (d)

LITERATURE SURVEY

Militante et al. (2019) studied and performed experiment on sugarcane leaf which has 13,842 images and were able to successfully classify between diseased and healthy image with accuracy of 95%. To expand the dataset, strategies for data augmentation were employed, encompassing actions such as rotating images by 25 degrees, flipping horizontally and vertically, and randomly shifting images. Training encompassed 60 epochs with a batch size of 32, utilizing the Adam optimizer in conjunction with a categorical cross-entropy loss function. A learning rate of 0.001 was initially set and decreased by a factor of 0.3. The training process incorporated early stopping, which observed the validation loss and halted training if an increase was detected. The computational tasks were executed on a Dell Inspiron 14-3476 equipped with an Intel Core i5 processor and 16GB memory.

TisenHuang et al. (2018) demonstrated an accuracy rate of 100% for the training set encompassing sugarcane with diseases, while the test set displayed an accuracy rate of 95.83%. The research uncovered a training set accuracy rate of 100% for sugarcane with diseases, alongside a test set accuracy rate of 95.83%. However, there were some limitations that affected the classification results, such as the randomness of the photo position, non-standard equipment lighting, physical damage to the sugarcane, and the presence of pseudo diseases. To overcome these limitations, the study used high exposure to acquire the image and removed regions with an area of 1. The study also compared the effectiveness of the Polynomial and RBF kernel functions in the SVM classifier and found that the RBF kernel function was more stable and reliable. The study suggests using the SVM classifier with the RBF kernel function to detect sugarcane borer disease. This approach can help reduce the planting of sugarcane seeds with diseases and improve sugarcane yield.

In the work by EK Ratnasari and M Mentari (2014), a model was put forward that demonstrated the capacity to ascertain spot disease types with an accuracy of 80% and an average error severity estimation of 5.73. The research introduces a model for the identification of sugarcane leaf diseases, encompassing both severity estimation and classification. The severity estimation is based on the size of the lesion, where a wider lesion indicates a higher severity. In the classification process, a fusion of texture and color feature extraction is employed in conjunction with an SVM classifier. The presented model has showcased notable accuracy in identifying sugarcane leaf diseases, accompanied by a comparatively low average error severity estimation, solely utilizing spot disease area data. Nevertheless, the model exhibits constraints in effectively distinguishing spot diseases from the entirety of the leaf, indicating a need for improved segmentation methods or pre-processing of the images.

S Srivastava et al. (2020) introduced a novel deep learning framework for detecting sugarcane plant diseases by analyzing various attributes such as leaves, stem, and color. An accuracy of 90.2% is achieved by utilizing VGG-16 for feature extraction and SVM for classification. The study employs three deep learning models—VGG-16, VGG-19, and Inception V3—to extract features from the sugarcane dataset. These features are then input to seven different classifiers—naive Bayes, AdaBoost, neural network, stochastic gradient descent, K-nearest neighbor, support vector machine, and logistic regression—to categorize the sugarcane as diseased or non-diseased. Model and classifier performance is assessed through classification accuracy (CA) and area under the curve (AUC) metrics.

Simões et al. (2023) built disease recognition models via RF, radial SVM, and KNN. Radial SVM with 9 predictive features excelled in classification. Complexities in plant disease image segmentation and classification were noted due to color variations. Spectral threshold-based methods faced challenges due to color variations. Object-oriented segmentation (OBIA) enhanced recognition and accuracy. Extracting 202 color, shape, and texture features, 25 were chosen based on color and intensity. RGB processing yielded satisfactory sugarcane disease recognition, radial SVM excelling. Potential for automated sugarcane disease diagnosis via RGB, requiring field validation. A lesion image database could extend this tech to other crop diseases. Proposed use of mobile apps for accessible disease diagnosis and sharing.

Thilagavathi et al. (2020) introduced an image processing-based approach for detecting diseases in sugarcane using Support Vector Machine (SVM). The process involves preprocessing diseased leaf images by eliminating unnecessary data, then enhancing them with adaptive histogram equalization (AHE). For segmentation, the approach employs Adaptive k-Means Clustering, while feature extraction is carried out using Grey Level Co-occurrence Matrix (GLCM) and Principal Component Analysis (PCA). The SVM algorithm is used for classification, implemented in MATLAB. Results for six sugarcane diseases are presented in figures 5 to 10. The proposed system addresses the challenge of manual disease detection by offering automated surveillance. Through a combination of GLCM, PCA feature extraction, and SVM classification, an impressive accuracy of 95% is achieved. This system proves valuable in identifying and categorizing the significant diseases affecting sugarcane yield, providing a promising tool for agricultural disease detection and management.

Umapathy Eaganathan et al. (2014) conducted a study employing K-means clustering and KNN classification to identify sugarcane leaf scorch disease. Gathering images from Madurai, India, they applied median filtering for preprocessing and Lab color model conversion to enhance accuracy. K-means algorithm enabled image segmentation, followed by K-NN classification. The Canon EOS 600D camera and MATLAB R2012a were used for data capture and processing. Disease symptoms encompassed red-brown spots, necrotic centers, and small blackish dots. K-means-based color segmentation was employed to segregate healthy and diseased areas. The study suggests exploring hybrid algorithms and neural networks to enhance recognition capabilities. Future research directions involve quantifying disease severity for a comprehensive assessment of its impact. This study serves as a valuable step toward automated disease detection in sugarcane plants, facilitating more effective disease management and agricultural productivity.

Tamilvizhi et al. (2022) introduced a Quantum-Behaved Particle Swarm Optimization-based deep transfer learning model designed for the detection and classification of sugarcane leaf diseases. The paper introduces a new QBPSO-DTL model for detecting and classifying sugarcane leaf diseases with high accuracy. The suggested method encompasses preprocessing, optimal region-growing segmentation, classification using DSAE, and QBPSO-based hyperparameter optimization. The SqueezeNet model is used as a feature extractor, and transfer learning is employed for training. The performance of the QBPSO-DTL model is evaluated using its own dataset, which consists of training and testing datasets with diseased and nondiseased classes. The presented methodology surpasses alternative techniques in various performance measures. While larger datasets are needed for training CNN models for recognizing plant leaf diseases, transfer learning can be used to adapt pretrained CNN models to recognize leaf diseases with small datasets. The proposed QBPSO-DTL model offers a novel method for detecting and classifying sugarcane leaf diseases.

Amarasingam Narmilan (2022) introduced an original approach to detect sugarcane white leaf disease (WLD) at an early stage, employing high-resolution multispectral sensors mounted on small unmanned aerial vehicles (UAVs) in conjunction with supervised machine learning classifiers. The validation of this method is conducted within a sugarcane field situated in Gal-Oya Plantation, Hingurana, Sri Lanka. The pixelwise segmented samples are categorized into classes like ground, shadow, healthy plant, early symptoms, and severe symptoms. Employing four machine learning algorithms, namely XGBoost (XGB), random forest (RF), decision tree (DT), and K-nearest neighbors (KNN), in combination with python libraries, vegetation indices (VIs), and five spectral bands, the study attains an impressive 94% accuracy rate in WLD detection. Notably, the most effective vegetation indices (VIs) for distinguishing between healthy and infected sugarcane crops are the modified soil-adjusted vegetation index (MSAVI), normalized difference vegetation index (NDVI), and excess green (ExG) within XGB, RF, and DT models. Additionally, optimal spectral bands are identified as red in XGB and RF, and green in DT.

Yiqi Huang et al. (2022) study addresses complex environment challenges by employing DeepLabV3+ for sugarcane leaf segmentation. To tackle limited sugarcane training images, two augmentation methods—supervised data augmentation and DCGANs—are adopted. Models like MobileNetV3-large, Alexnet, Resnet, and Densenet are trained across various datasets and augmentation strategies. The optimal network, MobileNetV3-large, is selected based on accuracy and training time. Initial classification using MobileNetV3-large achieved 53.5% accuracy with the original dataset. Substantial improvement to 99% accuracy resulted from background removal and inclusion of synthetic DCGAN-generated images. The recognition performance of trained models is compared using the same test set, highlighting the efficacy of the proposed approach.

MI Hossain and K Ahmad (2020) created models that were trained using 14,725 images of a healthy sugarcane leaves and infested sugarcane diseases and achieves a maximum 95.40% accuracy rate during training. Three architectures of CNN; StridedNet, LeNet, and VGGNet were used in the conduct of this study.

J. Sujithra and M. Ferni Ukrit (2022) introduced a novel approach, termed CRUN (Combining Regional-Based Convolutional Neural Networks and U-Net), for segmenting leaf diseases within augmented leaf datasets. Following segmentation, a morphological analysis is employed to assess disease severity, subsequently guiding the implementation of targeted fertilizer strategies to mitigate disease spread. The proposed method is tested on real-time images depicting sugarcane diseases like bacterial blight and red rot, as well as banana leaf diseases such as yellow and black sigatoka. Furthermore, the CRUN algorithm is applied to publicly available datasets from the Kaggle platform. The CRUN technique effectively delineates disease regions, while the morphological analysis aids in gauging disease severity and preventing further transmission. The combined CRUN approach, alongside the morphological analysis, emerges as a potent tool for automating leaf disease detection and prevention.

HS Malik and M Dwivedi (2021) developed models that underwent training with the sugarcane dataaset exhibited a notable accuracy of 93.40% on the test set and 76.40% on images sourced from various reliable online platforms. This underscores the approach's strength in effectively recognizing intricate patterns and variations encountered in real-world scenarios.

METHODOLOGY

Image Loading

Image loading step refers to the process of reading and loading an image into memory for further manipulation and analysis. This step commonly marks the outset of the process in most image processing workflows. When an image is loaded, its pixel values are read from a storage medium (e.g., disk storage, network storage, etc.) and stored in memory, forming a data structure that represents the image. The image can be in various formats such as JPEG, PNG, BMP, GIF, TIFF, etc., and the loading process varies depending on the format. Subsequently, the loaded image can undergo processing via diverse image processing methods, such as filtering, enhancement, transformation, feature extraction, object detection, and more. These processes allow us to modify or analyse the image to extract valuable information or to improve its quality for various applications like computer vision, medical imaging, surveillance, and photography (A. Esteva et al., 2021).

The image loading step is crucial as it serves as a foundation for all subsequent image processing operations. Accurate and efficient image loading is essential to ensure that the subsequent processing

Table 1. Performance measure from different studies

S.No.	Paper	Technique	Dataset	Accuracy
1	Militante et al. (2019)	Deep learning	Dataset from Phillipines	95%
2	Apan et al. (2004)	EO-1 Hyperion hyperspectral imagery	Australian Sugar Industry	96.9%
3	TisenHuang et al. (2018)	SVM	Guangxi	95.83%
4	EK Ratnasari and M Mentari (2014)	SVM	Sugarcane fields in Mojokerto, Indonesia	80%
5	S Srivastava et al. (2020)	SVM	Mawana Sugar Mill Pvt. Ltd.	90.2%
6	MI Hossain and K Ahma (2020)	CNN	Bangladesh & India	95.40%
7	Suresha M et al. (2017)	KNN	India	76.59%
8	Sandino et al. (2018)	XGBoost	Sri Lanka	97%
9	Prince Kumar et al. (2021)	YOLO, Faster R-CNN	India	58.13
10	Y Huang et al. (2022)	MobileNetV3-large	Guangxi University	53.5
11	R Aruna et al. (2023)	NLRGD	India	96.75

Figure 2. Flowchart of proposed methodology

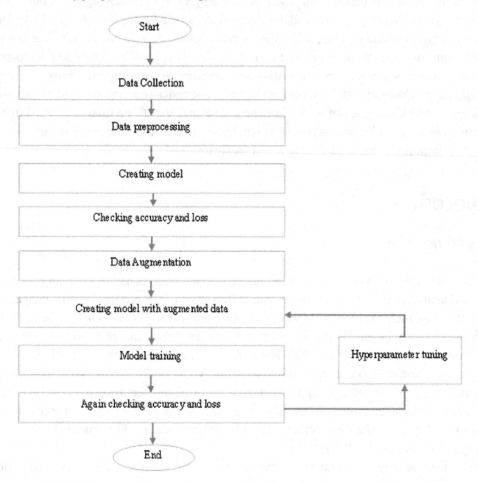

steps produce reliable and meaningful results. Additionally, handling image data efficiently is particularly important when dealing with large datasets or real-time applications.

Image Preprocessing

It takes the dataset and separates it into features and labels or dependent and independent variables. Computer Vision (CV) was used for this purpose and all images were also resized so that all images will have same shape, here 180*180. CV converts the image into BGR hence we need to convert it back into RGB. Label encoder was used to convert the string label into integer label. The dataset underwent partitioning into training, testing, and validation subsets with a random state of 23, where training set has 1462 images, testing set has 315 and validation set has 322 images. In TensorFlow for preprocessing and caching image data to optimize its use during training. This caches the training dataset in memory or on disk (depending on the available memory) to speed up training (S. W. D. Chien et al., 2021). By caching the dataset, the images can be loaded faster and with less overhead during each epoch of training. Caching the dataset is particularly useful when the dataset fits in memory and when the data loading and preprocessing steps are expensive (R. Macedo et al., 2021). Prefetch prepares the training dataset to be prefetched in a background thread while the model is training on the current batch. Prefetching reduces the idle time of the GPU by loading and preprocessing the next batch of data in the background while the current batch is being processed, which can improve the overall training performance.

Data Augmentation

Data augmentation is a technique used in machine learning and computer vision to artificially increase the size and diversity of a dataset by applying various transformations to the existing data (A. Mikołajczyk et al., 2018). The goal of data augmentation is to create additional variations of the original data, making the model more robust and better able to generalize to unseen examples. The set of augmentations(transformations) applied are randomflip with horizontal as the input parameter, randombrightness with value 0.2, randomcontrast with value 0.2, randomrotation with value 0.1, randomzoom with value 0.1, and gaussiannoise with value 0.2, here the value tells the percentage of images on which these augmentation techniques are applied randomly. These augmentation techniques are shown in Figure 3. The training parameter controls whether the augmentations should be applied or not. During training, this parameter is set to True, while during validation and testing, it is set to False to ensure that the model is not learning from augmented data.

1. RandomFlip: This layer performs random horizontal flipping of the input images. It randomly decides whether to flip each image horizontally (left to right) or vertically (right to left). Here the argument "horizontal" is used which specifies the type of flip to be applied.
2. RandomBrightness: This layer randomly adjusts the brightness of the input images. The brightness adjustment is performed by adding a random value to the pixel values of the images. The brightness adjustment is usually within a certain range to control the maximum amount of brightness change.

Figure 3. Visualization of data augmentation techniques used

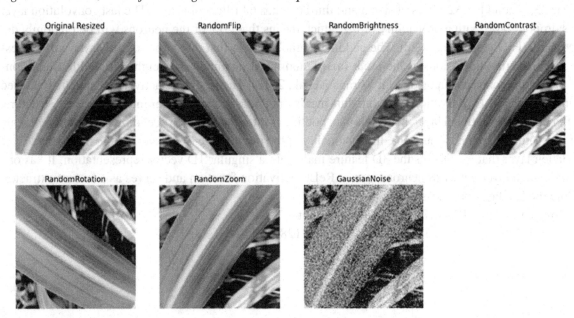

3. RandomContrast: This layer randomly adjusts the contrast of the input images. The contrast adjustment is achieved by scaling the pixel values of the images are perturbed using random variations. The contrast adjustment is typically within a certain range to control the maximum amount of contrast change.

4. RandomRotation: This layer randomly rotates the input images. It applies a random rotation to each image. The rotation angle is usually within a certain range to control the maximum angle of rotation.

5. RandomZoom: This layer randomly zooms the input images. It applies a random zoom to each image. The zoom level is typically within a certain range to control the maximum amount of zooming.

6. GaussianNoise: This layer adds random Gaussian noise to the input images. The noise is generated following a Gaussian distribution and subsequently added to the pixel values of the images on an element-wise basis. The amount of noise is usually controlled by specifying Gaussian distribution's standard deviation.

These data augmentation layers are utilized for introducing diversity within the training data, thus aiding the model in better generalization for unseen data and reduces the risk of overfitting. By introducing stochastic alterations to input images during the training phase, the model learns to be invariant to such transformations during inference, making it more robust and adaptable to real-world scenarios. Data augmentation is a crucial technique to elevate the efficacy of deep learning models, particularly in tasks involving image data.

CREATING CNN MODEL

The first layer of the model is a pre-processing layer that resizes and normalizes the input images. Subsequently, a sequence of convolutional layers is employed, utilizing learned convolutional filters to extract distinctive features from the input image. There are three convolution layers, first has 16 filters of size 3, second has 32 filters of size 3 and third one has 64 filters of size 3. The last convolution layer has dropout layer with a probability of 0.2 which means that 20% of the neurons will be randomly deactivated (P. Dileep et al., 2020). The padding 'same' ensures that the output of this layer will possess identical spatial dimensions as the input image, and it will maintain the height and width dimensions of the feature maps unchanged (Aldi Wiranata et al., 2018). The filters are activated using the Rectified Linear Unit (ReLU) activation function, thus inculcating non-linear behavior into the model's structure. After each convolutional layer, a layer of max pooling is introduced which accomplish reduction in scale of the feature maps and reduce the dimensionality of the output. The final layers of the model consist of a flatten layer that transforms the 3D feature maps into a singular 1D vector representation. It has one fully hidden layer with 128 neurons, uses a ReLU activation function and serves as a feature extractor, while the last layer produces the output classes.

Image size Conv1 Conv2 Conv3 Dense Output
180*180*3 180*180*16 90*90*34 45*45*64 128 4

Figure 4. Architecture of CNN model build

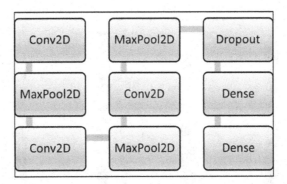

Figure 5. Convolutional layer architecture

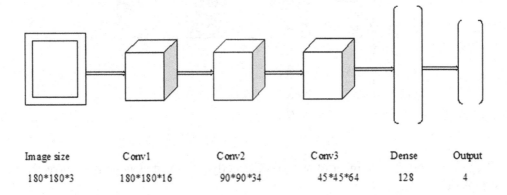

Image size	Conv1	Conv2	Conv3	Dense	Output
180*180*3	180*180*16	90*90*34	45*45*64	128	4

EXPERIMENTAL STUDIES

The research paper focuses on a study involving sugarcane leaf images, where four distinct types of leaves were analysed red rust, bacterial blight, red rot, and healthy sugarcane. These images, as depicted in Figure 1, were used to develop a classification system relying on methodologies from computer vision and machine learning disciplines. The objective was to automatically identify and differentiate between the various sugarcane leaf diseases and healthy leaves. Employed dataset was downloaded from Kaggle. It consists of 2099 images, and it was segmented into three segments training, testing and validation as shown in Figure 6.

Evaluation Metrics

Accuracy, Precision, and Recall are essential evaluation criteria employed to assess the performance of classification models. These metrics furnish valuable perspectives into how well the model is performing in terms of making correct and incorrect predictions for different classes.

- True Positive (TP): The number of samples correctly predicted as positive (correctly classified positive samples).

Figure 6. Division of dataset

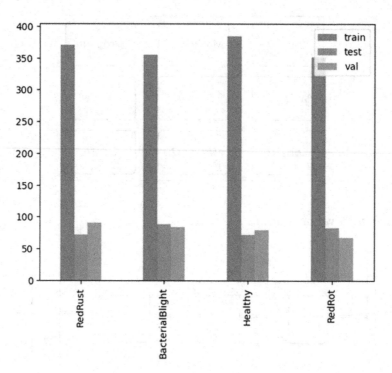

- True Negative (TN): The number of samples correctly predicted as negative (correctly classified negative samples).

- False Positive (FP): The number of samples incorrectly predicted as positive (false alarms).

- False Negative (FN): The number of samples incorrectly predicted as negative (misses).

1. Accuracy: Among the numerous metrics available for evaluation, accuracy stands as a prevalent indicator for assessing the overall effectiveness of a classification model. It quantifies the ratio of correctly categorized instances to the overall number of instances in the dataset. The accuracy is computed using the subsequent formula:

Accuracy = (TN + TP) / (TN + TP + FN + FP)

While accuracy is useful, however, in scenarios involving imbalanced datasets, where there exists a substantial disparity in the sample counts across various classes, accuracy might not be the optimal metric.

2. Precision: Precision is a measure that gauges the ratio of true positive predictions relative to all positive predictions projected by the model. It aids in evaluating the model's capacity to minimize false positive occurrences. The precision is computed through the utilization of the subsequent formula:

Precision = TP / (FP + TP)

Higher precision indicates fewer false positives, implying that the model's positive class predictions are more likely to be accurate.

3. Recall: Recall quantifies the ratio of true positive predictions to the entire set of actual positive samples present within the dataset. It helps assess the model's ability to capture all positive samples without missing any. The recall is computed using the ensuing formula:

Recall = TP / (TP + FN)

A higher recall signifies that the model can accurately recognize a greater number of positive samples.

4. F1 Score: The F1 score serves as another vital metric in classification tasks, particularly when confronted with imbalanced datasets. By merging precision and recall into a singular score, the F1 score offers a well-rounded assessment of a model's effectiveness. The F1 score represents the harmonic mean of precision and recall, determined through the subsequent formula:

F1 Score = 2 * (Precision * Recall) / (Precision + Recall)

Ranging between 0 and 1, the F1 score attains 1 in cases of a flawless model performance and 0 indicates poor performance. The F1 score proves valuable when there's a desire to achieve equilibrium between precision and recall. It penalizes the model for either low precision or low recall. For instance, when a model exhibits high precision while maintaining low recall, it means it is good at avoiding false positives but misses many true positives. On the other hand, if a model has high recall but low precision, it means it captures most of the true positives but also has many false positives. The F1 score considers both cases and offers a singular metric that encapsulates the compromise between precision and recall.

COMPARATIVE STUDY

A comparative analysis was conducted employing diverse machine learning algorithms and their performance is shown in Table 2.

1. k-Nearest Neighbors (k-NN)

The k-Nearest Neighbors algorithm is a simple and versatile classification algorithm (G. Guo., et al., 2003). By analyzing the class labels of its k nearest neighbors within the feature space, it assigns a classification to an input sample. The chosen value for k is a user-defined parameter, and the algorithm makes predictions through a collective consensus among the k neighbors. k-NN is easy to understand and implement but may suffer from computational inefficiency and vulnerability to the selection of k. The value of k is chosen to be 5, weights are set to be uniform which assign equal weights to all neighbors, algorithm is set to be auto which automatically selects the best algorithm based on input data and other parameters. Euclidean distance was used to calculate distance between data points.

2. Support Vector Machine (SVM)

Support Vector Machine (SVM) (V, Jakkula et al., 2006) stands as a potent and extensively employed supervised learning technique catering to classification and regression objectives. SVM's objective is to identify the optimal hyperplane that maximizes the separation between data points belonging to distinct classes within the feature space. It is effective in handling high-dimensional data and can handle non-linear data through the use of kernel functions. SVM performs well with proper tuning of hyperparameters but can be computationally expensive for large datasets. C serves as a regularization parameter that manages the equilibrium between achieving minimal training error and minimizing testing error. Smaller values of C create a wider margin but might misclassify some training examples. Here C is set to be 1. RBF as a kernel was used. It designates the kernel function utilized to convert the data into a space with a higher dimensionality. 'rbf' stands for Radial Basis Function (Gaussian) kernel. In Gamma value scale was passed, it employs the value of gamma as $1 / (n\_features * X.var())$.

3. Naive Bayes

Naive Bayes (I. Rish, 2001) operates as a probabilistic classification technique founded on Bayes' theorem. It operates under the assumption that given the class label, the features exhibit conditional independence, hence the "naive" assumption. Despite this simplicity, Naive Bayes can perform surprisingly well, especially on text and NLP tasks. It is computationally efficient, requires minimal data preparation, and is less prone to overfitting. However, its independence assumption might limit its performance on more complex data distributions. Priors are set to be none which means priors are calculated from the training data. The value of var_smoothing is 1e-9. It represents the proportion of the maximum variance across all features that is augmented to variances for the sake of enhancing computational stability.

4. Decision Tree

Decision Trees (Y. Y. Song et al., 2015) are a class of non-parametric supervised learning methods that formulate a tree-like model to make decisions contingent on the values of features. It recursively splits the data based on the most informative feature at each node, leading to a tree structure that can be used for classification. Decision Trees are easy to interpret and visualize, and they possess the capability to handle both numerical and categorical data. Nevertheless, they are susceptible to overfitting, especially with deep trees. Gini Index was used for measuring the quality of the split. A "splitter" is employed to select the division at every node. In this case, the "best" option was utilized. The criterion of splitting an internal node necessitated a minimum of 2 samples, while a leaf node was mandated to have at least 1 sample.

5. Random Forest

Random Forest (A. Cutler et al., 2012) is an ensemble learning method based on decision trees. The method creates numerous decision trees by leveraging bootstrapped samples from the dataset and employing randomized subsets of features at each decision node. The final prediction is determined by aggregating the individual tree predictions using either a majority vote or an averaging approach. Random Forest is robust, less prone to overfitting, and often performs well on a wide range of datasets. The number of trees used was 100. Gini impurity was used to measure the quality of split. The minimum number of samples required to split an internal node was 2 and the minimum number of samples required to be at a leaf node was 1.

6. XGBoost

XGBoost (T. Chem et al., 2015) stands for "Extreme Gradient Boosting" and is an optimized implementation of Gradient Boosting. It stands as a robust ensemble learning technique that sequentially adds weak learners to improve predictive performance. XGBoost is known for its efficiency, scalability, and high predictive accuracy. It also provides regularization techniques to prevent overfitting. Maximum depth of the individual trees in the boosting process is 3. Learning rate is 1. The model is designed to construct 10 boosting rounds (trees). The learning task pertains to binary logistic regression, with a corresponding objective function. The employed boosting model type is gbtree.

7. AdaBoost (Adaptive Boosting)

AdaBoost (R. E. Schapire, 2013) is ensemble learning approach that aggregates weak learners to create a strong classifier. It gives more importance to incorrectly classified data points by assigning them higher weights and trains subsequent models to focus on those misclassified samples. By iteratively adjusting the weights, AdaBoost aims to correct misclassifications and achieve better performance. Decision tree as base estimator or weak learner is used. The maximum number of boosting rounds (weak learners) to build is 30. The step size at which the boosting learns is 1. Another adaboost model used has three weak learners' decision tree, svm and linear regression. No of weak learners are 10 with learning rate of 1.

As illustrated in Figure 7, the substantial gap between the training and validation curves indicates a notable instance of overfitting in our model. Overfitting, a prevalent issue in machine learning, transpires when a model exhibits proficient performance on the training dataset but falters in its ability to generalize effectively to fresh, unfamiliar data. This arises when the model captures extraneous noise or incidental fluctuations present in the training data, rather than acquiring the fundamental patterns that should be applicable to any dataset. Overfitting can result in inadequate performance on unseen test or validation data, diminishing the model's practical applicability.

Causes of Overfitting

1. Model Complexity: Models characterized by their intricate structures and numerous parameters possess greater potential to memorize the training data, including noise and outliers, which can lead to overfitting.
2. Small Training Dataset: In cases where the training dataset is limited in size, the model might lack a sufficient range of diverse examples for effective learning the underlying patterns properly and can memorize the few samples, causing overfitting.
3. Lack of Regularization: Regularization techniques like L1 or L2 regularization can help control model complexity and reduce overfitting. Without regularization, the model might become too flexible and fit the noise in the data.
4. Data Imbalance: In situations where there is an imbalance in class distribution within the training data, the model could tend to overfit the more dominant class, resulting in suboptimal performance on the minority class.
5. Incorrect Hyperparameter Tuning: Incorrect choices of hyperparameters like learning rate, batch size, or number of layers can cause overfitting. Poor hyperparameter tuning may lead to the model getting stuck in local minima.

Figure 7. Graph before using data augmentation

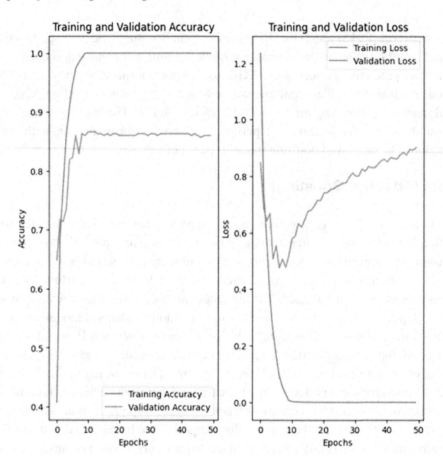

Ways to Avoid Overfitting

1. Use More Data: Expanding the training dataset with more diverse examples can aid in improving the model's generalization capabilities and reduce overfitting.
2. Split Data Properly: Divide the dataset into three subsets: training, validation, and test sets. Utilize the training set for model training, the validation set for hyperparameter tuning, and the test set for assessing the ultimate model performance.
3. Regularization: Apply L1 or L2 regularization to penalize large weight values and reduce model complexity.
4. Cross-Validation: Apply techniques such as k-fold cross-validation to evaluate the model's performance across various partitions of the dataset. This provides a comprehensive assessment of the model's capabilities on different data subsets.
5. Feature Selection: Select relevant features and remove irrelevant or noisy ones from the input data.
6. Early Stopping: Keep track of the model's performance on the validation set throughout the training process. Cease training when you observe a decline in performance, as this can help prevent overfitting and ensure that the model doesn't become overly specialized to the training data.

7. Dropout: Implement dropout layers during training to randomly deactivate neurons, preventing the model from becoming overly dependent on specific neurons.
8. Ensemble Methods: Combine multiple models (e.g., Random Forest, Gradient Boosting) to reduce overfitting by leveraging the wisdom of the crowd.

By addressing these factors and employing proper regularization and validation techniques, we can effectively mitigate overfitting and build models that generalize well to new data.

Confusion matrix is used in machine learning to gauge a classification model's effectiveness. It is a way to show the proportion of correct and incorrect examples based on the model's forecast. Classification models are designed to predict a categorical label for each event they are frequently used to gauge their effectiveness. The images were classified using a basic CNN model prior to the use of data augmentation. A confusion matrix was plotted, with the diagonal value representing the right predictions and the off diagonal representing our model's mistake, to provide a clear picture of the areas where our model failed to identify the images correctly. Figure 8 displays the confusion matrix. Its high number of off diagonal values indicates a less accurate model. To ensure that our algorithm could accurately classify the photos, the confusion matrix was projected on a test dataset.

Before implementing data augmentation, our model exhibited respectable performance with an accuracy score of 88.88%, precision at 89.02%, recall standing at 88.88%, and an F1 score of 88.82%. Figure 8 shows the confusion matrix before using data augmentation. These results were promising, indicating that our model could effectively identify sugarcane leaf diseases, yet we saw potential for improvement. To bolster our model's capabilities and further enhance its accuracy, we turned to the technique of data augmentation. With data augmentation, we sought to diversify our dataset by introducing variations and additional instances of our training data. This augmented dataset was carefully crafted to include varia-

Figure 8. Confusion matrix before using data augmentation

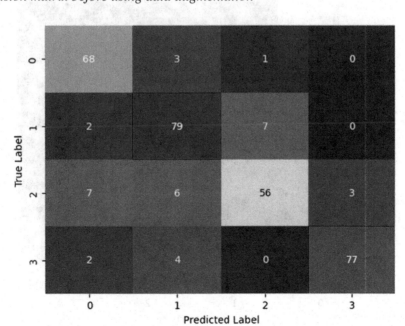

tions in lighting conditions, angles, and other factors that could be encountered in real-world scenarios. Subsequently, we fed this enriched dataset into our Convolutional Neural Network (CNN) model, aiming to capitalize on the increased diversity and quantity of training data to boost our model's accuracy and robustness. This strategic use of data augmentation was a pivotal step in refining our model and fine-tuning its ability to accurately detect sugarcane leaf diseases.

After applying data augmentation, the original dataset underwent various transformations, including adjustments to contrast, brightness, and other factors. This augmentation process introduced increased complexity to the dataset in a randomized manner. Subsequently, the augmented dataset was utilized to train the Convolutional Neural Network (CNN) model. The resulting confusion matrix exhibits notable improvements, characterized by a reduction in off-diagonal elements and an increase in diagonal values. Upon using augmentation our model generalizes well and captures complex patterns present in the dataset. Augmentation is done on training data only. Upon comparison between the confusion matrices of the simple model and the augmented model, it is evident that the number of correct predictions (diagonal values) has increased, while the number of incorrect predictions (off-diagonal values) has decreased in the augmented model. Additionally, the augmented model exhibits higher accuracy, precision, and recall compared to the simple model. The evaluation demonstrates that the augmented model outperforms its predecessor, boasting an enhanced overall accuracy, precision, and recall rate, reaching an impressive 98%. In Figure 9, the impact of data augmentation on our model's classification capabilities is vividly demonstrated through the confusion matrix. The discernible transformation in our model's performance is striking. Notably, there has been a substantial reduction in the number of false predictions, a testament to the effectiveness of the augmentation techniques employed. This visual representation underscores

Figure 9. Confusion matrix after using data augmentation

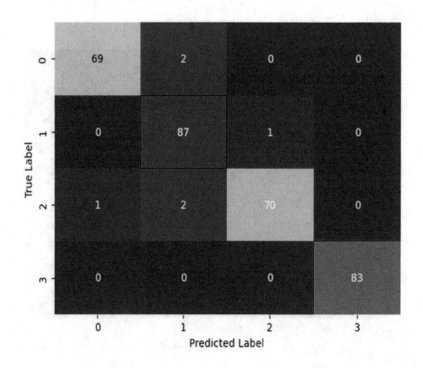

how data augmentation has substantially improved our model's ability to classify accurately, minimizing the instances of misclassification and bolstering its overall reliability.

Figure 10 illustrates a significant observation of the convergence of both lines in close proximity, indicative of the absence of overfitting. This alignment underscores the model's commendable learning capability, a conclusion further supported by its impressive performance on the validation dataset, as evident in the graphical representation. The oscillatory pattern in the lines demonstrates the model's on-going learning process. Notably, the accuracy graph consistently ascends, signifying favorable progress, while the loss graph consistently descends, reflecting an encouraging trend. This graphical depiction underscores the model's effective training and its ability to enhance both accuracy and minimize loss during the learning process.

Figure 11 is a visual representation of the successful outcomes generated by our model when applied to the testing dataset. It vividly portrays the instances where our model has effectively and accurately classified the diseases present in the images. Each image in the figure corresponds to a case where the model's prediction aligns with the actual disease diagnosis. This visual confirmation underscores the model's reliability and proficiency in correctly identifying diseases in the testing dataset, reaffirming its effectiveness as a valuable tool for disease recognition in the context of our research.

Figure 10. Graph after using data augmentation

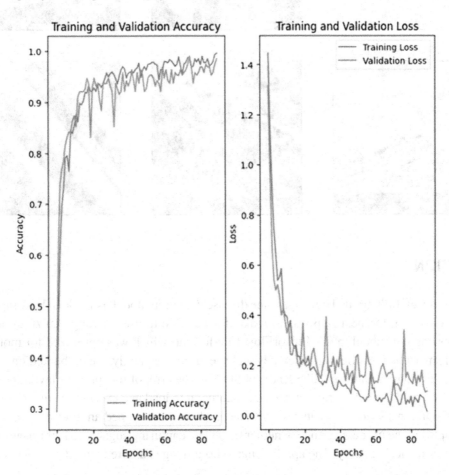

Figure 11. Output predicted on test dataset

APPLICATION

Once we had successfully trained our sugarcane disease detection model using deep learning techniques and a suitable dataset, the next step was to make it accessible to users through an Android app. This entailed exporting our model to the TensorFlow Lite format, which was optimized for mobile devices like Android smartphones, offering efficiency and speed. Subsequently, we embarked on Android app development, leveraging platforms like Android Studio. The crux of this process lay in integrating our TensorFlow Lite model into the app's codebase, enabling it to load and execute the model seamlessly. A key aspect of our app's success was its user interface, where we designed an intuitive and user-friendly GUI that simplified the user experience, whether they were capturing sugarcane leaf images or selecting them from their device's gallery. The app facilitated both image capture using the device's camera and image selection from the gallery with clear instructions. Within the app, we implemented the model inference process, preprocessing images as needed, and passed them through the TensorFlow Lite model for disease prediction. The app then presented the results to users, providing information on the detected disease, its severity, and recommended actions. It was crucial to optimize both the model and the app's code for mobile devices, as they had limited computational resources compared to desktops or servers. Rigorous testing on a variety of Android devices was essential to ensure consistent and accurate performance under different conditions. By choosing TensorFlow Lite, we benefited from its efficiency, compatibility, reduced app size, and user-friendliness. This app works offline which is a plus point where internet facilities are not available or have network issues, making it a valuable tool for sugarcane farmers in disease detection and crop management.

Above is the given approach followed while creating the app. After the training has been done and we've achieved the highest accuracy, we saved the model as tflite. The saved model was then deployed into an android app, which is written in java language. Then we saved the app and installed into the phone poco m4 pro and then downloaded some diseased sugarcane images from the internet and then we used our app to predict the disease. The app worked fine and results were accurate. The app and installed into the phone poco m4 pro and then downloaded some diseased sugarcane images from the internet and then we used our app to predict the disease. The app worked fine and results were accurate.

Within Figure 13, a collection of screenshots from our Android application is thoughtfully presented. These screenshots serve as a tangible testament to the seamless functionality and precision of our application. It becomes evident upon closer inspection that our app functions admirably, delivering accurate predictions as intended. Moreover, we've prioritized an intuitively designed user interface (UI), one that prioritizes simplicity and ease of use. There's a deliberate avoidance of unnecessary frills or superfluous features, opting instead for a minimalist approach that distills the essential components for an effortless user experience. This dedication to user-friendliness ensures that our application can be readily utilized by a broad spectrum of users, making it an accessible and indispensable tool for disease prediction and diagnosis.

Figure 12. Approach of implementing model into app

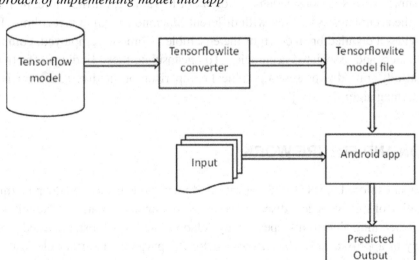

Figure 13. Screenshots of the Android app

RESULTS AND ANALYSIS

The pinnacle of accuracy reached in our experimentation was an impressive 98.09%, discernible in Figure 10. It's worth noting that this achievement was realized after an exhaustive training regimen spanning 60 epochs, although the model was initially trained over 90 epochs. For a comprehensive overview of accuracy across various epochs, kindly refer to Table 2. Furthermore, in Table 4, one can readily observe the accuracies associated with different Machine Learning algorithms. Table 4, on the other hand, provides a detailed breakdown of the ensemble techniques employed, complete with their respective parameters and associated accuracies. To encapsulate these findings effectively, Figure 14 has been thoughtfully crafted to present a graphical comparison of the diverse accuracies exhibited by our Machine Learning algorithms.

CONCLUSION AND FUTURE WORK

This research paper explored the effective utilization of machine learning and deep learning techniques for the classification of sugarcane leaf diseases using a comprehensive dataset. The initial experimentation with machine learning algorithms, specifically Adaboost and XGBoost, provided promising results with an accuracy of approximately 70%. However, for the purpose of further elevating accuracy and

Table 2. Accuracies in different epochs

Epochs	Accuracies
40	97.40
50	95.61
60	98.09
70	97.61
80	95.23
90	96.96

Table 3. ML algorithms and their accuracies

Algorithm	Accuracy
K Nearest Neighbors	64.57
Support Vector Machine	70.47
Decision Tree	53.52
Random Forest	73.90
Gaussian Naïve Bayes	65.90

Table 4. Ensemble learning and accuracies

Name	N_estimators	Base_estimator	Accuracy	Learning Rate
XGBoost	10		70.97	1
Adaboost	10	Decision tree, SVM and Logistic Regression	64.20	1
Adaboost	50	SVM	72.57	1
Adaboost	50	Decision Tree	55.42	1

robustness of the classification process, a Convolutional Neural Network (CNN) model was employed, yielding a significant improvement to an accuracy of 88%.

Recognizing the potential for even greater accuracy, data augmentation techniques were introduced to the CNN model. This strategic augmentation of the dataset resulted in a remarkable accuracy of 98%. This outcome underscores the importance of data preprocessing and augmentation in enhancing the performance of deep learning models, especially in scenarios with limited available data. The progression from traditional machine learning techniques to the advanced CNN architecture, coupled with data augmentation, demonstrates the power of modern approaches in tackling complex agricultural challenges like sugarcane leaf disease classification. It is evident that the adoption of deep learning techniques, particularly CNNs, combined with careful dataset curation and augmentation, can substantially elevate the accuracy of disease detection systems in the agriculture sector. The trained model was successfully deployed within an Android application, enhancing its accessibility and user-friendliness. The outcomes of this investigation not only make a valuable contribution to the domain of sugarcane disease detection but also underscore the broader potential of machine learning and deep learning in transforming agri-

Figure 14. Comparison of different ML algorithms

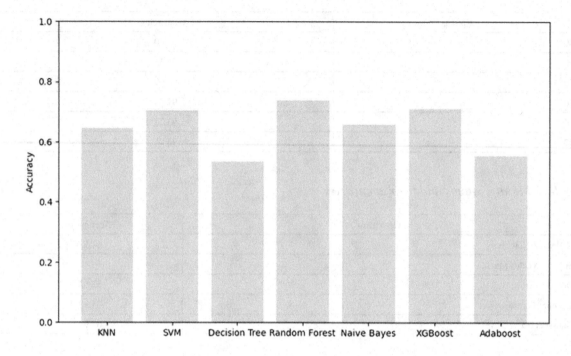

cultural practices and ensuring food security. As technology continues to evolve, there is ample room for further exploration and refinement of these techniques to address even more intricate challenges in the realm of plant pathology and beyond. As for future work we can improve the model and achieve even higher accuracy with more no of classes.

REFERENCES

Abayomi-Alli, O. O., Damaševičius, R., Misra, S., & Maskeliūnas, R. (2021). Cassava disease recognition from low-quality images using enhanced data augmentation model and deep learning. *Expert Systems: International Journal of Knowledge Engineering and Neural Networks*, *38*(7), e12746. doi:10.1111/exsy.12746

Addy, H. S., Nurmalasari, Wahyudi, A., Sholeh, A., Anugrah, C., Iriyanto, F., Darmanto, W., & Sugiharto, B. (2017). Detection and response of sugarcane against the infection of Sugarcane mosaic virus (SCMV) in Indonesia. *Agronomy (Basel)*, *7*(3), 50. doi:10.3390/agronomy7030050

Adem, K., Ozguven, M. M., & Altas, Z. (2023). A sugar beet leaf disease classification method based on image processing and deep learning. *Multimedia Tools and Applications*, *82*(8), 12577–12594. doi:10.1007/s11042-022-13925-6

Ahmad Loti, N. N., Mohd Noor, M. R., & Chang, S. W. (2021). Integrated analysis of machine learning and deep learning in chili pest and disease identification. *Journal of the Science of Food and Agriculture*, *101*(9), 3582–3594. doi:10.1002/jsfa.10987 PMID:33275806

Almadhor, A., Rauf, H. T., Lali, M. I. U., Damaševičius, R., Alouffi, B., & Alharbi, A. (2021). AI-driven framework for recognition of guava plant diseases through machine learning from DSLR camera sensor based high resolution imagery. *Sensors (Basel)*, *21*(11), 3830. doi:10.3390/s21113830 PMID:34205885

Apan, A., Held, A., Phinn, S., & Markley, J. (2004). Detecting sugarcane 'orange rust'disease using EO-1 Hyperion hyperspectral imagery. *International Journal of Remote Sensing*, *25*(2), 489–498. doi:10.1080/01431160310001618031

Aruna, R., Devi, M. S., Anand, A., Dutta, U., & Sagar, C. N. S. (2023, January). Inception Nesterov Momentum Adam L2 Regularized Learning Rate CNN for Sugarcane Disease Classification. In *2023 Third International Conference on Advances in Electrical, Computing, Communication and Sustainable Technologies (ICAECT)* (pp. 1-4). IEEE. 10.1109/ICAECT57570.2023.10117792

Brahimi, M., Boukhalfa, K., & Moussaoui, A. (2017). Deep learning for tomato diseases: Classification and symptoms visualization. *Applied Artificial Intelligence*, *31*(4), 299–315. doi:10.1080/08839514.2017.1315516

Chen, T., He, T., Benesty, M., Khotilovich, V., Tang, Y., Cho, H., ... Zhou, T. (2015). Xgboost: extreme gradient boosting. *R package version 0.4-2, 1*(4), 1-4.

Chien, S. W., Markidis, S., Sishtla, C. P., Santos, L., Herman, P., Narasimhamurthy, S., & Laure, E. (2018, November). Characterizing deep-learning I/O workloads in TensorFlow. In *2018 IEEE/ACM 3rd International Workshop on Parallel Data Storage & Data Intensive Scalable Computing Systems (PDSW-DISCS)* (pp. 54-63). IEEE.

Cutler, A., Cutler, D. R., & Stevens, J. R. (2012). Random forests. *Ensemble machine learning: Methods and applications*, 157-175.

Dileep, P., Das, D., & Bora, P. K. (2020, February). Dense layer dropout based CNN architecture for automatic modulation classification. In 2020 national conference on communications (NCC) (pp. 1-5). IEEE. doi:10.1109/NCC48643.2020.9055989

Elsharif, A. A., & Abu-Naser, S. S. (2019). An expert system for diagnosing sugarcane diseases. *International Journal of Academic Engineering Research*, *3*(3), 19–27.

Esteva, A., Chou, K., Yeung, S., Naik, N., Madani, A., Mottaghi, A., Liu, Y., Topol, E., Dean, J., & Socher, R. (2021). Deep learning-enabled medical computer vision. *NPJ Digital Medicine*, *4*(1), 5. doi:10.1038/s41746-020-00376-2 PMID:33420381

Garg, K., Bhugra, S., & Lall, B. (2021). Automatic quantification of plant disease from field image data using deep learning. In *Proceedings of the IEEE/CVF winter conference on applications of computer vision* (pp. 1965-1972). 10.1109/WACV48630.2021.00201

Guo, A., Huang, W., Dong, Y., Ye, H., Ma, H., Liu, B., Wu, W., Ren, Y., Ruan, C., & Geng, Y. (2021). Wheat yellow rust detection using UAV-based hyperspectral technology. *Remote Sensing (Basel)*, *13*(1), 123. doi:10.3390/rs13010123

Guo, G., Wang, H., Bell, D., Bi, Y., & Greer, K. (2003). KNN model-based approach in classification. In *On The Move to Meaningful Internet Systems 2003: CoopIS, DOA, and ODBASE: OTM Confederated International Conferences, CoopIS, DOA, and ODBASE 2003, Catania, Sicily, Italy, November 3-7, 2003. Proceedings* (pp. 986-996). Springer Berlin Heidelberg. 10.1007/978-3-540-39964-3_62

Guo, Y., Li, J. Y., & Zhan, Z. H. (2020). Efficient hyperparameter optimization for convolution neural networks in deep learning: A distributed particle swarm optimization approach. *Cybernetics and Systems*, *52*(1), 36–57. doi:10.1080/01969722.2020.1827797

Hemalatha, N. K., Brunda, R. N., Prakruthi, G. S., Prabhu, B. B., Shukla, A., & Narasipura, O. S. J. (2022). Sugarcane leaf disease detection through deep learning. In *Deep Learning for Sustainable Agriculture* (pp. 297–323). Academic Press. doi:10.1016/B978-0-323-85214-2.00003-3

Hoy, J. W., Grisham, M. P., & Damann, K. E. (1999). Spread and increase of ratoon stunting disease of sugarcane and comparison of disease detection methods. *Plant Disease*, *83*(12), 1170–1175. doi:10.1094/PDIS.1999.83.12.1170 PMID:30841145

Huang, T., Yang, R., Huang, W., Huang, Y., & Qiao, X. (2018). Detecting sugarcane borer diseases using support vector machine. *Information Processing in Agriculture*, *5*(1), 74–82. doi:10.1016/j.inpa.2017.11.001

Huang, Y., Li, R., Wei, X., Wang, Z., Ge, T., & Qiao, X. (2022). Evaluating Data Augmentation Effects on the Recognition of Sugarcane Leaf Spot. *Agriculture*, *12*(12), 1997. doi:10.3390/agriculture12121997

Jakkula, V. (2006). Tutorial on support vector machine (svm). School of EECS, Washington State University, 37(2.5), 3.

Jiang, P., Chen, Y., Liu, B., He, D., & Liang, C. (2019). Real-time detection of apple leaf diseases using deep learning approach based on improved convolutional neural networks. *IEEE Access : Practical Innovations, Open Solutions*, *7*, 59069–59080. doi:10.1109/ACCESS.2019.2914929

Kosamkar, P. K., Kulkarni, V. Y., Mantri, K., Rudrawar, S., Salmpuria, S., & Gadekar, N. (2018, August). Leaf disease detection and recommendation of pesticides using convolution neural network. In *2018 fourth international conference on computing communication control and automation (ICCUBEA)* (pp. 1-4). IEEE. 10.1109/ICCUBEA.2018.8697504

Kumar, A., & Tiwari, A. (2019). Detection of Sugarcane Disease and Classification using Image Processing. *International Journal for Research in Applied Science and Engineering Technology*, *7*(5), 2023–2030. doi:10.22214/ijraset.2019.5338

Kumar, P. (2021). Research Paper On Sugarcane Diseaese Detection Model. *Turkish Journal of Computer and Mathematics Education*, *12*(6), 5167–5174.

Lei, S., Luo, J., Tao, X., & Qiu, Z. (2021). Remote sensing detecting of yellow leaf disease of Arecanut based on UAV multisource sensors. *Remote Sensing (Basel)*, *13*(22), 4562. doi:10.3390/rs13224562

Li, L., Zhang, S., & Wang, B. (2021). Plant disease detection and classification by deep learning—A review. *IEEE Access : Practical Innovations, Open Solutions*, *9*, 56683–56698. doi:10.1109/ACCESS.2021.3069646

Liang, W. J., Zhang, H., Zhang, G. F., & Cao, H. X. (2019). Rice blast disease recognition using a deep convolutional neural network. *Scientific Reports*, *9*(1), 2869. doi:10.1038/s41598-019-38966-0 PMID:30814523

Lin, K., Gong, L., Huang, Y., Liu, C., & Pan, J. (2019). Deep learning-based segmentation and quantification of cucumber powdery mildew using convolutional neural network. *Frontiers in Plant Science*, *10*, 155. doi:10.3389/fpls.2019.00155 PMID:30891048

Liu, B., Tan, C., Li, S., He, J., & Wang, H. (2020). A data augmentation method based on generative adversarial networks for grape leaf disease identification. *IEEE Access : Practical Innovations, Open Solutions*, *8*, 102188–102198. doi:10.1109/ACCESS.2020.2998839

Macedo, R., Correia, C., Dantas, M., Brito, C., Xu, W., Tanimura, Y., ... Paulo, J. (2021, September). The Case for Storage Optimization Decoupling in Deep Learning Frameworks. In *2021 IEEE International Conference on Cluster Computing (CLUSTER)* (pp. 649-656). IEEE. 10.1109/Cluster48925.2021.00096

Mikołajczyk, A., & Grochowski, M. (2018, May). *Data augmentation for improving deep learning in image classification problem. In 2018 international interdisciplinary PhD workshop (IIPhDW)*. IEEE.

Militante, S. V., Gerardo, B. D., & Medina, R. P. (2019, October). Sugarcane disease recognition using deep learning. In 2019 IEEE Eurasia conference on IOT, communication and engineering (ECICE) (pp. 575-578). IEEE. doi:10.1109/ECICE47484.2019.8942690

Narmilan, A., Gonzalez, F., Salgadoe, A. S. A., & Powell, K. (2022). Detection of white leaf disease in sugarcane using machine learning techniques over UAV multispectral images. *Drones (Basel)*, *6*(9), 230. doi:10.3390/drones6090230

Padilla, D. A., Magwili, G. V., Marohom, A. L. A., Co, C. M. G., Gaño, J. C. C., & Tuazon, J. M. U. (2019, April). Portable yellow spot disease identifier on sugarcane leaf via image processing using support vector machine. In *2019 5th International Conference on Control, Automation and Robotics (ICCAR)* (pp. 901-905). IEEE. 10.1109/ICCAR.2019.8813495

Ratnasari, E. K., Mentari, M., Dewi, R. K., & Ginardi, R. H. (2014, September). Sugarcane leaf disease detection and severity estimation based on segmented spots image. In *Proceedings of International Conference on Information, Communication Technology and System (ICTS) 2014* (pp. 93-98). IEEE. 10.1109/ICTS.2014.7010564

Rish, I. (2001, August). An empirical study of the naive Bayes classifier. In IJCAI 2001 workshop on empirical methods in artificial intelligence (Vol. 3, No. 22, pp. 41-46). Academic Press.

Sandino, J., Pegg, G., Gonzalez, F., & Smith, G. (2018). Aerial mapping of forests affected by pathogens using UAVs, hyperspectral sensors, and artificial intelligence. *Sensors (Basel)*, *18*(4), 944. doi:10.3390/s18040944 PMID:29565822

Schapire, R. E. (2013). Explaining adaboost. In *Empirical Inference: Festschrift in Honor of Vladimir N. Vapnik* (pp. 37–52). Springer Berlin Heidelberg. doi:10.1007/978-3-642-41136-6_5

Sharma, R., & Tamta, S. (2015). A review on red rot: the cancer of sugarcane. *J Plant Pathol Microbiol*, *1*, 3.

SimõesI. O. P. D. S.de FreitasR. G.CursiD. E.ChapolaR. G.AmaralL. R. D. Recognition of Sugar Cane Orange and Brown Rust Through Leaf Image Processing. *Available at* SSRN 4305400. doi:10.2139/ssrn.4305400

Singh, A. K., Sreenivasu, S. V. N., Mahalaxmi, U. S. B. K., Sharma, H., Patil, D. D., & Asenso, E. (2022). Hybrid feature-based disease detection in plant leaf using convolutional neural network, bayesian optimized SVM, and random forest classifier. *Journal of Food Quality*, *2022*, 1–16. doi:10.1155/2022/2845320

Srivastava, S., Kumar, P., Mohd, N., Singh, A., & Gill, F. S. (2020). A novel deep learning framework approach for sugarcane disease detection. *SN Computer Science*, *1*(2), 1–7. doi:10.1007/s42979-020-0094-9

Strachan, S., Bhuiyan, S. A., Thompson, N., Nguyen, N. T., Ford, R., & Shiddiky, M. J. (2022). Latent potential of current plant diagnostics for detection of sugarcane diseases. *Current Research in Biotechnology*, *4*, 475–492. doi:10.1016/j.crbiot.2022.10.002

Sujithra, J., & Ukrit, M. F. (2022). CRUN-Based Leaf Disease Segmentation and Morphological-Based Stage Identification. *Mathematical Problems in Engineering*, *2022*, 2022. doi:10.1155/2022/2546873

Suresha, M., Shreekanth, K. N., & Thirumalesh, B. V. (2017, April). Recognition of diseases in paddy leaves using knn classifier. In *2017 2nd International Conference for Convergence in Technology (I2CT)* (pp. 663-666). IEEE. 10.1109/I2CT.2017.8226213

Tamilvizhi, T., Surendran, R., Anbazhagan, K., & Rajkumar, K. (2022). Quantum behaved particle swarm optimization-based deep transfer learning model for sugarcane leaf disease detection and classification. *Mathematical Problems in Engineering*, *2022*, 2022. doi:10.1155/2022/3452413

Thilagavathi, K., Kavitha, K., Praba, R. D., Arina, S. V., & Sahana, R. C. (2020). Detection of diseases in sugarcane using image processing techniques. *Bioscience Biotechnology Research Communications*, *13*(11), 109–115. doi:10.21786/bbrc/13.11/24

Tiwari, V., Joshi, R. C., & Dutta, M. K. (2021). Dense convolutional neural networks based multiclass plant disease detection and classification using leaf images. *Ecological Informatics*, *63*, 101289. doi:10.1016/j.ecoinf.2021.101289

Umapathy Eaganathan, D. J. S., Lackose, V., & Benjamin, F. J. (2014). Identification of sugarcane leaf scorch disease using K-means clustering segmentation and KNN based classification. *International Journal of Advances in Computer Science and Technology*, *3*(12), 11–16.

Viswanathan, R., & Rao, G. P. (2011). Disease scenario and management of major sugarcane diseases in India. *Sugar Tech*, *13*(4), 336–353. doi:10.1007/s12355-011-0102-4

Wiranata, A., Wibowo, S. A., Patmasari, R., Rahmania, R., & Mayasari, R. (2018, December). Investigation of padding schemes for faster R-CNN on vehicle detection. In *2018 International Conference on Control, Electronics, Renewable Energy and Communications (ICCEREC)* (pp. 208-212). IEEE. 10.1109/ICCEREC.2018.8712086

Zamani, A. S., Anand, L., Rane, K. P., Prabhu, P., Buttar, A. M., Pallathadka, H., Raghuvanshi, A., & Dugbakie, B. N. (2022). Performance of machine learning and image processing in plant leaf disease detection. *Journal of Food Quality*, *2022*, 1–7. doi:10.1155/2022/1598796

Chapter 14

Oil and Gas Industry Challenges for the Next Decade:
Strategies to Face Them From the Education of Future Petroleum Engineers

Rosario Cruz
UAT UAMRR, Mexico

ABSTRACT

Hydrocarbons are one of the most important sources of energy globally. The processing, use, and commercialization of these resources are the basis of the world economy, even in an era of energy transition like the one experienced today, in which alternative energies are developing rapidly. Activities carried out in the hydrocarbon industry contribute a large amount of energy-related CO2 emissions, in addition to other environmental risks such as hydrocarbon spills, soil and groundwater contamination, and fires. As a result, the importance of the industry has been overshadowed, even though because of these same activities, engineering and scientific advances have been achieved to optimize the production of hydrocarbons to satisfy global demand. Consequently, it is expected that the oil and gas industry will face challenges in the environmental, operational, and social context during the next decade.

INTRODUCTION

Hydrocarbons are non-renewable natural resources whose derivates are used in most of the daily use products, specially in fuels for different means of transportation and industrial machinery, as well as raw products for plastics, pharmaceutical, textiles, solvents, among others.

The hydrocarbon world trading is one of the major economic driving forces across the globe, as it controls the development of importing and exporting countries by contributing to the balance of payments and currency generation, which in turn allows the improvement of each country infrastructure. Further, the oil and gas industry is a significant source of employment and taxes.

DOI: 10.4018/979-8-3693-1487-6.ch014

Despite the great importance of hydrocarbons in the global socioeconomic context, in recent years important debates had arisen about the imminent depletion of oil and gas reservoirs and the increasing demand for them, and with it, the question of how the world is using them. Also, the necessary activities for hydrocarbon exploration and production have proven to cause sever environmental problems such as marine oil spills, ground water contamination, soil contamination, explosions and fires, among several others.

The fact that hydrocarbons continue to be essential in the social, economic and industrial development of the world and the fact that their use carries environmental risks and their imminent depletion, requires the modern oil industry to face challenges, including the effective regulation of oil activities, the development of technologies that allow safe and sound hydrocarbon production to satisfy the global demand, and the responsible exploration and production of challenging fields such as non-conventional reservoirs or deep and extra-deep waters reservoirs.

The challenges can be faced if all sectors related to hydrocarbon production work together and focus on a common objective. These sectors are governmental, economic, operational, and academic.

From the academia, educational programs aimed at training professionals who can develop in the hydrocarbon and energy industry in general, must consider the current problems and the future panorama of the oil industry in order to raise awareness among their students of the skills and attitudes that this important industry currently requires, and that allow them to successfully perform in the future.

This work briefly describes some of the challenges that the oil industry deals with at a global level, as well as some recommendations to strengthen academic plans in petroleum engineering so that future professionals acquire the necessary skillset to face three specific challenges in the industry during the next decade: digital transformation, energy transition and challenging specialized technical operations.

THE CHALLENGES OF THE OIL INDUSTRY FOR THE NEXT DECADE USING NEW TECHNOLOGY TRENDS

The International Society of Petroleum Engineers (SPE International) held the "SPE Workshop: Oil and Gas Technology for a Net-Zero World – Defining Our Grand Challenges for the Next Decade" workshop in January 2023, an event in which Panelists from international oil operating and service companies met, as well as financial and environmental stakeholders related to energy development. In this workshop, the technical development and research challenges for the global energy industry over the next decade were defined. Additionally, social or non-technical challenges related to industry education and advocacy are identified. The mentioned challenges will be briefly described below.

Enhanced Recovery from Non-Conventional Resources

Despite the accelerated development of non-fossil energies and their use, it is expected that the demand for oil and gas will continue to increase, at least until 2050 (EIA, 2013). The previous decade, the extraction of hydrocarbons from unconventional reservoirs, through horizontal drilling and hydraulic fracturing, helped meet global demand for hydrocarbons. However, production in this type of reservoir declines rapidly, and therefore the final recovery on average is 10% (Halsey et al., 2023).

Non-conventional reservoirs are interestingly challenging because of the nature of their characteristics such as ultra-low permeability, high fluid absorption and extremely low diffusion flow rates. Due to these characteristics, most of traditional enhanced oil and gas recovery techniques such as waterflooding and well-to-well injection methods become difficult to apply successfully. Therefore, single-well strategies as well as reservoir stimulation using injection of miscible and immiscible gases such as CO2, CH4 and N2, and other surfactant chemicals, solvents and nanoparticles must be improved and optimized. In addition, thermal recovery methods allow control of fluid viscosity and reservoir pressure. Challenges with these methods include understanding the flow of stimulant substances through the rock matrix, their interaction with fractures, and methodologies for optimally finding the stimulant and application parameters of each method. Moreover, these gas injection techniques include additional benefits such as the storage of greenhouse gases.

Net-Zero Upstream Operations

According to the EIA in 2020, emissions from operations and energy purchases accounted for about 15% of energy-related greenhouse gas emissions globally. Most of these emissions are attributed to the release of methane, the venting of CO_2 and flaring, in addition to the contribution generated by other industry operations such as gas and oil production and hydrocarbon transportation (Helsey, 2023).

Today there are technologies that allow fugitive CO_2 emissions to be detected ready for application. However, detecting these is not enough; the industry will require an infrastructure upgrade to minimize them, and an improvement in its monitoring processes. To do this, operational staff will need to be informed and aware to carry out a conscious effort throughout the hydrocarbon value chain.

CO2 Capture, Use, and Storage

Carbon capture, utilization and storage refers to a range of applications through which carbon dioxide (CO2) from industrial activities is captured and used directly or indirectly in different products, for example, in enhanced hydrocarbons recovery methods (EIA, 2023). This represents opportunities for the oil industry to be participant in activities that significantly reduce emissions, while increasing hydrocarbon recovery.

Geothermal Energy

Geothermal energy is a renewable source because is thermal energy extracted from the Earth's crust where it naturally occurs. This energy can be used directly for heating and cooling, or it can be transformed into electricity. The benefits of geothermal energy are its low cost, year-round availability and that it is independent of other meteorological variables, as well as low CO2 emissions, to mention a few. Typically, hot spots where the heat from the subsurface can be used are found in tectonically active zones where hot water or steam escapes to the surface or is found at shallow depths.

Its relationship with the oil industry is since drilling technologies that allow the extraction of hydrocarbons can be applied to the use of geothermal energy and underground thermal water. However, some adaptations must be made as the depths are greater, which increases the cost of drilling, in addition to the technologies and tools facing the challenge of very hard rocks and extreme temperatures.

On the other hand, the production of geothermal energy is based on the flow of fluids through rocks that provide heat through convection. Due to the depth at which they are found, the permeabilities of these rocks tend to be low, so they need to be fractured to achieve the necessary production rates. The challenge in enhanced geothermal systems lies in improving permeability through rock stimulation, while taking care of the risk of seismicity. Significant advances in enhanced oil and gas recovery techniques, such as hydraulic fracturing, can be applied to geothermal systems.

Digital Transformation

Digital transformation (Ortiz et al, 2020) in the oil industry, as in many others, leads to optimization not only in operational processes, but also in the reduction of risks of all kinds, and the improvement of the industry's business model.

Among the technologies currently used, artificial intelligence (Sanju et al, 2023) and machine learning (Jabbar et al, 2022) stand out for the automation of processes such as drilling, development, pipelines and refining (Kumar, 2019); Big Data and Analytics (Quintero et al, 2018, Quintero et al 2022) providing tools for processing enormous amounts of data, for modeling, simulation and forecasting the behavior of reservoirs, contributing to opportune decision-making for the appropriate depletion of reserves; robotic technologies used in the upstream and downstream stages, focused primarily on the inspection, maintenance and repair of surface facilities, allowing compliance with health, safety and environmental standards to be monitored, while increasing economic efficiency through the reduction of personnel necessary for maintenance activities, production handling and floor space requirements (Amit Shukla, Hamad Karki, 2016).

However, many challenges remain in combining expertise, data science, new analytics, and new computational models, especially to support computationally intensive workflows in seismic processing and reservoir modeling and simulation.

Education and Advocacy

It has already been mentioned that the oil industry provides the main sources of energy worldwide, which significantly impacts the global economy. However, one facet that is limitedly observed in the industry are the great engineering, scientific and commercial developments that had been achieved to provide global energy security. All these benefits have been overshadowed by the accusations against the oil industry due to the operational, environmental and safety risks that its activities represent.

Therefore, it is necessary to educate global society and opinion leaders about the importance and realities of energy production, increase the number of scientists and engineers to develop innovative projects in the oil industry, and educate members of the energy industry about the approaches and elements of the energy transition, and their role in it (Halsey et al., 2023).

Aligned with the global challenges, in Mexico the production in mature fields and their rapid decline, offshore exploration and production operations, the characterization and evaluation of reserves in unconventional fields, and digital transformation, including real-time information sensors, intelligent operations and data mining are some of the current challenges that must be faced. On the other hand, in the socioeconomic context, the Mexican oil industry represents a challenge due to its environmental regulatory policies, the lack of infrastructure, and the investment protocols of foreign companies, to mention a few (Ferreira, 2023).

QUALITY PETROLEUM ENGINEERING EDUCATION IN THE PRESENT TO AFFORD THE FUTURE

Since its beginnings at the beginning of the 19th century, petroleum engineering education has been based on study plans whose scope and contents are dictated by the needs of the petroleum industry, both in technical and interpersonal skills.

Petroleum engineering has unique characteristics, for example, that the entire process is oriented towards obtaining a raw material, that is, hydrocarbons, through a process that is executed remotely, since it is not possible to completely know the reservoir, nor the fluid conditions in situ. On the other hand, the design and installation of equipment for extraction is carried out virtually, since it is done underground from the surface, and cannot be directly observed, measured, or monitored, in addition to the changing factors in the subsurface environment which affect the result of each operation.

In addition to the technical characteristics described above, one more singularity of petroleum engineering is its industry, demand, and employment market. We are talking about an industry that not only has higher profits compared to others, but also its practices are more complex and high risk. Economic and technical risks and very high uncertainty due to lack of data are just some of the usual challenges faced by a petroleum engineer.

The same cyclical nature of the oil industry, which changes according to various socioeconomic factors, impacts the enrollment statistics of educational programs related to the hydrocarbon industry, in which a decrease in enrollment is observed after every recession the industry has experienced (Babadagli, 2023). Consequently, justifying the relevance and feasibility of academic programs becomes difficult.

In addition to the situations that the decrease in enrollment implies, academic petroleum engineering programs also face the problem of adapting to the panorama of the energy transition, in which one of the main difficulties is maintaining the fundamental identity of these programs, whilst attempting to train future professionals with the skillset that allow them to perform according to the trends of the following years.

To aim these challenges, de proposed action plan consists of an integral curriculum, in which not only the technical foundations of petroleum engineering are taught and updated, but also is complemented with disciplines such as geosciences, digital technologies, engineering skills, and courses that allow the development of critical thinking, decision-making, as well as their soft skills like collaborative work, communication skills, among others.

The technical contents are divided into cores according to the oil activity: geosciences, drilling, and production. In the discipline of geosciences, it is proposed to strengthen the areas of reservoir characterization through different sources of information such as seismic surveys, geological correlation and well logs, including in each of the topics the technological breakthroughs that are applied currently in the industry, for example, 3D modeling, with special emphasis on the fact that, by understanding the subsurface and the fluid flow through porous media, it is a skill that is not only applied in the oil industry, but also in geothermal energy production, or the recovery of groundwater.

On the other hand, in the drilling core, it is necessary to raise students' awareness not only of the technical importance of carrying out drilling operations properly, but also of operational safety, environmental and economic risks that this activity represents. Moreover, it is important to train future engineers in intelligent drilling through remote sensors, as well as machine learning and 3D modeling applied nowadays in the drilling engineering, and the role of human resources in this digital transformation era.

The approach of the production core courses are all those activities that are carried out on the surface with the objective of producing, managing, and transporting hydrocarbons. In them, the problem that must be addressed is the social and operational responsibility that these activities deserve, with the aim of minimizing work accidents and environmental risks. Also, in this group of courses it will be necessary to update those enhanced recovery techniques that can be applied to challenging reservoirs, such as non-conventional ones and those with ultra-low permeabilities. In this same group, contents about the capture and use of CO_2 can be included.

To maintain the fundamental essence of petroleum engineering, while preparing future professionals for the new technical challenges of the industry and the energy transition, it is advisable to include, as optional subjects, basic courses in geothermal energy and other alternative energies, as well as the use of other resources found in the subsurface, for example, groundwater. At the same time, it is advisable to prepare students not only for the operational side of the industry, but also to perform management positions whose functions include the administration of resources for the safe and reliable development of technical projects.

Additionally, subjects should be included that allow the student to develop critical thinking and analytical skills, with the aim of making decisions or seeking solutions to technical and engineering problems. To achieve the above, it is necessary for students to learn ways of learning, but also ways of applying and transmitting the knowledge they acquire, from a global vision of social and environmental responsibility. It is important to make students aware of the importance of acquiring and applying these skills, especially in an era whose technology develops rapidly because, regardless of the technological resources they use in their work or the scenario in which they find themselves, this is the very essence of an engineer.

Adequate technical training may not be sufficient in an environment such as petroleum engineering, where, as mentioned above, activities are carried out remotely and virtually. Therefore, it is important that future engineers are trained in resilience, adaptability and, also of utmost importance, collaboration. That said, it is appropriate to include in the curriculum courses aimed at the development and practice of soft skills, for example, emotional intelligence to manage stress and frustration, communication skills to transmit ideas, indications and results, and social interaction skills, not just interpersonal ones, but with the whole environment.

The result of updating the petroleum engineering educational programs would be professionals prepared with sufficient technical and soft skills to operate successfully in the petroleum industry, as well as achieve future projection in management positions, which are the objectives of any program. However, the added value that must be sought is to prepare students who are suitable to develop in any other industry that includes the extraction and use of natural resources. By achieving this, it would be possible to reduce the impact that industry fluctuations have on the enrollment in academic petroleum engineering programs.

The above can only be possible if the pillars of education work in synergy. These pillars are the educational program, students, teachers, and the oil industry.

An excellent curriculum design would be useless without the appropriate means to execute it; therefore, teachers and their experience are one of the key elements in the preparation of future engineers. Teachers are not only entrusted with transferring knowledge, but they also have the responsibility of encouraging independent thinking in students through exercises, practices and teaching strategies that develop problem solving through critical analysis. As if that were not enough, teachers must also motivate their students to develop soft skills such as collaborative work, communication skills and the willingness to learn as much new as possible.

The implementation and success of an updated academic plan not only depends on raising awareness among teachers and students but will also depend on the resources available to educational institutions. Equipping specialized laboratories, purchasing computer equipment with enough capacity, and specific software for different oil activities, represent a large investment that not all institutions can afford, especially if the number of enrollments in that program does not justify it. To compensate for the previous situation, it is necessary to work very closely with national and international oil companies, seeking agreements for professional practices, stays and additional courses for students and teachers, resulting in highly qualified elements for working life.

AN ACADEMIC PROGRAM ALIGNED TO ACTUAL GLOBAL QUALITY STANDARDS.

Academic programs, as any other operational process, must be evaluated based on the obtained results, which provides the opportunity to formulate judgments that allow adjustments to be made, all focused on the process improvement and optimization.

There are agencies in charge of certificate the quality of processes according to different standards. In the case of engineering academic programs, the results and operability are evaluated, with the aim of accreditation. By accrediting an academic program, this means ensuring that the necessary quality standards of the profession for which the program prepares students are met.

The Accreditation Board for Engineering and Technology (ABET) is a nonprofit, non-governmental international organization, dedicated to evaluate and accredit educational programs related to applied sciences, natural sciences, computer technology, engineering and technology.

Among the items that are evaluated for this purpose are student results, curricular design, teaching staff and facilities.

Programs willing accreditation through the ABET, among other things, must demonstrate and support that the results of their students meet the objectives of the academic program, since their achievement prepares graduates for their entry into work practice. The results requested for the ABET are cited below:

1. an ability to identify, formulate, and solve complex engineering problems by applying principles of engineering, science, and mathematics.
2. an ability to apply engineering design to produce solutions that meet specified needs with consideration of public health, safety, and welfare, as well as global, cultural, social, environmental, and economic factors.
3. an ability to communicate effectively with a range of audiences.
4. an ability to recognize ethical and professional responsibilities in engineering situations and make informed judgments, which must consider the impact of engineering solutions in global, economic, environmental, and societal contexts.
5. an ability to function effectively on a team whose members together provide leadership, create a collaborative and inclusive environment, establish goals, plan tasks, and meet objectives.
6. an ability to develop and conduct appropriate experimentation, analyze, and interpret data, and use engineering judgment to draw conclusions.

7.   an ability to acquire and apply new knowledge as needed, using appropriate learning strategies.

By knowing the expected results described above, it is possible to operate petroleum engineering programs according to a framework that ensures that the program is feasible and relevant.

CONCLUSION

Reinforcing, updating, and improving Petroleum Engineering education today is a feasible way to face the challenges that the industry currently demands, and the challenges that are anticipated to have to be assumed in the future.

Achieving quality education in petroleum engineering is possible if there is a suitable academic plan, and the means and actors necessary to implement it. In other words, students, teachers, educational institutions, government and industry must work synergistically to achieve this goal.

The oil industry is extremely important for the global economy, so professionals who work in the numerous activities it involves must be aware of the great operational, social, and environmental responsibility that carrying out these operations successfully represents.

Training professionals today, through quality education, can represent success in the energy industry of tomorrow.

REFERENCES

About ABET. (2023). ABET. https://www.abet.org/about-abet/

Babadagli, T. (2023). Reassessment of petroleum engineering education: Is it the end of an era or a new start? *Education for Chemical Engineers*, *43*, 1–9. doi:10.1016/j.ece.2023.01.003

Balhasan, S., & Musbah, I. (2021). The next generation of petroleum engineering students: Challenges and needs. *Journal of Positive School Psychology*, *6*(8), 4450–4457.

CO2 Capture and Utilization - Energy System. (n.d.). IEA. https://www.iea.org/energy-system/carbon-capture-utilisation-and-storage/co2-capture-and-utilisation

Fahes, M., Hosein, R., Zeynalov, G., Sedlar, D. K., Srivastava, M., Swindell, G. S., Kokkinos, N. C., & Willhite, G. (2023). The Impact of the Energy Transition on Petroleum Engineering Departments: The Faculty Perspective. *Paper Presented At The SPE Annual Technical Conference And Exhibition*. 10.2118/215086-MS

Ferreira, H. (2023, 12 mayo). What does the future hold for the oil industry in Mexico? (P. Velasco). *Mexico Bussiness News*. https://www.irena.org/Energy-Transition/Technology/Geothermal-energy

Halsey, T., Agrawal, G., Bailey, J. R., Balhoff, M., Borglum, S. J., Mohanty, K. K., & Traver, M. (2023). *Grand Challenges for the Oil and Gas Industry for the Next Decade and Beyond*. JPT. https://jpt.spe.org/grand-challenges-for-the-oil-and-gas-industry-for-the-next-decade-and-beyond

Jabbar, M. A., Ortiz-Rodríguez, F., Tiwari, S., & Siarry, P. (2022). *Applied Machine Learning and Data Analytics: 5th International Conference, AMLDA 2022, Reynosa, Tamaulipas, Mexico, December 22–23, 2022, Revised Selected Papers.* CCIS. 10.1007/978-3-031-34222-6

Kamal, M. M. (2021). *Future Need of Petroleum Engineering.* One Petro. doi:10.2118/200771-MS

Kumar, A. (2019). *A Machine Learning Application for Field Planning Offshore Technology Conference.* 10.4043/29224-MS

Mathur, A. (2023). Moving upstream with digital technology in the oil and gas industry. *World Oil.* https://www.worldoil.com/magazine/2023/august-2023/features/moving-upstream-with-digital-technology-in-the-oil-and-gas-industry/

Moving upstream with digital technology in the oil and gas industry. (n.d.). https://www.worldoil.com/magazine/2023/august-2023/features/moving-upstream-with-digital-technology-in-the-oil-and-gas-industry/

Ortiz-Rodríguez, F., Palma, R., & Villazón-Terrazas, B. (2006). Semantic based P2P System for local e-Government. In Proceedings of Informatik 2006. GI-Edition- Lecture Notes in Informatics (LNI).

Quintero, J. M., Abrego-Almazán, D., & Ortiz-Rodríguez, F. (2018). Use and usefulness of the information systems measurement. a quality approach at the mexican northeastern region. *Cuadernos Americanos, 31*(56), 7–30. doi:10.11144/Javeriana.cao.31-56.ubwm

Quintero, J. M. M., Echeverría, O. R., & Rodríguez, F. O. (2022). Trust and information quality for the customer satisfaction and loyalty in e-Banking with the use of the mobile phone. *Contaduría y Administración, 67*(1), 283–304.

Shukla, A., & Karki, H. (2016). Application of robotics in onshore oil and gas industry—A review Part I. *Robotics and Autonomous Systems, 75,* 490–507. doi:10.1016/j.robot.2015.09.012

Tiwari, S., Ortiz-Rodríguez, F., Mishra, S., Vakaj, E., & Kotecha, K. (2023). Artificial Intelligence: Towards Sustainable Intelligence. *First International Conference, AI4S 2023, Pune, India, September 4-5, 2023, Proceedings, Communications in Computer and Information Science.* 10.1007/978-3-031-47997-7

Villazón-Terrazas, B., Ortiz-Rodríguez, F., Tiwari, S. M., & Shandilya, S. K. (2020). Knowledge graphs and semantic web. *Communications in Computer and Information Science, 1232,* 1–225. doi:10.1007/978-3-030-65384-2

Chapter 15
Classification of Indian Native English Accents

A. Aadhitya
Anna University, Chennai, India

K. N. Balasubramanian
Anna University, Chennai, India

J. Dhalia Sweetlin
(iD) https://orcid.org/0000-0002-3718-8006
Anna University, Chennai, India

ABSTRACT

The accent spoken by the people is generally influenced by their native mother tongue language. People located at various geographical locations speak by adding flavors to their native language. Various Indian native English accents are classified to bring out a classic difference between these accents. To bring a solution to this problem, a comparative classification model has been built to classify the accents of five distinct native Indian languages such as Tamil, Malayalam, Odia, Telugu, and Bangla from English accents. Firstly, the features of the five-second audio samples each from different accents are obtained and converted to images. The consolidated attributes are gathered. The VGG16 pre-trained model is fused with support vector model to classify accents accurately. Secondly, along with these features, mel frequency cepstral coefficient is added and trained. Then, the features obtained from VGG16 were reduced using principal component analysis. Highest accuracy obtained was 98.46%. Further analysis could be made to produce automated speech recognition for various aspects.

1. INTRODUCTION

Understanding accents has been a major issue in recent days, such that the Human-Machine interaction can be built to do the same. Accents are the speech patterns or pronunciations that are found in different languages. A person's pronunciation of words or usage of rhythm, intonation, and stress in speech are all

DOI: 10.4018/979-8-3693-1487-6.ch015

examples of what is generally referred to as their accent. The same kind of accents are identified among people of an identical national background or ethnic group (Tarun et al., 2022). Accent classification is a multidisciplinary field that involves the identification and categorization of accents based on various phonetic, linguistic, and sociolinguistic features. Accents can be classified along a dialect continuum, which is a range of dialects spoken across a large area or based on unique speech patterns. By listening to a speech of the person one could get to know more about their origin. However, humans can not accurately categorize the accents for the first time. Speech recognition (Mridha et al., 2022) is one of the important issues for many investigative agents because of the accented speech. There would be different kinds of pronunciations within the same language that cannot be recognized with ease. The way a person speaks, including their accent, is influenced by a complex interplay between various factors, including biological, environmental, and cultural factors. Certain methods can be done to modify or adjust the accent of a person such as speech therapy, mimicking native language speakers, immersion in language or dialect by living in a community, training in phonetics of the language and exposure to media.

The Speech Recognition System (Caballero et al., 2006) comes into play to detect the accent of the speaker when the accent spoken by the other is different from others. The accurate identification of the accent is very important and such a model that clearly distinguishes between each of the Indian accents is required. This system can be used by the telephone or call centres to forward the call to the respective support person based on the language and the accent spoken. English is the global language which is spoken by most people around the globe. On the other hand, many people find it difficult to understand the English spoken by the opposite person because of the accent that they are using. Such that to reduce the work of translation a model is developed to perform accent recognition of five different native languages.

The Python package librosa (Suman et al., 2022; McFee et al., 2015) is used to visualize the audio samples and the matplotlib package is used to convert the audio samples to wave plots. The wave plots have been constructed using the amplitude and the time feature of each frame respectively. Such that they could be transformed into features after passing through VGG16 layers. This is one of the pre-trained models such that this VGG16 model has been used to produce the features.

The features retrieved from the model were reduced further using the method of principal component analysis (Bodine & Hochbaum, 2022) to decrease the curse of dimensionality. The most widely used feature, Mel Frequency Cepstral Coefficient (MFCC) is a feature extractor which is used to provide the best representation of the frequency components in the form of waves. The machine learning algorithm Support vector Machine (SVM) is used to classify the features belonging to the different classes. This is best suited to regression and classification-type problems. The kernels present in SVM are used to work with large dimensional features. As the speech features might be very huge, such that this model can be very effective in this case.

2. RELATED WORK

Deshpande et al (2005) focused on developing a GMM classifier model to categorize between standard Indian accent and American accent. The formatted frequencies from the respective accents were used and achieved a higher accuracy. However, the GMM classifier model has disadvantages such as being prone to overfitting, no support for high-dimensional data, being sensitive towards initial model conditions, expensive to train. Upadhyay & Lui (2018) have developed a model to classify different non-native English accents spoken by people from six different countries. They have used MFCC to extract the features and a Deep Belief Network to make the classification. The model attained an accuracy of about 71.9%. Ahmed et al (2019) aimed to classify accents of the same language VFNet, which is a CNN-based architecture. The trained model captured the audio features more elegantly when compared with other techniques. Guntur et al (2022) developed a Mother Tongue Influence system to categorize three different South Indian English Accents. This yielded an accuracy of about 86%. Honnavalli & Shylaja (2019) created a model which classifies the Indian and American accents by extracting the sample features using the MFCC method and this model achieved an accuracy score of about 76% on average.

Guntur et al (2022) made a model which classifies the English speech spoken in three distinct kinds of Dravidian languages from most of the states of India. GMM-UBM model was designed to classify the accents properly and with the metrics as 87.6%. The accuracy of predicting Kannada was greater than the rest of the two accents. Krishna et al (2020) developed an automated system to identify the speaker's native language by using MFCC to get the features. GMM-UBM and I-vector are used to train the model and attained an accuracy of about 84%. Parikh et al (2020) developed a model using CNN fused with DNN along with RNN to classify the speaker's native language. GAN was also used to convert the audio to output accent. Purwar et al (2022) developed a model to classify fellow citizens based on their accents and dialect. CNN and LSTM showed less accuracy when this model was compared. Duduka et al (2020) developed an automatic Speech Recognition system to perform a comparison survey on various machine learning models to classify accents accordingly.

Pedersen & Diederich (2007) developed a model to classify two accents of English. Features of one to four seconds samples are extracted using MFCC and these were trained using the SVM model. The accuracy metrics were around 75% for the trained model. Badhon et al (2021) classified nine different regional languages of Bengal by extracting the audio features using Mel Frequency Cepstral Coefficient. This method produced an accuracy of about 86% after training it with different Machine Learning and Deep Learning techniques. Mannepalli et al (2016) produced a recognition system that could categorize each of the accents in the Telugu language using MFCC as its feature extractor. This method provided a metric of 91% only with this classification. Duduka et al (2021) created a network to classify English accents as American and British using MFCC as the feature extractor. A CNN model was used to classify the accents accurately. Hossain et al (2022) proposed a model to classify seven different dialects of the Bangla language. This is built using a Stacked Convolutional Autoencoder and a Sequence of Multi-Label Extreme Learning machines to produce the classifications.

3. PROPOSED WORK

From the literature survey conducted, it is observed that to classify the accent, one should take into considering features like Amplitude, Frequency which in turn would help in classifying the Indian accent. Amplitude refers to the height of a sound wave, which determines how much energy the wave contains. But Volume is a subjective perception of loudness, which is influenced by several factors, including the amplitude. Several factors related to amplitude (loudness) and frequency (pitch) can influence the perception of accents such as Vowel Amplitude, Increased Speech emphasis and Frequency excursions. The change of a periodic variable over a period is measured by amplitude. A sound wave's amplitude is connected to the energy it carries. A wave with a high amplitude carries a lot of energy, while one with a low amplitude carries less energy. A CNN model trained on amplitude mel-spectrograms was employed in a study to categorise accented English in the context of accent classification through measuring amplitude. Modern classification outcomes were made possible by amplitude mel-spectrograms on a linear scale, which are the correlates of the energy of the audio stream. It is also vital to keep in mind that an oscillating signal's amplitude changes over its period, so it is usually not useful to estimate the energy at any given instant of time, but only the energy over some time-period window.

VGG16 is used for extracting the features from the audio spectrograms obtained from the WAV files and LinearSVC to classify the accent from the obtained features. Along with the features obtained from VGG16, MFCC features are also added. Normal accuracy scores are used since it is a classification problem, unlike regression. For the experiment, 5 Indian English accents are taken: Telugu, Malayalam, Bangla, Odiya and Tamil. The accents were taken with the help of a dataset called "AccentDB" maintained by Ahamad et al (2020), while for Tamil audio, manual scraping of the data from YouTube videos is done. The overall architecture of the model is also mentioned in Figure 1.

3.1 About the Dataset

AccentDB is used as the main dataset for this scenario as not many audio datasets are widely available that solely focus on Indian accent classification. The AccentDB dataset consists of two variants: Core and Extended. The Core type consists of WAV files which have 4 types of Indian accents: Telugu, Ma-

Table 1. Literature survey in summary

Study	Method Proposed / Followed	Contribution and Performance Metrics Obtained	Type
Tarun et al (2022)	Analysis methods to classify Indian English Accents	Core differences in vocabulary were identified which are different from other country's English accents	Analysis
Mridha et al (2022)	Automatic Speech Recognition for Bengali language	Analysis on existing ASR systems for parsing Bengali language is done	Survey
Suman et al (2022)	-	Demonstrated audio Visualization using Librosa library available in Python	Study & Research
Deshpande et al (2005)	GMM Classifier	Developed a GMM Classifier model to differentiate between Indian and American accent	Research
Upadhyay & Lui (2018)	MFCC, Deep Belief Networks	Developed a model to classify non native English accents spoken by people from 6 countries. Obtained Accuracy: 71.9%	Research
Ahamed et al (2019)	VFNet (CNN Based)	Created a model to classify accents of the same language	Research
Honnavalli & Shylaja (2021)	MFCC	Developed a model to clas sify Indian and American English accents. Accuracy obtained: 76%	Research
Guntur et al (2022)	GMM-UBM	Developed a model to classify 3 accents of Kannada language. Accuracy: 87.6%	Research
Krishna et al (2020)	MFCC, GMM- UBM with I-vector	Developed an automated system to identify a speaker's ethnicity via accent	Research
Parikh et al (2020)	CNN fused with DNN and RNN, GAN	Developed a model to classify a speaker's native language	Research
Pedersen & Diederich (2007)	MFCC, SVM	Made a model to classify two English accents. Accuracy obtained: 75%	Research
Badhon et al (2021)	MFCC	Developed a model to classify 9 different Bengali accents from given audio. Accuracy Obtained: 86%	Research
Duduka et al (2021)	CNN, MFCC	Made a CNN model to classify between American and British accents in audio.	Research

Figure 1. Architecture for accent classification model

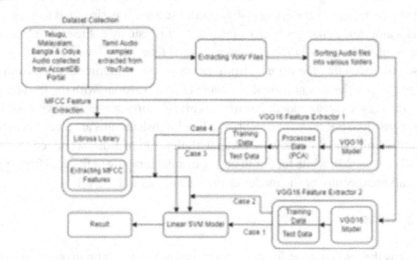

layalam, Bangla and Odiya, while the extended type consists of 5 English accents in addition to 4 Indian accents. The audio samples are obtained from 11 raw and unprocessed WAV files, in which they are split into 5-second audio samples in the dataset. Since the focus is on classifying the Indian accents alone, the Core type of dataset is taken which is around 2.8GB in size (compressed) and has 6500 WAV files in it. Each file in the dataset consists of 2 speakers in each accent folder. For the Tamil accent, manual scraping of the data from YouTube videos is done and stored in a folder with each WAV file having a 5-second delay. All WAV audio files have 44100 Hz as the sample rate which is of high quality.

3.2 Tools Used

The tools used in the proposed work are mentioned below:

- Language:
  - Python
- Frameworks
  - TensorFlow
  - Keras
  - Flask
- Platform
  - Google Colab
- Audio Analysis
  - Librosa
- Audio Extraction and Splitting (for external sources)
  - Wondershare Filmora 11
- Dataset Downloader
  - GDown library

4. EXPERIMENTAL ANALYSIS

For the experiment, Python is used mainly for data pre-processing, feature extraction and model training. For deployment, Flask is used to create a website where people can upload their audio files which in turn would return the accent as the result. In this section, the major parts of the experiment work are described. The implementation is done using Google Colab with GPU as a hardware accelerator.

4.1 Dataset Collection

Collecting data is the first and foremost step in the machine-learning process. To extract the dataset from Google Cloud (both AccentDB and Custom data) in which the WAV files are stored, the GDown library is used present in Python to download the tar files. After that, the tar file is extracted and the WAV files are obtained. Each file is 5 seconds in length and it is chosen as it is suitable as it reduces the workload of the system. They are used as they are not computationally intensive to convert them into Waveform images and analyse the features for a large dataset of 6500 WAV audio samples.

4.2 Data Sorting

After obtaining the WAV files, the files are stored in separate folders which represent the class. In this case, it is the Indian language. Since the file names are known in this case, it is easy to sort them into folders with the language as the respective folder name. After sorting the WAV data, they are sent to convert as Waveform images.

4.3 Waveform Images

From the WAV data sorted, they are made to pass through a function present in the librosa library called "waveshow" which will convert the amplitude values to image format. This is done for VGG16 model to easily segregate

features present in the waveform image of the audio file. The waveshow function is applied to a group of audio files instead of every file in the dataset. This is done to reduce the load of the system as the system gets to peak RAM limit when made to convert images from 6500 WAV files during the experiment. From every language, 200-300 audio files are taken and they are made to convert into images to avoid the load on the system. These images are then sent to the VGG16 model for extracting relevant features (shown in Figure 2). Each image is of 22.05 kHz bandwidth (assuming audio bandwidth is 44.1 kHz)

4.4 VGG16 Model

The VGG16 model is a Convolution Neural Network model created in 2014 to solve the ImageNet challenge. When compared to the GoogLeNet architecture, the model performed well during the challenge. VGG16 comprises 13 convolutional layers, 5 max-pooling layers, and 3 dense layers, which sums up a total of 21 levels, but only 16 of those layers are learnable parameters layers. This is also a reason for the number 16 in the VGG16 model. Small 3x3 filters that are piled on top of one another in increasing depths make up the design of VGG16. Small filters enable the network to learn more intricate characteristics while using fewer parameters. The convolutional layer uses a set of filters that it has learned

Figure 2. Wave plot image of a Telugu WAV audio file

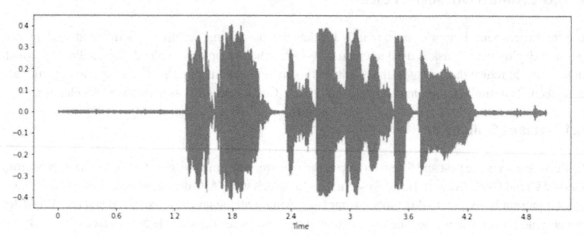

during training to perform a convolution operation on the input image. The rectified linear unit (ReLU) activation function adds nonlinearity to the model by passing the output of the convolutional layer through it. The maximum value in each pooling region is taken by the max pooling layer to reduce the spatial dimensions of the convolutional layer's output. The dense layer then adds a bias term and an activation function before applying a matrix multiplication operation to the output of the preceding layer. However, the model is slow in terms of training speed and large, making it only suitable for certain applications such as image classification. The model is also available as a pre-trained variant which makes it suitable for transfer learning. The architecture of VGG16 is shown in Figure 3.

The pre-trained variant of VGG16 from Keras is taken for the implementation as the main objective is to extract relevant features from the waveform images. The features extracted are then stored on a list which will be later converted to a data frame for further processing.

Figure 3. Architecture of VGG16 model

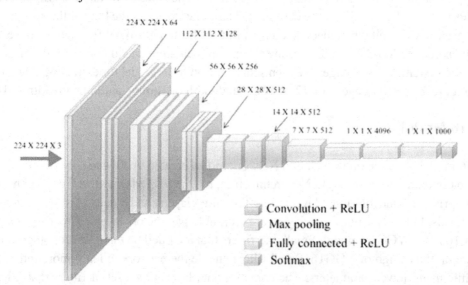

There are many other CNN architectures available such as AlexNet, GoogleNet, ResNet-50, and Inception-ResNet-v2 in which all are pre-trained. Except for AlexNet, other models such as GoogleNet, and ResNet are deep networks which are suitable only for training larger datasets. For smaller datasets, there is a risk of overfitting. So, a suitable network must be chosen in this case. Compared with AlexNet, VGG16 has a lower error rate and 16 layers; also, VGG16 is not as deep as compared with other networks, which makes it suitable for the proposed work though it has many parameters. The comparison table is given in Table 2 for clarity.

4.5 MFCC Features

Mel Frequency Cepstral Coefficients (MFCCs) are a characteristic that is commonly employed in artificial speech and speaker recognition. Before the introduction of MFCCs, the main feature type for automated speech recognition (ASR) was linear prediction coefficients (LPCs) and linear prediction cepstral coefficients (LPCCs), particularly used with HMM classifiers.

To obtain the MFCC features, the basic algorithm is followed below:

- The audio is divided into 20-40ms frames (25ms is preferred). Then the frames are passed through a filter.
- The frames are made to pass through a function which applies the Fast Fourier Transform (FFT) to convert them from the time domain to the frequency domain. FFT is similar as the Discrete Fourier Transform (DFT) but the complexity is reduced ($O(Nlog_2N)$) compared with DFT ($O(N^2)$). DFT is measured using the formula

$$x[k] = \Sigma \; x[n]e^{(-j2\pi kn)/N}$$

- After conversion, the Mel scale is applied to the filters to get a smooth spectrum which also reduces the size of features. The Mel scale is measured using the formula $M(f) = 1125 * ln(1 + f/700)$
- Finally, a discrete cosine transform is applied and the respective coefficients are plotted.

To obtain the MFCC features from the WAV audio, Librosa is used, which is a Python library made for music and audio analysis (not for processing and training models). In this implementation, 40 MFCC features (n_mfcc=40 is used in mfcc function from librosa library) are selected from each audio and the

Table 2. Comparison of CNN architectures

CNN Architecture	Year	Number of Layers	Number of Parameters	Error Rate	Type
VGG16	2014	16	138M	7.3%	Deep
AlexNet	2012	16	61M	15.3%	Shallow
GoogleNet	2014	22	62.3M	7.3%	Deep
ResNet-50	2015	50	23M	3.6%	Deep
Inception-ResNet-v2	2016	164	56M	4.9%	Deep
Inception-v4	2016	22	43M	5.0%	Deep

features are stored in the list (same as the previous method) and then later converted into a data frame for further processing.

The sample plot for MFCC is shown in Figure 4

4.6 LinearSVC Model

Support vector machines (SVMs) are supervised learning algorithms used for classification, regression, and outlier detection. However, it is most often used for classification. It operates on the principle of constructing a hyperplane that can segregate most of the points on the graph according to their class. Here, the LinearSVC (SVM with Linear Kernel) model is used with the help of the scikit-learn module, and the model is trained using the training data generated in the previous stage. As it is a classification model, the accuracy of the model for testing data is calculated using the accuracy score. The architecture is shown in Figure 5.

4.7 VGG16 + SVM Model

For image classification tasks, the VGG16 model, a convolutional neural network (CNN) architecture, is frequently used. However, by transforming sound data into spectrogram images, it can also be used for tasks involving sound classification. A spectrogram is a graphic representation of a sound signal's frequency content over time. It is produced by performing the Fourier transform on a sound signal within a small-time window and plotting the resulting spectrum against the passing of time. The spectrogram images are fed into the VGG16 model as input for sound accent classification. The model then learns to extract pertinent details from the images and categorise them into various classes of accent. The VGG16 model produces a set of high-level features that correspond to the input image's content. The VGG16 model's output is fed into a support vector machine (SVM) classifier to increase classification accuracy even further. The SVM is a machine learning algorithm that categorises data by locating the hyperplane that maximises the margin between the classes. The SVM classifies sound accents into various accent

Figure 4. Sample plot of MFCC for a WAV file

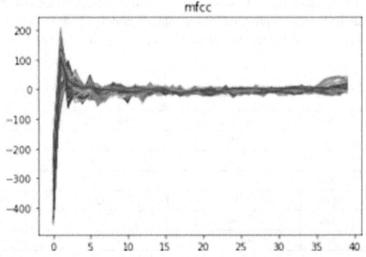

Figure 5. Architecture of SVM model

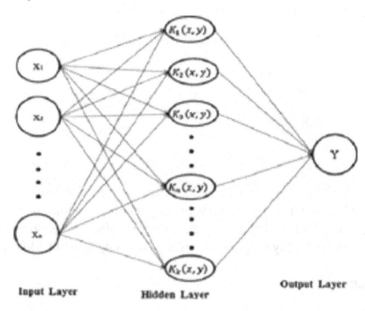

classes using the high-level features that the VGG16 model extracted as input. The combined architecture of the proposed model is shown in Figure 6. The advantages of the proposed model are as follows.

- SVM is effective in cases where the number of dimensions is greater than the number of samples. This is useful in accent classification tasks where there are many features to consider.
- VGG16 has a deeper architecture with 13 convolutional layers, followed by 3 fully-connected layers. This allows it to extract more complex features from the input data, which can improve classification accuracy.
- VGG16 uses smaller filter sizes (3×3) compared to other CNNs, which allows it to use a higher number of non-linear activations with a reduced number of parameters. This can improve the model's ability to capture complex patterns in the input data.
  - Both VGG16 and SVM provide high accuracy in scenarios where classification is required.

4.8 Data Processing and Training

The lists are created to store extracted features of audio via VGG16 and MFCC features are then converted to data frames via Pandas library. As the VGG16 feature vector is of huge size for one audio (nearly 25088 features in total for 5 seconds), the Principal Component Analysis (PCA) method is applied on every feature vector to reduce the overall feature size to 40 in the data frame. Then, the converted data frame is concatenated with the MFCC feature data frame and the respective classes are labelled manually in a list which ends the step. This processed dataset is now sent for a train-test split which is done in the 75:25 method. The obtained training and testing data is sent to the LinearSVC Model. Currently, the model is trained and tested with audio files having a bandwidth of up to 44.1 kHz. The proposed model can handle higher bandwidths as well, however, will use a lot of resources and hence can become computationally intensive. For example, to improvise the audio processing, Bandwidth Extension (BWE)

Figure 6. Architecture of VGG16 + SVM model

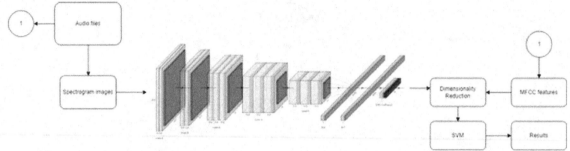

techniques can be employed to improve the audio quality and increase the frequency. Owing to their intensive processing nature, those techniques are not suitable for the case of processing audio files at a fast rate. Hence, the model currently supports processing files only up to 44.1 kHz bandwidth.

4.9 Testing Phase

In this phase, first, the model is made to be tested with the testing data split earlier during the testing phase. The overall accuracy of the model is recorded with different kinds of features and required tweaks are done to improve the accuracy rate. Finally, the model is tested with real audio datasets which are obtained from random videos available on YouTube. Before giving the data, the audio data is converted to WAV format with a 5-second slice format. Finally, the data is made to pass into the model. The model was able to predict the target language provided that the audio is free of background noise such that the features can be captured easily.

4.10 Deployment

For the deployment phase, the Flask library is used to create a web app in which users can send the audio data and view the accent type as the result. For saving VGG16 model parameters, the model is made to export to HDF5 format while the LinearSVC model parameters are exported with the help of the pickle library in python. After importing the parameters, the Flask app is created and the model works well along with the web app. The sample app interface is shown in Figure 7.

5. OUTPUT AND END PRODUCT

Following the creation of the classification model and the web app, the models are tested with various data and it handles well provided that the accents are within the class range. Since the focus is not on native accents, the classification of non-native English Indian accents alone is made as the objective of the experiment. Even with real-time data, the models classified the audio data with good accuracy. The accuracies of the models are recorded for 2 epochs and from them, the accuracy of the reduced VGG16 and MFCC features was recorded as the highest. The comparison table is also made in Table 3.

Figure 7. Result of model in flask application

Table 3. Accuracies of the features taken

Features Taken	Accuracy (in Percent)	Number of Features Taken
Unreduced VGG16	86.46	25088
Unreduced VGG16 and MFCC	96.46	25128
Reduced VGG16	71.46	40
Reduced VGG16 and MFCC	98.46	80

The final feature was finalized based on the accuracy patterns. Such that to find out the best fitting model a comparative analysis between four different approaches was carried out. First, the pre-trained model VGG16 was used as a feature extractor to get the features of the audio samples such as time for audio. The number of features obtained from this model is 25088. All these features were fed into the SVM classifier model and this yielded an accuracy of 86.4%. Secondly, the previously obtained VGG16 features were combined with the Mel Frequency Cepstral Coefficient (MFCC) features which collectively produced 25128 features. When these many features were trained using the SVM model and yielded 96.46% accuracy. The third observation is that the features obtained from the first method were reduced to 40 features using Principal Component Analysis. This was done to cut down the curse of dimensionality issue, but this model yielded the lowest accuracy of 71.46% percentage when compared with other approaches. The final method was conducted with the addition of reduced VGG16 features and MFCC, it totals up to 80 features. When these features were fed into the SVM model, it gave a maximum accuracy of 98.46%. From these observations, the model having the maximum accuracy can be used to categorize the audio files of respective accents. Table 4 shows the comparison of the proposed work with the existing works in accent classification.

Table 4. Comparison with existing works and models

Type of Model	Dataset Used	Features Taken	Accuracy
DBN	Customised	MFCC	71.9%
GMM-UBM + I-vector	Customised	-	93.9%
Random Forest	Customised	MFCC	86%
CNN	AccentDB	MFCC	96.85%
Proposed	AccentDB + Customised	VGG16 + MFCC	98.46%

6. CONCLUSION

The VGG16-SVC model is developed such that it classifies the five native Indian languages spoken in English. The features were extracted using the WAVfile package from SciPy such that the amplitude and time at each frame are returned from the function and are made to visualize as wave plots. These images are stored and given as input to the VGG16 pre-trained model and the features are extracted accordingly. The acquired features are used as the inputs along with MFCC Features to the Support Vector Machine Classifier and the model is trained. When the trained model was validated, it attained an accuracy of about 98.46%. This model would be useful to classify Indian Native languages based on English accents. The number of data samples for each class can be increased and a few more native languages can be added and classified. These may be considered as future works accordingly.

CONFLICT OF INTEREST

On behalf of all authors, the corresponding author states that there is no conflict of interest.

REFERENCES

Ahamad, A., Anand, A., & Bhargava, P. (2020). Accentdb: A database of non-native english accents to assist neural speech recognition. *arXiv preprint arXiv:2005.07973*.

Ahmed, A., Tangri, P., Panda, A., Ramani, D., & Karmakar, S. (2019, December). Vfnet: A convolutional architecture for accent classification. In *2019 IEEE 16th India Council International Conference (INDICON)* (pp. 1-4). IEEE. 10.1109/INDICON47234.2019.9030363

Al-Jumaili, Z., Bassiouny, T., Alanezi, A., Khan, W., Al-Jumeily, D., & Hussain, A. J. (2022, August). Classification of Spoken English Accents Using Deep Learning and Speech Analysis. In *International Conference on Intelligent Computing* (pp. 277-287). Cham: Springer International Publishing. 10.1007/978-3-031-13832-4_24

Badhon, S. S. I., Rahaman, H., Rupon, F. R., & Abujar, S. (2021). Bengali accent classification from speech using different machine learning and deep learning techniques. In *Soft Computing Techniques and Applications: Proceeding of the International Conference on Computing and Communication (IC3 2020)* (pp. 503-513). Springer Singapore. 10.1007/978-981-15-7394-1_46

Bodine, J., & Hochbaum, D. S. (2022). A Better Decision Tree: The Max-Cut Decision Tree with Modified PCA Improves Accuracy and Running Time. *SN Computer Science, 3*(4), 313. doi:10.1007/s42979-022-01147-4

Caballero, M., Moreno, A., & Nogueiras, A. (2006). Multidialectal acoustic modeling: A comparative study. Multilingual Speech and Language Processing.

Deshpande, S., Chikkerur, S., & Govindaraju, V. (2005, October). Accent classification in speech. In *Fourth IEEE Workshop on Automatic Identification Advanced Technologies (AutoID'05)* (pp. 139-143). IEEE. 10.1109/AUTOID.2005.10

Duduka, S., Jain, H., Jain, V., Prabhu, H., & Chawan, P. M. (2021). A neural network approach to accent classification. *International Research Journal of Engineering and Technology, 8*(03), 1175–1177.

Duduka, S., Jain, H., Jain, V., Prabhu, H., & Chawan, P. P. M. (2020). Accent classification using machine learning. *International Research Journal of Engineering and Technology (IRJET), 7*(11).

Guntur, R. K., Ramakrishnan, K., & Mittal, V. K. (2022). Foreign Accent Recognition Using a Combination of Native and Non-native Speech. In *Intelligent Sustainable Systems: Selected Papers of WorldS4 2021* (Vol. 1, pp. 713–721). Springer Nature Singapore. doi:10.1007/978-981-16-6309-3_67

Guntur, R. K., Ramakrishnan, K., & Vinay Kumar, M. (2022). An automated classification system based on regional accent. *Circuits, Systems, and Signal Processing, 41*(6), 3487–3507. doi:10.1007/s00034-021-01948-7

Honnavalli, D., & Shylaja, S. S. (2019, May). Supervised machine learning model for accent recognition in English speech using sequential MFCC features. In *International Conference on Artificial Intelligence and Data Engineering* (pp. 55-66). Singapore: Springer Nature Singapore.

Hossain, P. S., Chakrabarty, A., Kim, K., & Piran, M. J. (2022). Multi-Label Extreme Learning Machine (MLELMs) for Bangla Regional Speech Recognition. *Applied Sciences (Basel, Switzerland), 12*(11), 5463. doi:10.3390/app12115463

Krishna, G. R., Krishnan, R., & Mittal, V. K. (2020, December). A system for automatic regional accent classification. In *2020 IEEE 17th India Council International Conference (INDICON)* (pp. 1-5). IEEE. 10.1109/INDICON49873.2020.9342577

Mannepalli, K., Sastry, P. N., & Suman, M. (2016). MFCC-GMM based accent recognition system for Telugu speech signals. *International Journal of Speech Technology, 19*(1), 87–93. doi:10.1007/s10772-015-9328-y

McFee, B., Raffel, C., Liang, D., Ellis, D. P., McVicar, M., Battenberg, E., & Nieto, O. (2015, July). librosa: Audio and music signal analysis in python. In *Proceedings of the 14th python in science conference* (Vol. 8, pp. 18-25). 10.25080/Majora-7b98e3ed-003

Mridha, M. F., Ohi, A. Q., Hamid, M. A., & Monowar, M. M. (2022). A study on the challenges and opportunities of speech recognition for Bengali language. *Artificial Intelligence Review*, *55*(4), 1–25. doi:10.1007/s10462-021-10083-3

Parikh, P., Velhal, K., Potdar, S., Sikligar, A., & Karani, R. (2020, May). English language accent classification and conversion using machine learning. *Proceedings of the International Conference on Innovative Computing & Communications (ICICC)*. 10.2139/ssrn.3600748

Pedersen, C., & Diederich, J. (2007, July). Accent classification using support vector machines. In *6th IEEE/ACIS International Conference on Computer and Information Science (ICIS 2007)* (pp. 444-449). IEEE.

Purwar, A., Sharma, H., Sharma, Y., Gupta, H., & Kaur, A. (2022, April). Accent classification using machine learning and deep learning models. In *2022 1st international conference on informatics (ICI)* (pp. 13-18). IEEE. 10.1109/ICI53355.2022.9786885

Suman, S., Sahoo, K. S., Das, C., Jhanjhi, N. Z., & Mitra, A. (2022, June). Visualization of audio files using librosa. In *Proceedings of 2nd International Conference on Mathematical Modeling and Computational Science: ICMMCS 2021* (pp. 409-418). Singapore: Springer Nature Singapore. 10.1007/978-981-19-0182-9_41

Tarun, M., Israr, A., & Gajwal, D. (2022). Analysis of the factors influence Indian English accents, and how pronunciation and articulation fill the accent gap. *EPRA International Journal of Environmental Economics, Commerce and Educational Management*, *9*(4), 43–49.

Upadhyay, R., & Lui, S. (2018, January). Foreign English accent classification using deep belief networks. In *2018 IEEE 12th international conference on semantic computing (ICSC)* (pp. 290-293). IEEE. 10.1109/ICSC.2018.00053

Chapter 16

Analyzing Fuel Cell Vehicles Through Intelligent Battery Management Systems (BMS):
AI and ML Technologies for E–Mobility

Putchakayala Yanna Reddy

Department of Electrical & Electronics Engineering Department, Bharath Institute of Engineering and Technology, India

Balpreet Singh Madan

Department of Art and Design, School of Design, Architecture, and Planning, Sharda University, Greater Noida, India

Harishchander Anandaram

https://orcid.org/0000-0003-2993-5304

Department of Artificial Intelligence, Amrita Vishwa Vidyapeetham, Coimbatore, India

Praveen Rathod

Department of Mechanical Engineering, Vishwakarma Institute of Information Technology, Pune, India

S. Vasanthaseelan

https://orcid.org/0000-0003-1174-4497

Department of Mechanical Engineering, Sri Krishna College of Technology, Coimbatore, India

S. Boopathi

Muthayammal Engineering College, India

ABSTRACT

Integrating artificial intelligence (AI), internet of things (IoT), and machine learning (ML) technologies into fuel cell systems offers numerous benefits, applications, and opportunities for advancement across various sectors. This chapter explores the synergistic potential of AI, IoT, and ML in fuel cell integration, outlining their advantages, applications, challenges, and potential solutions. By leveraging AI for predictive maintenance, optimizing operating conditions through IoT sensors, and employing ML algorithms for efficiency enhancements, fuel cell systems can achieve higher performance and reliability. Real-world case studies and examples demonstrate successful integration in sectors such as transportation, energy production, and manufacturing. Moreover, this chapter discusses future prospects, including advancements in data analytics, system optimization, and scalability, driving innovation in fuel cell technology integration with AI, IoT, and ML.

DOI: 10.4018/979-8-3693-1487-6.ch016

INTRODUCTION

Fuel cells are a promising technology that convert chemical energy into electrical energy through electrochemical reactions. They offer high energy efficiency, low emissions, and quiet operation. However, successful integration requires advanced technologies like Artificial Intelligence (AI), Internet of Things (IoT), and Machine Learning (ML). These technologies can enhance efficiency, reliability, and performance in fuel cell integration. This article explores the role of AI, IoT, and ML in fuel cell integration, their benefits, applications, challenges, opportunities, and case studies. It also examines future trends and their potential impact on various industries (R. Kumar et al., 2021).

Fuel cells convert hydrogen or other fuel sources into electrical energy through an electrochemical reaction. They consist of an electrolyte, two catalyst-coated electrodes, and an external circuit. Fuel is supplied to the anode, which reacts with the catalyst, creating electrons and positively charged ions. These electrons flow through the circuit, producing electrical energy. The positively charged ions migrate to the cathode, where they combine with oxygen, creating water or other byproducts. Fuel cells have potential applications in transportation, residential and industrial power generation, and portable electronics (Exner et al., 2020; S. Kumar et al., 2023; Olivares-Rojas et al., 2020).

AI can significantly enhance fuel cell integration by enabling predictive maintenance, optimizing operating conditions, and improving system efficiency. By analyzing large amounts of data, AI algorithms can detect potential failures and performance degradation, reducing downtime and maximizing system availability. They can also optimize fuel cell operating conditions by adjusting parameters like temperature and humidity based on real-time inputs and environmental conditions. Applications of AI in fuel cell integration include fault detection, energy management, and system optimization, resulting in higher reliability, efficiency, and longevity, making it a more attractive energy solution (Exner et al., 2020; S. Kumar et al., 2023).

The IoT is a network of interconnected devices and sensors that collect and exchange data. By integrating fuel cells with IoT technologies, real-time monitoring and control of fuel cell systems can be achieved, enabling remote monitoring of system performance, fault detection, and efficient maintenance coordination. Benefits of IoT in fuel cell integration include enhanced system monitoring, early fault detection, remote control and operation, and improved maintenance planning. Applications of IoT in fuel cell integration include remote monitoring, predictive maintenance, and fleet management in transportation (Biswas & Wang, 2023; Exner et al., 2020).

ML algorithms can analyze large amounts of data from fuel cell systems, identify patterns, and make predictions or recommendations. This can optimize fuel cell operation, detect faults or anomalies, and improve system performance. By learning from historical data and adapting to changing conditions, ML algorithms can identify common patterns or trends, enabling system-wide optimization and performance improvement. Applications of ML in fuel cell integration include optimizing operating conditions, fault detection and diagnosis, and system performance improvement. By harnessing the power of ML, fuel cell integration can achieve higher efficiency, reliability, and performance, making it a more sustainable and viable energy solution (Moniruzzaman et al., 2023).

AI, IoT, and ML are revolutionizing fuel cell integration by enabling predictive maintenance, optimizing operating conditions, and improving system efficiency. This makes fuel cell integration a viable energy solution for various industries. This section explores the advantages, applications, challenges, opportunities, real-world implementations, and future trends in the field. The chapter discusses the potential of AI, IoT, and ML in fuel cell integration. Fuel cells, which generate electricity through chemical reactions, are highly efficient and produce zero emissions. By integrating these technologies with other technologies, they can improve their performance, efficiency, and monitoring capabilities. AI, IoT, and ML can optimize operating conditions, detect faults, predict maintenance needs, and enhance system monitoring and control. This results in fuel cells operating at peak performance, with improved efficiency and reduced downtime. The chapter highlights the benefits, applications, challenges, and opportunities of these technologies in fuel cell integration (Hussain et al., 2023).

Implementing AI, IoT, and ML in fuel cell integration faces challenges such as data availability, computational complexity, and infrastructure integration. However, real-world case studies show successful implementations in transportation, residential, and industrial power generation. Future advancements in AI, IoT, and ML technologies, along with renewable energy sources, are expected to enhance fuel cell integration. Expansion into aerospace and marine sectors also presents exciting opportunities for fuel cell integration. The chapter's objectives are depicted in Figure 1 and discussed below.

- To outline the benefits of integrating AI, IoT, and ML technologies in fuel cell systems
- To highlight the various applications of AI, IoT, and ML in fuel cell integration
- To discuss the challenges and potential solutions for implementing AI, IoT, and ML in fuel cell integration
- To explore the opportunities and potential advancements for fuel cell integration with AI, IoT, and ML technologies
- To provide real-world case studies and examples of successful fuel cell integration with AI, IoT, and ML technologies in various sectors

Figure 1. Objectives of the chapter

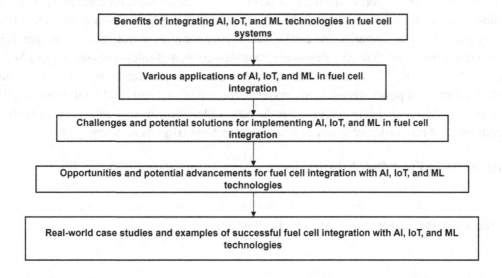

FUEL CELL TECHNOLOGY

Fuel cell technology is a promising and sustainable alternative to traditional power generation, converting fuel's chemical energy into electrical energy through an electrochemical reaction. It offers high energy efficiency, minimal greenhouse gas emissions, and versatile applications, making it a promising alternative (Feng et al., 2022).

A fuel cell is a device that converts fuel into electricity, heat, and water through the electrochemical reaction of fuel and oxidant gases. Its structure consists of an electrolyte, an anode, and a cathode, which allow ions to pass and prevent gas mixing. The anode is the electrode where fuel is oxidized, while the cathode is the electrode where oxidant is reduced. Fuel cells offer high energy efficiency, converting up to 60% of the energy in fuel into usable electricity, reducing wasted energy and fuel consumption.

Fuel cells offer a low environmental impact compared to fossil fuel-burning power plants, producing minimal harmful emissions. The only byproducts are water vapor and small amounts of carbon dioxide when hydrocarbon fuels like natural gas or diesel are used. This makes fuel cells a cleaner and more sustainable option for power generation, reducing greenhouse gas emissions and improving air quality (Rewatkar et al., 2022). Fuel cell technology is versatile and can be applied in various sectors, including transportation, stationary power applications, and renewable energy sources. For example, fuel cells can be used in electric vehicles, backup power systems, remote off-grid sites, and clean electricity sources for homes and businesses.

Fuel cell technology presents a promising and sustainable alternative to traditional power generation methods due to its high energy efficiency, minimal emissions, and versatile applications. However, challenges such as high costs and manufacturing processes need to be addressed for widespread adoption. Research and development efforts are focused on reducing costs and improving fuel cell durability and reliability. Despite these challenges, ongoing research and development efforts are continuously improving fuel cell technology and driving its integration into the energy landscape.

ARTIFICIAL INTELLIGENCE IN FUEL CELL INTEGRATION

AI has the potential to revolutionize the integration of fuel cell technology. By leveraging AI algorithms and machine learning techniques, it is possible to optimize fuel cell performance, improve efficiency, and enhance overall system operation. AI can be used to monitor and control various parameters in real-time, allowing for better predictive maintenance, fault detection, and mitigation strategies (Al-Othman et al., 2022). Additionally, AI can analyze complex data sets and optimize system configurations, such as load management and power dispatch, to maximize the use of fuel cells and minimize energy losses. The integration of AI in fuel cell technology has the potential to significantly enhance the reliability and cost-effectiveness of this sustainable power generation method (Biswas & Wang, 2023).

Benefits of AI in Fuel Cell Integration

The several benefits of integrating AI in fuel cell technology are explained below (Chen et al., 2020). Figure 2 illustrates the advantages of AI in fuel cell integration.

Figure 2. Benefits of AI in fuel cell integration

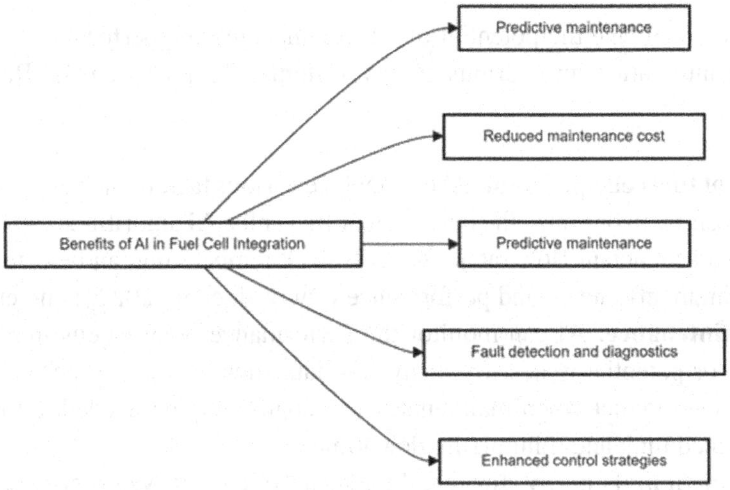

- **Improved efficiency:** AI algorithms can optimize the operation of fuel cells by continuously analyzing real-time data and adjusting various parameters. This leads to improved efficiency and performance, ensuring that fuel cells operate at their maximum potential.
- **Predictive maintenance:** AI can monitor and analyze fuel cell performance, detecting any anomalies or potential issues in real-time. By doing so, it can provide early alerts and predictive maintenance recommendations, minimizing downtime and reducing maintenance costs.
- **Fault detection and mitigation:** AI algorithms can quickly identify and diagnose faults or malfunctions in fuel cells. By detecting these issues early, AI can initiate mitigation strategies to prevent system failures and ensure continuous operation.
- **Energy management and optimization:** AI can analyze complex data sets, including energy demand patterns, weather forecasts, and electricity prices. Based on this analysis, AI can optimize the operation of fuel cells by determining the most efficient power dispatch and load management strategies (Ugandar et al., 2023; Venkateswaran et al., 2023).
- **Improved system reliability:** By continuously monitoring and analyzing fuel cell performance, AI can identify potential reliability issues and suggest improvements. This can lead to increased system reliability and reduced downtime, enhancing the overall performance of fuel cell systems.
- **Cost savings:** AI optimization techniques can maximize the use of fuel cells, reducing energy losses and improving overall system efficiency. This can result in significant cost savings in terms of fuel consumption and energy bills.
- **Enhanced sustainability:** Fuel cells are already a sustainable energy generation technology, but integrating AI can further enhance their sustainability. By optimizing their operation and improving efficiency, AI can help reduce greenhouse gas emissions and reliance on fossil fuels.

Overall, the integration of AI in fuel cell technology has the potential to enhance performance, reduce costs, and improve the sustainability of fuel cell systems.

Applications of Artificial Intelligence in Fuel Cell Integration

These applications demonstrate the potential of AI in enhancing the performance, efficiency, and reliability of fuel cell integration into various energy systems (Boopathi, 2024a; Ramudu et al., 2023; Zekrifa et al., 2023).

- **Optimization of fuel cell operation:** AI can analyze various factors such as temperature, humidity, and fuel composition to optimize the operation of fuel cells. AI algorithms can continuously adjust parameters such as reactant flow rates, fuel cell stack temperature, and electrolyte concentration to ensure maximum efficiency and performance (Dwivedi et al., 2022; Feng et al., 2022).
- **Predictive maintenance:** AI can monitor the performance of fuel cells in real-time and detect any anomalies or potential issues. By analyzing data such as voltage, current, and temperature, AI algorithms can predict when maintenance or repairs may be needed, allowing for proactive maintenance scheduling and minimizing downtime.
- **Load management and energy storage:** AI algorithms can analyze energy demand patterns and prioritize load management strategies. They can also integrate with energy storage systems, such as batteries or supercapacitors, to optimize the distribution of power and ensure efficient use of fuel cells (Satav et al., 2023; Syamala et al., 2023).
- **Fault detection and diagnostics:** AI can automatically detect and diagnose faults or malfunctions in fuel cell systems. By analyzing sensor data and comparing it to historical data, AI algorithms can identify patterns and deviations that may indicate a problem. This allows for early intervention and mitigation strategies to prevent system failures.
- **Energy management and optimization:** AI can analyze data from various sources, such as weather forecasts, electricity prices, and energy demand patterns, to optimize the operation of fuel cells. AI algorithms can determine the most efficient power dispatch strategies, taking into account factors such as energy availability, cost, and environmental impact (Naveeenkumar et al., 2024; Paul et al., 2024; Vanitha et al., 2023).
- **Remote monitoring and control:** AI can enable remote monitoring and control of fuel cell systems, allowing for real-time performance analysis and adjustment. This is particularly useful for large-scale installations or installations in remote locations, where it may be impractical to have personnel on site at all times.
- **System integration and interoperability:** AI can facilitate the integration of fuel cell systems with other energy generation technologies, such as solar panels or wind turbines. By analyzing and optimizing the operation of these integrated systems, AI can maximize overall efficiency and power output.

INTERNET OF THINGS IN FUEL CELL INTEGRATION

IoT plays a crucial role in fuel cell integration by providing real-time data monitoring, remote control, and optimization capabilities (Pourrahmani et al., 2022). IoT integration in fuel cell systems enhances efficiency, reduces maintenance costs, enables predictive maintenance, improves fault detection, and facilitates advanced control strategies for performance optimization.

- IoT sensors are placed within the fuel cell system to collect real-time data on various parameters such as temperature, pressure, voltage, current, and gas flow rate. This data is continuously transmitted to a centralized platform for monitoring and analysis (Malathi et al., 2024; Pachiappan et al., 2024).
- With IoT, fuel cell systems can be remotely controlled and monitored. This allows operators to monitor the system's performance, check for any anomalies, and make adjustments as needed from a remote location. It helps in reducing the need for on-site interventions and improves operational efficiency (Malathi et al., 2024; Subha et al., 2023).
- IoT enables predictive maintenance by analyzing the real-time data collected from the fuel cell system. Through machine learning algorithms, the IoT platform can detect patterns and trends in the data to predict equipment failures or maintenance needs. This helps in proactively addressing potential issues and minimizing system downtime (Pachiappan et al., 2024; Rahamathunnisa et al., 2024).
- IoT can detect faults in the fuel cell system by analyzing the data obtained from various sensors. It can identify abnormalities or deviations from the normal operating conditions, which could indicate potential faults or performance degradation. This enables early detection and timely maintenance actions (Ali et al., 2024; Boopathi, 2024b).
- IoT integration enables advanced control strategies for optimizing the performance of fuel cell systems. Real-time data and analytics help in adjusting operating parameters, such as airflow and fuel supply, to maximize energy efficiency, reduce emissions, and extend the lifespan of the fuel cells.
- IoT platforms can integrate fuel cell systems with other energy generation and storage devices, such as solar panels and batteries. This allows for optimized energy management, where surplus power from the fuel cells can be stored or supplied to the grid based on demand and availability.

Benefits of Internet of Things in Fuel Cell Integration

The IoT in fuel cell integration offers numerous benefits, including real-time data monitoring, remote control, predictive maintenance, fault detection, and diagnostics. These technologies enhance control strategies, energy management, cost reduction, efficiency, reliability, monitoring, reporting, scalability, sustainability, and decision-making (Chou et al., 2020; Sethusubramanian et al., 2021). Real-time data monitoring provides accurate information on system performance, while remote control allows operators to monitor and control fuel cell systems from a remote location. Fault detection and diagnostics help identify abnormalities and performance degradation early.

Fuel cell systems can be optimized for energy efficiency and reduced emissions, extending their lifespan. Integrating fuel cell systems with other energy devices reduces operational expenses and costs through proactive maintenance and early fault detection. IoT offers scalability and flexibility, allowing easy integration with existing infrastructure. Sustainability and environmental benefits are achieved through optimized energy usage and renewable energy sources integration.

Applications of Internet of Things in Fuel Cell Integration

The integration of the IoT with fuel cells presents a myriad of applications that contribute to enhanced efficiency, sustainability, and management of fuel cell systems. From real-time monitoring to predictive

Figure 3. Various applications of IoT in fuel cell integration

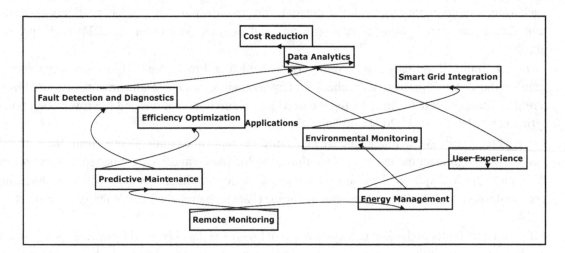

maintenance, the applications of IoT in fuel cell integration are diverse and impactful. Figure 3 depicts various applications of IoT in fuel cell integration (Pourrahmani et al., 2022; Rewatkar et al., 2022).

- One of the primary applications of IoT in fuel cell integration is remote monitoring and control. IoT sensors embedded within fuel cell systems continuously collect data on various parameters such as temperature, pressure, voltage, and current. This real-time monitoring enables operators to assess the health and performance of fuel cells from a remote location. Additionally, remote control capabilities allow operators to make adjustments and optimize the system without the need for physical presence, resulting in improved operational efficiency.
- IoT-enabled predictive maintenance is a crucial application in fuel cell integration. By analyzing the data collected from sensors, the system can predict potential issues and maintenance needs before they lead to system failures. This proactive approach reduces downtime, increases the reliability of fuel cell systems, and extends their overall lifespan.
- IoT plays a pivotal role in intelligent energy management for fuel cells. Sensors gather data on energy production, consumption, and storage. This information is then analyzed to optimize the distribution of energy within a network. Real-time adjustments based on demand and supply conditions result in improved energy utilization, cost savings, and a more sustainable operation (Karthik et al., 2023; Maguluri et al., 2023).
- IoT sensors facilitate the early detection of anomalies and faults within fuel cell systems. Continuous monitoring of performance metrics allows for timely intervention and prevents major issues. Moreover, the diagnostic capabilities of IoT help operators identify the root causes of problems, enabling efficient troubleshooting and maintenance.
- Through the integration of IoT, fuel cell systems can benefit from data-driven insights into their performance. Operators can use this information to optimize operating conditions, ensuring that the fuel cells operate at their maximum efficiency. Continuous monitoring and real-time adjustments lead to improved overall energy efficiency.

- IoT sensors can measure emissions and environmental conditions associated with fuel cell operation. This data is crucial for assessing the environmental impact of fuel cells and ensuring compliance with regulatory standards. Environmental monitoring contributes to sustainability efforts and the development of cleaner energy solutions (Boopathi, 2022; Boopathi et al., 2023).
- The integration of IoT provides a user-friendly interface for monitoring and controlling fuel cell systems. Users can access data and control features through web interfaces or mobile applications, enhancing the overall user experience. This accessibility improves the ease of operation and allows for better decision-making.
- Accumulated data from IoT sensors can be analyzed using advanced analytics tools. This analysis helps operators identify patterns, trends, and opportunities for further optimization of fuel cell performance. The insights gained from data analytics contribute to continuous improvement and innovation in fuel cell technology.
- Fuel cell systems integrated with IoT seamlessly connect with smart grids. This integration facilitates better coordination between energy producers and consumers, leading to improved grid stability and reliability. The synergy between fuel cells and smart grids contributes to the development of a more robust and flexible energy infrastructure (Hema et al., 2023; Kavitha et al., 2023).
- Through efficient monitoring and control enabled by IoT, fuel cell systems can be operated more effectively, resulting in reduced operational costs. Predictive maintenance and optimized energy management contribute to resource and cost savings over the long term (Malathi et al., 2024).

The integration of IoT in fuel cells enhances monitoring, control, and optimization, contributing to clean and efficient energy systems. As technology advances, the synergy between IoT and fuel cells holds potential for innovative applications and improvements in energy sustainability.

MACHINE LEARNING IN FUEL CELL INTEGRATION

ML applications in fuel cell integration offer advanced capabilities for optimizing performance, predicting maintenance needs, and enhancing overall efficiency. ML algorithms leverage data generated by sensors and other sources within the fuel cell system to make predictions, identify patterns, and adapt to changing conditions (Wang et al., 2020). Here are several key applications of ML in fuel cell integration. The integration of machine learning (ML) in fuel cell systems improves performance, reliability, and efficiency by leveraging data analytics and adaptive learning. This makes fuel cell technology more adaptable to dynamic conditions, paving the way for smart energy systems.

- ML algorithms can analyze vast amounts of data from fuel cell systems to identify patterns and correlations that may not be apparent through traditional methods. This analysis helps optimize operating conditions, improve energy conversion efficiency, and enhance overall performance.
- ML models excel in predictive maintenance by analyzing historical and real-time data to identify trends and patterns indicative of potential system failures. This enables operators to predict when maintenance is needed, reducing downtime and preventing unexpected breakdowns (M. Kumar et al., 2023; Pachiappan et al., 2024; Sathish et al., 2023).
- ML algorithms can be trained to detect anomalies and diagnose faults in fuel cell systems. By continuously monitoring various parameters, ML models can identify deviations from normal op-

Figure 4. Benefits of ML in fuel cell integration

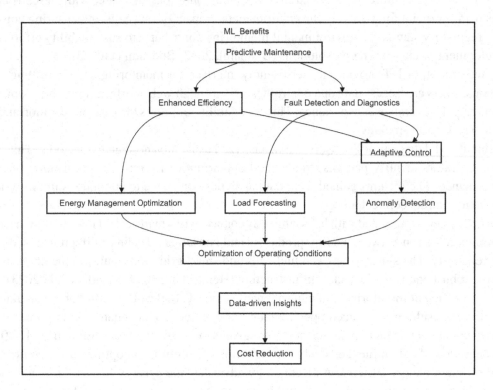

erating conditions, helping operators pinpoint the root causes of issues and enabling more effective troubleshooting.

- ML techniques can analyze complex relationships between input variables and fuel cell efficiency. By learning from historical data, ML models can recommend adjustments to operating parameters to maximize efficiency under different operating conditions.
- ML algorithms can play a crucial role in optimizing energy management within fuel cell systems. By analyzing data on energy production, consumption, and storage, ML models can dynamically adjust the distribution of energy to meet demand, leading to improved energy utilization and cost savings.
- ML models can be trained to forecast energy demand based on historical data, weather patterns, and other relevant factors. This capability is particularly valuable in fuel cell systems integrated with smart grids, allowing for better coordination and planning of energy production and distribution.
- ML algorithms enable adaptive control strategies by continuously learning and adjusting the control parameters of fuel cell systems in response to changing operating conditions. This adaptability improves the system's ability to respond to fluctuations in demand and environmental factors.
- ML models can detect abnormal behavior or unexpected events in fuel cell systems. This is valuable for early identification of potential issues, enabling proactive maintenance and preventing system failures.
- ML algorithms can optimize the operating conditions of fuel cells by considering various factors such as temperature, pressure, and humidity. This results in improved overall system efficiency and performance.

- ML provides data-driven insights into complex relationships within fuel cell systems. These insights can inform decision-making processes, guide system improvements, and contribute to the ongoing development of fuel cell technology.

Benefits of Machine Learning in Fuel Cell Integration

ML significantly enhances fuel cell integration performance, efficiency, and overall system management, offering key benefits such as improved system management and system efficiency as shown in Figure 4. The integration of ML in fuel cell systems offers a range of benefits, from predictive maintenance to enhanced efficiency and innovation. These applications empower fuel cell technology to become more adaptive, reliable, and efficient in meeting the demands of clean and sustainable energy solutions (Li & Yu, 2021).

- ML algorithms analyze historical and real-time data from fuel cell systems to predict maintenance needs. By identifying patterns and anomalies, ML models can forecast potential issues, enabling proactive maintenance and minimizing downtime (Tian et al., 2021).
- ML models optimize the operating conditions of fuel cells by learning from data patterns. This results in improved energy conversion efficiency and overall system performance. ML algorithms can dynamically adjust parameters for varying operating conditions, maximizing efficiency.
- ML enables the early detection of faults and anomalies within fuel cell systems. By continuously monitoring parameters, ML models can identify deviations from normal behavior, diagnose issues, and assist in troubleshooting, leading to improved reliability.
- ML allows for the development of adaptive control strategies. By learning from data and adjusting control parameters in real-time, fuel cell systems can adapt to changing conditions, optimizing their response to fluctuations in demand, weather, or other factors.
- ML applications optimize energy management within fuel cell systems by analyzing data on energy production, consumption, and storage. This results in dynamic adjustments to energy distribution, contributing to better energy utilization and cost savings.
- ML models forecast energy demand based on historical data and external factors. This capability is crucial for fuel cell systems integrated with smart grids, allowing for better planning and coordination of energy production to meet predicted demand.
- ML algorithms excel in anomaly detection, identifying abnormal behavior or unexpected events in fuel cell systems. This proactive identification helps in early intervention, preventing potential system failures and ensuring continuous operation.
- ML applications optimize various operating conditions of fuel cells, including temperature, pressure, and humidity. By learning from data patterns, ML models recommend adjustments that result in improved overall system efficiency and performance.
- ML provides data-driven insights into complex relationships within fuel cell systems. This information guides decision-making processes, helping operators and engineers make informed choices for system improvements and optimization.
- ML fosters a culture of continuous improvement by constantly learning from new data. This adaptability contributes to ongoing innovation in fuel cell technology, allowing for the implementation of cutting-edge solutions and advancements.

- Through predictive maintenance, optimized energy management, and efficient fault detection, ML contributes to cost reduction by minimizing downtime, extending the lifespan of fuel cell components, and improving overall system reliability.

Applications of Machine Learning in Fuel Cell Integration

ML applications in fuel cell integration span various aspects, enhancing the performance, reliability, and efficiency of fuel cell systems. The specific applications of ML in the integration of fuel cells (Chou et al., 2020; Wang et al., 2020).

- ML models excel in detecting anomalies and faults within fuel cell systems. By continuously monitoring various parameters, ML algorithms can identify deviations from normal behavior, helping operators diagnose issues and perform targeted maintenance.
- ML applications optimize the performance of fuel cells by analyzing data on operating conditions, efficiency, and environmental factors. These models can recommend adjustments to parameters, ensuring that the fuel cells operate at their maximum efficiency under different conditions.
- ML contributes to intelligent energy management within fuel cell systems. By analyzing data on energy production, consumption, and storage, ML models optimize the distribution of energy to meet demand, resulting in improved energy efficiency and cost savings.
- ML models can forecast energy demand based on historical data, weather patterns, and other relevant factors. This capability is particularly valuable in fuel cell systems integrated with smart grids, allowing for better planning and coordination of energy production.
- ML enables the development of adaptive control strategies. By continuously learning from data and adjusting control parameters in real-time, fuel cell systems can adapt to changing conditions, optimizing their response to fluctuations in demand and external factors.
- ML algorithms are effective in detecting abnormal behavior or unexpected events in fuel cell systems. This capability allows for early identification of potential issues, facilitating proactive maintenance and preventing system failures.
- ML applications optimize various operating conditions of fuel cells, such as temperature, pressure, and humidity. By learning from data patterns, ML models recommend adjustments that result in improved overall system efficiency and performance.
- ML provides valuable data-driven insights into the complex relationships within fuel cell systems. This information can guide the design process, helping engineers make informed decisions and fostering continuous innovation in fuel cell technology.
- ML contributes to cost reduction by minimizing downtime through predictive maintenance, extending the lifespan of fuel cell components, and improving overall system reliability. These factors lead to lower operational costs and increased return on investment.
- ML can analyze data related to emissions and environmental conditions associated with fuel cell operation. This information aids in assessing the environmental impact of fuel cells and ensuring compliance with regulatory standards (Sharma et al., 2024; Sundaramoorthy et al., 2024).
- ML can be utilized to enhance the user experience by optimizing interfaces and control systems. Personalized user interfaces, informed by ML insights, make it easier for operators to monitor and control fuel cell systems.

ML's diverse applications in fuel cell integration contribute to cleaner, more efficient energy systems. These applications enable fuel cells to operate intelligently, adapt to changing conditions, and contribute to sustainability and energy efficiency goals.

CHALLENGES AND OPPORTUNITIES IN FUEL CELL INTEGRATION

Fuel cell integration, while holding great promise for clean energy solutions, comes with its own set of challenges and opportunities. Addressing these challenges can unlock the full potential of fuel cell technology and contribute to its widespread adoption (Vishnumurthy & Girish, 2021; Zehir & Zehir, 2022).

Challenges

Costs and Economics

- Challenge: High upfront costs associated with fuel cell technology, including manufacturing and installation expenses, hinder widespread adoption.
- Opportunity: Continued research, technological advancements, and economies of scale have the potential to drive down costs, making fuel cell systems more economically viable.

Infrastructure Development

- Challenge: Insufficient infrastructure, including a lack of refueling stations for hydrogen fuel cells, limits the practicality and convenience of widespread adoption.
- Opportunity: Investment in infrastructure development, both for hydrogen production and distribution, can facilitate the growth of fuel cell technology and create a supportive ecosystem.

Hydrogen Production and Storage

- Challenge: Current methods of hydrogen production often rely on fossil fuels, reducing the environmental benefits of fuel cells. Additionally, efficient and cost-effective hydrogen storage solutions are needed.
- Opportunity: Advancements in green hydrogen production through electrolysis powered by renewable energy sources and improvements in hydrogen storage technologies can enhance the sustainability of fuel cell systems.

Durability and Lifespan

- Challenge: The durability and lifespan of fuel cell components, such as membranes and catalysts, can be limiting factors, especially in harsh operating conditions.
- Opportunity: Research and development efforts aimed at improving the durability and longevity of fuel cell components will contribute to increased reliability and reduced maintenance costs.

Supply Chain and Raw Materials

- Challenge: Dependence on rare materials, such as platinum for catalysts, can pose supply chain risks and increase costs.
- Opportunity: Research into alternative materials and recycling methods can mitigate supply chain vulnerabilities and reduce dependence on scarce resources.

Standardization and Regulations

- Challenge: Lack of standardized testing methods and regulatory frameworks can slow down the certification process and impede market acceptance.
- Opportunity: Industry collaboration, along with the development of clear and standardized regulations, can create a more favorable environment for fuel cell integration.

Prospects

- Fuel cells offer a clean, efficient, and sustainable energy source, producing electricity with water and heat as primary byproducts, aligning with global efforts for low-carbon energy (Feng et al., 2022).
- Fuel cells offer decentralized power generation, enabling off-grid applications and distributed energy systems, thereby enhancing energy resilience and reducing reliance on centralized power plants.
- Fuel cells offer potential for electrification of transportation, particularly in fuel cell vehicles (FCVs), due to their longer ranges and shorter refueling times compared to electric batteries.
- Hybrid systems combine fuel cells with renewable energy sources like solar or wind, offering a reliable, continuous power supply, overcoming intermittency issues in certain renewables.
- The ongoing advancements in fuel cell technology, including improvements in materials, designs, and manufacturing processes, present an opportunity for more efficient and cost-effective systems.
- Fuel cells offer potential for energy storage and grid balancing, providing power during peak demand or when renewable sources are unavailable.
- Green hydrogen production, utilizing renewable energy sources and electrolysis, offers a sustainable pathway for fuel cells, promoting a transition towards a carbon-neutral energy landscape.
- Research and innovation in fuel cell technology, supported by public and private investments, presents an opportunity to address current challenges and unlock new applications.
- Fuel cells offer a potential solution for energy security and resilience, providing backup power during grid outages or emergencies, especially in critical infrastructure and mission-critical applications.

The integration of fuel cells faces challenges, but ongoing research, technological advancements, and supportive policies offer numerous opportunities for widespread adoption, contributing to a more sustainable and resilient energy ecosystem.

FUTURE TRENDS IN FUEL CELL INTEGRATION

Fuel cell integration is expected to undergo significant advancements in the coming years due to technological innovation, market demands, and the global shift towards sustainable energy solutions, with several future trends shaping the landscape as Figure 5. Future fuel cell integration trends will focus on cost reduction, infrastructure development, green hydrogen production, technological advancements, decentralized power generation, electrification, smart grid integration, IoT and data analytics, and regulatory support, contributing to widespread adoption of fuel cell technology for a sustainable energy future (Dhanya et al., 2023; Ingle et al., 2023; Ravisankar et al., 2023).

- Future trends in fuel cell integration will focus on reducing manufacturing costs and improving economies of scale to make fuel cell technology more commercially viable. Increased production volumes and technological advancements will drive down the costs of fuel cell components, making them competitive with conventional energy sources (Chou et al., 2020).
- The expansion of hydrogen infrastructure, including production, storage, and distribution facilities, will be a key trend in fuel cell integration. Governments, industries, and stakeholders are investing in the development of hydrogen refueling stations and distribution networks to support the widespread adoption of fuel cell vehicles and stationary fuel cell systems.
- Future trends will see a shift towards green hydrogen production methods, such as electrolysis powered by renewable energy sources. Green hydrogen offers a sustainable pathway for fuel cell integration, aligning with global efforts to decarbonize energy systems and reduce greenhouse gas emissions (Dhanalakshmi et al., 2024a, 2024b).
- Fuel cell systems will increasingly be integrated with renewable energy sources like solar and wind power to create hybrid energy systems. These hybrid systems combine the benefits of fuel cells with intermittent renewable energy generation, providing reliable and continuous power supply.
- Future trends will witness significant advancements in fuel cell technology, including improvements in efficiency, durability, and power density. Research and development efforts will focus on developing next-generation fuel cell materials, membranes, catalysts, and system designs to enhance performance and reliability.
- Fuel cell integration will enable decentralized power generation, allowing for distributed energy systems that are resilient and adaptable. Small-scale fuel cell systems will be deployed in residential, commercial, and industrial settings, providing backup power, grid support, and off-grid energy solutions.
- Fuel cell integration will play a crucial role in the electrification of transportation, particularly in heavy-duty vehicles, buses, and marine applications. Fuel cell vehicles (FCVs) offer long-range capabilities and shorter refueling times compared to electric batteries, making them suitable for various transportation sectors.
- Future trends will focus on integrating fuel cell systems with smart grids to enhance grid stability, reliability, and efficiency. Fuel cells will provide grid balancing services, energy storage, and demand response capabilities, contributing to the optimization of energy distribution and consumption.
- The integration of IoT technology and data analytics will enable real-time monitoring, predictive maintenance, and optimization of fuel cell systems. IoT sensors will collect data on performance metrics, while ML algorithms will analyze the data to identify trends, anomalies, and opportunities for optimization.

Figure 5. Future trends in fuel cell integration

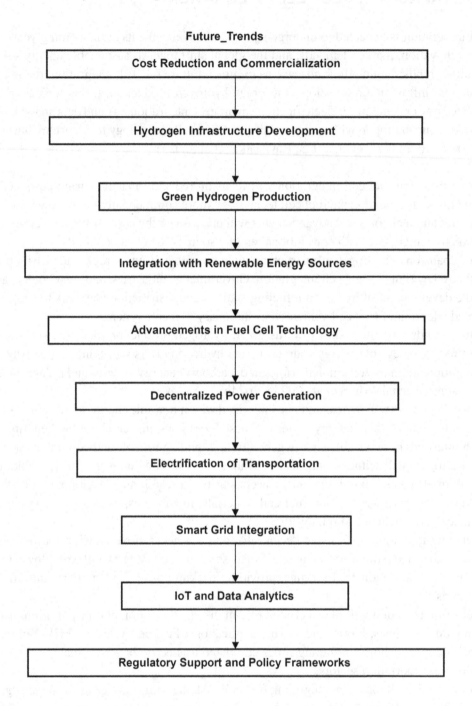

- Governments and regulatory agencies will play a crucial role in shaping the future of fuel cell integration through supportive policies, incentives, and regulatory frameworks. Measures such as carbon pricing, emissions targets, and R&D funding will drive investments and innovation in fuel cell technology (Saravanan et al., 2022).

CONCLUSION

Fuel cell integration offers a clean, efficient, and sustainable energy solution for various applications, including transportation and power generation. Despite challenges like high upfront costs, infrastructure limitations, and technological barriers, the future of fuel cell integration presents numerous opportunities for advancement. Future trends in fuel cell integration include cost reduction, commercialization, hydrogen infrastructure development, green hydrogen production, renewable energy integration, advancements in fuel cell technology, decentralized power generation, electrification, smart grid integration, IoT, data analytics, and regulatory support.

Fuel cell integration can significantly contribute to a sustainable, low-carbon energy future by addressing challenges and leveraging emerging opportunities. With continued research, innovation, and stakeholder collaboration, fuel cell technology can revolutionize energy systems, reduce greenhouse gas emissions, mitigate climate change impacts, and foster economic growth and energy security.

ABBREVIATIONS

AI - Artificial Intelligence
IoT - Internet of Things
ML - Machine Learning

REFERENCES

Al-Othman, A., Tawalbeh, M., Martis, R., Dhou, S., Orhan, M., Qasim, M., & Olabi, A. G. (2022). Artificial intelligence and numerical models in hybrid renewable energy systems with fuel cells: Advances and prospects. *Energy Conversion and Management*, *253*, 115154. doi:10.1016/j.enconman.2021.115154

Ali, M. N., Senthil, T., Ilakkiya, T., Hasan, D. S., Ganapathy, N. B. S., & Boopathi, S. (2024). IoT's Role in Smart Manufacturing Transformation for Enhanced Household Product Quality. In *Advanced Applications in Osmotic Computing* (pp. 252–289). IGI Global. doi:10.4018/979-8-3693-1694-8.ch014

Biswas, A., & Wang, H.-C. (2023). Autonomous vehicles enabled by the integration of IoT, edge intelligence, 5G, and blockchain. *Sensors (Basel)*, *23*(4), 1963. doi:10.3390/s23041963 PMID:36850560

Boopathi, S. (2022). An investigation on gas emission concentration and relative emission rate of the near-dry wire-cut electrical discharge machining process. *Environmental Science and Pollution Research International*, *29*(57), 86237–86246. doi:10.1007/s11356-021-17658-1 PMID:34837614

Boopathi, S. (2024a). Advancements in Machine Learning and AI for Intelligent Systems in Drone Applications for Smart City Developments. In *Futuristic e-Governance Security With Deep Learning Applications* (pp. 15–45). IGI Global. doi:10.4018/978-1-6684-9596-4.ch002

Boopathi, S. (2024b). Sustainable Development Using IoT and AI Techniques for Water Utilization in Agriculture. In Sustainable Development in AI, Blockchain, and E-Governance Applications (pp. 204–228). IGI Global. doi:10.4018/979-8-3693-1722-8.ch012

Boopathi, S., Alqahtani, A. S., Mubarakali, A., & Panchatcharam, P. (2023). Sustainable developments in near-dry electrical discharge machining process using sunflower oil-mist dielectric fluid. *Environmental Science and Pollution Research International*, •••, 1–20. doi:10.1007/s11356-023-27494-0 PMID:37199846

Chen, X., Cao, W., Zhang, Q., Hu, S., & Zhang, J. (2020). Artificial intelligence-aided model predictive control for a grid-tied wind-hydrogen-fuel cell system. *IEEE Access : Practical Innovations, Open Solutions*, 8, 92418–92430. doi:10.1109/ACCESS.2020.2994577

Chou, C.-J., Jiang, S.-B., Yeh, T.-L., Tsai, L.-D., Kang, K.-Y., & Liu, C.-J. (2020). A portable direct methanol fuel cell power station for long-term internet of things applications. *Energies*, *13*(14), 3547. doi:10.3390/en13143547

Dhanalakshmi, M., Tamilarasi, K., Saravanan, S., Sujatha, G., Boopathi, S., & Associates. (2024a). Fog Computing-Based Framework and Solutions for Intelligent Systems: Enabling Autonomy in Vehicles. In Computational Intelligence for Green Cloud Computing and Digital Waste Management (pp. 330–356). IGI Global.

Dhanalakshmi, M., Tamilarasi, K., Saravanan, S., Sujatha, G., Boopathi, S., & Associates. (2024b). Fog Computing-Based Framework and Solutions for Intelligent Systems: Enabling Autonomy in Vehicles. In Computational Intelligence for Green Cloud Computing and Digital Waste Management (pp. 330–356). IGI Global.

Dhanya, D., Kumar, S. S., Thilagavathy, A., Prasad, D., & Boopathi, S. (2023). Data Analytics and Artificial Intelligence in the Circular Economy: Case Studies. In Intelligent Engineering Applications and Applied Sciences for Sustainability (pp. 40–58). IGI Global.

Dwivedi, K. A., Huang, S.-J., & Wang, C.-T. (2022). Integration of various technology-based approaches for enhancing the performance of microbial fuel cell technology: A review. *Chemosphere*, *287*, 132248. doi:10.1016/j.chemosphere.2021.132248 PMID:34543899

Exner, J.-P., Bauer, S., Novikova, K., Ludwig, J., & Werth, D. (2020). Connected E-Mobility, IoT and its Emerging Requirements for Planning and Infrastructures. *Shaping Urban Change–Livable City Regions for the 21st Century. Proceedings of Real Corp 2020, 25th International Conference on Urban Development, Regional Planning and Information Society*, 175–181.

Feng, Z., Huang, J., Jin, S., Wang, G., & Chen, Y. (2022). Artificial intelligence-based multi-objective optimisation for proton exchange membrane fuel cell: A literature review. *Journal of Power Sources*, *520*, 230808. doi:10.1016/j.jpowsour.2021.230808

Hema, N., Krishnamoorthy, N., Chavan, S. M., Kumar, N., Sabarimuthu, M., & Boopathi, S. (2023). A Study on an Internet of Things (IoT)-Enabled Smart Solar Grid System. In *Handbook of Research on Deep Learning Techniques for Cloud-Based Industrial IoT* (pp. 290–308). IGI Global. doi:10.4018/978-1-6684-8098-4.ch017

Hussain, Z., Babe, M., Saravanan, S., Srimathy, G., Roopa, H., & Boopathi, S. (2023). Optimizing Biomass-to-Biofuel Conversion: IoT and AI Integration for Enhanced Efficiency and Sustainability. In N. Cobîrzan, R. Muntean, & R.-A. Felseghi (Eds.), Advances in Finance, Accounting, and Economics (pp. 191–214). IGI Global. doi:10.4018/978-1-6684-8238-4.ch009

Ingle, R. B., Swathi, S., Mahendran, G., Senthil, T., Muralidharan, N., & Boopathi, S. (2023). Sustainability and Optimization of Green and Lean Manufacturing Processes Using Machine Learning Techniques. In *Circular Economy Implementation for Sustainability in the Built Environment* (pp. 261–285). IGI Global. doi:10.4018/978-1-6684-8238-4.ch012

Karthik, S., Hemalatha, R., Aruna, R., Deivakani, M., Reddy, R. V. K., & Boopathi, S. (2023). Study on Healthcare Security System-Integrated Internet of Things (IoT). In Perspectives and Considerations on the Evolution of Smart Systems (pp. 342–362). IGI Global.

Kavitha, C., Varalatchoumy, M., Mithuna, H., Bharathi, K., Geethalakshmi, N., & Boopathi, S. (2023). Energy Monitoring and Control in the Smart Grid: Integrated Intelligent IoT and ANFIS. In Applications of Synthetic Biology in Health, Energy, and Environment (pp. 290–316). IGI Global.

Kumar, M., Kumar, K., Sasikala, P., Sampath, B., Gopi, B., & Sundaram, S. (2023). Sustainable Green Energy Generation From Waste Water: IoT and ML Integration. In Sustainable Science and Intelligent Technologies for Societal Development (pp. 440–463). IGI Global.

Kumar, R., Lamba, K., & Raman, A. (2021). Role of zero emission vehicles in sustainable transformation of the Indian automobile industry. *Research in Transportation Economics*, *90*, 101064. doi:10.1016/j.retrec.2021.101064

Kumar, S., Rathore, R. S., Dohare, U., Kaiwartya, O., Lloret, J., Kumar, N., & ... (2023). BEET: Blockchain Enabled Energy Trading for E-Mobility Oriented Electric Vehicles. *IEEE Transactions on Mobile Computing*.

Li, J., & Yu, T. (2021). A novel data-driven controller for solid oxide fuel cell via deep reinforcement learning. *Journal of Cleaner Production*, *321*, 128929. doi:10.1016/j.jclepro.2021.128929

Maguluri, L. P., Ananth, J., Hariram, S., Geetha, C., Bhaskar, A., & Boopathi, S. (2023). Smart Vehicle-Emissions Monitoring System Using Internet of Things (IoT). In Handbook of Research on Safe Disposal Methods of Municipal Solid Wastes for a Sustainable Environment (pp. 191–211). IGI Global.

Malathi, J., Kusha, K., Isaac, S., Ramesh, A., Rajendiran, M., & Boopathi, S. (2024). IoT-Enabled Remote Patient Monitoring for Chronic Disease Management and Cost Savings: Transforming Healthcare. In Advances in Explainable AI Applications for Smart Cities (pp. 371–388). IGI Global.

Moniruzzaman, M., Yassine, A., & Hossain, M. S. (2023). Energizing Charging Services for Next-Generation Consumers E-Mobility With Reinforcement Learning and Blockchain. *IEEE Transactions on Consumer Electronics*.

Naveeenkumar, N., Rallapalli, S., Sasikala, K., Priya, P. V., Husain, J., & Boopathi, S. (2024). Enhancing Consumer Behavior and Experience Through AI-Driven Insights Optimization. In *AI Impacts in Digital Consumer Behavior* (pp. 1–35). IGI Global. doi:10.4018/979-8-3693-1918-5.ch001

Olivares-Rojas, J. C., Reyes-Archundia, E., Gutièrrez-Gnecchi, J. A., & Molina-Moreno, I. (2020). A survey on smart metering systems using blockchain for E-Mobility. *arXiv Preprint arXiv:2009.09075*.

Pachiappan, K., Anitha, K., Pitchai, R., Sangeetha, S., Satyanarayana, T., & Boopathi, S. (2024). Intelligent Machines, IoT, and AI in Revolutionizing Agriculture for Water Processing. In *Handbook of Research on AI and ML for Intelligent Machines and Systems* (pp. 374–399). IGI Global.

Paul, A., Thilagham, K., KG, J., Reddy, P. R., Sathyamurthy, R., & Boopathi, S. (2024). Multi-criteria Optimization on Friction Stir Welding of Aluminum Composite (AA5052-H32/B4C) using Titanium Nitride Coated Tool. Engineering Research Express.

Pourrahmani, H., Yavarinasab, A., Zahedi, R., Gharehghani, A., Mohammadi, M. H., Bastani, P., & Van herle, J. (2022). The applications of Internet of Things in the automotive industry: A review of the batteries, fuel cells, and engines. *Internet of Things : Engineering Cyber Physical Human Systems*, *19*, 100579. doi:10.1016/j.iot.2022.100579

Rahamathunnisa, U., Sudhakar, K., Padhi, S., Bhattacharya, S., Shashibhushan, G., & Boopathi, S. (2024). Sustainable Energy Generation From Waste Water: IoT Integrated Technologies. In Adoption and Use of Technology Tools and Services by Economically Disadvantaged Communities: Implications for Growth and Sustainability (pp. 225–256). IGI Global.

Ramudu, K., Mohan, V. M., Jyothirmai, D., Prasad, D., Agrawal, R., & Boopathi, S. (2023). Machine Learning and Artificial Intelligence in Disease Prediction: Applications, Challenges, Limitations, Case Studies, and Future Directions. In Contemporary Applications of Data Fusion for Advanced Healthcare Informatics (pp. 297–318). IGI Global.

Ravisankar, A., Sampath, B., & Asif, M. M. (2023). Economic Studies on Automobile Management: Working Capital and Investment Analysis. In Multidisciplinary Approaches to Organizational Governance During Health Crises (pp. 169–198). IGI Global.

Rewatkar, P., Nath, D., Kumar, P. S., Suss, M. E., & Goel, S. (2022). Internet of Things enabled environmental condition monitoring driven by laser ablated reduced graphene oxide based Al-air fuel cell. *Journal of Power Sources*, *521*, 230938. doi:10.1016/j.jpowsour.2021.230938

Saravanan, A., Venkatasubramanian, R., Khare, R., Surakasi, R., Boopathi, S., Ray, S., & Sudhakar, M. (2022). Policy trends of renewable energy and non. *Renewable Energy*.

Satav, S. D., Lamani, D., Harsha, K., Kumar, N., Manikandan, S., & Sampath, B. (2023). Energy and Battery Management in the Era of Cloud Computing: Sustainable Wireless Systems and Networks. In Sustainable Science and Intelligent Technologies for Societal Development (pp. 141–166). IGI Global.

Sathish, T., Sunagar, P., Singh, V., Boopathi, S., Al-Enizi, A. M., Pandit, B., Gupta, M., & Sehgal, S. S. (2023). Characteristics estimation of natural fibre reinforced plastic composites using deep multi-layer perceptron (MLP) technique. *Chemosphere*, *337*, 139346. doi:10.1016/j.chemosphere.2023.139346 PMID:37379988

Sethusubramanian, C., Vigneshpoopathy, M., Chamundeeswari, V., & Pradeep, J. (2021). Implementation of PI-controlled converter and monitoring of fuel cell on an IoT—Cloud platform. *Recent Trends in Renewable Energy Sources and Power Conversion: Select Proceedings of ICRES 2020*, 215–228.

Sharma, M., Sharma, M., Sharma, N., & Boopathi, S. (2024). Building Sustainable Smart Cities Through Cloud and Intelligent Parking System. In *Handbook of Research on AI and ML for Intelligent Machines and Systems* (pp. 195–222). IGI Global.

Subha, S., Inbamalar, T., Komala, C., Suresh, L. R., Boopathi, S., & Alaskar, K. (2023). A Remote Health Care Monitoring system using internet of medical things (IoMT). *IEEE Explore*, 1–6.

Sundaramoorthy, K., Singh, A., Sumathy, G., Maheshwari, A., Arunarani, A., & Boopathi, S. (2024). A Study on AI and Blockchain-Powered Smart Parking Models for Urban Mobility. In *Handbook of Research on AI and ML for Intelligent Machines and Systems* (pp. 223–250). IGI Global.

Syamala, M., Komala, C., Pramila, P., Dash, S., Meenakshi, S., & Boopathi, S. (2023). Machine Learning-Integrated IoT-Based Smart Home Energy Management System. In *Handbook of Research on Deep Learning Techniques for Cloud-Based Industrial IoT* (pp. 219–235). IGI Global. doi:10.4018/978-1-6684-8098-4.ch013

Tian, P., Liu, X., Luo, K., Li, H., & Wang, Y. (2021). Deep learning from three-dimensional multiphysics simulation in operational optimization and control of polymer electrolyte membrane fuel cell for maximum power. *Applied Energy*, 288, 116632. doi:10.1016/j.apenergy.2021.116632

Ugandar, R., Rahamathunnisa, U., Sajithra, S., Christiana, M. B. V., Palai, B. K., & Boopathi, S. (2023). Hospital Waste Management Using Internet of Things and Deep Learning: Enhanced Efficiency and Sustainability. In Applications of Synthetic Biology in Health, Energy, and Environment (pp. 317–343). IGI Global.

Vanitha, S., Radhika, K., & Boopathi, S. (2023). Artificial Intelligence Techniques in Water Purification and Utilization. In *Human Agro-Energy Optimization for Business and Industry* (pp. 202–218). IGI Global. doi:10.4018/978-1-6684-4118-3.ch010

Venkateswaran, N., Vidhya, K., Ayyannan, M., Chavan, S. M., Sekar, K., & Boopathi, S. (2023). A Study on Smart Energy Management Framework Using Cloud Computing. In 5G, Artificial Intelligence, and Next Generation Internet of Things: Digital Innovation for Green and Sustainable Economies (pp. 189–212). IGI Global. doi:10.4018/978-1-6684-8634-4.ch009

Vishnumurthy, K., & Girish, K. (2021). A comprehensive review of battery technology for E-mobility. *Journal of the Indian Chemical Society*, 98(10), 100173. doi:10.1016/j.jics.2021.100173

Wang, Y., Seo, B., Wang, B., Zamel, N., Jiao, K., & Adroher, X. C. (2020). Fundamentals, materials, and machine learning of polymer electrolyte membrane fuel cell technology. *Energy and AI*, 1, 100014. doi:10.1016/j.egyai.2020.100014

Zehir, C., & Zehir, M. (2022). Emerging blockchain solutions in the mobility ecosystem: Associated risks and areas for applications. *Bussecon Review of Social Sciences, 4*(2), 1–14.

Zekrifa, D. M. S., Kulkarni, M., Bhagyalakshmi, A., Devireddy, N., Gupta, S., & Boopathi, S. (2023). Integrating Machine Learning and AI for Improved Hydrological Modeling and Water Resource Management. In *Artificial Intelligence Applications in Water Treatment and Water Resource Management* (pp. 46–70). IGI Global. doi:10.4018/978-1-6684-6791-6.ch003

Chapter 17
AI–Enabled Data Processing for Real–World Applications of IoT:
A Review–Based Approach

Suresh Santhanagopalan
ⓘD https://orcid.org/0000-0002-9011-8031
St. Joseph's College (Autonomous), India

Murali Ramachandran
ⓘD https://orcid.org/0000-0002-9011-8031
St. Joseph's College (Autonomous), India

A. Pappu Rajan
ⓘD https://orcid.org/0000-0002-5110-9802
St. Joseph's College (Autonomous), India

ABSTRACT

This is a digitally inclined era. The government support across all the countries in the globe and its associated initiatives on this IoT are commendable. In this chapter, the authors studied the research papers related to big data, IoT, and AI. The research papers were fetched from the Scopus database using Boolean operators (AND, OR) with the keywords, "IoT", "Big Data", "H IoT", and "AI". The chapter is presented in two parts. The first part is about the synthesis of the major papers related to this study. The second part is about the leverage of AI in various sectors like healthcare, education, finance, smart cities, energy, telecommunication, and agriculture. After studying from the vast literature, it shows that that IoT, big data, and ML are indispensable in the years to come. In this chapter, the authors call for government, industries, and academicians to collaborate together for conferences, seminars, and joint projects to digitalize all the premises and bring a data driven decisions.

INTRODUCTION

The (IoT) stands as the most difficult platform poised to connect physical objects in the upcoming future. Numerous review studies have been undertaken to assess and consolidate the utilization of IoT across

DOI: 10.4018/979-8-3693-1487-6.ch017

diverse domains. However, there is a notable gap in research, as there has been a lack of comprehensive review studies exploring the application of IoT in the field of education. (Ahaidous et al., 2023) The retail sector leads the way in adopting IoT, anticipating a transformation in the customer shopping experience. Rooted in the service-dominant logic, it is suggested that engaging with IoT retail technology enhances the co-creation of value by customers. (Balaji & Roy, 2017). The circular economy stands to benefit from the integration of advancing digital technologies like big data, artificial intelligence (AI), blockchain, and the Internet of Things (IoT).The integration of digital technologies along with innovative business models is expected to offer solutions to various global challenges, including those associated with the transformation to a circular economy(Chauhan et al., 2022). In the dynamic era, organizations leverage advanced technologies like Artificial Intelligence (AI), Internet of Things (IoT), and Big Data to enhance customer loyalty. By synergistically integrating these technologies, businesses aim to elevate customer satisfaction, engagement, relationships, and overall experiences, fostering stronger customer allegiance and maintaining a competitor (Rane, 2023a). The integration of Artificial Intelligence (AI) with the Internet of Things (IoT) revolutionizes technology, imbuing machines with emotions and enabling remote operations, reflecting the ongoing evolution in our lives and surroundings (Sharma et al., 2021).

APPLICATIONS OF H-IOT

Healthcare Internet of Things (H-IoT) advancements offer opportunities for remote patient treatment and monitoring, emphasizing the critical need for securing personal health data during transmission.

Figure 1. Conceptual framework based on the scholarly articles synthesized

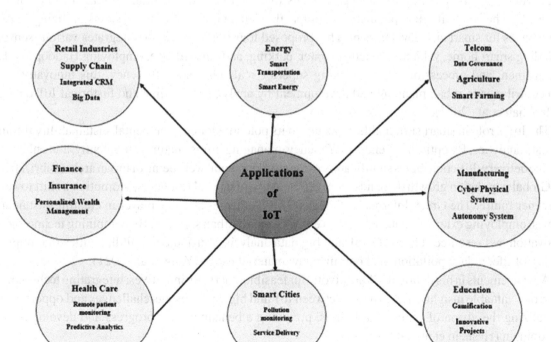

This tackles security challenges within H-IoT, probing into cryptographic solutions within big data, blockchain, machine learning, edge computing, and software-defined networks. It discusses current trends like remote patient monitoring, predictive analytics, and anticipates future prospects, while critically analysing limitations in H-IoT systems, providing valuable insights for future researchers aiming to enhance healthcare system efficiency and security (M. Kumar et al., 2023).

The use of H-IOT systems ensures that IoT and AI, among the fastest-growing technologies globally, converge in the concept of smart cities to revolutionize healthcare. Leveraging these technologies for remote healthcare monitoring in smart city frameworks enhances efficiency, reduces costs, and prioritizes improved patient care (Alshamrani, 2022).

Deploying a multi-agent approach enhanced by machine learning, H-IoT has improved the advanced persistent threat detection process. This includes predictive analytics for identifying security vulnerabilities, recognizing patterns, and predicting and identifying outliers, leading to more effective results (MacDermott et al., 2019).

(H-IoT), a vital component of healthcare automation, integrates machine learning (ML) algorithms for data processing and accurate predictions. ML applications in H-IoT span domains such as diagnosis, prognosis, assistive systems, monitoring, and logistics, showcasing practical usability with experimental evidence of accuracy. Ensuring high accuracy and robust security measures, these applications contribute to the growing healthcare technology (Bharadwaj et al., 2021).

ROLE OF IOT IN SMART CITIES

Smart cities encounter global challenges in implementation, yet untapped potential lies in the synergy of IoT and big data, opening promising horizons for development and future research (Talebkhah et al., 2021). The surge in urban population prompts the demand for IoT-based systems, utilizing sensors and devices for smart city development. This proposed four-tier architecture integrates various sensors, including smart home, vehicular, weather, water, parking, and surveillance, employing Hadoop for data management and processing. Demonstrating superior scalability and efficiency, this innovative system contributes to urban planning and development by analyzing real-time and historical IoT datasets (Talebkhah et al., 2021).

The IoT's role in smart sustainable cities lies in its potential for environmental sustainability through big data analytics. By optimizing energy efficiency, managing infrastructure intelligently, and enhancing service delivery, IoT contributes significantly to the environmental well-being of urban areas (Bibri, 2018).

Global population growth demands more efficient use of natural resources, prompting a shift towards a greener future. The Green Internet of Things (G-IoT) emerges as a key player in creating sustainable homes, employing extensive data analysis to enhance smart urban services. By combining technological innovation and resource sharing, G-IoT and big data analysis contribute to building cities that improve quality of life, reduce pollution, and optimize raw material usage (Yang et al., 2021).

Advancements in big data and IoT are pivotal for feasible smart city initiatives, integrating technologies to extract valuable insights. The synergy between IoT and big data presents challenges and opportunities in realizing the vision of future smart cities, providing a benchmark for progress and development in this domain (Hashem et al., 2016).

The integration of IoT and big data analytics offers a novel disaster-resilient smart city architecture, enhancing real-time and offline disaster management activities. Utilizing the Hadoop Ecosystem and

Table 1. Background of the study

Theme	Author	Key Findings
AI in Agriculture	(Talaviya et al., 2020)	Agriculture's economic significance has spurred a global shift towards automating farming to meet out the rising food demands. Traditional methods are insufficient, leading to the introduction of AI in agriculture, revolutionizing practices to address challenges like climate changes, population growth, employment, and food security.
Cloud Computing	(Rajagopal et al., 2020)	Addressing the challenge of network intrusion detection is a substantial concern for the researchers, industry personnel, and commercial sectors. The ongoing threat of cyber-attacks requires resilient approaches to tackle this persistent issue. Traditional machine learning algorithms prove ineffective in handling the vast network traffic.
IoT Technologies	(Swamy & Kota, 2020)	Integration of Sensor, Embedded, Computing, and Communication technologies to provide seamless services; Impact on society and industries; Addressing system-level design aspects for a potential IoT system.
IoT Security	(Wazid et al., 2019)	Challenges in IoT communication environment; Focus on malware attacks and their impact on data confidentiality, integrity, authenticity, and availability; Review of existing schemes for malware detection and prevention.
Agriculture 4.0	(Pathan et al., 2020)	Fourth agricultural revolution using digital technologies for smarter, more efficient, and environmentally responsible agriculture; Impact of technologies like Big Data, AI, robots, IoT, and virtual reality; Focus on precision agriculture and digitized equipment.
ML in Healthcare	(Javaid et al., 2022)	ML applications in healthcare for improved speed and accuracy; Use of healthcare data for optimal trial sample, data points collection, and epidemic detection; Impact on clinical decision support, illness detection, and personalized treatment approaches.
Text Mining in Finance	(Gupta et al., 2020)	Influence of text-mining technologies on financial sector looks commendable. The finance domain involves a large amount of data which requires a data driven decision making. The collaboration of text mining and data analytics shall bring a solution to the existing text mining challenges.
Smart Farming	(Aliyu & Liu, 2023)	Introduces a framework designed to enhance the security and privacy of smart farms by leveraging the decentralized nature of blockchain technology. The framework securely stores and manages data obtained from IoT devices within smart farms, guaranteeing the integrity and validity of the data.
Smart Farming Security	(Selvarajan et al., 2020)	Enhanced machine learning model for attack prediction and classification in supervisory control and data acquisition (SCADA) systems; Use of mean-shift clustering and genetically seeded flora optimization algorithm; Evaluation of performance metrics.
Industry 5.0 and Blockchain	(Verma et al., 2022)	Industry 5.0 marks a shift from intensive automation to customer driven focus, integrating hyper-cognitive systems, AI, and blockchain for secure transfer of data. The author outlined about the key drivers, potential applications, and proposes an architectural vision, guiding industry practitioners and researchers in BC (block chain) assisted solutions for diverse verticals.

Spark, the environment efficiently processes data for activities like fire detection, pollution monitoring, and emergency departure, showcasing superior performance in processing time and throughput. Identified challenges in the system further highlight the potential for advancing disaster resilience in smart cities (Shah et al., 2019).

Smart Cities, driven by the infusion of Big Data and IoT, aim to create a futuristic urban environment prioritizing citizen well-being, ensuring rights, and adopting sustainable industry and urban planning. Despite implementation challenges, a surge in global efforts and funded research projects emphasizes the integration of Smart City features, leveraging the power of Big Data and IoT to enhance services and elevate the quality of life for citizens worldwide (Sánchez-Corcuera et al., 2019).

Future smart cities, driven by advanced information and communication technologies, address citizens' growing needs through sustainable urban planning, industry engagement, and well-being assurance. Governments globally tackle challenges posed by rapid urbanization to create environmentally sustainable urban spaces. These emerging technologies emphasizes cybersecurity integration for robust smart city development, encompassing existing frameworks, technological challenges, and future dimensions, prioritizing smart living (Javed et al., 2022).

EDUCATION

AI catalyzes education's evolution from Education 4.0 to 5.0, integrating personalized and adaptive learning with the aid of Big Data and IoT. Education 4.0 employs AI for tailored learning, and Education 5.0 dynamically adjusts based on real-time data, enhancing outcomes (Rane et al., 2023).

The synergy of (IoT), cloud, and fog computing is shaping a smart world, influencing the evolution of traditional educational institutions. This study proposes a smart institution framework comprising five elements, endorsing the integration of cloud computing, fog and IoT to tackle issues of the learners in learning and administration. Advancements in student attendance, academic progress shows the transformative impact of smart technologies on educational outcomes and institutional efficiency (Badshah et al., 2023).

Education 4.0, aligned with the fourth industrial revolution, emphasizes experiential learning through innovative projects in Portuguese higher education. Adoption of serious games, with less than 20% of projects incorporating gamification approaches (Almeida & Simoes, 2019). A transformative strategy is required for higher education leverages IoT, Big Data & Cloud Computing, and Learning Analytics to create personalized curricula solutions (Moreira et al., 2017).

MANUFACTURING SECTOR

The digitization of the physical world through IoT has led to continuous global connectivity. The Industrial Internet of Things (IIoT), part of the fourth revolution, prioritizes interconnectivity, automation, autonomy, real-time data, and leverages big data in the manufacturing sector. Connecting over 30 billion devices, IoT presents growth opportunities but faces primary challenges in security and privacy (Munirathinam, 2020).

The IoT evolution has paved the way for Industrial IoT (IIoT), especially significant in manufacturing, where it automates real-time sensing, capturing, communication, and processing. This article explores 5G-enabled IIoT emergence, research trends, security measures, and the revolutionary framework meeting IIoT application demands, incorporating IoT and big data for comprehensive insights (Atharvan et al., 2022).

A methodology for crafting a smart Production Planning and Control (PPC) system, leveraging IoT, big-data analytics, and machine learning is presented to enhance operational efficiency. Highlighting dynamic, real-time decision-making, it addresses scalability and flexibility through a service-oriented architecture (Oluyisola et al., 2022).

In response to the transition from mass production to customization, this proposal introduces a model for a Smart Cyber-Physical Manufacturing System .Aligned with Fourth industrial era (i.e AI evolution) principles, the Smart-CPMS exhibits features stimulated by biology, featuring self-organization and adaptability. Each resource on the shop floor operates as an autonomous cyber-physical system, utilizing cognitive agent technology and IoT infrastructure to dynamically respond to evolving manufacturing requirements without external intervention (Tran et al., 2019).

In the era of rapid industrialization, embodied by Germany's Industry 4.0 and India's Made-in-India 2025 initiatives, the transformative potential is hitched through the integration of emerging technologies like cyber-physical systems, IoT, and cloud computing in manufacturing. Yet, the realization of Industry 4.0's full potential faces challenges due to the scarcity of robust tools, particularly in the domain of formal methods and systems, delaying the comprehensive utilization of IoT and big data (Tran et al., 2019).

In the fourth industrial revolution, predictive maintenance is crucial for sustainable manufacturing, utilizing digital methods to minimize downtime, extend machine life, and enhance production quality (Achouch et al., 2022).

RETAIL INDUSTRIES

The synergy between Internet of Things (IoT) and big data is reshaping global manufacturing supply chains, emphasizing optimized operational coordination and leveraging smart connected product data for informed decision-making. The integration addresses governance challenges and aims to drive advancements in data-driven supply chain management while providing insights for regulatory frameworks in IoT and big data industries (He et al., 2020).

Exploring big data analytics' impact on retail supply chains, TODIM is employed to select optimal practices among nine alternatives. The study highlights a common challenge for retail firms, navigating the trade-off between customer loyalty and cost in implementing big data practices. It outlines the need for emerging retail companies to assess and adopt effective big data strategies based on key supply chain performance measures (He et al., 2020).

In the dynamic business environment, organizations leverage AI, IoT, and Big Data to boost customer loyalty. Emphasizing real-time data gathering through IoT, customization of offerings using AI, and the secure integration of Blockchain with IoT, this highlights the collaborative use of these technologies for enhanced customer satisfaction and lasting relationships (Rane, 2023b).

In the retail sector, big data tools and applications find relevance through connected devices, sensors, and mobile apps. Examining their impact, four key themes emerge: availability, assortment, pricing, and layout planning. Insights from historical sales data, loyalty schemes, and external factors like competitor prices and weather conditions inform operational planning, but challenges such as skill shortages and IT integration issues are the few complexities in fully leveraging big data (Aktas & Meng, 2017).

Integrating CRM and IoT, big data has a big role in transforming customer experiences and service personalization., illustrated by dynamic approaches like push notifications on smartphones, intensifying businesses' targeted outreach efforts(Anshari et al., 2019).

The retail sector is undergoing an intense transformation with the pervasive use of mobile apps. Retailers are now poised to actively shape the entire consumer decision making process which leads to customer driven shopping experience.(Faulds et al., 2018).Retail managers adopting a comprehensive strategy approach categorized at market, firm, store, and customer levels (V. Kumar et al., 2017).

The substantial impact of relationship commitment on AI-enabled customer experiences is featured by emphasizing the mediating roles played by trust and perceived sacrifice (Reinartz et al., 2019).

FINANCE

Financial technology (fintech) has significantly transformed the global financial industry by incorporating big data, cloud computing, IoT, artificial intelligence, and block chain. The focus is on how big data plays a crucial role in shaping new business models and improving financial transactions, creating benefits that extend beyond socioeconomic and geographic boundaries in the financial sector (Awotunde et al., 2021).

Cutting-edge digital technologies such as Big Data, Machine Learning, Artificial Intelligence (AI), and blockchain are having a positive impact on the financial sector. The findings highlight real-world applications in areas such as Know Your Customer (KYC), Personalized Wealth Management, Asset Management, Portfolio Risk Assessment, and Usage-based Insurance leveraging IoT data (Soldatos & Kyriazis, 2022).

The dynamic banking sector involves addressing challenges in managing vast data, real-time fraud monitoring and bringing imnovations in payment processes. Leveraging the Internet of Things (IoT), an architecture is explored to efficiently handle massive datasets from diverse devices, meeting the industry's evolving demands (Boumlik & Bahaj, 2018).

Industry 4.0 adoption in Indian BFSI, emphasizing Cyber Security and the study reflecting medium to low maturity, provide insights into the application of IoT and big data in the BFSI sector, contributing to understanding their usage in Industry 4.0 (Boumlik & Bahaj, 2018).

The global insurance sector is in a transformative erae, utilizing advanced data-processing tools like ML with real-time data from mobile devices, IoT, and wearables. Empowered by cloud computing and 5G networks, these technologies are reshaping insurance mechanics. Traditionally risk-averse, insurance enterprises are now adapting to digitization, unlocking new opportunities and addressing challenges posed by these advancements (King et al., 2021).

In the era of big data, the banking sector utilizes advanced Data Mining techniques for strategic management and enhanced customer satisfaction. This review addresses the research gap by providing an updated overview of DM implementations in banking, highlighting trends, technological aids, and key obstacles. It serves as a comprehensive reference for future developments in both DM and the banking sector (King et al., 2021).

The banking industry, amid daily changes, faces substantial challenges in managing vast data and real-time fraud monitoring from diverse devices. Innovations in payment processes aim to bolster security and digital skills. Recognizing customer behaviors' significance, the Internet of Things (IoT) emerges as a potential solution for efficient data collection and sharing. However, conventional database systems struggle with real-time processing, prompting exploration of alternative architectures to handle massive datasets in IoT-enabled banking (King et al., 2021).

Blockchain and big data are transformative technologies expected to revolutionize business operations. Their integration offers ideal solutions for addressing challenges in big data management and analytics. Blockchain provides a secure consensus method, creating an audit trail that verifies transaction correctness and integrity, ensuring adherence to agreements. As an added layer for big data analytics, Blockchain enhances security within network architecture. This authors explored the synergy between Blockchain and big data, emphasizing their role in securing banking operations (Muheidat et al., 2022).

AI IN ENERGY SECTOR

Harmonizing artificial intelligence, big data, IoT, and blockchain is essential for comprehensive smart energy management. AI models, fueled by big data, predict and optimize energy use, while IoT platforms connect devices for improved data access. This seamless integration is pivotal for advancing the energy sector toward a lower-carbon system (Li et al., 2023).

Integration of IoT in the energy sector, particularly in smart grids, enhances energy efficiency and facilitates the adoption of renewable sources. IoT applications covers technologies like cloud computing and data analysis platforms (Li et al., 2023).

Machine learning algorithms identify appliances, and in practical scenarios, the demand-response program substantially reduces power costs based on time-of-use considerations (Dhaou, 2023). Strategies into smart home management, smart cities, smart grids, smart environmental systems, and smart transportation systems will address the challenges and identifying open research directions to enhance energy consumption efficiency and improve life in metropolitan areas (Dhaou, 2023).

AI IN AGRICULTURE

Examining the role of Internet of Things (IoT) in agriculture, this design addresses challenges related to storing and analysing diverse sensor data. Utilizing cloud computing, the proposed architecture ensures efficient data handling without specifying particular technologies (Wang et al., 2014).

Leveraging big data technology, an Agricultural Internet of Things system is established for precise data acquisition through sensor, image, and meteorological modules. Achieving less than 1% prediction error, the model provides effective guidance for enhancing agricultural product quality and yield (Wang et al., 2014).

Utilizing soil moisture sensors, the system allows automatic or manual control of watering through a smartphone application, enhancing agricultural productivity and reducing costs. The results demonstrate effective soil moisture maintenance for vegetable growth in Thailand (Wang et al., 2014).

The ongoing transition to agriculture-specific solutions highlights the need for a practical engineering approach and a holistic systems-thinking perspective to ensure effective problem- solving in this domain (Wang et al., 2014).

Smart Farming, powered by IoT, Cloud Computing, and Big Data, revolutionizes the food supply chain. Big Data drives predictive insights, reshapes business models, and alters power dynamics among stakeholders. The future hinges on a choice between closed, proprietary systems or open, collaborative approaches, emphasizing the need for research on governance and effective data-sharing business models (Wolfert et al., 2017).

IoT is reshaping agriculture through automated land management, minimizing human intervention (Wolfert et al., 2017).

Big data analytics in agriculture provides valuable insights for well-informed weather decisions, enhanced yield productivity, and reduced costs in harvesting and pesticide use. The examination identifies diverse sources of big data in precision agriculture, discusses ICT components, and addresses associated challenges, emphasizing potential applications in weather forecasting through a programming model and distributed algorithm (Wolfert et al., 2017).

AI IN TELECOM

Amid increased data traffic driven by shifts in customer behaviour, especially due to Covid-19, telecommunications operators have a golden chance to generate new revenues using Big Data Analytics (BDA) solutions. Challenges in selecting technical solutions and governance methodologies during BDA project initiation are prominent. This exploration focuses on key aspects of BDA telecommunications projects such as governance, architecture, data governance, and project teams, providing insights and use cases to streamline implementation and guide telecommunications operators towards revenue creation and cost optimization (Wolfert et al., 2017).

5G's rapid growth revolutionizes industries with its high-speed connectivity and low latency, especially benefiting the Internet of Things (IoT) market. The integration of technologies like data mining and AI in 5G enhances efficiency and real-time analytics, signifying a substantial leap in technological advancement for automated device management (Aggarwal et al., 2021).

The growth of low-cost, internet-connected sensors in smart cities is shaping data-driven decisions in various industries (Mukherjee et al., 2022). Big data improves human and organizational capacity for effective smart city governance (Sarker et al., 2020).

The overlooked role of IoT in e-government is significant, as it offers political, strategic, tactical, and operational benefits (Brous & Janssen, 2015). Presenting a citizen-centred big data analysis framework for smart city governance intelligence, the three-layered structure outlines a practical path for implementing citizen-focused data in governance decision-making, considering urban governance issues and data-analysis algorithms (Ju et al., 2018).

As advancements in Artificial Intelligence (AI) and the Internet of Things (IoT) reshape industries, the pursuit for a greener future. The fusion of Green IoT (G-IoT) and big data analysis becomes instrumental in creating sustainable cities, contributing to smarter, safer urban environments with improved quality of life and resource efficiency (Maksimovic, 2017).

CONCLUSION

From the articles reviewed in this chapter, one can understand the importance of integration between IoT, AI, and big data in enhancing the customization and personalization of business systems. Data-driven decision-making in all sectors, including retail, pharma, health care, and FMCG, leads to efficiency in their business operations. The retail sector is at the forefront and setting a new frontier in adopting the IoT, enhancing a seamless shopping experience for the customer through the integration of technology. Category management is one important area in retail management that enhances customer experience in the retail sector, which aligns with the results given by the authors (Rajan & Suresh, 2016). Industry-wise utilization and integration of technologies were discussed, which shows that smart manufacturing, finance, and agri-transformation have happened in recent years. Because of this technology, predictive maintenance, data-driven decision-making, and customization were possible. The IoT-based smart cities provide a planned urban ecosystem with sustainable operations like energy savings, traffic control, and better urban planning. Sustainable urbanization looks possible and gives new confidence to developing countries. Especially energy management and optimization of low-carbon systems show smart energy management systems. Most importantly, IoT-based agriculture has been developed a lot in India; however, in the developing economy, it is still in the development stage. (Narwane et al., 2022). The IoT usage in the agri-supply chain could forecast food needs and reduce food waste. (Luthra et al., 2018). The central government of India has already taken measures to boost big data in agriculture, higher education, and governance, which is a good move. However, the leverage of big data and IoT by the state governments of India is still in the emerging stage. The study shows that food security and climate change are the major issues that will be tackled using AI in agriculture. Also, machine learning applications in healthcare and personalised treatment Efficient business operations, sustainable cities, zero-error inventories, and data-driven decisions are made easier using big data and IoT models. Data-driven decision-making is imperative for retail, pharma, healthcare, and FMCG as lots of data are involved, and the leverage of these techniques would bring operational efficiency to the nature of the business. However, emerging economies like India are still in the developing stage, and state governments should implement the IoT and big data approaches to create a sustainable and inclusive environment, making this technology possible for retailers, farmers, and business owners at all levels. The central government shall initiate an urgent call for the state IT ministries to enhance corporate governance and sustainability operations using AI, IoT, and big data through conferences, seminars, and paper presentations. The government agencies, like ICSSR, shall call for proposals and projects to merge the educational and corporate sectors into this segment. The FDI support and the potential of IIM's, NIT's, Central and State universities, and affiliated institutions shall ease the education and practise of this IoT. The management institutes shall provide mandatory courses on this technical subject, which gives budding managers a technical touch on this concept. It is in the hands of academicians, practitioners, and the government to implement it very quickly and provide a sustainable and inclusive future in India. The integration of blockchain, IoT, and big data provides a positive shift across all industries, which provides a sustainable way in terms of a secure, optimized, and efficient way of performing business.

REFERENCES

Achouch, M., Dimitrova, M., Ziane, K., Sattarpanah Karganroudi, S., Dhouib, R., Ibrahim, H., & Adda, M. (2022). On Predictive Maintenance in Industry 4.0: Overview, Models, and Challenges. *Applied Sciences (Basel, Switzerland)*, *12*(16), 8081. doi:10.3390/app12168081

Aggarwal, P. K., Jain, P., Mehta, J., Garg, R., Makar, K., & Chaudhary, P. (2021). Machine Learning, Data Mining, and Big Data Analytics for 5G-Enabled IoT. In Blockchain for 5G-Enabled IoT (pp. 351–375). Springer International Publishing. doi:10.1007/978-3-030-67490-8_14

Ahaidous, K., Tabaa, M., & Hachimi, H. (2023). Towards IoT-Big Data architecture for future education. *Procedia Computer Science*, *220*, 348–355. doi:10.1016/j.procs.2023.03.045

Aktas, E., & Meng, Y. (2017). An Exploration of Big Data Practices in Retail Sector. *Logistics*, *1*(2), 12. doi:10.3390/logistics1020012

Aliyu, A. A., & Liu, J. (2023). Blockchain-Based Smart Farm Security Framework for the Internet of Things. *Sensors (Basel)*, *23*(18), 7992. doi:10.3390/s23187992 PMID:37766046

Almeida, F., & Simoes, J. (2019). The Role of Serious Games, Gamification and Industry 4.0 Tools in the Education 4.0 Paradigm. *Contemporary Educational Technology*, *10*(2), 120–136. doi:10.30935/cet.554469

Alshamrani, M. (2022). IoT and artificial intelligence implementations for remote healthcare monitoring systems: A survey. *Journal of King Saud University. Computer and Information Sciences*, *34*(8), 4687–4701. doi:10.1016/j.jksuci.2021.06.005

Anshari, M., Almunawar, M. N., Lim, S. A., & Al-Mudimigh, A. (2019). Customer relationship management and big data enabled: Personalization & customization of services. *Applied Computing and Informatics*, *15*(2), 94–101. doi:10.1016/j.aci.2018.05.004

Atharvan, G., Koolikkara Madom Krishnamoorthy, S., Dua, A., & Gupta, S. (2022). A way forward towards a technology-driven development of industry 4.0 using big data analytics in 5G-enabled IIoT. *International Journal of Communication Systems*, *35*(1), e5014. Advance online publication. doi:10.1002/dac.5014

Awotunde, J. B., Adeniyi, E. A., Ogundokun, R. O., & Ayo, F. E. (2021). *Application of Big Data with Fintech in Financial Services*. doi:10.1007/978-981-33-6137-9_3

Badshah, A., Rehman, G. U., Farman, H., Ghani, A., Sultan, S., Zubair, M., & Nasralla, M. M. (2023). Transforming Educational Institutions: Harnessing the Power of Internet of Things, Cloud, and Fog Computing. *Future Internet*, *15*(11), 367. doi:10.3390/fi15110367

Balaji, M. S., & Roy, S. K. (2017). Value co-creation with Internet of things technology in the retail industry. *Journal of Marketing Management*, *33*(1–2), 7–31. doi:10.1080/0267257X.2016.1217914

Ben Dhaou, I. (2023). Design and Implementation of an Internet-of-Things-Enabled Smart Meter and Smart Plug for Home-Energy-Management System. *Electronics (Basel)*, *12*(19), 4041. doi:10.3390/electronics12194041

Bharadwaj, H. K., Agarwal, A., Chamola, V., Lakkaniga, N. R., Hassija, V., Guizani, M., & Sikdar, B. (2021). A Review on the Role of Machine Learning in Enabling IoT Based Healthcare Applications. *IEEE Access : Practical Innovations, Open Solutions*, *9*, 38859–38890. doi:10.1109/ACCESS.2021.3059858

Bibri, S. E. (2018). The IoT for smart sustainable cities of the future: An analytical framework for sensor-based big data applications for environmental sustainability. *Sustainable Cities and Society*, *38*, 230–253. doi:10.1016/j.scs.2017.12.034

Boumlik, A., & Bahaj, M. (2018). *Big Data and IoT: A Prime Opportunity for Banking Industry*. doi:10.1007/978-3-319-69137-4_35

Brous, P., & Janssen, M. (2015). *Advancing e-Government Using the Internet of Things: A Systematic Review of Benefits*. doi:10.1007/978-3-319-22479-4_12

Chauhan, C., Parida, V., & Dhir, A. (2022). Linking circular economy and digitalisation technologies: A systematic literature review of past achievements and future promises. *Technological Forecasting and Social Change*, *177*, 121508. doi:10.1016/j.techfore.2022.121508

Faulds, D. J., Mangold, W. G., Raju, P. S., & Valsalan, S. (2018). The mobile shopping revolution: Redefining the consumer decision process. *Business Horizons*, *61*(2), 323–338. doi:10.1016/j.bushor.2017.11.012

Gupta, A., Dengre, V., Kheruwala, H. A., & Shah, M. (2020). Comprehensive review of text-mining applications in finance. *Financial Innovation*, *6*(1), 39. Advance online publication. doi:10.1186/s40854-020-00205-1

Hashem, I. A. T., Chang, V., Anuar, N. B., Adewole, K., Yaqoob, I., Gani, A., Ahmed, E., & Chiroma, H. (2016). The role of big data in smart city. *International Journal of Information Management*, *36*(5), 748–758. doi:10.1016/j.ijinfomgt.2016.05.002

He, L., Xue, M., & Gu, B. (2020). Internet-of-things enabled supply chain planning and coordination with big data services: Certain theoretic implications. *Journal of Management Science and Engineering*, *5*(1), 1–22. doi:10.1016/j.jmse.2020.03.002

Javaid, M., Haleem, A., Pratap Singh, R., Suman, R., & Rab, S. (2022). Significance of machine learning in healthcare: Features, pillars and applications. *International Journal of Intelligent Networks*, *3*, 58–73. doi:10.1016/j.ijin.2022.05.002

Javed, A. R., Shahzad, F., Rehman, S., Zikria, Y. B., Razzak, I., Jalil, Z., & Xu, G. (2022). Future smart cities: Requirements, emerging technologies, applications, challenges, and future aspects. *Cities (London, England)*, *129*, 103794. doi:10.1016/j.cities.2022.103794

Ju, J., Liu, L., & Feng, Y. (2018). Citizen-centered big data analysis-driven governance intelligence framework for smart cities. *Telecommunications Policy*, *42*(10), 881–896. doi:10.1016/j.telpol.2018.01.003

King, M. R. N., Timms, P. D., & Rubin, T. H. (2021). Use of Big Data in Insurance. In *The Palgrave Handbook of Technological Finance* (pp. 669–700). Springer International Publishing. doi:10.1007/978-3-030-65117-6_24

Kumar, M., Kumar, A., Verma, S., Bhattacharya, P., Ghimire, D., Kim, S., & Hosen, A. S. M. S. (2023). Healthcare Internet of Things (H-IoT): Current Trends, Future Prospects, Applications, Challenges, and Security Issues. *Electronics (Basel)*, *12*(9), 2050. doi:10.3390/electronics12092050

Kumar, V., Anand, A., & Song, H. (2017). Future of Retailer Profitability: An Organizing Framework. *Journal of Retailing*, *93*(1), 96–119. doi:10.1016/j.jretai.2016.11.003

Li, J., Herdem, M. S., Nathwani, J., & Wen, J. Z. (2023). Methods and applications for Artificial Intelligence, Big Data, Internet of Things, and Blockchain in smart energy management. *Energy and AI*, *11*, 100208. doi:10.1016/j.egyai.2022.100208

Luthra, S., Mangla, S. K., Garg, D., & Kumar, A. (2018). *Internet of Things (IoT) in Agriculture Supply Chain Management: A Developing Country Perspective.* doi:10.1007/978-3-319-75013-2_16

MacDermott, A., Kendrick, P., Idowu, I., Ashall, M., & Shi, Q. (2019). Securing Things in the Healthcare Internet of Things. *2019 Global IoT Summit (GIoTS)*, 1–6. doi:10.1109/GIOTS.2019.8766383

Maksimovic, M. (2017). The Role of Green Internet of Things (G-IoT) and Big Data in Making Cities Smarter, Safer and More Sustainable. *International Journal of Computing and Digital Systemss*, *6*(4), 175–184. doi:10.12785/IJCDS/060403

Moreira, F., Ferreira, M. J., & Cardoso, A. (2017). *Higher Education Disruption Through IoT and Big Data: A Conceptual Approach*. doi:10.1007/978-3-319-58509-3_31

Muheidat, F., Patel, D., Tammisetty, S., Tawalbeh, L. A., & Tawalbeh, M. (2022). Emerging Concepts Using Blockchain and Big Data. *Procedia Computer Science*, *198*, 15–22. doi:10.1016/j.procs.2021.12.206

Mukherjee, S., Gupta, S., Rawlley, O., & Jain, S. (2022). Leveraging big data analytics in 5G-enabled IoT and industrial IoT for the development of sustainable smart cities. *Transactions on Emerging Telecommunications Technologies*, *33*(12), e4618. Advance online publication. doi:10.1002/ett.4618

Munirathinam, S. (2020). *Industry 4.0: Industrial Internet of Things*. IIOT. doi:10.1016/bs.adcom.2019.10.010

Narwane, V. S., Gunasekaran, A., & Gardas, B. B. (2022). Unlocking adoption challenges of IoT in Indian Agricultural and Food Supply Chain. *Smart Agricultural Technology*, *2*, 100035. doi:10.1016/j.atech.2022.100035

Oluyisola, O. E., Bhalla, S., Sgarbossa, F., & Strandhagen, J. O. (2022). Designing and developing smart production planning and control systems in the industry 4.0 era: A methodology and case study. *Journal of Intelligent Manufacturing*, *33*(1), 311–332. doi:10.1007/s10845-021-01808-w

Pathan, M., Patel, N., Yagnik, H., & Shah, M. (2020). Artificial cognition for applications in smart agriculture: A comprehensive review. *Artificial Intelligence in Agriculture*, *4*, 81–95. doi:10.1016/j.aiia.2020.06.001

Rajagopal, S., Kundapur, P. P., & Hareesha, K. S. (2020). A Stacking Ensemble for Network Intrusion Detection Using Heterogeneous Datasets. *Security and Communication Networks*, *2020*, 1–9. Advance online publication. doi:10.1155/2020/4586875

Rajan.Suresh, A. P. (2016). Application of Retail Analytics Using Association Rule Mining In Data Mining Techniques With Respect To Retail Supermarket. *Archers & Elevators Publishing House*, *01*(1), 1–23.

Rane, N. (2023a). Enhancing Customer Loyalty through Artificial Intelligence (AI), Internet of Things (IoT), and Big Data Technologies: Improving Customer Satisfaction, Engagement, Relationship, and Experience. SSRN *Electronic Journal*. doi:10.2139/ssrn.4616051

Rane, N. (2023b). Enhancing Customer Loyalty through Artificial Intelligence (AI), Internet of Things (IoT), and Big Data Technologies: Improving Customer Satisfaction, Engagement, Relationship, and Experience. SSRN *Electronic Journal*. doi:10.2139/ssrn.4616051

Rane, N., Choudhary, S., & Rane, J. (2023). Education 4.0 and 5.0: Integrating Artificial Intelligence (AI) for Personalized and Adaptive Learning. SSRN *Electronic Journal*. doi:10.2139/ssrn.4638365

Reinartz, W., Wiegand, N., & Imschloss, M. (2019). The impact of digital transformation on the retailing value chain. *International Journal of Research in Marketing*, *36*(3), 350–366. doi:10.1016/j.ijresmar.2018.12.002

Sánchez-Corcuera, R., Nuñez-Marcos, A., Sesma-Solance, J., Bilbao-Jayo, A., Mulero, R., Zulaika, U., Azkune, G., & Almeida, A. (2019). Smart cities survey: Technologies, application domains and challenges for the cities of the future. *International Journal of Distributed Sensor Networks*, *15*(6). doi:10.1177/1550147719853984

Sarker, M. N. I., Khatun, M. N., Alam, G. M., & Islam, M. S. (2020). Big Data Driven Smart City: Way to Smart City Governance. *2020 International Conference on Computing and Information Technology (ICCIT-1441)*, 1–8. 10.1109/ICCIT-144147971.2020.9213795

Selvarajan, S., Shaik, M., Ameerjohn, S., & Kannan, S. (2020). Mining of intrusion attack in SCADA network using clustering and genetically seeded flora-based optimal classification algorithm. *IET Information Security*, *14*(1), 1–11. doi:10.1049/iet-ifs.2019.0011

Shah, S. A., Seker, D. Z., Rathore, M. M., Hameed, S., Ben Yahia, S., & Draheim, D. (2019). Towards Disaster Resilient Smart Cities: Can Internet of Things and Big Data Analytics Be the Game Changers? *IEEE Access : Practical Innovations, Open Solutions*, *7*, 91885–91903. doi:10.1109/ACCESS.2019.2928233

Sharma, D., Singh, A., & Singhal, S. (2021). The Technological Shift: AI in Big Data and IoT. In The Smart Cyber Ecosystem for Sustainable Development (pp. 69–90). Wiley. doi:10.1002/9781119761655.ch4

Soldatos, J., & Kyriazis, D. (Eds.). (2022). *Big Data and Artificial Intelligence in Digital Finance*. Springer International Publishing. doi:10.1007/978-3-030-94590-9

Swamy, S. N., & Kota, S. R. (2020). An Empirical Study on System Level Aspects of Internet of Things (IoT). *IEEE Access : Practical Innovations, Open Solutions*, *8*, 188082–188134. doi:10.1109/ACCESS.2020.3029847

Talaviya, T., Shah, D., Patel, N., Yagnik, H., & Shah, M. (2020). Implementation of artificial intelligence in agriculture for optimisation of irrigation and application of pesticides and herbicides. *Artificial Intelligence in Agriculture*, *4*, 58–73. doi:10.1016/j.aiia.2020.04.002

Talebkhah, M., Sali, A., Marjani, M., Gordan, M., Hashim, S. J., & Rokhani, F. Z. (2021). IoT and Big Data Applications in Smart Cities: Recent Advances, Challenges, and Critical Issues. *IEEE Access : Practical Innovations, Open Solutions*, *9*, 55465–55484. doi:10.1109/ACCESS.2021.3070905

Tran, P., Park, Nguyen, & Hoang. (2019). Development of a Smart Cyber-Physical Manufacturing System in the Industry 4.0 Context. *Applied Sciences (Basel, Switzerland)*, *9*(16), 3325. doi:10.3390/app9163325

Verma, A., Bhattacharya, P., Madhani, N., Trivedi, C., Bhushan, B., Tanwar, S., Sharma, G., Bokoro, P. N., & Sharma, R. (2022). Blockchain for Industry 5.0: Vision, Opportunities, Key Enablers, and Future Directions. *IEEE Access : Practical Innovations, Open Solutions*, *10*, 69160–69199. doi:10.1109/ACCESS.2022.3186892

Wang, H. Z., Lin, G. W., Wang, J. Q., Gao, W. L., Chen, Y. F., & Duan, Q. L. (2014). Management of Big Data in the Internet of Things in Agriculture Based on Cloud Computing. *Applied Mechanics and Materials*, *548–549*, 1438–1444. . doi:10.4028/www.scientific.net/AMM.548-549.1438

Wazid, M., Das, A. K., Rodrigues, J. J. P. C., Shetty, S., & Park, Y. (2019). IoMT Malware Detection Approaches: Analysis and Research Challenges. *IEEE Access : Practical Innovations, Open Solutions*, 7, 182459–182476. doi:10.1109/ACCESS.2019.2960412

Wolfert, S., Ge, L., Verdouw, C., & Bogaardt, M.-J. (2017). Big Data in Smart Farming – A review. *Agricultural Systems*, 153, 69–80. doi:10.1016/j.agsy.2017.01.023

Yang, Z., Jianjun, L., Faqiri, H., Shafik, W., Talal Abdulrahman, A., Yusuf, M., & Sharawy, A. M. (2021). Green Internet of Things and Big Data Application in Smart Cities Development. *Complexity*, *2021*, 1–15. doi:10.1155/2021/4922697

Chapter 18
Advancements in Electric Vehicle Management System:
Integrating Machine Learning and Artificial Intelligence

D. Godwin Immanuel

Department of Electrical and Electronics Engineering, Sathyabama Institute of Science and Technology, India

Gautam Solaimalai

U.S. Bank, USA

B. M. Chandrakala

Department of Information Science and Engineering, Dayananda Sagar College of Engineering, Bengaluru, India

V. G. Bharath

iD https://orcid.org/0000-0002-2468-9143

Vessels Engineers, Bangalore, India

Mukul Kumar Singh

Department of Electrical Engineering, MJP Rohilkhand University, Bareilly, India

Sampath Boopathi

iD https://orcid.org/0000-0002-2065-6539

Department of Mechanical Engineering, Muthayammal Engineering College, Namakkal, India

ABSTRACT

The chapter discusses the advancement of electric vehicle (EV) management systems, emphasizing the role of machine learning and artificial intelligence in optimizing vehicle dynamics, battery management, charging infrastructure, and user preferences. These technologies can enhance performance, efficiency, and user experience by adapting to dynamic driving conditions, optimizing energy consumption, and providing personalized experiences. The chapter also addresses challenges like data privacy, computational complexity, and interoperability, suggesting solutions and highlighting the need for collaborative research initiatives and regulatory frameworks for responsible ML and AI deployment in the EV industry.

DOI: 10.4018/979-8-3693-1487-6.ch018

INTRODUCTION

The evolution of electric vehicle (EV) management systems has been a transformative journey, marked by significant advancements in technology, regulations, and consumer preferences. From rudimentary control mechanisms to sophisticated integrated systems powered by machine learning and artificial intelligence, this evolution reflects a convergence of innovation, sustainability, and user-centric design. Initially, electric vehicles were equipped with basic management systems aimed at ensuring operational safety and efficiency. These early systems primarily focused on monitoring battery status, controlling motor functions, and regulating charging processes. However, the limited computing power and simplistic algorithms restricted their adaptability to dynamic driving conditions and user behavior (Liu et al., 2022a).

As the demand for EVs surged and technological innovations accelerated, the evolution of management systems gained momentum. The introduction of more powerful onboard computers enabled the integration of advanced sensors, actuators, and communication modules, laying the foundation for intelligent control architectures. Moreover, advancements in battery technology, such as lithium-ion cells, facilitated higher energy densities and faster charging capabilities, necessitating more sophisticated management strategies (Hasan et al., 2021). One of the key milestones in the evolution of EV management systems was the adoption of predictive analytics and diagnostic algorithms. By leveraging historical usage data and real-time sensor inputs, these algorithms enabled predictive maintenance, fault detection, and performance optimization. This proactive approach not only improved reliability and safety but also reduced operational costs and downtime, enhancing the overall ownership experience for EV users (Yang et al., 2020).

The integration of machine learning (ML) and artificial intelligence (AI) represented a quantum leap in the evolution of EV management systems. ML algorithms, such as neural networks and decision trees, revolutionized energy management, route optimization, and user-centric features. These algorithms continuously learn from vast datasets, including driving patterns, environmental conditions, and user preferences, to dynamically adjust vehicle parameters and optimize performance in real-time (Ibrahim & Jiang, 2021). Furthermore, AI-powered features, such as adaptive cruise control and autonomous driving assistance, redefined the concept of vehicle autonomy and safety. By analyzing sensor data from onboard cameras, radars, and lidars, AI systems can anticipate potential hazards, predict traffic patterns, and autonomously adjust driving behavior to ensure optimal efficiency and safety. Moreover, AI algorithms enable personalized driving experiences through voice recognition, gesture control, and intelligent infotainment systems, enhancing user comfort and convenience (İnci et al., 2021).

The evolution of EV management systems has also been shaped by regulatory frameworks and industry standards aimed at promoting interoperability, safety, and environmental sustainability. Initiatives such as the ISO 15118 standard for vehicle-to-grid communication and the OCPP protocol for charging infrastructure interoperability have facilitated seamless integration and interoperability between EVs and charging stations, fostering the growth of a robust electric mobility ecosystem (Pandiyan et al., 2023). Looking ahead, the evolution of EV management systems is poised to continue on an exponential trajectory, driven by advancements in data analytics, connectivity, and autonomous technologies. Emerging trends such as vehicle-to-everything (V2X) communication, cloud-based analytics, and edge computing hold the promise of further enhancing the efficiency, reliability, and intelligence of EV management systems (Liu et al., 2022b).

The evolution of electric vehicle management systems is a result of technological innovation, regulatory initiatives, and consumer demand for sustainable mobility solutions. This evolution, from basic control mechanisms to intelligent, data-driven systems powered by ML and AI, focuses on efficiency, safety, and user-centric design.

Traditional Approaches vs. ML and AI Integration

The study contrasts traditional methods with the integration of machine learning and artificial intelligence in electric vehicle management, highlighting the shift towards more adaptive, intelligent, and user-centric systems. Table 1 shows the performance of traditional methods (Ahmed et al., 2021; Pandiyan et al., 2023; Shibl et al., 2020).

MACHINE LEARNING IN ELECTRIC VEHICLE MANAGEMENT

The implementation of machine learning methods in electric vehicle energy management systems involves several steps and descriptive points (Du et al., 2020). The figure 1 depicts the various aspects of machine learning in electric vehicle management.

- **Data Collection and Preprocessing**: Collect relevant data from various sources such as vehicle sensors, GPS, weather forecasts, and historical driving patterns. Preprocess the data to remove noise, handle missing values, and normalize features for consistency (Basso et al., 2021).
- **Feature Selection and Engineering**: Identify relevant features related to energy consumption, driving behavior, environmental factors, and vehicle characteristics. Engineer new features or transform existing ones to extract meaningful insights for energy management.
- **Model Selection and Training**: Choose appropriate machine learning models such as regression, classification, or reinforcement learning based on the specific energy management objectives. Split the dataset into training and testing sets to evaluate model performance. Train the selected models

Table 1. Performance of traditional approaches and the integration of machine learning and artificial intelligence (ML) in electric vehicles

Performance Aspect	Traditional Approaches in EV	ML and AI Integrations in EV
1. Energy Efficiency	Limited Optimization	Dynamic Optimization
2. Range	Static Estimations	Adaptive Range Prediction
3. Battery Life	Basic Monitoring	Advanced Health Management
4. Driving Dynamics	Fixed Parameters	Adaptive Control
5. Charging Speed	Fixed Charging Rates	Adaptive Charging Strategies
6. Route Optimization	Manual Planning	Dynamic Route Adjustment
7. Fault Detection	Reactive Maintenance	Predictive Maintenance
8. Safety Systems Performance	Basic Functionality	Adaptive Safety Features
9. User Experience	Limited Personalization	Personalized Features
10. Overall System Efficiency	Static Performance Metrics	Dynamic System Optimization

Figure 1. The various aspects of machine learning in electric vehicle management

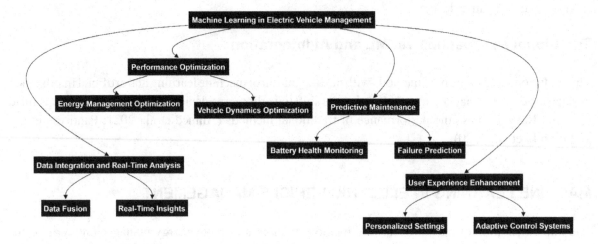

using the training dataset to learn patterns and relationships between input features and energy consumption.

- **Model Validation and Evaluation**: Validate the trained models using the testing dataset to ensure generalization and avoid overfitting. Evaluate model performance metrics such as accuracy, precision, recall, and F1-score to assess the effectiveness of energy management predictions.
- **Optimization and Control Strategies**: Develop optimization algorithms or control strategies based on the trained machine learning models to optimize energy consumption and enhance efficiency. Implement dynamic control strategies that adapt to real-time driving conditions, battery health, and user preferences (Paul et al., 2024; Sampath et al., 2023; Vanitha et al., 2023; Veeranjaneyulu et al., 2023).
- **Integration with Vehicle Systems**: Integrate the machine learning-based energy management system with onboard vehicle systems to enable seamless communication and control. Develop interfaces or APIs for data exchange between the energy management system and other vehicle components such as powertrain, battery management system, and infotainment system (Babu et al., 2022; Boopathi et al., 2021; Chandrika et al., 2023).
- **Real-time Monitoring and Adaptation**: Implement real-time monitoring of energy consumption, battery status, and environmental conditions to enable adaptive energy management decisions. Continuously update and retrain machine learning models using new data to improve prediction accuracy and adaptability (Basso et al., 2021).
- **Testing and Validation**: Conduct extensive testing and validation of the integrated energy management system in simulated and real-world driving scenarios. Validate the system's performance under various conditions including different driving patterns, terrain, weather conditions, and traffic scenarios.
- **Deployment and Maintenance**: Deploy the machine learning-based energy management system in production vehicles while ensuring compatibility with existing vehicle platforms and infrastructure. Establish a maintenance and update schedule to address any issues, incorporate new features, and improve system performance over time.

The process involves user feedback, new features, performance monitoring, and data collection to refine machine learning models and optimize strategies for electric vehicle systems, thereby enhancing efficiency and performance, and thereby enhancing overall efficiency (Tang et al., 2021a).

Energy Management and Optimization

The table 2 provides a comprehensive overview of the various factors that contribute to effective energy management and optimization.

Route Optimization and Adaptive Decision-Making

Advanced data analytics, machine learning, and real-time decision-making algorithms will be utilized in electric vehicle energy management systems to optimize route planning, enhance energy efficiency, and improve user experience (Tang et al., 2021a)

- Gather data on traffic conditions, road infrastructure, weather forecasts, and vehicle parameters.
- Cleanse and preprocess the collected data to remove outliers, handle missing values, and ensure data consistency.
- Utilize algorithms to generate optimal driving routes considering factors such as distance, traffic congestion, road gradient, and charging station availability.
- Integrate real-time data feeds to dynamically adjust planned routes based on current traffic conditions and road closures.

Table 2. Factors for energy management and optimization

Factors	Energy Management and Optimization
Energy Monitoring	Utilize sensors to monitor energy consumption in real-time, including motor, battery, and auxiliary systems.
Predictive Modeling	Develop predictive models using historical data and machine learning algorithms to forecast energy usage and optimize performance.
Dynamic Route Optimization	Incorporate GPS data and real-time traffic information to dynamically optimize driving routes for energy efficiency.
Regenerative Braking Systems	Implement regenerative braking systems to capture and store energy during deceleration, thus improving overall efficiency.
Adaptive Cruise Control	Utilize adaptive cruise control systems that adjust speed and acceleration based on traffic conditions and energy efficiency goals.
Battery Management	Implement advanced battery management systems to optimize charging and discharging cycles, prolonging battery life and efficiency.
Eco-Driving Assistance	Provide eco-driving assistance features, such as real-time feedback on driving behavior and suggestions for energy-efficient driving techniques.
Vehicle-to-Grid Integration	Explore vehicle-to-grid (V2G) integration, allowing EVs to participate in grid services and optimize energy usage based on grid demand and pricing.
Smart Charging Infrastructure	Develop smart charging infrastructure that optimizes charging schedules based on energy grid demand, renewable energy availability, and cost.
Energy Recovery Systems	Integrate energy recovery systems, such as solar panels or kinetic energy recovery systems, to supplement vehicle power and increase efficiency

- Use historical driving data and machine learning models to predict energy consumption along different route options.
- Incorporate information about charging station locations, availability, and charging speeds into route planning to optimize charging stops.
- Factor in battery health and state of charge (SoC) when planning routes to minimize battery degradation and ensure optimal performance.
- Incorporate user preferences such as preferred charging times, route preferences, and desired travel duration into route optimization algorithms.
- Implement a feedback loop to continuously improve route optimization algorithms based on user feedback and performance metrics.
- Develop algorithms that dynamically adjust route recommendations based on real-time data, user feedback, and changing environmental conditions.

ARTIFICIAL INTELLIGENCE FOR ENHANCED PERFORMANCE

AI can enhance electric vehicle performance and battery capacity by utilizing advanced algorithms and data analytics, optimizing various vehicle operation aspects as illustrated in a flowchart(Tang et al., 2021b). The figure 2 depicts various aspects of artificial intelligence that can improve the performance of electric vehicles.

a. **Battery Management and Optimization**:
   ◦ **Battery Health Monitoring**: AI algorithms analyze battery data in real-time to assess its health status, detect degradation patterns, and predict remaining useful life (Kushwah et al., 2024; Malathi et al., 2024).
   ◦ **Optimal Charging Strategies**: AI optimizes charging schedules based on factors like battery state of charge (SoC), temperature, and degradation, maximizing battery lifespan and performance.

Figure 2. Various aspects of artificial intelligence for enhanced performance in electric vehicles

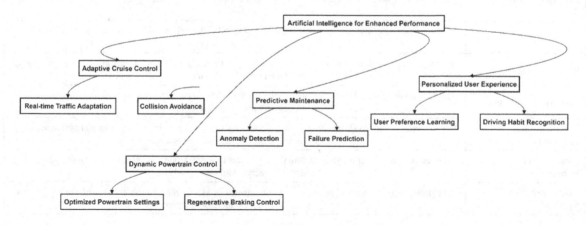

    ◦   **Energy Consumption Prediction**: AI models predict energy consumption based on driving patterns, traffic conditions, and environmental factors, allowing for more accurate range estimation and efficient energy management.

b.   **Driving Dynamics and Performance**:
    ◦   **Adaptive Cruise Control**: AI-powered adaptive cruise control systems adjust vehicle speed and acceleration based on real-time traffic conditions, optimizing energy usage while maintaining safety.
    ◦   **Dynamic Powertrain Control**: AI algorithms optimize powertrain settings (e.g., motor torque, regenerative braking) in response to driving conditions, improving efficiency and performance.
    ◦   **Driver Assistance Systems**: AI-enhanced driver assistance systems provide real-time feedback on driving behavior, promoting energy-efficient driving practices and optimizing performance.

c.   **Predictive Maintenance**:
    ◦   **Component Health Monitoring**: AI algorithms analyze sensor data to detect anomalies and predict potential failures in vehicle components, enabling proactive maintenance and minimizing downtime.
    ◦   **Fault Detection and Diagnostics**: AI identifies and diagnoses faults in real-time, providing early warnings to prevent breakdowns and ensuring optimal vehicle performance.

d.   **User Experience Enhancement**:
    ◦   **Personalized Settings**: AI learns user preferences and driving habits to personalize vehicle settings, such as climate control, seat positions, and infotainment options, optimizing comfort and convenience.
    ◦   **Voice and Gesture Control**: AI-powered interfaces enable intuitive interaction with vehicle systems through voice commands and gestures, enhancing user experience and minimizing distractions.

e.   **Battery Capacity Enhancement**:
    ◦   **Battery Chemistry Optimization**: AI algorithms optimize battery chemistry and materials to increase energy density, improve charging efficiency, and extend battery lifespan.
    ◦   **Energy Storage Solutions**: AI designs and optimizes energy storage solutions, such as solid-state batteries and supercapacitors, to enhance battery capacity and performance (Rahamathunnisa et al., 2024; Revathi et al., 2024).

Deep Learning and Neural Network Architectures

Deep learning and neural network architectures play a crucial role in electric vehicle (EV) energy management by leveraging complex algorithms to analyze large datasets, model nonlinear relationships, and make accurate predictions. It provides a detailed explanation of how deep learning and neural network architectures can be effectively utilized in EV energy management (Lipu et al., 2021a). Neural network architectures such as LSTM, CNN, RNN, DQN, DDPG, autoencoders, and DNNs can be trained using large datasets of EV performance data, sensor readings, driving patterns, and environmental conditions to optimize various aspects of EV energy management. These architectures leverage the power of deep learning to model complex relationships and make accurate predictions, ultimately enhancing EV performance, efficiency, and battery capacity (Satav et al., 2023; Verma et al., 2024).

a. **Battery Health Monitoring**: LSTM networks are effective for analyzing time-series data, making them suitable for predicting battery degradation patterns over time based on historical battery performance data.

b. **Optimal Charging Strategies**: CNNs can analyze various charging parameters such as battery temperature, state of charge (SoC), and charging rate to optimize charging strategies and minimize degradation.

c. **Energy Consumption Prediction**: RNNs are well-suited for sequential data analysis and can accurately predict future energy consumption based on past driving patterns, traffic conditions, and environmental factors.

d. **Adaptive Cruise Control**: DQNs are reinforcement learning algorithms that can learn optimal control policies for adaptive cruise control systems, adjusting vehicle speed and acceleration in real-time to optimize energy usage while ensuring safety.

e. **Dynamic Powertrain Control**: DDPG is a deep reinforcement learning algorithm that can optimize powertrain settings such as motor torque and regenerative braking based on real-time driving conditions and energy efficiency goals.

f. **Predictive Maintenance**: Autoencoders can be used for anomaly detection in sensor data, identifying deviations from normal operating conditions and predicting potential failures in vehicle components.

g. **Personalized Settings**: DNNs can learn user preferences and driving habits from historical data, allowing for personalized settings such as climate control, seat positions, and infotainment options to enhance user experience.

h. **Battery Chemistry Optimization**: GANs can generate synthetic data to simulate different battery chemistry configurations, allowing for optimization of battery materials and chemistry to increase energy density and performance.

Adaptive Cruise Control Systems

Adaptive Cruise Control (ACC) systems in electric vehicles (EVs) enhance safety and convenience by using advanced sensors and artificial intelligence algorithms to automatically adjust vehicle speed and maintain a safe following distance from the vehicle ahead, unlike traditional cruise control systems (Jayakumar et al., 2021).

ACC systems in electric vehicles (EVs) are based on sensors like radar, lidar, and cameras that continuously scan the environment to detect nearby vehicles and obstacles. These sensors provide real-time data on the distance, relative speed, and trajectory of vehicles ahead, allowing the ACC system to dynamically adjust the vehicle's speed to match traffic flow and maintain a safe distance. This proactive approach to driving reduces the likelihood of accidents and improves overall road safety by adjusting speed and following distance faster than human drivers (Babu et al., 2022; Chandrika et al., 2023).

ACC systems in electric vehicles (EVs) improve efficiency and energy management by optimizing acceleration and deceleration patterns based on real-time traffic conditions. This minimizes unnecessary energy consumption and maximizes range, crucial for EVs' battery life and driving range. ACC systems can be integrated with regenerative braking technology to enhance energy efficiency. Regenerative braking converts kinetic energy into electrical energy, stored in the battery for later use. By coordinating with ACC systems, EVs can maximize energy regeneration and reduce reliance on traditional friction brakes, extending battery life and improving overall efficiency.

Adaptive Cruise Control (ACC) systems in electric vehicles (EVs) enhance safety, efficiency, and driving comfort by automating speed control and maintaining a safe distance from other vehicles. This reduces the need for constant acceleration and deceleration, providing a smoother driving experience. ACC systems are particularly beneficial in stop-and-go traffic situations, reducing fatigue and stress. They use advanced sensors and artificial intelligence algorithms to automatically adjust speed and maintain a safe following distance, improving road safety, energy management, and overall driving experience.

Cognitive Capabilities in EV Management

Cognitive capabilities in electric vehicle management involve the use of advanced AI algorithms to mimic human-like cognitive functions like reasoning, problem-solving, and decision-making. These capabilities are crucial for optimizing EV operation, enhancing efficiency, safety, and user experience, and include key cognitive capabilities (Chandran et al., 2021; Ji et al., 2020).

- **Adaptive Learning**: EVs equipped with cognitive capabilities can continuously learn and adapt to changing driving conditions, user preferences, and environmental factors. By analyzing vast amounts of data collected from sensors, onboard systems, and external sources, cognitive algorithms can identify patterns, predict future events, and optimize vehicle performance accordingly.
- **Predictive Maintenance**: Cognitive algorithms can analyze sensor data from various vehicle components to predict potential failures or maintenance issues before they occur. By monitoring factors such as battery health, motor performance, and cooling system efficiency, EVs can schedule proactive maintenance tasks to prevent costly breakdowns and maximize uptime.
- **Dynamic Energy Management**: Cognitive capabilities enable EVs to dynamically manage energy usage based on real-time data and user preferences. By considering factors such as driving patterns, traffic conditions, and energy grid availability, cognitive algorithms can optimize energy consumption, extend battery life, and maximize driving range.
- **Intelligent Route Planning**: Cognitive algorithms can analyze traffic patterns, road conditions, and user preferences to generate optimal driving routes. By incorporating real-time data feeds and predictive analytics, EVs can dynamically adjust route plans to avoid congestion, minimize energy consumption, and optimize travel time.
- **Adaptive Cruise Control**: Cognitive capabilities enhance adaptive cruise control systems by enabling the vehicle to intelligently adjust speed and acceleration based on traffic conditions, road topology, and user preferences. By analyzing sensor data and predicting the behavior of surrounding vehicles, cognitive algorithms can optimize driving dynamics for safety and efficiency (Boopathi, 2024).
- **Context-Aware Decision Making**: Cognitive algorithms enable EVs to make context-aware decisions by considering various factors such as weather conditions, road hazards, and user preferences. By integrating data from external sources such as weather forecasts and traffic reports, EVs can make informed decisions to ensure safe and efficient operation.
- **Personalized User Experience**: Cognitive capabilities allow EVs to personalize the driving experience based on individual user preferences and behavior. By learning from past interactions and user feedback, cognitive algorithms can adjust vehicle settings, infotainment options, and driving dynamics to enhance comfort and satisfaction.

Figure 3. Integrated management framework for electric vehicles

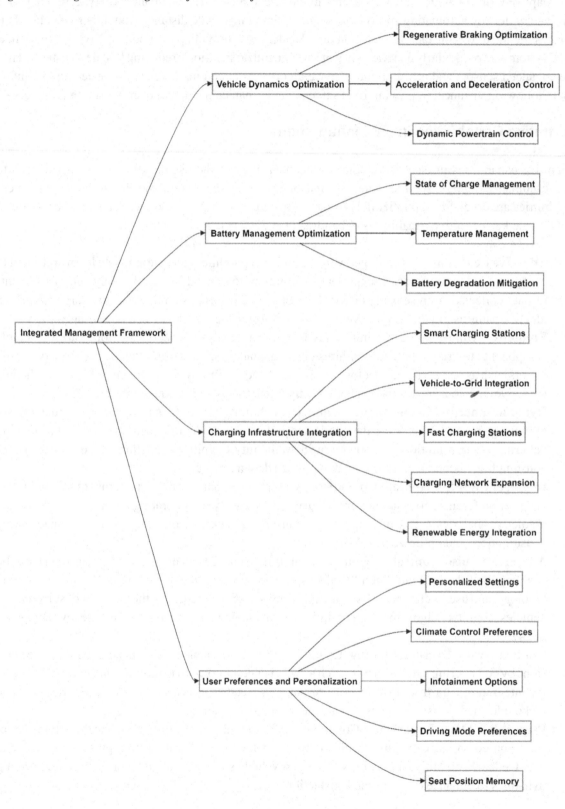

Cognitive capabilities enhance electric vehicle management by enabling intelligent decision-making, adaptive learning, and personalized user experiences. Advanced artificial intelligence algorithms optimize energy usage, improve safety, and provide a seamless driving experience for users.

INTEGRATED MANAGEMENT FRAMEWORK

Cognitive capabilities enhance electric vehicle management by enabling intelligent decision-making, adaptive learning, and personalized user experiences. Advanced artificial intelligence algorithms optimize energy usage, improve safety, and provide a seamless driving experience for users (Venegas et al., 2021). The integration of machine learning and artificial intelligence in electric vehicle management enhances performance, resulting in more efficient, adaptive, and user-friendly systems compared to traditional methods, as depicted in figure 3. The integrated management framework for electric vehicles combines various functionalities and technologies to enhance performance, efficiency, and user experience. It utilizes advanced technologies like data analytics, machine learning, and smart charging infrastructure, enabling EVs to operate more efficiently, extend battery life, and provide a seamless driving experience (Das et al., 2020).

a) **Vehicle Dynamics Optimization**:
   ◦ Integrated control systems that optimize vehicle dynamics, including acceleration, braking, and steering, to improve efficiency and driving performance.
   ◦ Adaptive cruise control and regenerative braking systems that adjust vehicle speed and energy regeneration based on real-time traffic conditions and driving behavior.
b) **Battery Management System (BMS)**:
   ◦ Advanced BMS that monitors battery health, state of charge (SoC), and temperature to optimize charging and discharging cycles, prolong battery life, and ensure safe operation.
   ◦ Predictive maintenance algorithms that analyze battery data to detect and address potential issues before they affect performance or safety.
c) **Charging Infrastructure Integration**:
   ◦ Smart charging infrastructure that integrates with the EV's onboard systems to optimize charging schedules based on energy grid demand, renewable energy availability, and user preferences.
   ◦ Vehicle-to-grid (V2G) integration that enables bidirectional energy flow between EVs and the grid, allowing EVs to provide grid services and participate in demand response programs.
d) **Route Optimization and Navigation**:
   ◦ Intelligent route planning and navigation systems that optimize driving routes based on factors such as traffic conditions, road topology, energy consumption, and charging station availability.
   ◦ Real-time updates and adaptive routing algorithms that dynamically adjust routes to avoid congestion, minimize energy consumption, and optimize travel time.
e) **User Preferences and Personalization**:
   ◦ Personalized user profiles and preferences that adjust vehicle settings, climate control, infotainment options, and driving dynamics to enhance comfort and convenience.

      ○   Voice recognition and natural language processing (NLP) systems that enable intuitive interaction with the vehicle and customization of user preferences.

f)   **Data Integration and Analysis**:

      ○   Integration of data from onboard sensors, GPS, weather forecasts, and charging stations to provide real-time insights into vehicle performance, energy consumption, and driving patterns.

      ○   Data analytics and machine learning algorithms that analyze large datasets to optimize energy management, predict maintenance needs, and improve overall system efficiency.

g)   **Safety and Security Features**:

      ○   Advanced driver assistance systems (ADAS) that provide collision avoidance, lane-keeping assistance, and emergency braking to enhance safety and reduce the risk of accidents.

      ○   Cybersecurity measures to protect vehicle systems from cyber threats and ensure the integrity and confidentiality of data transmitted between the vehicle and external systems.

Data Integration and Real-Time Analysis

Data integration and real-time analysis are crucial in electric vehicle management systems, facilitating the seamless integration of diverse data sources and providing immediate actionable insights (Tran et al., 2020). Data integration and real-time analysis are crucial in electric vehicle management systems for efficient energy management, user experience enhancement, predictive maintenance, and charging management, resulting in improved performance, efficiency, and user satisfaction.

- **Comprehensive Data Utilization**: Data integration allows EV management systems to access and utilize a wide range of data sources, including vehicle telemetry data, GPS information, weather forecasts, charging infrastructure status, and user preferences. By integrating these disparate data sources, EV management systems can gain a comprehensive understanding of the operating environment and make more informed decisions.

- **Optimized Energy Management**: Real-time analysis of integrated data enables EV management systems to optimize energy consumption and maximize efficiency. By analyzing factors such as driving patterns, traffic conditions, terrain, and battery status in real-time, these systems can dynamically adjust vehicle parameters such as speed, acceleration, and route to minimize energy consumption and extend driving range.

- **Enhanced User Experience**: Real-time analysis of integrated data allows EV management systems to provide personalized and context-aware user experiences. By considering factors such as user preferences, driving habits, and environmental conditions, these systems can tailor vehicle settings, climate control, and navigation routes to meet the specific needs and preferences of individual users, thereby enhancing the overall driving experience.

- **Predictive Maintenance**: Real-time analysis of integrated data facilitates predictive maintenance by enabling EV management systems to monitor the health and performance of vehicle components in real-time. By analyzing sensor data from various vehicle systems, these systems can detect anomalies, predict potential failures, and schedule proactive maintenance tasks to prevent breakdowns and maximize vehicle uptime.

- **Efficient Charging Management**: Real-time analysis of integrated data allows EV management systems to optimize charging infrastructure utilization and maximize charging efficiency. By monitoring factors such as charging station availability, energy grid demand, and renewable energy availability in real-time, these systems can dynamically adjust charging schedules and prioritize charging sessions to minimize wait times and optimize energy usage.

Optimization of Vehicle Dynamics and Battery Management

The optimization of vehicle dynamics and battery management in electric vehicles (EVs) involves various methods to enhance efficiency, performance, and overall driving experience (Hussain et al., 2021; Tran et al., 2020).

Vehicle Dynamics Optimization

a. **Regenerative Braking Optimization**:
   - Approach: Regenerative braking systems capture kinetic energy during deceleration and convert it into electrical energy to recharge the battery.
   - Method: Adjusting regenerative braking levels based on driving conditions, such as traffic density and road gradient, to maximize energy regeneration without compromising safety.
b. **Acceleration and Deceleration Control**:
   - Approach: Optimizing acceleration and deceleration patterns to minimize energy consumption and maximize efficiency.
   - Method: Implementing intelligent control algorithms that adjust acceleration and deceleration rates based on real-time traffic conditions and driver behavior to optimize energy usage.
c. **Dynamic Powertrain Control**:
   - Approach: Dynamically adjusting powertrain settings, such as motor torque and gear ratios, to optimize performance and efficiency.
   - Method: Utilizing adaptive control algorithms that optimize powertrain parameters based on driving conditions, user preferences, and energy consumption goals.

Battery Management Optimization

By employing these various approaches and methods for optimizing vehicle dynamics and battery management, electric vehicles can achieve improved efficiency, performance, and overall driving experience, contributing to their widespread adoption and sustainability (Zhang et al., 2020).

a. **State of Charge (SoC) Management**:
   - Approach: Optimizing the battery's state of charge to balance energy storage capacity and longevity.
   - Method: Implementing predictive algorithms that analyze driving patterns, route characteristics, and energy consumption to dynamically adjust charging and discharging rates to maintain optimal SoC levels.
b. **Temperature Management**:
   - Approach: Maintaining optimal battery temperature to improve performance and extend battery life.

      ○ Method: Utilizing thermal management systems that monitor battery temperature and adjust cooling or heating mechanisms to prevent overheating or overcooling, thereby optimizing battery performance.

c. **Battery Degradation Mitigation**:
      ○ Approach: Minimizing battery degradation to prolong battery lifespan and maintain performance.
      ○ Method: Implementing adaptive charging strategies, such as limiting fast charging or adjusting charging rates based on battery health indicators, to mitigate degradation and optimize battery longevity.

Integrated Approach

a. **Predictive Analytics**:
      ○ Approach: Using predictive analytics to anticipate future driving conditions and optimize vehicle dynamics and battery management accordingly.
      ○ Method: Incorporating machine learning algorithms that analyze historical data, weather forecasts, and traffic patterns to predict future driving scenarios and adjust vehicle parameters in advance for optimal efficiency and performance.

b. **Real-time Feedback and Control**:
      ○ Approach: Providing real-time feedback to drivers and dynamically adjusting vehicle dynamics and battery management based on feedback and external factors.
      ○ Method: Integrating sensors and onboard systems that provide real-time feedback to drivers on energy consumption, driving behavior, and battery status, while also enabling adaptive control algorithms to adjust vehicle parameters in response to changing conditions.

Charging Infrastructure and User Preferences

Table 3 presents information on charging infrastructure and user preferences. This table provides a comprehensive overview of charging infrastructure and user preferences in electric vehicles, detailing potential changes and adaptations based on user references, with each aspect listed with specific implementations and presented in a structured table format for clarity (Illmann & Kluge, 2020; Lee et al., 2020).

CHALLENGES AND FUTURE DIRECTIONS

Data Privacy and Interoperability Challenges: Data privacy in electric vehicles (EVs) involves protecting sensitive information like location data, driving patterns, and performance metrics. Interoperability challenges arise from integrating data from various sources, such as EVs, charging infrastructure, and grid systems, while ensuring seamless communication. Addressing these requires robust encryption and access control mechanisms, as well as standardized communication protocols and data formats for interoperability between systems and stakeholders. The figure 4 and Table 4 depicts the intersection of technological advancements and challenges (Lipu et al., 2021b).

Table 4 presents the challenges and future directions for the project (Husain et al., 2021).

Table 3. Charging infrastructure and user preferences

CHARGING INFRASTRUCTURE	USER PREFERENCES
Smart Charging Stations	**Personalized Settings**
- Implement smart charging stations equipped with communication capabilities to optimize charging schedules based on energy grid demand, renewable energy availability, and user preferences.	- Develop user profiles that allow customization of vehicle settings such as charging times, preferred charging locations, and charging rates based on individual user preferences.
Vehicle-to-Grid Integration	**Climate Control Preferences**
- Enable bidirectional energy flow between EVs and the grid, allowing EVs to provide grid services and participate in demand response programs, thereby optimizing energy usage and grid stability.	- Incorporate user preferences for climate control settings, including temperature, fan speed, and airflow direction, to ensure personalized comfort during driving.
Fast Charging Stations	**Infotainment Options**
- Install fast charging stations along major travel routes to minimize charging time and enable long-distance travel with EVs.	- Customize infotainment options such as music playlists, navigation preferences, and voice command settings to align with individual user preferences and enhance the driving experience.
Charging Network Expansion	**Driving Mode Preferences**
- Expand the charging network coverage to increase accessibility and convenience for EV owners, ensuring widespread adoption and support for electric vehicles.	- Allow users to customize driving mode preferences, including eco-mode, sport mode, and comfort mode, to suit different driving scenarios and personal preferences for driving dynamics.
Renewable Energy Integration	**Seat Position Memory**
- Integrate renewable energy sources such as solar panels into charging infrastructure to promote sustainable charging practices and reduce reliance on fossil fuels.	- Implement seat position memory settings that automatically adjust seat positions, including seat height, angle, and lumbar support, based on individual user profiles, enhancing comfort and convenience for drivers and passengers.
Wireless Charging Technology	**Charging Profile Customization**
- Implement wireless charging technology to eliminate the need for physical cables and enable convenient charging without manual intervention.	- Allow users to customize charging profiles, including charging speed, maximum charge limit, and preferred charging duration, to accommodate individual preferences and requirements.
Charging Station Availability Monitoring	**Preferred Charging Locations**
- Develop systems to monitor charging station availability in real-time and provide users with information on nearby stations, availability status, and expected wait times.	- Enable users to specify preferred charging locations such as home, workplace, or public charging stations, and prioritize these locations in route planning and charging recommendations.
Charging Payment Integration	**Payment and Billing Preferences**
- Integrate payment systems with charging infrastructure to facilitate seamless payment processing for charging services, including pay-per-use, subscription-based, or pre-paid options.	- Offer flexible payment and billing options for charging services, allowing users to choose preferred payment methods, billing cycles, and expense tracking features for managing charging expenses.
Charging Session Scheduling	**Charging Time Window Selection**
- Enable users to schedule charging sessions in advance, allowing them to specify preferred charging times based on energy tariff rates, off-peak hours, or personal schedules.	- Provide options for selecting charging time windows within user-defined preferences, such as overnight charging, mid-day charging, or opportunistic charging during low-demand periods, to optimize cost savings and convenience.
Emergency Charging Assistance	**Emergency Contact Integration**
- Implement emergency charging assistance services to provide support in case of unexpected battery depletion or charging emergencies, including on-demand charging assistance or emergency charging access.	- Integrate emergency contact information into vehicle systems, allowing users to specify emergency contacts for notification in case of charging-related issues or emergencies, ensuring prompt assistance and support when needed.

Computational Complexity and Scalability: The integration of artificial intelligence (AI) and machine learning (ML) algorithms with electric vehicle (EV) battery management systems (BMS)

Table 4. Challenges and future directions

Challenges	Future Directions
Data Complexity: Battery systems generate vast amounts of complex data, including temperature, voltage, current, and state of charge (SoC), which must be accurately captured and processed for effective management.	**Advanced Data Analytics**: Develop advanced data analytics techniques, including machine learning algorithms, to analyze and interpret complex battery data in real-time, enabling precise monitoring and control of battery performance.
Modeling Complexity: Battery behavior is nonlinear and influenced by various factors such as temperature, aging, and usage patterns, making it challenging to develop accurate predictive models for battery performance and degradation.	**Advanced Modeling Techniques**: Utilize advanced modeling techniques, such as physics-based models, neural networks, and reinforcement learning algorithms, to capture the nonlinear behavior of batteries and accurately predict performance and degradation over time.
Real-time Optimization: Achieving real-time optimization of battery operation and charging requires fast and efficient algorithms capable of processing large volumes of data and making timely decisions to optimize battery performance while ensuring safety and reliability.	**Real-time Control Systems**: Develop real-time control systems that integrate AI and ML algorithms with battery management systems to optimize charging and discharging strategies, adapt to dynamic operating conditions, and maximize battery lifespan and performance.
Safety and Reliability: Ensuring the safety and reliability of battery systems is paramount, requiring robust algorithms and control strategies to prevent overcharging, overheating, and other safety hazards that could compromise battery integrity.	**Safety Assurance**: Implement advanced safety assurance mechanisms, including fault detection and mitigation algorithms, redundant sensor systems, and fail-safe control strategies, to ensure the safe operation of battery systems under all operating conditions.
Scalability and Compatibility: Integrating AI and ML capabilities with existing BMS platforms and EV architectures poses challenges related to scalability, compatibility, and integration with legacy systems and hardware.	**Scalable Solutions**: Develop scalable AI and ML solutions that can be seamlessly integrated with existing BMS platforms and EV architectures, ensuring compatibility and interoperability while enabling future scalability and expansion.
Energy Efficiency: Optimizing energy efficiency and minimizing energy losses during charging and discharging cycles require advanced algorithms that can accurately predict energy consumption and optimize charging/discharging strategies accordingly.	**Energy-aware Algorithms**: Design energy-aware algorithms that leverage AI and ML techniques to predict energy consumption, optimize charging/discharging schedules, and minimize energy losses, thereby improving overall energy efficiency and extending battery life.

Figure 4. Technological advancements and challenges

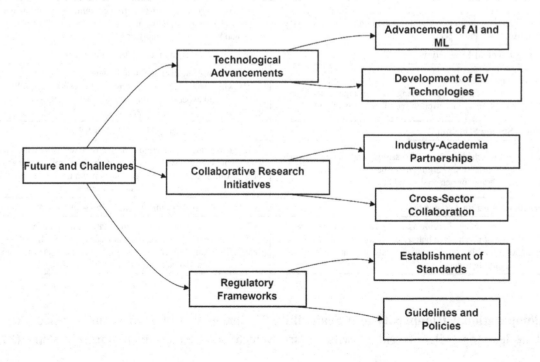

introduces computational complexity and scalability challenges. These challenges stem from the need to process large volumes of data in real-time, develop complex predictive models for battery behavior, and ensure scalability to accommodate increasing data volumes and computational demands. Overcoming these challenges involves leveraging high-performance computing resources, optimizing algorithm efficiency, and implementing scalable architectures that can accommodate the growing computational requirements of AI and ML algorithms in EV BMS applications (Liu et al., 2022a).

Collaborative Research and Regulatory Frameworks: Collaborative research and regulatory frameworks are essential for promoting innovation and ensuring the safe and responsible deployment of electric vehicles (EVs) and associated technologies. Collaborative research initiatives bring together industry stakeholders, research institutions, and government agencies to address key challenges, share knowledge and resources, and drive technological advancements in the EV ecosystem. Regulatory frameworks play a crucial role in establishing standards, guidelines, and policies to govern the development, deployment, and operation of EVs, ensuring safety, security, and compliance with applicable regulations (Hasan et al., 2021; Hussain et al., 2021). By fostering collaboration and establishing clear regulatory guidelines, stakeholders can work together to accelerate the adoption of EVs and promote the development of sustainable transportation solutions.

CONCLUSION

The chapter on integrated management for electric vehicles (EVs) discusses the use of advanced technologies like machine learning, artificial intelligence (AI), and data analytics to optimize performance, efficiency, and user experience. It covers the evolution of EV management systems, AI's application in enhancing performance and battery capacity, challenges and future directions, charging infrastructure, and user preferences. AI and machine learning play a crucial role in EV operations, enabling EVs to adapt to changing driving conditions, optimize energy consumption, and enhance efficiency. Integrating AI with battery management systems improves performance and battery longevity.

The integration of AI and machine learning in electric vehicle (EV) management systems presents challenges like data privacy, computational complexity, and interoperability. To overcome these, robust data encryption, optimized algorithms, and standardized communication protocols are needed. Collaborative research initiatives and regulatory frameworks will drive innovation and establish guidelines for responsible EV deployment. This collaboration among industry stakeholders, research institutions, and government agencies can accelerate EV adoption and promote sustainable transportation solutions.

The integration of machine learning, artificial intelligence, and data analytics can significantly improve electric vehicle management systems, enhancing performance, efficiency, and user experience. Despite challenges, collaborative efforts and regulatory frameworks will facilitate the continued adoption of electric vehicles as a sustainable transportation solution.

ABBREVIATIONS

ACC Adaptive Cruise Control
ADAS Advanced Driver Assistance Systems
AI Artificial Intelligence

BMS Battery Management System
CNN Convolutional Neural Network
DDPG Deep Deterministic Policy Gradient
DNN Deep Neural Network
DQN Deep Q-Network
GANs Generative Adversarial Networks
LSTM Long Short-Term Memory
ML Machine Learning
NLP Natural Language Processing
RNN Recurrent Neural Network
SoC State of Charge
V2G Vehicle-to-Grid
V2X Vehicle-to-Everything

REFERENCES

Ahmed, M., Zheng, Y., Amine, A., Fathiannasab, H., & Chen, Z. (2021). The role of artificial intelligence in the mass adoption of electric vehicles. *Joule*, *5*(9), 2296–2322. doi:10.1016/j.joule.2021.07.012

Babu, B. S., Kamalakannan, J., Meenatchi, N., Karthik, S., & Boopathi, S. (2022). Economic impacts and reliability evaluation of battery by adopting Electric Vehicle. *IEEE Explore*, 1–6.

Basso, R., Kulcsár, B., & Sanchez-Diaz, I. (2021). Electric vehicle routing problem with machine learning for energy prediction. *Transportation Research Part B: Methodological*, *145*, 24–55. doi:10.1016/j.trb.2020.12.007

Boopathi, S. (2024). Sustainable Development Using IoT and AI Techniques for Water Utilization in Agriculture. In Sustainable Development in AI, Blockchain, and E-Governance Applications (pp. 204–228). IGI Global. doi:10.4018/979-8-3693-1722-8.ch012

Boopathi, S., Gavaskar, T., Dogga, A. D., Mahendran, R. K., Kumar, A., Kathiresan, G., N., V., Ganesan, M., Ishwarya, K. R., & Ramana, G. V. (2021). *Emergency medicine delivery transportation using unmanned aerial vehicle (Patent Grant)*.

Chandran, V., Patil, C. K., Karthick, A., Ganeshaperumal, D., Rahim, R., & Ghosh, A. (2021). State of charge estimation of lithium-ion battery for electric vehicles using machine learning algorithms. *World Electric Vehicle Journal*, *12*(1), 38. doi:10.3390/wevj12010038

Chandrika, V., Sivakumar, A., Krishnan, T. S., Pradeep, J., Manikandan, S., & Boopathi, S. (2023). Theoretical Study on Power Distribution Systems for Electric Vehicles. In *Intelligent Engineering Applications and Applied Sciences for Sustainability* (pp. 1–19). IGI Global. doi:10.4018/979-8-3693-0044-2.ch001

Das, H. S., Rahman, M. M., Li, S., & Tan, C. (2020). Electric vehicles standards, charging infrastructure, and impact on grid integration: A technological review. *Renewable & Sustainable Energy Reviews*, *120*, 109618. doi:10.1016/j.rser.2019.109618

Du, G., Zou, Y., Zhang, X., Liu, T., Wu, J., & He, D. (2020). Deep reinforcement learning based energy management for a hybrid electric vehicle. *Energy*, *201*, 117591. doi:10.1016/j.energy.2020.117591

Hasan, M. K., Mahmud, M., Habib, A. A., Motakabber, S., & Islam, S. (2021). Review of electric vehicle energy storage and management system: Standards, issues, and challenges. *Journal of Energy Storage*, *41*, 102940. doi:10.1016/j.est.2021.102940

Husain, I., Ozpineci, B., Islam, M. S., Gurpinar, E., Su, G.-J., Yu, W., Chowdhury, S., Xue, L., Rahman, D., & Sahu, R. (2021). Electric drive technology trends, challenges, and opportunities for future electric vehicles. *Proceedings of the IEEE*, *109*(6), 1039–1059. doi:10.1109/JPROC.2020.3046112

Hussain, M. T., Sulaiman, N. B., Hussain, M. S., & Jabir, M. (2021). Optimal Management strategies to solve issues of grid having Electric Vehicles (EV): A review. *Journal of Energy Storage*, *33*, 102114. doi:10.1016/j.est.2020.102114

Ibrahim, A., & Jiang, F. (2021). The electric vehicle energy management: An overview of the energy system and related modeling and simulation. *Renewable & Sustainable Energy Reviews*, *144*, 111049. doi:10.1016/j.rser.2021.111049

Illmann, U., & Kluge, J. (2020). Public charging infrastructure and the market diffusion of electric vehicles. *Transportation Research Part D, Transport and Environment*, *86*, 102413. doi:10.1016/j.trd.2020.102413

İnci, M., Büyük, M., Demir, M. H., & İlbey, G. (2021). A review and research on fuel cell electric vehicles: Topologies, power electronic converters, energy management methods, technical challenges, marketing and future aspects. *Renewable & Sustainable Energy Reviews*, *137*, 110648. doi:10.1016/j.rser.2020.110648

Jayakumar, J., Nagaraj, B., Chacko, S., & Ajay, P. (2021). Conceptual implementation of artificial intelligent based E-mobility controller in smart city environment. *Wireless Communications and Mobile Computing*, *2021*, 1–8. doi:10.1155/2021/5325116

Ji, H., Alfarraj, O., & Tolba, A. (2020). Artificial intelligence-empowered edge of vehicles: Architecture, enabling technologies, and applications. *IEEE Access : Practical Innovations, Open Solutions*, *8*, 61020–61034. doi:10.1109/ACCESS.2020.2983609

Kushwah, J. S., Gupta, M., Shrivastava, S., Saxena, N., Saini, R., & Boopathi, S. (2024). Psychological Impacts, Prevention Strategies, and Intervention Approaches Across Age Groups: Unmasking Cyberbullying. In Change Dynamics in Healthcare, Technological Innovations, and Complex Scenarios (pp. 89–109). IGI Global.

Lee, J. H., Chakraborty, D., Hardman, S. J., & Tal, G. (2020). Exploring electric vehicle charging patterns: Mixed usage of charging infrastructure. *Transportation Research Part D, Transport and Environment*, *79*, 102249. doi:10.1016/j.trd.2020.102249

Lipu, M. H., Hannan, M., Karim, T. F., Hussain, A., Saad, M. H. M., Ayob, A., Miah, M. S., & Mahlia, T. I. (2021a). Intelligent algorithms and control strategies for battery management system in electric vehicles: Progress, challenges and future outlook. *Journal of Cleaner Production*, *292*, 126044. doi:10.1016/j.jclepro.2021.126044

Lipu, M. H., Hannan, M., Karim, T. F., Hussain, A., Saad, M. H. M., Ayob, A., Miah, M. S., & Mahlia, T. I. (2021b). Intelligent algorithms and control strategies for battery management system in electric vehicles: Progress, challenges and future outlook. *Journal of Cleaner Production*, *292*, 126044. doi:10.1016/j.jclepro.2021.126044

Liu, W., Placke, T., & Chau, K. (2022). Overview of batteries and battery management for electric vehicles. *Energy Reports*, *8*, 4058–4084. doi:10.1016/j.egyr.2022.03.016

Malathi, J., Kusha, K., Isaac, S., Ramesh, A., Rajendiran, M., & Boopathi, S. (2024). IoT-Enabled Remote Patient Monitoring for Chronic Disease Management and Cost Savings: Transforming Healthcare. In Advances in Explainable AI Applications for Smart Cities (pp. 371–388). IGI Global.

Pandiyan, P., Saravanan, S., Usha, K., Kannadasan, R., Alsharif, M. H., & Kim, M.-K. (2023). Technological advancements toward smart energy management in smart cities. *Energy Reports*, *10*, 648–677. doi:10.1016/j.egyr.2023.07.021

Paul, A., Thilagham, K., KG, J., Reddy, P. R., Sathyamurthy, R., & Boopathi, S. (2024). Multi-criteria Optimization on Friction Stir Welding of Aluminum Composite (AA5052-H32/B4C) using Titanium Nitride Coated Tool. Engineering Research Express.

Rahamathunnisa, U., Sudhakar, K., Padhi, S., Bhattacharya, S., Shashibhushan, G., & Boopathi, S. (2024). Sustainable Energy Generation From Waste Water: IoT Integrated Technologies. In Adoption and Use of Technology Tools and Services by Economically Disadvantaged Communities: Implications for Growth and Sustainability (pp. 225–256). IGI Global.

Revathi, S., Babu, M., Rajkumar, N., Meti, V. K. V., Kandavalli, S. R., & Boopathi, S. (2024). Unleashing the Future Potential of 4D Printing: Exploring Applications in Wearable Technology, Robotics, Energy, Transportation, and Fashion. In Human-Centered Approaches in Industry 5.0: Human-Machine Interaction, Virtual Reality Training, and Customer Sentiment Analysis (pp. 131–153). IGI Global.

Sampath, B., Sasikumar, C., & Myilsamy, S. (2023). Application of TOPSIS Optimization Technique in the Micro-Machining Process. In Trends, Paradigms, and Advances in Mechatronics Engineering (pp. 162–187). IGI Global.

Satav, S. D., Lamani, D., Harsha, K., Kumar, N., Manikandan, S., & Sampath, B. (2023). Energy and Battery Management in the Era of Cloud Computing: Sustainable Wireless Systems and Networks. In Sustainable Science and Intelligent Technologies for Societal Development (pp. 141–166). IGI Global.

Shibl, M., Ismail, L., & Massoud, A. (2020). Machine learning-based management of electric vehicles charging: Towards highly-dispersed fast chargers. *Energies*, *13*(20), 5429. doi:10.3390/en13205429

Tang, X., Guo, Q., Li, M., Wei, C., Pan, Z., & Wang, Y. (2021). Performance analysis on liquid-cooled battery thermal management for electric vehicles based on machine learning. *Journal of Power Sources*, *494*, 229727. doi:10.1016/j.jpowsour.2021.229727

Tran, D.-D., Vafaeipour, M., El Baghdadi, M., Barrero, R., Van Mierlo, J., & Hegazy, O. (2020). Thorough state-of-the-art analysis of electric and hybrid vehicle powertrains: Topologies and integrated energy management strategies. *Renewable & Sustainable Energy Reviews*, *119*, 109596. doi:10.1016/j.rser.2019.109596

Vanitha, S., Radhika, K., & Boopathi, S. (2023). Artificial Intelligence Techniques in Water Purification and Utilization. In *Human Agro-Energy Optimization for Business and Industry* (pp. 202–218). IGI Global. doi:10.4018/978-1-6684-4118-3.ch010

Veeranjaneyulu, R., Boopathi, S., Kumari, R. K., Vidyarthi, A., Isaac, J. S., & Jaiganesh, V. (2023). Air Quality Improvement and Optimisation Using Machine Learning Technique. *IEEE- Explore*, 1–6.

Venegas, F. G., Petit, M., & Perez, Y. (2021). Active integration of electric vehicles into distribution grids: Barriers and frameworks for flexibility services. *Renewable & Sustainable Energy Reviews*, *145*, 111060. doi:10.1016/j.rser.2021.111060

Verma, R., Christiana, M. B. V., Maheswari, M., Srinivasan, V., Patro, P., Dari, S. S., & Boopathi, S. (2024). Intelligent Physarum Solver for Profit Maximization in Oligopolistic Supply Chain Networks. In *AI and Machine Learning Impacts in Intelligent Supply Chain* (pp. 156–179). IGI Global. doi:10.4018/979-8-3693-1347-3.ch011

Yang, C., Zha, M., Wang, W., Liu, K., & Xiang, C. (2020). Efficient energy management strategy for hybrid electric vehicles/plug-in hybrid electric vehicles: Review and recent advances under intelligent transportation system. *IET Intelligent Transport Systems*, *14*(7), 702–711. doi:10.1049/iet-its.2019.0606

Zhang, F., Wang, L., Coskun, S., Pang, H., Cui, Y., & Xi, J. (2020). Energy management strategies for hybrid electric vehicles: Review, classification, comparison, and outlook. *Energies*, *13*(13), 3352. doi:10.3390/en13133352

Chapter 19
A Comprehensive Exploration of Mathematical Programming and Optimization Techniques in Electrical and Electronics Engineering

S. Nagarani

(iD) https://orcid.org/0000-0001-6009-5599

Department of Mathematics, Sri Ramakrishna Institute of Technology, Coimbatore, India

A. Arivarasi

Department of Electronics and Communication Engineering, Sri Sairam College of Engineering, Bangalore, India

L. Ancelin

Department of Mathematics, Madras Christian College, Chennai, India

R. Naveeth Kumar

Department of Biomedical Engineering, Dr. NGP Institute of Technology, Coimbatore, India

Arvind Sharma

Department of Electronics and Communication Engineering, Government Women Engineering College, Ajmer, India

Sureshkumar Myilsamy

Bannari Amman Institute of Technology, India

ABSTRACT

This chapter delves into the use of mathematical programming techniques in electrical and electronics engineering, highlighting their significance in enhancing efficiency, resource allocation, and decision-making processes. Techniques like linear programming, nonlinear programming, and integer programming are utilized for optimal power system resource allocation, design optimization, and discrete decision variables in circuit design. Mixed-integer programming is used for network optimization, dynamic programming for trajectory optimization, quadratic programming for control strategies, stochastic programming for uncertainties in electrical grid operations, and convex programming for structural optimization.

DOI: 10.4018/979-8-3693-1487-6.ch019

INTRODUCTION

In the dynamic landscape of Electrical and Electronics Engineering, the integration of mathematical programming techniques has become increasingly crucial for optimizing complex systems, enhancing efficiency, and addressing multifaceted challenges. This comprehensive exploration aims to unravel the diverse applications of mathematical programming in this field, shedding light on methodologies such as Linear Programming, Nonlinear Programming, Integer Programming, Mixed-Integer Programming, Dynamic Programming, Quadratic Programming, Stochastic Programming, Convex Programming, Meta-heuristic Algorithms, Multi-Objective Programming, and Game Theory. By delving into these techniques, we uncover their roles in revolutionizing resource allocation, design optimization, and decision-making processes within electrical and electronic systems (Vagaská et al., 2022).

The foundation of this exploration lies in recognizing the pivotal role played by mathematical programming in the field of Electrical and Electronics Engineering. As technological advancements accelerate, the complexity of systems grows, necessitating sophisticated tools to tackle intricate problems. Mathematical programming, with its diverse set of techniques, emerges as a powerful ally in optimizing these systems, ensuring they operate with maximum efficiency and effectiveness. Linear Programming (LP), a foundational technique in mathematical programming, is a key focus in the application domain of power systems. By optimizing resource allocation in electrical grids and addressing challenges related to load balancing and economic dispatch, LP contributes significantly to the seamless operation of power networks. This section of the exploration delves into the nuances of LP in power systems, showcasing its role in achieving optimal utilization of resources and minimizing operational costs (Ayalew et al., 2018).

Moving beyond linear constraints, the exploration navigates into the realm of Nonlinear Programming, where its applications in circuit design within the Electronics domain take center stage. Nonlinear Programming facilitates the optimization of electronic circuits, ensuring they meet stringent performance and efficiency criteria. This section uncovers the intricacies of employing Nonlinear Programming techniques to model and optimize electronic components, highlighting their significance in pushing the boundaries of circuit design (Bordin, 2015).

The exploration extends its reach to Integer Programming, emphasizing its relevance in network optimization. With a particular focus on communication networks, this section showcases how Integer Programming aids in addressing discrete decision variables, enhancing system reliability, and fortifying network robustness. By providing solutions to challenges associated with discrete decision-making, Integer Programming emerges as a valuable tool in optimizing network performance and resilience (Antoniou & Lu, 2007). The synthesis of discrete and continuous decision variables takes center stage in the discussion of Mixed-Integer Programming. This section unveils its applications in system design, where the integration of both discrete and continuous decision variables becomes crucial. With an emphasis on reliability-centered design principles, Mixed-Integer Programming emerges as a technique that harmonizes disparate elements in system design, ensuring a holistic and robust approach (Rao, 2019).

Dynamic Programming steps into the spotlight as the exploration unfolds the applications of this technique in the realm of control systems. From trajectory optimization for electronic devices to the formulation of optimal control strategies, Dynamic Programming proves instrumental in enhancing the efficiency and responsiveness of control systems within Electrical and Electronics Engineering (Cafieri et al., 2013). As the exploration progresses, it will delve deeper into Quadratic Programming, Stochastic Programming, Convex Programming, Metaheuristic Algorithms, Multi-Objective Programming, and Game Theory, providing a holistic understanding of their applications and impact in the diverse facets of Electrical and Electronics Engineering. This comprehensive examination aims to equip researchers, engineers, and students with insights into the transformative power of mathematical programming techniques in navigating the challenges and opportunities within this rapidly evolving field.

Background and Significance

Electrical and Electronics Engineering (EEE) stands at the forefront of technological innovation, playing a pivotal role in shaping the modern world. With the ever-increasing complexity of systems and the need for optimal resource utilization, the integration of mathematical programming techniques has become indispensable in addressing the multifaceted challenges inherent in this field. Historically, traditional methods in EEE primarily relied on deterministic models and empirical approaches. However, the inherent complexity of electrical and electronic systems, coupled with the demand for increased efficiency and performance, necessitated a paradigm shift towards more systematic and rigorous optimization methodologies. This shift led to the incorporation of mathematical programming, a field that leverages mathematical models and algorithms to find optimal solutions to complex problems (Mouassa & Bouktir, 2018).

The significance of mathematical programming in EEE lies in its ability to provide systematic and efficient tools for decision-making, design optimization, and resource allocation. One of the key techniques, Linear Programming (LP), has proven invaluable in the optimization of resource allocation in power systems. By formulating linear relationships among variables, LP aids in achieving optimal energy distribution, load balancing, and economic dispatch within electrical grids. This application alone demonstrates the transformative impact of mathematical programming on the foundational aspects of power systems. Moreover, the introduction of Nonlinear Programming (NLP) has revolutionized the design process in electronic circuits. Traditional circuit design methods often fell short when dealing with intricate nonlinear relationships. NLP allows engineers to model and optimize electronic components with nonlinear characteristics, enabling the creation of circuits that push the boundaries of performance and efficiency (Mouassa & Bouktir, 2018).

Integer Programming (IP) and Mixed-Integer Programming (MIP) have emerged as indispensable tools for addressing discrete decision variables in network optimization and system design. In communication networks, where decisions often involve discrete elements, IP ensures robustness and reliability. MIP extends this capability by harmonizing both discrete and continuous decision variables, presenting a comprehensive approach to system design in EEE. As technological systems become more interconnected and data-driven, stochastic elements and uncertainties pose significant challenges. This is where Stochastic Programming (SP) steps in, providing a framework to manage uncertainties in electrical grid operations and environmental impacts. SP enhances decision-making processes by accounting for the inherent variability in factors such as energy demand and supply (Shuaibu Hassan et al., 2020; Su et al., 2020).

The integration of mathematical programming techniques in Electrical and Electronics Engineering (EEE) is crucial for precision, efficiency, and innovation. These methodologies provide a systematic and quantitative approach to problem-solving, fostering advancements in power systems, circuit design, and network optimization. Their significance remains paramount in ensuring EEE stays at the forefront of technological progress.

Objectives

i. This chapter provides an in-depth analysis of various mathematical programming techniques, including linear, nonlinear, integer, dynamic, quadratic, stochastic, convex, metaheuristic, multi-objective, and game theory.

ii. Chapter highlights the various applications of mathematical programming in Electrical and Electronics Engineering, highlighting how each technique optimizes various system aspects, including power grids, circuit design, control systems, and communication networks.

iii. This chapter aims to demonstrate the effective use of mathematical programming techniques in Electrical and Electronics Engineering through real-world case studies and practical examples, providing insights into their effectiveness.

iv. This study explores the interdisciplinary integration of mathematical programming with other fields in Electrical and Electronics Engineering, highlighting its synergy with emerging technologies and addressing challenges in real-world engineering scenarios.

v. It explores the current trends and future directions in mathematical programming techniques in Electrical and Electronics Engineering, their potential impact, and their role in addressing future challenges and opportunities in the rapidly evolving technological landscape.

LINEAR PROGRAMMING IN POWER SYSTEMS

Linear Programming (LP) stands as a powerful mathematical tool that finds widespread application in the domain of power systems engineering. Its core strength lies in optimizing resource allocation within electrical grids, offering solutions to complex challenges related to load balancing and economic dispatch. This section provides a comprehensive exploration of the applications of Linear Programming in these critical areas of power systems (Khodr et al., 2002).

Optimal Resource Allocation in Electrical Grids

Optimal resource allocation is a paramount concern in electrical grids, where the efficient utilization of resources directly impacts system performance, cost-effectiveness, and sustainability. Linear Programming, with its ability to handle linear relationships among variables, becomes instrumental in achieving optimal resource allocation within the grid (Delson & Shahidehpour, 1992; Stott et al., 1979).

Various Elements and Functions

i.   **Generation Units:** Linear Programming aids in determining the optimal output levels of different generation units to meet electricity demand while minimizing costs. By formulating linear relationships among generation capacities, fuel costs, and environmental constraints, LP ensures an efficient utilization of resources.

ii.   **Renewable Energy Integration:** LP facilitates the integration of renewable energy sources into the grid by optimizing their contribution in conjunction with conventional sources. This includes considering factors like weather conditions, generation capacity, and storage capabilities to achieve an optimal mix (J. Nishanth et al., 2023).

iii. **Transmission Network:** Linear Programming addresses the optimal utilization of the transmission network by determining the most economical and efficient way to transmit electricity from generation units to load centers. This involves minimizing transmission losses and congestion while meeting demand constraints.

Load Balancing and Economic Dispatch

Load balancing is a critical aspect of power system operation, ensuring that the electricity demand is met while maintaining the stability and reliability of the grid. Economic dispatch complements this by determining the most cost-effective way to allocate generation resources to meet the load (Mouassa & Bouktir, 2018).

Various Elements and Functions

i. **Demand Forecasting:** LP incorporates demand forecasting data to optimize the allocation of generation resources. By considering forecasted demand patterns, the system can proactively balance the load, preventing under or overutilization of resources.

ii. **Cost Minimization:** Economic dispatch involves minimizing the overall cost of generation, considering factors such as fuel costs, operational constraints, and environmental considerations. Linear Programming models these factors to find the optimal dispatch strategy that meets demand at the lowest possible cost (Babu et al., 2022; Ingle et al., 2023; Mohanty et al., 2023; Ravisankar et al., 2023).

iii. **Renewable Energy Variability:** LP addresses the variability of renewable energy sources, such as wind and solar, by dynamically adjusting their contribution to the economic dispatch. This ensures that the grid remains stable despite the intermittent nature of these sources.

Linear Programming is a crucial tool in power systems, particularly in resource allocation, load balancing, and economic dispatch, which significantly improves the efficiency, reliability, and sustainability of electrical grids. Its ability to model complex relationships and optimize decision variables makes it an invaluable tool.

NONLINEAR PROGRAMMING IN CIRCUIT DESIGN

Circuit design within the realm of Electrical and Electronics Engineering demands meticulous optimization to achieve superior performance and efficiency. Nonlinear Programming (NLP) emerges as a powerful methodology to address the complexities inherent in electronic circuits, offering a sophisticated approach to both overall circuit optimization and the modeling of nonlinear electronic components (Mehmood, Zameer, Ling, et al., 2020).

Optimization of Electronic Circuits for Performance and Efficiency

i. **Parameter Tuning for Performance Enhancement:** Nonlinear Programming allows engineers to fine-tune various parameters within electronic circuits, optimizing the performance of individual components. This includes adjusting resistor values, capacitor sizes, and other parameters to meet specific performance criteria, such as frequency response, gain, or signal-to-noise ratio (Boopathi, 2019a; Boopathi et al., 2017; Boopathi & Sivakumar, 2016).

ii. **Trade-off Analysis for Efficient Designs:** NLP facilitates trade-off analyses, considering conflicting objectives in circuit design. Engineers can balance trade-offs between power consumption, speed, and other performance metrics to achieve an optimal compromise that aligns with the intended application and design constraints.

iii. **Sensitivity Analysis for Robustness:** Nonlinear Programming enables sensitivity analysis, helping designers understand how changes in component values or external conditions impact circuit performance. This capability is crucial for ensuring robust designs that can withstand variations in operating conditions.

iv. **Integration of Advanced Technologies:** NLP accommodates the integration of advanced technologies, such as integrated circuits and nanoelectronics, by optimizing the placement and configuration of these technologies within the overall circuit. This ensures that the benefits of cutting-edge technologies are fully harnessed in the design process (Boopathi, 2023; Venkateswaran et al., 2023).

v. **Dynamic Optimization for Time-Varying Signals:** In circuits handling time-varying signals, NLP can be applied dynamically to optimize the performance over different operating conditions. This is particularly valuable in communication systems or signal processing applications where signal characteristics may change dynamically.

Figure 1. Various factors considered for the nonlinear modeling for electronic components

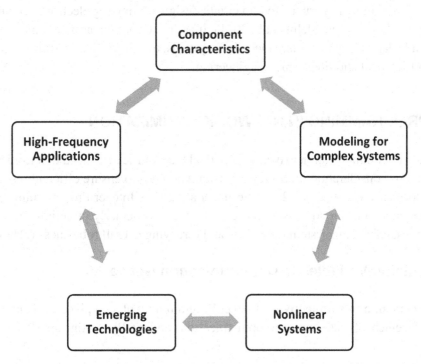

Nonlinear Modeling for Electronic Components

The nonlinear modeling for electronic components is influenced by various factors, as shown in Figure 1.

i. **Accurate Representation of Component Characteristics:** NLP enables accurate modeling of nonlinear characteristics exhibited by electronic components such as diodes, transistors, and amplifiers. This modeling ensures that the behavior of these components is faithfully represented, allowing for precise predictions during the design phase (Mehmood, Zameer, Aslam, et al., 2020).

ii. **Behavioral Modeling for Complex Systems:** Electronic circuits often involve complex systems with nonlinear behaviors. NLP facilitates behavioral modeling, capturing the intricate interactions among components and providing a realistic representation of the circuit's response to different input conditions.

iii. **Optimization of Nonlinear Systems:** By extending beyond linear relationships, NLP is well-suited for optimizing circuits with nonlinear elements. It accommodates the complexities arising from nonlinearities, ensuring that the design process considers the full range of operating conditions and component behaviors (Boopathi, Pandey, et al., 2023; Kumara et al., 2023; J. Nishanth et al., 2023).

iv. **Adaptability to Emerging Technologies:** NLP's flexibility allows it to adapt to emerging technologies and materials in electronic components. This adaptability ensures that circuit designers can explore innovative solutions without being constrained by traditional linear modeling approaches.

v. **Precision in High-Frequency Applications:** In high-frequency circuits where nonlinear effects can significantly impact performance, NLP provides a precise framework for optimization. This is crucial in applications like RF (Radio Frequency) circuits and microwave systems, where signal integrity and efficiency are paramount.

Nonlinear Programming is a crucial tool in circuit design, optimizing electronic circuits for superior performance and efficiency (Vendelin et al., 2021). It addresses nonlinear modeling challenges, ensuring precision and adaptability in modern electronic systems, meeting the increasing demands of diverse applications in Electrical and Electronics Engineering.

INTEGER PROGRAMMING IN NETWORK OPTIMIZATION

The optimization of communication networks, a critical facet of Electrical and Electronics Engineering, requires meticulous consideration of discrete decision variables to ensure efficient resource allocation and robust performance (Satav et al., 2023; Verma et al., 2024). Integer Programming (IP) emerges as a potent mathematical tool for addressing these challenges, particularly in optimizing communication network structures, enhancing system reliability, and fortifying overall robustness (Nair et al., 2020).

Discrete Decision Variables in Communication Networks

i. **Node Placement and Connectivity:** Integer Programming plays a pivotal role in determining the optimal placement of nodes within a communication network. By treating node locations as discrete decision variables, IP allows for the strategic positioning of network nodes to minimize latency, improve coverage, and enhance overall connectivity.

ii. **Routing Strategies:** In communication networks, the selection of optimal routing paths is crucial. IP facilitates the discrete selection of routes by considering different pathways, avoiding congestion, and optimizing data flow. This ensures efficient utilization of network resources and minimizes packet loss or delays.

iii. **Resource Allocation:** IP is employed to address discrete decision variables related to resource allocation, such as bandwidth assignment and channel allocation. By formulating these decisions as integer variables, IP optimizes the allocation process, preventing conflicts and congestion while enhancing the overall efficiency of communication networks.

iv. **Optimal Placement of Network Components:** Beyond node placement, IP addresses the discrete decisions associated with the placement of network components such as routers, switches, and access points. This optimization ensures an optimal layout that minimizes hardware costs, reduces latency, and enhances the network's overall performance.

v. **Security Measures:** Discrete decisions related to security measures, such as firewall placements or intrusion detection system configurations, are critical in communication networks. IP models these decisions to fortify the network against potential cyber threats while minimizing the impact on overall performance (Agrawal et al., 2023; Anitha et al., 2023; Karthik et al., 2023).

System Reliability and Robustness

i. **Redundancy Planning:** Integer Programming aids in the strategic allocation of redundant components within the network to enhance reliability. By formulating redundancy decisions as discrete variables, IP ensures that backup systems are optimally placed to minimize the impact of failures and maintain continuous network operation (Hubara et al., 2020).

ii. **Failure Recovery Strategies:** In the event of a network component failure, IP can be utilized to determine the optimal recovery strategy. This involves decisions on how to reroute traffic, activate backup systems, or redistribute loads, with a focus on minimizing downtime and ensuring seamless service continuity.

iii. **Load Balancing for Robust Performance:** IP addresses discrete decisions related to load balancing strategies, optimizing the distribution of network traffic to prevent congestion and enhance overall robustness. By considering various load scenarios as discrete variables, IP ensures that the network remains resilient under varying demand conditions.

iv. **Optimization of Backup Systems:** Integer Programming extends its application to optimizing backup systems, including decisions related to the placement and capacity of backup components. This ensures that backup resources are strategically positioned to provide effective support during network disruptions or emergencies.

v. **Sensitivity Analysis for Reliability Enhancement:** IP facilitates sensitivity analysis, allowing engineers to explore how changes in discrete variables impact network reliability. This capability is vital for understanding the trade-offs between reliability, cost, and performance, guiding decisions that enhance the robustness of communication networks (Akay et al., 2021).

Integer Programming is a crucial tool in Electrical and Electronics Engineering for network optimization, addressing discrete decision variables in communication networks to create robust, reliable, and efficient systems, ensuring optimal performance in dynamic and challenging network conditions.

MIXED-INTEGER PROGRAMMING IN SYSTEM DESIGN

System design within Electrical and Electronics Engineering involves intricate decision-making processes where both discrete and continuous variables play pivotal roles. Mixed-Integer Programming (MIP) provides a powerful framework for addressing the complexities of system design by simultaneously optimizing discrete and continuous decision variables(Akay et al., 2021; Hubara et al., 2020). This section outlines the procedural steps of applying MIP in system design, particularly focusing on the integration of both variable types and adherence to reliability-centered design principles. The procedure of mixed-integer programming in system design is illustrated in Figure 2.

i. **Formulation of Objective Function:** Begin by formulating an objective function that captures the overarching goal of the system design. This could include minimizing costs, maximizing performance, or achieving a balance between conflicting objectives. The objective function should incorporate both continuous and discrete variables, reflecting the multidimensional nature of the design problem (Boopathi, 2022e; Boopathi & Sivakumar, 2013a; Paul et al., 2024).
ii. **Identification of Decision Variables:** Clearly define the decision variables, distinguishing between those that are discrete and continuous. Discrete variables may represent choices such as component

Figure 2. Procedure of mixed-integer programming in system design

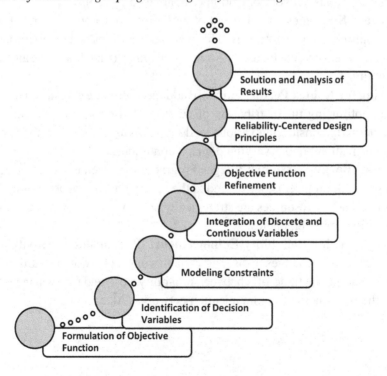

selection, system configuration, or on/off states, while continuous variables could include parameters like dimensions, capacities, or resource allocations. Ensure that the decision variables align with the specific requirements and constraints of the system being designed.

iii. **Modeling Constraints:** Establish a set of constraints that represent the physical, operational, and functional requirements of the system. These constraints should incorporate both discrete and continuous variables, reflecting the interdependencies and limitations within the design space. Constraints may include capacity constraints, performance requirements, reliability thresholds, and other system-specific criteria.

iv. **Integration of Discrete and Continuous Variables:** MIP excels in handling both discrete and continuous variables simultaneously. Formulate the mathematical model to incorporate these variables, recognizing that certain decisions may be best represented discreetly while others are more appropriately modeled as continuous. This integration allows for a more realistic representation of the decision-making process in system design.

v. **Objective Function Refinement:** Refine the objective function to balance the trade-offs between discrete and continuous decisions. Consider the impact of discrete choices on overall system performance and reliability. For instance, the selection of discrete components may affect the continuous parameters of the system, such as efficiency or response time. Optimize the objective function to achieve the desired system performance while respecting reliability-centered design principles (Boopathi, 2013; Boopathi & Sivakumar, 2013a; Paul et al., 2024).

vi. **Reliability-Centered Design Principles:** Integrate reliability-centered design principles into the optimization model. This involves explicitly incorporating reliability objectives and constraints into the mathematical formulation. Define reliability metrics, failure modes, and acceptable risk levels. MIP allows for the inclusion of discrete decisions related to redundancy, backup systems, and maintenance schedules, ensuring a robust and reliable system design.

vii. **Solver Configuration:** Utilize a MIP solver to find the optimal solution to the formulated mathematical model. Configure the solver settings to accommodate the mixed nature of the variables. Advanced MIP solvers employ sophisticated algorithms to efficiently explore the solution space, providing an optimal combination of discrete and continuous decisions that meet the defined objectives and constraints.

viii. **Analysis of Results:** Analyze the results obtained from the MIP solver, interpreting the optimal values for both discrete and continuous variables. Evaluate the implications of the design choices on system performance, cost-effectiveness, and reliability. Perform sensitivity analyses to understand how changes in discrete decisions impact overall system behavior.

Mixed-Integer Programming is a versatile system design approach that integrates discrete and continuous decision variables. Engineers can create systems that meet performance objectives and demonstrate resilience and reliability amidst uncertainties and operational challenges, using reliability-centered design principles.

DYNAMIC PROGRAMMING IN CONTROL SYSTEMS

Dynamic Programming (DP) is a powerful mathematical optimization technique that finds extensive application in the field of control systems engineering. This section explores the procedural aspects of applying DP specifically to trajectory optimization for electronic devices and the formulation of optimal control strategies. Through the lens of DP, engineers can dynamically optimize the behavior of electronic devices, ensuring efficient trajectories and control strategies that maximize performance (Nair et al., 2020).

Trajectory Optimization for Electronic Devices

i.   **Dynamic System Modeling:** Begin by developing a dynamic model that represents the behavior of the electronic device. This model should capture the interplay of variables, such as voltage, current, and temperature, over time. Accurate modeling is crucial for trajectory optimization, as it forms the basis for predicting how the device responds to control inputs (Hubara et al., 2020).

ii.   **Cost Function Definition:** Formulate a cost function that quantifies the performance goals for trajectory optimization. This function incorporates key parameters such as energy consumption, response time, or any other relevant metrics that characterize the desired trajectory. The objective is to minimize or maximize this cost function based on the system's specifications (Boopathi et al., 2018).

iii.   **Discretization of Time:** DP typically involves the discretization of time into smaller intervals. Break down the overall trajectory optimization problem into a series of subproblems by dividing time into discrete steps. This allows for a sequential decision-making process, where optimal decisions at each step contribute to the overall optimized trajectory.

iv.   **Value Function Iteration:** Apply the principle of value iteration, a hallmark of DP, to iteratively update a value function associated with each time step. The value function represents the cumulative cost or reward over time. The iterative process refines the value function, converging towards an optimal solution that minimizes the overall cost of the trajectory.

v.   **Backward Recursion:** Utilize backward recursion to compute optimal control inputs at each time step. Start from the final time step and work backward, determining the optimal control actions that contribute to minimizing the cost function. This backward recursion process ensures that decisions made earlier in the trajectory are consistent with the overall optimization objective.

vi.   **Dynamic Programming Equations:** Develop dynamic programming equations that relate the value function, state transitions, and control inputs. These equations encapsulate the dynamics of the electronic device, linking the current state to the next state based on the applied control input. Solving these equations iteratively yields the optimal trajectory for the electronic device.

Optimal Control Strategies

i.   **State-Space Representation:** Represent the control system in a state-space framework, capturing the relationship between system states, control inputs, and disturbances. This representation forms the basis for formulating optimal control strategies using DP (Akay et al., 2021).

ii.   **Formulation:** Define an objective function that encapsulates the goals of the control strategy. This could involve minimizing energy consumption, achieving a specific response time, or ensuring stability. The objective function guides the DP algorithm towards identifying the optimal control actions.

iii.   **Discretization of Control Inputs:** Discretize the space of possible control inputs to facilitate the application of DP. By breaking down the continuous range of control inputs into discrete values,

DP explores the solution space more effectively, identifying the optimal control actions within the defined constraints (Babu et al., 2022; Boopathi, 2021).

iv. **Value Iteration and Policy Improvement:** Apply the principles of value iteration and policy improvement to iteratively refine the control strategy. Value iteration refines the value function associated with different control inputs, while policy improvement determines the optimal control actions at each state. This iterative process converges towards an optimal control strategy.

v. **Implementation of Feedback Control:** Implement the derived control strategy as a feedback control system. The optimal control actions, determined through DP, serve as the basis for real-time adjustments in response to the evolving state of the electronic device. This feedback mechanism ensures that the control system adapts dynamically to changing conditions.

vi. **Performance Evaluation:** Evaluate the performance of the implemented control strategy under various operating conditions. This may involve simulation studies, testing in a controlled environment, or monitoring the electronic device's behavior in real-time. Assess the achieved objectives, such as trajectory optimization and overall system performance, against the defined metrics.

Dynamic Programming is a systematic approach used for trajectory optimization and control strategy formulation in electronic devices. It enhances performance, efficiency, and responsiveness of devices, ensuring optimal operation in diverse conditions by dynamically optimizing trajectories and control actions.

STOCHASTIC PROGRAMMING IN ELECTRICAL GRID OPERATIONS

Stochastic Programming (SP) is a crucial tool in managing uncertainties in power system planning in electrical grid operations. It accounts for fluctuating demand, renewable energy variability, and unforeseen events, enabling robust decision-making and effective environmental impact assessment and mitigation (Zakaria et al., 2020). The figure 3 illustrates the use of stochastic programming to manage uncertainties in power system planning.

Managing Uncertainties in Power System Planning

a) **Scenario Generation:** Begin by generating a set of scenarios that represent various possible future states of the power system. These scenarios should encompass uncertainties in factors such as demand, renewable energy generation, and equipment failures. Use historical data, probabilistic models, or a combination of both to create a representative set of scenarios (Mansouri et al., 2020).

b) **Stochastic Optimization Formulation:** Formulate the power system planning problem as a stochastic optimization model. Integrate the generated scenarios into the optimization framework, treating uncertain parameters as stochastic variables. The objective is to optimize decision variables under each scenario to achieve robust and reliable solutions.

c) **Decision Variables and Constraints:** Define decision variables related to power generation, transmission, and distribution, considering both continuous and discrete aspects. Formulate constraints that reflect the physical, operational, and regulatory constraints of the power system. These constraints should be adaptable to the uncertainties present in each scenario (Boopathi, 2019b, 2021; Boopathi & Sivakumar, 2016; Vignesh et al., 2018).

d) **Robust Optimization:** Leverage robust optimization techniques within the stochastic programming framework. This involves optimizing decisions not only with respect to the expected values

Figure 3. Stochastic programming for managing uncertainties in power system planning

of uncertain parameters but also considering the worst-case scenarios. Robust optimization ensures that the power system remains resilient and effective under a wide range of potential conditions.

e) **Real-Time Adaptive Strategies:** Implement real-time adaptive strategies based on the outcomes of stochastic optimization. Continuously update decision variables and operational plans as new information becomes available. This adaptive approach allows the power system to respond dynamically to unfolding uncertainties, maintaining stability and efficiency.

Environmental Impact Assessment and Mitigation

f) **Incorporating Environmental Variables:** Extend the stochastic programming model to incorporate environmental variables that impact power system operations. This may include uncertainties related to renewable energy availability, emissions, and environmental regulations. Treat these variables as stochastic parameters within the optimization model (Y. Li et al., 2022).

g) **Environmental Impact Metrics:** Define metrics that quantify the environmental impact of power system operations. These metrics could include carbon emissions, air quality indices, or other relevant environmental indicators. Formulate the objective function to minimize the environmental impact, aligning with sustainability goals (Boopathi, 2022b, 2022c; Boopathi, Alqahtani, et al., 2023; Gowri et al., 2023a).

h) **Emission Mitigation Strategies:** Develop mitigation strategies for emissions and environmental impacts within the stochastic programming framework. These strategies may involve optimizing the utilization of renewable energy sources, scheduling maintenance activities to minimize emissions, or implementing demand response programs. Stochastic programming enables the exploration of diverse mitigation options (Boopathi, 2022b; Sampath, 2021).

i) **Regulatory Compliance:** Incorporate regulatory constraints and environmental compliance requirements into the stochastic optimization model. Ensure that decision variables and operational plans adhere to environmental regulations, fostering a sustainable and responsible approach to power system operations.

j) **Trade-off Analysis:** Conduct trade-off analyses between economic objectives and environmental impact. Stochastic programming allows for the exploration of trade-offs, providing insights into the compromises and synergies between economic efficiency and environmental sustainability. This analysis aids decision-makers in finding optimal solutions that balance competing objectives.

Stochastic Programming is a method used in electrical grid operations to manage uncertainties and assess environmental impact, providing a comprehensive and adaptive approach for decision-makers to navigate complex challenges, ensuring power system resilience, sustainability, and efficiency in an ever-changing landscape.

ALGORITHM FOR METAHEURISTIC ALGORITHMS IN SIGNAL PROCESSING

Metaheuristic algorithms like Evolutionary Algorithms (EAs) and Swarm-based approaches are powerful optimization techniques in signal processing applications. They efficiently explore solution spaces, making them valuable tools for optimizing signal processing tasks. This article provides a general algorithmic framework for applying metaheuristic algorithms in signal optimization (Pal et al., 2022). The figure 4 depicts the steps of Evolutionary Algorithms (EAs) in signal optimization.

Algorithm for Evolutionary Algorithms (EAs) in Signal Optimization

a) **Initialization:** Generate an initial population of potential solutions, each representing a candidate signal optimization strategy. Define the objective function that quantifies the quality of a solution, capturing the optimization goals in signal processing (Qaisar et al., 2022).

b) **Evaluation:** Evaluate the fitness of each solution in the population using the defined objective function. Assess how well each solution satisfies the optimization criteria for signal processing.

c) **Selection:** Use a selection mechanism (e.g., roulette wheel or tournament selection) to choose individuals from the population based on their fitness. Favor solutions with higher fitness values for reproduction.

d) **Crossover:** Apply crossover operators to recombine selected individuals, generating new solutions that inherit characteristics from both parent solutions. Mimic genetic recombination to explore potential improvements in signal optimization strategies.

e) **Mutation:** Introduce random changes to selected individuals through mutation operators, introducing diversity to the population. Encourage exploration by introducing small, random alterations to the signal optimization strategies (Boopathi & Kumar, 2024; Boopathi & Sivakumar, 2013a).

f) **Replacement:** Replace the old population with the newly generated offspring, ensuring the population size remains constant. Maintain a diverse set of solutions to explore a broader range of signal optimization possibilities.

Figure 4. Steps of evolutionary algorithms (EAs) in signal optimization

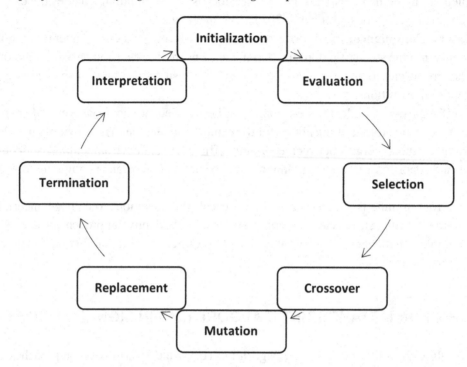

g) **Termination:** Repeat the evaluation, selection, crossover, mutation, and replacement steps for a predefined number of iterations or until convergence criteria are met. Convergence criteria may include reaching a target fitness level or a plateau in improvement.

h) **Output:** Output the best solution found during the optimization process as the optimized signal processing strategy.

Algorithm for Swarm-Based Approaches in Artificial Intelligence

This algorithmic framework provides a generic structure for applying metaheuristic algorithms, specifically Evolutionary Algorithms and Swarm-based approaches, to signal processing optimization. The adaptability and exploration capabilities of these algorithms make them effective tools for finding optimal solutions in diverse signal processing applications (Boopathi et al., 2022; Boopathi & Sivakumar, 2013a; Sampath, Pandian, et al., 2022).

a) **Initialization:** Initialize a swarm of agents (particles) representing potential solutions to the signal optimization problem. Define the objective function that measures the quality of a solution in signal processing (El-Kenawy et al., 2022).

b) **Velocity and Position Updates:** Update the velocity and position of each particle based on its current state, previous velocity, and the influence of the best solution found by the particle and the best solution found by the entire swarm. Simulate the particles' movements through the solution space, guiding them toward promising signal optimization strategies.

c) **Evaluation:** Evaluate the fitness of each particle by applying the defined objective function to their current positions. Assess how well each particle's current position satisfies the signal processing optimization criteria.

d) **Local and Global Best Updates:** Update the local best position for each particle, considering its historical best and the current evaluation. Update the global best position for the entire swarm, considering the best positions found by all particles (Boopathi et al., 2022; Boopathi & Sivakumar, 2013a; Sampath, Pandian, et al., 2022).

e) **Termination:** Repeat the velocity and position updates, evaluation, and best position updates for a predefined number of iterations or until convergence criteria are met. Convergence criteria may include reaching a target fitness level or a plateau in improvement.

f) **Output:** Output the best solution found during the optimization process as the optimized signal processing strategy.

EVOLUTIONARY MULTI-OBJECTIVE PROGRAMMING (EMOP) IN RESOURCE ALLOCATION

Evolutionary Multi-Objective Programming (EMOP) is a powerful optimization approach that addresses resource allocation problems involving conflicting objectives. In the context of system design and network optimization with multiple objectives, EMOP offers a systematic framework for finding solutions that balance competing goals (Boopathi, 2022f; Boopathi et al., 2021; Gowri et al., 2023b). The following outlines how EMOP can be applied to resource allocation, particularly focusing on balancing conflicting objectives and optimizing networks with multiple criteria (El-Kenawy et al., 2022).

Balancing Conflicting Objectives in System Design

1. **Problem Formulation:** Define the system design problem, specifying the multiple conflicting objectives that need to be balanced. These objectives could include minimizing costs, maximizing performance, and ensuring reliability (Ojstersek et al., 2020).

2. **Objective Function Definitions:** Formulate the objective functions, each representing one of the conflicting objectives. These functions should capture the quantitative measures of system performance related to the specified objectives.

3. **Decision Variables:** Identify the decision variables related to system design. These variables may involve discrete choices, such as selecting components, as well as continuous variables, like parameters for tuning system parameters.

4. **Pareto Dominance:** Utilize the concept of Pareto dominance to compare and evaluate solutions. A solution is considered Pareto dominant if it is better than another solution in at least one objective without being worse in any other objective. This allows for the identification of trade-offs and optimal compromises (Behmanesh et al., 2021).

5. **Initialization:** Generate an initial population of potential solutions, each representing a different configuration of the system design with varying levels of compromise between conflicting objectives.

6. **Evolutionary Operators:** Apply evolutionary operators such as crossover and mutation to create new solutions in subsequent generations. These operators should be designed to preserve Pareto dominance and explore the trade-off space efficiently.
7. **Population Update:** Use a selection mechanism that favors solutions not yet explored or those that contribute to a diverse representation of the Pareto front. This ensures the exploration of the entire trade-off space.
8. **Termination Criteria:** Set termination criteria, such as the number of generations or convergence of the Pareto front, to determine when to stop the evolutionary process (J. R. Nishanth et al., 2023; Sampath, C., et al., 2022).
9. **Output:** Output the set of Pareto-optimal solutions discovered during the EMOP process. These solutions represent different compromises between conflicting objectives in the system design.

Network Optimization With Multiple Objectives

i. **Problem Formulation:** Formulate the network optimization problem considering multiple conflicting objectives, such as minimizing latency, maximizing throughput, and minimizing energy consumption (Janardhana et al., 2023; Kannan et al., 2022).
ii. **Objective Function Definitions:** Define objective functions that quantify the performance metrics associated with the network optimization objectives. These could include measures like delay, packet loss, and energy efficiency.
iii. **Decision Variables:** Identify decision variables related to network configuration, including parameters such as routing paths, bandwidth allocation, and node placements.
iv. **Pareto Dominance:** Apply Pareto dominance to evaluate solutions, allowing for the identification of trade-offs and optimal solutions that balance conflicting objectives.
v. **Initialization:** Initialize a population of potential network configurations, considering various trade-offs between conflicting objectives.
vi. **Evolutionary Operators:** Employ evolutionary operators that respect Pareto dominance, allowing for the creation of new solutions that explore different regions of the trade-off space.
vii. **Population Update:** Use a selection mechanism that promotes diversity and exploration of the Pareto front. This ensures a comprehensive exploration of the multiple-objective optimization landscape.
viii. **Termination Criteria:** Define termination criteria for the EMOP process, determining when to stop the evolution. This could be based on the number of generations, convergence of the Pareto front, or other specified conditions.
ix. **Output:** Output the Pareto-optimal solutions found during the optimization process. These solutions represent the network configurations that provide the best trade-offs between conflicting objectives.

Evolutionary Multi-Objective Programming is a versatile and effective approach for resource allocation problems involving conflicting objectives. Whether applied to system design or network optimization, EMOP facilitates the discovery of Pareto-optimal solutions that represent the optimal compromises in the face of multiple conflicting objectives (Boopathi et al., 2021; Boopathi & Sivakumar, 2013b; Gowri et al., 2023b; Sathish et al., 2023).

GAME THEORY APPLICATIONS IN DECISION-MAKING

Game Theory provides a powerful framework for understanding and modeling decision-making in scenarios where multiple entities, or players, interact. In the context of communication networks, both competitive and cooperative scenarios are prevalent. This section explores the applications of Game Theory in decision-making within communication networks, addressing competitive situations where entities strive to maximize their individual gains and cooperative situations where entities collaborate for mutual benefits (Palafox-Alcantar et al., 2020). The figure 5 illustrates various competitive scenarios that can be addressed using game theory.

Competitive Scenarios

i.   **Player Definition:** Identify the players in the communication network, which may include service providers, users, or devices. Each player has its own objectives and strategies (Hang et al., 2020).
ii.   **Utility Functions:** Define utility functions for each player, representing their individual preferences and goals. These functions quantify the payoff or benefit that each player receives based on the chosen strategies and the actions of other players.
iii. **Strategic Interactions:** Model the strategic interactions among players in the communication network. Players make decisions to maximize their own utility, taking into account the decisions made by others. This may involve issues like bandwidth allocation, pricing strategies, or resource utilization.
iv.   **Nash Equilibrium:** Analyze the game to identify Nash Equilibrium, where no player has an incentive to unilaterally deviate from their chosen strategy given the strategies of others. Nash Equilibrium provides insights into stable states in competitive scenarios.
v.   **Network Security:** Apply Game Theory to model scenarios related to network security, where malicious entities may attempt to compromise the integrity or availability of the network. Players make decisions about intrusion detection, prevention, and response strategies to protect their interests.

Figure 5. The carious competitive scenarios problem for applying game theory

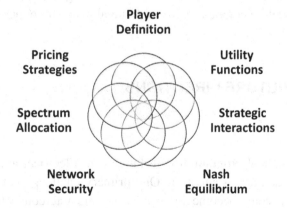

vi. **Spectrum Allocation:** In wireless communication networks, model the competition among users or service providers for spectrum allocation. Game Theory can help optimize the allocation of limited frequency bands, considering factors like interference and user demand.

vii. **Pricing Strategies:** Explore competitive pricing strategies in communication networks where service providers aim to attract users while maximizing their revenue. Game Theory can guide the analysis of price competition, bundling strategies, and market equilibrium.

Cooperative Scenarios

a) **Coalition Formation:** Define cooperative scenarios where players form coalitions to achieve common goals. This could involve the collaboration of communication devices to improve network efficiency or the cooperation of service providers for mutual benefits (He et al., 2020).

b) **Cooperative Game Models:** Use cooperative game models, such as the Shapley value or the core, to allocate benefits among cooperating players. These models provide fair and stable solutions to cooperative scenarios, considering the contributions of each player.

c) **Resource Sharing:** Model resource-sharing scenarios, where entities in the communication network collaborate to share resources efficiently. This could include bandwidth sharing, load balancing, or cooperative caching to enhance overall network performance.

d) **Distributed Antenna Systems:** Apply Game Theory to optimize the deployment of Distributed Antenna Systems (DAS) in cooperative scenarios. Players, such as mobile operators, may collaborate to jointly deploy and share DAS infrastructure to improve coverage and capacity.

e) **Quality of Service Improvement:** Explore cooperative scenarios aimed at enhancing Quality of Service (QoS) in communication networks. Players may cooperate to manage network congestion, prioritize traffic, or collectively invest in infrastructure upgrades to improve overall service quality.

f) **Collaborative Spectrum Sensing:** In cognitive radio networks, use Game Theory to model collaborative spectrum sensing among users. Players collaborate to detect and share information about available spectrum bands, optimizing spectrum utilization and minimizing interference.

g) **Network Virtualization:** Model cooperative scenarios in network virtualization, where multiple operators collaborate to share virtualized resources. Game Theory can assist in allocating virtual resources efficiently, maximizing overall network performance.

Game Theory is a crucial tool for decision-making in communication networks, addressing both competitive and cooperative scenarios. It enhances understanding and optimization of decision-making processes, whether it's modeling competition for individual gains or cooperation for shared objectives (T. Li et al., 2022).

CHALLENGES AND FUTURE DIRECTIONS

Challenges

The application of mathematical programming techniques in Electrical and Electronics Engineering faces several challenges that warrant attention. One primary challenge is the complexity of modern engineering systems. As systems become more intricate and interconnected, mathematical models need to evolve to capture the multidimensional aspects of these systems accurately. The incorporation of uncertainties, nonlinearities, and dynamic behaviors poses additional challenges, requiring advanced mathematical programming approaches to handle these complexities (He et al., 2020; Ojstersek et al., 2020; Palafox-Alcantar et al., 2020).

Another challenge is the scalability of optimization models. As the size and complexity of engineering problems grow, traditional optimization algorithms may struggle to find solutions within acceptable timeframes. Addressing scalability challenges necessitates the development of innovative algorithms and optimization techniques capable of handling large-scale problems efficiently (Palaniappan et al., 2023; Senthil et al., 2023). Interdisciplinary collaboration is crucial, yet challenging, as mathematical programming techniques need to be seamlessly integrated with domain-specific knowledge. Bridging the gap between mathematical modeling and engineering expertise is essential for the successful application of optimization techniques in real-world engineering problems.

Future Directions

The future of mathematical programming techniques in Electrical and Electronics Engineering holds promising avenues for advancement and innovation. One key direction is the integration of machine learning techniques with mathematical optimization. Combining the learning capabilities of machine learning models with the precision of optimization techniques can enhance the adaptability and intelligence of engineering systems (Ojstersek et al., 2020; Stott et al., 1979).

Advancements in metaheuristic algorithms and nature-inspired optimization techniques, such as genetic algorithms and simulated annealing, offer potential breakthroughs in solving complex engineering optimization problems. The exploration of hybrid algorithms, combining the strengths of different optimization approaches, can provide robust solutions to multifaceted challenges. Embracing real-time optimization and control strategies is another future direction. As engineering systems become more dynamic, the ability to adapt and optimize in real-time becomes paramount. Developing optimization algorithms capable of continuous adaptation to changing conditions will be crucial for achieving optimal performance in dynamic environments (J. Nishanth et al., 2023; Sampath et al., 2023; Yupapin et al., 2023).

Furthermore, addressing the challenges of sustainability and resilience in engineering systems will be a focal point. Optimization techniques can play a pivotal role in designing eco-friendly and resilient systems, considering factors such as energy efficiency, environmental impact, and robustness to uncertainties (Boopathi, 2022a, 2022d). The application of mathematical programming techniques in Electrical and Electronics Engineering requires a collaborative effort from researchers, practitioners, and interdisciplinary collaborators. By enhancing algorithmic capabilities, embracing emerging technologies, and aligning optimization strategies, the field can unlock new possibilities and solve complex engineering problems.

CONCLUSION

In conclusion, the chapter provides a comprehensive exploration of the application of mathematical programming techniques in Electrical and Electronics Engineering. The versatility of mathematical programming, encompassing linear programming, nonlinear programming, integer programming, mixed-integer programming, dynamic programming, quadratic programming, stochastic programming, convex programming, metaheuristic algorithms, multi-objective programming, and game theory, is highlighted throughout various engineering domains.

The chapter emphasizes the significance of these techniques in addressing diverse challenges, ranging from optimal resource allocation and system design to network optimization and decision-making in competitive and cooperative scenarios. The effectiveness of mathematical programming in navigating complex, real-world problems is evident, offering systematic approaches for optimizing solutions, managing uncertainties, and achieving desired objectives.

However, the chapter also acknowledges the challenges that the field faces, such as handling the increasing complexity of modern engineering systems, scalability issues, and the need for interdisciplinary collaboration. Overcoming these challenges requires continuous innovation, advancements in algorithmic capabilities, and the integration of emerging technologies.

Looking forward, the chapter identifies promising future directions, including the integration of machine learning techniques, advancements in metaheuristic algorithms, real-time optimization, and a focus on sustainability and resilience. These directions aim to further enhance the adaptability, intelligence, and eco-friendliness of engineering systems, aligning them with the evolving demands of the contemporary landscape.

In essence, the chapter underscores the integral role of mathematical programming techniques in shaping the present and future of Electrical and Electronics Engineering. By providing a foundation for systematic problem-solving, optimization, and decision-making, these techniques contribute significantly to the advancement and innovation within the field. As research and technological advancements continue, the integration of mathematical programming techniques is poised to play a pivotal role in addressing the evolving challenges and complexities of engineering systems.

ABBREVIATIONS

- DP - Dynamic Programming
- Eas - Evolutionary Algorithms
- EEE - Electrical and Electronics Engineering
- EMOP - Evolutionary Multi-Objective Programming
- IP - Integer Programming
- LP - Linear Programming
- MIP - Mixed-Integer Programming
- NLP - Nonlinear Programming

REFERENCES

Agrawal, A. V., Magulur, L. P., Priya, S. G., Kaur, A., Singh, G., & Boopathi, S. (2023). Smart Precision Agriculture Using IoT and WSN. In *Handbook of Research on Data Science and Cybersecurity Innovations in Industry 4.0 Technologies* (pp. 524–541). IGI Global. doi:10.4018/978-1-6684-8145-5.ch026

Akay, B., Karaboga, D., Gorkemli, B., & Kaya, E. (2021). A survey on the artificial bee colony algorithm variants for binary, integer and mixed integer programming problems. *Applied Soft Computing*, *106*, 107351. doi:10.1016/j.asoc.2021.107351

Anitha, C., Komala, C., Vivekanand, C. V., Lalitha, S., & Boopathi, S. (2023). Artificial Intelligence driven security model for Internet of Medical Things (IoMT). *IEEE Explore*, 1–7.

Antoniou, A., & Lu, W.-S. (2007). *Practical optimization: Algorithms and engineering applications* (Vol. 19). Springer.

Ayalew, M. F., Hussen, S., & Pasam, G. (2018). Optimization techniques in power system. *International Journal of Engineering Applied Sciences and Technology*, *3*(10), 2455–2143.

Babu, B. S., Kamalakannan, J., Meenatchi, N., Karthik, S., & Boopathi, S. (2022). Economic impacts and reliability evaluation of battery by adopting Electric Vehicle. *IEEE Explore*, 1–6.

Behmanesh, R., Rahimi, I., & Gandomi, A. H. (2021). Evolutionary many-objective algorithms for combinatorial optimization problems: A comparative study. *Archives of Computational Methods in Engineering*, *28*(2), 673–688. doi:10.1007/s11831-020-09415-3

Boopathi, S. (2013). *Experimental study and multi-objective optimization of near-dry wire-cut electrical discharge machining process* [PhD Thesis]. http://hdl.handle.net/10603/16933

Boopathi, S. (2019). Experimental investigation and parameter analysis of LPG refrigeration system using Taguchi method. *SN Applied Sciences*, *1*(8), 892. doi:10.1007/s42452-019-0925-2

Boopathi, S. (2021). *Experimental Evaluation of a Domestic Refrigerator Working With LPG*. Academic Press.

Boopathi, S. (2022a). An experimental investigation of Quench Polish Quench (QPQ) coating on AISI 4150 steel. *Engineering Research Express*, *4*(4), 045009. doi:10.1088/2631-8695/ac9ddd

Boopathi, S. (2022b). An investigation on gas emission concentration and relative emission rate of the near-dry wire-cut electrical discharge machining process. *Environmental Science and Pollution Research International*, *29*(57), 86237–86246. doi:10.1007/s11356-021-17658-1 PMID:34837614

Boopathi, S. (2022c). Cryogenically treated and untreated stainless steel grade 317 in sustainable wire electrical discharge machining process: A comparative study. *Springer :Environmental Science and Pollution Research*, 1–10.

Boopathi, S. (2022e). Experimental investigation and multi-objective optimization of cryogenic Friction-stir-welding of AA2014 and AZ31B alloys using MOORA technique. *Materials Today. Communications*, *33*, 104937. doi:10.1016/j.mtcomm.2022.104937

Boopathi, S. (2023). Deep Learning Techniques Applied for Automatic Sentence Generation. In Promoting Diversity, Equity, and Inclusion in Language Learning Environments (pp. 255–273). IGI Global. doi:10.4018/978-1-6684-3632-5.ch016

Boopathi, S., Alqahtani, A. S., Mubarakali, A., & Panchatcharam, P. (2023). Sustainable developments in near-dry electrical discharge machining process using sunflower oil-mist dielectric fluid. *Environmental Science and Pollution Research International*, 1–20. doi:10.1007/s11356-023-27494-0 PMID:37199846

Boopathi, S., & Kumar, P. (2024). Advanced bioprinting processes using additive manufacturing technologies: Revolutionizing tissue engineering. *3D Printing Technologies: Digital Manufacturing, Artificial Intelligence, Industry 4.0*, 95.

Boopathi, S., Kumaresan, A., & Manohar, N., & KrishnaMoorthi, R. (2017). Review on Effect of Process Parameters—Friction Stir Welding Process. *International Research Journal of Engineering and Technology*, 4(7), 272–278.

Boopathi, S., Myilsamy, S., & Sukkasamy, S. (2021). *Experimental Investigation and Multi-Objective Optimization of Cryogenically Cooled Near-Dry Wire-Cut EDM Using TOPSIS Technique*. IJAMT.

Boopathi, S., Pandey, B. K., & Pandey, D. (2023). Advances in Artificial Intelligence for Image Processing: Techniques, Applications, and Optimization. In Handbook of Research on Thrust Technologies' Effect on Image Processing (pp. 73–95). IGI Global.

Boopathi, S., Saranya, A., Raghuraman, S., & Revanth, R. (2018). Design and Fabrication of Low Cost Electric Bicycle. *International Research Journal of Engineering and Technology*, 5(3), 146–147.

Boopathi, S., & Sivakumar, K. (2013). Experimental investigation and parameter optimization of near-dry wire-cut electrical discharge machining using multi-objective evolutionary algorithm. *International Journal of Advanced Manufacturing Technology*, 67(9–12), 2639–2655. doi:10.1007/s00170-012-4680-4

Boopathi, S., & Sivakumar, K. (2016). Optimal parameter prediction of oxygen-mist near-dry wire-cut EDM. *Inderscience: International Journal of Manufacturing Technology and Management*, 30(3–4), 164–178. doi:10.1504/IJMTM.2016.077812

Boopathi, S., Sureshkumar, M., & Sathiskumar, S. (2022). Parametric Optimization of LPG Refrigeration System Using Artificial Bee Colony Algorithm. *International Conference on Recent Advances in Mechanical Engineering Research and Development*, 97–105.

Bordin, C. (2015). *Mathematical optimization applied to thermal and electrical energy systems*. Academic Press.

Cafieri, S., Liberti, L., Messine, F., & Nogarede, B. (2013). Optimal design of electrical machines: Mathematical programming formulations. *COMPEL-The International Journal for Computation and Mathematics in Electrical and Electronic Engineering*, 32(3), 977–996.

Delson, J. K., & Shahidehpour, S. (1992). Linear programming applications to power system economics, planning and operations. *IEEE Transactions on Power Systems*, 7(3), 1155–1163. doi:10.1109/59.207329

El-Kenawy, E.-S. M., Mirjalili, S., Alassery, F., Zhang, Y.-D., Eid, M. M., El-Mashad, S. Y., Aloyaydi, B. A., Ibrahim, A., & Abdelhamid, A. A. (2022). Novel meta-heuristic algorithm for feature selection, unconstrained functions and engineering problems. *IEEE Access : Practical Innovations, Open Solutions*, 10, 40536–40555. doi:10.1109/ACCESS.2022.3166901

Gowri, N. V., Dwivedi, J. N., Krishnaveni, K., Boopathi, S., Palaniappan, M., & Medikondu, N. R. (2023). Experimental investigation and multi-objective optimization of eco-friendly near-dry electrical discharge machining of shape memory alloy using Cu/SiC/Gr composite electrode. *Environmental Science and Pollution Research International*, *30*(49), 1–19. doi:10.1007/s11356-023-26983-6 PMID:37126160

Hang, P., Lv, C., Xing, Y., Huang, C., & Hu, Z. (2020). Human-like decision making for autonomous driving: A noncooperative game theoretic approach. *IEEE Transactions on Intelligent Transportation Systems*, *22*(4), 2076–2087. doi:10.1109/TITS.2020.3036984

He, J., Li, Y., Li, H., Tong, H., Yuan, Z., Yang, X., & Huang, W. (2020). Application of game theory in integrated energy system systems: A review. *IEEE Access : Practical Innovations, Open Solutions*, *8*, 93380–93397. doi:10.1109/ACCESS.2020.2994133

Hubara, I., Nahshan, Y., Hanani, Y., Banner, R., & Soudry, D. (2020). Improving post training neural quantization: Layer-wise calibration and integer programming. *arXiv Preprint arXiv:2006.10518*.

Ingle, R. B., Swathi, S., Mahendran, G., Senthil, T., Muralidharan, N., & Boopathi, S. (2023). Sustainability and Optimization of Green and Lean Manufacturing Processes Using Machine Learning Techniques. In *Circular Economy Implementation for Sustainability in the Built Environment* (pp. 261–285). IGI Global. doi:10.4018/978-1-6684-8238-4.ch012

Janardhana, K., Anushkannan, N., Dinakaran, K., Puse, R. K., & Boopathi, S. (2023). Experimental Investigation on Microhardness, Surface Roughness, and White Layer Thickness of Dry EDM. *Engineering Research Express*, *5*(2), 025022. doi:10.1088/2631-8695/acce8f

Kannan, E., Trabelsi, Y., Boopathi, S., & Alagesan, S. (2022). Influences of cryogenically treated work material on near-dry wire-cut electrical discharge machining process. *Surface Topography : Metrology and Properties*, *10*(1), 015027. doi:10.1088/2051-672X/ac53e1

Karthik, S., Hemalatha, R., Aruna, R., Deivakani, M., Reddy, R. V. K., & Boopathi, S. (2023). Study on Healthcare Security System-Integrated Internet of Things (IoT). In Perspectives and Considerations on the Evolution of Smart Systems (pp. 342–362). IGI Global.

Khodr, H., Gomez, J., Barnique, L., Vivas, J., Paiva, P., Yusta, J., & Urdaneta, A. (2002). A linear programming methodology for the optimization of electric power-generation schemes. *IEEE Transactions on Power Systems*, *17*(3), 864–869. doi:10.1109/TPWRS.2002.800982

Kumara, V., Mohanaprakash, T., Fairooz, S., Jamal, K., Babu, T., & Sampath, B. (2023). Experimental Study on a Reliable Smart Hydroponics System. In *Human Agro-Energy Optimization for Business and Industry* (pp. 27–45). IGI Global. doi:10.4018/978-1-6684-4118-3.ch002

Li, T., Peng, G., Zhu, Q., & Başar, T. (2022). The confluence of networks, games, and learning a game-theoretic framework for multiagent decision making over networks. *IEEE Control Systems*, *42*(4), 35–67. doi:10.1109/MCS.2022.3171478

Li, Y., Wang, B., Yang, Z., Li, J., & Chen, C. (2022). Hierarchical stochastic scheduling of multi-community integrated energy systems in uncertain environments via Stackelberg game. *Applied Energy*, *308*, 118392. doi:10.1016/j.apenergy.2021.118392

Mansouri, S., Ahmarinejad, A., Ansarian, M., Javadi, M., & Catalao, J. (2020). Stochastic planning and operation of energy hubs considering demand response programs using Benders decomposition approach. *International Journal of Electrical Power & Energy Systems*, *120*, 106030. doi:10.1016/j.ijepes.2020.106030

Mehmood, A., Zameer, A., Aslam, M. S., & Raja, M. A. Z. (2020). Design of nature-inspired heuristic paradigm for systems in nonlinear electrical circuits. *Neural Computing & Applications*, *32*(11), 7121–7137. doi:10.1007/s00521-019-04197-7

Mehmood, A., Zameer, A., Ling, S. H., Rehman, A. U., & Raja, M. A. Z. (2020). Integrated computational intelligent paradigm for nonlinear electric circuit models using neural networks, genetic algorithms and sequential quadratic programming. *Neural Computing & Applications*, *32*(14), 10337–10357. doi:10.1007/s00521-019-04573-3

Mohanty, A., Venkateswaran, N., Ranjit, P., Tripathi, M. A., & Boopathi, S. (2023). Innovative Strategy for Profitable Automobile Industries: Working Capital Management. In Handbook of Research on Designing Sustainable Supply Chains to Achieve a Circular Economy (pp. 412–428). IGI Global.

Mouassa, S., & Bouktir, T. (2018). Mathematics in electrical and electronic engineering. *COMPEL*, 208.

Nair, V., Bartunov, S., Gimeno, F., Von Glehn, I., Lichocki, P., Lobov, I., O'Donoghue, B., Sonnerat, N., Tjandraatmadja, C., Wang, P., & Associates. (2020). Solving mixed integer programs using neural networks. *arXiv Preprint arXiv:2012.13349*.

Nishanth, J., Deshmukh, M. A., Kushwah, R., Kushwaha, K. K., Balaji, S., & Sampath, B. (2023). Particle Swarm Optimization of Hybrid Renewable Energy Systems. In *Intelligent Engineering Applications and Applied Sciences for Sustainability* (pp. 291–308). IGI Global. doi:10.4018/979-8-3693-0044-2.ch016

Nishanth, J. R., Deshmukh, M. A., Kushwah, R., Kushwaha, K. K., Balaji, S., & Sampath, B. (2023). Particle Swarm Optimization of Hybrid Renewable Energy Systems. In B. K. Mishra (Ed.), Advances in Civil and Industrial Engineering (pp. 291–308). IGI Global. doi:10.4018/979-8-3693-0044-2.ch016

Ojstersek, R., Brezocnik, M., & Buchmeister, B. (2020). Multi-objective optimization of production scheduling with evolutionary computation: A review. *International Journal of Industrial Engineering Computations*, *11*(3), 359–376. doi:10.5267/j.ijiec.2020.1.003

Pal, H. S., Kumar, A., Vishwakarma, A., & Ahirwal, M. K. (2022). Electrocardiogram signal compression using tunable-Q wavelet transform and meta-heuristic optimization techniques. *Biomedical Signal Processing and Control*, *78*, 103932. doi:10.1016/j.bspc.2022.103932

Palafox-Alcantar, P., Hunt, D., & Rogers, C. (2020). The complementary use of game theory for the circular economy: A review of waste management decision-making methods in civil engineering. *Waste Management (New York, N.Y.)*, *102*, 598–612. doi:10.1016/j.wasman.2019.11.014 PMID:31778971

Palaniappan, M., Tirlangi, S., Mohamed, M. J. S., Moorthy, R. S., Valeti, S. V., & Boopathi, S. (2023). Fused Deposition Modelling of Polylactic Acid (PLA)-Based Polymer Composites: A Case Study. In Development, Properties, and Industrial Applications of 3D Printed Polymer Composites (pp. 66–85). IGI Global.

Paul, A., Thilagham, K. KG, J., Reddy, P. R., Sathyamurthy, R., & Boopathi, S. (2024). Multi-criteria Optimization on Friction Stir Welding of Aluminum Composite (AA5052-H32/B4C) using Titanium Nitride Coated Tool. Engineering Research Express.

Qaisar, S. M., Khan, S. I., Dallet, D., Tadeusiewicz, R., & Pławiak, P. (2022). Signal-piloted processing metaheuristic optimization and wavelet decomposition based elucidation of arrhythmia for mobile healthcare. *Biocybernetics and Biomedical Engineering*, 42(2), 681–694. doi:10.1016/j.bbe.2022.05.006

Rao, S. S. (2019). *Engineering optimization: Theory and practice.* John Wiley & Sons. doi:10.1002/9781119454816

Ravisankar, A., Sampath, B., & Asif, M. M. (2023). Economic Studies on Automobile Management: Working Capital and Investment Analysis. In Multidisciplinary Approaches to Organizational Governance During Health Crises (pp. 169–198). IGI Global.

Sampath, B. (2021). *Sustainable Eco-Friendly Wire-Cut Electrical Discharge Machining: Gas Emission Analysis.* Academic Press.

Sampath, B., Pandian, M., Deepa, D., & Subbiah, R. (2022). Operating parameters prediction of liquefied petroleum gas refrigerator using simulated annealing algorithm. *AIP Conference Proceedings*, 2460(1), 070003. doi:10.1063/5.0095601

Sampath, B., Sasikumar, C., & Myilsamy, S. (2023). Application of TOPSIS Optimization Technique in the Micro-Machining Process. In Trends, Paradigms, and Advances in Mechatronics Engineering (pp. 162–187). IGI Global.

Sampath, B. C. S., & Myilsamy, S. (2022). Application of TOPSIS Optimization Technique in the Micro-Machining Process. In M. A. Mellal (Ed.), Advances in Mechatronics and Mechanical Engineering (pp. 162–187). IGI Global. doi:10.4018/978-1-6684-5887-7.ch009

Satav, S. D., Lamani, D., Harsha, K., Kumar, N., Manikandan, S., & Sampath, B. (2023). Energy and Battery Management in the Era of Cloud Computing: Sustainable Wireless Systems and Networks. In Sustainable Science and Intelligent Technologies for Societal Development (pp. 141–166). IGI Global.

Sathish, T., Sunagar, P., Singh, V., Boopathi, S., Al-Enizi, A. M., Pandit, B., Gupta, M., & Sehgal, S. S. (2023). Characteristics estimation of natural fibre reinforced plastic composites using deep multi-layer perceptron (MLP) technique. *Chemosphere*, *337*, 139346. doi:10.1016/j.chemosphere.2023.139346 PMID:37379988

Senthil, T., Puviyarasan, M., Babu, S. R., Surakasi, R., Sampath, B., & Associates. (2023). Industrial Robot-Integrated Fused Deposition Modelling for the 3D Printing Process. In Development, Properties, and Industrial Applications of 3D Printed Polymer Composites (pp. 188–210). IGI Global.

Shuaibu Hassan, A., Sun, Y., & Wang, Z. (2020). Optimization techniques applied for optimal planning and integration of renewable energy sources based on distributed generation: Recent trends. *Cogent Engineering*, 7(1), 1766394. doi:10.1080/23311916.2020.1766394

Stott, B., Marinho, J., & Alsac, O. (1979). Review of linear programming applied to power system rescheduling. *IEEE Conference Proceedings Power Industry Computer Applications Conference, 1979. PICA-79.*, 142–154. 10.1109/PICA.1979.720058

Su, W., Yu, S. S., Li, H., Iu, H. H.-C., & Fernando, T. (2020). An MPC-based dual-solver optimization method for DC microgrids with simultaneous consideration of operation cost and power loss. *IEEE Transactions on Power Systems, 36*(2), 936–947. doi:10.1109/TPWRS.2020.3011038

Vagaská, A., Gombár, M., & Straka, L. (2022). Selected Mathematical Optimization Methods for Solving Problems of Engineering Practice. *Energies, 15*(6), 2205. doi:10.3390/en15062205

Vendelin, G. D., Pavio, A. M., Rohde, U. L., & Rudolph, M. (2021). *Microwave circuit design using linear and nonlinear techniques.* John Wiley & Sons. doi:10.1002/9781119741725

Venkateswaran, N., Vidhya, R., Naik, D. A., Raj, T. M., Munjal, N., & Boopathi, S. (2023). Study on Sentence and Question Formation Using Deep Learning Techniques. In *Digital Natives as a Disruptive Force in Asian Businesses and Societies* (pp. 252–273). IGI Global. doi:10.4018/978-1-6684-6782-4.ch015

Verma, R., Christiana, M. B. V., Maheswari, M., Srinivasan, V., Patro, P., Dari, S. S., & Boopathi, S. (2024). Intelligent Physarum Solver for Profit Maximization in Oligopolistic Supply Chain Networks. In *AI and Machine Learning Impacts in Intelligent Supply Chain* (pp. 156–179). IGI Global. doi:10.4018/979-8-3693-1347-3.ch011

Vignesh, S., Arulshri, K., SyedSajith, S., Kathiresan, S., Boopathi, S., & Dinesh Babu, P. (2018). Design and development of ornithopter and experimental analysis of flapping rate under various operating conditions. *Materials Today: Proceedings, 5*(11), 25185–25194. doi:10.1016/j.matpr.2018.10.320

Yupapin, P., Trabelsi, Y., Nattappan, A., & Boopathi, S. (2023). Performance improvement of wire-cut electrical discharge machining process using cryogenically treated super-conductive state of Monel-K500 alloy. *Iranian Journal of Science and Technology. Transaction of Mechanical Engineering, 47*(1), 267–283. doi:10.1007/s40997-022-00513-0

Zakaria, A., Ismail, F. B., Lipu, M. H., & Hannan, M. A. (2020). Uncertainty models for stochastic optimization in renewable energy applications. *Renewable Energy, 145*, 1543–1571. doi:10.1016/j.renene.2019.07.081

Compilation of References

. Kaykova, O., Khriyenko, O., Kovtun, D., Naumenko, A., Terziyan, V., & Zharko, A. (2007). Challenges of General Adaptation Framework for Industrial Semantic Web. *Semantic Web-Based Information Systems: State-of-the-Art Applications, CyberTech Publishing*, 61-97.

Abayomi-Alli, O. O., Damaševičius, R., Misra, S., & Maskeliūnas, R. (2021). Cassava disease recognition from low-quality images using enhanced data augmentation model and deep learning. *Expert Systems: International Journal of Knowledge Engineering and Neural Networks*, *38*(7), e12746. doi:10.1111/exsy.12746

Abdulsalam, Y. S., & Hedabou, M. (2021). Security and privacy in cloud computing: Technical review. *Future Internet*, *14*(1), 11. doi:10.3390/fi14010011

About ABET. (2023). ABET. https://www.abet.org/about-abet/

Abraham, A., Hörandner, F., Zefferer, T., & Zwattendorfer, B. (2020). E-government in the public cloud: Requirements and opportunities. *Electronic Government, an International Journal, 16*(3), 260–280.

Achouch, M., Dimitrova, M., Ziane, K., Sattarpanah Karganroudi, S., Dhouib, R., Ibrahim, H., & Adda, M. (2022). On Predictive Maintenance in Industry 4.0: Overview, Models, and Challenges. *Applied Sciences (Basel, Switzerland)*, *12*(16), 8081. doi:10.3390/app12168081

ACTIVAGE. (2021). *About ACTIVAGE*. Retrieved May 11, 2021 from https://www.activageproject.eu/activage-project/#About-ACTIVAGE

Addy, H. S., Nurmalasari, Wahyudi, A., Sholeh, A., Anugrah, C., Iriyanto, F., Darmanto, W., & Sugiharto, B. (2017). Detection and response of sugarcane against the infection of Sugarcane mosaic virus (SCMV) in Indonesia. *Agronomy (Basel)*, *7*(3), 50. doi:10.3390/agronomy7030050

Adem, K., Ozguven, M. M., & Altas, Z. (2023). A sugar beet leaf disease classification method based on image processing and deep learning. *Multimedia Tools and Applications*, *82*(8), 12577–12594. doi:10.1007/s11042-022-13925-6

Adli, H. K., Remli, M. A., Wan Salihin Wong, K. N. S., Ismail, N. A., González-Briones, A., Corchado, J. M., & Mohamad, M. S. (2023). Recent Advancements and Challenges of AIoT Application in Smart Agriculture: A Review. *Sensors (Basel)*, *23*(7), 3752. doi:10.3390/s23073752 PMID:37050812

Adly, A. S., Adly, A. S., & Adly, M. S. (2020). Approaches based on artificial intelligence and the internet of intelligent things to prevent the spread of COVID-19: Scoping review. *Journal of Medical Internet Research*, *22*(8), e19104. doi:10.2196/19104 PMID:32584780

Aggarwal, P. K., Jain, P., Mehta, J., Garg, R., Makar, K., & Chaudhary, P. (2021). Machine Learning, Data Mining, and Big Data Analytics for 5G-Enabled IoT. In Blockchain for 5G-Enabled IoT (pp. 351–375). Springer International Publishing. doi:10.1007/978-3-030-67490-8_14

Agrawal, A. V., Pitchai, R., Senthamaraikannan, C., Balaji, N. A., Sajithra, S., & Boopathi, S. (2023). Digital Education System During the COVID-19 Pandemic. In Using Assistive Technology for Inclusive Learning in K-12 Classrooms (pp. 104–126). IGI Global. doi:10.4018/978-1-6684-6424-3.ch005

Agrawal, A. V., Shashibhushan, G., Pradeep, S., Padhi, S., Sugumar, D., & Boopathi, S. (2023). Synergizing Artificial Intelligence, 5G, and Cloud Computing for Efficient Energy Conversion Using Agricultural Waste. In Sustainable Science and Intelligent Technologies for Societal Development (pp. 475–497). IGI Global.

Agrawal, A. V., Magulur, L. P., Priya, S. G., Kaur, A., Singh, G., & Boopathi, S. (2023). Smart Precision Agriculture Using IoT and WSN. In *Handbook of Research on Data Science and Cybersecurity Innovations in Industry 4.0 Technologies* (pp. 524–541). IGI Global. doi:10.4018/978-1-6684-8145-5.ch026

Ahaidous, K., Tabaa, M., & Hachimi, H. (2023). Towards IoT-Big Data architecture for future education. *Procedia Computer Science*, *220*, 348–355. doi:10.1016/j.procs.2023.03.045

Ahamad, A., Anand, A., & Bhargava, P. (2020). Accentdb: A database of non-native english accents to assist neural speech recognition. *arXiv preprint arXiv:2005.07973*.

Ahmad Loti, N. N., Mohd Noor, M. R., & Chang, S. W. (2021). Integrated analysis of machine learning and deep learning in chili pest and disease identification. *Journal of the Science of Food and Agriculture*, *101*(9), 3582–3594. doi:10.1002/jsfa.10987 PMID:33275806

Ahmed, A., Tangri, P., Panda, A., Ramani, D., & Karmakar, S. (2019, December). Vfnet: A convolutional architecture for accent classification. In *2019 IEEE 16th India Council International Conference (INDICON)* (pp. 1-4). IEEE. 10.1109/INDICON47234.2019.9030363

Ahmed, A. A., & Alshandoli, A. S. (2020). Using of neural network controller and fuzzy pid control to improve electric vehicle stability based on a14-dof model. *2020 International Conference on Electrical Engineering (ICEE)*, 1–6. 10.1109/ICEE49691.2020.9249784

Ahmed, M., Zheng, Y., Amine, A., Fathiannasab, H., & Chen, Z. (2021). The role of artificial intelligence in the mass adoption of electric vehicles. *Joule*, *5*(9), 2296–2322. doi:10.1016/j.joule.2021.07.012

Akay, B., Karaboga, D., Gorkemli, B., & Kaya, E. (2021). A survey on the artificial bee colony algorithm variants for binary, integer and mixed integer programming problems. *Applied Soft Computing*, *106*, 107351. doi:10.1016/j.asoc.2021.107351

Akkiraju, R., Farrell, J., Miller, J., Nagarajan, M., Schmidt, M., Sheth, A., & Verma, K. (2005). *Web Service Semantics - WSDL-S*. A joint UGA-IBM Technical Note, version 1.0. http://lsdis.cs.uga.edu/projects/METEOR-S/WSDL-S

Aktas, E., & Meng, Y. (2017). An Exploration of Big Data Practices in Retail Sector. *Logistics*, *1*(2), 12. doi:10.3390/logistics1020012

Al Abdulwahid, A., Clarke, N., Stengel, I., Furnell, S., & Reich, C. (2016). Continuous and transparent multimodal authentication: Reviewing the state of the art. *Cluster Computing*, *19*(1), 455–474. doi:10.1007/s10586-015-0510-4

Al Sumarmad, K. A., Sulaiman, N., Wahab, N. I. A., & Hizam, H. (2022). Energy management and voltage control in microgrids using artificial neural networks, PID, and fuzzy logic controllers. *Energies*, *15*(1), 303. doi:10.3390/en15010303

Alahi, M. E. E., Sukkuea, A., Tina, F. W., Nag, A., Kurdthongmee, W., Suwannarat, K., & Mukhopadhyay, S. C. (2023). Integration of IoT-Enabled Technologies and Artificial Intelligence (AI) for Smart City Scenario: Recent Advancements and Future Trends. *Sensors (Basel)*, *23*(11), 5206. doi:10.3390/s23115206 PMID:37299934

Al-Amin, M., Karim, D. Z., & Bushra, T. A. (2019, December). Prediction of rice disease from leaves using deep convolution neural network towards a digital agricultural system. In *2019 22nd International Conference on Computer and Information Technology (ICCIT)* (pp. 1-5). IEEE. 10.1109/ICCIT48885.2019.9038229

Alamsyah, A., Kusuma, G. N. W., & Ramadhani, D. P. (2024, February 26). A Review on Decentralized Finance Ecosystems. *Future Internet*, *16*(3), 76. doi:10.3390/fi16030076

Aldwairi, M., & Aldhanhani, S. (2017, August). Multi-factor authentication system. In *The 2017 International Conference on Research and Innovation in Computer Engineering and Computer Sciences (RICCES'2017)*. Malaysia Technical Scientist Association.

Ali, M. N., Senthil, T., Ilakkiya, T., Hasan, D. S., Ganapathy, N. B. S., & Boopathi, S. (2024). IoT's Role in Smart Manufacturing Transformation for Enhanced Household Product Quality. In *Advanced Applications in Osmotic Computing* (pp. 252–289). IGI Global. doi:10.4018/979-8-3693-1694-8.ch014

Ali, O., & Osmanaj, V. (2020). The role of government regulations in the adoption of cloud computing: A case study of local government. *Computer Law & Security Report*, *36*, 105396. doi:10.1016/j.clsr.2020.105396

Aliyu, A. A., & Liu, J. (2023). Blockchain-Based Smart Farm Security Framework for the Internet of Things. *Sensors (Basel)*, *23*(18), 7992. doi:10.3390/s23187992 PMID:37766046

Al-Jumaili, Z., Bassiouny, T., Alanezi, A., Khan, W., Al-Jumeily, D., & Hussain, A. J. (2022, August). Classification of Spoken English Accents Using Deep Learning and Speech Analysis. In *International Conference on Intelligent Computing* (pp. 277-287). Cham: Springer International Publishing. 10.1007/978-3-031-13832-4_24

Almadhor, A., Rauf, H. T., Lali, M. I. U., Damaševičius, R., Alouffi, B., & Alharbi, A. (2021). AI-driven framework for recognition of guava plant diseases through machine learning from DSLR camera sensor based high resolution imagery. *Sensors (Basel)*, *21*(11), 3830. doi:10.3390/s21113830 PMID:34205885

Almeida, F., & Simoes, J. (2019). The Role of Serious Games, Gamification and Industry 4.0 Tools in the Education 4.0 Paradigm. *Contemporary Educational Technology*, *10*(2), 120–136. doi:10.30935/cet.554469

Al-Othman, A., Tawalbeh, M., Martis, R., Dhou, S., Orhan, M., Qasim, M., & Olabi, A. G. (2022). Artificial intelligence and numerical models in hybrid renewable energy systems with fuel cells: Advances and prospects. *Energy Conversion and Management*, *253*, 115154. doi:10.1016/j.enconman.2021.115154

Alouffi, B., Hasnain, M., Alharbi, A., Alosaimi, W., Alyami, H., & Ayaz, M. (2021). A systematic literature review on cloud computing security: Threats and mitigation strategies. *IEEE Access : Practical Innovations, Open Solutions*, *9*, 57792–57807. doi:10.1109/ACCESS.2021.3073203

Alrubayyi, H., Alshareef, M. S., Nadeem, Z., Abdelmoniem, A. M., & Jaber, M. (2024, February 29). Security Threats and Promising Solutions Arising from the Intersection of AI and IoT: A Study of IoMT and IoET Applications. *Future Internet*, *16*(3), 85. doi:10.3390/fi16030085

Alsanad, H., Sadik, A., Ucan, O., Ilyas, M., & Bayat, O. (2022). YOLO-V3 based real-time drone detection algorithm. *Multimedia Tools and Applications*, *81*, 26185–26198.

Alshamrani, M. (2022). IoT and artificial intelligence implementations for remote healthcare monitoring systems: A survey. *Journal of King Saud University. Computer and Information Sciences*, *34*(8), 4687–4701. doi:10.1016/j.jksuci.2021.06.005

Al-Sudairy, M. T., & Vasista, T. G. K. (2011). Semantic Data Integration Approaches. *International Journal of Web & Semantic Technology*, *2*(1), 12. doi:10.5121/ijwest.2011.2101

Alto, V. (2019). Face recognition with opencv: Haar cascade. *DataSeries Imagine the future of data*.

Altulaihan, E., Almaiah, M. A., & Aljughaiman, A. (2024, January 22). Anomaly Detection IDS for Detecting DoS Attacks in IoT Networks Based on Machine Learning Algorithms. *Sensors (Basel), 24*(2), 713. doi:10.3390/s24020713 PMID:38276404

Alvi, A. N., Ali, M., Saleh, M. S., Alkhathami, M., Alsadie, D., Alghamdi, B., & Alenzi, B. (2024, February 5). TM-PAD: Time-Slot-Based Medium Access Control Protocol to Meet Adaptive Data Requirements for Trusted Nodes in Fog-Enabled Smart Cities. *Applied Sciences (Basel, Switzerland), 14*(3), 1319. doi:10.3390/app14031319

Amara, F. Z., Hemam, M., Djezzar, M., & Maimour, M. (2022). Semantic web technologies for internet of things semantic interoperability. *Advances in Information, Communication and Cybersecurity: Proceedings of ICI2C'21*, 133–143.

Anand, G., & Kumawat, A. (2021). Object detection and position tracking in real time using Raspberry Pi. *Materials Today: Proceedings, 47*, 3221–3226. doi:10.1016/j.matpr.2021.06.437

Angundjaja, C. Y., Wang, Y., & Jiang, W. (2021). Power management for connected EVs using a fuzzy logic controller and artificial neural network. *Applied Sciences (Basel, Switzerland), 12*(1), 52. doi:10.3390/app12010052

Anitha, C., Komala, C., Vivekanand, C. V., Lalitha, S., & Boopathi, S. (2023). Artificial Intelligence driven security model for Internet of Medical Things (IoMT). *IEEE Explore*, 1–7.

Anshari, M., Almunawar, M. N., Lim, S. A., & Al-Mudimigh, A. (2019). Customer relationship management and big data enabled: Personalization & customization of services. *Applied Computing and Informatics, 15*(2), 94–101. doi:10.1016/j.aci.2018.05.004

Antoniou, A., & Lu, W.-S. (2007). *Practical optimization: Algorithms and engineering applications* (Vol. 19). Springer.

Antoniou, G., & Harmelen, F. V. (2008). *A Semantic Web Primer*. The MIT Press.

Anwar, A. A. (2022). A survey of semantic web (Web 3.0), its applications, challenges, future and its relation with Internet of things (IoT). *Web Intelligence, Preprint*, 1–30.

Apan, A., Held, A., Phinn, S., & Markley, J. (2004). Detecting sugarcane 'orange rust'disease using EO-1 Hyperion hyperspectral imagery. *International Journal of Remote Sensing, 25*(2), 489–498. doi:10.1080/01431160310001618031

Arafeh, M., Wazzeh, M., Ould-Slimane, H., Talhi, C., Mourad, A., & Otrok, H. (2023, October 16). Efficient Privacy-Preserving ML for IoT: Cluster-Based Split Federated Learning Scheme for Non-IID Data. *2023 7th Cyber Security in Networking Conference (CSNet)*. 10.1109/CSNet59123.2023.10339772

Archana, K. S., & Sahayadhas, A. (2018). Automatic rice leaf disease segmentation using image processing techniques. *Int. J. Eng. Technol, 7*(3.27), 182-185.

Arita, Y., Nozaki, N., & Demizu, K. (2012). Mechanical design platform on Engineering Cloud. *Fujitsu Scientific and Technical Journal*, 422–427.

Aruna, R., Devi, M. S., Anand, A., Dutta, U., & Sagar, C. N. S. (2023, January). Inception Nesterov Momentum Adam L2 Regularized Learning Rate CNN for Sugarcane Disease Classification. In *2023 Third International Conference on Advances in Electrical, Computing, Communication and Sustainable Technologies (ICAECT)* (pp. 1-4). IEEE. 10.1109/ICAECT57570.2023.10117792

Asaad, R. R., Ali, R. I., Ali, Z. A., & Shaaban, A. A. (2023). Image Processing with Python Libraries. *Academic Journal of Nawroz University, 12*(2), 410–416. doi:10.25007/ajnu.v12n2a1754

Atharvan, G., Koolikkara Madom Krishnamoorthy, S., Dua, A., & Gupta, S. (2022). A way forward towards a technology-driven development of industry 4.0 using big data analytics in 5G-enabled IIoT. *International Journal of Communication Systems*, *35*(1), e5014. Advance online publication. doi:10.1002/dac.5014

Atieh, A. T. (2021). The next generation cloud technologies: A review on distributed cloud, fog and edge computing and their opportunities and challenges. *ResearchBerg Review of Science and Technology*, *1*(1), 1–15.

Awotunde, J. B., Adeniyi, E. A., Ogundokun, R. O., & Ayo, F. E. (2021). *Application of Big Data with Fintech in Financial Services*. doi:10.1007/978-981-33-6137-9_3

Ayalew, M. F., Hussen, S., & Pasam, G. (2018). Optimization techniques in power system. *International Journal of Engineering Applied Sciences and Technology*, *3*(10), 2455–2143.

Azrour, M., Mabrouki, J., Guezzaz, A., & Farhaoui, Y. (2021). New enhanced authentication protocol for internet of things. *Big Data Mining and Analytics*, *4*(1), 1–9. doi:10.26599/BDMA.2020.9020010

Baader, F., & Nutt, W. (2003). *Basic Description Logics, The description logic handbook*. Cambridge University Press.

Babadagli, T. (2023). Reassessment of petroleum engineering education: Is it the end of an era or a new start? *Education for Chemical Engineers*, *43*, 1–9. doi:10.1016/j.ece.2023.01.003

Babangida, L., Perumal, T., Mustapha, N., & Yaakob, R. (2022). Internet of Things (IoT) Based Activity Recognition Strategies in Smart Homes: A Review. *IEEE Sensors Journal*, *22*(9), 8327–8336. doi:10.1109/JSEN.2022.3161797

Babu, B. S., Kamalakannan, J., Meenatchi, N., Karthik, S., & Boopathi, S. (2022). Economic impacts and reliability evaluation of battery by adopting Electric Vehicle. *IEEE Explore*, 1–6.

Badhon, S. S. I., Rahaman, H., Rupon, F. R., & Abujar, S. (2021). Bengali accent classification from speech using different machine learning and deep learning techniques. In *Soft Computing Techniques and Applications: Proceeding of the International Conference on Computing and Communication (IC3 2020)* (pp. 503-513). Springer Singapore. 10.1007/978-981-15-7394-1_46

Badshah, A., Rehman, G. U., Farman, H., Ghani, A., Sultan, S., Zubair, M., & Nasralla, M. M. (2023). Transforming Educational Institutions: Harnessing the Power of Internet of Things, Cloud, and Fog Computing. *Future Internet*, *15*(11), 367. doi:10.3390/fi15110367

Bakhshi, T., Ghita, B., & Kuzminykh, I. (2024, January 22). A Review of IoT Firmware Vulnerabilities and Auditing Techniques. *Sensors (Basel)*, *24*(2), 708. doi:10.3390/s24020708 PMID:38276399

Balaji, M. S., & Roy, S. K. (2017). Value co-creation with Internet of things technology in the retail industry. *Journal of Marketing Management*, *33*(1–2), 7–31. doi:10.1080/0267257X.2016.1217914

Balhasan, S., & Musbah, I. (2021). The next generation of petroleum engineering students: Challenges and needs. *Journal of Positive School Psychology*, *6*(8), 4450–4457.

Banane, M., & Belangour, A. (2019). A survey on RDF data stores based on NoSQL systems for the Semantic Web applications. In Advanced Intelligent Systems for Sustainable Development (AI2SD'2018) Volume 5: Advanced Intelligent Systems for Computing Sciences (pp. 444-451). Springer International Publishing. doi:10.1007/978-3-030-11928-7_40

Barbosa, A. T., da Silva, C. C., Caetano, R. L., da Silva, D. P. S., Barbosa, J. V., & Pinto, Z. T. (2022). Agile methodologies: And its applicability in the marketing area. *Revista Ibero-Americana de Humanidades. Ciência & Educação (Bauru)*, *8*(3), 1659–1669.

Barnaghi, P., Wang, W., Henson, C., & Taylor, K. (2012). Semantics for the Internet of Things: Early progress and back to the future. *International Journal on Semantic Web and Information Systems*, 8(1), 1–21. doi:10.4018/jswis.2012010101

Barrera, R. M., Martinez-Rodriguez, J. L., Tiwari, S., & Barrera, V. (2023). Political Marketing App Based on Citizens. In *Global Perspectives on the Strategic Role of Marketing Information Systems* (pp. 118–147). IGI Global. doi:10.4018/978-1-6684-6591-2.ch008

Bashir, K., Rehman, M., & Bari, M. (2019). Detection and classification of rice diseases: An automated approach using textural features. *Mehran University Research Journal of Engineering & Technology*, 38(1), 239–250. doi:10.22581/muet1982.1901.20

Basso, R., Kulcsár, B., & Sanchez-Diaz, I. (2021). Electric vehicle routing problem with machine learning for energy prediction. *Transportation Research Part B: Methodological*, 145, 24–55. doi:10.1016/j.trb.2020.12.007

Behmanesh, R., Rahimi, I., & Gandomi, A. H. (2021). Evolutionary many-objective algorithms for combinatorial optimization problems: A comparative study. *Archives of Computational Methods in Engineering*, 28(2), 673–688. doi:10.1007/s11831-020-09415-3

Beiderbeck, D., Frevel, N., von der Gracht, H. A., Schmidt, S. L., & Schweitzer, V. M. (2021). Preparing, conducting, and analyzing Delphi surveys: Cross-disciplinary practices, new directions, and advancements. *MethodsX*, 8, 101401. Advance online publication. doi:10.1016/j.mex.2021.101401 PMID:34430297

Ben Dhaou, I. (2023). Design and Implementation of an Internet-of-Things-Enabled Smart Meter and Smart Plug for Home-Energy-Management System. *Electronics (Basel)*, 12(19), 4041. doi:10.3390/electronics12194041

Benjamin Argyle-Ross. (2018). *Agile Methodology: An Overview, The art of iterative and incremental software development.* https://zenkit.com/en/blog/agile-methodology-an-overview/

Bergamaschi, S., Beneventano, D., Guerra, F., & Vincini, M. (2004). Building a tourism information provider with the MOMIS system. *Information Technology & Tourism*, 7(3-4), 221–238.

Bergmann, R., & Schaaf, M. (2003). Structural Case-Based Reasoning and Ontology-Based Knowledge Management: A Perfect Match? *Journal of Universal Computer Science, UCS*, 9(7), 608–626.

Berners-Lee, T., Hendler, J., & Lassila, O. (2001). The Semantic Web. *Scientific American*, 284(May), 34–43. doi:10.1038/scientificamerican0501-34 PMID:11323639

Berners-Lee, T., Hendler, J., & Lassila, O. (2001). The Semantic Web: A new form of Web content that is meaningful to computers will unleash a revolution of new possibilities. *Scientific American*, 284(5), 34–43.

Bharadwaj, H. K., Agarwal, A., Chamola, V., Lakkaniga, N. R., Hassija, V., Guizani, M., & Sikdar, B. (2021). A Review on the Role of Machine Learning in Enabling IoT Based Healthcare Applications. *IEEE Access : Practical Innovations, Open Solutions*, 9, 38859–38890. doi:10.1109/ACCESS.2021.3059858

Bhartiya, V. P., Janghel, R. R., & Rathore, Y. K. (2022, March). Rice Leaf Disease Prediction Using Machine Learning. In *2022 Second International Conference on Power, Control and Computing Technologies (ICPC2T)* (pp. 1-5). IEEE. 10.1109/ICPC2T53885.2022.9776692

Bianchini, D., Antonellis, V. A., Melchiori, M., & Salvi, D. (2006). Semantic Enriched Service Discovery. *International Conference in Data Engineering Workshop,* 38.

Bibri, S. E. (2018). The IoT for smart sustainable cities of the future: An analytical framework for sensor-based big data applications for environmental sustainability. *Sustainable Cities and Society*, 38, 230–253. doi:10.1016/j.scs.2017.12.034

Bibri, S. E., Krogstie, J., Kaboli, A., & Alahi, A. (2024). Smarter eco-cities and their leading-edge artificial intelligence of things solutions for environmental sustainability: A comprehensive systematic review. *Environmental Science and Ecotechnology*, *19*, 100330. doi:10.1016/j.ese.2023.100330 PMID:38021367

Biswas, A., & Wang, H.-C. (2023). Autonomous vehicles enabled by the integration of IoT, edge intelligence, 5G, and blockchain. *Sensors (Basel)*, *23*(4), 1963. doi:10.3390/s23041963 PMID:36850560

Bizer, C., Volz, J., Kobilarov, G., & Gaedke, M. (2009, April). Silk-a link discovery framework for the web of data. In *18th International World Wide Web Conference* (Vol. 122). Academic Press.

Bizer, C., Heese, R., Mochol, M., Oldakowski, R., Tolksdorf, R., & Eckstein, R. (2005). The impact of semantic web technologies on job recruitment processes. In *Wirtschaftsinformatik 2005: eEconomy, eGovernment, eSociety* (pp. 1367–1381). Physica-Verlag HD. doi:10.1007/3-7908-1624-8_72

Blomqvist, E. (2014). The use of Semantic Web technologies for decision support–a survey. *Semantic Web*, *5*(3), 177–201. doi:10.3233/SW-2012-0084

Bobde, Y., Narayanan, G., Jati, M., Raj, R. S. P., Cvitić, I., & Peraković, D. (2024, February 7). Enhancing Industrial IoT Network Security through Blockchain Integration. *Electronics (Basel)*, *13*(4), 687. doi:10.3390/electronics13040687

Bodine, J., & Hochbaum, D. S. (2022). A Better Decision Tree: The Max-Cut Decision Tree with Modified PCA Improves Accuracy and Running Time. *SN Computer Science*, *3*(4), 313. doi:10.1007/s42979-022-01147-4

Boopathi, S. (2013). *Experimental study and multi-objective optimization of near-dry wire-cut electrical discharge machining process* [PhD Thesis]. http://hdl.handle.net/10603/16933

Boopathi, S. (2021). *Experimental Evaluation of a Domestic Refrigerator Working With LPG*. Academic Press.

Boopathi, S. (2021). *Pollution monitoring and notification: Water pollution monitoring and notification using intelligent RC boat*. Academic Press.

Boopathi, S. (2022). Cryogenically treated and untreated stainless steel grade 317 in sustainable wire electrical discharge machining process: A comparative study. *Environmental Science and Pollution Research*, 1–10.

Boopathi, S. (2022). Performance Improvement of Eco-Friendly Near-Dry wire-Cut Electrical Discharge Machining Process Using Coconut Oil-Mist Dielectric Fluid. *Journal of Advanced Manufacturing Systems*.

Boopathi, S. (2022c). Cryogenically treated and untreated stainless steel grade 317 in sustainable wire electrical discharge machining process: A comparative study. *Springer :Environmental Science and Pollution Research*, 1–10.

Boopathi, S. (2023). Deep Learning Techniques Applied for Automatic Sentence Generation. In Promoting Diversity, Equity, and Inclusion in Language Learning Environments (pp. 255–273). IGI Global. doi:10.4018/978-1-6684-3632-5.ch016

Boopathi, S. (2024a). Balancing Innovation and Security in the Cloud: Navigating the Risks and Rewards of the Digital Age. In Improving Security, Privacy, and Trust in Cloud Computing (pp. 164–193). IGI Global.

Boopathi, S. (2024b). Balancing Innovation and Security in the Cloud: Navigating the Risks and Rewards of the Digital Age. In Improving Security, Privacy, and Trust in Cloud Computing (pp. 164–193). IGI Global.

Boopathi, S. (2024c). Sustainable Development Using IoT and AI Techniques for Water Utilization in Agriculture. In Sustainable Development in AI, Blockchain, and E-Governance Applications (pp. 204–228). IGI Global. doi:10.4018/979-8-3693-1722-8.ch012

Boopathi, S., & Kumar, P. (2024). Advanced bioprinting processes using additive manufacturing technologies: Revolutionizing tissue engineering. *3D Printing Technologies: Digital Manufacturing, Artificial Intelligence, Industry 4.0*, 95.

Boopathi, S., Gavaskar, T., Dogga, A. D., Mahendran, R. K., Kumar, A., Kathiresan, G., N., V., Ganesan, M., Ishwarya, K. R., & Ramana, G. V. (2021). *Emergency medicine delivery transportation using unmanned aerial vehicle (Patent Grant).*

Boopathi, S., Karthikeyan, K. R., Jaiswal, C., Dabi, R., Sunagar, P., & Malik, S. (2024). *IoT based Automatic Cooling Tower.* Academic Press.

Boopathi, S., Kumar, P. K. S., Meena, R. S., Sudhakar, M., & Associates. (2023). Sustainable Developments of Modern Soil-Less Agro-Cultivation Systems: Aquaponic Culture. In Human Agro-Energy Optimization for Business and Industry (pp. 69–87). IGI Global.

Boopathi, S., Pandey, B. K., & Pandey, D. (2023). Advances in Artificial Intelligence for Image Processing: Techniques, Applications, and Optimization. In Handbook of Research on Thrust Technologies' Effect on Image Processing (pp. 73–95). IGI Global.

Boopathi, S. (2019). Experimental investigation and parameter analysis of LPG refrigeration system using Taguchi method. *SN Applied Sciences, 1*(8), 892. doi:10.1007/s42452-019-0925-2

Boopathi, S. (2022). An extensive review on sustainable developments of dry and near-dry electrical discharge machining processes. *ASME: Journal of Manufacturing Science and Engineering, 144*(5), 050801–1.

Boopathi, S. (2022). An investigation on gas emission concentration and relative emission rate of the near-dry wire-cut electrical discharge machining process. *Environmental Science and Pollution Research International, 29*(57), 86237–86246. doi:10.1007/s11356-021-17658-1 PMID:34837614

Boopathi, S. (2022a). An experimental investigation of Quench Polish Quench (QPQ) coating on AISI 4150 steel. *Engineering Research Express, 4*(4), 045009. doi:10.1088/2631-8695/ac9ddd

Boopathi, S. (2022e). Experimental investigation and multi-objective optimization of cryogenic Friction-stir-welding of AA2014 and AZ31B alloys using MOORA technique. *Materials Today. Communications, 33*, 104937. doi:10.1016/j.mtcomm.2022.104937

Boopathi, S. (2023). Internet of Things-Integrated Remote Patient Monitoring System: Healthcare Application. In *Dynamics of Swarm Intelligence Health Analysis for the Next Generation* (pp. 137–161). IGI Global. doi:10.4018/978-1-6684-6894-4.ch008

Boopathi, S. (2024a). Advancements in Machine Learning and AI for Intelligent Systems in Drone Applications for Smart City Developments. In *Futuristic e-Governance Security With Deep Learning Applications* (pp. 15–45). IGI Global. doi:10.4018/978-1-6684-9596-4.ch002

Boopathi, S., Alqahtani, A. S., Mubarakali, A., & Panchatcharam, P. (2023). Sustainable developments in near-dry electrical discharge machining process using sunflower oil-mist dielectric fluid. *Environmental Science and Pollution Research International*, 1–20. doi:10.1007/s11356-023-27494-0 PMID:37199846

Boopathi, S., Balasubramani, V., Kumar, R. S., & Singh, G. R. (2021). The influence of human hair on kenaf and Grewia fiber-based hybrid natural composite material: An experimental study. *Functional Composites and Structures, 3*(4), 045011. doi:10.1088/2631-6331/ac3afc

Boopathi, S., & Khang, A. (2023). AI-Integrated Technology for a Secure and Ethical Healthcare Ecosystem. In *AI and IoT-Based Technologies for Precision Medicine* (pp. 36–59). IGI Global. doi:10.4018/979-8-3693-0876-9.ch003

Boopathi, S., Kumaresan, A., & Manohar, N., & KrishnaMoorthi, R. (2017). Review on Effect of Process Parameters—Friction Stir Welding Process. *International Research Journal of Engineering and Technology, 4*(7), 272–278.

Boopathi, S., Myilsamy, S., & Sukkasamy, S. (2021). *Experimental Investigation and Multi-Objective Optimization of Cryogenically Cooled Near-Dry Wire-Cut EDM Using TOPSIS Technique*. IJAMT.

Boopathi, S., Saranya, A., Raghuraman, S., & Revanth, R. (2018). Design and Fabrication of Low Cost Electric Bicycle. *International Research Journal of Engineering and Technology*, *5*(3), 146–147.

Boopathi, S., & Sivakumar, K. (2012). Experimental Analysis of Eco-friendly Near-dry Wire Electrical Discharge Machining Process. *Archives des Sciences*, *65*(10), 334–346.

Boopathi, S., & Sivakumar, K. (2013). Experimental investigation and parameter optimization of near-dry wire-cut electrical discharge machining using multi-objective evolutionary algorithm. *International Journal of Advanced Manufacturing Technology*, *67*(9–12), 2639–2655. doi:10.1007/s00170-012-4680-4

Boopathi, S., & Sivakumar, K. (2016). Optimal parameter prediction of oxygen-mist near-dry wire-cut EDM. *Inderscience: International Journal of Manufacturing Technology and Management*, *30*(3–4), 164–178. doi:10.1504/IJMTM.2016.077812

Boopathi, S., Sureshkumar, M., & Sathiskumar, S. (2022). Parametric Optimization of LPG Refrigeration System Using Artificial Bee Colony Algorithm. *International Conference on Recent Advances in Mechanical Engineering Research and Development*, 97–105.

Bordin, C. (2015). *Mathematical optimization applied to thermal and electrical energy systems*. Academic Press.

Borges, L. O., Hernández Quintana, A., & Roche, S. R. (2017). Curricular production academic stages on Digital Humanities: Towards a necessary diagnosis. *Ciencias de la Información*, *48*(1), 19–26.

Boumlik, A., & Bahaj, M. (2018). *Big Data and IoT: A Prime Opportunity for Banking Industry*. doi:10.1007/978-3-319-69137-4_35

Brahimi, M., Boukhalfa, K., & Moussaoui, A. (2017). Deep learning for tomato diseases: Classification and symptoms visualization. *Applied Artificial Intelligence*, *31*(4), 299–315. doi:10.1080/08839514.2017.1315516

Brickley, D. (n.d.). *Geospatial ontology*. Available. https://www.w3.org/2005/Incubator/geo/XGR-geo-ont-20071023/

Brickley, D., & Guha, R. (2015). RDFa Lite 1.1 - Third Edition. W3C Recommendation.

Bronner, W., Gebauer, H., Lamprecht, C., & Wortmann, F. (2021). Sustainable AIoT: how artificial intelligence and the internet of things affect profit, people, and planet. *Connected Business: Create Value in a Networked Economy*, 137–154.

Brous, P., & Janssen, M. (2015). *Advancing e-Government Using the Internet of Things: A Systematic Review of Benefits*. doi:10.1007/978-3-319-22479-4_12

Butt, U. A., Mehmood, M., Shah, S. B. H., Amin, R., Shaukat, M. W., Raza, S. M., Suh, D. Y., & Piran, M. J. (2020). A review of machine learning algorithms for cloud computing security. *Electronics (Basel)*, *9*(9), 1379. doi:10.3390/electronics9091379

Byrnes, L., & Etter, S. J. (2008). Student Response Systems for Active Learning. In *Encyclopedia of Information Technology Curriculum Integration* (pp. 803–807). IGI Global. doi:10.4018/978-1-59904-881-9.ch126

C., Qureshi, A., Awan, I., & Konur, S. (2024, February 23). Enhancing Zero Trust Models in the Financial Industry through Blockchain Integration: A Proposed Framework. *Electronics*, *13*(5), 865. doi:10.3390/electronics13050865

Caballero, M., Moreno, A., & Nogueiras, A. (2006). Multidialectal acoustic modeling: A comparative study. Multilingual Speech and Language Processing.

Cafieri, S., Liberti, L., Messine, F., & Nogarede, B. (2013). Optimal design of electrical machines: Mathematical programming formulations. *COMPEL-The International Journal for Computation and Mathematics in Electrical and Electronic Engineering, 32*(3), 977–996.

Cai, M. Zhang, W. Y., Zhang, K. & Li, S. T. (2010). SWMRD: A Semantic Web-based manufacturing resource discovery system for cross-enterprise collaboration. *International Journal of Production Research, 48*(120), 3445-3460.

Cai, L., Tian, Y., Liu, Z., Cheng, Q., Xu, J., & Ning, Y. (2016). Application of cloud computing to simulation of a heavy-duty machine tool. *International Journal of Advanced Manufacturing Technology, 84*(1-4), 291–303. doi:10.1007/s00170-015-7916-2

Calvanese, D., Cogrel, B., Kalayci, E. G., Komla-Ebri, S., Kontchakov, R., Lanti, D., . . . Xiao, G. (2015, June). OBDA with the Ontop Framework. In SEBD (pp. 296-303). Academic Press.

Canavese, D., Mannella, L., Regano, L., & Basile, C. (2024, January 17). Security at the Edge for Resource-Limited IoT Devices. *Sensors (Basel), 24*(2), 590. doi:10.3390/s24020590 PMID:38257680

Cao, Q., Zanni-Merk, C., Samet, A., Reich, C., De Beuvron, F. D. B., Beckmann, A., & Giannetti, C. (2022). KSPMI: A knowledge-based system for predictive maintenance in industry 4.0. *Robotics and Computer-integrated Manufacturing, 74*, 102281. doi:10.1016/j.rcim.2021.102281

Cardoso, J. (2006). Discovering Semantic Web Services with and without a Common Ontology Commitment. *IEEE Service Computing Workshop*, 183-190.

Cardoso, J., & Sheth, A. (2003). Semantic e-Workflow Composition. *Journal of Intelligent Information Systems, 21*(3), 191–225. doi:10.1023/A:1025542915514

Centres for Disease Control and Prevention. (2015, May 29). *Definition of policy*. Retrieved March 19, 2023, from https://www.cdc.gov/policy/opaph/process/definition.html

Chandran, V., Patil, C. K., Karthick, A., Ganeshaperumal, D., Rahim, R., & Ghosh, A. (2021). State of charge estimation of lithium-ion battery for electric vehicles using machine learning algorithms. *World Electric Vehicle Journal, 12*(1), 38. doi:10.3390/wevj12010038

Chandrika, V., Sivakumar, A., Krishnan, T. S., Pradeep, J., Manikandan, S., & Boopathi, S. (2023). Theoretical Study on Power Distribution Systems for Electric Vehicles. In *Intelligent Engineering Applications and Applied Sciences for Sustainability* (pp. 1–19). IGI Global. doi:10.4018/979-8-3693-0044-2.ch001

Chang, W. J., Chen, L. B., Chen, M. C., Lin, J. Y., Su, J. P., Hsu, C. H., & Ou, Y. K. (2020, October 13). A Deep Learning-Based Intelligent Anti-Collision System for Car Door. *2020 IEEE 9th Global Conference on Consumer Electronics (GCCE)*. 10.1109/GCCE50665.2020.9291741

Chang, J., Ong, H., Wang, T., & Chen, H. H. (2022). A Fully Automated Intelligent Medicine Dispensary System Based on AIoT. *IEEE Internet of Things Journal, 9*(23), 23954–23966. doi:10.1109/JIOT.2022.3188552

Chang, W. J., Chen, L. B., Chen, M. C., Chiu, Y. C., & Lin, J. Y. (2020). ScalpEye: A Deep Learning-Based Scalp Hair Inspection and Diagnosis System for Scalp Health. *IEEE Access : Practical Innovations, Open Solutions, 8*, 134826–134837. doi:10.1109/ACCESS.2020.3010847

Chashyn, D., Khurudzhi, Y., & Daukšys, M. (2023). *Integration of Building Information Modeling and Artificial Intelligence of Things in Post-War Renovation and Retrofitting of Historical Buildings*. Academic Press.

Chauhan, C., Parida, V., & Dhir, A. (2022). Linking circular economy and digitalisation technologies: A systematic literature review of past achievements and future promises. *Technological Forecasting and Social Change, 177*, 121508. doi:10.1016/j.techfore.2022.121508

Chaves-Fraga, D., Ruckhaus, E., Priyatna, F., Vidal, M. E., & Corcho, O. (2021). Enhancing virtual ontology based access over tabular data with Morph-CSV. *Semantic Web, 12*(6), 869–902. doi:10.3233/SW-210432

Chen, T., He, T., Benesty, M., Khotilovich, V., Tang, Y., Cho, H., ... Zhou, T. (2015). Xgboost: extreme gradient boosting. *R package version 0.4-2, 1*(4), 1-4.

Chen, J., Zhang, D., Nanehkaran, Y. A., & Li, D. (2020). Detection of rice plant diseases based on deep transfer learning. *Journal of the Science of Food and Agriculture, 100*(7), 3246–3256. doi:10.1002/jsfa.10365 PMID:32124447

Chen, K.-T., Huang, C.-Y., & Hsu, C.-H. (2014). Cloud gaming onward: Research opportunities and outlook. *2014 IEEE International Conference on Multimedia and Expo Workshops (ICMEW)*, 1–4. 10.1109/ICMEW.2014.6890683

Chen, X., Cao, W., Zhang, Q., Hu, S., & Zhang, J. (2020). Artificial intelligence-aided model predictive control for a grid-tied wind-hydrogen-fuel cell system. *IEEE Access : Practical Innovations, Open Solutions, 8*, 92418–92430. doi:10.1109/ACCESS.2020.2994577

Chen, Y., Dong, G., Xu, C., Hao, Y., & Zhao, Y. (2023). EStore: A User-Friendly Encrypted Storage Scheme for Distributed File Systems. *Sensors (Basel), 23*(20), 8526. doi:10.3390/s23208526 PMID:37896619

Chien, S. W., Markidis, S., Sishtla, C. P., Santos, L., Herman, P., Narasimhamurthy, S., & Laure, E. (2018, November). Characterizing deep-learning I/O workloads in TensorFlow. In *2018 IEEE/ACM 3rd International Workshop on Parallel Data Storage & Data Intensive Scalable Computing Systems (PDSW-DISCS)* (pp. 54-63). IEEE.

Choobineh, M., Arab, A., Khodaei, A., & Paaso, A. (2022). Energy innovations through blockchain: Challenges, opportunities, and the road ahead. *The Electricity Journal, 35*(1), 107059. doi:10.1016/j.tej.2021.107059

Chou, C.-J., Jiang, S.-B., Yeh, T.-L., Tsai, L.-D., Kang, K.-Y., & Liu, C.-J. (2020). A portable direct methanol fuel cell power station for long-term internet of things applications. *Energies, 13*(14), 3547. doi:10.3390/en13143547

CO2 Capture and Utilization - Energy System. (n.d.). IEA. https://www.iea.org/energy-system/carbon-capture-utilisation-and-storage/co2-capture-and-utilisation

Cob-Parro, A. C., Lalangui, Y., & Lazcano, R. (2024, January 25). Fostering Agricultural Transformation through AI: An Open-Source AI Architecture Exploiting the MLOps Paradigm. *Agronomy (Basel), 14*(2), 259. doi:10.3390/agronomy14020259

Čolaković, A., & Hadžialić, M. (2018). Internet of Things (IoT): A review of enabling technologies, challenges, and open research issues. *Computer Networks, 144*, 17–39. doi:10.1016/j.comnet.2018.07.017

Copacino, W., & Anderson, D. (2003). Connecting with the Bottom Line: A Global Study of Supply Chain Leadership and its Contribution to the High Performance Business. *Accenture*, 1.

Costa Lima, V., Alves, D., Andrade Bernardi, F., & Charters Lopes Rijo, R. P. (2023). Security approaches for electronic health data handling through the Semantic Web: A scoping review. *Semantic Web, 14*(4), 771–784. doi:10.3233/SW-223088

Cutler, A., Cutler, D. R., & Stevens, J. R. (2012). Random forests. *Ensemble machine learning: Methods and applications*, 157-175.

Dadkhah, M., Araban, S., & Paydar, S. (2020a). A systematic literature review on semantic web enabled software testing. *Journal of Systems and Software, 162*, 110485. doi:10.1016/j.jss.2019.110485

Daniya, T., & Srinivasan, V. (2023). Shuffled shepherd social optimization based deep learning for rice leaf disease classification and severity percentage prediction. *Concurrency and Computation*, *35*(4), e7523. doi:10.1002/cpe.7523

Das, S., Lekhya, G., Shreya, K., Shekinah, K. L., Babu, K. K., & Boopathi, S. (2024). Fostering Sustainability Education Through Cross-Disciplinary Collaborations and Research Partnerships: Interdisciplinary Synergy. In Facilitating Global Collaboration and Knowledge Sharing in Higher Education With Generative AI (pp. 60–88). IGI Global.

Das, A., Dutta, R., Das, S., & Sengupta, S. (2020). Feature selection using graph-based clustering for rice disease prediction. *Computational Intelligence in Pattern Recognition Proceedings of CIPR*, *2019*, 589–598.

Das, A., Mallick, C., & Dutta, S. (2020). Deep learning-based automated feature engineering for rice leaf disease prediction. *Computational Intelligence in Pattern Recognition Proceedings of CIPR*, *2020*, 133–141.

Dasgupta, D., Roy, A., & Nag, A. (2017). *Advances in user authentication*. Springer International Publishing. doi:10.1007/978-3-319-58808-7

Das, H. S., Rahman, M. M., Li, S., & Tan, C. (2020). Electric vehicles standards, charging infrastructure, and impact on grid integration: A technological review. *Renewable & Sustainable Energy Reviews*, *120*, 109618. doi:10.1016/j.rser.2019.109618

Das, S., Sengupta, S., & Das, P. (2022). Feature Selection Using Louvain Clustering Algorithm for Rice Disease Prediction. *Computational Intelligence in Pattern Recognition Proceedings of CIPR*, *2021*, 99–108.

Daud, S. M., Jozani, H. J., & Arab, F. (2013). A review on predicting outbreak of tungro disease in rice fields based on epidemiological and biophysical factors. *International Journal of Innovation, Management and Technology*, *4*(4), 447–450. doi:10.7763/IJIMT.2013.V4.439

Davies, H. C., Eynon, R., & Salveson, C. (2021). The mobilisation of AI in education: A Bourdieusean field analysis. *Sociology*, *55*(3), 539–560. doi:10.1177/0038038520967888

Davies, J., Studer, R., & Warren, P. (Eds.). (2006). *Semantic Web technologies: trends and research in ontology-based systems*. John Wiley & Sons. doi:10.1002/047003033X

de Campos Souza, P. V. (2020). Fuzzy neural networks and neuro-fuzzy networks: A review the main techniques and applications used in the literature. *Applied Soft Computing*, *92*, 106275. doi:10.1016/j.asoc.2020.106275

de Freitas, M. P., Piai, V. A., Farias, R. H., Fernandes, A. M., de Moraes Rossetto, A. G., & Leithardt, V. R. Q. (2022). Artificial intelligence of things applied to assistive technology: A systematic literature review. *Sensors (Basel)*, *22*(21), 8531. doi:10.3390/s22218531 PMID:36366227

Dell'Olio, L., Ibeas, A., de Ona, J., & de Ona, R. (2017). *Public transportation quality of service: Factors, models, and applications*. Elsevier.

Delson, J. K., & Shahidehpour, S. (1992). Linear programming applications to power system economics, planning and operations. *IEEE Transactions on Power Systems*, *7*(3), 1155–1163. doi:10.1109/59.207329

Deshpande, S., Chikkerur, S., & Govindaraju, V. (2005, October). Accent classification in speech. In *Fourth IEEE Workshop on Automatic Identification Advanced Technologies (AutoID'05)* (pp. 139-143). IEEE. 10.1109/AUTOID.2005.10

Dhanalakshmi, M., Tamilarasi, K., Saravanan, S., Sujatha, G., Boopathi, S., & Associates. (2024). Fog Computing-Based Framework and Solutions for Intelligent Systems: Enabling Autonomy in Vehicles. In Computational Intelligence for Green Cloud Computing and Digital Waste Management (pp. 330–356). IGI Global.

Dhanalakshmi, M., Tamilarasi, K., Saravanan, S., Sujatha, G., Boopathi, S., & Associates. (2024a). Fog Computing-Based Framework and Solutions for Intelligent Systems: Enabling Autonomy in Vehicles. In Computational Intelligence for Green Cloud Computing and Digital Waste Management (pp. 330–356). IGI Global.

Dhanalakshmi, M., Tamilarasi, K., Saravanan, S., Sujatha, G., Boopathi, S., & Associates. (2024b). Fog Computing-Based Framework and Solutions for Intelligent Systems: Enabling Autonomy in Vehicles. In Computational Intelligence for Green Cloud Computing and Digital Waste Management (pp. 330–356). IGI Global.

Dhanapalan, L., & Chen, J. Y. (2007). A case study of integrating protein interaction data using semantic web technology. *International Journal of Bioinformatics Research and Applications*, *3*(3), 286–302. doi:10.1504/IJBRA.2007.015004 PMID:18048193

Dhanya, D., Kumar, S. S., Thilagavathy, A., Prasad, D., & Boopathi, S. (2023). Data Analytics and Artificial Intelligence in the Circular Economy: Case Studies. In Intelligent Engineering Applications and Applied Sciences for Sustainability (pp. 40–58). IGI Global.

Dileep, P., Das, D., & Bora, P. K. (2020, February). Dense layer dropout based CNN architecture for automatic modulation classification. In 2020 national conference on communications (NCC) (pp. 1-5). IEEE. doi:10.1109/NCC48643.2020.9055989

Diwan, T., Anirudh, G., & Tembhurne, J. (2023). Object detection using YOLO: Challenges, architectural successors, datasets and applications. *Multimedia Tools and Applications*, *82*, 9243–9275.

Dlamini, N. N., & Johnston, K. (2016, November). The use, benefits and challenges of using the Internet of Things (IoT) in retail businesses: A literature review. In *2016 international conference on advances in computing and communication engineering (ICACCE)* (pp. 430-436). IEEE.

Domakonda, V. K., Farooq, S., Chinthamreddy, S., Puviarasi, R., Sudhakar, M., & Boopathi, S. (2022). Sustainable Developments of Hybrid Floating Solar Power Plants: Photovoltaic System. In Human Agro-Energy Optimization for Business and Industry (pp. 148–167). IGI Global.

Domingue, J., Cabral, L., Galizia, S., Tanasescu, V., Gugliotta, A., Norton, B., & Pedrinaci, C. (2008). IRS-III: A Broker-based Approach to Semantic Web Service. *Journal of Web Semantics*, *6*(2), 109–132. doi:10.1016/j.websem.2008.01.001

Domingue, J., Fensel, D., & Hendler, J. A. (Eds.). (2011). *Handbook of semantic web technologies*. Springer Science & Business Media. doi:10.1007/978-3-540-92913-0

Donkers, A., Yang, D., de Vries, B., & Baken, N. (2022). Semantic web technologies for indoor environmental quality: A review and ontology design. *Buildings*, *12*(10), 1522. doi:10.3390/buildings12101522

Duduka, S., Jain, H., Jain, V., Prabhu, H., & Chawan, P. P. M. (2020). Accent classification using machine learning. *International Research Journal of Engineering and Technology (IRJET)*, *7*(11).

Duduka, S., Jain, H., Jain, V., Prabhu, H., & Chawan, P. M. (2021). A neural network approach to accent classification. *International Research Journal of Engineering and Technology*, *8*(03), 1175–1177.

Du, G., Zou, Y., Zhang, X., Liu, T., Wu, J., & He, D. (2020). Deep reinforcement learning based energy management for a hybrid electric vehicle. *Energy*, *201*, 117591. doi:10.1016/j.energy.2020.117591

Du, H., Wang, J., Hu, Z., Yao, X., & Zhang, X. (2008). Prediction of fungicidal activities of rice blast disease based on least-squares support vector machines and project pursuit regression. *Journal of Agricultural and Food Chemistry*, *56*(22), 10785–10792. doi:10.1021/jf8022194 PMID:18950187

Dumbrava, C. (2021). *Artificial intelligence at EU borders. Overview of applications and key issues.* Brussels, Belgium: European Parliamentary Research Service. Retrieved 12 21, 2021, from https://www. europarl. europa. eu/RegData/etudes/IDAN/2021/690706/EPRS_IDA (2021) 690706_EN.pdf

Durán, C. G., & Ramírez, C. M. (2021). Integration of open educational resources using semantic platform. *IEEE Access : Practical Innovations, Open Solutions, 9*, 93079–93088. doi:10.1109/ACCESS.2021.3092315

Dwivedi, K. A., Huang, S.-J., & Wang, C.-T. (2022). Integration of various technology-based approaches for enhancing the performance of microbial fuel cell technology: A review. *Chemosphere, 287*, 132248. doi:10.1016/j.chemosphere.2021.132248 PMID:34543899

El Naqa, I., & Murphy, M. J. (2015). What is machine learning? In *Machine Learning in Radiation Oncology* (pp. 3–11). Springer International Publishing. doi:10.1007/978-3-319-18305-3_1

Elagib, N. A., & Al-Saidi, M. (2020). Balancing the benefits from the water–energy–land–food nexus through agroforestry in the Sahel. *The Science of the Total Environment, 742*, 140509. doi:10.1016/j.scitotenv.2020.140509 PMID:33167296

El-Haddadeh, R. (2020). Digital innovation dynamics influence on organisational adoption: The case of cloud computing services. *Information Systems Frontiers, 22*(4), 985–999. doi:10.1007/s10796-019-09912-2

El-Kenawy, E.-S. M., Mirjalili, S., Alassery, F., Zhang, Y.-D., Eid, M. M., El-Mashad, S. Y., Aloyaydi, B. A., Ibrahim, A., & Abdelhamid, A. A. (2022). Novel meta-heuristic algorithm for feature selection, unconstrained functions and engineering problems. *IEEE Access : Practical Innovations, Open Solutions, 10*, 40536–40555. doi:10.1109/ACCESS.2022.3166901

Elsaleh, T., Bermudez-Edo, M., Enshaeifar, S., Acton, S.T., Rezvani, R., & Barnaghi, P. (2019). IoT -Stream: A Lightweight Ontology for Internet of Things Data Streams. *2019 Global IoT Summit (GIoTS).* doi:10.1109/giots.2019.8766367

Elsharif, A. A., & Abu-Naser, S. S. (2019). An expert system for diagnosing sugarcane diseases. *International Journal of Academic Engineering Research, 3*(3), 19–27.

EPSPARQL: A Unified Language for Event Processing and Stream Reasoning. (n.d.). In *The 20th International Conference.* ACM Press. doi:10.1145/1963405.1963495

Esteva, A., Chou, K., Yeung, S., Naik, N., Madani, A., Mottaghi, A., Liu, Y., Topol, E., Dean, J., & Socher, R. (2021). Deep learning-enabled medical computer vision. *NPJ Digital Medicine, 4*(1), 5. doi:10.1038/s41746-020-00376-2 PMID:33420381

Exner, J.-P., Bauer, S., Novikova, K., Ludwig, J., & Werth, D. (2020). Connected E-Mobility, IoT and its Emerging Requirements for Planning and Infrastructures. *Shaping Urban Change–Livable City Regions for the 21st Century. Proceedings of Real Corp 2020, 25th International Conference on Urban Development, Regional Planning and Information Society*, 175–181.

Fahes, M., Hosein, R., Zeynalov, G., Sedlar, D. K., Srivastava, M., Swindell, G. S., Kokkinos, N. C., & Willhite, G. (2023). The Impact of the Energy Transition on Petroleum Engineering Departments: The Faculty Perspective. *Paper Presented At The SPE Annual Technical Conference And Exhibition.* 10.2118/215086-MS

Faulds, D. J., Mangold, W. G., Raju, P. S., & Valsalan, S. (2018). The mobile shopping revolution: Redefining the consumer decision process. *Business Horizons, 61*(2), 323–338. doi:10.1016/j.bushor.2017.11.012

Feng, Z., Huang, J., Jin, S., Wang, G., & Chen, Y. (2022). Artificial intelligence-based multi-objective optimisation for proton exchange membrane fuel cell: A literature review. *Journal of Power Sources, 520*, 230808. doi:10.1016/j.jpowsour.2021.230808

Fensel, D., & Bussler, C. (2002). The Web Service Modeling Framework WSMF. *Electronic Commerce Research and Applications*, *1*(2), 113–137. doi:10.1016/S1567-4223(02)00015-7

Fera, F. T., & Spandonidis, C. (2024, February 6). An Artificial Intelligence and Industrial Internet of Things-Based Framework for Sustainable Hydropower Plant Operations. *Smart Cities*, *7*(1), 496–517. doi:10.3390/smartcities7010020

Fernández-Breis, J. T., Maldonado, J. A., Marcos, M., Legaz-García, M. D. C., Moner, D., Torres-Sospedra, J., Esteban-Gil, A., Martínez-Salvador, B., & Robles, M. (2013). Leveraging electronic healthcare record standards and semantic web technologies. *Journal of the American Medical Informatics Association : JAMIA*, *20*(e2), e288–e296. doi:10.1136/amiajnl-2013-001923 PMID:23934950

Ferreira, H. (2023, 12 mayo). What does the future hold for the oil industry in Mexico? (P. Velasco). *Mexico Bussiness News*. https://www.irena.org/Energy-Transition/Technology/Geothermal-energy

Franco da Silva, A. C., & Hirmer, P. (2020). Models for internet of things environments—A survey. *Information (Basel)*, *11*(10), 487. doi:10.3390/info11100487

Franco, P., Martínez, J. M., Kim, Y., & Ahmed, M. (2021). IoT Based Approach for Load Monitoring and Activity Recognition in Smart Homes. *IEEE Access : Practical Innovations, Open Solutions*, *9*, 45325–45339. doi:10.1109/ACCESS.2021.3067029

Franklin, K. K., & Hart, J. K. (2006). Influence of web-based distance education on the academic department chair role. *Journal of Educational Technology & Society, 9*(1), 213-228. doi:https://www.jstor.org/stable/jeductechsoci.9.1.213

Fry, A. (2022, January 31). *What is an LMS? Learning management systems explained.* Retrieved from MOODLE: https://moodle.com/news/what-is-an-lms-learning-management-systems-explained/

Fugate, B., Sahin, F., & Mentzer, J. T. (2006). Supply Chain Management Coordination Mechanisms. *Journal of Business Logistics*, *27*(2), 129–161. doi:10.1002/j.2158-1592.2006.tb00220.x

Gagnon, J. C., & Barber, B. R. (2018). Feasibility. In *The SAGE encyclopaedia of educational research, measurement, and evaluation* (p. 668). SAGE. doi:10.4135/9781506326139.n259

Gandomi, A., & Haider, M. (2015). Beyond the hype: Big data concepts, methods, and analytics. *International Journal of Information Management*, *35*(2), 137–144. doi:10.1016/j.ijinfomgt.2014.10.007

Ganeshan, R., & Harrison, T. P. (1995). *An introduction to supply chain management.* Supply Chain Management, Version 1. Available from http://silmaril.smeal.psu.edu/misc/supply_chain_ intro.html

Garg, K., Bhugra, S., & Lall, B. (2021). Automatic quantification of plant disease from field image data using deep learning. In *Proceedings of the IEEE/CVF winter conference on applications of computer vision* (pp. 1965-1972). 10.1109/WACV48630.2021.00201

Garud, K. S., Jayaraj, S., & Lee, M.-Y. (2021). A review on modeling of solar photovoltaic systems using artificial neural networks, fuzzy logic, genetic algorithm and hybrid models. *International Journal of Energy Research*, *45*(1), 6–35. doi:10.1002/er.5608

Ghani, U., Bajwa, I. S., & Ashfaq, A. (2018). A fuzzy logic based intelligent system for measuring customer loyalty and decision making. *Symmetry*, *10*(12), 761. doi:10.3390/sym10120761

Gharaibeh, A., Salahuddin, M. A., Hussini, S. J., Khreishah, A., Khalil, I., Guizani, M., & Al-Fuqaha, A. (2017). Smart cities: A survey on data management, security, and enabling technologies. *IEEE Communications Surveys and Tutorials*, *19*(4), 2456–2501. doi:10.1109/COMST.2017.2736886

Giunchiglia, F., Shvaiko, P., & Yatskevich, M. (2004). S-Match: an algorithm and an implementation of semantic matching. *Proceedings of 1st European Semantic Web Symposium (ESWS)*, 3053, 61-75. 10.1007/978-3-540-25956-5_5

Gnanaprakasam, C., Vankara, J., Sastry, A. S., Prajval, V., Gireesh, N., & Boopathi, S. (2023). Long-Range and Low-Power Automated Soil Irrigation System Using Internet of Things: An Experimental Study. In Contemporary Developments in Agricultural Cyber-Physical Systems (pp. 87–104). IGI Global.

Goosen, L. (2018). Ethical Data Management and Research Integrity in the Context of e-Schools and Community Engagement. In C. Sibinga (Ed.), *Ensuring Research Integrity and the Ethical Management of Data* (pp. 14–45). IGI Global. doi:10.4018/978-1-5225-2730-5.ch002

Gordon, T. J. (2009). The real-time Delphi method. *Futures Research Methodology Version 3, 19*. Retrieved from https://millennium-project.org/wp-content/uploads/2022/01/05-Real-Time-Delphi.pdf

Gowri, N. V., Dwivedi, J. N., Krishnaveni, K., Boopathi, S., Palaniappan, M., & Medikondu, N. R. (2023). Experimental investigation and multi-objective optimization of eco-friendly near-dry electrical discharge machining of shape memory alloy using Cu/SiC/Gr composite electrode. *Environmental Science and Pollution Research International, 30*(49), 1–19. doi:10.1007/s11356-023-26983-6 PMID:37126160

Grimm, S., Monk, B., & Preist, C. (2006). Matching Semantic Service Descriptions with Local Closed-World Reasoning. *European Semantic Web Conference*, 575-589. 10.1007/11762256_42

Gruber, T. R. (1993). *A Translation Approach to Portable Ontology Specifications*. Stanford University, Computer Science Department, Knowledge Systems Laboratory, Technical Report KSL 92-71.

Guarino, N., & Giaretta, P. (1995). *Ontologies and Knowledge Base: Towards a Terminological Classification Toward Very Large Knowledge Base: Knowledge Building and Knowledge Sharing*. IOS Press.

Guntur, R. K., Ramakrishnan, K., & Mittal, V. K. (2022). Foreign Accent Recognition Using a Combination of Native and Non-native Speech. In *Intelligent Sustainable Systems: Selected Papers of WorldS4 2021* (Vol. 1, pp. 713–721). Springer Nature Singapore. doi:10.1007/978-981-16-6309-3_67

Guntur, R. K., Ramakrishnan, K., & Vinay Kumar, M. (2022). An automated classification system based on regional accent. *Circuits, Systems, and Signal Processing, 41*(6), 3487–3507. doi:10.1007/s00034-021-01948-7

Guo, G., Wang, H., Bell, D., Bi, Y., & Greer, K. (2003). KNN model-based approach in classification. In *On The Move to Meaningful Internet Systems 2003: CoopIS, DOA, and ODBASE: OTM Confederated International Conferences, CoopIS, DOA, and ODBASE 2003, Catania, Sicily, Italy, November 3-7, 2003. Proceedings* (pp. 986-996). Springer Berlin Heidelberg. 10.1007/978-3-540-39964-3_62

Guo, A., Huang, W., Dong, Y., Ye, H., Ma, H., Liu, B., Wu, W., Ren, Y., Ruan, C., & Geng, Y. (2021). Wheat yellow rust detection using UAV-based hyperspectral technology. *Remote Sensing (Basel), 13*(1), 123. doi:10.3390/rs13010123

Guo, J., Li, K., Fan, J., Luo, Y., & Wang, J. (2021). Neural-fuzzy-based adaptive sliding mode automatic steering control of vision-based unmanned electric vehicles. *Chinese Journal of Mechanical Engineering, 34*(1), 1–13. doi:10.1186/s10033-021-00597-w

Guo, Y., Li, J. Y., & Zhan, Z. H. (2020). Efficient hyperparameter optimization for convolution neural networks in deep learning: A distributed particle swarm optimization approach. *Cybernetics and Systems, 52*(1), 36–57. doi:10.1080/01969722.2020.1827797

Gupta, A., Dengre, V., Kheruwala, H. A., & Shah, M. (2020). Comprehensive review of text-mining applications in finance. *Financial Innovation, 6*(1), 39. Advance online publication. doi:10.1186/s40854-020-00205-1

Gurney, K. (2018). *An introduction to neural networks*. CRC Press. doi:10.1201/9781315273570

Gutiérrez, C., & Sequeda, J. F. (2021). Knowledge graphs. *Communications of the ACM, 64*(3), 96–104. doi:10.1145/3418294

Hadad, M., Attarsharghi, S., Dehghanpour Abyaneh, M., Narimani, P., Makarian, J., Saberi, A., & Alinaghizadeh, A. (2024, February 14). Exploring New Parameters to Advance Surface Roughness Prediction in Grinding Processes for the Enhancement of Automated Machining. *Journal of Manufacturing and Materials Processing, 8*(1), 41. doi:10.3390/jmmp8010041

Haller, A., Janowicz, K., Cox, S. J., Lefrançois, M., Taylor, K., Le Phuoc, D., Lieberman, J., García-Castro, R., Atkinson, R., & Stadler, C. (2019). The modular SSN ontology: A joint W3C and OGC standard specifying the semantics of sensors, observations, sampling, and actuation. *Semantic Web, 10*(1), 9–32. doi:10.3233/SW-180320

Halsey, T., Agrawal, G., Bailey, J. R., Balhoff, M., Borglum, S. J., Mohanty, K. K., & Traver, M. (2023). *Grand Challenges for the Oil and Gas Industry for the Next Decade and Beyond*. JPT. https://jpt.spe.org/grand-challenges-for-the-oil-and-gas-industry-for-the-next-decade-and-beyond

Hang, P., Lv, C., Xing, Y., Huang, C., & Hu, Z. (2020). Human-like decision making for autonomous driving: A non-cooperative game theoretic approach. *IEEE Transactions on Intelligent Transportation Systems, 22*(4), 2076–2087. doi:10.1109/TITS.2020.3036984

Han, H., & Trimi, S. (2022). Towards a data science platform for improving SME collaboration through Industry 4.0 technologies. *Technological Forecasting and Social Change, 174*, 121242. doi:10.1016/j.techfore.2021.121242

Hansen, E. B., & Bøgh, S. (2021). Artificial intelligence and internet of things in small and medium-sized enterprises: A survey. *Journal of Manufacturing Systems, 58*, 362–372. doi:10.1016/j.jmsy.2020.08.009

Han, T., Muhammad, K., Hussain, T., Jaime, L., & Wook Baik, S. (2021). An Efficient Deep Learning Framework for Intelligent Energy Management in IoT Networks. *IEEE Internet of Things Journal, 8*(5), 3170–3179. doi:10.1109/JIOT.2020.3013306

Harris, C. R., Millman, K. J., Van Der Walt, S. J., Gommers, R., Virtanen, P., Cournapeau, D., Wieser, E., Taylor, J., Berg, S., Smith, N. J., Kern, R., Picus, M., Hoyer, S., van Kerkwijk, M. H., Brett, M., Haldane, A., del Río, J. F., Wiebe, M., Peterson, P., ... Oliphant, T. E. (2020). Array programming with NumPy. *Nature, 585*(7825), 357–362. doi:10.1038/s41586-020-2649-2 PMID:32939066

Hasan, M. J., Mahbub, S., Alom, M. S., & Nasim, M. A. (2019, May). Rice disease identification and classification by integrating support vector machine with deep convolutional neural network. In *2019 1st international conference on advances in science, engineering and robotics technology (ICASERT)* (pp. 1-6). IEEE. 10.1109/ICASERT.2019.8934568

Hasan, M. K., Mahmud, M., Habib, A. A., Motakabber, S., & Islam, S. (2021). Review of electric vehicle energy storage and management system: Standards, issues, and challenges. *Journal of Energy Storage, 41*, 102940. doi:10.1016/j.est.2021.102940

Hashem, I. A. T., Chang, V., Anuar, N. B., Adewole, K., Yaqoob, I., Gani, A., Ahmed, E., & Chiroma, H. (2016). The role of big data in smart city. *International Journal of Information Management, 36*(5), 748–758. doi:10.1016/j.ijinfomgt.2016.05.002

He, F., Zhang, Y., Chen, H., Zhang, Z., & Peng, Y. L. (2008). The prediction of protein-protein interaction networks in rice blast fungus. *BMC Genomics, 9*(1), 1–12. doi:10.1186/1471-2164-9-519 PMID:18976500

Heiler, S. (1995). Semantic interoperability. *ACM Computing Surveys, 27*(2), 271–273. doi:10.1145/210376.210392

He, J., Li, Y., Li, H., Tong, H., Yuan, Z., Yang, X., & Huang, W. (2020). Application of game theory in integrated energy system systems: A review. *IEEE Access : Practical Innovations, Open Solutions*, 8, 93380–93397. doi:10.1109/ACCESS.2020.2994133

He, L., Xue, M., & Gu, B. (2020). Internet-of-things enabled supply chain planning and coordination with big data services: Certain theoretic implications. *Journal of Management Science and Engineering*, 5(1), 1–22. doi:10.1016/j.jmse.2020.03.002

Hemalatha, N. K., Brunda, R. N., Prakruthi, G. S., Prabhu, B. B., Shukla, A., & Narasipura, O. S. J. (2022). Sugarcane leaf disease detection through deep learning. In *Deep Learning for Sustainable Agriculture* (pp. 297–323). Academic Press. doi:10.1016/B978-0-323-85214-2.00003-3

Hema, N., Krishnamoorthy, N., Chavan, S. M., Kumar, N., Sabarimuthu, M., & Boopathi, S. (2023). A Study on an Internet of Things (IoT)-Enabled Smart Solar Grid System. In *Handbook of Research on Deep Learning Techniques for Cloud-Based Industrial IoT* (pp. 290–308). IGI Global. doi:10.4018/978-1-6684-8098-4.ch017

Hendler, J., Gandon, F., & Allemang, D. (2020). *Semantic web for the working ontologist: Effective modeling for linked data, RDFS, and OWL*. Morgan & Claypool.

Hernández-Quintana, A. (2014a). *Folksonomies: the most recent ecological evidence in the information industry*. Instituto de Información Científica y Tecnológica (IDICT).

Hernández-Quintana, A. (2014b). *The philosophy of information and document convergence: inserting a theoretical paradigm in the archive science*. Instituto de Información Científica y Tecnológica (IDICT).

Hernández-Quintana, A., & Trinquete, A. T. (2022, May). TAXChe: An Online Taxonomy for Che's Marginalias: A Proposal from the Digital Humanities. In Knowledge Organization across Disciplines, Domains, Services and Technologies (pp. 111-120). Ergon-Verlag.

Hitzler, P., Krotzsch, M., & Rudolph, S. (2009). *Foundations of semantic web technologies*. CRC Press. doi:10.1201/9781420090512

Honnavalli, D., & Shylaja, S. S. (2019, May). Supervised machine learning model for accent recognition in English speech using sequential MFCC features. In *International Conference on Artificial Intelligence and Data Engineering* (pp. 55-66). Singapore: Springer Nature Singapore.

Hossain, M., Kayas, G., Hasan, R., Skjellum, A., Noor, S., & Islam, S. M. R. (2024, January 24). A Holistic Analysis of Internet of Things (IoT) Security: Principles, Practices, and New Perspectives. *Future Internet*, 16(2), 40. doi:10.3390/fi16020040

Hossain, P. S., Chakrabarty, A., Kim, K., & Piran, M. J. (2022). Multi-Label Extreme Learning Machine (MLELMs) for Bangla Regional Speech Recognition. *Applied Sciences (Basel, Switzerland)*, 12(11), 5463. doi:10.3390/app12115463

Hou, K. M., Diao, X., Shi, H., Ding, H., Zhou, H., & de Vaulx, C. (2023). Trends and Challenges in AIoT/IIoT/IoT Implementation. *Sensors (Basel)*, 23(11), 5074. doi:10.3390/s23115074 PMID:37299800

Hou, S., Fang, D., Pan, Y., Li, Y., & Yin, G. (2021). Hybrid Pyramid Convolutional Network for Multiscale Face Detection. *Computational Intelligence and Neuroscience*, 2021, 1–15. doi:10.1155/2021/9963322 PMID:34035802

Hoy, J. W., Grisham, M. P., & Damann, K. E. (1999). Spread and increase of ratoon stunting disease of sugarcane and comparison of disease detection methods. *Plant Disease*, 83(12), 1170–1175. doi:10.1094/PDIS.1999.83.12.1170 PMID:30841145

Hsieh, J. Y., Huang, W., Yang, H. T., Lin, C. C., Fan, Y. C., & Chen, H. (2019). *Building the rice blast disease prediction model based on machine learning and neural networks*. EasyChair.

Hu, X., & Huang, B. (2020, December). Face Detection based on SSD and CamShift. In *2020 IEEE 9th Joint International Information Technology and Artificial Intelligence Conference (ITAIC)* (Vol. 9, pp. 2324-2328). IEEE. 10.1109/ITAIC49862.2020.9339094

Huang, T., Yang, R., Huang, W., Huang, Y., & Qiao, X. (2018). Detecting sugarcane borer diseases using support vector machine. *Information Processing in Agriculture*, *5*(1), 74–82. doi:10.1016/j.inpa.2017.11.001

Huang, Y., Li, R., Wei, X., Wang, Z., Ge, T., & Qiao, X. (2022). Evaluating Data Augmentation Effects on the Recognition of Sugarcane Leaf Spot. *Agriculture*, *12*(12), 1997. doi:10.3390/agriculture12121997

Huang, Y., Xue, X., & Jiang, C. (2020). Semantic integration of sensor knowledge on artificial internet of things. *Wireless Communications and Mobile Computing*, *2020*, 1–8. doi:10.1155/2020/8815001

Hubara, I., Nahshan, Y., Hanani, Y., Banner, R., & Soudry, D. (2020). Improving post training neural quantization: Layer-wise calibration and integer programming. *arXiv Preprint arXiv:2006.10518*.

Hui, E., Feng, B., Lee, C., Yang, J., & Chen, J. (2019). A design of CNC architecture based on cloud computing. *Proceedings of the Institution of Mechanical Engineers. Part B, Journal of Engineering Manufacture*, *233*(4), 1260–1268. doi:10.1177/0954405418774601

Hu, M., Cao, E., Huang, H., Zhang, M., Chen, X., & Chen, M. (2023). AIoTML: A Unified Modeling Language for AIoT-Based Cyber-Physical Systems. *IEEE Transactions on Computer-Aided Design of Integrated Circuits and Systems*, *42*(11), 3545–3558. doi:10.1109/TCAD.2023.3264786

Hung, L. L. (2021, November 16). Adaptive Devices for AIoT Systems. *2021 International Symposium on Intelligent Signal Processing and Communication Systems (ISPACS)*. 10.1109/ISPACS51563.2021.9651095

Hunter, J., Little, S., & Schroeter, R. (2008). The application of semantic web technologies to multimedia data fusion within escience. In *Semantic Multimedia and Ontologies: Theory and Applications* (pp. 207–226). Springer London. doi:10.1007/978-1-84800-076-6_8

Husain, I., Ozpineci, B., Islam, M. S., Gurpinar, E., Su, G.-J., Yu, W., Chowdhury, S., Xue, L., Rahman, D., & Sahu, R. (2021). Electric drive technology trends, challenges, and opportunities for future electric vehicles. *Proceedings of the IEEE*, *109*(6), 1039–1059. doi:10.1109/JPROC.2020.3046112

Hussain, Z., Babe, M., Saravanan, S., Srimathy, G., Roopa, H., & Boopathi, S. (2023). Optimizing Biomass-to-Biofuel Conversion: IoT and AI Integration for Enhanced Efficiency and Sustainability. In Circular Economy Implementation for Sustainability in the Built Environment (pp. 191–214). IGI Global.

Hussain, M. T., Sulaiman, N. B., Hussain, M. S., & Jabir, M. (2021). Optimal Management strategies to solve issues of grid having Electric Vehicles (EV): A review. *Journal of Energy Storage*, *33*, 102114. doi:10.1016/j.est.2020.102114

Hussain, Z., Babe, M., Saravanan, S., Srimathy, G., Roopa, H., & Boopathi, S. (2023). Optimizing Biomass-to-Biofuel Conversion: IoT and AI Integration for Enhanced Efficiency and Sustainability. In N. Cobîrzan, R. Muntean, & R.-A. Felseghi (Eds.), Advances in Finance, Accounting, and Economics (pp. 191–214). IGI Global. doi:10.4018/978-1-6684-8238-4.ch009

Hyvönen, E. (2020). Using the Semantic Web in digital humanities: Shift from data publishing to data-analysis and serendipitous knowledge discovery. *Semantic Web*, *11*(1), 187–193. doi:10.3233/SW-190386

Ibrahim, A., & Jiang, F. (2021). The electric vehicle energy management: An overview of the energy system and related modeling and simulation. *Renewable & Sustainable Energy Reviews, 144*, 111049. doi:10.1016/j.rser.2021.111049

IETF RFC 4226. (2015). *HOTP: An HMAC-Based One-Time Password Algorithm, Anti Phishing Group, "Phishing Activity rends Report"*. http://www.antiphishing.org

Illmann, U., & Kluge, J. (2020). Public charging infrastructure and the market diffusion of electric vehicles. *Transportation Research Part D, Transport and Environment, 86*, 102413. doi:10.1016/j.trd.2020.102413

İnci, M., Büyük, M., Demir, M. H., & İlbey, G. (2021). A review and research on fuel cell electric vehicles: Topologies, power electronic converters, energy management methods, technical challenges, marketing and future aspects. *Renewable & Sustainable Energy Reviews, 137*, 110648. doi:10.1016/j.rser.2020.110648

Ingle, R. B., Swathi, S., Mahendran, G., Senthil, T., Muralidharan, N., & Boopathi, S. (2023). Sustainability and Optimization of Green and Lean Manufacturing Processes Using Machine Learning Techniques. In *Circular Economy Implementation for Sustainability in the Built Environment* (pp. 261–285). IGI Global. doi:10.4018/978-1-6684-8238-4.ch012

Ishak, N. M., & Abu Bakar, A. Y. (2014). Developing Sampling Frame for Case Study: Challenges and Conditions. *World Journal of Education, 4*(3), 29-35. Retrieved from https://files.eric.ed.gov/fulltext/EJ1158705.pdf

Jaatun, M. G., Pearson, S., Gittler, F., Leenes, R., & Niezen, M. (2020). Enhancing accountability in the cloud. *International Journal of Information Management, 53*, 101498. doi:10.1016/j.ijinfomgt.2016.03.004

Jabbar, M. A., Ortiz-Rodríguez, F., Tiwari, S., & Siarry, P. (2022). *Applied Machine Learning and Data Analytics: 5th International Conference, AMLDA 2022, Reynosa, Tamaulipas, Mexico, December 22–23, 2022, Revised Selected Papers*. CCIS. 10.1007/978-3-031-34222-6

Jain, S., & Ramesh, D. (2021, July). AI based hybrid CNN-LSTM model for crop disease prediction: An ML advent for rice crop. In *2021 12th International Conference on Computing Communication and Networking Technologies (ICCCNT)* (pp. 1-7). IEEE.

Jain, S., Sahni, R., Khargonkar, T., Gupta, H., Verma, O. P., Sharma, T. K., Bhardwaj, T., Agarwal, S., & Kim, H. (2022). Automatic rice disease detection and assistance framework using deep learning and a Chatbot. *Electronics (Basel), 11*(14), 2110. doi:10.3390/electronics11142110

Jaiswal, A. (2023). *Guide to Haar Cascade Algorithm with Object Detection Example*. https://www.analyticsvidhya.com/blog/2022/04/object-detection-using-haar-cascade-opencv/

Jakkula, V. (2006). Tutorial on support vector machine (svm). School of EECS, Washington State University, 37(2.5), 3.

Jan Saleem, T., & Ahsan Chishti, M. (2021). Deep learning for the internet of things: Potential benefits and use-cases. *Digital Communications and Networks, 7*(4), 526–542. doi:10.1016/j.dcan.2020.12.002

Janardhana, K., Anushkannan, N., Dinakaran, K., Puse, R. K., & Boopathi, S. (2023). Experimental Investigation on Microhardness, Surface Roughness, and White Layer Thickness of Dry EDM. *Engineering Research Express, 5*(2), 025022. doi:10.1088/2631-8695/acce8f

Jane, J. B., & Ganeshi, E. (2019). A review on big data with machine learning and fuzzy logic for better decision making. *Int. J. Sci. Technol. Res, 8*, 1121–1125.

Janowicz, K., Haller, A., Cox, S., Phuoc, D. L., & Lefrancois, M. (2018). SOSA: A Lightweight Ontology for Sensors, Observations, Samples, and Actuators. *Journal of Web Semantics*. doi:10.2139/ssrn.3248499

Janowicz, K., Haller, A., Cox, S. J., Le Phuoc, D., & Lefrançois, M. (2019). SOSA: A lightweight ontology for sensors, observations, samples, and actuators. *Journal of Web Semantics*, *56*, 1–10. doi:10.1016/j.websem.2018.06.003

Javaid, M., Haleem, A., Pratap Singh, R., Suman, R., & Rab, S. (2022). Significance of machine learning in healthcare: Features, pillars and applications. *International Journal of Intelligent Networks*, *3*, 58–73. doi:10.1016/j.ijin.2022.05.002

Javed, A. R., Shahzad, F., Rehman, S., Zikria, Y. B., Razzak, I., Jalil, Z., & Xu, G. (2022). Future smart cities: Requirements, emerging technologies, applications, challenges, and future aspects. *Cities (London, England)*, *129*, 103794. doi:10.1016/j.cities.2022.103794

Jayakumar, J., Nagaraj, B., Chacko, S., & Ajay, P. (2021). Conceptual implementation of artificial intelligent based E-mobility controller in smart city environment. *Wireless Communications and Mobile Computing*, *2021*, 1–8. doi:10.1155/2021/5325116

Jeevanantham, Y. A., Saravanan, A., Vanitha, V., Boopathi, S., & Kumar, D. P. (2022). Implementation of Internet-of Things (IoT) in Soil Irrigation System. *IEEE Explore*, 1–5.

Jiang, H., & Learned-Miller, E. (2017, May). Face detection with the faster R-CNN. In *2017 12th IEEE International Conference on Automatic Face & Gesture Recognition (FG 2017)* (pp. 650-657). IEEE. 10.1109/FG.2017.82

Jiang, J. J., & Conrath, D. W. (1997). Semantic Similarity Based on Corpus Statistics and Lexical Taxonomy. *Proceedings of International Conference Research on Computational Lingustics*.

Jiang, P., Chen, Y., Liu, B., He, D., & Liang, C. (2019). Real-time detection of apple leaf diseases using deep learning approach based on improved convolutional neural networks. *IEEE Access : Practical Innovations, Open Solutions*, *7*, 59069–59080. doi:10.1109/ACCESS.2019.2914929

Jiang, X., Gao, T., Zhu, Z., & Zhao, Y. (2021). Real-Time Face Mask Detection Method Based on YOLOv3. *Electronics*, *10*, 837.

Jiang, Z., Gu, J., Liu, M., & Pan, D. Z. (2023, July). Delving into effective gradient matching for dataset condensation. In *2023 IEEE International Conference on Omni-layer Intelligent Systems (COINS)* (pp. 1-6). IEEE. 10.1109/COINS57856.2023.10189244

Jia, X., Hu, N., Su, S., Yin, S., Zhao, Y., Cheng, X., & Zhang, C. (2020, April 11). IRBA: An Identity-Based Cross-Domain Authentication Scheme for the Internet of Things. *Electronics (Basel)*, *9*(4), 634. doi:10.3390/electronics9040634

Ji, H., Alfarraj, O., & Tolba, A. (2020). Artificial intelligence-empowered edge of vehicles: Architecture, enabling technologies, and applications. *IEEE Access : Practical Innovations, Open Solutions*, *8*, 61020–61034. doi:10.1109/ACCESS.2020.2983609

Joshua, S. R., Park, S., & Kwon, K. (2024, January 8). Knowledge-Based Modeling Approach: A Schematic Design of Artificial Intelligence of Things (AIoT) for Hydrogen Energy System. *2024 IEEE 14th Annual Computing and Communication Workshop and Conference (CCWC)*. 10.1109/CCWC60891.2024.10427681

Judith, A., Kathrine, G. J. W., Silas, S., & J, A. (2023, December 24). Efficient Deep Learning-Based Cyber-Attack Detection for Internet of Medical Things Devices. *RAiSE-2023*. doi:10.3390/engproc2023059139

Ju, J., Liu, L., & Feng, Y. (2018). Citizen-centered big data analysis-driven governance intelligence framework for smart cities. *Telecommunications Policy*, *42*(10), 881–896. doi:10.1016/j.telpol.2018.01.003

Juliette, E. (2023). *Data Privacy and Security: Safeguarding*. https://www.ironhack.com/gb/blog/data-privacy-and-security-safeguarding-information-in-the-digital-age

Junghanns, M., Petermann, A., Gómez, K., & Rahm, E. (2015). Gradoop: Scalable graph data management and analytics with hadoop. *arXiv preprint arXiv:1506.00548.*

Ju, S., & Park, Y. (2023, December 11). Provably Secure Lightweight Mutual Authentication and Key Agreement Scheme for Cloud-Based IoT Environments. *Sensors (Basel)*, *23*(24), 9766. doi:10.3390/s23249766 PMID:38139612

Justinha. (2023). *Authentication methods in Microsoft Entra ID - security questions.* https://learn.microsoft.com/en-us/entra/identity/authentication/conceptauthentication-security-questions

Kalakota, R., & Whiston, A. (1997). *Electronic commerce: a manager's guide.* Addison Wesley.

Kamal, M. M. (2021). *Future Need of Petroleum Engineering.* One Petro. doi:10.2118/200771-MS

Kang, Ho., & Kim, Y. (2023). *Real-time object detection and segmentation technology: an analysis of the YOLO algorithm.* JMST Advances.

Kannan, E., Trabelsi, Y., Boopathi, S., & Alagesan, S. (2022). Influences of cryogenically treated work material on near-dry wire-cut electrical discharge machining process. *Surface Topography : Metrology and Properties*, *10*(1), 015027. doi:10.1088/2051-672X/ac53e1

Kaplan, A., & Haenlein, M. (2019). Siri, Siri, in my hand: Who's the fairest in the land? On the interpretations, illustrations, and implications of artificial intelligence. *Business Horizons*, *62*(1), 15–25. doi:10.1016/j.bushor.2018.08.004

Karthik, S., Hemalatha, R., Aruna, R., Deivakani, M., Reddy, R. V. K., & Boopathi, S. (2023). Study on Healthcare Security System-Integrated Internet of Things (IoT). In Perspectives and Considerations on the Evolution of Smart Systems (pp. 342–362). IGI Global.

Katsantonis, D., Kadoglidou, K., Dramalis, C., & Puigdollers, P. (2017). Rice blast forecasting models and their practical value: A review. *Phytopathologia Mediterranea*, ●●●, 187–216.

Katuu, S. (2021). Trends in the enterprise resource planning market landscape. *Journal of Information and Organizational Sciences*, *45*(1), 55–75. doi:10.31341/jios.45.1.4

Kaufer, F., & Klusch, M. (2006). WSMO-MX: A Logic Programming Based Hybrid Service Matchmaker. *European Conference on Web Services*, 161-170. 10.1109/ECOWS.2006.39

Kaundal, R., Kapoor, A. S., & Raghava, G. P. (2006). Machine learning techniques in disease forecasting: A case study on rice blast prediction. *BMC Bioinformatics*, *7*(1), 1–16. doi:10.1186/1471-2105-7-485 PMID:17083731

Kaur, J., & Singh, W. (2022). Tools, techniques, datasets and application areas for object detection in an image: A review. *Multimedia Tools and Applications*, *81*(27), 38297–38351. doi:10.1007/s11042-022-13153-y PMID:35493415

KAV, R. P., Pandraju, T. K. S., Boopathi, S., Saravanan, P., Rathan, S. K., & Sathish, T. (2023). Hybrid Deep Learning Technique for Optimal Wind Mill Speed Estimation. *2023 7th International Conference on Electronics, Communication and Aerospace Technology (ICECA)*, 181–186.

Kavitha, C., Varalatchoumy, M., Mithuna, H., Bharathi, K., Geethalakshmi, N., & Boopathi, S. (2023). Energy Monitoring and Control in the Smart Grid: Integrated Intelligent IoT and ANFIS. In Applications of Synthetic Biology in Health, Energy, and Environment (pp. 290–316). IGI Global.

Kerrison, S., Jusak, J., & Huang, T. (2023, May 6). Blockchain-Enabled IoT for Rural Healthcare: Hybrid-Channel Communication with Digital Twinning. *Electronics (Basel)*, *12*(9), 2128. doi:10.3390/electronics12092128

Khodr, H., Gomez, J., Barnique, L., Vivas, J., Paiva, P., Yusta, J., & Urdaneta, A. (2002). A linear programming methodology for the optimization of electric power-generation schemes. *IEEE Transactions on Power Systems*, *17*(3), 864–869. doi:10.1109/TPWRS.2002.800982

Kiefer, C., & Bernstein, A. (2008). The Creation and Evaluation of iSPARQL Strategies for Matchmaking. *European Semantic Web Conference*, 463-477. 10.1007/978-3-540-68234-9_35

Kim, H., Park, S., Hong, H., Park, J., & Kim, S. (2024, February 28). A Transferable Deep Learning Framework for Improving the Accuracy of Internet of Things Intrusion Detection. *Future Internet*, *16*(3), 80. doi:10.3390/fi16030080

Kim, Y., Roh, J. H., & Kim, H. Y. (2017). Early forecasting of rice blast disease using long short-term memory recurrent neural networks. *Sustainability (Basel)*, *10*(1), 34. doi:10.3390/su10010034

King, M. R. N., Timms, P. D., & Rubin, T. H. (2021). Use of Big Data in Insurance. In *The Palgrave Handbook of Technological Finance* (pp. 669–700). Springer International Publishing. doi:10.1007/978-3-030-65117-6_24

Kiratiratanapruk, K., Temniranrat, P., Sinthupinyo, W., Marukatat, S., & Patarapuwadol, S. (2022). Automatic Detection of Rice Disease in Images of Various Leaf Sizes. *arXiv preprint arXiv:2206.07344*.

Klusch, M., Fries, B., & Sycara, K. (2008). OWLS-MX: A Hybrid Semantic Web Service Matchmaker for OWL-S Services. *Journal of Web Semantics*.

Kong, S. M., Yoo, C., Park, J., Park, J. H., & Lee, S. W. (2024, January 25). AIoT Monitoring Technology for Optimal Fill Dam Installation and Operation. *Applied Sciences (Basel, Switzerland)*, *14*(3), 1024. doi:10.3390/app14031024

Korstjens, I., & Moser, A. (2018). Series: Practical guidance to qualitative research. Part 4: Trustworthiness and publishing. *The European Journal of General Practice*, *24*(1), 120–124. doi:10.1080/13814788.2017.1375092 PMID:29202616

Kosamkar, P. K., Kulkarni, V. Y., Mantri, K., Rudrawar, S., Salmpuria, S., & Gadekar, N. (2018, August). Leaf disease detection and recommendation of pesticides using convolution neural network. In *2018 fourth international conference on computing communication control and automation (ICCUBEA)* (pp. 1-4). IEEE. 10.1109/ICCUBEA.2018.8697504

Koshariya, A. K., Kalaiyarasi, D., Jovith, A. A., Sivakami, T., Hasan, D. S., & Boopathi, S. (2023). AI-Enabled IoT and WSN-Integrated Smart Agriculture System. In *Artificial Intelligence Tools and Technologies for Smart Farming and Agriculture Practices* (pp. 200–218). IGI Global. doi:10.4018/978-1-6684-8516-3.ch011

Koshariya, A. K., Khatoon, S., Marathe, A. M., Suba, G. M., Baral, D., & Boopathi, S. (2023). Agricultural Waste Management Systems Using Artificial Intelligence Techniques. In *AI-Enabled Social Robotics in Human Care Services* (pp. 236–258). IGI Global. doi:10.4018/978-1-6684-8171-4.ch009

Krishna, G. R., Krishnan, R., & Mittal, V. K. (2020, December). A system for automatic regional accent classification. In *2020 IEEE 17th India Council International Conference (INDICON)* (pp. 1-5). IEEE. 10.1109/INDICON49873.2020.9342577

Krishnamoorthy, N., Prasad, L. N., Kumar, C. P., Subedi, B., Abraha, H. B., & Sathishkumar, V. E. (2021). Rice leaf diseases prediction using deep neural networks with transfer learning. *Environmental Research*, *198*, 111275. doi:10.1016/j.envres.2021.111275 PMID:33989629

Kumar Sahu, A., Sharma, S., Tanveer, M., & Raja, R. (2021). Internet of Things attack detection using hybrid Deep Learning Model. *Computer Communications*, *176*, 146–154. doi:10.1016/j.comcom.2021.05.024

Kumar, A. (2019). *A Machine Learning Application for Field Planning Offshore Technology Conference*. 10.4043/29224-MS

Kumar, M., Kumar, K., Sasikala, P., Sampath, B., Gopi, B., & Sundaram, S. (2023). Sustainable Green Energy Generation From Waste Water: IoT and ML Integration. In Sustainable Science and Intelligent Technologies for Societal Development (pp. 440–463). IGI Global.

Kumar, P. R., Meenakshi, S., Shalini, S., Devi, S. R., & Boopathi, S. (2023). Soil Quality Prediction in Context Learning Approaches Using Deep Learning and Blockchain for Smart Agriculture. In Effective AI, Blockchain, and E-Governance Applications for Knowledge Discovery and Management (pp. 1–26). IGI Global. doi:10.4018/978-1-6684-9151-5.ch001

Kumar, A. A. (2021). Semantic memory: A review of methods, models, and current challenges. *Psychonomic Bulletin & Review*, *28*(1), 40–80. doi:10.3758/s13423-020-01792-x PMID:32885404

Kumar, A., & Tiwari, A. (2019). Detection of Sugarcane Disease and Classification using Image Processing. *International Journal for Research in Applied Science and Engineering Technology*, *7*(5), 2023–2030. doi:10.22214/ijraset.2019.5338

Kumara, V., Mohanaprakash, T., Fairooz, S., Jamal, K., Babu, T., & Sampath, B. (2023). Experimental Study on a Reliable Smart Hydroponics System. In *Human Agro-Energy Optimization for Business and Industry* (pp. 27–45). IGI Global. doi:10.4018/978-1-6684-4118-3.ch002

Kumar, M., Kumar, A., Verma, S., Bhattacharya, P., Ghimire, D., Kim, S., & Hosen, A. S. M. S. (2023). Healthcare Internet of Things (H-IoT): Current Trends, Future Prospects, Applications, Challenges, and Security Issues. *Electronics (Basel)*, *12*(9), 2050. doi:10.3390/electronics12092050

Kumar, P. (2021). Research Paper On Sugarcane Diseaese Detection Model. *Turkish Journal of Computer and Mathematics Education*, *12*(6), 5167–5174.

Kumar, R., Lamba, K., & Raman, A. (2021). Role of zero emission vehicles in sustainable transformation of the Indian automobile industry. *Research in Transportation Economics*, *90*, 101064. doi:10.1016/j.retrec.2021.101064

Kumar, S., Chandra, J., Alshamrani, S., Chaudhari, V., Dumka, A., Singh, R., Rashid, M., Gehlot, A., & AlGhamdi, S. (2022). Automatic Vehicle Identification and Classification Model Using the YOLOv3 Algorithm for a Toll Management System. *Sustainability*, *14*, 9163.

Kumar, S., Rathore, R. S., Dohare, U., Kaiwartya, O., Lloret, J., Kumar, N., & ... (2023). BEET: Blockchain Enabled Energy Trading for E-Mobility Oriented Electric Vehicles. *IEEE Transactions on Mobile Computing*.

Kumar, V., Anand, A., & Song, H. (2017). Future of Retailer Profitability: An Organizing Framework. *Journal of Retailing*, *93*(1), 96–119. doi:10.1016/j.jretai.2016.11.003

Kunal Jain, K. (2021). *BCrypt Algorithm*. https://www.topcoder.com/thrive/articles/bcrypt-algorithm

Kushwah, J. S., Gupta, M., Shrivastava, S., Saxena, N., Saini, R., & Boopathi, S. (2024). Psychological Impacts, Prevention Strategies, and Intervention Approaches Across Age Groups: Unmasking Cyberbullying. In Change Dynamics in Healthcare, Technological Innovations, and Complex Scenarios (pp. 89–109). IGI Global.

Kuzlu, M., Fair, C., & Guler, O. (2021). Role of artificial intelligence in the Internet of Things (IoT) cybersecurity. *Discover Internet of Things*, *1*(1), 1–14. doi:10.1007/s43926-020-00001-4

Kwon, B. W., Sharma, P. K., & Park, J. H. (2019). CCTV-based multi-factor authentication system. *Journal of Information Processing Systems*, *15*(4), 904–919.

Lajmi, S., Ghedira, C., & Ghedira, K. (2006a). How to apply CBR method in web service composition. *Second International Conference on Signal-Image Technology and Internet Based Systems (SITI'2006)*. Springer Verlag.

Lajmi, S., Ghedira, C., Ghedira, K., & Benslimane, D. (2006b). Web_CBR: How to compose web service via case based reasoning. *IEEE International Symposium on Service-Oriented Applications, Integration and Collaboration held with the IEEE International Conference on eBusiness Engineering (ICEBE 2006)*.

Laliwala, Z., Khosla, R., Majumdar, P., & Chaudhary, S. (2006). Semantic and Rule Based Event-Driven Dynamic Web Service Composition for Automation of Business Processes. *Proceedings of the IEEE Service Computing Workshop (SCW06)*.

Lambert, D. M., & Cooper, M. C. (2000). Issues in Supply Chain Management. *Industrial Marketing Management*, 29(1), 65–83. doi:10.1016/S0019-8501(99)00113-3

Lampropoulos, G., Garzón, J., Misra, S., & Siakas, K. (2024, February 7). The Role of Artificial Intelligence of Things in Achieving Sustainable Development Goals: State of the Art. *Sensors (Basel)*, 24(4), 1091. doi:10.3390/s24041091 PMID:38400249

Lampropoulos, G., Keramopoulos, E., & Diamantaras, K. (2020). Enhancing the functionality of augmented reality using deep learning, semantic web and knowledge graphs: A review. *Visual Informatics*, 4(1), 32–42. doi:10.1016/j.visinf.2020.01.001

Lauria, M., & Azzalin, M. (2024, February 1). Digital Twin Approach in Buildings: Future Challenges via a Critical Literature Review. *Buildings*, 14(2), 376. doi:10.3390/buildings14020376

Lee, H. M., Ham, S. M., Moon, H., Kwon, H. M., Rho, J. H., & Seo, J. (2023, June). A Metaverse Emotion Mapping System with an AIoT Facial Expression Recognition Device. *2023 IEEE International Conference on Metaverse Computing, Networking and Applications (MetaCom)*. 10.1109/MetaCom57706.2023.00132

Lee, J. H., Chakraborty, D., Hardman, S. J., & Tal, G. (2020). Exploring electric vehicle charging patterns: Mixed usage of charging infrastructure. *Transportation Research Part D, Transport and Environment*, 79, 102249. doi:10.1016/j.trd.2020.102249

Lei, S., Luo, J., Tao, X., & Qiu, Z. (2021). Remote sensing detecting of yellow leaf disease of Arecanut based on UAV multisource sensors. *Remote Sensing (Basel)*, 13(22), 4562. doi:10.3390/rs13224562

Le-Thanh, L., Nguyen-Thi-Viet, H., Lee, J., & Nguyen-Xuan, H. (2022). Machine learning-based real-time daylight analysis in buildings. *Journal of Building Engineering*, 52, 104374. doi:10.1016/j.jobe.2022.104374

Li, S. H. (2002). *An Integrated Model for Supply Chain Management Practice, Performance and Competitive Advantage* [PhD Dissertation]. University of Toledo, Toledo, OH.

Liang, T., & Konsynski, B. R. (1993). Modeling by analogy: Use of analogical reasoning in model management systems. *Decision Support Systems*, 9(1), 113–125. doi:10.1016/0167-9236(93)90026-Y

Liang, W. J., Zhang, H., Zhang, G. F., & Cao, H. X. (2019). Rice blast disease recognition using a deep convolutional neural network. *Scientific Reports*, 9(1), 2869. doi:10.1038/s41598-019-38966-0 PMID:30814523

Li, J., Herdem, M. S., Nathwani, J., & Wen, J. Z. (2023). Methods and applications for Artificial Intelligence, Big Data, Internet of Things, and Blockchain in smart energy management. *Energy and AI*, 11, 100208. doi:10.1016/j.egyai.2022.100208

Li, J., Sikora, R., Shaw, M. J., & Woo Tan, G. A. (2006). Strategic analysis of inter-organizational information sharing. *Decision Support Systems*, 42(1), 251–266. doi:10.1016/j.dss.2004.12.003

Li, J., & Yu, T. (2021). A novel data-driven controller for solid oxide fuel cell via deep reinforcement learning. *Journal of Cleaner Production*, 321, 128929. doi:10.1016/j.jclepro.2021.128929

Li, L., & Horrocks, I. (2003). A Software Framework for Matchmaking Based on Semantic Web Technology. *International Conference in World Wide Web*, 331-339. 10.1145/775152.775199

Li, L., Zhang, S., & Wang, B. (2021). Plant disease detection and classification by deep learning—A review. *IEEE Access : Practical Innovations, Open Solutions*, 9, 56683–56698. doi:10.1109/ACCESS.2021.3069646

Li, M., Yu, B., Rana, O. F., & Wang, Z. (2008). Grid Service Discovery with Rough Sets. *IEEE Transactions on Knowledge and Data Engineering*, 20(6), 851–862. doi:10.1109/TKDE.2007.190744

Limkar, S., Kulkarni, S., Chinchmalatpure, P., Sharma, D., Desai, M., Angadi, S., & Jadhav, P. (2020). Classification and prediction of rice crop diseases using CNN and PNN. In *Intelligent Data Engineering and Analytics: Frontiers in Intelligent Computing: Theory and Applications (FICTA 2020)* (Vol. 2, pp. 31–40). Springer Singapore.

Lin, K., Gong, L., Huang, Y., Liu, C., & Pan, J. (2019). Deep learning-based segmentation and quantification of cucumber powdery mildew using convolutional neural network. *Frontiers in Plant Science*, 10, 155. doi:10.3389/fpls.2019.00155 PMID:30891048

Lin, S., Cui, L., & Ke, N. (2024, January 10). End-to-End Encrypted Message Distribution System for the Internet of Things Based on Conditional Proxy Re-Encryption. *Sensors (Basel)*, 24(2), 438. doi:10.3390/s24020438 PMID:38257530

Lipu, M. H., Hannan, M., Karim, T. F., Hussain, A., Saad, M. H. M., Ayob, A., Miah, M. S., & Mahlia, T. I. (2021a). Intelligent algorithms and control strategies for battery management system in electric vehicles: Progress, challenges and future outlook. *Journal of Cleaner Production*, 292, 126044. doi:10.1016/j.jclepro.2021.126044

Li, T., Peng, G., Zhu, Q., & Başar, T. (2022). The confluence of networks, games, and learning a game-theoretic framework for multiagent decision making over networks. *IEEE Control Systems*, 42(4), 35–67. doi:10.1109/MCS.2022.3171478

Liua, S., Xua, Y., Guoa, L., Shaoa, M., Yuea, G., & An, D. (2021). Multi-scale personnel deep feature detection algorithm based on Extended-YOLOv3. *Journal of Intelligent & Fuzzy Systems*, 40(1), 773–786. doi:10.3233/JIFS-200778

Liu, B., Tan, C., Li, S., He, J., & Wang, H. (2020). A data augmentation method based on generative adversarial networks for grape leaf disease identification. *IEEE Access : Practical Innovations, Open Solutions*, 8, 102188–102198. doi:10.1109/ACCESS.2020.2998839

Liu, W., Placke, T., & Chau, K. (2022). Overview of batteries and battery management for electric vehicles. *Energy Reports*, 8, 4058–4084. doi:10.1016/j.egyr.2022.03.016

Liu, X., Kong, J., Peng, L., Luo, D., Xu, G., Chen, X., & Liu, X. (2023, December 1). A Secure Multi-Party Computation Protocol for Graph Editing Distance against Malicious Attacks. *Mathematics*, 11(23), 4847. doi:10.3390/math11234847

Li, X., Yang, Z., & Wu, H. (2020). *Face detection based on receptive field enhanced multi-task cascaded convolutional neural networks*. IEEE. doi:10.1109/ACCESS.2020.3023782

Li, Y., Wang, B., Yang, Z., Li, J., & Chen, C. (2022). Hierarchical stochastic scheduling of multi-community integrated energy systems in uncertain environments via Stackelberg game. *Applied Energy*, 308, 118392. doi:10.1016/j.apenergy.2021.118392

Li, Y., Wang, L., & Li, W. (2019). Key technologies of mechanical fault diagnosis system based on cloud computing. *International Journal of Mechatronics and Applied Mechanics*, 6, 107–119.

Lork, C., Choudhary, V., Hassan, N. U., Tushar, W., Yuen, C., Ng, B. K. K., Wang, X., & Liu, X. (2019). An ontology-based framework for building energy management with IoT. *Electronics (Basel)*, 8(5), 485. doi:10.3390/electronics8050485

Luthra, S., Mangla, S. K., Garg, D., & Kumar, A. (2018). *Internet of Things (IoT) in Agriculture Supply Chain Management: A Developing Country Perspective.* doi:10.1007/978-3-319-75013-2_16

Ma, Q., & Huang, X. (2022). Research on recognizing required items based on opencv and machine learning. In *SHS Web of Conferences* (Vol. 140, p. 01016). EDP Sciences. 10.1051/shsconf/202214001016

Maarala, A. I., Su, X., & Riekki, J. (2016). Semantic reasoning for context-aware Internet of Things applications. *IEEE Internet of Things Journal*, *4*(2), 461–473. doi:10.1109/JIOT.2016.2587060

MacDermott, A., Kendrick, P., Idowu, I., Ashall, M., & Shi, Q. (2019). Securing Things in the Healthcare Internet of Things. *2019 Global IoT Summit (GIoTS)*, 1–6. doi:10.1109/GIOTS.2019.8766383

Macedo, R., Correia, C., Dantas, M., Brito, C., Xu, W., Tanimura, Y., ... Paulo, J. (2021, September). The Case for Storage Optimization Decoupling in Deep Learning Frameworks. In *2021 IEEE International Conference on Cluster Computing (CLUSTER)* (pp. 649-656). IEEE. 10.1109/Cluster48925.2021.00096

Madan, A. (2021). Face recognition using Haar cascade classifier. *Int. J. Mod. Trends Sci. Technol*, *7*(01), 85–87. doi:10.46501/IJMTST070119

Madruga, G. O., Roche, S. R., & Hernández Quintana, A. (2017). Citizen Information in the local press. A content analysis in the Tribuna de La Habanas Newspaper in the period 2008-2014. *Ciencias de la Información*, *48*(1), 11–18.

Maguluri, L. P., Ananth, J., Hariram, S., Geetha, C., Bhaskar, A., & Boopathi, S. (2023). Smart Vehicle-Emissions Monitoring System Using Internet of Things (IoT). In Handbook of Research on Safe Disposal Methods of Municipal Solid Wastes for a Sustainable Environment (pp. 191–211). IGI Global.

Maksimovic, M. (2017). The Role of Green Internet of Things (G-IoT) and Big Data in Making Cities Smarter, Safer and More Sustainable. *International Journal of Computing and Digital Systemss*, *6*(4), 175–184. doi:10.12785/IJCDS/060403

Malathi, J., Kusha, K., Isaac, S., Ramesh, A., Rajendiran, M., & Boopathi, S. (2024). IoT-Enabled Remote Patient Monitoring for Chronic Disease Management and Cost Savings: Transforming Healthcare. In Advances in Explainable AI Applications for Smart Cities (pp. 371–388). IGI Global.

Malicdem, A. R., & Fernandez, P. L. (2015). Rice blast disease forecasting for northern Philippines. *WSEAS Trans. Inf. Sci. Appl*, *12*, 120–129.

Malik, N., & Malik, S. K. (2020). Using IoT and semantic web technologies for the healthcare and medical sector. *Ontology-Based Information Retrieval for Healthcare Systems*, 91-115.

Maneesha, A., Suresh, C., & Kiranmayee, B. V. (2021). Prediction of rice plant diseases based on soil and weather conditions. In *Proceedings of International Conference on Advances in Computer Engineering and Communication Systems: ICACECS 2020* (pp. 155-165). Springer Singapore. 10.1007/978-981-15-9293-5_14

Mannepalli, K., Sastry, P. N., & Suman, M. (2016). MFCC-GMM based accent recognition system for Telugu speech signals. *International Journal of Speech Technology*, *19*(1), 87–93. doi:10.1007/s10772-015-9328-y

Mansouri, S., Ahmarinejad, A., Ansarian, M., Javadi, M., & Catalao, J. (2020). Stochastic planning and operation of energy hubs considering demand response programs using Benders decomposition approach. *International Journal of Electrical Power & Energy Systems*, *120*, 106030. doi:10.1016/j.ijepes.2020.106030

Margaret, R. (2018). *False Acceptance Ratio.* https://www.techopedia.com/definition/27569/false-acceptance-ratio-far

Martin, D., Burstein, M., Mcdermott, D., Mcilraith, S., Paolucci, M., Sycara, K., Mcguinness, D. L., Sirin, E., & Srinivasan, N. (2007). Bringing Semantics to Web Services with OWL-S. *World Wide Web (Bussum), 10*(3), 243–277. doi:10.1007/s11280-007-0033-x

Martin, D., Paolucci, M., McIlraith, S., Burstein, M., McDermott, D., McGunness, D., Barsia, B., Payne, T., Sabou, M., Solanki, M., Srinivasan, N., & Sycara, K. (2004). Bringing Semantics to Web Services: The OWL-S Approach , *Proceeding of First International Workshop Semantic Web Services and Web Process Composition.*

Martinez-Rodriguez, J. L., Hogan, A., & Lopez-Arevalo, I. (2020). Information extraction meets the semantic web: A survey. *Semantic Web, 11*(2), 255–335. doi:10.3233/SW-180333

Masood, A., Lakew, D. S., & Cho, S. (2020). Security and privacy challenges in connected vehicular cloud computing. *IEEE Communications Surveys and Tutorials, 22*(4), 2725–2764. doi:10.1109/COMST.2020.3012961

Mathulaprangsan, S., Lanthong, K., Jetpipattanapong, D., Sateanpattanakul, S., & Patarapuwadol, S. (2020, March). Rice diseases recognition using effective deep learning models. In *2020 Joint International Conference on Digital Arts, Media and Technology with ECTI Northern Section Conference on Electrical, Electronics, Computer and Telecommunications Engineering (ECTI DAMT & NCON)* (pp. 386-389). IEEE. 10.1109/ECTIDAMTNCON48261.2020.9090709

Mathur, A. (2023). Moving upstream with digital technology in the oil and gas industry. *World Oil.* https://www.worldoil.com/magazine/2023/august-2023/features/moving-upstream-with-digital-technology-in-the-oil-and-gas-industry/

Matskin, M., Maigre, R., & Tyugu, E. (2007). Computational logical semantics for business process language. *Proceedings of second international conference on Internet and Web applications and services (ICIW 2007),* 526-531.

Matthews, B. (2005). Semantic web technologies. *E-learning, 6*(6), 8.

Mayring, P. (2014). *Qualitative content analysis: theoretical foundation, basic procedures and software solution.* Retrieved from Klagenfurt: https://www.ssoar.info/ssoar/bitstream/handle/document/39517/ssoar-2014-mayring-Qualitative_content_analysis_theoretical_foundation.pdf

McFee, B., Raffel, C., Liang, D., Ellis, D. P., McVicar, M., Battenberg, E., & Nieto, O. (2015, July). librosa: Audio and music signal analysis in python. In *Proceedings of the 14th python in science conference* (Vol. 8, pp. 18-25). 10.25080/Majora-7b98e3ed-003

McIlraith, S., & Martin, D. (2003). Bringing Semantics to Web Services. *IEEE Intelligent Systems, 18*(1), 90–93. doi:10.1109/MIS.2003.1179199

Medina-Quintero, J. M., Ortiz-Rodriguez, F., Tiwari, S., & Saenz, F. I. (2023). Trust in Electronic Banking With the Use of Cell Phones for User Satisfaction. In *Global Perspectives on the Strategic Role of Marketing Information Systems* (pp. 87–106). IGI Global. doi:10.4018/978-1-6684-6591-2.ch006

Medina-Quintero, J. M., Sahagun, M. A., Alfaro, J., & Ortiz-Rodriguez, F. (Eds.). (2023). *Global Perspectives on the Strategic Role of Marketing Information Systems.* IGI Global. doi:10.4018/978-1-6684-6591-2

Mehmood, A., Zameer, A., Aslam, M. S., & Raja, M. A. Z. (2020). Design of nature-inspired heuristic paradigm for systems in nonlinear electrical circuits. *Neural Computing & Applications, 32*(11), 7121–7137. doi:10.1007/s00521-019-04197-7

Mehmood, A., Zameer, A., Ling, S. H., Rehman, A. U., & Raja, M. A. Z. (2020). Integrated computational intelligent paradigm for nonlinear electric circuit models using neural networks, genetic algorithms and sequential quadratic programming. *Neural Computing & Applications, 32*(14), 10337–10357. doi:10.1007/s00521-019-04573-3

Mehta, S., Tiwari, S., Siarry, P., & Jabbar, M. A. (Eds.). (2022). *Tools, Languages, Methodologies for Representing Semantics on the Web of Things.* John Wiley & Sons. doi:10.1002/9781394171460

Melin, P., Sánchez, D., Monica, J. C., & Castillo, O. (2023). Optimization using the firefly algorithm of ensemble neural networks with type-2 fuzzy integration for COVID-19 time series prediction. *Soft Computing*, 27(6), 3245–3282. doi:10.1007/s00500-020-05549-5 PMID:33456340

Miao, F., Holmes, W., Huang, R., & Zhang, H. (2021). AI and education: A guidance for policymakers. United Nations Educational, Scientific and Cultural Organization (UNESCO).

Middleton, F. (2020, June 26). *Reliability vs Validity in Research\ Differences, Types and Examples*. Retrieved from Scribbr: https://www.scribbr.com/author/fionamiddleton/

Mikołajczyk, A., & Grochowski, M. (2018, May). *Data augmentation for improving deep learning in image classification problem. In 2018 international interdisciplinary PhD workshop (IIPhDW)*. IEEE.

Militante, S. V., Gerardo, B. D., & Medina, R. P. (2019, October). Sugarcane disease recognition using deep learning. In 2019 IEEE Eurasia conference on IOT, communication and engineering (ECICE) (pp. 575-578). IEEE. doi:10.1109/ECICE47484.2019.8942690

Mimboro, P., Lumban Gaol, F., Lesie Hendric Spits Warnars, H., & Soewito, B. (2021, November 24). Weather Monitoring System AIoT Based for Oil Palm Plantation Using Recurrent Neural Network Algorithm. *2021 IEEE 5th International Conference on Information Technology, Information Systems and Electrical Engineering (ICITISEE)*. 10.1109/ICITISEE53823.2021.9655818

Ministry of Education. (2005, March). *ICT Policy for Education*. Windhoek: John Meinert Publications. Retrieved from https://www.moe.gov.na/files/downloads/155_Published%20ICT%20Policy%202005%20-%2015%20March%202005.pdf

Mohanty, A., Venkateswaran, N., Ranjit, P., Tripathi, M. A., & Boopathi, S. (2023). Innovative Strategy for Profitable Automobile Industries: Working Capital Management. In Handbook of Research on Designing Sustainable Supply Chains to Achieve a Circular Economy (pp. 412–428). IGI Global.

Mohanty, A., Jothi, B., Jeyasudha, J., Ranjit, P., Isaac, J. S., & Boopathi, S. (2023). Additive Manufacturing Using Robotic Programming. In *AI-Enabled Social Robotics in Human Care Services* (pp. 259–282). IGI Global. doi:10.4018/978-1-6684-8171-4.ch010

Mokhtar, S. S. S., Mahomed, A. S. B., Aziz, Y. A., & Rahman, S. A. (2020). Industry 4.0: The importance of innovation in adopting cloud computing among SMEs in Malaysia. *Polish Journal of Management Studies, 22*.

Moniruzzaman, M., Yassine, A., & Hossain, M. S. (2023). Energizing Charging Services for Next-Generation Consumers E-Mobility With Reinforcement Learning and Blockchain. *IEEE Transactions on Consumer Electronics*.

Morales-Sáenz, F. I., Medina-Quintero, J. M., & Ortiz-Rodriguez, F. (2023). Bibliometrics Study of Organizational Cybersecurity. In *Emerging Technologies and Digital Transformation in the Manufacturing Industry* (pp. 115–139). IGI Global. doi:10.4018/978-1-6684-8088-5.ch008

Moreira, F., Ferreira, M. J., & Cardoso, A. (2017). *Higher Education Disruption Through IoT and Big Data: A Conceptual Approach*. doi:10.1007/978-3-319-58509-3_31

Mouassa, S., & Bouktir, T. (2018). Mathematics in electrical and electronic engineering. *COMPEL*, 208.

Moutsos, J. (2022). *Why You Need to Stop Using Single-Factor Authentication*. https://dynamixsolutions.com/stop-using-single-factor-authentication

Moving upstream with digital technology in the oil and gas industry. (n.d.). https://www.worldoil.com/magazine/2023/august-2023/features/moving-upstream-with-digital-technology-in-the-oil-and-gas-industry/

Mridha, M. F., Ohi, A. Q., Hamid, M. A., & Monowar, M. M. (2022). A study on the challenges and opportunities of speech recognition for Bengali language. *Artificial Intelligence Review*, *55*(4), 1–25. doi:10.1007/s10462-021-10083-3

Muheidat, F., Patel, D., Tammisetty, S., Tawalbeh, L. A., & Tawalbeh, M. (2022). Emerging Concepts Using Blockchain and Big Data. *Procedia Computer Science*, *198*, 15–22. doi:10.1016/j.procs.2021.12.206

Mukherjee, S., Gupta, S., Rawlley, O., & Jain, S. (2022). Leveraging big data analytics in 5G-enabled IoT and industrial IoT for the development of sustainable smart cities. *Transactions on Emerging Telecommunications Technologies*, *33*(12), e4618. Advance online publication. doi:10.1002/ett.4618

Munirathinam, S. (2020). *Industry 4.0: Industrial Internet of Things*. IIOT. doi:10.1016/bs.adcom.2019.10.010

M, V. K., Venkatachalam, K., P, P., Almutairi, A., & Abouhawwash, M. (2021, July 30). Secure biometric authentication with de-duplication on distributed cloud storage. *PeerJ. Computer Science*, *7*, e569. doi:10.7717/peerj-cs.569

Nabilla, R. (2023). *9 best WordPress LMS plugins for your eLearning site*. Retrieved from Hostinger: https://www.hostinger.com/tutorials/wordpress-lms-plugins

Nadhan, A. S., & Jacob, I. J. (2023, December 12). A Secure Lightweight Cryptographic Algorithm for the Internet of Things (IoT) Based on Deoxyribonucleic Acid (DNA) Sequences. *RAiSE*, *2023*, 31. Advance online publication. doi:10.3390/engproc2023059031

Nahr, J. G., Nozari, H., & Sadeghi, M. E. (2021). Green supply chain based on artificial intelligence of things (AIoT). *International Journal of Innovation in Management. Economics and Social Sciences*, *1*(2), 56–63.

Nair, V., Bartunov, S., Gimeno, F., Von Glehn, I., Lichocki, P., Lobov, I., O'Donoghue, B., Sonnerat, N., Tjandraatmadja, C., Wang, P., & Associates. (2020). Solving mixed integer programs using neural networks. *arXiv Preprint arXiv:2012.13349*.

Nanda, A. K., Sharma, A., Augustine, P. J., Cyril, B. R., Kiran, V., & Sampath, B. (2024). Securing Cloud Infrastructure in IaaS and PaaS Environments. In Improving Security, Privacy, and Trust in Cloud Computing (pp. 1–33). IGI Global. doi:10.4018/979-8-3693-1431-9.ch001

Narmilan, A., Gonzalez, F., Salgadoe, A. S. A., & Powell, K. (2022). Detection of white leaf disease in sugarcane using machine learning techniques over UAV multispectral images. *Drones (Basel)*, *6*(9), 230. doi:10.3390/drones6090230

Narwane, V. S., Gunasekaran, A., & Gardas, B. B. (2022). Unlocking adoption challenges of IoT in Indian Agricultural and Food Supply Chain. *Smart Agricultural Technology*, *2*, 100035. doi:10.1016/j.atech.2022.100035

Narwane, V. S., Raut, R. D., Mangla, S. K., Gardas, B. B., Narkhede, B. E., Awasthi, A., & Priyadarshinee, P. (2020). Mediating role of cloud of things in improving performance of small and medium enterprises in the Indian context. *Annals of Operations Research*, 1–30.

Nauck, D., & Kruse, R. (2020). Neuro–Fuzzy Systems. In *Handbook of Fuzzy Computation* (pp. 319–D2). CRC Press. doi:10.1201/9780429142741-50

Naveeenkumar, N., Rallapalli, S., Sasikala, K., Priya, P. V., Husain, J., & Boopathi, S. (2024). Enhancing Consumer Behavior and Experience Through AI-Driven Insights Optimization. In *AI Impacts in Digital Consumer Behavior* (pp. 1–35). IGI Global. doi:10.4018/979-8-3693-1918-5.ch001

Nettleton, D. F., Katsantonis, D., Kalaitzidis, A., Sarafijanovic-Djukic, N., Puigdollers, P., & Confalonieri, R. (2019). Predicting rice blast disease: Machine learning versus process-based models. *BMC Bioinformatics*, *20*(1), 1–16. doi:10.1186/s12859-019-3065-1 PMID:31640541

Ngugi, J. K., & Goosen, L. (2021). Innovation, Entrepreneurship, and Sustainability for ICT Students Towards the Post-COVID-19 Era. In L. C. Carvalho, L. Reis, & C. Silveira (Eds.), *Handbook of Research on Entrepreneurship, Innovation, Sustainability, and ICTs in the Post-COVID-19 Era* (pp. 110–131). IGI Global. doi:10.4018/978-1-7998-6776-0.ch006

Ni, M., Chen, L., Hao, X., Sun, H., Liu, C., Zhang, Z., Wu, L., & Pan, L. (2020, October 24). A Novel Prefetching Scheme for Non-Volatile Cache in the AIoT Processor. *2020 5th International Conference on Universal Village (UV)*. 10.1109/UV50937.2020.9426214

Nishanth, J., Deshmukh, M. A., Kushwah, R., Kushwaha, K. K., Balaji, S., & Sampath, B. (2023). Particle Swarm Optimization of Hybrid Renewable Energy Systems. In *Intelligent Engineering Applications and Applied Sciences for Sustainability* (pp. 291–308). IGI Global. doi:10.4018/979-8-3693-0044-2.ch016

Nita, S. L., & Mihailescu, M. I. (2023). *Advances to Homomorphic and Searchable Encryption.* Springer., doi:10.1007/978-3-031-43214-9

Noble, H., & Smith, J. (2015). Issues of validity and reliability in qualitative research. *Evidence-Based Nursing, 18*(2), 34–35. doi:10.1136/eb-2015-102054 PMID:25653237

Nowell, L. S., Norris, J. M., White, D. E., & Moules, N. J. (2017). Thematic analysis: Striving to meet the trustworthiness criteria. *International Journal of Qualitative Methods, 16*(1). Advance online publication. doi:10.1177/1609406917733847

Nozaki, S., Serizawa, A., Yoshihira, M., Fujita, M., Shibata, Y., Yamanaka, T., ... Nishigaki, M. (2022, August). Multi-observed Multi-factor Authentication: A Multi-factor Authentication Using Single Credential. In *International Conference on Network-Based Information Systems* (pp. 201-211). Cham: Springer International Publishing. 10.1007/978-3-031-14314-4_20

OASIS. (2004). *Introduction to UDDI: Important Features and Functional Concepts.* Organization for the Advancement of Structured Information Standards.

Oh, J., Lee, J., Park, Y., & Park, Y. (2022, December 18). A Secure Data Processing System in Edge Computing-Powered AIoT. *2022 IEEE Asia-Pacific Conference on Computer Science and Data Engineering (CSDE)*. 10.1109/CSDE56538.2022.10089302

Ojstersek, R., Brezocnik, M., & Buchmeister, B. (2020). Multi-objective optimization of production scheduling with evolutionary computation: A review. *International Journal of Industrial Engineering Computations, 11*(3), 359–376. doi:10.5267/j.ijiec.2020.1.003

Olivares-Rojas, J. C., Reyes-Archundia, E., Gutièrrez-Gnecchi, J. A., & Molina-Moreno, I. (2020). A survey on smart metering systems using blockchain for E-Mobility. *arXiv Preprint arXiv:2009.09075.*

Oluyisola, O. E., Bhalla, S., Sgarbossa, F., & Strandhagen, J. O. (2022). Designing and developing smart production planning and control systems in the industry 4.0 era: A methodology and case study. *Journal of Intelligent Manufacturing, 33*(1), 311–332. doi:10.1007/s10845-021-01808-w

OMG. (2009). *Business Process Model and Notation.* http://www.omg.org/spec/BPMN/1.2/(2009)

Optimal IdM. (2022). *Security Question Best Practices.* https://optimalidm.com/resources/blog/security-question-best-practices/

Ortiz-Rodríguez, F., Palma, R., & Villazón-Terrazas, B. (2006). Semantic based P2P System for local e-Government. In Proceedings of Informatik 2006. GI-Edition- Lecture Notes in Informatics (LNI).

Ortiz-Rodriguez, F., Tiwari, S., Amara, F. Z., & Sahagun, M. A. (2023). E-Government Success: An End-User Perspective. In Global Perspectives on the Strategic Role of Marketing Information Systems (pp. 168-186). IGI Global.

Ortiz-Rodriguez, F., Medina-Quintero, J. M., Tiwari, S., & Villanueva, V. (2022). EGODO ontology: sharing, retrieving, and exchanging legal documentation across e-government. In *Futuristic Trends for Sustainable Development and Sustainable Ecosystems* (pp. 261–276). IGI Global. doi:10.4018/978-1-6684-4225-8.ch016

Osman, T., Thakker, D., & Al-Dabass, D. (2006a). *Semantic-Driven Matching of Web services using Case-Based Reasoning*. In The Fourth IEEE International Conference on Web Services (ICWS 2006), Chicago, USA.

Osman, T., Thakker, D., & Al-Dabass, D. (2006b). S-CBR: Semantic Case Based Reasoner for Web services discovery and matchmaking. *20th European Conference on Modeling and Simulation (ECMS2006)*, 723-729.

Ożadowicz, A. (2024, February 3). Generic IoT for Smart Buildings and Field-Level Automation—Challenges, Threats, Approaches, and Solutions. *Computers*, *13*(2), 45. doi:10.3390/computers13020045

P., Saini, N., Gulzar, Y., Turaev, S., Kaur, A., Nisa, K. U., & Hamid, Y. (2024, February 19). A Review and Comparative Analysis of Relevant Approaches of Zero Trust Network Model. *Sensors, 24*(4), 1328. https://doi.org/ doi:10.3390/s24041328Daah

Pachiappan, K., Anitha, K., Pitchai, R., Sangeetha, S., Satyanarayana, T., & Boopathi, S. (2024). Intelligent Machines, IoT, and AI in Revolutionizing Agriculture for Water Processing. In *Handbook of Research on AI and ML for Intelligent Machines and Systems* (pp. 374–399). IGI Global.

Padilla, D. A., Magwili, G. V., Marohom, A. L. A., Co, C. M. G., Gaño, J. C. C., & Tuazon, J. M. U. (2019, April). Portable yellow spot disease identifier on sugarcane leaf via image processing using support vector machine. In *2019 5th International Conference on Control, Automation and Robotics (ICCAR)* (pp. 901-905). IEEE. 10.1109/ICCAR.2019.8813495

Paek, S., & Kim, N. (2021). Analysis of worldwide research trends on the impact of artificial intelligence in education. *Sustainability (Basel)*, *13*(14), 7941. doi:10.3390/su13147941

Pal, K., & Karakostas, B. (2014). A Multi Agent-based Service Framework for supply Chain Management. *Procedia Computer Science, 32*, 53-60.

Palafox-Alcantar, P., Hunt, D., & Rogers, C. (2020). The complementary use of game theory for the circular economy: A review of waste management decision-making methods in civil engineering. *Waste Management (New York, N.Y.)*, *102*, 598–612. doi:10.1016/j.wasman.2019.11.014 PMID:31778971

Palaniappan, M., Tirlangi, S., Mohamed, M. J. S., Moorthy, R. S., Valeti, S. V., & Boopathi, S. (2023). Fused Deposition Modelling of Polylactic Acid (PLA)-Based Polymer Composites: A Case Study. In Development, Properties, and Industrial Applications of 3D Printed Polymer Composites (pp. 66–85). IGI Global.

Pal, H. S., Kumar, A., Vishwakarma, A., & Ahirwal, M. K. (2022). Electrocardiogram signal compression using tunable-Q wavelet transform and meta-heuristic optimization techniques. *Biomedical Signal Processing and Control*, *78*, 103932. doi:10.1016/j.bspc.2022.103932

Pal, K., & Palmer, O. (2000). A decision-support systems for business acquisition. *Decision Support Systems*, *27*(4), 411–429. doi:10.1016/S0167-9236(99)00083-4

Pallathadka, H., Ravipati, P., Sajja, G. S., Phasinam, K., Kassanuk, T., Sanchez, D. T., & Prabhu, P. (2022). Application of machine learning techniques in rice leaf disease detection. *Materials Today: Proceedings*, *51*, 2277–2280. doi:10.1016/j.matpr.2021.11.398

Pal, S., Pramanik, A., Maiti, J., & Pabitra, M. (2021). Deep learning in multi-object detection and tracking: State of the art. *Applied Intelligence*, *51*(9), 6400–6429. doi:10.1007/s10489-021-02293-7

Pandiyan, P., Saravanan, S., Usha, K., Kannadasan, R., Alsharif, M. H., & Kim, M.-K. (2023). Technological advancements toward smart energy management in smart cities. *Energy Reports*, *10*, 648–677. doi:10.1016/j.egyr.2023.07.021

Papazoglou, M. (2012). *Web Services and SOA: Principles and Technology*. Pearson.

Parikh, P., Velhal, K., Potdar, S., Sikligar, A., & Karani, R. (2020, May). English language accent classification and conversion using machine learning. *Proceedings of the International Conference on Innovative Computing & Communications (ICICC)*. 10.2139/ssrn.3600748

Patel, A., & Jain, S. (2021). Present and future of semantic web technologies: A research statement. *International Journal of Computers and Applications*, *43*(5), 413–422. doi:10.1080/1206212X.2019.1570666

Patel, B., & Sharaff, A. (2021). Rice crop disease prediction using machine learning technique. *International Journal of Agricultural and Environmental Information Systems*, *12*(4), 1–15. doi:10.4018/IJAEIS.20211001.oa5

Pathak, J., Koul, N., Caragea, D., & Honavar, V. G. (2005). A Framework for Semantic Web Services Discovery. *ACM International Workshop on Web Information and Data Management*, 45-50. 10.1145/1097047.1097057

Pathan, M., Patel, N., Yagnik, H., & Shah, M. (2020). Artificial cognition for applications in smart agriculture: A comprehensive review. *Artificial Intelligence in Agriculture*, *4*, 81–95. doi:10.1016/j.aiia.2020.06.001

Patil, A., Oundhaka, S., Sheth, A., & Verma, K. (2004). METEOR-S Web service Annotation Framework. *Proceedings of the Thirteenth International World Wide Web Conference*, 553-562.

Patil, R. R., & Kumar, S. (2021). Predicting rice diseases across diverse agro-meteorological conditions using an artificial intelligence approach. *PeerJ. Computer Science*, *7*, e687. doi:10.7717/peerj-cs.687 PMID:34604518

Patil, R. R., & Kumar, S. (2022). Rice-fusion: A multimodality data fusion framework for rice disease diagnosis. *IEEE Access : Practical Innovations, Open Solutions*, *10*, 5207–5222. doi:10.1109/ACCESS.2022.3140815

Paul, A., Thilagham, K. KG, J., Reddy, P. R., Sathyamurthy, R., & Boopathi, S. (2024). Multi-criteria Optimization on Friction Stir Welding of Aluminum Composite (AA5052-H32/B4C) using Titanium Nitride Coated Tool. Engineering Research Express.

Paul, A., Thilagham, K., KG, J., Reddy, P. R., Sathyamurthy, R., & Boopathi, S. (2024). Multi-criteria Optimization on Friction Stir Welding of Aluminum Composite (AA5052-H32/B4C) using Titanium Nitride Coated Tool. Engineering Research Express.

Pauwels, P., Zhang, S., & Lee, Y. C. (2017). Semantic web technologies in the AEC industry: A literature overview. *Automation in Construction*, *73*, 145–165. doi:10.1016/j.autcon.2016.10.003

Pedersen, C., & Diederich, J. (2007, July). Accent classification using support vector machines. In *6th IEEE/ACIS International Conference on Computer and Information Science (ICIS 2007)* (pp. 444-449). IEEE.

Perera, C., Zaslavsky, A., Christen, P., & Georgakopoulos, D. (2014). Sensing as a service model for smart cities supported by the internet of things. *Transactions on Emerging Telecommunications Technologies*, *25*(1), 81–93. doi:10.1002/ett.2704

Peter, O., Pradhan, A., & Mbohwa, C. (2023). Industrial internet of things (IIoT): Opportunities, challenges, and requirements in manufacturing businesses in emerging economies. *Procedia Computer Science*, *217*, 856–865. doi:10.1016/j.procs.2022.12.282

Phan, D., Bab-Hadiashar, A., Fayyazi, M., Hoseinnezhad, R., Jazar, R. N., & Khayyam, H. (2020). Interval type 2 fuzzy logic control for energy management of hybrid electric autonomous vehicles. *IEEE Transactions on Intelligent Vehicles*, *6*(2), 210–220. doi:10.1109/TIV.2020.3011954

Phan, D., Bab-Hadiashar, A., Hoseinnezhad, R. N., Jazar, R., Date, A., Jamali, A., Pham, D. B., & Khayyam, H. (2020). Neuro-fuzzy system for energy management of conventional autonomous vehicles. *Energies, 13*(7), 1745. doi:10.3390/en13071745

Pise, A. A., Almuzaini, K. K., Ahanger, T. A., Farouk, A., Pareek, P. K., Nuagah, S. J., & ... (2022). Enabling artificial intelligence of things (AIoT) healthcare architectures and listing security issues. *Computational Intelligence and Neuroscience, 2022*, 2022. doi:10.1155/2022/8421434 PMID:36911247

Pliatsios, A., Goumopoulos, C., & Kotis, K. (2020). A review on iot frameworks supporting multi-level interoperability—The semantic social network of things framework. *Int. J. Adv. Internet Technol, 13*(1), 46–64.

Pourrahmani, H., Yavarinasab, A., Zahedi, R., Gharehghani, A., Mohammadi, M. H., Bastani, P., & Van herle, J. (2022). The applications of Internet of Things in the automotive industry: A review of the batteries, fuel cells, and engines. *Internet of Things : Engineering Cyber Physical Human Systems, 19*, 100579. doi:10.1016/j.iot.2022.100579

Prabhuswamy, M., Tripathi, R., Vijayakumar, M., Thulasimani, T., Sundharesalingam, P., & Sampath, B. (2024). A Study on the Complex Nature of Higher Education Leadership: An Innovative Approach. In *Challenges of Globalization and Inclusivity in Academic Research* (pp. 202–223). IGI Global. doi:10.4018/979-8-3693-1371-8.ch013

Pramila, P., Amudha, S., Saravanan, T., Sankar, S. R., Poongothai, E., & Boopathi, S. (2023). Design and Development of Robots for Medical Assistance: An Architectural Approach. In Contemporary Applications of Data Fusion for Advanced Healthcare Informatics (pp. 260–282). IGI Global.

Prudhomme, C., Homburg, T., Ponciano, J. J., Boochs, F., Cruz, C., & Roxin, A. M. (2020). Interpretation and automatic integration of geospatial data into the Semantic Web: Towards a process of automatic geospatial data interpretation, classification and integration using semantic technologies. *Computing, 102*(2), 365–391. doi:10.1007/s00607-019-00701-y

Puranik, T. A., Shaik, N., Vankudoth, R., Kolhe, M. R., Yadav, N., & Boopathi, S. (2024). Study on Harmonizing Human-Robot (Drone) Collaboration: Navigating Seamless Interactions in Collaborative Environments. In Cybersecurity Issues and Challenges in the Drone Industry (pp. 1–26). IGI Global.

Purwar, A., Sharma, H., Sharma, Y., Gupta, H., & Kaur, A. (2022, April). Accent classification using machine learning and deep learning models. In *2022 1st international conference on informatics (ICI)* (pp. 13-18). IEEE. 10.1109/ICI53355.2022.9786885

Qaisar, S. M., Khan, S. I., Dallet, D., Tadeusiewicz, R., & Pławiak, P. (2022). Signal-piloted processing metaheuristic optimization and wavelet decomposition based elucidation of arrhythmia for mobile healthcare. *Biocybernetics and Biomedical Engineering, 42*(2), 681–694. doi:10.1016/j.bbe.2022.05.006

Qiao, Y., Song, Y., & Huang, K. (2019). A novel control algorithm design for hybrid electric vehicles considering energy consumption and emission performance. *Energies, 12*(14), 2698. doi:10.3390/en12142698

Qiu, J., Lu, X., Wang, X., & Hu, X. (2021, March). Research on rice disease identification model based on migration learning in VGG network. *IOP Conference Series. Earth and Environmental Science, 680*(1), 012087. doi:10.1088/1755-1315/680/1/012087

Quintero, J. M., Abrego-Almazán, D., & Ortiz-Rodríguez, F. (2018). Use and usefulness of the information systems measurement. a quality approach at the Mexican northeastern region. *Cuadernos de Administración, 31*(56), 7-30. doi:10.11144/javeriana.cao.31-56.ubwm

Quintero, J. M. M., Echeverría, O. R., & Rodríguez, F. O. (2022). Trust and information quality for the customer satisfaction and loyalty in e-Banking with the use of the mobile phone. *Contaduría y Administración, 67*(1), 283–304.

Quintero, J. M., Abrego-Almazán, D., & Ortiz-Rodríguez, F. (2018). Use and usefulness of the information systems measurement. a quality approach at the mexican northeastern region. *Cuadernos Americanos*, *31*(56), 7–30. doi:10.11144/Javeriana.cao.31-56.ubwm

Qu, Q., Hatami, M., Xu, R., Nagothu, D., Chen, Y., Li, X., Blasch, E., Ardiles-Cruz, E., & Chen, G. (2024, February 13). The Microverse: A Task-Oriented Edge-Scale Metaverse. *Future Internet*, *16*(2), 60. doi:10.3390/fi16020060

Rahamathunnisa, U., Sudhakar, K., Padhi, S., Bhattacharya, S., Shashibhushan, G., & Boopathi, S. (2024). Sustainable Energy Generation From Waste Water: IoT Integrated Technologies. In Adoption and Use of Technology Tools and Services by Economically Disadvantaged Communities: Implications for Growth and Sustainability (pp. 225–256). IGI Global.

Rahamathunnisa, U., Subhashini, P., Aancy, H. M., Meenakshi, S., Boopathi, S., & ... (2023). Solutions for Software Requirement Risks Using Artificial Intelligence Techniques. In *Handbook of Research on Data Science and Cybersecurity Innovations in Industry 4.0 Technologies* (pp. 45–64). IGI Global.

Rahamathunnisa, U., Sudhakar, K., Murugan, T. K., Thivaharan, S., Rajkumar, M., & Boopathi, S. (2023). Cloud Computing Principles for Optimizing Robot Task Offloading Processes. In *AI-Enabled Social Robotics in Human Care Services* (pp. 188–211). IGI Global. doi:10.4018/978-1-6684-8171-4.ch007

Raja, G., Essaky, S., Ganapathisubramaniyan, A., & Baskar, Y. (2023, August). Nexus of Deep Reinforcement Learning and Leader–Follower Approach for AIoT Enabled Aerial Networks. *IEEE Transactions on Industrial Informatics*, *19*(8), 9165–9172. doi:10.1109/TII.2022.3226529

Rajagopal, S., Kundapur, P. P., & Hareesha, K. S. (2020). A Stacking Ensemble for Network Intrusion Detection Using Heterogeneous Datasets. *Security and Communication Networks*, *2020*, 1–9. Advance online publication. doi:10.1155/2020/4586875

Rajan.Suresh, A. P. (2016). Application of Retail Analytics Using Association Rule Mining In Data Mining Techniques With Respect To Retail Supermarket. *Archers & Elevators Publishing House*, *01*(1), 1–23.

Ramesh, B. N., Amballi, A. R., & Mahanta, V. (2018). Django the python web framework. *International Journal of Computer Science and Information Technology Research*, *6*(2), 59–63.

Ramos, E. J., Montpetit, M. J., Skarmeta, A. F., Boussard, M., Angelakis, V., & Kutscher, D. (2022, November 29). Architecture Framework for Intelligence Orchestration in AIoT and IoT. *2022 International Conference on Smart Applications, Communications and Networking (SmartNets)*. 10.1109/SmartNets55823.2022.9994029

Ramudu, K., Mohan, V. M., Jyothirmai, D., Prasad, D., Agrawal, R., & Boopathi, S. (2023). Machine Learning and Artificial Intelligence in Disease Prediction: Applications, Challenges, Limitations, Case Studies, and Future Directions. In Contemporary Applications of Data Fusion for Advanced Healthcare Informatics (pp. 297–318). IGI Global.

Rane, N. (2023a). Enhancing Customer Loyalty through Artificial Intelligence (AI), Internet of Things (IoT), and Big Data Technologies: Improving Customer Satisfaction, Engagement, Relationship, and Experience. SSRN *Electronic Journal*. doi:10.2139/ssrn.4616051

Rane, N., Choudhary, S., & Rane, J. (2023). Education 4.0 and 5.0: Integrating Artificial Intelligence (AI) for Personalized and Adaptive Learning. SSRN *Electronic Journal*. doi:10.2139/ssrn.4638365

Rani, C. J., & Munnisa, S. S. (2016). A survey on web authentication methods for web applications. *International Journal of Computer Science and Information Technologies*, *7*(4), 1678–1680.

Ranjan, R., Patel, V. M., & Chellappa, R. (2017). Hyperface: A deep multi-task learning framework for face detection, landmark localization, pose estimation, and gender recognition. *IEEE Transactions on Pattern Analysis and Machine Intelligence*, *41*(1), 121–135. doi:10.1109/TPAMI.2017.2781233 PMID:29990235

Rao, S. S. (2019). *Engineering optimization: Theory and practice*. John Wiley & Sons. doi:10.1002/9781119454816

Rathore, N. P. S., & Prasad, L. (2020). Automatic rice plant disease recognition and identification using convolutional neural network. *Journal of Critical Reviews, 7*(15), 6076-6086.

Ratnasari, E. K., Mentari, M., Dewi, R. K., & Ginardi, R. H. (2014, September). Sugarcane leaf disease detection and severity estimation based on segmented spots image. In *Proceedings of International Conference on Information, Communication Technology and System (ICTS) 2014* (pp. 93-98). IEEE. 10.1109/ICTS.2014.7010564

Ravisankar, A., Sampath, B., & Asif, M. M. (2023). Economic Studies on Automobile Management: Working Capital and Investment Analysis. In Multidisciplinary Approaches to Organizational Governance During Health Crises (pp. 169–198). IGI Global.

Reategui, E. B., & Campbell, J. A. (1995). A Classification System for Credit Card Transactions. *Advances in Case-Based Reasoning: Second European Workshop (EWCBR-94),* 280-291. 10.1007/3-540-60364-6_43

Rebecca, B., Kumar, K. P. M., Padmini, S., Srivastava, B. K., Halder, S., & Boopathi, S. (2024). Convergence of Data Science-AI-Green Chemistry-Affordable Medicine: Transforming Drug Discovery. In *Handbook of Research on AI and ML for Intelligent Machines and Systems* (pp. 348–373). IGI Global.

Reddy, M. A., Reddy, B. M., Mukund, C., Venneti, K., Preethi, D., & Boopathi, S. (2023). Social Health Protection During the COVID-Pandemic Using IoT. In *The COVID-19 Pandemic and the Digitalization of Diplomacy* (pp. 204–235). IGI Global. doi:10.4018/978-1-7998-8394-4.ch009

Rehman, H. U., & Atiq, R. (2022). A disease predictive model based on epidemiological factors for the management of bacterial leaf blight of rice. *Brazilian Journal of Biology*, 84. PMID:35293481

Reinartz, W., Wiegand, N., & Imschloss, M. (2019). The impact of digital transformation on the retailing value chain. *International Journal of Research in Marketing*, *36*(3), 350–366. doi:10.1016/j.ijresmar.2018.12.002

Rejeb, A., Rejeb, K., & Keogh, J. G. (2021). Cryptocurrencies in modern finance: A literature review. *Etikonomi*, *20*(1), 93–118. doi:10.15408/etk.v20i1.16911

Rekeraho, A., Cotfas, D. T., Cotfas, P. A., Tuyishime, E., Balan, T. C., & Acheampong, R. (2024, February 13). Enhancing Security for IoT-Based Smart Renewable Energy Remote Monitoring Systems. *Electronics (Basel)*, *13*(4), 756. doi:10.3390/electronics13040756

Republic of Namibia. (2020). *Public Sector Innovation Policy*. Office of the Prime Minister.

Revathi, A., & Poonguzhali, S. (2023). IoT and Machine Learning Algorithm in Smart Agriculture. In *Futuristic Communication and Network Technologies: Select Proceedings of VICFCNT 2021, Volume 1* (pp. 355-369). Singapore: Springer Nature Singapore. 10.1007/978-981-19-8338-2_29

Revathi, A., & Poonguzhali, S. (2023). The Role of AIoT-Based Automation Systems Using UAVs in Smart Agriculture. In Revolutionizing Industrial Automation Through the Convergence of Artificial Intelligence and the Internet of Things (pp. 100-117). IGI Global.

Revathi, S., Babu, M., Rajkumar, N., Meti, V. K. V., Kandavalli, S. R., & Boopathi, S. (2024). Unleashing the Future Potential of 4D Printing: Exploring Applications in Wearable Technology, Robotics, Energy, Transportation, and Fashion. In Human-Centered Approaches in Industry 5.0: Human-Machine Interaction, Virtual Reality Training, and Customer Sentiment Analysis (pp. 131–153). IGI Global.

Rewatkar, P., Nath, D., Kumar, P. S., Suss, M. E., & Goel, S. (2022). Internet of Things enabled environmental condition monitoring driven by laser ablated reduced graphene oxide based Al-air fuel cell. *Journal of Power Sources, 521*, 230938. doi:10.1016/j.jpowsour.2021.230938

Rezaee, M. J., Jozmaleki, M., & Valipour, M. (2018). Integrating dynamic fuzzy C-means, data envelopment analysis and artificial neural network to online prediction performance of companies in stock exchange. *Physica A, 489*, 78–93. doi:10.1016/j.physa.2017.07.017

Rhayem, A., Mhiri, M. B. A., & Gargouri, F. (2020). Semantic web technologies for the internet of things: Systematic literature review. *Internet of Things: Engineering Cyber Physical Human Systems, 11*, 100206. doi:10.1016/j.iot.2020.100206

Rijal, S., & Devkota, Y. (2020). A review on various management method of rice blast disease. *Malaysian Journal of Sustainable Agriculture, 4*(1), 14–18.

Rish, I. (2001, August). An empirical study of the naive Bayes classifier. In IJCAI 2001 workshop on empirical methods in artificial intelligence (Vol. 3, No. 22, pp. 41-46). Academic Press.

Rodríguez Molina, J. (2012). *Semantic middleware development for the Internet of Things*. Academic Press.

Roman, D., Keller, U., Lausen, H., de Bruijn, J., Lara, R., Stollberg, M., Polleres, A., Feier, C., Bussler, C., & Fensel, D. (2005). Web service modeling ontology. *Applied Ontology, 1*(1), 77–106.

Roman, D., Kopecky, J., Vitvar, T., Domingue, J., & Fensel, D. (2015). WSMO-Lite and hRESTS: Lightweight semantic annotations for Web services and RESTful APIs. *Journal of Web Semantics, 31*, 39–58. doi:10.1016/j.websem.2014.11.006

Rowland, A., Folmer, E., & Beek, W. (2020). Towards self-service gis—Combining the best of the semantic web and web gis. *ISPRS International Journal of Geo-Information, 9*(12), 753. doi:10.3390/ijgi9120753

Sabou, M. (2016). An introduction to semantic web technologies. *Semantic Web Technologies for Intelligent Engineering Applications*, 53-81.

Sacco, F. M. (2020). The Evolution of the Telecom Infrastructure Business: Unchartered Waters Ahead of Great Opportunities. *Disruption in the Infrastructure Sector: Challenges and Opportunities for Developers, Investors and Asset Managers*, 87–148.

Sahagun, M. A., Ortiz-Rodriguez, F., & Medina-Quintero, J. M. (2023). The Salary and Wage Inequality Effect on Productivity on the Mexico-US Border: Mexican Middle Management Supervisor Perspective. In Emerging Technologies and Digital Transformation in the Manufacturing Industry (pp. 193-212). IGI Global.

Sampath, B. (2021). *Sustainable Eco-Friendly Wire-Cut Electrical Discharge Machining: Gas Emission Analysis*. Academic Press.

Sampath, B., Sasikumar, C., & Myilsamy, S. (2023). Application of TOPSIS Optimization Technique in the Micro-Machining Process. In Trends, Paradigms, and Advances in Mechatronics Engineering (pp. 162–187). IGI Global.

Sampath, B. C. S., & Myilsamy, S. (2022). Application of TOPSIS Optimization Technique in the Micro-Machining Process. In M. A. Mellal (Ed.), Advances in Mechatronics and Mechanical Engineering (pp. 162–187). IGI Global. doi:10.4018/978-1-6684-5887-7.ch009

Sampath, B., Pandian, M., Deepa, D., & Subbiah, R. (2022). Operating parameters prediction of liquefied petroleum gas refrigerator using simulated annealing algorithm. *AIP Conference Proceedings*, *2460*(1), 070003. doi:10.1063/5.0095601

Sampath, B., Sureshkumar, T., Yuvaraj, M., & Velmurugan, D. (2021). Experimental Investigations on Eco-Friendly Helium-Mist Near-Dry Wire-Cut EDM of M2-HSS Material. *Materials Research Proceedings*, *19*, 175–180.

Sánchez-Corcuera, R., Nuñez-Marcos, A., Sesma-Solance, J., Bilbao-Jayo, A., Mulero, R., Zulaika, U., Azkune, G., & Almeida, A. (2019). Smart cities survey: Technologies, application domains and challenges for the cities of the future. *International Journal of Distributed Sensor Networks*, *15*(6). doi:10.1177/1550147719853984

Sandino, J., Pegg, G., Gonzalez, F., & Smith, G. (2018). Aerial mapping of forests affected by pathogens using UAVs, hyperspectral sensors, and artificial intelligence. *Sensors (Basel)*, *18*(4), 944. doi:10.3390/s18040944 PMID:29565822

Sangeetha, M., Kannan, S. R., Boopathi, S., Ramya, J., Ishrat, M., & Sabarinathan, G. (2023). Prediction of Fruit Texture Features Using Deep Learning Techniques. *2023 4th International Conference on Smart Electronics and Communication (ICOSEC)*, 762–768.

Santipantakis, G. M., Kotis, K. I., Vouros, G. A., & Doulkeridis, C. (2018, June). Rdf-gen: Generating RDF from streaming and archival data. In *Proceedings of the 8th International Conference on Web Intelligence, Mining and Semantics* (pp. 1-10). 10.1145/3227609.3227658

Saravanan, A., Venkatasubramanian, R., Khare, R., Surakasi, R., Boopathi, S., Ray, S., & Sudhakar, M. (2022). Policy trends of renewable energy and non. *Renewable Energy*.

Saravanan, M., Vasanth, M., Boopathi, S., Sureshkumar, M., & Haribalaji, V. (2022). Optimization of Quench Polish Quench (QPQ) Coating Process Using Taguchi Method. *Key Engineering Materials*, *935*, 83–91. doi:10.4028/p-z569vy

Sarker, M. N. I., Khatun, M. N., Alam, G. M., & Islam, M. S. (2020). Big Data Driven Smart City: Way to Smart City Governance. *2020 International Conference on Computing and Information Technology (ICCIT-1441)*, 1–8. 10.1109/ICCIT-144147971.2020.9213795

Satav, S. D., Lamani, D., Harsha, K., Kumar, N., Manikandan, S., & Sampath, B. (2023). Energy and Battery Management in the Era of Cloud Computing: Sustainable Wireless Systems and Networks. In Sustainable Science and Intelligent Technologies for Societal Development (pp. 141–166). IGI Global.

Satav, S. D., Hasan, D. S., Pitchai, R., Mohanaprakash, T., Sultanuddin, S., & Boopathi, S. (2023). Next generation of internet of things (ngiot) in healthcare systems. In *Sustainable Science and Intelligent Technologies for Societal Development* (pp. 307–330). IGI Global.

Sathish, T., Sunagar, P., Singh, V., Boopathi, S., Al-Enizi, A. M., Pandit, B., Gupta, M., & Sehgal, S. S. (2023). Characteristics estimation of natural fibre reinforced plastic composites using deep multi-layer perceptron (MLP) technique. *Chemosphere*, *337*, 139346. doi:10.1016/j.chemosphere.2023.139346 PMID:37379988

Sawat, D.D., & Hegadi, R.S. (2017). Unconstrained face detection: a deep learning and machine learning combined approach. *CSI Transactions on ICT, 5*(2), 195-199.

Schapire, R. E. (2013). Explaining adaboost. In *Empirical Inference: Festschrift in Honor of Vladimir N. Vapnik* (pp. 37–52). Springer Berlin Heidelberg. doi:10.1007/978-3-642-41136-6_5

Selvakumar, S., Shankar, R., Ranjit, P., Bhattacharya, S., Gupta, A. S. G., & Boopathi, S. (2023). E-Waste Recovery and Utilization Processes for Mobile Phone Waste. In *Handbook of Research on Safe Disposal Methods of Municipal Solid Wastes for a Sustainable Environment* (pp. 222–240). IGI Global. doi:10.4018/978-1-6684-8117-2.ch016

Selvarajan, S., Shaik, M., Ameerjohn, S., & Kannan, S. (2020). Mining of intrusion attack in SCADA network using clustering and genetically seeded flora-based optimal classification algorithm. *IET Information Security*, *14*(1), 1–11. doi:10.1049/iet-ifs.2019.0011

Sengeni, D., Padmapriya, G., Imambi, S. S., Suganthi, D., Suri, A., & Boopathi, S. (2023). Biomedical waste handling method using artificial intelligence techniques. In *Handbook of Research on Safe Disposal Methods of Municipal Solid Wastes for a Sustainable Environment* (pp. 306–323). IGI Global. doi:10.4018/978-1-6684-8117-2.ch022

Seng, K. P., Ang, L. M., & Ngharamike, E. (2022). Artificial intelligence Internet of Things: A new paradigm of distributed sensor networks. *International Journal of Distributed Sensor Networks*, *18*(3), 15501477211062835. doi:10.1177/15501477211062835

Sengupta, S., Dutta, A., Abdelmohsen, S. A., Alyousef, H. A., & Rahimi-Gorji, M. (2022). Development of a Rice Plant Disease Classification Model in Big Data Environment. *Bioengineering (Basel, Switzerland)*, *9*(12), 758. doi:10.3390/bioengineering9120758 PMID:36550964

Senthil, T., Puviyarasan, M., Babu, S. R., Surakasi, R., Sampath, B., & Associates. (2023). Industrial Robot-Integrated Fused Deposition Modelling for the 3D Printing Process. In Development, Properties, and Industrial Applications of 3D Printed Polymer Composites (pp. 188–210). IGI Global.

Sepasgozar, S., Karimi, R., Farahzadi, L., Moezzi, F., Shirowzhan, S. M., Ebrahimzadeh, S., Hui, F., & Aye, L. (2020). A systematic content review of artificial intelligence and the internet of things applications in smart home. *Applied Sciences (Basel, Switzerland)*, *10*(9), 3074. doi:10.3390/app10093074

Sequeda, J. F. (2013, October). On the Semantics of R2RML and its Relationship with Direct Mapping. In ISWC (Posters & Demos) (pp. 193-196). Academic Press.

Sethusubramanian, C., Vigneshpoopathy, M., Chamundeeswari, V., & Pradeep, J. (2021). Implementation of PI-controlled converter and monitoring of fuel cell on an IoT—Cloud platform. *Recent Trends in Renewable Energy Sources and Power Conversion: Select Proceedings of ICRES 2020*, 215–228.

Sethy, P. K., Barpanda, N. K., Rath, A. K., & Behera, S. K. (2020). Nitrogen deficiency prediction of rice crop based on convolutional neural network. *Journal of Ambient Intelligence and Humanized Computing*, *11*(11), 5703–5711. doi:10.1007/s12652-020-01938-8

Shah, S. A., Seker, D. Z., Rathore, M. M., Hameed, S., Ben Yahia, S., & Draheim, D. (2019). Towards Disaster Resilient Smart Cities: Can Internet of Things and Big Data Analytics Be the Game Changers? *IEEE Access : Practical Innovations, Open Solutions*, *7*, 91885–91903. doi:10.1109/ACCESS.2019.2928233

Sham, S. (2021). *Security Questions: Best Practices, Examples, and Ideas*. https://www.okta.com/blog/2021/03/security-questions/

Sharma, A., & Jain, S. (2021). Multilingual Semantic Representation of Smart Connected World Data. *Smart Connected World: Technologies and Applications Shaping the Future*, 125-138.

Sharma, D. M., Ramana, K. V., Jothilakshmi, R., Verma, R., Maheswari, B. U., & Boopathi, S. (2024). Integrating Generative AI Into K-12 Curriculums and Pedagogies in India: Opportunities and Challenges. *Facilitating Global Collaboration and Knowledge Sharing in Higher Education With Generative AI*, 133–161.

Sharma, D., Singh, A., & Singhal, S. (2021). The Technological Shift: AI in Big Data and IoT. In The Smart Cyber Ecosystem for Sustainable Development (pp. 69–90). Wiley. doi:10.1002/9781119761655.ch4

Sharma, R., & Tamta, S. (2015). A review on red rot: the cancer of sugarcane. *J Plant Pathol Microbiol, 1*, 3.

Sharma, M., Gupta, R., & Acharya, P. (2020). Analysing the adoption of cloud computing service: A systematic literature review. *Global Knowledge. Memory and Communication, 70*(1/2), 114–153.

Sharma, M., Sharma, M., Sharma, N., & Boopathi, S. (2024). Building Sustainable Smart Cities Through Cloud and Intelligent Parking System. In *Handbook of Research on AI and ML for Intelligent Machines and Systems* (pp. 195–222). IGI Global.

Sharma, R., & Kukreja, V. (2021, March). Rice diseases detection using convolutional neural networks: a survey. In *2021 International Conference on Advance Computing and Innovative Technologies in Engineering (ICACITE)* (pp. 995-1001). IEEE. 10.1109/ICACITE51222.2021.9404620

Sharma, V., & Naaz Mir, R. (2020). A comprehensive and systematic look up into deep learning based object detection techniques: A review. *Computer Science Review, 38*, 100301.

Sheikh, M. S., Liang, J., & Wang, W. (2020). Security and privacy in vehicular ad hoc network and vehicle cloud computing: A survey. *Wireless Communications and Mobile Computing, 2020*, 1–25. doi:10.1155/2020/5129620

Shen, C., Yu, T., Yuan, S., Li, Y., & Guan, X. (2016, March 9). Performance Analysis of Motion-Sensor Behavior for User Authentication on Smartphones. *Sensors (Basel), 16*(3), 345. doi:10.3390/s16030345 PMID:27005626

Sheth, A. P., & Ramakrishnan, C. (2003). Semantic (Web) technology in action: Ontology driven information systems for search, integration, and analysis. *A Quarterly Bulletin of the Computer Society of the IEEE Technical Committee on Data Engineering, 26*(4), 40.

Shibl, M., Ismail, L., & Massoud, A. (2020). Machine learning-based management of electric vehicles charging: Towards highly-dispersed fast chargers. *Energies, 13*(20), 5429. doi:10.3390/en13205429

Shin, D. H., Han, S. J., Kim, Y. B., & Euom, I. C. (2024, January 29). Research on Digital Forensics Analyzing Heterogeneous Internet of Things Incident Investigations. *Applied Sciences (Basel, Switzerland), 14*(3), 1128. doi:10.3390/app14031128

Shingo, S. (1988). *Non-Stock Production*. Productivity Press.

Shipepe, A., Uwu-Khaeb, L., Kolog, E. A., Apiola, M., Mufeti, K., & Sutinen, E. (2021, October). Towards the Fourth Industrial Revolution in Namibia: An Undergraduate AI Course Africanized. *Frontiers in Education (FIE) Conference* (pp. 1-8). IEEE.

Shi, Q., Zhang, Z., Yang, Y., Shan, X., Salam, B., & Lee, C. (2021). Artificial intelligence of things (AIoT) enabled floor monitoring system for smart home applications. *ACS Nano, 15*(11), 18312–18326. doi:10.1021/acsnano.1c07579 PMID:34723468

Shteingart, H., Gordon, A. N., & Gazit, J. (2016). Two-factor authentication. In Microsoft technology licensing. LLC.

Shuaibu Hassan, A., Sun, Y., & Wang, Z. (2020). Optimization techniques applied for optimal planning and integration of renewable energy sources based on distributed generation: Recent trends. *Cogent Engineering, 7*(1), 1766394. doi:10.1080/23311916.2020.1766394

Shukla, A., & Karki, H. (2016). Application of robotics in onshore oil and gas industry—A review Part I. *Robotics and Autonomous Systems, 75*, 490–507. doi:10.1016/j.robot.2015.09.012

Silva, B. N., Khan, M., & Han, K. (2018). Internet of things: A comprehensive review of enabling technologies, architecture, and challenges. *IETE Technical Review, 35*(2), 205–220. doi:10.1080/02564602.2016.1276416

SimõesI. O. P. D. S.de FreitasR. G.CursiD. E.ChapolaR. G.AmaralL. R. D. Recognition of Sugar Cane Orange and Brown Rust Through Leaf Image Processing. *Available at* SSRN 4305400. doi:10.2139/ssrn.4305400

Singh, A. K., Sreenivasu, S. V. N., Mahalaxmi, U. S. B. K., Sharma, H., Patil, D. D., & Asenso, E. (2022). Hybrid feature-based disease detection in plant leaf using convolutional neural network, bayesian optimized SVM, and random forest classifier. *Journal of Food Quality*, *2022*, 1–16. doi:10.1155/2022/2845320

Singh, B., & Kapoor, M. (2021). A Framework for the Generation of Obstacle Data for the Study of Obstacle Detection by Ultrasonic Sensors. *IEEE Sensors Journal*, *21*(7), 1558–1748. doi:10.1109/JSEN.2021.3055515

Singh, C., & Singh, D. (2019). A 3-level multifactor Authentication scheme for cloud computing. *International Journal of Computer Engineering and Technology*, *10*(1). Advance online publication. doi:10.34218/IJCET.10.1.2019.020

Singh, G., Bhardwaj, G., Singh, S. V., Chaturvedi, P., Kumar, V., & Gupta, S. (2021). Industry 4.0: The industrial revolution and future landscape in Indian Market. *2021 International Conference on Technological Advancements and Innovations (ICTAI)*, 500–505. 10.1109/ICTAI53825.2021.9673154

Singh, G., & Singh, R. (2023, April). Rice Leaf Disease Prediction: A Survey. In *2023 International Conference on Inventive Computation Technologies (ICICT)* (pp. 582-587). IEEE. 10.1109/ICICT57646.2023.10134267

Skanda, C., Srivatsa, B., & Premananda, B. S. (2022, November). Secure Hashing using BCrypt for Cryptographic Applications. In *2022 IEEE North Karnataka Subsection Flagship International Conference (NKCon)* (pp. 1-5). IEEE. 10.1109/NKCon56289.2022.10126956

Skoutas, D., Simitsis, A., & Sellis, T. (2007). A Ranking Mechanism for Semantic Web Service Discovery. *IEEE Congress on Services*, 41-48.

Sobhkhiz, S., Taghaddos, H., Rezvani, M., & Ramezanianpour, A. M. (2021). Utilization of semantic web technologies to improve BIM-LCA applications. *Automation in Construction*, *130*, 103842. doi:10.1016/j.autcon.2021.103842

Soldatos, J., & Kyriazis, D. (Eds.). (2022). *Big Data and Artificial Intelligence in Digital Finance*. Springer International Publishing. doi:10.1007/978-3-030-94590-9

Soroceanu, T., Buchmann, N., & Margraf, M. (2023, October 6). On Multiple Encryption for Public-Key Cryptography. *Cryptography*, *7*(4), 49. doi:10.3390/cryptography7040049

Sowmyalakshmi, R., & Jayasankar, T., Pillai, V. A., Subramaniyan, K., Pustokhina, I. V., Pustokhin, D. A., & Shankar, K. (2021). An optimal classification model for rice plant disease detection. *Computers, Materials & Continua*, *68*, 1751–1767. doi:10.32604/cmc.2021.016825

Sporny, Longley, Kellogg, & Lehn. (2018). *JSON-LD 1.1*. W3C Recommendation.

Srinath, K. R. (2017). Python–the fastest growing programming language. *International Research Journal of Engineering and Technology*, *4*(12), 354–357.

Srinivas, B., Maguluri, L. P., Naidu, K. V., Reddy, L. C. S., Deivakani, M., & Boopathi, S. (2023). Architecture and Framework for Interfacing Cloud-Enabled Robots. In *Handbook of Research on Data Science and Cybersecurity Innovations in Industry 4.0 Technologies* (pp. 542–560). IGI Global. doi:10.4018/978-1-6684-8145-5.ch027

Srivastava, S., Kumar, P., Mohd, N., Singh, A., & Gill, F. S. (2020). A novel deep learning framework approach for sugarcane disease detection. *SN Computer Science*, *1*(2), 1–7. doi:10.1007/s42979-020-0094-9

Sriwanna, K. (2022). Weather-based rice blast disease forecasting. *Computers and Electronics in Agriculture*, *193*, 106685. doi:10.1016/j.compag.2022.106685

Stephen, A., Punitha, A., & Chandrasekar, A. (2023). Optimal deep generative adversarial network and convolutional neural network for rice leaf disease prediction. *The Visual Computer*, 1–18.

Stephens, S. (2007). The enterprise semantic web: technologies and applications for the real world. In *The Semantic Web: Real-World Applications from Industry* (pp. 17–37). Springer US. doi:10.1007/978-0-387-48531-7_2

Stott, B., Marinho, J., & Alsac, O. (1979). Review of linear programming applied to power system rescheduling. *IEEE Conference Proceedings Power Industry Computer Applications Conference, 1979. PICA-79.*, 142–154. 10.1109/PICA.1979.720058

Strachan, S., Bhuiyan, S. A., Thompson, N., Nguyen, N. T., Ford, R., & Shiddiky, M. J. (2022). Latent potential of current plant diagnostics for detection of sugarcane diseases. *Current Research in Biotechnology*, 4, 475–492. doi:10.1016/j.crbiot.2022.10.002

Studer, R., Benjamins, V. R., & Fensel, D. (1998). Knowledge engineering: Principles and methods. *Data & Knowledge Engineering*, 25(1-2), 161–197. doi:10.1016/S0169-023X(97)00056-6

Subha, S., Inbamalar, T., Komala, C., Suresh, L. R., Boopathi, S., & Alaskar, K. (2023). A Remote Health Care Monitoring system using internet of medical things (IoMT). *IEEE Explore*, 1–6.

Subramanian, G., Patil, B. T., & Gardas, B. B. (2021). Evaluation of enablers of cloud technology to boost industry 4.0 adoption in the manufacturing micro, small and medium enterprises. *Journal of Modelling in Management*, 16(3), 944–962. doi:10.1108/JM2-08-2020-0207

Suhail, M., Akhtar, I., Kirmani, S., & Jameel, M. (2021). Development of progressive fuzzy logic and ANFIS control for energy management of plug-in hybrid electric vehicle. *IEEE Access : Practical Innovations, Open Solutions*, 9, 62219–62231. doi:10.1109/ACCESS.2021.3073862

Su, J. (1668). H., Ali, S., & Salman, M. (2024, March 4). Research on Blockchain-Enabled Smart Grid for Anti-Theft Electricity Securing Peer-to-Peer Transactions in Modern Grids. *Sensors (Basel)*, 24(5), 1668. Advance online publication. doi:10.3390/s24051668

Sujith, A., Sekhar Sajja, G., Mahalakshmi, V., Nuhmani, S., & Prasanalakshmi, B. (2022). Systematic review of smart health monitoring using deep learning and Artificial intelligence. *Neuroscience Informatics (Online)*, 2(3), 100028. doi:10.1016/j.neuri.2021.100028

Sujithra, J., & Ukrit, M. F. (2022). CRUN-Based Leaf Disease Segmentation and Morphological-Based Stage Identification. *Mathematical Problems in Engineering*, 2022, 2022. doi:10.1155/2022/2546873

Suman, S., Sahoo, K. S., Das, C., Jhanjhi, N. Z., & Mitra, A. (2022, June). Visualization of audio files using librosa. In *Proceedings of 2nd International Conference on Mathematical Modeling and Computational Science: ICMMCS 2021* (pp. 409-418). Singapore: Springer Nature Singapore. 10.1007/978-981-19-0182-9_41

Sun, Z., Zhu, M., Zhang, Z., Chen, Z., Shi, Q., Shan, X., & Lee, C. (2021, January 25). Smart Soft Robotic Manipulator for Artificial Intelligence of Things (AIOT) Based Unmanned Shop Applications. *2021 IEEE 34th International Conference on Micro Electro Mechanical Systems (MEMS)*. 10.1109/MEMS51782.2021.9375221

Sundaramoorthy, K., Singh, A., Sumathy, G., Maheshwari, A., Arunarani, A., & Boopathi, S. (2024). A Study on AI and Blockchain-Powered Smart Parking Models for Urban Mobility. In *Handbook of Research on AI and ML for Intelligent Machines and Systems* (pp. 223–250). IGI Global.

Sung, W. T., Devi, I. V., & Hsiao, S. J. (2022). Early warning of impending flash flood based on AIoT. *EURASIP Journal on Wireless Communications and Networking*, 2022(1), 15. doi:10.1186/s13638-022-02096-5

Sun, Z., Zhu, M., Zhang, Z., Chen, Z., Shi, Q., Shan, X., Yeow, R. C. H., & Lee, C. (2021). Artificial Intelligence of Things (AIoT) enabled virtual shop applications using self-powered sensor enhanced soft robotic manipulator. *Advancement of Science*, 8(14), 2100230. doi:10.1002/advs.202100230 PMID:34037331

Suresha, M., Shreekanth, K. N., & Thirumalesh, B. V. (2017, April). Recognition of diseases in paddy leaves using knn classifier. In *2017 2nd International Conference for Convergence in Technology (I2CT)* (pp. 663-666). IEEE. 10.1109/I2CT.2017.8226213

Suresh, S., Natarajan, E., Boopathi, S., & Kumar, P. (2024). Processing of smart materials by additive manufacturing and 4D printing. In A. Kumar, P. Kumar, N. Sharma, & A. K. Srivastava (Eds.), *Digital Manufacturing, Artificial Intelligence, Industry 4.0* (pp. 181–196). De Gruyter. doi:10.1515/9783111215112-008

Su, W., Yu, S. S., Li, H., Iu, H. H.-C., & Fernando, T. (2020). An MPC-based dual-solver optimization method for DC microgrids with simultaneous consideration of operation cost and power loss. *IEEE Transactions on Power Systems*, 36(2), 936–947. doi:10.1109/TPWRS.2020.3011038

Swamy, S. N., & Kota, S. R. (2020). An Empirical Study on System Level Aspects of Internet of Things (IoT). *IEEE Access : Practical Innovations, Open Solutions*, 8, 188082–188134. doi:10.1109/ACCESS.2020.3029847

Syamala, M., Komala, C., Pramila, P., Dash, S., Meenakshi, S., & Boopathi, S. (2023). Machine Learning-Integrated IoT-Based Smart Home Energy Management System. In *Handbook of Research on Deep Learning Techniques for Cloud-Based Industrial IoT* (pp. 219–235). IGI Global. doi:10.4018/978-1-6684-8098-4.ch013

Sycara, K. P., Paolucci, M., Ankolekar, A., & Srinivasan, N. (2003). Automated Discovery, Interaction and Computation of Semanticmweb Services. *Journal of Web Semantics*, 1(1), 27–46. doi:10.1016/j.websem.2003.07.002

Sycara, K., Widoff, S., Klusch, M., & Lu, J. (2002). LARKS: Dynamic Matching Among Heterogeneous Software Agents in Cyberspace. *Autonomous Agents and Multi-Agent Systems*, 5(2), 173–203. doi:10.1023/A:1014897210525

Tabbussum, R., & Dar, A. Q. (2021). Performance evaluation of artificial intelligence paradigms—Artificial neural networks, fuzzy logic, and adaptive neuro-fuzzy inference system for flood prediction. *Environmental Science and Pollution Research International*, 28(20), 25265–25282. doi:10.1007/s11356-021-12410-1 PMID:33453033

Tabrizchi, H., & Kuchaki Rafsanjani, M. (2020). A survey on security challenges in cloud computing: Issues, threats, and solutions. *The Journal of Supercomputing*, 76(12), 9493–9532. doi:10.1007/s11227-020-03213-1

Tabuenca, B., Uche-Soria, M., Greller, W., Hernández-Leo, D., Balcells-Falgueras, P., Gloor, P., & Garbajosa, J. (2024). Greening smart learning environments with Artificial Intelligence of Things. *Internet of Things : Engineering Cyber Physical Human Systems*, 25, 101051. doi:10.1016/j.iot.2023.101051

Taghavifar, H., Hu, C., Qin, Y., & Wei, C. (2020). EKF-neural network observer based type-2 fuzzy control of autonomous vehicles. *IEEE Transactions on Intelligent Transportation Systems*, 22(8), 4788–4800. doi:10.1109/TITS.2020.2985124

Talaviya, T., Shah, D., Patel, N., Yagnik, H., & Shah, M. (2020). Implementation of artificial intelligence in agriculture for optimisation of irrigation and application of pesticides and herbicides. *Artificial Intelligence in Agriculture*, 4, 58–73. doi:10.1016/j.aiia.2020.04.002

Talebkhah, M., Sali, A., Marjani, M., Gordan, M., Hashim, S. J., & Rokhani, F. Z. (2021). IoT and Big Data Applications in Smart Cities: Recent Advances, Challenges, and Critical Issues. *IEEE Access : Practical Innovations, Open Solutions*, 9, 55465–55484. doi:10.1109/ACCESS.2021.3070905

Tamilvizhi, T., Surendran, R., Anbazhagan, K., & Rajkumar, K. (2022). Quantum behaved particle swarm optimization-based deep transfer learning model for sugarcane leaf disease detection and classification. *Mathematical Problems in Engineering*, *2022*, 2022. doi:10.1155/2022/3452413

Tamura, Y., Kawakami, M., & Yamada, S. (2013). Reliability modeling and analysis for open source cloud computing. *Proceedings of the Institution of Mechanical Engineers. Part O, Journal of Risk and Reliability*, *227*(2), 179–186. doi:10.1177/1748006X12475110

Tang, C., Cui, Z., Chu, M., Lu, Y., Zhou, F., & Gao, S. (2022). Piezoelectric and Machine Learning Based Keystroke Dynamics for Highly Secure User Authentication. *IEEE Sensors Journal*.

Tang, X., Guo, Q., Li, M., Wei, C., Pan, Z., & Wang, Y. (2021). Performance analysis on liquid-cooled battery thermal management for electric vehicles based on machine learning. *Journal of Power Sources*, *494*, 229727. doi:10.1016/j.jpowsour.2021.229727

Tan, L., Yu, K., Ming, F., Cheng, X., & Srivastava, G. (2021). Secure and resilient artificial intelligence of things: A HoneyNet approach for threat detection and situational awareness. *IEEE Consumer Electronics Magazine*, *11*(3), 69–78. doi:10.1109/MCE.2021.3081874

Tanque, M. (2021). Knowledge Representation and Reasoning in AI-Based Solutions and IoT Applications. In *Artificial Intelligence to Solve Pervasive Internet of Things Issues* (pp. 13–49). Elsevier. doi:10.1016/B978-0-12-818576-6.00002-2

Tao, F., Zhang, L., Venkatesh, V., Luo, Y., & Cheng, Y. (2011). Cloud manufacturing: A computing and service-oriented manufacturing model. *Proceedings of the Institution of Mechanical Engineers. Part B, Journal of Engineering Manufacture*, *225*(10), 1969–1976. doi:10.1177/0954405411405575

Tarun, M., Israr, A., & Gajwal, D. (2022). Analysis of the factors influence Indian English accents, and how pronunciation and articulation fill the accent gap. *EPRA International Journal of Environmental Economics, Commerce and Educational Management*, *9*(4), 43–49.

Taylor, S. J., Kiss, T., Terstyanszky, G., Kacsuk, P., & Fantini, N. (2014). Cloud computing for simulation in manufacturing and engineering: Introducing the CloudSME simulation platform. *ANSS 14, Annual Simulation Symposium 2014, in Conjunction with 2014 Spring Simulation Multi-Conference (SpringSim'14)*, *46*(2).

Taylor, S., Surridge, M., & Pickering, B. (2021, May 10). Regulatory Compliance Modelling Using Risk Management Techniques. *2021 IEEE World AI IoT Congress (AIIoT)*. 10.1109/AIIoT52608.2021.9454188

Terziyan, V., & Kononenko, O. (2003, September). Semantic Web enabled Web services: State-of-art and industrial challenges. In *International Conference on Web Services* (pp. 183-197). Springer Berlin Heidelberg. 10.1007/978-3-540-39872-1_15

Thantharate, P., & Thantharate, A. (2023, October 17). ZeroTrustBlock: Enhancing Security, Privacy, and Interoperability of Sensitive Data through ZeroTrust Permissioned Blockchain. *Big Data and Cognitive Computing*, *7*(4), 165. doi:10.3390/bdcc7040165

Thilagavathi, K., Kavitha, K., Praba, R. D., Arina, S. V., & Sahana, R. C. (2020). Detection of diseases in sugarcane using image processing techniques. *Bioscience Biotechnology Research Communications*, *13*(11), 109–115. doi:10.21786/bbrc/13.11/24

Thomas, P. A., & Preetha Mathew, K. (2023). A broad review on non-intrusive active user authentication in biometrics. *Journal of Ambient Intelligence and Humanized Computing*, *14*(1), 339–360. doi:10.1007/s12652-021-03301-x PMID:34109006

Thomas, S., & Pachaiyappan, P. (2022). Role of E-Learning in Seconday Teacher Education. In P. Pachaiyappan (Ed.), *Current Trends in ICT and Education* (Vol. 1, pp. 67–77). AkiNik Publications.

Tian, P., Liu, X., Luo, K., Li, H., & Wang, Y. (2021). Deep learning from three-dimensional multiphysics simulation in operational optimization and control of polymer electrolyte membrane fuel cell for maximum power. *Applied Energy*, *288*, 116632. doi:10.1016/j.apenergy.2021.116632

Tiwari, S., Ortiz-Rodríguez, F., Mishra, S., Vakaj, E., & Kotecha, K. (2023). Artificial Intelligence: Towards Sustainable Intelligence. *First International Conference, AI4S 2023, Pune, India, September 4-5, 2023, Proceedings, Communications in Computer and Information Science.* 10.1007/978-3-031-47997-7

Tiwari, V., Joshi, R. C., & Dutta, M. K. (2021). Dense convolutional neural networks based multiclass plant disease detection and classification using leaf images. *Ecological Informatics*, *63*, 101289. doi:10.1016/j.ecoinf.2021.101289

Tortoise Media. (2021). *The Global AI Index*. Retrieved March 4, 2023, from https://www.tortoisemedia.com/intelligence/global-ai/

Totschnig, W. (2020). Fully autonomous AI. *Science and Engineering Ethics*, *26*(5), 2473–2485. doi:10.1007/s11948-020-00243-z PMID:32725298

Toulni, H., Nsiri, B., Boulmalf, M., & Sadiki, T. (2015). An ontology based approach to traffic management in urban areas. *International Journal of Systems Applications, Engineering & Development*, 9.

Tran, D.-D., Vafaeipour, M., El Baghdadi, M., Barrero, R., Van Mierlo, J., & Hegazy, O. (2020). Thorough state-of-the-art analysis of electric and hybrid vehicle powertrains: Topologies and integrated energy management strategies. *Renewable & Sustainable Energy Reviews*, *119*, 109596. doi:10.1016/j.rser.2019.109596

Tran, P., Park, Nguyen, & Hoang. (2019). Development of a Smart Cyber-Physical Manufacturing System in the Industry 4.0 Context. *Applied Sciences (Basel, Switzerland)*, *9*(16), 3325. doi:10.3390/app9163325

Tran, Q. N., Turnbull, B. P., & Hu, A. J. (2021). Biometrics and Privacy-Preservation: How Do They Evolve? *IEEE Open Journal of the Computer Society*, *2*, 179–191. doi:10.1109/OJCS.2021.3068385

Trialog. (2021). *IoT systems and interoperability*. Retrieved June 5, 2021 from https://www.trialog.com/en/IoT-systems-and-interoperability

Triantafyllou, A., Sarigiannidis, P., & Bibi, S. (2019). Precision agriculture: A remote sensing monitoring system architecture. *Information (Basel)*, *10*(11), 348. doi:10.3390/info10110348

Tsai, C. H., & Su, P. C. (2021). The application of multi-server authentication scheme in internet banking transaction environments. *Information Systems and e-Business Management*, *19*(1), 77–105. doi:10.1007/s10257-020-00481-5

Ugandar, R., Rahamathunnisa, U., Sajithra, S., Christiana, M. B. V., Palai, B. K., & Boopathi, S. (2023). Hospital Waste Management Using Internet of Things and Deep Learning: Enhanced Efficiency and Sustainability. In Applications of Synthetic Biology in Health, Energy, and Environment (pp. 317–343). IGI Global.

Ülkü, M. A., Bookbinder, J. H., & Yun, N. Y. (2024, February 4). Leveraging Industry 4.0 Technologies for Sustainable Humanitarian Supply Chains: Evidence from the Extant Literature. *Sustainability (Basel)*, *16*(3), 1321. doi:10.3390/su16031321

Umapathy Eaganathan, D. J. S., Lackose, V., & Benjamin, F. J. (2014). Identification of sugarcane leaf scorch disease using K-means clustering segmentation and KNN based classification. *International Journal of Advances in Computer Science and Technology*, *3*(12), 11–16.

Umer, M. A., Belay, E. G., & Gouveia, L. B. (2024, February 5). Leveraging Artificial Intelligence and Provenance Blockchain Framework to Mitigate Risks in Cloud Manufacturing in Industry 4.0. *Electronics (Basel)*, *13*(3), 660. doi:10.3390/electronics13030660

United Nations Educational, Scientific and Cultural Organisation (UNESCO). (2022). *Windhoek statement on Artificial Intelligence in Southern Africa*. UNESCO.

Upadhyay, R., & Lui, S. (2018, January). Foreign English accent classification using deep belief networks. In *2018 IEEE 12th international conference on semantic computing (ICSC)* (pp. 290-293). IEEE. 10.1109/ICSC.2018.00053

Uunona, G. N., & Goosen, L. (2023). Leveraging Ethical Standards in Artificial Intelligence Technologies: A Guideline for Responsible Teaching and Learning Applications. In M. Garcia, M. Lopez Cabrera, & R. de Almeida (Eds.), *Handbook of Research on Instructional Technologies in Health Education and Allied Disciplines* (pp. 310–330). IGI Global. doi:10.4018/978-1-6684-7164-7.ch014

Vagaská, A., Gombár, M., & Straka, L. (2022). Selected Mathematical Optimization Methods for Solving Problems of Engineering Practice. *Energies*, *15*(6), 2205. doi:10.3390/en15062205

Vagizov, M., Potapov, A., Konzhgoladze, K., Stepanov, S., & Martyn, I. (2021, October). Prepare and analyze taxation data using the Python Pandas library. *IOP Conference Series. Earth and Environmental Science*, *876*(1), 012078. doi:10.1088/1755-1315/876/1/012078

Vandervelden, T., Deac, D., Van Glabbeek, R., De Smet, R., Braeken, A., & Steenhaut, K. (2023, December 22). Evaluation of 6LoWPAN Generic Header Compression in the Context of an RPL Network. *Sensors (Basel)*, *24*(1), 73. doi:10.3390/s24010073 PMID:38202935

Vanitha, S., Radhika, K., & Boopathi, S. (2023). Artificial Intelligence Techniques in Water Purification and Utilization. In *Human Agro-Energy Optimization for Business and Industry* (pp. 202–218). IGI Global. doi:10.4018/978-1-6684-4118-3.ch010

Varelas, G., Voutsakis, E., Raftopoulou, P., Petrakis, E. G. M., & Milios, E. (2005). Semantic Similarity methods in WordNet and their application to information retrieval on the Web. *Proceedings of the 7th annual ACM international workshop on web information and data management*. 10.1145/1097047.1097051

Veeranjaneyulu, R., Boopathi, S., Kumari, R. K., Vidyarthi, A., Isaac, J. S., & Jaiganesh, V. (2023). Air Quality Improvement and Optimisation Using Machine Learning Technique. *IEEE Explore*, 1–6.

Veeranjaneyulu, R., Boopathi, S., Kumari, R. K., Vidyarthi, A., Isaac, J. S., & Jaiganesh, V. (2023). Air Quality Improvement and Optimisation Using Machine Learning Technique. *IEEE- Explore*, 1–6.

Veeranjaneyulu, R., Boopathi, S., Narasimharao, J., Gupta, K. K., Reddy, R. V. K., & Ambika, R. (2023). Identification of Heart Diseases using Novel Machine Learning Method. *IEEE Explore*, 1–6.

Velásquez, I., Caro, A., & Rodríguez, A. (2018). Authentication schemes and methods: A systematic literature review. *Information and Software Technology*, *94*, 30–37. doi:10.1016/j.infsof.2017.09.012

Velasquez, M., Andre, C., Shanks, S. J., & Meyer, M. (1992). Ethical relativism. *Issues in Ethics*, *5*(2). https://edward-wimberley.com/courses/IntroEnvPol/ethicalreal.pdf

Venâncio Adriano, P., Lisboa, A., & Barbosa, A. (2022). An automatic fire detection system based on deep convolutional neural networks for low-power, resource-constrained devices. *Neural Computing & Applications*, *34*(18), 15349–15368. doi:10.1007/s00521-022-07467-z

Vendelin, G. D., Pavio, A. M., Rohde, U. L., & Rudolph, M. (2021). *Microwave circuit design using linear and nonlinear techniques*. John Wiley & Sons. doi:10.1002/9781119741725

Venegas, F. G., Petit, M., & Perez, Y. (2021). Active integration of electric vehicles into distribution grids: Barriers and frameworks for flexibility services. *Renewable & Sustainable Energy Reviews*, *145*, 111060. doi:10.1016/j.rser.2021.111060

Venkatasubramanian, V., Chitra, M., Sudha, R., Singh, V. P., Jefferson, K., & Boopathi, S. (2024). Examining the Impacts of Course Outcome Analysis in Indian Higher Education: Enhancing Educational Quality. In Challenges of Globalization and Inclusivity in Academic Research (pp. 124–145). IGI Global.

Venkateswaran, N., Vidhya, K., Ayyannan, M., Chavan, S. M., Sekar, K., & Boopathi, S. (2023). A Study on Smart Energy Management Framework Using Cloud Computing. In 5G, Artificial Intelligence, and Next Generation Internet of Things: Digital Innovation for Green and Sustainable Economies (pp. 189–212). IGI Global. doi:10.4018/978-1-6684-8634-4.ch009

Venkateswaran, N., Kumar, S. S., Diwakar, G., Gnanasangeetha, D., & Boopathi, S. (2023). Synthetic Biology for Waste Water to Energy Conversion: IoT and AI Approaches. *Applications of Synthetic Biology in Health. Energy & Environment*, 360–384.

Venkateswaran, N., Vidhya, R., Naik, D. A., Raj, T. M., Munjal, N., & Boopathi, S. (2023). Study on Sentence and Question Formation Using Deep Learning Techniques. In *Digital Natives as a Disruptive Force in Asian Businesses and Societies* (pp. 252–273). IGI Global. doi:10.4018/978-1-6684-6782-4.ch015

Verma, A., Bhattacharya, P., Madhani, N., Trivedi, C., Bhushan, B., Tanwar, S., Sharma, G., Bokoro, P. N., & Sharma, R. (2022). Blockchain for Industry 5.0: Vision, Opportunities, Key Enablers, and Future Directions. *IEEE Access : Practical Innovations, Open Solutions*, *10*, 69160–69199. doi:10.1109/ACCESS.2022.3186892

Verma, K., Sivashanmugam, K., Sheth, A., Patil, A., Oundhakar, S., & Miller, J. (2005). METEOR-S WSDI: A Scalable P2P Infrastructure of Registries for Semantic Publication and Discovery of Web Services. *Information Technology and Management*, *6*(1), 17–39. doi:10.1007/s10799-004-7773-4

Verma, R., Christiana, M. B. V., Maheswari, M., Srinivasan, V., Patro, P., Dari, S. S., & Boopathi, S. (2024). Intelligent Physarum Solver for Profit Maximization in Oligopolistic Supply Chain Networks. In *AI and Machine Learning Impacts in Intelligent Supply Chain* (pp. 156–179). IGI Global. doi:10.4018/979-8-3693-1347-3.ch011

Verma, T., & Dubey, S. (2021). Prediction of diseased rice plant using video processing and LSTM-simple recurrent neural network with comparative study. *Multimedia Tools and Applications*, *80*(19), 29267–29298. doi:10.1007/s11042-021-10889-x

Vignesh, S., Arulshri, K., SyedSajith, S., Kathiresan, S., Boopathi, S., & Dinesh Babu, P. (2018). Design and development of ornithopter and experimental analysis of flapping rate under various operating conditions. *Materials Today: Proceedings*, *5*(11), 25185–25194. doi:10.1016/j.matpr.2018.10.320

Villazón-Terrazas, B., Ortiz-Rodríguez, F., Tiwari, S. M., & Shandilya, S. K. (2020). Knowledge graphs and semantic web. *Communications in Computer and Information Science*, *1232*, 1–225.

Vimala, S., Gladiss Merlin, N. R., Ramanathan, L., & Cristin, R. (2021). Optimal routing and deep regression neural network for rice leaf disease prediction in IoT. *International Journal of Computational Methods*, *18*(07), 2150014. doi:10.1142/S0219876221500146

Vishnumurthy, K., & Girish, K. (2021). A comprehensive review of battery technology for E-mobility. *Journal of the Indian Chemical Society*, *98*(10), 100173. doi:10.1016/j.jics.2021.100173

Viswanathan, R., & Rao, G. P. (2011). Disease scenario and management of major sugarcane diseases in India. *Sugar Tech*, *13*(4), 336–353. doi:10.1007/s12355-011-0102-4

Vrijhoef, R., & Koskela, L. (1999). Role of supply chain management in construction. *Proceedings of the Seventh Annual Conference of the International Group for Lean Construction*, 133-146.

W3C. (2013). *SPARQL Query Language for RDF*. Retrieved June 9, 2021 from https://www.w3.org/TR/rdf-sparql-query/

W3C. (n.d.-a). *Semantic Sensor Network Ontology*. Available. https://www.w3.org/TR/vocab-ssn/

W3C. (n.d.-b). *SSN*. Available at https://bioportal.bioontology.org/ontologies/SSN

Wagner, A., Bonduel, M., Pauwels, P., & Rüppel, U. (2020). Representing construction-related geometry in a semantic web context: A review of approaches. *Automation in Construction*, *115*, 103130. doi:10.1016/j.autcon.2020.103130

Wang, H. Z., Lin, G. W., Wang, J. Q., Gao, W. L., Chen, Y. F., & Duan, Q. L. (2014). Management of Big Data in the Internet of Things in Agriculture Based on Cloud Computing. *Applied Mechanics and Materials*, *548–549*, 1438–1444. . doi:10.4028/www.scientific.net/AMM.548-549.1438

Wang, L., & Cao, J. (2007). Web Services Semantic Searching enhanced by Case Based Reasoning. *18th International Workshop on Database and Expert Systems Applications*.

Wang, P., Gao, R. X., & Fan, Z. (2015). Cloud computing for cloud manufacturing: Benefits and limitations. *Journal of Manufacturing Science and Engineering*, *137*(4), 040901. doi:10.1115/1.4030209

Wang, P., Jin, Z., Liu, L., & Cai, G. (2008). Building Toward Capability Specifications of Web Services Based on an Environment Ontology. *IEEE Transactions on Knowledge and Data Engineering*, *20*(4), 547–561. doi:10.1109/TKDE.2007.190719

Wang, X., Chen, Y., Zhu, X., Li, C., & Fang, K. (2024, January 18). A Redactable Blockchain Scheme Supporting Quantum-Resistance and Trapdoor Updates. *Applied Sciences (Basel, Switzerland)*, *14*(2), 832. doi:10.3390/app14020832

Wang, Y., Seo, B., Wang, B., Zamel, N., Jiao, K., & Adroher, X. C. (2020). Fundamentals, materials, and machine learning of polymer electrolyte membrane fuel cell technology. *Energy and AI*, *1*, 100014. doi:10.1016/j.egyai.2020.100014

Wang, Y., Zhang, B., Ma, J., & Jin, Q. (2023). Artificial intelligence of things (AIoT) data acquisition based on graph neural networks: A systematical review. *Concurrency and Computation*, *35*(23), e7827. doi:10.1002/cpe.7827

Warren, K. (2020, May). *Qualitative data analysis methods 101: The "Big 6" methods + examples*. Retrieved March 12, 2023, from Grad Coach: https://gradcoach.com/qualitative-data-analysis-methods/

Watson, I. (1997). *Applying Case-Based Reasoning: Techniques for Enterprise Systems*. Morgan Kaufman.

Wazid, M., Das, A. K., Rodrigues, J. J. P. C., Shetty, S., & Park, Y. (2019). IoMT Malware Detection Approaches: Analysis and Research Challenges. *IEEE Access : Practical Innovations, Open Solutions*, *7*, 182459–182476. doi:10.1109/ACCESS.2019.2960412

Weyrich & Ebert. (2016). Reference Architectures for the Internet of Things. *IEEE Software, 33*(1), 112–116. . 1109/MS.2016.20 doi:https://doi.org/10

What is Linked Data? (2015). Retrieved June 9, 2021 from https://www.w3.org/standards/semanticweb/data

Wikipedia. (2023). *Dataset*. Wikipedia The Free Encyclopedia.

Wilamowski, B. M. (2018). Neural networks and fuzzy systems. In *Microelectronics* (pp. 18–1). CRC Press. doi:10.1201/9781315220482-18

Williams, K., & Griffin, J. A. (2019). Better security and encryption within cloud computing systems. In Cloud Security: Concepts, Methodologies, Tools, and Applications (pp. 812–823). IGI Global. doi:10.4018/978-1-5225-8176-5.ch041

Wiranata, A., Wibowo, S. A., Patmasari, R., Rahmania, R., & Mayasari, R. (2018, December). Investigation of padding schemes for faster R-CNN on vehicle detection. In *2018 International Conference on Control, Electronics, Renewable Energy and Communications (ICCEREC)* (pp. 208-212). IEEE. 10.1109/ICCEREC.2018.8712086

Wiryasaputra, R., Huang, C. Y., Lin, Y. J., & Yang, C. T. (2024, February 11). An IoT Real-Time Potable Water Quality Monitoring and Prediction Model Based on Cloud Computing Architecture. *Sensors (Basel)*, *24*(4), 1180. doi:10.3390/s24041180 PMID:38400338

Wolfert, S., Ge, L., Verdouw, C., & Bogaardt, M.-J. (2017). Big Data in Smart Farming – A review. *Agricultural Systems*, *153*, 69–80. doi:10.1016/j.agsy.2017.01.023

Wooldridge, M., & Jennings, N. (1995). Intelligent Agents: Theory and Practice. *The Knowledge Engineering Review*, *10*(2), 115–152. doi:10.1017/S0269888900008122

World Economic Forum. (2022). *Regulatory Technology for the 21st Century*. Retrieved from https://www3.weforum.org/docs/WEF_Regulatory_Tech_for_the_21st_Century_2022.pdf

WSDL-S. (2005). https://www.w3.org/Submission/WSDL-S/

Wu, V. (2021). *Hashing passwords and authenticating users with bcrypt*. https://medium.com/@wu.victor.95/hashing-passwords-and-authenticating-users-with-bcrypt-dc2fdd978568

Wu, B., Cheng, T., Yip, T. L., & Wang, Y. (2020). Fuzzy logic based dynamic decision-making system for intelligent navigation strategy within inland traffic separation schemes. *Ocean Engineering*, *197*, 106909. doi:10.1016/j.oceaneng.2019.106909

Wu, H., Han, H., Wang, X., & Sun, S. (2020). Research on artificial intelligence enhancing internet of things security: A survey. *IEEE Access : Practical Innovations, Open Solutions*, *8*, 153826–153848. doi:10.1109/ACCESS.2020.3018170

Xie, M., Li, Y., Yoshigoe, K., Seker, R., & Bian, J. (2015, January). CamAuth: securing web authentication with camera. In *2015 IEEE 16th International Symposium on High Assurance Systems Engineering* (pp. 232-239). IEEE. 10.1109/HASE.2015.41

Xiong, Z., Cai, Z., Takabi, D., & Li, W. (2021). Privacy threat and defense for federated learning with non-iid data in AIoT. *IEEE Transactions on Industrial Informatics*, *18*(2), 1310–1321. doi:10.1109/TII.2021.3073925

Xu, J., Liu, X., Pan, W., Li, X., Yao, A., & Yang, Y. (2023, September 11). EXPRESS 2.0: An Intelligent Service Management Framework for AIoT Systems in the Edge. *2023 38th IEEE/ACM International Conference on Automated Software Engineering (ASE)*. 10.1109/ASE56229.2023.00020

Yahya, M., Breslin, J. G., & Ali, M. I. (2021). Semantic web and knowledge graphs for industry 4.0. *Applied Sciences (Basel, Switzerland)*, *11*(11), 5110. doi:10.3390/app11115110

Yang, C. T., Chen, H. W., Chang, E. J., Kristiani, E., Nguyen, K. L. P., & Chang, J. S. (2021). Current advances and future challenges of AIoT applications in particulate matters (PM) monitoring and control. *Journal of Hazardous Materials*, *419*, 126442. doi:10.1016/j.jhazmat.2021.126442 PMID:34198222

Yang, C., Zha, M., Wang, W., Liu, K., & Xiang, C. (2020). Efficient energy management strategy for hybrid electric vehicles/plug-in hybrid electric vehicles: Review and recent advances under intelligent transportation system. *IET Intelligent Transport Systems*, *14*(7), 702–711. doi:10.1049/iet-its.2019.0606

Yang, Z., Jianjun, L., Faqiri, H., Shafik, W., Talal Abdulrahman, A., Yusuf, M., & Sharawy, A. M. (2021). Green Internet of Things and Big Data Application in Smart Cities Development. *Complexity*, *2021*, 1–15. doi:10.1155/2021/4922697

Yang, Z., Xiong, B., Chen, K., Yang, L. T., Deng, X., Zhu, C., & He, Y. (2024, January 1). Differentially Private Federated Tensor Completion for Cloud–Edge Collaborative AIoT Data Prediction. *IEEE Internet of Things Journal*, *11*(1), 256–267. doi:10.1109/JIOT.2023.3314460

Ye, Y., Yang, D., Jiang, Z., & Tong, L. (2008). An ontology-based architecture for implementing semantic integration of supply chain management. *International Journal of Computer Integrated Manufacturing*, *21*(1), 1–18. doi:10.1080/09511920601182225

Yuan, C., Zhang, Q., & Wu, S. (2023). A real time fingerprint liveness detection method for fingerprint authentication systems. *Advances in Computers*, *131*, 149–180. doi:10.1016/bs.adcom.2023.04.004

Yupapin, P., Trabelsi, Y., Nattappan, A., & Boopathi, S. (2023). Performance improvement of wire-cut electrical discharge machining process using cryogenically treated super-conductive state of Monel-K500 alloy. *Iranian Journal of Science and Technology. Transaction of Mechanical Engineering*, *47*(1), 267–283. doi:10.1007/s40997-022-00513-0

Zaidi, A. Z., Chong, C. Y., Jin, Z., Parthiban, R., & Sadiq, A. S. (2021). Touch-based continuous mobile device authentication: State-of-the-art, challenges and opportunities. *Journal of Network and Computer Applications*, *191*, 103162. doi:10.1016/j.jnca.2021.103162

Zainuddin, A. A., Zakirudin, M. A. Z., Zulkefli, A. S. S., Mazli, A. M., Wardi, M. A. S. M., Fazail, M. N., Razali, M. I. Z. M., & Yusof, M. H. (2024). Artificial Intelligence: A New Paradigm for Distributed Sensor Networks on the Internet of Things: A Review. *International Journal on Perceptive and Cognitive Computing*, *10*(1), 16–28. doi:10.31436/ijpcc. v10i1.414

Zakaria, A., Ismail, F. B., Lipu, M. H., & Hannan, M. A. (2020). Uncertainty models for stochastic optimization in renewable energy applications. *Renewable Energy*, *145*, 1543–1571. doi:10.1016/j.renene.2019.07.081

Zamani, A. S., Anand, L., Rane, K. P., Prabhu, P., Buttar, A. M., Pallathadka, H., Raghuvanshi, A., & Dugbakie, B. N. (2022). Performance of machine learning and image processing in plant leaf disease detection. *Journal of Food Quality*, *2022*, 1–7. doi:10.1155/2022/1598796

Zeadally, S., & Bello, O. (2021). Harnessing the power of Internet of Things based connectivity to improve healthcare. *Internet of Things : Engineering Cyber Physical Human Systems*, *14*, 100074. doi:10.1016/j.IoT.2019.100074

Zehir, C., & Zehir, M. (2022). Emerging blockchain solutions in the mobility ecosystem: Associated risks and areas for applications. *Bussecon Review of Social Sciences, 4*(2), 1–14.

Zekrifa, D. M. S., Kulkarni, M., Bhagyalakshmi, A., Devireddy, N., Gupta, S., & Boopathi, S. (2023). Integrating Machine Learning and AI for Improved Hydrological Modeling and Water Resource Management. In *Artificial Intelligence Applications in Water Treatment and Water Resource Management* (pp. 46–70). IGI Global. doi:10.4018/978-1-6684-6791-6.ch003

Zhang, L., Dabipi, I. K., & Brown Jr, W. L. (2018). Internet of Things applications for agriculture. *Internet of things A to Z: Technologies and applications*, 507-528.

Zhang, C., Liang, Y., Tavares, A., Wang, L., Gomes, T., & Pinto, S. (2024, February 21). An Improved Public Key Cryptographic Algorithm Based on Chebyshev Polynomials and RSA. *Symmetry*, *16*(3), 263. doi:10.3390/sym16030263

Zhang, F., Wang, L., Coskun, S., Pang, H., Cui, Y., & Xi, J. (2020). Energy management strategies for hybrid electric vehicles: Review, classification, comparison, and outlook. *Energies*, *13*(13), 3352. doi:10.3390/en13133352

Zhang, J., & Tao, D. (2020). Empowering things with intelligence: A survey of the progress, challenges, and opportunities in artificial intelligence of things. *IEEE Internet of Things Journal*, *8*(10), 7789–7817. doi:10.1109/JIOT.2020.3039359

Zhang, R., Liu, L., Dong, M., & Ota, K. (2024, February 2). On-Demand Centralized Resource Allocation for IoT Applications: AI-Enabled Benchmark. *Sensors (Basel)*, *24*(3), 980. doi:10.3390/s24030980 PMID:38339696

Zhang, T., Li, J., Jia, W., Sun, J., & Yang, H. (2018). Fast and robust occluded face detection in ATM surveillance. *Pattern Recognition Letters*, *107*, 33–40. doi:10.1016/j.patrec.2017.09.011

Zhang, W. Y., Cai, M., Qiu, J., & Yin, J. W. (2009). Managing distributed manufacturing knowledge through multi-perspective modelling for Semantic Web applications. *International Journal of Production Research*, *47*(23), 6525–6542. doi:10.1080/00207540802311114

Zhou, C., Zhong, Y., Zhou, S., Song, J., & Xiang, W. (2023). Rice leaf disease identification by residual-distilled transformer. *Engineering Applications of Artificial Intelligence*, *121*, 106020. doi:10.1016/j.engappai.2023.106020

Zhu, H., Tiwari, P., Ghoneim, A., & Hossain, M. S. (2022, May). A Collaborative AI-Enabled Pretrained Language Model for AIoT Domain Question Answering. *IEEE Transactions on Industrial Informatics*, *18*(5), 3387–3396. doi:10.1109/TII.2021.3097183

Zhu, S., Ota, K., & Dong, M. (2022). Energy-efficient artificial intelligence of things with intelligent edge. *IEEE Internet of Things Journal*, *9*(10), 7525–7532. doi:10.1109/JIOT.2022.3143722

About the Contributors

Fernando Ortiz-Rodriguez is a Full Professor and Head of the Artificial Intelligence and Innovation Lab at Tamaulipas Autonomous University. He was the Executive Director at the International Institute of Studies (IIES). He created the First Business School in Tamaulipas, Mexico. He worked as the Information Technology Manager at Emerson Electric, where he developed more than 40 pieces of software, some of them used globally in Emerson and achieved technology convergence by implementing the first efforts on IoT and Industry 4.0. Fernando is a member of National Systems Researchers (SNI) Level 1 of the National Council of Science and Technology (CONACYT) and INDEX IT Advisor.

Sanju Tiwari is a Sr. Researcher at Universidad Autonoma de Tamaulipas, Mexico. She is a DAAD Post-Doc-Net AI Fellow for 2021-2022. Prior to this she was a Post-Doctoral Fellow at Universidad Politecnica de Madrid, Spain. She is one of the General Chair of KGSWC-2021 Conference and Editor of Elsevier Books.

Ania Hernández Quintana is a full time professor at Information Science Department, University of Havana. Former Deputy Director of National Archive of the Republic of Cuba. More than twenty years of experience in Knowledge Organization and Documentary Linguistics teaching and research.

Jose L. Martinez-Rodriguez received his Ph.D. in Computer Science from Cinvestav Tamaulipas, Mexico (2018). He is an Associate Professor in the Faculty of Engineering and Science at the Autonomous University of Tamaulipas. His research interests include Semantic Web representation, Data Mining, Information Extraction, and Cloud Computing.

* * *

Pappurajan A. has specialized in Information Technology and Data Science. He has 20 years of teaching experience. Prior to academics he had 1 year and 4 months of experience in IT Industry using Visual Basic and Oracle. He has done his Doctorate in Computer Applications from Manonmaniam Sundaranar University, Tirunelveli. He teaches Quantitative Techniques, ICT Skills, Management Information System, Data Mining, Machine Learning, Big data analytics and Deep Learning. His area of interest include programming languages, analytical tools like SPSS, MS Excel, Weka, R and PYTHON. He has published more than 40 International articles with more than 70 citations. Currently, he is the Chair of Accreditation and Documentation at JIM.

Ouwafemi Samson Balogun is a Lecturer at the Department of Statistics and Operations Research, Modibbo Adama University of Technology, Yola, Adamawa State, Nigeria, and he is currently a Post-Doctoral Researcher at the School of Computing, University of Eastern Finland. He holds a Ph.D. in Statistics from the Department of Statistics, University of Ilorin, Kwara State, Nigeria. He is a Senior Research Fellow at Centre for Multidisciplinary Research and Innovation (CEMRI) and He is a member of International Biometric Society (IBS), International Statistical Institute (ISI), Nigerian Statistical Association (NSA), Nigerian Mathematical Society (NMS). He has several conference and journal papers in reputable international bodies, and he is also served as guest reviewers for several journals. His research interest is data science, machine learning, Data Mining, biostatistics, categorical data analysis, modeling and probability distribution models.

Marwa Ben Arab is an engineer and holds a doctorate from the National Engineering School Of Sfax (ENIS) in Tunisia, Sfax. She is a member of the Electric System and Renewable Energy Laboratory (LSEER) within the Electric Department.

Smpath Boopathi is an accomplished individual with a strong academic background and extensive research experience. He completed his undergraduate studies in Mechanical Engineering and pursued his postgraduate studies in the field of Computer-Aided Design. Dr. Boopathi obtained his Ph.D. from Anna University, focusing his research on Manufacturing and optimization. Throughout his career, Dr. Boopathi has made significant contributions to the field of engineering. He has authored and published over 155 research articles in internationally peer-reviewed journals, highlighting his expertise and dedication to advancing knowledge in his area of specialization. His research output demonstrates his commitment to conducting rigorous and impactful research. In addition to his research publications, Dr. Boopathi has also been granted one patent and has three published patents to his name. This indicates his innovative thinking and ability to develop practical solutions to real-world engineering challenges. With 17 years of academic and research experience, Dr. Boopathi has enriched the engineering community through his teaching and mentorship roles.

Lkshmi D. is presently designated as a Senior Associate Professor in the School of Computing Science and Engineering (SCSE) & Assistant Director, at the Centre for Innovation in Teaching & Learning (CITL) at VIT Bhopal. She has 17 international conference presentations, and 21 international journal papers inclusive of SCOPUS & SCI (cumulative impact factor 31). 3 SCOPUS inee book chapters. A total of 24 patents are in various states and 18 patents have been granted at both national and international levels. One Edited book with Taylor & Francis (SCOPUS Indexed). She has won two Best Paper awards at international conferences, one at the IEEE conference and another one at EAMMIS 2021. She received two awards in the year 2022. She received two awards in the year 2022. She has addressed innumerable guest lectures, acted as a session chair, and was invited as a keynote speaker at several international conferences. She has conducted FDPs that cover approximately ~80,000 plus faculty members including JNTU, TEQIP, SERB, SWAYAM, DST, AICTE, MHRD, ATAL, ISTE, Madhya Pradesh Government-sponsored, and self-financed workshops across India on various titles.

Lila Goosen is a full professor in the Department of Science and Technology Education of the University of South Africa. Prof. Goosen was an Associate Professor in the School of Computing, and the module leader and head designer of the fully online signature module for the College for Science, Engineering and Technology, rolled out to over 92,000 registered students since the first semester of 2013. She also supervises ten Masters and Doctoral students, and has successfully completed supervision of 43 students at postgraduate level. Previously, she was a Deputy Director at the South African national Department of Education. In this capacity, she was required to develop ICT strategies for implementation. She also promoted, coordinated, managed, monitored and evaluated ICT policies and strategies, and drove the research agenda in this area. Before that, she had been a lecturer of Information Technology (IT) in the Department for Science, Mathematics and Technology Education in the Faculty of Education of the University of Pretoria. Her research interests have included cooperative work in IT, effective teaching and learning of programming and teacher professional development.

Ltfi Krichen was born in Sfax, TUNISIA. He received the Engineer Diploma, the Doctorate Degree and University Habilitation Diploma(HDR) in Electrical Engineering from the National School of Engineering of Sfax in 1989, 1995 and 2008, respectively. Currently, he is Professor of Electric Machines and Renewable Energy Systems in the Electrical Engineering Department of the National School of Engineering of Sfax. His research interests are motor drives, power electronic converters, renewable energy systems, plug in electric vehicle.

Ancelin L. received her M.Sc. and M.Phil. in Mathematics from Stella Maris College, Chennai in 2003 and 2004 respectively. She has more than 18 years experience in teaching and is currently serving as an Assistant Professor in the department of Mathematics (SFS) at Madras Christian College, Chennai. Her areas of interest are Optimization techniques, Fuzzy logic and Graph theory.

Amed Abel Leyva Mederos is a Doctor in Information Sciences at the University of Granada in Spain. Professor of the Department of Information Sciences and Computer Sciences of the Central University of Las Villas.

Lwal Olumuyiwa Mashood is an Assistant Lecturer in the Department of Statistics, Faculty of Science, Air Force Institute of Technology, Kaduna, Nigeria; with a passion for teaching, novelty research enthusiasm and openness to new challenges. He currently runs his PhD in Statistics from the Department of Statistics, Ahmadu Bello University, Zaria, Nigeria. His research interest includes Biostatistics, public health, infectious disease, statistical methods and mathematical statistics. He is married and blessed with a child.

Marius Iulian Mihailescu is Associate Professor at "Spiru Haret" University and CEO of Dapyx Solution Ltd., a company focused on security- and cryptography-related research. He has authored and co-authored more than 50 articles, journal contributions, and conference proceedings, and three books related to security and cryptography, including the International Journal of Applied Cryptography. He lectures at well-known national and international universities, teaching courses on programming, cryptography, information security, and other technical topics. He holds a PhD (thesis on applied cryptography over biometrics data) and two MSc in information security and software engineering.

Sreshkumar Myilsamy completed his undergraduate in Mechanical Engineering and postgraduate in the field of Engineering Design. He completed his Ph.D. from Anna University, Chennai, Tamil Nādu, India.

Sefania Loredana Nita, Ph.D., is a Senior Lecturer at Military Technical Academy "Ferdinand I", Bucharest, Romania, and a Software Developer at the Institute of for Computers from Bucharest, Romania. Her Ph.D. thesis is on advanced cryptographic schemes using searchable Searchable encryption Encryption and Homomorphic Encryption. She has worked for more than two years as an assistant lecturer at the University of Bucharest where she taught courses on subjects such as advanced programming techniques, simulation methods, and operating systems. She has authored and co-authored more than 32 papers at conferences and journals and has authored 7 books. She holds an MSc in Software engineering Engineering and two BSc in computer Computer Science and Mathematics.

Kamalendu Pal is currently associated with the Department of Computer Science, School of Science and Technology at City, University of London. He has a diverse academic background, having received a BSc (Hons) degree in Physics from Calcutta University, India, followed by a Postgraduate Diploma in Computer Science from Pune, India. He has also worked as a research assistant for the government of India's two research and development organizations, under the Council of Scientific and Industrial Research (CSIR). Later, Kamalendu graduated with his MSc in Software Systems Technology from the University of Sheffield, a Postgraduate Diploma in Artificial Intelligence from Kingston University, an MPhil in Computer Science from University College London, an MBA from the University of Hull, and a diploma in Higher Education teaching practice from City, University of London, United Kingdom. Kamalendu is an accomplished researcher, having published over a hundred international research articles (including book chapters) in the scientific community. His research papers have been published in prestigious journals such as the ACM SIGMIS Database, Expert Systems with Applications, Decision Support Systems, and international conferences. His research interests include various fields of computer science - such as knowledge-based systems, decision support systems, teaching and learning practices, blockchain technology, software engineering, service-oriented computing, sensor network simulation, and supply chain management. Kamalendu is also on the editorial board of an international computer science journal. He is a member of the British Computer Society, the Institution of Engineering and Technology, and the IEEE Computer Society.

Mrali Ramachandran is a highly competent and accomplished management professional with an extensive 11-year background in teaching and training, skillfully utilizing his exceptional interpersonal abilities to contribute to the overall prosperity of the institute. Holding a distinguished doctorate in management from the prestigious Bharathiar University, a renowned state-owned institution in Tamil Nadu, he has solidified his expertise in the field. Additionally, he completed a full-time MBA at Saranathan College of Engineering, affiliated with the esteemed Anna University. Dr Murali's expertise spans a wide array of subject areas, including Digital marketing, Managerial economics, Spreadsheets for managers, Advertising management, Research methodology, Statistical package for social sciences, and business communication. His comprehensive knowledge and effective delivery of lectures in these domains have garnered significant recognition. Furthermore, Dr Murali's commitment to continuous learning and professional growth is evident through his participation in Faculty Development Programs (FDP) conducted by esteemed institutions such as IIM Indore and

IIT Madras. These programs allowed him to further enhance his skills in areas such as case writing, simulation, and gamification, thus expanding his pedagogical repertoire. In line with his dedication to academic research, Dr. Murali has presented and published his insightful research papers in prestigious conferences organized by renowned institutions like IIM Nagpur and IIM Kozhikode. Moreover, his contributions have been acknowledged in reputable journals, further establishing his intellectual contributions to the field. Demonstrating his commitment to fostering student development, Dr Murali has successfully organized a funded program aimed at enhancing the soft skills and computer literacy of undergraduate students. This program, funded by RGNIYD (Rajiv Gandhi National Institute of Youth Development), showcased his passion for empowering and equipping students with essential skills for their future endeavours. Equipped with a profound understanding of data analysis tools, Dr Murali showcases his proficiency in SPSS, Jamovi, and the R Package (Bibliometrix). These skills enable him to employ robust methodologies and data-driven insights in his research and academic pursuits, ensuring a comprehensive and rigorous approach.

Muna Rekik is an Assistant Professor in the Department of Electrical Engineering at the National Engineering School of Sfax (ENIS). She is also a member in the Electrical Systems and Renewable Energy Laboratory.

Jse Senso has a Doctor in Information Sciences from the University of Granada. Full professor and member of the Doctorate team in Information Sciences.

Jgrati Singh is working as an Assistant Professor in the Department of Computer Science & Engineering at Indira Gandhi Delhi Technical University for Women, Delhi. She completed her Ph.D. from Motilal Nehru National Institute of Technology Allahabad in the field of Text Data Analysis. Her Thesis work deals with the Twitter Data Analytics using Machine Learning based Approaches. She has published Seven SCI/Scopus journal papers and ten Conference papers. She received her M.Tech and B.Tech both degrees from Banasthali Vidyapith Rajasthan. During her M.Tech, one year Internship program is done at IIIT Hyderabad in the field of Natural Language Processing. She has taken various hands-on training sessions in the Summer training programs named "Data Driven Computing and Networking" and "Data Analytics and Machine Learning in R (DAMLR)" organized by the Department of Computer Science & Engineering, MNNIT Allahabad.

Index

A

Accent Classification 320-324, 328-329, 331-334

Accessibility 97, 140, 187, 189-190, 192, 222, 305, 343

Adaptability 74, 104, 111, 120, 123, 162, 198-199, 207, 210-211, 221-222, 224, 257, 268, 271-274, 316, 344-345, 360, 372, 374, 398, 406, 411-412

Adoption Factors 219

AIoT Applications 133, 139, 141, 153-154, 164, 166-167, 187, 196-198, 200-202, 209, 211, 251-253, 256-259, 265-266, 268, 270-271, 277-278, 283

Application 2, 7, 33, 40, 46, 51, 53, 58, 64, 66-68, 70, 73, 81, 84, 86, 89-90, 92, 94, 99, 102, 112, 115-116, 119, 129, 136-137, 145, 149-150, 153-154, 159, 167-168, 174-177, 181, 185, 202, 208, 212, 217, 229, 235, 242, 248, 252-253, 256-260, 263, 267-268, 275, 278, 281, 302-303, 305, 313, 319, 331, 342, 357, 360, 362-363, 366, 368-370, 387, 390, 393-395, 397, 399, 401-402, 410-411, 415, 417

Artificial Intelligence (AI) 3, 13, 27, 122, 129, 131, 134, 138, 140, 146, 148, 157-158, 161-162, 173, 185, 187-191, 207, 232, 279, 335-336, 357, 362, 364, 368, 371-372, 385, 387

Artificial Intelligence in Education (AIED) 175, 185

Artificial Intelligence of Things (AIoT) 13-14, 19, 24, 26, 128-129, 131-132, 139-141, 143-144, 149-150, 153, 157, 166, 169, 171, 173, 186-188, 190-191, 196, 201, 204-207, 209

Audio Classification 320

Authentication 1, 3, 5-6, 16-17, 66-72, 74, 78, 80-85, 130, 134-136, 138, 143, 145, 148-151, 163, 169, 171, 200-202, 213, 228, 239

Autonomous Artificial Intelligence (AI) 185

Autonomous Electric Vehicles 104-111, 121, 123

B

Battery Management 126, 246, 335, 354, 371, 374, 376, 381, 383-385, 387-390, 417

Big Data

Big Data 8, 47, 53-54, 82, 125, 172, 175, 182, 185, 218, 259, 314, 356-370

Blockchain 22, 128, 165-168, 172, 200, 203-204, 233, 242-244, 249, 351, 353-355, 357-358, 361-363, 365, 367-369, 388

Building Information Modeling 208, 215, 248

C

Cepstral Coefficient 320-322, 331

Challenges 2-3, 9, 17, 21, 23-26, 30, 47, 74, 85, 102, 105, 111, 121, 125-127, 129-133, 138, 141, 146, 157-158, 162, 164, 170-171, 178, 180, 183, 186, 188-190, 193, 196, 198-199, 202, 205-208, 211-214, 219, 226-227, 231, 234, 236-237, 240, 243-246, 251-253, 256, 261-262, 264-265, 276-285, 287-288, 305-306, 311-316, 318, 334-338, 347-348, 351, 354, 357-365, 367-371, 384, 386-387, 389-390, 393-395, 398, 401, 405, 410-412

Circuit Design 392-398, 418

Cloud Computing 1-2, 6-9, 18-22, 24-25, 84, 87, 123, 126, 153, 172, 203, 219-224, 229-232, 234, 240-247, 352, 354-355, 360-363, 369, 390, 417

Cloud Infrastructure 9, 13, 18, 24, 188, 191, 198, 219-220, 224-227, 239-240, 244

Control Models 1-2, 5, 14-17, 19, 186-187, 189, 192-193, 195-197, 201-202, 248, 251, 254-256, 271-273

Cybersecurity 3, 17-18, 21, 23, 69, 123, 128-129, 141, 150, 161, 163, 177, 183, 199, 234, 236, 241, 245-246, 277, 359, 382, 412

D

Data Analytics 8, 14, 134, 163, 190, 210, 234, 248, 319, 335, 343, 349, 351-352, 358, 361-366, 368-369, 372, 375-376, 381-382, 387

Data Augmentation 113, 284-286, 288, 291-292, 298-301, 305-306, 308-309

Data Privacy 2-3, 10, 18-19, 67, 83, 128-130, 134, 136, 139-141, 164, 188, 198-199, 213, 253, 255, 371, 384, 387

Decision-making 2-3, 14, 18-19, 33, 87, 105-110, 114-115, 117, 120-123, 127-130, 132-134, 139, 143, 146, 153, 156-158, 164, 176, 187-198, 207, 209-211, 213, 221-224, 232, 235, 251-259, 261-262, 266-276, 314-315, 341, 343, 345, 360-361, 364-365, 375, 379, 381, 392-394, 400-403, 409-410, 412, 416

Deep Learning 13, 21, 23, 25, 84, 86, 88-89, 91-92, 94-95, 100-103, 125, 165, 170, 198, 203-204, 207, 210, 215-217, 243-247, 284-285, 287, 292, 302, 304-310, 322, 332-334, 351-352, 355, 377, 413, 418

Delphi Technique 177-178, 180-181, 185

Description Logic 27, 30, 37-38, 47-48

E

Educational Technology (EdTech) 176, 185

Efficiency 3, 7, 14, 17-19, 23, 33, 53, 57, 60, 64, 71, 74, 87, 92, 104-105, 110-111, 119-123, 125, 133-134, 140-141, 153, 161-162, 168, 188, 192, 197, 204, 208, 214, 219-222, 224-226, 229-230, 232, 234-235, 240-241, 247, 251-252, 255-256, 262-263, 265-266, 270-271, 273, 277-279, 297, 302-303, 314, 335-347, 349, 353, 355, 358, 360, 363-365, 371-375, 377-379, 381-384, 387, 392-394, 396, 398-399, 401, 403-405, 408, 410-411

E-Learning 173-176, 184-185, 281

Electric Vehicle (EV) 112, 371-372, 377, 385, 387

Emerging Economy 177, 356

Ethics 139, 167, 173-177, 179-180, 184-185, 188, 199

Experimentation 8, 89, 115, 233, 285, 304, 317

F

Fuel Cell Integration 335-351

Future Developments 122, 362

Fuzzy Logic Control 104, 123, 125, 274

H

Hashed Secure Question 66-67, 80-81

HVAC 249, 266

I

IIoT 265, 281-282, 360, 366, 368

Industry 4.0 24-26, 86-89, 101, 123, 172, 174, 214, 241, 243, 245-246, 280, 361-362, 365-366, 368-369, 412, 414

Innovation 1-3, 6-8, 10-14, 16-22, 24-25, 82, 106, 130-131, 162, 164, 166-168, 175, 177-178, 184-185, 187-189, 191-192, 197, 199, 202-204, 213-215, 219-220, 224-226, 229-230, 233-234, 236-237, 240-242, 247, 252, 261, 267, 279, 335, 343, 345-346, 348-351, 355, 358, 367, 372, 387, 394, 411-412

Integer Programming 392-394, 398-400, 411-413, 415

Integration 1-4, 7, 13, 15-16, 18-20, 23, 28, 30-32, 35, 37, 47, 49, 54, 63-64, 73, 86, 88-90, 92, 104, 106, 108-111, 116-118, 122-123, 125, 131, 134, 138, 142, 147, 153, 156-157, 160-162, 168, 182, 187-188, 190-198, 200, 203-204, 207-208, 211-215, 219-220, 222-223, 226, 230-232, 235-236, 240-241, 244, 248-249, 251-253, 255-270, 272-274, 276-279, 282-283, 335-353, 357-365, 372-374, 381-382, 385, 387-388, 391, 393-395, 397, 400-401, 411-412, 417

Interface Design 186-187, 189-190

Internet of Things (IoT) 3, 7, 13, 21, 23, 27, 54, 86-87, 101, 125, 129, 131, 134, 138, 140-141, 146, 150, 153-154, 157-158, 162, 164, 167, 169-170, 173, 187-191, 207, 212, 225, 280, 335-336, 353, 356-357, 361-364, 367-369, 415

Interoperability 1-4, 14, 16-21, 24, 32-33, 65, 139, 144, 150, 159, 167, 172, 187-190, 192-193, 196-198, 201-202, 211, 251-256, 258, 260-262, 268-269, 271-273, 277, 281, 340, 371-372, 384, 387

L

Learning Management System (LMS) 185

Line Delimited JSON 249

Linear Programming 392-396, 411-412, 414-415, 418

LMS Plugin 185

M

Machine Learning (ML) 122, 175, 185, 207, 232, 335-336, 343, 358, 372, 385

Management Systems 23, 29, 50, 74, 122, 152, 155, 173-176, 182, 335, 364, 371-373, 375, 382, 384-385, 387

Mechanical Engineering 1, 104, 124, 127, 186, 219-221, 223, 226-227, 229-234, 236-241, 335, 371, 414, 417-418

Mel Frequency 320-322, 327, 331

Mixed-Integer Programming 392-394, 400-401, 412

ML 23-24, 122-123, 125-126, 168, 175, 185, 204-

205, 207, 216, 232, 241, 244-246, 284, 305-306,
335-337, 343-347, 349, 351, 353-356, 358, 362,
371-373, 385, 387-388

N

Network Optimization 392-394, 398, 400, 407-408, 412
Neural Networks 26, 83, 103-104, 106-114, 117, 123-
125, 127, 206, 210, 216, 218, 274, 285, 287-288,
306, 308, 310, 372, 416
Nonlinear Programming 392-394, 396-398, 411-412

O

Object Detection 75, 82, 86-88, 92, 94, 101-102, 289
One Time Password 66-67, 70, 81
Ontology 2, 4, 14, 20, 27, 30, 32-34, 36-38, 40-42,
44-49, 51-52, 54-55, 64-65, 181, 184, 209, 211,
251-252, 257-264, 266-267, 271, 279-283
Opportunities 3, 8, 14, 16, 19-21, 25-26, 85, 121-122,
126, 128-129, 152, 162, 166, 174, 186, 188-189,
191-192, 197-199, 201-202, 205-206, 213-214,
220, 224-227, 241-243, 245, 269, 282, 284, 313,
334-337, 343, 347-349, 351, 357-358, 360, 362,
369, 389, 394-395
OWL 1-2, 4, 14, 16-17, 19-20, 33, 36-37, 40, 45-46, 186,
209, 211, 248-249, 251, 253, 256, 258-261, 281

P

Power Systems 338, 392-396, 414-415, 418
Principal Component Analysis 287, 320-321, 329, 331
Privacy 2-3, 5, 10, 17-21, 24, 67, 83, 128-132, 134-137,
139-144, 146-149, 154-159, 162-164, 166-168,
172, 188, 196, 198-203, 213, 219-220, 222, 227-
229, 240-242, 244, 246, 252-253, 255-257, 262,
275, 277-278, 283, 360, 371, 384, 387
Privacy-Preserving Techniques 128

Q

Query Language 2, 4, 14, 20, 60, 65, 248, 251, 253, 256

R

Raspberry Pi 86, 88-90, 94, 96-99, 101
RDF 1-2, 4-5, 14, 16-17, 19-20, 54, 57, 61, 63, 65, 186,
192, 202, 209, 211, 248-249, 251-253, 256-260,
263-264, 267, 271-272, 275, 277, 279, 282
RDF Query Language 2, 4, 14, 20, 248
Recognition 66-68, 71, 73-76, 79-85, 87, 101-102,

135, 149, 151, 170, 208, 210, 215-217, 267-268,
284, 287-288, 301, 306-310, 320-322, 327, 332-
334, 372, 382
Resource Description Framework 2, 4, 14, 20, 192,
202, 209, 248, 259, 271

S

Safety 29, 74, 104-105, 110-111, 118-123, 130, 155,
160, 163, 188, 208, 272, 275, 314-315, 317, 372-
373, 377-379, 381-383, 387
Security 1-3, 5-22, 24-26, 66-67, 69-71, 73-76, 80-81,
83-84, 86-87, 89, 124-125, 128-159, 161-169, 171-
172, 188, 196, 198, 200-203, 207, 213, 219-220,
222, 224, 227-230, 233, 236-242, 244, 246-247,
252-253, 255, 257, 262, 275, 278-280, 306, 314,
348, 351, 353, 358, 360, 362, 365, 367-369, 382,
387, 399, 409, 413, 415
Semantic Interoperability 1-2, 14, 16, 18-19, 21, 189,
192-193, 197-198, 202, 256, 260, 262, 268, 281
Semantic Web 1-6, 14-27, 30, 33-35, 37-40, 44-54,
64-65, 173-176, 180-181, 186-187, 189, 192-193,
195-202, 204-205, 207-209, 211-214, 248-273,
275-282, 319
Semantic Web Service 27, 30, 34-35, 38, 45-49, 51
Semantic Web Tech 248
Simulation 50, 98, 110-111, 115, 118, 120-121, 220-
221, 224, 226, 230, 233, 235, 240, 242, 247, 314,
355, 389, 403
Small and Medium Enterprises (SMEs) 219-221,
225, 234
Smart Farming 23, 243, 356, 363, 370
Smart Parking Systems 86, 89
SPARQL 2, 4, 14, 16, 19-20, 54-55, 58, 60-61, 65,
186, 248-249, 251-253, 256, 264, 267, 271-273
SPARQL Protocol 2, 4, 14, 20, 248
Sugarcane Leaf Disease 284-285, 305, 308-310
Supply Chain Management 16, 27-29, 37, 48-51, 235,
269, 283, 361, 367
Support Vector Classifier 320

T

Technologies and Applications 173-176, 180, 282-283
Transfer Learning 96, 114, 215-216, 288, 310, 326

U

Unauthorized 5, 9-10, 66-67, 69-71, 73, 130-131, 134-
135, 143, 145, 147-148, 150, 152, 156, 158, 161,
200-201, 227-228, 234, 236-237, 239, 275, 278

Usability 69-71, 73, 130, 174, 176, 186-190, 192-197, 199, 201, 358
User Experience 68, 71, 73, 150, 174, 176, 186-187, 190, 195, 212, 302-303, 343, 346, 371, 375, 377-379, 381-382, 387

V

Vehicle Dynamics 104, 108, 111, 113-114, 121, 123, 371, 381, 383-384

W

Web Data Security 128
Web Ontology Language 2, 4, 14, 20, 209, 248, 259
Web Protocol 248
World Wide Web Consortium 54, 248

Y

YOLOv3 86, 88, 92-93, 96, 99, 101-102

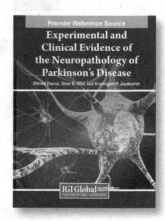
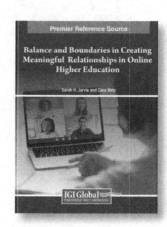

Are You Ready to
Publish Your Research

IGI Global offers book authorship and editorship opportunities across three major subject areas, including Business, STM, and Education.

Benefits of Publishing with IGI Global:

- Free one-on-one editorial and promotional support.

- Expedited publishing timelines that can take your book from start to finish in less than one (1) year.

- Choose from a variety of formats, including Edited and Authored References, Handbooks of Research, Encyclopedias, and Research Insights.

- Utilize IGI Global's eEditorial Discovery® submission system in support of conducting the submission and double-blind peer review process.

- IGI Global maintains a strict adherence to ethical practices due in part to our full membership with the Committee on Publication Ethics (COPE).

- Indexing potential in prestigious indices such as Scopus®, Web of Science™, PsycINFO®, and ERIC – Education Resources Information Center.

- Ability to connect your ORCID iD to your IGI Global publications.

- Earn honorariums and royalties on your full book publications as well as complimentary content and exclusive discounts.

Join Your Colleagues from Prestigious Institutions, Including:

Australian National University

Massachusetts Institute of Technology

JOHNS HOPKINS UNIVERSITY

HARVARD UNIVERSITY

COLUMBIA UNIVERSITY IN THE CITY OF NEW YORK

Learn More at: www.igi-global.com/publish

or Contact IGI Global's Aquisitions Team at: acquisition@igi-global.com

Printed in the United States
by Baker & Taylor Publisher Services